Central Asia, as it emerges from a political and economic system that was closed until the end of the twentieth century, is a textbook case for globalization. Its entry into the global arena must be understood not only through Central Asian states' interaction with numerous external players, but also in geo-economic terms. The region's natural resources compel the attention of rivalrous great powers and ambitious internal factions. Russia and China dominate the horizon, with other global players close behind. The local regimes are caught between the need for international collaborations to valorize their resources and the need to maintain control over them in the interest of state sovereignty. Local patterns of development thus become a key driver of external actors' involvement and shape the mechanisms by which the Central Asian states are forging a place for themselves in the globalized world.

This pathbreaking introduction to Central Asia in contemporary international economic and political context answers the needs of both academic and professional audiences.

Globalizing Central Asia

Geopolitics and the Challenges of Economic Development

Marlene Laruelle and Sebastien Peyrouse

Routledge
Taylor & Francis Group

LONDON AND NEW YORK

First published 2013 by M.E. Sharpe

Published 2015 by Routledge
2 Park Square, Milton Park, Abingdon, Oxon OX14 4RN
711 Third Avenue, New York, NY 10017, USA

Routledge is an imprint of the Taylor & Francis Group, an informa business

Library of Congress Cataloging-in-Publication Data

Laruelle, Marlene.
Globalizing Central Asia : geopolitics and the challenges of economic development / by Marlene
Laruelle and Sebastien Peyrouse.
    p. cm.
Includes bibliographical references and index.
ISBN 978-0-7656-3504-4 (hardcover : alk. paper)—ISBN 978-0-7656-3505-1 (pbk. : alk. paper)
    1. Economic development—Asia, Central. 2. Geopolitics—Asia, Central. 3. Asia, Central—
Foreign economic relations. 4. Globalization—Asia, Central. I. Peyrouse, Sibastien. II. Title.

HC420.3.L374 2012
338.958—dc23   2012011121

ISBN 13: 9780765635051 (pbk)
ISBN 13: 9780765635044 (hbk)

Contents

List of Maps, Figures, and Tables

Introduction

Globalization is now one of the most used words in the media, politics, and academia. This multifaceted concept has become a catchall into which anyone can read whatever he or she wants—often with a heavy dose of ideology. Advocates of complete deregulation of the economy may argue that the state has lost its regulatory role in a global era; some resist globalization on protectionist and nationalistic grounds; still others advocate alternative globalizations, whether based on "world citizenship" or on environmental or "degrowth" theories. In the end, however, when we separate the reality from the hype, we see that the history of man is a history of globalization: large population migrations in prehistoric and ancient times; the dissemination of culture through medieval scholars, world religions, or great voyages of discovery and colonial conquest; the establishment of international organizations such as the Red Cross or the League of Nations; the rise of communism as the first major ideology to transcend national boundaries. Contemporary globalization has therefore a long lineage.

Another exaggeration is the idea that globalization abolishes space and time. In actuality, only capital markets are truly globalized, transcending physical borders. Information, too, is immediate—at least some of it—although it is not yet borderless. But many other aspects of human life are still marked by time and space, and in most senses, the borders of nation-states continue to be as relevant—especially in some parts of the globe—as ever. The vast majority of the world's people never leave the territory where they were born; they may be able to connect to the wider world via Facebook, but their everyday experiences are still demarcated by space and bounded by access to transportation. The new interactions that arise between states, consumers, transnational corporations, and civil society entities do not mean the end of the state; the state is still the only formal political space in which the civil rights of individuals are expressed, or for which we fight.

Nor does globalization spell the end of geography. Economic activities—outside of finance—are still geographically located. The old geography of production, distribution, and consumption still functions, but it is being transformed. In Peter Dicken's description, economic globalization is characterized by "an increasingly complex geography of production, distribution and consumption whose scale has become, if not totally global, at least vastly more extensive, and whose choreography has become increasingly intricate."[1] The historic patterns of trade between Europe, North America, and Japan—with intensive commercial and financial flows and dense networks of transport and communications—are increasingly challenged by China, the Asian "tigers" and "dragons," and individual countries like Brazil or South Africa. Of course, there are still persistent peripheries: sub-Saharan Africa, a large part of Latin America, and Central Eurasia. Core–periphery geography is evolving dramatically, and the societies that are in the process of catching up are quite changed by the time they enter the globalized world. The Chinese workforce, for instance, will soon be too expensive for Chinese strategies of producing cheap goods, and sub-Saharan African countries attract Chinese businesses.

Globalization is also multi-scale. It impacts not only global flows, but also the events of everyday life, and it has a regional dimension. Archipelago economies are forming, focused on one or more economic powers that drive an entire region: the United States in North America; the European Union for Europe, the Mediterranean region, and Russia; and China for the Asia-Pacific. China, India, Brazil, and South Africa are the main emergent powers, grouped under the BRICS acronym. Russia is conventionally included in this group, but its membership is questionable. The Russian economy experienced significant growth in the beginning of the twenty-first century compared to its collapse in the previous decade, but on a longer scale Russia's economy compared to the Soviet one can be read as in decline. In many respects Russia is a former power; it is not emergent, but rather in a phase of withdrawal, like Europe.

This rise of "regionness" is an important aspect of globalization, not only in economic terms, but also increasingly in strategic and cultural ones. It is accompanied by a narrative that evokes a multipolar world in which the so-called American superpower is relegated to being a power among others. The phenomenon of regionness thus implies a potential geopolitical pluralism, which the BRICS countries promote loudly in international fora. It calls into question the "eurocentrism" of international relations, and it suggests that foreign policy is impacted by the cultures of international actors. Globalization is therefore not a teleological process that will result in uniform governance or some kind of world harmony.

Central Eurasia—defined as the immense area that spans from Siberia to Russia's Pacific coast, the three South Caucasus countries (Armenia, Georgia, Azerbaijan), the five Central Asian countries (Kazakhstan, Kyrgyzstan, Tajikistan, Turkmenistan, Uzbekistan), Mongolia, Afghanistan, Xinjiang, and Kashmir—is one of the world's persistent peripheries. This is immediately apparent if one looks at the Northern Corridor of Modern Activity (NCMA), which shows a dense belt circling the earth, tracing the flows of telecommunications activities during one twenty-four-hour period in the late 1990s. In it, Central Eurasia presents itself as an immense blank space—a Modern Activity Gap (MAG)—in which communications between Asia and the Atlantic vanish as if in a black hole.[2]

Central Eurasia has been home to centers of civilization for brief periods in history, in ancient and medieval times. In modern times, it has always been part of the periphery, whether of the Russian, Ottoman, Persian, British, or Chinese empire.

It has remained sparsely populated compared to the large concentrations of people nearby (the Mediterranean Basin, India, and China) and lacking in political unity. Historically, the region was a transit area for people, goods, and ideas—as successive "empires of the steppes" invaded Europe from the Altaic homelands, and to the south when the Silk Road trade linked China to the Mediterranean. These overland routes lost their raison d'être after the great maritime discoveries of the fifteenth century and as a result of changes to the local context, such as Iran's passing under Safavid domination. The disappearance of the Silk Roads preceded and cannot be explained by the colonial powers' "Great Game." By the seventeenth and eighteenth centuries, the Uzbek khanates, at the geographical heart of Central Eurasia, had been relegated to the distant peripheries of the Russian, British, and Chinese empires. Subsequently, Russian commercial domination, and then the imposition of the Soviet regime, almost entirely redirected the trade flows toward the north. Central Asia—with the South Caucasus and the Russian Far East—became a sort of cul-de-sac of the Soviet Union, closed off to trade with its southern neighbors. The rest of Central Eurasia was transformed into buffer states (Afghanistan, Mongolia) or marginalized regions with a peripheral status (Xinjiang, Kashmir). The twentieth century saw the erecting of new barriers, territorial and ideological, which profoundly altered the social fabric, bringing to an end the last elements of unity of this vast area.

For Central Asia this persistent peripheral status is not solely a product of tsarist imperial policy or the Soviet regime, but more one of history and geography. The region's extreme continental climate limits the potential for exploitation of the land and for human settlement. The landscape is either arid—from the sandy desert of Turkmenistan, which forms part of the Aralo-Caspian Depression, to the grassy steppes of Kazakhstan leading to Mongolia—or mountainous, with the Pamirs, the Tian-Shan, and the northern foothills of the Himalayas. The Karakum Desert covers 80 percent of Turkmen territory and the Kyzylkum a large part of Uzbekistan, while nearly half of Kyrgyzstan and Tajikistan is at an altitude of more than 3,000 meters. The Ferghana Valley is the main exception: its fertile soil and good provision of water make it the region's "garden."

Central Asia's population density has always been relatively low. The city-states of early antiquity developed in desert oases or the deltas of its great rivers, the Amu Darya and the Syr Darya. These city-states were linked by a system of caravan routes that enabled the circulation of commodities, people, and ideas between relatively isolated settlements. Even in the most prosperous eras, people were one of the region's most precious commodities precisely because they were so scarce. Today the total number of inhabitants for the five Central Asian states is only about 60 million.[3] However, despite its generally low human density, the region is heavily overpopulated in its agrarian zones.[4] In Turkmenistan, there are at most only 0.5 hectares of arable land per inhabitant (as compared with an average of 2.3 hectares for the rest of the former Soviet Union). The situation is particularly acute in the Ferghana Valley, with more than 10 million inhabitants (20 percent of the Central Asian population), and levels of human density reaching 559 persons per km^2 around Andijan.[5]

Although food has always been produced locally, Central Asian societies have historically been very dependent upon production from abroad. Artisanship remained limited (carpets, jewels, ceramics, pottery, textiles, objects made of iron, etc.), so that nearly all finished products (as well as tea, salt, and spices) had to be imported, principally from China, Iran, and India, via the famous Silk Roads. From the second half of the eighteenth century onward, imports came mainly from the north, from Russia. The tsarist authorities set up similar mechanisms to those that the Western powers used in Africa and Asia: they dispatched administrators and finished products, and they extracted primary products, thereby reinforcing local economic patterns.[6] From the end of the nineteenth century onward, Central Asia became one of the main zones of cotton production for Russia, while some mining extraction industries operated in the Kazakh steppes. The Soviet economic planning regime intensified this specialization in primary products: cotton in Uzbekistan and Turkmenistan, coal and all types of minerals in Kazakhstan, uranium in Uzbekistan, gold in Kyrgyzstan, and so on. The significant population flows generated by the Soviet system—with large European populations migrating to the region and "punished peoples" being forcibly resettled there—responded to the development of industrial complexes and the large cotton and sugar collective farms.[7]

Upon the collapse of Soviet Union at the end of 1991, Kazakhstan, Kyrgyzstan, Tajikistan, Turkmenistan, and Uzbekistan acquired political independence. Today they share many common patterns and features: the same cultural and political legacy; weak governance; loss of the economic linkages between Soviet republics; the logic of "transition" from planned to market economy; and limited connectivity to world markets. In economic terms, all have the advantage of being geographically at the crossroads of some of the world's fastest-growing economies, but they are landlocked (and in the case of Uzbekistan, doubly so). They are endowed with large reserves of oil (Kazakhstan); gas (Turkmenistan, and to a lesser extent Uzbekistan and Kazakhstan); potential hydropower (Tajikistan, Kyrgyzstan); uranium, precious minerals, and rare earths (mainly Kazakhstan), and gold (mainly in Uzbekistan); they also produce cotton (Uzbekistan and Turkmenistan, to a lesser extent Kazakhstan and Tajikistan). In addition, unlike many third world countries, they benefited from the advantages of the Soviet regime—a literacy rate of almost 100 percent and universal healthcare systems, both of which are now in decline due to lack of investments in human capital and citizens' well-being.

The region's unity stops here. Each of the Central Asian countries has elaborated its own exit from the Soviet system in terms of political regime, economic policies, opening to the world, cultural and social trends, and conceptions of nationhood. The key stakes they have to face are related to demography (generational changes and developmental prospects for societies with large youth populations like Uzbekistan and Tajikistan); economic development capacities (subsoil resources, transit and trade opportunities, workforce migrations); and the regional environment (proximity to three of the BRICS countries, drug routes, and Islamic insurgencies). Each country also has its own specific problems to resolve: energy, water, and food crises (Tajikistan,

Kyrgyzstan); fear of political Islam (Uzbekistan, Tajikistan); potential interethnic tensions (Kyrgyzstan, Kazakhstan); youth unemployment (Uzbekistan, Turkmenistan); and massive labor migrations (Tajikistan, Uzbekistan, Kyrgyzstan). Their degree of integration with the world is also very different. Turkmenistan is one of the world's most closed countries after North Korea, and has maintained both political and economic isolation; Kyrgyzstan has sought to be the most politically, socially, and economically open, and was the first country in the Commonwealth of Independent States (CIS) to join the World Trade Organization (WTO), in 1998.

The states are all members of major international organizations, except Turkmenistan, which pursues isolationist policies under a status of "permanent neutrality."[8] They enjoy the benefits offered by European banking institutions (the European Bank for Reconstruction and Development) as well as the Asian Development Bank and the Islamic Development Bank. That said, international financial institutions (IFIs) such as the World Bank and the International Monetary Fund (IMF) have difficulty working in Central Asia, especially in Turkmenistan and Uzbekistan, as do United Nations (UN) agencies. They are also members of many regional organizations, but these are rarely effective. Only those headed by Moscow or Beijing (the Eurasian Economic Community and the Customs Union, the Shanghai Cooperation Organization) can impact on local economic realities, while others (the Economic Cooperation Organization, Conference on Interaction and Confidence Building Measures in Asia, Organization of Islamic Cooperation, and so on) are essentially forums for discussion and international visibility, with no efficacy on the ground. In addition, regional cooperation between Central Asian states is impeded by multiple tensions between political leaders, border issues, and contradictory geopolitical and economic orientations, allowing external actors to play one country against another and reducing the ability of local governments to advance their own interests.

With independence came a return of the narrative about Central Asia as a crossroads, promulgated by the local governments as well as by international donors and external actors. But the geographical centrality that seems so obvious on the map bears little resemblance to the economic and cultural realities. "Only rarely do [geographically] central locations coincide with [actual] centers; very often, they are 'internal peripheries.'"[9] The fact remains that Central Asia continues to be a persistent periphery, poorly connected to the rest of the world in terms of trade statistics, communication and transport networks, and business and investment environment.[10] Nonetheless, Kazakhstan is the world's foremost uranium producer, the second-largest exporter of flour, and will become one of the ten largest exporters of petroleum in the next decade; Turkmenistan has the fourth or fifth largest reserves of gas in the world; Uzbekistan is the world's second-largest exporter of cotton and is globally well placed in exports of gold and uranium. Moreover, typical globalizing mechanisms are emerging there. The investment strategies of some of the large Kazakh metallurgical firms in sub-Saharan Africa, and the structure of the Kazakh sovereign wealth fund Samruk-Kazyna, exemplify the global trends of south-south investments and new developmental "state capitalism."

In addition, Central Asia can be considered well integrated into the world economy if one takes alternative criteria into account. Labor migration flows place Tajikistan and Kyrgyzstan above Central America in terms of dependence on remittances. Mafia-type networks, largely related to drug-trafficking and prostitution, link Central Asia, Europe and the Mediterranean, and the Gulf states. Groups of young Central Asian men in search of Islamic knowledge travel to Malaysia and Mecca and other destinations in a globalized Islamic world. Corrupt ruling elites stow millions of dollars in offshore havens like Cyprus, the Cayman Islands, and the British Virgin Islands, and acquire real estate in Switzerland or the French Riviera, in preparation for a comfortable retirement or sudden exile. The Central Asian states are thus in the process of strengthening their statehood in symbolic, political, and territorial terms, while at the same time their economies and societies follow some globalizing, sometimes denationalizing, trends.

Emerging from a political and economic system that was closed until the end of the twentieth century, Central Asia could be a "textbook case" for globalization, as the region adapts to a highly competitive world where the criteria for success are changing rapidly. The new states must manage the tensions between being formally independent and needing to be "open" to outsiders, whether states, investors, individuals, or legal norms. Globalization is thus reshaping statehood; it has increased the weight of the exogenous demands imposed on the elites and has profoundly transformed the normative definition of the state.[11] Yet most publications on contemporary Central Asia ignore this globalization question, focusing only on the geopolitical stakes to which the region is subject, with particular emphasis on the classic strategic balance among the major powers and their conflicting pressures on local governments. Questions of economic development are rarely correlated with geopolitical dimensions, except for the export of hydrocarbons. However, by shifting the focus onto the primary economic realities of Central Asia—the predominance of the agricultural sector, the overspecialization in primary resources, difficulties of access to energy, excessively landlocked character, and weak capabilities for a service-based economy—it becomes possible to better understand the mechanisms by which the Central Asian states are forging a place for themselves in the globalized world.

In the 1990s, analysts tended to see Central Asia in terms of geopolitical theories, especially the classic balance between the global maritime power (the United States) and the continental power (Russia); in the early twenty-first century, the emphasis has shifted toward economics. For the external actors in Central Asia, economic and political interests are intrinsically interlinked. Defense of their geopolitical interests (influence on local elites, strategic cooperation, and containment of competitors) is combined with promotion of their economic interests through multiple means, ranging from "good neighbor" policies (China) to aid and assistance (the European Union, United States, and Japan) and contracts for their state-run and private firms. For the Central Asian states, the major challenge is balancing external actors, and linking geopolitics and economic development. Moving beyond their 1990s quest for international recognition, they have reformulated their interests in more pragmatic terms and anchored their international positioning on the logics of access to resources and economic specialization. Local economic potentials, but also limitations, have worked to cement the balance in favor of China, and to a lesser extent, Russia; to give a larger role to Europe, and to partially dampen the influence of the major actors of the 1990s, namely the United States, Turkey, and Iran.

Western observers are accustomed to seeing Central Asia through the prism of the "Great Game," with too many actors competing over the region, but the Central Asian governments see things quite differently. There may be many players, but few of them are able to go beyond mere talk; numerous development projects are still waiting for a generous donor undeterred by investment conditions that are difficult and insecure. Over the course of twenty years of independence, the Central Asian states have been disappointed by most of the external actors on which they pinned their greatest hopes, namely, the United States, Europe, India, and Japan. They have limited the influence of other actors for reasons having more to do with perceived Islamist threats (Turkey, Iran, Pakistan, and the Gulf countries). Only one country, China, has not disappointed them in these ways, but it provokes anxieties concerning the sustainability of their long-term sovereignty toward their big neighbor.

The aim of this book is to provide keys to understanding Central Asia in an era of globalization by analyzing both the strategies of external actors and the local patterns of development. Topics that will not be explored here include the strategic balance of power, the legal frameworks in which the local economies are developing, the shadow economy, or the cultural globalization that is occurring in Central Asia via migration or the education of young people abroad.

In Part 1 of the book, we inquire into the place held by the various external actors on the Central Asian scene, their multiple "little games," and their economic presence in the region. In Part 2, we look at the economic realities of Central Asia and the main sectors of production and services. With this analytical framework we hope to highlight elements through which the Central Asian states are charting their political construction, their international place, and their development strategies in a globalized world. We are deeply grateful to all those who have helped us realize this project, especially Michelle Marie Smith, Alec Forss, Steve Corcoran, Gaël Raballand, Patricia Kolb, Ana Erlic, and Marlyn Miller.

Notes

1. P. Dicken, *Global Shift: Mapping the Changing Contours of the World Economy* (New York: Guilford Press, 2011), 3.

2. S. Benson, *The MAGAI™ Construct and the Northern Distribution Network* (Washington, DC: Center for Strategic and International Studies, November 2009), 3–4.

3. Uzbekistan, with about 27 million people, has close to half the population of the region; Kazakhstan has about 15 million people. The figures for the three other republics are much smaller: there are about 6 million inhabitants in Kyrgyzstan and in Turkmenistan, and about 7 million in Tajikistan. Uzbekistan's and Turkmenistan's demographic data, however, are based on estimates, given the lack of census-taking, not to mention data manipulation by the political authorities.

4. The data show 5.5 inhabitants per km² in Kazakhstan, 10 in Turkmenistan, 28 in Kyrgyzstan, 49 in Tajikistan, and 64 in Uzbekistan; detailed figures per year are available on Sherbrooke University's website: http://perspective.usherbrooke.ca/bilan/servlet/BMListeSta tSpecifique?codetheme=1.

5. *Chislennost' naseleniia Respubliki Uzbekistan na 1.1.2005* (Tashkent: Goskomstat, 2005), 5–15. We thank Olivier Ferrando for conveying this information to me.

6. S. Becker, *Russia's Protectorates in Central Asia: Bukhara and Khiva, 1865–1924* (London: RoutledgeCurzon, 2004); S. Abashin and S. Gorshenina, eds., *Le Turkestan russe, une colonie pas comme les autres?* (Brussels: Complexes, 2009).

7. I. Ohayon. "La déportation des peuples punis en Asie centrale," in *Le XXe siècle des guerres*, ed. P. Causarano, V. Galimi et al. (Paris: Éd. de l'Atelier, 2004), 172–81.

8. L. Anceschi, *Turkmenistan's Foreign Policy: Positive Neutrality and the Consolidation of the Turkmen Regime* (London: Routledge, 2008).

9. O. Dollfus, *La mondialisation* (Paris: Presses de Sciences Po, 2001), 57.

10. See the introduction to part 2 in this volume.

11. J. Heathershaw, "Tajikistan amidst Globalization: State Failure or State Transformation?" *Central Asian Survey* 30, no. 1 (2011): 147–68.

Globalizing
Central Asia

Part I

"Great Games" and "Small Games"

The Strategies and Outcomes
of External Actors

All parts of the world have given rise to meta-discourses fed by historical and geographical references, but some do so more than others. This is the case for Central Asia, where onlookers embed the realities of daily political, social, economic, and cultural existence in a globalizing narrative that is intended to make sense of contemporary developments. This is not only a sign of lack of knowledge about the region, but also of the lack of interpretative guides to the changes taking place there. Thus, since the collapse of the Soviet Union, Central Asia is variously cast as the "South" of the former Soviet Union, the eastern pole of Washington's "Greater Middle East," the new "Far West" of China, a "buffer zone" between continental and maritime powers, a "Greater Central Asia" linked to South Asia through Afghanistan, the "Caspian Basin" as a historical place of conflict between Russia and Iran, and as a "Central Eurasia" where Slavic, Turkic, Persian, and Chinese cultures meet. These familiar interpretations invite external actors to project their international identity on the region, each with their own set of normative principles, arguments in favor of rapprochement with Central Asia, and legitimacy strategies to influence the future of the region.

Among these metanarratives, the "Great Game" is probably the most popular.[1] It recalls the geopolitical competition between the Russian and British empires during the second half of the nineteenth century in the area stretching from the Kazakh and Turkmen steppes to the north of India, and from the Caspian Sea to the foothills of the Himalayas. It led to the birth of Afghanistan and the historic separation between Russian Turkestan and British India.[2] The current idea of the new "Great Game" is marked by the post–Cold War rediscovery of colonial adventures and revives the Orientalist fashions of the nineteenth century, as well as Romanticism's attraction to a mystical "East." The previous "Great Game" was not a typical armed conflict, but rather an indirect competition based on cultural and commercial sway, which used methods of disinformation and discrete struggles for influence, as well as the weapon of scientific knowledge. All these are standard strategies of the twenty-first-century post–Cold War world, hence the tendency to consider both situations similar.[3]

But the "Great Game" formula causes confusion on multiple levels. The contemporary Central Asian states are independent, legitimate international actors and recognized members of major organizations, which the nineteenth century khanates of Bukhara, Khiva, and Kokand were not. They cannot be reduced to simple objects

4

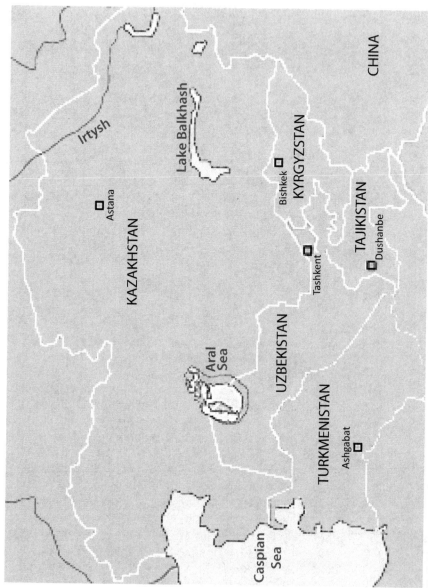

Political Map of Central Asia

of rivalry between great powers, and they have not been passive recipients of external influence, either under colonial domination in the nineteenth century, Soviet control in the twentieth century, or post–Cold War geopolitical contests in the twenty-first century. They are actors in their own right, with their own subjectivity and projection of identity on the international stage.

Most importantly, despite a power differential that is not in their favor, they are able to deploy strategies to force regional actors and global powers to compete with one another, and have the capacity to limit the impact of outsiders. Neither Russia nor China nor the United States can impose their rules of the game on Central Asia in a unilateral manner, and any of them may experience sudden losses of influence. Moscow has limited means by which to exert pressure on Turkmenistan or Uzbekistan, and it also has to manage the growing autonomy of Kazakhstan, as well as respond to the bargaining tactics used by Tajikistan and Kyrgyzstan. Beijing has been unable to enforce its own specific set of economic and strategic wishes, and the Central Asian states rejected its proposal to transform the Shanghai Cooperation Organization into a free trade zone. China also found itself at a loss, for example, when confronted with Tashkent's obstruction of the hydroelectric station projects it is financing in Tajikistan. The United States or the European Union cannot influence the nature of Central Asian regimes, which have managed to maintain political isolation when faced with democratizing pressures, and Washington has experienced several significant strategic setbacks in the region.

The notion of the "Great Game" also presupposes a set of binary oppositions whose relevance has not been demonstrated. While Russia and the United States appeared to dominate the Central Asian scene in the 1990s, now China has positioned itself as a new matrix for the region and potentially as a competitor with Russia. US-China competition in the region is not clearly apparent, but it exists. Yet multiple other powers, such as the European Union, Japan, South Korea, Turkey, Iran, India, have also entered the regional arena. Each seeks to project itself as a model for Central Asian development and to frame the legitimacy narratives of the Central Asian states.

Russia's and China's influence has been established over the long term, and both have territorial contiguity with several Central Asian countries. They are the only "total" players in the sense that they are able to partly shape politics, strategic orientations, economic development, and social issues in Central Asia. With the Soviet legacy, Russia has a cultural advantage, although China hopes to fill the gap with its economic dynamism. A second set of actors, the United States and the EU are both symbols of democratic values and a Western way of life that is both attractive and repellent. The differences between these two actors, however, are significant. Washington arrived in the region with the legitimacy of the sole superpower, but its distance from the Eurasian continent limits its level of interaction with Central Asian societies. For its part, Brussels is mobilizing its normative and soft power. It is more influential in economic terms than the United States, but less so in strategic terms; it has the potential to influence state-building in the region, but its foreign policy lacks impact. A third set of actors, Iran and Turkey, draw on cultural and linguistic proximity, which provides them with niches of influence but not first-tier status. A fourth group includes the more minor actors—Japan, South Korea, India, Pakistan, the United Arab Emirates, Malaysia, and Israel—and a fifth group of even less influential countries includes former Soviet "brothers" and newly rediscovered neighbors, Ukraine, Belarus, the South Caucasus, and Afghanistan.

Far from being binary, the relationships between Central Asian countries and each of these external actors, or among the external actors themselves, are flexible. Not all of them share the same objectives, strategies, or outcomes, and the "smaller" actors can sometimes impede the "greater" powers. None of these external actors wants to gain a monopoly over the region. It is too fragile domestically and too exposed to an unstable regional environment for outside powers to risk entering into conflict with the others to achieve a unilateral stranglehold over it. This situation is positive, since it limits greatly the risks of conflict between external actors. But it is also negative, since the main influential actors are involved mostly with defense strategies (to confine the risks of "instability" emanating from Central Asia), and no one is ready to pay too dearly for its presence in the region.

The diversity of Central Asia has also been reinforced since independence. The five states now have little in common in terms of economic capacity and development strategy. Each of them is autonomous in its foreign policy decisions, and has a very specific identity and its own views on the geopolitical environment. Kyrgyzstan and Turkmenistan each view China differently, and the same is true of Russia in Kazakhstan and Uzbekistan. The governments quite legitimately exploit international competition to their own advantage and are learning how to present different faces depending upon the partner with which they are dealing. When negotiating with Moscow and Beijing, they do not conceal the authoritarian nature of their decision making, but when meeting with the Europeans and Americans, they display concern for democratization and good governance. With Muslim countries they play the Islam card, and with Israel and Europe, that of the secular state. From the time of their independence, the states of Central Asia have promoted divergent conceptions of their place on the international stage, and these divergences have widened over time. Twenty years after the collapse of the Soviet Union, the Central Asian foreign policies share similar objectives—autonomy but recognition—but from it they draw very different strategies and outcomes. Indeed, the diversity of positions is extreme, going from Turkmen isolationism—so complete that it led to the country's often being placed alongside North Korea and Burma in various global rankings—to the far-reaching openness of Kyrgyzstan—the only country in the world to host a Russian and an American military base on its soil only a few kilometers from one another.

Kazakhstan is the only Central Asian state to have succeeded in implementing a positive multi-vectored policy vis-à-vis its international partners, by building links in multiple directions, rather than opposing the actors against one another. By openly displaying the hierarchy of its relationships—Russia first, China second, followed by the West (with the European Union taking precedence over the United States)[4]—

Table Part I.I

Main Economic Partners of Central Asia by Rank, Value of Trade, and Percentage in 2010

Rank	Country	Total trade in million US$	Percent of total Central Asian trade
1	China	28,388.7	26.1
2	EU	28,317.3	26
3	Russia	13,955.4	12.8
4	Turkey	6,204.8	5.7
5	United States	2,919.2	2.6
6	Ukraine	2,895.2	2.6
7	South Korea	2,739.1	2.5
8	Belarus	1,246.4	1.1
9	Japan	1,069.1	0.9
10	UAE	927.5	0.8
11	Iran	834.7	0.7
12	Azerbaijan	624.8	0.5
13	Afghanistan	531.5	0.4
14	India	476.6	0.4
15	Malaysia	208.4	0.19
16	Israel	129.4	0.11
17	Pakistan	34.5	0.03

Sources: 2011 European Commission statistics, http://ec.europa.eu/trade/creating-opportunities/bilateral-relations/countries-and-regions/.

Note: For 2010 the euro-dollar official exchange rate was 0.785.

Kazakh foreign policy has managed to build stable and consensual foreign policies. The multi-vectored policy of the other Central Asian states has proven more problematic.[5] Turkmenistan's stance of "permanent neutrality" can only be defined as multi-vectored by default, since it is more isolationist than internationalist. Uzbekistan has undergone several major strategic reversals, which makes its multi-vector orientation a sign of geopolitical instability, as it switches between pro-Western and anti-Russian, and anti-Western and pro-Russian stances. Kyrgyzstan, for its part, as well as Tajikistan to a lesser extent, are able to play on the oppositions between the major powers with a fair amount of success, but they do not have any established multi-vectored policy to speak of. They play one power against another, while Kazakhstan plays on all of the powers at the same time.

A realistic interpretation of the interaction between Central Asian countries and external actors is therefore not of a "Great Game," but rather of many "little games" that are modular, evolving, negotiable, complementary, and not exclusive of one another.

Notes

1. A. Sengupta, *Heartlands of Eurasia: The Geopolitics of Political Space* (Lanham, MD: Lexington Books, 2009); N. Megoran and S. Sharapova, eds., "On the Centenary of Halford Mackinder's Geographical Pivot of History," *Central Asia and the Caucasus* 34, no. 4 (2005).

2. P. Hopkirk, *The Great Game: The Struggle for Empire in Central Asia* (Tokyo: Kodansha International, 1992); G. Mogran, *Anglo-Russian Rivalry in Central Asia, 1810–1895* (London: Frank Cass, 1981); K. Meyer and S. B. Brisac, *Tournament of Shadows: The Great Game and the Race for Empire in Central Asia* (Washington, DC: Counterpoint, 1999).

3. J. Piatigorsky and J. Sapir, eds., *Le grand jeu—XIXe siècle, les enjeux géopolitiques de l'Asie centrale* (Paris: Autrement, 2009).

4. B. K. Sultanov and L. M. Muzaparova, eds., *Stanovlenie vneshnei politiki Kazakhstana: Istoriia, dostizheniia, vzgliad na budushchee* (Almaty: IWEP, 2005).

5. F. Tolipov, "The Foreign Policy Orientations of Central Asian States: Positive and Negative Diversification," in *Eager Eyes Fixed on Eurasia*, ed. Iwashita Akihiro (Sapporo: Hokkaido University, 2007), 23–40.

1

Russia in Central Asia

Old Patterns, New Challenges

Contemporary Central Asia cannot be understood without reference to Russia. Russia is a former colonial power whose cultural values and language are still in broad circulation; since the beginning of the twenty-first century, flows of migrant labor from Central Asia have reshaped cultural relations between the two spaces. The Kremlin is still a key strategic partner for soft and hard security issues: it provides political support to the Central Asian regimes and is an important economic player, in particular in energy, although Moscow increasingly is in competition with other external actors. Seen from Moscow, Central Asia makes up a central element of Russian energy policies and, strategically as much as politically, is a key component of the great-power image that the Kremlin is fostering.

After the implosion of the Soviet Union, Russia's standing as former colonial center presented it with many difficulties. In Central Asia, holding Moscow at bay became a top priority. Resounding critiques rang out about "Russian colonialism," but they lasted only for a brief period. During the mid-1990s, the newly independent states began attenuating their criticisms of Moscow as they started to experience social difficulties. It was a time when nostalgia for the Brezhnev years became an increasingly popular leitmotiv, and Russians could no longer be blamed for all evils.[1] In less than two decades, Russia has succeeded in inverting the Soviet past and turning it into an asset of shared proximity. Since 2000, it has once again become a respected power in Central Asia, where its economic and geopolitical revival is admired, but the drivers of that influence, especially in some countries, are fragile and short term.

Although the weight of history still influences certain Russian strategies, contemporary developments are forcing Moscow to readjust its view of Central Asia to be more forward-looking. The country is experiencing a growing strategic insecurity and fears the risks of destabilization at its southern borders. At the same time, control over Central Asian hydrocarbons, uranium, and electricity is part of the Russian state's key strategies in its mastery of the so-called Near Abroad. Politically, Moscow wants to have friendly regimes on its borders and to be able to exercise a certain right to oversee what it considers to be its sphere of influence. Russia may have regained some of its influence in the first decade of the twenty-first century, but it faces new domestic and international challenges, and needs to fundamentally redefine its policy toward Central Asia.

The Ebb and Flow of Russian Influence in Central Asia

Russia's global geopolitical interests have substantially changed since the end of Cold War. The Kremlin is still in the process of adjusting its perceptions of the international scene, and is having difficulties in identifying its long-term partners and competitors.[2] The ambivalent and sometimes hesitant character of Russian foreign policy remains particularly pronounced in Central Asia because Moscow's long-term challenges there are complex. Moreover, the Russian decision-makers who deal with Central Asia issues are diverse, reflecting the range of relations between the two zones that have emerged from the Soviet legacy. Several sets of actors—the presidential administration, the Ministry of Foreign Affairs and diplomatic channels, the Ministry of Defense, the security services, and major Russian firms (public and private)—may work in tandem, but also have conflicting interests and competing areas of influence.

During the first phase extending from the fall of the Soviet Union to the second half of the 1990s, the Kremlin failed to exhibit a defined policy in relation to Central Asia. The Commonwealth of Independent States (CIS) was presented as a mechanism to ensure a "civilized divorce," with no other objective than to avoid conflict situations arising from the dislocation of the links between republics.[3] The reasons behind Russia's disinterest in Central Asia were multiple—ideological, political, and economic. The elites in power during the liberal government of Egor Gaidar (1992–1993) thought that Russia's strategic interests lay in the West. Still harboring the Gorbachevian idea of the "Common European Home," many of them expected a rapid integration into European space, a relatively unproblematic transition to a market economy, and the establishment of Western democratic norms. The years of empire and Soviet power were decried as having "diverted" Russia from the European path. These assumptions ran counter to any potential desire Moscow may have had to maintain control over Central Asia, which was considered to be a backward, corrupt region symbolic of the Brezhnev stagnation, and one that would slow Russia's march toward Europe.[4]

On the economic level, the shock therapy that Russia experienced meant that the large companies, which were being rapidly privatized, no longer played any structural role in foreign policy. The drastic collapse of living standards for the majority of the population left Moscow with no way to influence the other republics through subsidies. Russia stopped being the locomotive of Central Asian integration and brutally expelled the republics from the ruble zone in 1993.[5] It refused a regional alliance suggested by Kazakh president Nursultan Nazarbayev in 1994, which would create a non-ideological Eurasian Union to maintain a high level of economic integration and aid the countries in their transition to a market economy.[6] Russia showed almost no reaction to NATO's Partnership for Peace, which integrated the former Soviet republics, and remained content with its observer status in the Central Asian Union (Kazakhstan, Kyrgyzstan, and Uzbekistan). Bilateral trade with Central Asia collapsed: in 1993 it was only one-tenth of its 1991 level (about US$6 billion compared to 60 billion two years previous) and remained unchanged until 1995.[7]

Moscow focused almost exclusively on strategic stakes: negotiating the rental of the Baikonur Cosmodrome in Kazakhstan; exerting pressure on the new states to make them join the CIS Collective Security Treaty; maintaining Russian troops in Kyrgyzstan, Tajikistan, and Turkmenistan along the former international Soviet borders with China, Afghanistan, and Iran; and involving the Russian army's 201st motorized division in Tajikistan during the civil war.[8] A decree issued in September 1995 declared the CIS an "area of vital interest," and Russia hoped to have others recognize what it deemed as its right to oversee the region.[9] The human and cultural potential created by the Soviet regime, however, remained largely ignored. Moscow seemed unwilling to go about defending the Russian minority in Central Asia, which numbered close to ten million people at the last Soviet census of 1989,[10] nor to maintain the Russophone infrastructures (schools, universities, media) that were crucial for long-term influence.[11] Moscow's foreign policy, both chaotic and contradictory, appeared bound to "lose" Central Asia,[12] while setting up much more elaborate mechanisms of influence in post-Soviet fractious areas such as Latvia, Estonia, the Crimea, Transnistria, South Ossetia, and Abkhazia.

The Russian domestic context changed rapidly and led to the birth of a second phase of Russian foreign policy in the second half of the 1990s. Only a few years after the collapse of the Soviet Union, assessments of the country could only be critical, even among liberals. The Russian state was weak and without resources, was unable to adequately finance an army, exerted a diminished influence on the international scene, and had no clearly defined geopolitical interests.[13] In 1996, Boris Yeltsin tried to revive Russia's great power status and replaced the foreign affairs minister at the time, Andrei Kozyrev, with Evgenii Primakov, a prominent Soviet diplomat whose political ascension to the post of prime minister (1998–1999) symbolized the Kremlin's political turnaround.[14] Upon assuming office, Primakov called for a balanced policy to continue the development of good neighborly relations with the West, in particular with the European Union, while simultaneously stressing cooperation with Asian countries, first and foremost China and India.[15] He said what the majority of the elite dared not declare publicly: to be recognized as a great power, Russia must resume its role as the linchpin of post-Soviet space. The country, however, no longer had the means to stage its "return." As the major enterprises had been largely privatized, the state lacked finances; the country was having difficulties in exiting the post-Soviet economic crisis—heightened by the stock market crash of summer 1998—and the elite were unable to resolve domestic problems linked to the war in Chechnya.[16] Lastly, the Kremlin remained divided over the final objectives of the new foreign policy: while the idea of returning to the status of a great power had almost unanimous support, many thought that Moscow could do so without having to reinvest in Central Asia.[17]

The Kremlin soon began to exhibit more concern with the deterioration of the situation on its southern borders. Despite the peace accords of 1997, which put an end to the civil war in Tajikistan, Central Asia seemed under increasing threat. After the defeat of the Northern Alliance in 1996, Kabul fell under the control of the Taliban, drug trafficking grew in the region, and in 1999 and 2000 Uzbekistan and Kyrgyzstan were in direct danger from the Islamic Movement of Uzbekistan.[18] Russia, however, had relinquished control of the former external borders of the Soviet Union. In 1999, the Russian army ceded management operations along the borders with China, Afghanistan, and Iran to the national armies of Kyrgyzstan and Turkmenistan, remaining present only in Tajikistan, which it left in 2005.[19] In the economic sphere, trade relations between Moscow and the Central Asian states dropped to an all-time low, collapsing to less than US$4 billion in 1999. Although trade levels were actually higher than this, the dearth of liquidities obliged the two sides to operate according to a barter system, which remained uncounted in official statistics.[20] Moscow also tried to reenter the oil sector in Kazakhstan and the gas sector in Turkmenistan, and did not hesitate to use the "energy weapon," for example by blocking transit across its territory. This forced the Central Asian states to establish strategies to bypass it: Astana managed this with China, and Ashgabat with Iran.

Despite resolute discourse on its natural role in post-Soviet space, at the end of the 1990s the former "elder brother" had no means to pursue its policies. On the institutional level, Russia could only operate bilaterally, thanks to signing friendship and cooperation treaties with the Central Asian states, but could not pursue any effective multilateral policies. The lack of financing allocated by member countries to the CIS confirmed the absence of any collective political will. The Kremlin's room to maneuver in its former territory was drastically reduced. On the other hand, NATO (the North Atlantic Treaty Organization) was particularly active in the region; the United States was advancing its pawns by supporting the birth of an anti-Russian axis called GUAM (Georgia-Ukraine-Armenia-Moldova)], and by financing the Baku-Tbilisi-Ceyhan (BTC) oil pipeline; the European Union saw its destiny as eastward enlargement through the integration of the Baltic states; and Ukraine and Georgia presented themselves as the bridgeheads of Western influence in their confrontation with Russia. Meanwhile, the new actors—the United States, European countries, China, Turkey, Iran, and Japan—firmly established themselves in Central Asia and thwarted all attempts made by Russian companies to set up monopolies in the region, with the partial exception of hydrocarbons.[21]

The third phase of Russian foreign policy began with Vladimir Putin's ascension to power. In November and December 1999, the Kremlin's new strongman visited Tajikistan and Uzbekistan, and revisited Uzbekistan, as well as Turkmenistan, in May 2000. In June of the same year, he laid out the major lines of his foreign policy, giving priority to the CIS[22] and to the development of active diplomacy vis-à-vis major Asian partners such as India, Iran, and China. Relations with the two Central Asian countries most averse to Russian influence, Turkmenistan and Uzbekistan, improved slowly, and observers viewed Putin's visit to the two capitals as a diplomatic success.[23] The three other states, which sought to pursue balanced policies between Russia and the West, also showed their receptiveness to the message of assertiveness coming from the Kremlin. The events of September 11, 2001, gave Moscow increased resolve in its will to reengage in Central Asia. The US military presence at Karshi-Khanabad in Uzbekistan and Manas in Kyrgyzstan, although approved by Putin, pushed the Kremlin to increase its ambitions in the region.[24]

Within a few years, Russia had once again become the leading bilateral partner of Kazakhstan, Kyrgyzstan, and Tajikistan. At the multilateral level it leads both the Eurasian Economic Community (EurAsEc),[25] and the Collective Security Treaty Organization (CSTO).[26] Only Turkmenistan has refused to join the two institutions; Uzbekistan remains a reticent member of the first, and withdrawn from the second in 2012. The Kremlin has attested its unfailing support for all the Central Asian regimes whose authoritarianism has contributed to a loosening of ties with the United States and the European Union, as well as to a decreasing involvement of international donors. The struggle against so-called Islamic terrorism was a powerful factor: the leitmotiv of the "war against terror" made it possible to weave new links between leadership circles and to claim that the Central Asian states and Russia were both victims of internationalized Jihadism. Central Asia supported Russia in its war in Chechnya in exchange for the Kremlin's support for its fight against the Islamic Movement of Uzbekistan, the Hizb ut-Tahrir, as well as the secular political opposition. The "color revolutions" in Georgia in 2003, in Ukraine in 2004, and in Kyrgyzstan in 2005, accelerated Central Asian feelings of encirclement by the United States and thus fostered rapprochement with Moscow. Presidents Nursultan Nazarbayev, Islam Karimov, and Emomali Rahmon felt they were potential targets and sought support from the Kremlin.[27] The Russian-Central Asian alliance reached its apogee during the Uzbek authorities' repression of the Andijan insurrection of May 13, 2005. While Western countries condemned the regime for its immoderate use of force and rejected the official theory of an Islamist coup d'état, Russia (and China) came unhesitatingly to the rescue of Islam Karimov.[28]

Nonetheless, despite undeniable success during Putin's first two presidential terms, Russia's power of persuasion in Central Asia remains limited.[29] Many factors have acted as a reminder that Russia's preeminent positions are far from guaranteed, even in seemingly Russophile countries like Kazakhstan. In 2008, for example, Moscow's recognition of the independence of South Ossetia and Abkhazia surprised Central Asian leaders, who refused to undermine the inviolability of borders inherited from the Soviet Union.[30] The notion of "friendly regimes," often used to describe political relations between the Russian regime and its Central Asian counterparts, is paradoxical: Tashkent and Ashgabat are the most suspicious of Moscow's reassertion of influence, but their lack of openness to foreign influences and their authoritarian orientations also serve Russian interests. Tajikistan is increasingly resistant to Russia's presence, but cannot do without the economic and security aid Moscow provides. For its part, Bishkek is able to advance pro-Western arguments (for instance after the establishment of parliamentary regime in 2010), while also remaining pro-Russian. The Kazakh elites are increasingly autonomous in relation to Russia, and although Nursultan Nazarbayev remains a major supporter of the Kremlin's strategies for regional integration, Kazakhstan is seeking to attain geopolitical autonomy and an equal status with Russia.

Western pundits tend to overestimate Moscow's ability to direct the orientation of the Central Asian states. The trend toward increasingly authoritarian forms of governance, although evidently influenced by the regional environment, cannot be explained by Russian leadership. It cannot be assumed that Kazakhstan, Tajikistan, Turkmenistan, and Uzbekistan have a spontaneous democratic character but have become "victims" of Russian—and Chinese—authoritarian pressures. Domestic issues and local political culture drive Central Asia's choices in terms of political regimes.[31] The political compatibility between the Kremlin and its Central Asian counterparts is therefore not a permanent given but an axis of convenience. Regime changes in one or another of the republics or in Moscow could put a rapid end to the circumstantial consensus of post-Soviet authoritarianism.[32]

Russia's Obsession with Security on Its Southern Borders

Russia's chief reason for involvement in Central Asia is security. Challenges are multiple, as any destabilization in the weakest (Kyrgyzstan, Tajikistan) or the most unpredictable (Uzbekistan) states could have immediate repercussions in Russia: Islamist infiltration in the Volga-Ural region and the North Caucasus; an increase in already considerable inflow of drugs reaching the Russian population; a loss of control over the export networks of hydrocarbons, uranium mines, strategic sites in the military-industrial complex, and electrical power stations; a drop in trade exchanges; or an uncontrollable surge of migrants, in particular refugees. That these repercussions are often overestimated is of little importance: myths and phobias are a part of decision-making processes. Although Kazakhstan is the only Central Asian state that shares borders with Russia, Moscow sees the security of its southern borders as a question of domestic security borne out not of "imperialism," but of pragmatism. The 7,000 kilometers of Russian-Kazakh border, in the heart of the steppes, are nearly impossible to secure, and clandestine flows are better controlled downstream along the former southern border of the Soviet Union. Moscow therefore thinks of Central Asia as a buffer zone with a "South" increasingly subjected to strategic uncertainty and non-traditional threats.

Russia's perceptions of its global security evolved throughout the first decade of the twenty-first century, and the new Concept of National Security for 2020, adopted in May 2009, advances more nuanced and subtle arguments, reflecting changes within the international security environment.[33] It defines security more broadly, and includes energy security, soft security challenges, the environment, health, education, migrations, technologies, living standards, and so on. The definition of enemies and dangers has also changed.[34] Even if some prisms inherited from the Cold War still shape Russian perceptions, today Moscow tries to take into account two categories of danger: non-traditional threats (failing states, drug-trafficking, migration, human security), and strategic uncertainties (potential rapid changes in the domestic or international orientation of its neighbors). Within this prism, the West is no longer really a danger; China is, in terms of strategic uncertainty, while the "South" (consisting of the new federal district of the North Caucasus, and of Transcaucasia, Central Asia, Iran, and Afghanistan) combines both non-traditional threats and strategic uncertainty. The

"South" is the zone where overlapping domestic and foreign stakes are strongest, where the borders are least stable, and where both conventional and non-conventional security are at play.

To address these challenges, Russia has positioned itself as a reliable partner of the Central Asian governments, ready to collaborate with all of them, even Tashkent and Ashgabat, when called for. Of the CIS institutions, only the Anti-Terrorist Center (ATC) is properly functional, inasmuch as it continues to provide Central Asian security services with training and offers joint exercises called "South Anti-Terror," administered by the Russian FSB (the former KGB, the Federal Security Service). Russian-Central Asian multilateral collaborations are mainly geared toward the CSTO.[35] Apart from its role in the elaboration of collective strategies to combat terrorism, transnational dangers, and drug trafficking, the CSTO is the only regional institution with a genuine military dimension.[36] The Collective Rapid Deployment Force (CRDF) for Central Asia is comprised of Kazakh, Kyrgyz, Russian, and Tajik units, and totals around 4,000 men. It is the only organization with trained armed forces capable of intervening in real time and could be upgraded to a force of 20,000 soldiers.[37] Joint military exercises, carried out annually in one of the member countries, simulate terrorist attacks and anti-narcotics operations, and are a growing axis of cooperation. Since 2005, the CSTO has also revived cooperation between the Russian and Central Asian military industrial complexes, and allows for the preferential sale of Russian military material to Central Asian states at domestic market prices.

However, bilateralism dominates in the domain of security. Since the early 1990s, Russia has held joint military exercises with Kazakhstan, Kyrgyzstan, and Tajikistan; exercises with Uzbekistan only began in 2005 and rapidly ceased, and none have been organized with the Turkmen army. Although there are no longer any Russian troops in Turkmenistan, Kyrgyzstan, or Tajikistan, bilateral consultations are still conducted on border securitization with Bishkek and Dushanbe. In addition, joint operations are organized that focus on drug-trafficking and illegal migrations, such as those undertaken with Kazakhstan on the Caspian Sea and along the length of the Chinese border. The FSB border service plays an advisory role and provides technical assistance in Kyrgyzstan and Tajikistan. Russian troops, who helped both countries create their own air defense systems in the 1990s, continue to train their air force personnel.[38] The Soviet legacy has also enabled Moscow to help train a majority of Central Asian military personnel.[39] Several hundred high-level Central Asian officers have studied at Russian military academies, which serve as models for the Central Asian military schools, and the two Russian military bases in Kyrgyzstan and Tajikistan offer specialized onsite training.[40]

The Russian authorities have succeeded in keeping or in regaining a number of military and research facilities in Kazakhstan, Kyrgyzstan, and Tajikistan.[41] Kazakhstan was the site of some of the most important military installations in the Soviet Union, and its territory constitutes a major element of the Russian defense system. Since the 1990s, Astana has allowed Russia the use of several firing ranges in exchange for military materiel, specialized maintenance, and officer training. Moscow rents the Baikonur space complex from Astana (70 percent of Russian rocket launches occur there), but also weapons and missile launch centers in the Atyrau and Western Kazakhstan regions. In Kyrgyzstan, under a CSTO agreement, Russia has the Kant base at its disposal, which opened in 2003 and can accommodate close to 800 men, as well as the Russian army's anti-submarine weapons test zone at Karakol on the shores of Lake Issyk Kul. In addition, plans were made in 2010 to open a small center in the Osh region under the control of the FSB in order to monitor both drug trafficking and Islamist movements.[42] Upon the signing of a 2004 treaty, Moscow opened its largest military base after Sevastopol outside the Federation's borders in Tajikistan, where about 7,000 troops are deployed.[43] Russia has been allowed to deploy other troop units at Kurgan-Tyube and Kulyab, to occupy the Ayni Airforce Base close to Dushanbe, which hosts Russian helicopter squadrons, and to use the Okno space surveillance center, home to an electronic and optic monitoring station of the Russian space forces. A 30-year lease of the base between both countries was signed in 2012. Russia does not have any military facilities in either Turkmenistan or Uzbekistan, but would like Tashkent to grant it access to the Ust-Yurt Plateau for ballistic missile tests.

Since the beginning of the twenty-first century, Russia has supplied the Central Asian states with large quantities of military equipment, either by selling it at preferential prices, notably to Kazakhstan and Uzbekistan (the only two states in the region able to finance their armies), or by supplying the material in return for the rental of sites (Kyrgyzstan and Tajikistan). Russia therefore equips the Central Asian armies with weapons, munitions, night-vision apparatus, planes, helicopters, anti-missile defense systems, and tanks, as well as ships for the Kazakh Caspian Fleet. It also provides after-sales service and repairs. Since 2005, Moscow's influence has further been enhanced by the revival of the Central Asia military-industrial complex.[44]

However this cooperation in hard security does not prepare Moscow to counter non-traditional threats coming from the "South." The Central Asian regimes consider soft security mechanisms to be a core element of their state sovereignty, and are reluctant to acquiesce to foreign interference; however, their level of preparedness is low and measures are rendered ineffective by the rampant corruption of law enforcement agencies. Yet Central Asia's soft security is crucial for Russia, especially as it considers itself a victim of the drug trafficking from Afghanistan. The Russian authorities are no longer hiding their intent to mercilessly oppose what they label "narco-aggression."[45] The country does have the unenviable status of being the world's leading consumer of heroin, using seventy tons per year, or around 21 percent of world consumption, according to the United Nations Office on Drugs and Crime (UNODC).[46] Russia has between four and six million drug users, mainly young people in both urban and rural areas, according to these calculations; this figure has increased by a factor of more than nine over the last decade.[47] The federal anti-drug agency estimates that each year 10,000 Russians die from overdoses and that another 70,000 deaths are drug-related.[48] Moreover, this consumption has a major effect on the spread of HIV/AIDS.[49] This situation is a part of a more general debate on the country's demographic crisis and the concomitant absence of efficient state policy to deal with poor public health, in particular male mortality from violent deaths.[50]

Since 2009, it appears that a fourth and new phase of Russian influence in Central Asia has been taking shape. A number of factors have weakened the Central Asian states, including the 2008 economic crisis; an increase in allegedly Islamist incursions in the Tajik Rasht Valley in 2009 and 2010; the ousting of Kurmanbek Bakiyev in Kyrgyzstan and interethnic riots in Osh in 2010; and the Arab Spring in 2011, all of which have necessitated a re-reading of the Central Asian situation. At least officially, the Kremlin does not advocate interference in the internal affairs of foreign countries; however, Russian experts are more and more cognizant of the fact that the absence of development prospects in Kyrgyzstan, Tajikistan, and Uzbekistan shapes global insecurity, and may have a destabilizing impact. In Moscow, some officials are starting discreetly to encourage Central Asian governments to undertake reforms for fear that Egyptian-type protests will occur there as the result of a poisonous "cocktail" of political repression, social and economic depression, and the capturing of their country's riches by a small elite. Russian Deputy Minister of Foreign Affairs Grigory Karasin expressed that very fear at a hearing devoted to Central Asian problems at the Duma in April 2011.[51] Drastically reshaping Russia's levers of influence in preparation for both the Western withdrawal from Afghanistan in 2014,[52] and the forthcoming possible crisis in Central Asia is becoming Moscow's main objective.

Russia's Economic Involvement: Hydrocarbons and Integrated Space

The second most important factor motivating Russian influence in the region is the economy. Although in the 1990s the major Russian companies pursued their own policies, which were often not consonant with those of the Kremlin, under Putin state interests and those of major firms have been reunified. This seems to have provided Russia with a single solution for its multiple objectives: first, to maintain political influence over the Central Asian regimes through the control of resources; second, to continue to collect considerable transit revenues from these landlocked countries; third, to slow down the emergence of competing export routes. Russia has therefore regained an important, but no longer monopolistic, economic position in Central Asia at the beginning of the twenty-first century.[53] Russian-Central Asian trade tripled between 2003 and 2007, skyrocketing from US$7 to US$21 billion.[54] In 2010, these commercial exchanges stood at almost US$14 billion, positioning Russia as the region's third-largest trading partner behind China and the European Union, although it remains first in imports for Kazakhstan and Turkmenistan, and first in exports for Kyrgyzstan.

More so than other international actors, Russia plays a structuring role in the development of the Central Asian hydrocarbon market. Its activities were initially limited to Kazakhstan, but around 2000, Gazprom also began to make significant inroads into Uzbekistan and Turkmenistan, and, since 2005, into Kyrgyzstan and Tajikistan as well. Gazprom, Rosneft, and Lukoil are involved in numerous energy projects, mainly in Kazakhstan and Uzbekistan: geological exploration; exploitation

Table 1.1

Russia's Place in Imports, Exports, and the Trade Total of Central Asian States in 2010 (in millions of US$)

	Imports	Rank	Exports	Rank	Total trade	Rank
Kazakhstan	5,399.2 (18.7%)	3	2,268.5 (4.9%)	3	7,667.7 (10.3%)	3
Kyrgyzstan	1,032.3 (15%)	2	342.2 (32.1%)	1	1,374.6 (17.3%)	2
Tajikistan	823.9 (32.2%)	1	97.9 (8.5%)	3	921.9 (24.9%)	1
Turkmenistan	765 (14.2%)	3	129.8 (4%)	8	894.9 (10.3%)	4
Uzbekistan	1,761.5 (21.4%)	1	1,334.7 (24.1%)	1	3,096.3 (22.5%)	1

Source: 2011 European Commission statistics, http://ec.europa.eu/trade/creating-opportunities/bilateral-relations/countries-and-regions/.

of deposits; construction or renovation of pipelines, refineries or plants; and sale of petroleum derivatives.[55] Always on the lookout for possibilities to export resources and collect transit rights, Russia contributes to the increase in export levels of Central Asian resources and to a reduction of internal trade among the five states.[56] It also reinforces the region's role as an exporter of primary resources by neglecting to develop Central Asia's hydrocarbon refining capacity, especially the manufacture of products with high added value, which is an inefficient trade pattern.[57] For two decades, Russia's energy strategies were based on the idea that Central Asia was a captive market. While the major oil and gas fields in western Siberia are being depleted, both Gazprom and Rosneft have delayed the large investments needed to exploit new Arctic and Siberian deposits, and preferred to meet growing European demand with exports from Central Asia.[58] This logic is no longer functional. The Central Asian markets are decreasingly captive; new export routes have been built and prices no longer allow Gazprom to reap substantial profits.

Despite the predominance of the energy issue, Russia's trade with Central Asia involves other important sectors of cooperation: uranium (reinforcement of nuclear integration between Moscow and Astana, creation of joint ventures for extraction and the building of reactors); electricity (the maintenance of the Soviet grid facilitates common projects); hydroelectricity (Russia finances Sangtuda in Tajikistan and Kambarata in Kyrgyzstan); construction (mainly in Kazakhstan); telecommunications (above all mobile telecommunications); transport (in particular freight services) and railways (but not the automobile market); banks (the Russo-Kazakh partnerships are multiplying); the military-industrial complex; and, lastly, certain agribusiness sectors (Russia and Kazakhstan are strengthening their cooperation in cereal production). Russia therefore remains a dominant economic actor in mineral resources, which are important for the heavy industry sector, and in infrastructure—the old Soviet specializations—but is a relatively limited and uncompetitive actor in terms of small and mid-size companies, new technologies, and the like. This stratification reflects a more general one in the Russian economy, which continues to be rent-seeking and is finding it hard to diversify. But it can also be explained by the equally restrictive state of the Central Asian economies, in which small and mid-size enterprises and new technologies struggle to find a place. The region's economies are destined to serve above all as transit zones for Sino-Russian-European trade, hence the emphasis on infrastructure and freight-related services.

Moscow indeed has lost its control over the Central Asian economies, especially with the rise of China as a major trading partner of the region. Only control over some hydrocarbons exports and strategic partnerships, for example in the civilian nuclear sector, seems set to continue over the long term. Moscow's strategy is therefore to rejuvenate the Soviet legacy by promoting with some republics an integrated space in terms of transport, electricity, and communications. Deemed to be "integrating" factors par excellence, these may slow down the economic dissociation between Russia and Central Asia as a result of Chinese pressure.[59] This has been a priority strategy since 2008. The Eurasian Economic Community has led to the simplification of customs procedures with Kazakhstan, Kyrgyzstan, and Tajikistan. Since 2010, the Russia-Belarus-Kazakhstan Custom Union has enabled Russia to maintain common dynamics in terms of trade. In July 2011, the three member states removed their customs borders and in January 2012, created a common market, the Eurasian Economic Space, of 170 million people.

The Customs Union does not actually slow China's progress, and will be partially transformed after accession of Russia and Kazakhstan to the World Trade Organization.[60] Nevertheless, the political message of regional integration has been clearly relayed. Putin's statements in October 2011, in favor of creating a new Eurasian Union, have further confirmed this. For the first time, the Kremlin is openly mulling the idea of creating a few joint, supranational mechanisms in specific areas—mainly the economic and financial domains, but also potentially the strategic sector—that would guarantee an integrative dynamic between Russia and some of its closest CIS neighbors: Kazakhstan, Belarus, potentially Kyrgyzstan and Tajikistan, perhaps Armenia, while Ukraine is increasingly targeted.[61]

Prospects for Russia's Long-Term Success in Central Asia

Russia is a power unlike any other in Central Asia: it is the region's former colonizer, a role that started in the nineteenth century (and as early as the eighteenth for some of the northern parts of Kazakhstan), and was the driver of Soviet political, social, and cultural engineering for seventy years. This legacy has its positive and negative aspects. It has been positive insofar as it has involved a long period of Russo-Central Asian collaboration that gave rise to a largely shared feeling of belonging to the same "civilization," sometimes named post-Soviet, or Eurasian; it has been negative insofar as it has accrued all the political resentment and cultural misinterpretation of the colonizer-colonized relationship. Russian-Central Asian relations are therefore complex, with each actor having a highly emotional perception of its relation to the other.[62]

People-to-people relation is a key component of Russia's influence. The Central Asian political and intellectual elite were educated either in Moscow or in Leningrad; prior to 1991 the Russian and Central Asian military and secret service personnel all belonged to the same bureaucratic entity; the patronage strategies of decision-making circles were formed in the same Soviet mold, and still operate according to very similar patterns. On the cultural level, the advantage is also clearly in Russia's favor. The most spoken language in the region is still Russian, which enjoys an official status in three states: Kyrgyzstan, which is officially bilingual, and Kazakhstan and Tajikistan, where Russian is a designated language of interethnic communication.[63] For the moment, English has not succeeded in affecting the predominance of Russian, and still less have Turkish, Arabic, or Chinese. Russian culture remains very present, in particular through cable television channels, pop music, fashions, and books. Labor migration also reinforces Russian's influence, enabling it to recover a certain cultural and linguistic sway in the region and provide a new pole of development for Central Asian societies. At least five million Tajiks, Kyrgyz, and Uzbeks now work seasonally in Russia, thereby re-creating, in all their complexity, economic and social relations with the former metropole.[64] In part, therefore, Central Asian societies continue to view the world through the Russian prism, regarded as a more familiar "West" than the more foreign Western Europe or the United States.

However, a form of post-colonial condescension still profoundly marks the Russian view of Central Asia. Since the nineteenth century, Russian elites have been much more concerned with ensuring the loyalty of the western margins of the empire, in particular of Ukraine, than with the eastern margins. The eastern areas, considered to be economically and culturally backward, were presented as an additional weight that Russia had shouldered, not as a culturally important region that it had proudly conquered. At the same time, Russia's imperial legitimacy relied directly on maintaining rule over Central Asia. The glorification of the land's vastness, of expansion into Asia, of the "Great Game" with the British empire, the idea of being the meeting point of the Christian and Muslim worlds—all these notions were made possible by the colonization of the steppes and of Turkistan. This asymmetrical relationship is indicative of the instrumental but key role that Central Asia plays in Russian identity-building. Even the Eurasianist movement is the same in this regard, though it is considered the most favorable avenue to a rapprochement with Asia.[65]

In the contemporary Russian debates about maintaining influence in Central Asia, the region is conceived of as part of its de jure sphere of influence. Political submission and economic control are desired, but not social proximity, since this provokes xenophobia. Central Asia is therefore asked to accept Russia's right to oversee it and to maintain the shared major economic axes in terms of energy and infrastructure, but not to mingle with Russian society through migration. In Russian public opinion, Central Asia is usually associated with notions of Islamism, terrorism, the mafia, and criminality, while positive references emphasizing the historical and cultural ties to Central Asian peoples are rare.[66] The region is said to have only three choices: remain in Russia's fold, sink into a state of chronic instability—whether due to Islamism or the criminalization of the state by mafia networks—or fall under Chinese domination. Russian elites believe that even if criticized by the Central Asians countries, they will choose Moscow for lack of better alternatives. This generalized disdain affects Russian academic and expert knowledge of Central Asia, which is now minimal. At the moment, therefore, Russia has almost no long-term vision of the relations it would like to entertain with its "South," nor any strategy to propose that would offer Central Asia any status other than that of Moscow's geographical and political appendix. Aware of Russia's inability to formulate a coherent plan for its partnership with the region, the Central Asian elites denounce it for simply riding on the inertia of its historical legacy, without any prospect of innovation, but the majority of them continue to see Moscow as a source of stability for all of Eurasia.

Moreover, Russia has been slow to prepare for the changes of generation that are taking shape in Central Asia. Once the Soviet generations have disappeared, it is uncertain what relations with Moscow will look like, or whether Moscow has the means to counter the influence of the West, China, or Islam on the young generations. On paper, Russia does have arguments in its favor. Although the young political generations educated outside the CIS, in particular in Kazakhstan or in Kyrgyzstan, may have a more critical view of Russia, this does not necessarily translate into power for Russophobic circles. On the contrary, a more peaceful reading of the Soviet past, including the idea that Russia remains a path to Europeanness and that there exists a post-Soviet or Eurasian "civilization," are all arguments with widespread currency among the young generations of the Central Asian middle and upper classes. Despite these assets, Moscow's development of its soft power has been slow. The existence of a Russophone space is celebrated in official narratives as one that unifies Central Asia and Russia, but in practice the budget that Moscow allocates to the maintenance of Russian language schools and universities, as well as to the development of a Russian-speaking media, is minimal.[67] Here again, the Kremlin is resting too passively on its Soviet legacy.

Russia could preserve its key role in Central Asia, especially its soft power influence, were it to attempt to do so. That would include such steps as complying with the Central Asian states' wishes for investments in economic sectors other than those of hydrocarbons; continuing to train Central Asian political and military cadres and to prepare them to face soft security challenges; promoting the Russian language, culture, and education among the local populations; creating a more secure working environment for the millions of Central Asian migrants settled in Russia; and forming lobbies among the younger generations who stand to inherit the reins of power. Future generations in Central Asia will have more mixed opinions on their international allies—pro-Western, pro-Chinese, pro-Turkish, and more nationalist and Islamic points of view will emerge. This will require that Moscow focus on increasing its networks of influence.

Measuring Russia's success, or lack thereof, in Central Asia is complex. Despite its "return" during the first decade of the twenty-first century, Moscow has well and truly lost the stranglehold it once had over the region. However, the Kremlin never actually envisaged recapturing its dominance or politically reintegrating the Central Asian states within the Russian Federation. Although Moscow wishes to remain Central Asia's main partner, it no longer envisions that its presence there will be exclusive.[68] The Kremlin has learned, sometimes to its detriment, to cooperate with or acquiesce to other external actors, as was shown by Vladimir Putin's acceptance of the installation of American military bases after September 11, and its cooperation with China within the Shanghai Cooperation Organization. It can therefore be concluded that Russia has succeeded in returning to the region, since it has again become a legitimate ally in a Central Asian market albeit one that is no longer monopolistic.

Russia is still the main power in Central Asia through its role as an interface with the West. It has thus been able to turn to its advantage—at least for the medium term—the continuity of processes of Soviet integration in economic infrastructure and institutional mechanisms, as well as the continued existence of people-to-people relations. Its co-optation of the local elite, its political legitimacy, and its role as a cultural mediator of Europeanness in Central Asia constitute elements of leverage. However, Moscow is not prepared for generational change in the region, has failed to adequately cultivate its soft power legitimacy, has no solution for the risks of instability that confront the region, and lacks a constructive image of Central Asia's future.

Moreover, Russia is in the process of becoming a power just like any other in Central Asia. First, its influence increasingly differs by country: it is expected to remain a key and global partner for Kazakhstan and Kyrgyzstan; a still important but more reluctant ally of Tajikistan; and to become a more minimal actor in Uzbekistan and Turkmenistan. As a regional entity, Central Asia no longer exists in Russian foreign policy. The multilateral structures—the CSTO, the Eurasian Economic Community, and the Customs Union—do not include the five states and are almost exclusively limited to Kazakhstan, Kyrgyzstan, and Tajikistan. Second, the Russian economic presence is in decline and faced with competition from China and the EU, and it specializes only in certain niches: hydrocarbons, uranium, electricity, and transport. Third, in the coming years, the Kremlin is likely to request growing involvement from other external actors and may develop a "Russia-first" strategy that limits its involvement in the region. The security management costs of Central Asia are high and Moscow no longer has the means or the willingness to go it alone. The official narrative of the "sphere of influence" has begun to be transformed into a narrative about a "sphere of responsibility."[69]

The success of Russian influence in Central Asia will also depend on how Russian society meets its own set of domestic challenges. Russian elites increasingly worry about non-traditional threats emanating from the "South" and Russia's domestic challenges, especially in the North Caucasus. These drastic changes in self-representation may push Russian society closer to the West—more likely Europe than the United States. They also propel Moscow to more seriously consider joint action with NATO in Central Asia or Afghanistan.[70] Moreover, labor migrations from Central Asia are changing the balance between the former metropole and its Near Abroad. These migrants are crucial to the dynamism of the Russian economy, but the authorities are at a loss at how to halt the rise of xenophobia and in fact, albeit somewhat ambiguously, have cultivated it by having opened the Pandora's box of Russian nationalism.[71] Demographic projections for 2025 show a Russia of about 130 million inhabitants and a Central Asia of about 75 million; by 2050, the gap will have narrowed further with a population of 116 million in Russia and 91 million in Central Asia. Though Central Asia is Russia's Near Abroad today, this post-imperial situation is bound to reverse thanks to migration patterns. Russia is compelled to become increasingly multicultural, and this element will be a key component of the evolving Russia-Central Asia relationship.

Notes

1. K. Syroezhkin, "Central Asia between the Gravitational Poles of Russia and China," in *Central Asia: A Gathering Storm?*, ed. B. Rumer (Armonk, NY: M.E. Sharpe, 2002), 169–207.

2. A. Tsygankov, *Russia's Foreign Policy: Change and Continuity in National Identity* (Lanham, MD: Rowman & Littlefield, 2006).

3. S. Crow, *The Making of Foreign Policy in Russia under Yeltsin* (Munich: RFE/RL Research Institute, 1993); P. Shearman, ed., *Russian Foreign Policy Since 1990* (Boulder, CO: Westview Press, 1995); F. S. Larrabee, *Foreign and Security Policy Decision-Making Under Yeltsin* (Washington, DC: Rand Corporation, 1997).

4. P. Reddaway and D. Glinski, *The Tragedy of Russia's Reforms: Market Bolshevism against Democracy* (Washington, DC: United States Institute of Peace Press, 2001).

5. M. Dabrowski, "The Reasons of the Collapse of the Ruble Zone," *CASE Network Studies and Analysis*, no. 58 (November 1995).

6. N. Nazarbaev, *Evraziiskii soiuz: Idei, praktika, perspektivy, 1994–1997* (Moscow: Fond sodeistviia razvitiia politicheskikh i sotsial'nykh nauk, 1997).

7. V. Paramonov and A. Strokov, *The Evolution of Russia's Central Asian Policy* (Shrivenham: Defence Academy of the United Kingdom, 2008), 4.

8. M. J. Orr, "The Russian Garrison in Tajikistan—201st Gachina Twice Red Banner Motor Rifle Division," *Conflict Studies Research Center Occasional Brief* 85 (2011).

9. On Russia's policy in the CIS, see N. J. Jackson, *Russian Foreign Policy and the CIS: Theories, Debates, and Actions* (London: Routledge, 2003).

10. S. Peyrouse, "The Russian Minority in Central Asia: Migration, Politics, and Language," *Kennan Occasional Papers* 297 (2008).

11. D. Laitin, *Identity in Formation: The Russian-Speaking Populations in the Near Abroad* (Ithaca: Cornell University Press, 1998); C. King and N. J. Melvin, eds., *Nations Abroad: Diaspora Politics and International Relations in the Former Soviet Union* (Boulder, CO: Westview Press, 1999).

12. D. Trenin, "Southern Watch: Russia's Policy in Central Asia," *Journal of International Affairs* 56, no. 2 (2003): 119–31.

13. On the revival of great power narratives in Russia in the 1990s, see F. Hill, *In Search of Great Russia: Elites, Ideas, Power, the State, and the Pre-Revolutionary Past in the New Russia, 1991–1996* (PhD diss., Harvard University, 1998).

14. On the main figures of this self-assertive narrative, see M. Laruelle, *In the Name of the Nation: Nationalism and Politics in Contemporary Russia* (New York: Palgrave Macmillan, 2009), 122–31.

15. P. Rangsimaporn, *Russia as an Aspiring Great Power in East Asia: Perceptions and Policies from Yeltsin to Putin* (New York: Palgrave Macmillan, 2009).

16. A. Lieven, *Chechnya: Tombstone of Russian Power* (New Haven, CO: Yale University Press, 1998).

17. More in Hill, *In Search of Great Russia.*

18. V. V. Naumkin, *Radical Islam in Central Asia: Between Pen and Rifle* (Lanham, MD: Rowman & Littlefield, 2005).

19. On the Russian military presence in Tajikistan, see M. Makhonina, *Voenno-politicheskoe sotrudnichestvo mezhdu Rossiei i Tadzhikistanom, 1993–1999* (Dushanbe: Akademiia Nauk, 1999).

20. Paramonov and Strokov, *The Evolution of Russia's Central Asian Policy,* 8.

21. D. Trenin, *The End of Eurasia: Russia on the Border between Geopolitics and Globalization* (Washington, DC: Carnegie Endowment for International Peace, 2002); Jackson, *Russian Foreign Policy.*

22. K. Crane, D.J. Peterson, and O. Oliker, "Russian Investment in the Commonwealth of Independent States," *Eurasian Geography and Economics* 46, no. 6 (2005): 405–44.

23. L. Jonson, *Vladimir Putin and Central Asia: The Shaping of Russian Foreign Policy* (London: I.B. Tauris, 2004); J. Dunlop, "Reintegrating 'Post-Soviet Space,'" *Journal of Democracy* 11, no. 3 (2000): 39–47.

24. B. Lo, *Vladimir Putin and the Evolution of Russian Foreign Policy: Reality, Illusion and Mythmaking* (London: Royal Institute of International Affairs, 2003); B. Nygren, *The Rebuilding of Greater Russia: Putin's Foreign Policy Towards the CIS Countries* (London: Routledge, 2007).

25. The EurAsEC was created in 2000. In October 2005 it was decided that Uzbekistan would join, but Tashkent has always been a reluctant participant and has never implemented the common legal system.

26. Founded in 2002, the CSTO includes Russia, four Central Asian states (Turkmenistan is not a member of it), Belarus, and Armenia.

27. J. L. Wilson, "The Legacy of the Color Revolutions for Russian Politics and Foreign Policy," *Problems of Post-Communism* 57, no. 2 (2010): 21–36.

28. F. Hill and K. Jones, "Fear of Democracy or Revolution: The Reaction to Andijan," *Washington Quarterly* 29, no. 3 (2006): 111–25; M. Brill Olcott and M. Barnett, "The Andijan Uprising, Akramiya and Akram Yuldashev," The Carnegie Endowment for International Peace, June 22, 2006, http://www.carnegieendowment.org/publications/index.cfm?fa=view&id=18453&prog=zru.

29. M. Kramer, "Russian Policy Toward the Commonwealth of Independent States: Recent Trends and Future Prospects," *Problems of Post-Communism* 55, no. 6 (2008): 3–19; D. Averre, "Russian Foreign Policy and the Global Political Environment," *Problems of Post-Communism* 55, no. 5 (2008): 28–39.

30. N. Swanström, "Shanghai Cooperation Organization and the Aftermath of the Russian Invasion of Georgia," *China and Eurasia Forum Quarterly* 6, no. 3 (2008): 3–7.

31. On the need to analyze political authoritarianism in the local culture, see for the Turkmen case, M. Denison, "The Art of the Impossible: Political Symbolism and the Creation of National Identity and Collective Memory in Post-Soviet Turkmenistan," *Europe-Asia Studies* 61, no. 7 (2009): 1167–87.

32. On political systems and regime changes, see H. E. Hale, "Regime Cycles. Democracy, Autocracy, and Revolution in Post-Soviet Eurasia," *World Politics* 58 (October): 133–65.

33. On the "National Security Strategy of the Russian Federation until 2020," see M. de Haas and H. Schröder, "Russia's National Security Strategy," *Russian Analytical Digest*, no. 62 (2009), http://www.isn.ethz.ch/isn/Digital-Library/Publications/Detail/?id=101960&lng=en.

34. J. W. Parker, "Russia's Revival: Ambitions, Limitations, and Opportunities for the United States," *INSS Strategic Perspectives*, no. 3 (2011).

35. A. Nikitin, "Post-Soviet Military-Political Integration: The Collective Security Treaty

Organization and Its Relations with the EU and NATO," *China and Eurasia Forum Quarterly* 5, no. 1 (2007): 35–44.

36. V. Paramonov and O. Stopovski, *Russia and Central Asia: Multilateral Security Cooperation* (Shrivenham: Defence Academy of the United Kingdom, 2008).

37. K. Marten, "Central Asia: Military Modernization and the Great Game," in *Strategic Asia 2005–06: Military Modernization in an Era of Uncertainty*, ed. A. J. Tellis and M. Wills (Seattle: National Bureau of Asian Research, 2005), 210–35.

38. More details in S. Peyrouse, "Russia-Central Asia: Advances and Shortcomings of the Military Partnership," in *Central Asian Security Trends: Views from Europe and Russia*, ed. S. Blank (Carlisle, PA: Strategic Studies Institute, US Army War College, 2011), 1–34.

39. E. Marat, "Soviet Military Legacy and Regional Security Cooperation in Central Asia," *The China and Eurasia Forum Quarterly* 5, no. 1 (2007): 83–114.

40. More details in S. Peyrouse, "The Central Asian Armies Facing the Challenge of Formation," *Journal of Power Institutions in Post-Soviet Societies*, no. 11 (2010): 2–16.

41. V. Paramonov and O. Stolpovski, *Russia and Central Asia: Bilateral Cooperation in the Defence Sector* (Shrivenham: Defence Academy of the United Kingdom, 2008).

42. E. Marat, "Russia Plans to Open Military Training Facility in Kyrgyzstan," *Eurasia Daily Monitor* 7, no. 166, September 16, 2010, http://www.jamestown.org/programs/edm/single/?tx_ttnews%5Btt_news%5D=36855&tx_ttnews%5BbackPid%5D=27&cHash=340e59e20d.

43. M. Klein, "Russia's Military Capabilities: 'Great Power' Ambitions and Reality," *SW Research Paper*, no. 12, October 2009, http://www.swp-berlin.org/fileadmin/contents/products/research_papers/2009_RP12_kle_ks.pdf.

44. For more details, see chapter 13.

45. S. Blagov, "Moscow Accuses West of 'Narco-Aggression'," *ISN Security Watch*, April 1, 2010, http://www.isn.ethz.ch/isn/Current-Affairs/Security-Watch/Detail/?lng=en&id=114434.

46. "World Drug Report 2010," Special Report, UN Office on Drugs and Crime, Vienna, 2010, 41, 45.

47. "Illicit Drug Trends in the Russian Federation," Special Report, UN Office on Drugs and Crime, Vienna, April 2008, 10.

48. "International Narcotics Control Strategy Report—2008," Special Report, US Department of State, March 2008, http://moscow.usembassy.gov/incsr2008.html.

49. "Illicit Drug Trends in the Russian Federation," 6.

50. N. Eberstadt, "Russia's Peacetime Demographic Crisis: Dimensions, Causes, Implications," Report of the National Bureau of Asian Research, May 2010.

51. "Stranam Tsentral'noi Azii nuzhny reformy, chtoby izbezhat' povtoreniia sobytii v Severnoi Afrike," *Regnum News Agency*, April 13, 2011.

52. M. Laruelle, "Beyond the Afghan Trauma: Russia's Return to Afghanistan," *Jamestown Occasional Paper* (August 2009); M. Laruelle, "Russia's Perceptions and Strategies in Afghanistan and their Consequences for NATO," *NATO Research Paper*, no. 69 (November 2011).

53. J. Perovic, "From Disengagement to Active Economic Competition: Russia's Return to the South Caucasus and Central Asia," *Demokratizatsiya. The Journal of Post-Soviet Democratization*, no. 1 (2005): 61–85.

54. V. Paramonov and A. Strokov, *Ekonomicheskoe prisutstvie Rossii i Kitaia v Tsentral'noi Azii* (Shrivenham: Defence Academy of the United Kingdom, 2007), 3–4.

55. More details in V. Paramonov and A. Strokov, *Russia-Central Asia: Existing and Potential Oil and Gas Trade* (Shrivenham: Defence Academy of the United Kingdom, 2008).

56. Ibid., 9.

57. V. Paramonov and A. Strokov, *Russian Oil and Gas Projects and Investments in Central Asia* (Shrivenham: Defence Academy of the United Kingdom, 2008).

58. More on Gazprom's strategies in J. Stern, *The Future of Russian Gas and Gazprom* (Oxford: Oxford University Press, 2005).

59. See Report of the Eurasian Development Bank, for example, E. Vinokurov, ed., "Obshchii

elektroenergeticheskii rynok SNG," 2008; E. Vinokurov, ed., "Mezhdunarodnye transportnye korridory EvrAsES," 2009; and the journal *Evraziiskaia ekonomicheskaia integratsiia*.

60. A. Aslund, "Why Doesn't Russia Join the WTO?," *Washington Quarterly* 33, no. 2 (2010): 49–63.

61. "The Eurasian Union Project," *Russian Analytical Digest*, no. 112, April 20, 2012.

62. More details in M. Laruelle, *Russian Policy on Central Asia and the Role of Russian Nationalism*, (Washington, DC: The Central Asia-Caucasus Institute Silk Road Studies Program, 2008).

63. The Russian language lost its official status in Turkmenistan and Uzbekistan in the early 1990s.

64. M. Laruelle, ed., *Migration and Social Upheaval as the Face of Globalization in Central Asia* (London: Brill, 2012).

65. On Kazakh Eurasianism, see M. Laruelle, *Russian Eurasianism: An Ideology of Empire* (Washington, DC: Woodrow Wilson Center Press/Johns Hopkins University Press, 2008), 171–88.

66. More in M. Laruelle, "Russian Policy on Central Asia."

67. J. Hedenskog and R. L. Larsson, *Russian Leverage on the CIS and the Baltic States* (Stockholm: Swedish Defense Research Agency, 2007).

68. J. Boonstra, "Russia and Central Asia: From Disinterest to Eager Leadership," *EU-Russia Centre Review*, no. 8 (2008): 70–79.

69. D. Trenin, "Russia's Spheres of Interest, not Influence," *Washington Quarterly* 32, no. 4 (2009): 3–22.

70. More in Laruelle, "Russia's Perceptions and Strategies."

71. More in Laruelle, *In the Name of the Nation*.

72. See Population Reference Bureau statistics, https://www.prb.org/pdf09/09wpds_eng.pdf.

2
China
The Newcomer That Made a Difference

At the collapse of the Soviet Union, China arrived in Central Asia with few assets. Prior to this date, the generally poor state of Sino-Soviet relations, as well as Moscow's control on the federated republics' access to the outside world had impeded bilateral relations with China. For newly independent Central Asian states, establishing direct relations with Beijing has therefore required overcoming the extremely negative clichés about China disseminated in Soviet propaganda, clichés that reinforced Central Asian societies' already long-standing apprehensions of their large neighbor.[1]

Chinese interests in Central Asia have been structured in phases. In the first half of the 1990s, Beijing's concern was primarily to sign demarcation treaties, demilitarize the borders, and prevent the strengthening of Uyghur separatism. In the second half of the 1990s and early years of the twenty-first century, it aimed to create a platform for discussion and mutual discovery, and to build a collective security framework through the Shanghai Cooperation Organization.[2] From 2000 to 2005, China moved to establish itself vigorously on the Central Asian market, mainly in hydrocarbons, extractive industries, infrastructures, and communications. Finally, since 2005, Beijing has been trying—albeit timidly—to establish ways to promote its language and culture and to train Central Asian elites according to the Chinese model. Despite China's initially negative overall image in Central Asia, the Middle Kingdom has succeeded in improving its reputation with soft-power diplomacy, and drastically impacted the economic and strategic situation in Central Asia. It has positioned itself as the second most influential external actor in the region, surpassing Russia in economic terms, but not in strategic or cultural terms.

Central Asia on the Chinese Global Radar

China's key foreign policy strategies are driven by factors far removed from Central Asia: they favor the stability of relations with the United States;[3] the improvement of still difficult relations with Japan and other Asian neighbors; the maintenance of China's right of influence on the North Korean issue; and the development of part-nership with the European Union and improved relations with India.[4] In this foreign policy framework, establishing relations with the new post-Soviet neighbors occupies a relatively minor place. Once the Soviet Union disappeared, China's primary objective was to maintain stability on its north and northwest border by addressing the issue of territorial boundaries with Russia, Kazakhstan, Kyrgyzstan, and Tajikistan, and seeking confirmation that they would respect the "One China" discourse.[5]

Yet in the Chinese perception of its environment, Central Asia is not only a part of the post-Soviet world, but also a part of West Asia. Beijing has positively reappraised continental routes to the detriment of maritime routes as part of a long-term historical evolution. Since the nineteenth century and its confrontation with Europe during the Opium Wars, China has concentrated on its maritime development. However, today's ruling elites know that domestic unity and stability, not to mention great power status, will require a rebalancing in favor of the continent.[6] Beijing is therefore increasingly looking toward building a privileged partnership with the Muslim world, continuing its already established strategic relationship with Pakistan. Despite their very distant relations throughout the twentieth century, China has been rapidly establishing itself in Afghanistan over the last few years.[7] Iran and Saudi Arabia are the main focal points for China in West Asia and the Gulf countries. But it is also advancing just as rapidly into the rest of the Arab world, in a bid to link up with its interests in Africa, in particular those in Sudan.[8]

Moreover, seen from Beijing Central Asia is unique in terms of its direct interference with domestic issues. The cultural, linguistic, and religious similarities between the Central Asian and Uyghur populations are not only important, but are also regularly revived. The Soviet Union was a key political and economic partner of Xinjiang in the 1930s and 1940s, before the founding of the People's Republic of China. The world as seen from the capital of Xinjiang, Urumqi, was oriented more toward Moscow than Beijing.[9] In the 1950s and 1960s, tens of thousands of Chinese citizens from Xinjiang emigrated to the Soviet Union; the Uyghur intelligentsia predominantly moved to Kazakhstan, and to a lesser extent to Kyrgyzstan and Russia itself.[10] In 1991, the sudden appearance on the international stage of five new states reinforced Chinese concerns about the claims of Uyghurs, that can be seen as the "sixth people of Central Asia," still waiting for independence.[11] Central Asia's ethnic contiguity with the Uyghur world is therefore perceived by Beijing more as a danger than as an opportunity; nonetheless the region is also conceived as a key engine for Xinjiang's current economic development and future stabilization. Beijing's "open door policy" and "Far West Development Program" have indeed helped to transform this landlocked region into a site of major subsoil resource exploitation and an outpost for the advancement of Chinese trade in Central Asia, Afghanistan, and Pakistan.[12] The Chinese policy is thus double-sided: it is repressive in political terms when it comes to pressuring the Central Asian governments to eliminate Uyghur associations, but constructive in economic terms when it comes to offering development aid on the principle that the improvement of living standards defuses political conflict.

Finally, China has come to see Central Asia as a partial solution to two concerns: securing continental energy supplies that are not subject to global geopolitical complications, especially in the Straits of Malacca; and appearing as a peacefully rising power able to play the card of multilateralism.[13] In Chinese energy strategies, Kazakhstan has emerged as an exporter of oil and uranium, and Turkmenistan as an exporter of gas, while Tajikistan and Kyrgyzstan have the potential, still unrealized, to export hydroelectricity and water. As for the second concern, through the Shanghai Cooperation Organization (SCO) China is experimenting with new platforms for discussion between powers and ensuring its "peaceful rise" (*heping jueqi*) in order to allay international concerns.[14] However, the importance of these elements should not be overestimated. In 2009, Central Asia represented less than 1 percent of the foreign trade of the People's Republic of China,[15] and will not prove an alternative to the Middle East in terms of hydrocarbon supplies. The SCO is a preferred venue for Beijing on the international stage, but its potential failure, or at least weakening, would have no direct consequences for China, as it can support other multilateral mechanisms to enhance its strategy of "peaceful rise."[16]

Even if energy and multilateralism remain important components of Chinese international positioning, Beijing's interest in Central Asia is primarily driven by the goal of domestic stability in Xinjiang, supported by good neighborly relations with governments, and the transformation of Xinjiang and Central Asia into areas of transit trade for the conquest of new markets.[17] Central Asia is therefore, paradoxically, fundamental in terms of domestic stability because of the Uyghur issue and marginal to the preoccupations of Chinese foreign policy as a whole. The region is not related to Japan, North Korea, or even to Taiwan since the Central Asian governments have not sought to challenge the "One China" policy. Central Asia also remains a secondary matter when compared to the issues of trade, currency, and human rights that occupy China-United States everyday negotiations. It seems thus that a gap does exist between Chinese global foreign policy strategies and its specific interest in Central Asia.[18]

Settled Border Disputes, but Contentious Issues Remain

With the collapse of the Soviet Union, China quickly became aware of the unique opportunities that arose with the new geopolitical situation, which was not however without new risks, particularly in relation to its north and northwest borders. In 1991, Chinese economic power was still a shadow of what it was to become two decades later, and the idea that the post-Soviet states were new markets to be conquered had yet to play a major role in Chinese strategies. Despite the satisfaction of seeing a superpower state like the Soviet Union disappear, and with it the historical Sino-Soviet conflict, Beijing was above all concerned about the impact of Central Asia's independence on the situation in Xinjiang, as well as about the risks of conflict linked to the non-delimitation of borders.

Although China immediately recognized the independence of the five states, it considered itself to have been a victim of the "unequal treaties" signed in the nineteenth century with European powers. According to Mao's rhetoric, these treaties excised some 1,500,000 km^2 gained from China to the advantage of tsarist and then Soviet Russia. Close to two-thirds of this surface area, or 910,000 km^2, were situated in Central Asia, while the other third under contest was in Siberia and the Far East.[19] Still under international sanctions after the violent repression in Tiananmen in June 1989, the Chinese authorities agreed to reduce their territorial claims to "only" 34,000 km², chiefly out of a desire to secure political allies in Central Asia.[20] They also agreed to receive only part of the area they requested and eventually signed border demarcation treaties with Kazakhstan in 1994 (some still-disputed zones were settled in 1999), with Kyrgyzstan in 1996 (here also, resolutions over disputed areas were settled in 1999), and with Tajikistan in 2002 (it was not until 2011 that the Tajik senate ratified transfer of 1 percent of territory to China[21]). Beijing has remained content with the cession of territories far smaller than those stipulated in its original claims, but the territorial areas it has acquired nonetheless do have a real economic and strategic viability, including access to rivers, subsoil resources, and high mountain passes.

Initially, the Chinese authorities, no longer having to negotiate with a powerful Soviet Union, had thought that their economic and geopolitical differential over the new states would make negotiations easier and procure them greater advantage—especially as the Central Asian governments were in search of partners and needed to find alternatives for the loss of Soviet subsidies. The negotiations, however, turned out to be more complicated than Beijing had expected. The Central Asian authorities, concerned about a future Chinese hegemony after more than a century of Russo-Soviet domination, would not yield easily. The pride of having recently acquired independence made them loath to cede any territory lightly, especially with Sinophobe feelings running high. The threat of international terrorism also impeded negotiations concerning border demilitarization. Although the negotiations were more difficult than Beijing expected, in comparison with its highly charged dispute with the Soviet regime, the ten-year period it took China to resolve its border disputes with Kazakhstan, Kyrgyzstan, and Tajikistan was relatively short and peaceful.

This cession of territory was viewed very negatively by part of the population, especially in Kyrgyzstan, where citizens accused Askar Akayev's regime of capitulating to China; it was also suspected that the Chinese would soon lay down additional claims.[22] Even today, Central Asian public opinion fears that this peaceful solution might only be provisional. Not one of the territorial treaties has been published, a fact that fuels speculation about the existence of possible secret clauses. Legal imprecision is rife and the question remains open as to whether the treaties are definitive or if they have been established only for a period of twenty years, as were some of the Sino-Russian treaties signed in early years of the twenty-first century.[23] The possibility of having to renegotiate some territories in the decades to come, when the power differential in favor of China will be even greater, is a legitimate public concern in Kazakhstan, Kyrgyzstan, and Tajikistan.

Furthermore, the Sino-Kazakh issue of cross-border river management still remains unresolved. Both of Kazakhstan's main rivers, the Ili and the Irtysh, have their sources in Xinjiang and in the Chinese Altay. In the framework of the "Far West development program," Beijing has increased its withdrawal of water upstream from both rivers. The Kara Irtysh-Karamay canal, constructed at the end of the 1990s, is set to divert between

10 and 40 percent of the river flow of the Irtysh, and draws about 450 million m³ per year, a figure that is likely to reach more than one billion m³ as it attains maximum capacity in 2020. For the Kazakh authorities, the withdrawals upstream spell economic and ecological disaster.[24] The Ili feeds the Kapchagay hydroelectric station, which supplies energy to the southern regions of the country. Important towns in the northeast, such as Karaganda, Semey, and Pavlodar are supplied with fresh water by the Irtysh, and the expansion of the capital, Astana, itself also requires increasingly substantial contributions of water. The ecological situation of Lake Balkhash, made precarious by the Kapchagay Reservoir, would also reach catastrophic proportions in case of further reductions to its water input. According to the UNDP (United Nations Development Programme), the decrease in contributions of water to Lake Balkhash could result in "an environmental tragedy comparable to the disaster of the Aral Sea."[25]

This question of cross-border rivers has been a topic of negotiations since Kazakhstan's independence. Murat Auezov, the first Kazakh ambassador to Beijing, as well as a famous Orientalist and opponent of President Nazarbayev, raised the problem but did not succeed in attracting the attention of the Chinese authorities. After many years of debate, in 2001, a framework agreement on the protection and the utilization of cross-border rivers was finally signed between the two countries. Nevertheless, the document remains vague, failing to mention any specific treatment for the Ili and the Irtysh, and only makes provision for a "reasoned" usage of common waters. Only in 2010 did both countries finally declare themselves ready to sign an agreement for the protection of both cross-border rivers.[26] In 2011 an intergovernmental agreement on the protection of water quality of cross-border rivers was signed, according to which both parties are strictly obligated to monitor water quality, but Beijing and Astana have failed to develop a unified position with respect to water intake limits. The problem has therefore yet to be properly addressed, and China's attitude reinforces already prevalent concerns within Kazakh society about its intentions in the region.[27]

Relations between Central Asia and China have not been built solely on the resolution of old border issues, but have also been concerned with managing the difficult Uyghur question. The Uyghur diaspora in Central Asia totals about 300,000, residing mainly in Kazakhstan and Kyrgyzstan.[28] In 1995, the Friendship Declaration between Kazakhstan and the People's Republic of China invoked the common struggle against separatism; both states pledged to make unwelcome on their soil forces opposed to the territorial integrity of the other. In 1996, as tensions became more acute in Xinjiang, Beijing compelled both the Kazakh and Kyrgyz governments to dissolve all the autonomist Uyghur associations.[29] Pressure seems to have been applied at the highest levels, on the presidents directly. Both governments liquidated the most radical associations and tried to infiltrate those that still existed by co-opting some local Uyghur leaders.[30] The Chinese secret services also reportedly entered Kazakh territory, more or less with the consent of the authorities, in order to track down Uyghur dissidents and expel them to China.

Beijing's reducing its territorial demands seems to have been directly linked to the settling of the Uyghur question in Kazakhstan and Kyrgyzstan. The Central Asian governments were therefore under no illusions as to Beijing's determination regarding the Uyghur issue and of course that of Taiwan, threatening to undermine the very foundation of the new states if they refused to adhere to the "One China" discourse or to solve the Uyghur problem in Beijing's favor. The Central Asian elites came out of this experience with a feeling that China could simultaneously show itself to be a pragmatic economic and diplomatic partner, ready to foster regional development, and also a neighbor with whom certain limits could not be crossed when dealing with sensitive domestic affairs.

China's Building of Strategic and Political Legitimacy

Once the border question was resolved and the Uyghur problem brought under control, China mounted a large economic offensive in Central Asia and invested in questions of security. Created in 1996, the Shanghai Group set itself the primary goal of demilitarizing the Sino-Soviet border zones and of facilitating the delimitation of border lines, but was quick to envisage creating a commitment to a more global vision of regional stability.[31] In 2001, the creation out of the Shanghai Group of the Shanghai Cooperation Organization, which included the membership of Uzbekistan, did not go unnoticed. It today brings together three-fifths of the Eurasian continent and a quarter of the world's population, and even more if one adds to this the states with observer status such as India, Pakistan, Iran, and Mongolia, who joined in 2004–2005. While some experts saw the SCO as a first mechanism of cooperation between countries with a long tradition of enmity, others saw it as the formation of a new anti-Western alliance between Beijing, Moscow, and four of the Central Asian states (Kazakhstan, Kyrgyzstan, Uzbekistan, and Tajikistan), and even as the expression of Sino-Russian hegemony at the heart of the Old World.[32]

The SCO has helped to ease long-standing tensions between the Russian and Chinese worlds by putting in place cooperative mechanisms for former Soviet states to engage with China. A cornerstone has been the establishment of a collective discourse on the common threats members of the organization face, based on the Chinese narrative of the "three evils" (*san gu shili*, also called the three extremisms, *sange jiduanzhuyi*) of fundamentalism, extremism, and secessionism. Its greatest successes in this regard have arguably been the signing of extradition treaty between member states and the formation of a terrorist "black list" containing some one thousand individuals and forty organizations.[33] Now that this threshold of development and institutionalization has been reached, the organization faces new challenges. Beyond the rhetoric of cooperation and the declarations of good intentions, it has experienced many difficulties. The member states often have very divergent interests, which may undermine the credibility of the organization in the mid- to long term. The extension of the SCO's competencies to the economic sector, for instance, initiated a debate among member states, revealing their often contradictory interests. Security and economic agendas now compete. They are obviously not mutually exclusive, but faced with limited budgets it is impossible to give priority to both. China is unambiguously the main driver of any sort of economic reorientation of the SCO; however, both Moscow and the Central Asian states fear that they will fall under Chinese economic domination and argue that free trade zones are only possible between countries that are on the same economic level. Only the energy sector, particularly oil, is recognized as an engine of regional cooperation, and distant sights have been set on an "energy club" that would wield influence on the international stage.[34] The SCO also serves as a multilateral framework for negotiations that are actually bilateral, for example in the case of Chinese loans to Tajikistan or Kyrgyzstan.

Even in its area of emphasis, security, the SCO is relatively inactive in practice and unable to compete with Russian influence. As it was not designed to be a supranational organization, implying the reduced sovereignty of its members, it does not have a defined military structure like the Collective Security Treaty Organization (CSTO). Neither is it a military defense alliance like NATO, nor does it seek to create multilateral military or police units. Despite the establishment in 2004 of an anti-terrorist center in Tashkent—the Regional Anti-Terrorist Structure (RATS), designed to develop common approaches to combat terrorist movements—any multilateral security dynamic remains embryonic.[35] Moreover, neither Russia nor China is inclined to disclose sensitive information about new technologies and their respective military complexes. While the two capitals do not officially see themselves as potential enemies, a history of distrust and a sense of inevitable rivalry dominate.[36] SCO activities largely remain at the stage of declarations of intent. A lack of coordination between member states is evident, the desire to exchange information is restrained, the financial resources are far too few, and the bureaucratic structures are too weak. Furthermore, the absence of actual common jurisdiction in most areas considerably weakens the scope for potential action.[37]

If the SCO is viewed as a mechanism to reinforce confidence, it has been a historical success. But if it is viewed as an organization that attempts to influence Central Asian security realities, for the time being at least, it appears to be no more than a "paper tiger," with the sole exception of the management of the Uyghur question.[38] The gap between the organization's narrative about the fight against non-traditional threats and its mechanisms to enable collective, or at least concerted, action is immense. The SCO does not provide any military guarantees in cases of domestic crisis. Nor does it offer any structure such as a "rapid intervention force" or a collective troop force like that of the Ministry of Emergency Situations in Russia, which would enable it to intervene in situations such as natural or industrial catastrophes, sudden population displacements, refugee crises, and so on. The SCO has never managed to react to a large-scale crisis within one of its member states. Its silence during the Kyrgyz events of 2010 weakened its legitimacy, as does its incapacity to offer collective assistance to a state that, albeit a non-member, is as key in the region as Afghanistan.[39]

The obsession for consensus and for maintaining the status quo has hampered the SCO's effectiveness. Since 2008, the organization seems to have entered a growth crisis: it has not defined any positive long-term goals, has no well-defined priorities, and refuses to discuss divergences in its members' priorities. It has, in particular, failed to coordinate joint activities against drug-trafficking or to become a forum for discussion on the water issue. Despite calls issued by Dushanbe, Bishkek, and Tashkent for the SCO to mediate in their water conflict, China has steadfastly refused to become involved. The SCO seems therefore primarily to be a reflection of Chinese willingness to support a so-called healthy Central Asian order, free from any of the "three evils," and devoid of pro-Western forces that might act to destabilize the region.[40]

For the time being, Chinese bilateral military presence in Central Asia is also limited, unable to rival Russia's preeminent role. Its aid is restricted to electronic materials, automobiles, and textiles, and includes almost no military sales properly speaking. However, Astana has expressed its intention to obtain military equipment from the Chinese People's Liberation Army (PLA) and hopes to take advantage of free transfers of decommissioned military assets when the Chinese army engages in modernizing its equipment.[41] Finally, aid for training military cadres—albeit modest—has started to develop with a number of exchanges organized; the language barrier, however, has hindered prospects: Courses for Central Asian officers in Chinese military academies are taught in Russian, as Chinese instructors are unable to speak Central Asian languages and vice versa. For the Central Asian governments, equipment and training from the PLA remains more of a theoretical possibility with aid focused primarily on non-military material and little of it being devoted to training, and they therefore continue to rely on largely outdated Soviet supplies.[42]

Western observers often overestimate Chinese political influence over the Central Asian regimes. Even if the SCO partially limits the Central Asian states' room to maneuver, in particular relative to the West, it provides them with an ideological framework with which to shore up their legitimacy on both the domestic and international fronts. The Central Asian governments have subscribed to the Chinese narrative on the need to combat the "three evils," which reinforces their own quest for political legitimacy founded on the definition of external and internal enemies. The China-Central Asia global political rapprochement has had an impact on Central Asian societies: Beijing, for instance, is appreciated by governments for providing technology that restricts access to the Internet and software that can block dissident sites.[43] But as with Moscow, this is primarily an axis of convenience for the Central Asian regimes, not a strategy that Beijing imposes by force. The China-Kazakhstan partnership is termed "strategic"— the highest of diplomatic modifiers—confirming that Astana is one of Beijing's major political allies in the post-Soviet space. However, although the SCO undeniably attempts to counter Western influence in the Old World, no country in the region wishes to pursue an aggressive policy aimed directly against US interests.[44] The Central Asian states consider Western presence in the region to be a guarantee of balance, and agree that the exclusive, dual grip of Russia and China would be dangerous.[45]

Chinese Inroads in Central Asia: Trade and Investments

Growing Chinese influence has an impact not only on the political and geopolitical situation of Central Asia, but also has profoundly changed the economic status quo in the region. As in the other areas of the world where Beijing is establishing itself, its settlement strategies respond to many objectives, seen by the Chinese authorities as intrinsically related. First, China consolidates its geopolitical influence in Central Asia by creating economically based good neighborly relations that work to defuse potential tensions. Second, it contributes to regional development in order to avoid political and social destabilization that could have domestic consequences in Xinjiang and slow down Chinese economic growth. Lastly, the Central Asian states provide new markets for Chinese products, markets that could open up to the whole of Russia, Iran, and Turkey. For landlocked Central Asia, the Chinese economic engine opens up the prospect of new trans-Eurasian corridors and is thus seen as a unique historical opportunity.

Since the fall of the Soviet Union, China-Central Asia trade has gone through three principal phases. The first period, covering the years 1992–1996, was marked by the opening of the first Sino-Kazakh border post at Dostyk-Alashankou and the signing of multiple friendship treaties and agreements for cooperation. The volume of trade exchanges at that time ranged between US$350 and US$700 million per year, much less than Central Asia's trade—albeit in free fall—with Russia, or its growing trade with Turkey and Iran.[46] During the second period, between 1997 and 2001, exchanges doubled.[47] However after a phase of promises and hopes, the setting up of Chinese firms was somewhat hindered by the global crisis that impacted the Central Asian economies, which was further exacerbated by the Russian crash in the summer of 1998. Despite the success of the border negotiations, renewed separatist claims in Xinjiang also negated the desire of the Central Asian and Chinese authorities to simplify customs regulations.

The third phase began in 2002. With the two main problems either resolved (border issues) or obviated (Uyghur separatism), dealings henceforth became much more pragmatic and based on mutually advantageous economic cooperation. The trade boom was accompanied by the first Chinese economic ventures into Central Asia in key sectors such as hydrocarbons and infrastructure; profound economic changes in Xinjiang thanks to the "Far West development program"; and the strengthening of the role of the SCO. Between 2002 and 2003, trade increased about 300 percent, going from about US$ 1 billion per year to more than 3 billion. An increase of 150 percent followed between 2004 and 2006, with trade reaching more than US$10 billion according to Central Asian figures,[48] or US$13 billion, according to Chinese figures.[49] In the latter half of the decade, China closely trailed Russia. In 2008, before the world economic downturn, trade between China and Central Asia exceeded US$25 billion, while trade between Russia and Central Asia stood at US$27 billion.[50] Since then, China has clearly gained the upper hand while Russia has stagnated, with US$28 billion for Beijing compared to less than 14 billion for Moscow in 2010.

Each Central Asian state occupies a distinct position in trade with China. Kazakhstan accounts for about two-thirds of the Sino-Central Asian trade total, which is primarily trade with Xinjiang. Astana has quickly risen to become the second largest of China's trading partners in the CIS after Russia and has held the mantle of Xinjiang's largest

Table 2.1

China's Place in Imports, Exports, and the Trade Total of Central Asian States in 2010 (in millions of US$)

	Imports	Rank	Exports	Rank	Total trade	Rank
Kazakhstan	9,839.8 (34.1%)	1	9,655.6 (21.1%)	2	19,495.5 (26.1%)	2
Kyrgyzstan	4,320 (62.7%)	1	61.1 (5.7%)	4	4,381.2 (55%)	1
Tajikistan	230 (9%)	4	427.3 (37.3%)	1	657.4 (17.8%)	2
Turkmenistan	553.6 (10.2%)	4	920.2 (28.4%)	1	1,473.8 (17%)	2
Uzbekistan	1,247 (15.2%)	4	1,133.3 (20.5%)	2	2,380.3 (17.3%)	2

Source: 2011 European Commission statistics, http://ec.europa.eu/trade/trade-statistics/; http://ec.europa.eu/trade/creating-opportunities/bilateral-relations/countries-and-regions/.

foreign trading partner for quite some time. This trade is particularly effective in the northern part of Xinjiang, which accounts for only 23 percent of the province's territory and half its population, but 70 percent of regional production due to its considerable resources, including the Karamay deposits, the Koktagay mines, and fertile agricultural areas.[51] For Astana, the partnership with China has been mostly focused on the extractive industries (hydrocarbons, uranium, and precious metals), communications technologies, and trade of consumer staples.

For Kyrgyzstan, the stakes are different. China accounts for about two-thirds of its imports and largely overshadows trade with Russia or the EU. Despite its intrinsic economic weakness, Kyrgyzstan is the second-largest country in Central Asia in terms of trade exchanges with China, as it serves as a platform for the reexport of Chinese products. According to World Bank calculations, Bishkek reexports close to three quarters of incoming Chinese products, mainly to Kazakhstan and Uzbekistan, enabling it to generate substantial revenues.[52] The value of these reexports is allegedly equivalent to the country's GDP, and today constitutes the Kyrgyz state's main source of foreign currency, ahead of the gold mine at Kumtor; however, Bishkek's trade deficit with Beijing in 2008 was more than 250 percent of its GDP.[53] Kyrgyzstan offers a very advantageous system for the payment of customs taxes, which are calculated on the basis of product volume and not value. Chinese traders, preferring to negotiate with the easily corruptible Kyrgyz customs officers rather than with the Kazakh authorities, who are much stricter on imports, thus see the country as a particularly attractive, but unstable option.[54] However, this changed abruptly in 2011 when the Customs Union, of which Kyrgyzstan is not a part, came into force. The Russian-led new regional integration strategy drastically reduces Kyrgyzstan's role as a platform for the reexport of Chinese goods to Kazakhstan, and accentuates the Kyrgyz recurrent economic crisis.

On paper, trade between China and Uzbekistan, the most populous country of Central Asia with 27 million inhabitants, remains abnormally low. The absence of shared borders and Uzbekistan's isolationist stance partly explain this situation. However, Chinese products reach the Uzbek market through neighboring Kyrgyzstan (mainly via the Karasuu bazaar), and often by clandestine means, in order to escape Uzbek customs. As direct calculations are impossible, an idea of the significance of this trade, which is bound to grow in scope in the coming years, can only be made through the approximate figures of Kyrgyz reexports.[55]

Tajikistan was obliged to wait until the opening of the border post at Kulma-Kalasu in 2004 before it could seek to emulate Kyrgyzstan in terms of reexports. Today, the wholesale Chinese bazaars that have opened on Tajik territory serve not just the national market but also the neighboring Uzbek and Afghan ones. Chinese credit institutions give their preference to Tajikistan, in part because it is seen by Beijing as the missing link in its access to Afghanistan. Accordingly, Dushanbe accounts for two-thirds of the Chinese loans offered to Central Asia as a whole. Tajikistan's largest creditor is China and its indebtedness toward its neighbor has reached dramatic proportions: about two-third of Tajik debt is tied to Chinese credits.[56] More than 80 percent of Chinese investments in the country are offered in the form of credit, which Tajikistan risks having to pay back in some way.

Turkmenistan was the last to come onto China's radar, but their bilateral relationship has rapidly developed in scale. Almost absent from the trade figures at the time of the visit of President Saparmurat Niyazov to Beijing in 2006, the most closed country in post-Soviet space has since opened itself up to trade with China. However, with no common border, the countries exchange mainly gas and raw materials, while petty trade is still very weak. Turkmenistan is now the only remaining Central Asian country that receives its food products and basic goods mostly from Turkey and Iran instead of from China.[57]

The Central Asian states, as well as China, have every interest in developing their mutual relations as their economies are more complementary to than in direct competition with one another. China has the capacity to export consumer products to Central Asia at low prices, which suits the low living standards of the local populations, whereas Russian, Turkish, and Iranian, not to mention Western, products remain too expensive. It is also able to provide technological goods to the middle and upper classes, whose consumption patterns are constantly rising, in particular in Kazakhstan. Between 80 and 90 percent of Chinese exports to Central Asia consist of finished, diversified goods: consumer products, machinery, processed foodstuffs, textiles, shoes, electronic goods, pharmaceutical products, automobile parts, and so on.[58] Conversely, about three quarters of Central Asian exports to China consist of raw materials, petrol, and ferrous and nonferrous metals.[59]

Hydrocarbons—mainly gas from Turkmenistan and oil from Kazakhstan—are at the forefront of Chinese activity in Central Asia, as is Kazakh uranium. But it also aims at a multitude of other sectors, in particular those linked to infrastructure and communications.[60] China is one of the only external actors present in Central Asia that attaches enough importance to the frequently neglected banking sector to enable the Central Asian states to pursue large-scale projects. Chinese aid for development is granted either by subsidies, which are generally paid in kind in order to reduce the risks of corruption, or by preferential or concessional credit paid by the Export-Import Bank of China (Eximbank), the Development Bank, or the State Bank. They offer higher lines of credits than those extended by Islamic or European banks, and at lower interest rates than those of the main international lenders.[61] Though the money from loans is, on paper, granted to the beneficiary country, it is generally transferred to the company in charge of the project, which makes it possible to keep the money inside the Chinese system.[62] This gives China a certain advantage over countries with privatized economies. Kyrgyzstan and Tajikistan were among the first to receive Chinese assistance, mainly to finance infrastructure projects: in 2004, China announced a loan of US$900 million to Central Asia, most of which was given to Dushanbe; and in 2009, a few weeks before the SCO summit in Yekaterinburg, China extended US$10 billion in credit to Kazakhstan, half of the sum being made up by a loan from Eximbank to its counterpart, the Development Bank of Kazakhstan.[63] And in 2012 President Hu Jintao relaunched his 2009 proposal to provide a new US$10 billion loan under SCO auspices.

It seems very likely that China's trade domination over Central Asia will be confirmed in the coming decades. Beijing will remain the foremost economic partner of the five states. Central Asian consumers will follow Chinese trends in everyday consumption goods, as well as in high-tech products, but also partially in foodstuffs. Despite an appearance to the contrary, Chinese control over Kazakh oil is not established, and control over Turkmen gas and Kazakh uranium will be more critical. But the real locus of Chinese power resides in its massive investments in Central Asian infrastructure, communications, and potentially new technologies, and in its still-to-be-developed control of industrial structures and electricity production.

China has become a major, structural actor in Central Asia. It plays a negative role by transforming the local economies into raw material support bases, and by destroying, through mechanisms of competition, the already very limited post-Soviet industrial fabric, which is a creator of employment. But Beijing also becomes a key positive element in Central Asia's transition to the service economy and to that of new technologies. Its proximity has proven a guarantee of development and participation in world markets. As Kyrgyzstan has shown, the reexport of Chinese products throughout the rest of Central Asia, and to Russia and potentially the Middle East, makes it possible to set up new dynamics that transform the social fabric. A whole range of new professions are being created, all linked to the service economy: transport, freight, logistics, translation, legal and commercial services, foreign sales networks, and so on. Central Asian younger generations have entered this niche as a way to meet their own aspirations. It presupposes mastery of market-economy principles, emphasizes knowledge that is at once individual (foreign languages) and institutional (university diplomas), and enables an opening up to foreign countries and the earning of much higher revenues than those provided by traditional tertiary, state-dependent professions (teaching, medicine).

New economic niches with China are also gradually assuming cultural connotations. Among the young generations of all backgrounds—elites, middle classes, or small merchants—all things Chinese are in fashion, especially in Kazakhstan and Kyrgyzstan. Chinese language education is growing, as are stints at Chinese universities.[64] National minorities with links to China, like the Dungans (Muslim Hans) seek to position themselves as cultural and commercial go-betweens.[65] Fear of Chinese migrants and the myth of the "yellow peril" are still widespread, but Beijing has put in place timid strategies of co-optation in order to deal with Central Asians' identity worries. At the 12th Heads of State Summit (SCO) in 2012, Hu Jintao fostered China's newly acquired soft power by offering thousands of scholarships for Central Asian civil servants. In years to come, China will need to elaborate a more active cultural presence, promote "Chineseness" (*zhonghuaxing*), and take the cultural fears it provokes into account in its decision-making.

Although Central Asia remains marked by numerous phobias regarding its Chinese neighbor and impressed by the differences in power and demography, Beijing's Central Asian policy aims to be pragmatic. The border disputes have been settled, the Uyghur dissidents muzzled, and the local political regimes won over to the Chinese discourse on the fight against the "three evils," the unity of the People's Republic of China and Taiwan, and on the danger of Western interference. China has skillfully managed asymmetric relationships and consolidated its security governance mechanisms. Its commercial involvement in the region is in full bloom and its stranglehold over the energy resources is increasing. The Chinese authorities, aware of their limits in managing their own national peripheries, have therefore little interest in getting too involved in a region they see as unstable. They have no interest in highlighting too visibly their pressures on Central Asia and prefer to promote the idea of a partnership in which each actor is a winner. Beijing therefore supports the Russian strategic presence and willingly plays "second fiddle" to Moscow on security issues, while seeking to dominate in the economic sphere. It increasingly worries about the loss of Russian influence in the region and growing domestic instability, since no global or regional power seems to be willing or able to take the Central Asian states under its wing. Above all else, Beijing is seeking stability on its borders in order to calmly manage domestic issues and does not conceal its reluctance to become more involved in Central Asia's security.

Notes

1. An old Central Asian tradition, handed down through centuries-old oral epics, presents China as a distant but recurrent enemy of Turkic peoples and as a historical opponent of Islam.

2. On the China-Central Asia relationship during the 1990s, see T. Kellner, *L'Occident de la Chine: Pékin et la nouvelle Asie centrale, 1991–2001* (Paris: PUF, 2008).

3. R. Foot, "Chinese Strategies in a US-Hegemonic Global Order: Accommodating and Hedging," *International Affairs* 82, no. 1 (2006): 77–94.

4. H. Lai, *The Domestic Sources of China's Foreign Policy: Regimes, Leadership, Priorities, and Process* (London: Routledge, 2010); R. S. Ross and A. I. Johnston, eds., *New Directions in the Study of China's Foreign Policy* (Stanford: Stanford University Press, 2006).

5. J. Cabestan, *La Politique internationale de la Chine: Entre intégration et volonté de puissance* (Paris: Presses de Sciences Po, 2010).

6. B. Gill, *Rising Star: China's New Security Diplomacy* (Washington, DC: Brookings Institution Press, 2007).

7. T. Kellner, "Le Dragon et la tulipe: Les relations sino-afghanes dans la période post-9/11," Brussels Institute of Contemporary China Studies, *Asia Paper* 4, no. 1, 2009.

8. See the special issue of the *China Quarterly*, J. C. Strauss and M. Saavedra, eds., "China and Africa: Emerging Patterns in Globalization and Development," no. 199 (September 2009).

9. J. A. Millward, *Eurasian Crossroads: A History of Xinjiang* (New York: Columbia University Press, 2007). See also M. Dickens, *The Soviets in Xinjiang, 1911–1949*, http://www.oxuscom.com/sovinxj.htm.

10. On the migration flows between Xinjiang and Kazakhstan, see G. M. Mendikulova and B. Zh. Atanbaeva, *Istoriia migratsii mezhdu Kazakhstanom i Kitaem v 1860–1960-e gg.* (Almaty: Izd-vo SaGa, 2008).

11. On contemporary challenges in Xinjiang, see S. Frederick Starr, ed., *Xinjiang: China's Muslim Borderland* (Armonk, NY: M.E. Sharpe, 2004).

12. J. W. Garver, "Development of China's Overland Transportation Links with Central, South-West, and South Asia," *China Quarterly*, no. 185 (2006): 1–22.

13. R. Ong, "China's Security Interests in Central Asia," *Central Asian Survey* 24, no. 4 (2005): 425–39.

14. A. Goldstein, *Rising to the Challenge: China's Grand Strategy and International Security* (Stanford: Stanford University Press, 2005).

15. Statistics from the US-China Business Council, www.uschina.org.

16. M. Leonard, *What Does China Think?* (London: Fourth Estate, 2008); B. Courmont, *Chine: La grande séduction; Essai sur le soft power chinois* (Paris: Editions Choiseul, 2009); R. S. Ross and F. Zhu, eds., *China's Ascent: Power, Security, and the Future of International Politics* (Ithaca, NY: Cornell University Press, 2008).

17. C. Mackerras and M. Clarke, eds., *China, Xinjiang, and Central Asia: History, Transition, and Crossborder Interaction into the Twenty-First Century* (New York: Routledge, 2009).

18. H. Zhao, "Central Asia in China's Diplomacy," in *Central Asia: Views from Washington, Moscow, and Beijing*, ed. E. Rumer, D. Trenin, and H. Zhao (Armonk, NY: M.E. Sharpe, 2007), 137.

19. Y. Pi, "China's Boundary Issues with the Former Soviet Union," *Issues and Studies* 28, no. 7 (1992): 63–75.

20. China claimed 2,235 km^2 of territory in Kazakhstan, divided into eleven zones, some of which comprised only tens of km^2. In Kyrgyzstan it claimed 3,728 km^2 divided into five zones, but originally continued to insist on nearly all of its claims in Tajikistan, from which it demanded a large part of the Pamir (28,430 km^2), equal to one-fifth of the country's overall surface area.

21. S. Smirnov, "Kitai otshchepil chast' Tadzhikistana," *Gazeta.ru*, January 12, 2011, http://www.gazeta.ru/politics/2011/01/12_kz_3489206.shtml.

22. For more on Sinophobia in Central Asia, see M. Laruelle and S. Peyrouse, *The "Chinese Question" in Central Asia: Domestic Order, Social Change and the Chinese Factor* (New York, London: Columbia University Press, 2012), 97–116.

23. N. Maxwell, "How the Sino-Russian Boundary Conflict was Finally Settled: From Nerchinsk 1689 to Vladivostok 2005 via Zhenbao Island 1969," in *Eager Eyes Fixed on Eurasia*, ed. A. Iwashita (Hokkaido: Slavic Research Center, Hokkaido University, 2007), 47–73.

24. S. Peyrouse, "Flowing Downstream: The Sino-Kazakh Water Dispute," *China Brief* 7, no. 10 (2007): 7–10.

25. "Water Resources of Kazakhstan in the New Millennium," Report of the United Nations Development Programme, UNDPKAZ 07, Almaty, 2004, 41.

26. "Kazakhstan nameren podpisat' soglashenie s Kitaem o transgranichnykh rekakh," *RIA Novosti*, February 24, 2010, http://www.rian.ru/world/20100224/210592367.html.

27. A.D. Riabtsev, "Ugrozy vodnoi bezopasnosti v Respublike Kazakhstan v transgranich-nom kontekste i vozmozhnye puti ikh ustraneniia," Report of the Interstate Commission for Water Coordination of Central Asia, 2008, http://www.icwc-aral.uz/workshop_march08/pdf/ryabtsev_ru.pdf.

28. M. Laruelle and S. Peyrouse, "Cross-Border Minorities as Cultural and Economic Mediators between China and Central Asia," *China and Eurasia Forum Quarterly* 7, no. 1 (2009): 93–119.

29. Anonymous interviews carried out at the Institute of Uyghur Studies (Institute of Oriental Studies, Academy of Sciences, Almaty), March 2005.

30. R. Castets, "Opposition politique, nationalisme et islam chez les Ouïghours du Xinjiang," *Les Etudes du CERI*, no. 110, 2004.

31. S. Aris, *Eurasian Regionalism: The Shanghai Cooperation Organisation* (New York: Palgrave Macmillan, 2011).

32. S. Hanova, "Perspectives on the SCO: Images and Discourses," *China and Eurasia Forum Quarterly* 7, no. 3 (2009): 63–82.

33. A. Cooley, *Great Games, Local Rules: The New Great Power Contest in Central Asia* (Oxford: Oxford University Press, 2012).

34. B. Sultanov and R. Krumm, eds., *Problemy ekonomicheskogo i finansovogo sotrudni-chestva v ramkakh ShOS* (Almaty: Kazakhstanskii institut strategicheskikh issledovanii, 2006); M. Ashimbaev and G. Chufrin, eds., *ShOS: Stanovlenie i perspektivy razvitiia* (Almaty: Institut mirovoi ekonomiki, 2005); V. S. Frolenkov, *Sovremennye torgovo-ekonomicheskie otnosheniia KNR s tsentral'no-aziatskimi gosudarstvami-chlenami ShOS i Turkmenistanom* (Moscow: Institut Dal'nego Vostoka RAN, 2009).

35. H. Zhao, "Kitai, Tsentral'naia Aziia i Shankhaiskaia Organizatsiia sotrudnichestva," Carnegie Moscow Center Working Paper, no. 5, 2005.

36. Lo, *Axis of Convenience*.

37. More details in Laruelle and Peyrouse, *The "Chinese Question" in Central Asia*, 27–44.

38. A. Cooley, "The Stagnation of the SCO: Competing Agendas and Divergent Interests in Central Asia," PONARS Eurasia Policy Memo, no. 85, September 2009.

39. M. Singh Roy, "Shanghai Cooperation Organisation and Afghanistan: Scope and Limita-tion," *Strategic Analysis* 34, no. 4 (2010): 545–61.

40. M. Oresman, "Catching the Shanghai Spirit," *Journal of Social Sciences*, no. 12, De-cember 2003, republished in *Foreign Policy*: http://www.foreignpolicy.com/articles/2004/05/01/catching_the_shanghai_spirit.

41. S. Peyrouse, "Sino-Kazakh Relations: A Nascent Strategic Partnership," *China Brief* 8, no. 21 (2008): 11–15.

42. S. Peyrouse, "Military Cooperation between China and Central Asia: Breakthrough, Limits, and Prospects," *China Brief* 10, no. 5 (2010): 10–14.

43. For instance, when the second Turkmen president, Gurbanguly Berdymukhammedov, reopened Internet cafes in February 2007, he signed contracts with Chinese companies for software designed to control access to sites. Authors' fieldwork in Internet cafes in Ashgabat, March 2008.

44. A. Iwashita, "The Shanghai Cooperation Organization and Its Implications for Eurasian Security: A New Dimension of 'Partnership' After the Post-Cold War Period," in *Slavic Eurasia's Integration into the World Economy and Community*, ed. S. Tabata and A. Iwashita (Sapporo: Slavic Research Center, Hokkaido University, 2004), 259–81.

45. K. L. Syroezhkin, *Problemy sovremennogo Kitaia i bezopasnost' v Tsentral'noi Azii* (Almaty: KISI, 2006); A. Bukhanov, "Aktual'nye voprosy kazakhstansko-rossiiskikh otnoshenii glazami kazakhstanskikh ekspertov," *Kazakhstan v global'nykh protsessakh*, no. 4 (2006): 92–99;

A. Abdrakhmanov and A. Kaukenov, "Otnosheniia Kitaia i stran Tsentral'noi Azii glazami kazakhstanskikh ekspertov," *Kazakhstan v global'nykh protsessakh*, no. 3 (2007): 119–28.

46. Paramonov and Strokov, *Ekonomicheskoe prisutstvie*, 2.

47. Ibid., 4.

48. G. Raballand and A. Andrésy, "Why Should Trade between Central Asia and China Continue to Expand?" *Asia-Europe Journal* 5, no. 2 (2007): 235–52.

49. G. Raballand and B. Kaminski, "La Déferlante économique chinoise et ses conséquences en Asie centrale," *Monde chinois*, no. 11 (2007): 129–34.

50. 2009 European Commission's statistics, http://ec.europa.eu/trade/trade-statistics/.

51. Sh. Nadyrov, "Sin'tszian-uigurskii avtonomnyi raion v dinamike ekonomicheskikh i politicheskikh otnoshenii RK i KNR," *Kazakhstan-Spektr*, no. 1 (2006): 14–25.

52. G. Raballand and B. Kaminski, "Entrepôt for Chinese Consumer Goods in Central Asia: The Puzzle of Re-Exports through Kyrgyz Bazaars," *Eurasian Geography and Economics* 50, no. 5 (2009): 581–90.

53. Ibid., 582.

54. Anonymous interviews with Kazakh and Kyrgyz experts in Chinese business, Bishkek, February 2008, Almaty, September 2010.

55. B. Kaminski, and G. Raballand, "Re-export Flows through Bazaars in Kyrgyzstan: Magnitude and Implications for Country's External Performance," unpublished paper, 2010.

56. A. Sodiqov, "Tajikistan attracts more Chinese funds," *Asia Times*, June 19, 2012, http://www.atimes.com/atimes/Central_Asia/NF19Ag01.html.

57. More details in S. Peyrouse, *Turkmenistan: Strategies of Power, Dilemmas of Development* (Armonk, NY: M.E. Sharpe, 2011), 193–217.

58. For a break-down by product, see H. Wu, and C. Chen, "The Prospects for Regional Economic Integration between China and the Five Central Asian Countries," *Europe-Asia Studies* 56, no. 7 (2004): 1069–80.

59. V. Paramonov and A. Strokov, *Economic Involvement of Russia and China in Central Asia* (Swindon: Defence Academy of the United Kingdom, 2007), 6. See also M. Myant and J. Drahokoupil, "International Integration and the Structure of Exports in Central Asian Republics," *Eurasian Geography and Economics* 49, no. 5 (2009): 604–22.

60. For more details, see chapters 12 and 13.

61. R. Pomfret, "Turkmenistan's Foreign Policy," *China and Eurasia Forum Quarterly* 6, no. 4 (2008): 29.

62. N. Kassenova, "Aide au développement: La percée chinoise au Tadjikistan et au Kirghizstan," Report of the Institut français des relations internationales (IFRI), Russie.NEI.Visions, no. 36, January 2009, 11.

63. "China Loans 10 bln dlrs to Kazakhstan," *Energy Daily*, April 17, 2009, http://www.energy-daily.com/reports/China_loans_10_bln_dlrs_to_Kazakhstan_state_media_999.html.

64. More details in Laruelle and Peyrouse, *The "Chinese Question" in Central Asia*, 133–142.

65. Laruelle and Peyrouse, "Cross-Border Minorities."

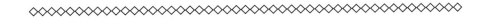

3

The United States

The Too Distant, but Unavoidable Partner

Washington's long-term objectives in Central Asia were established at the beginning of the 1990s and have not changed significantly since then: avert the return of Russian domination, prevent the emergence of a new hegemonic power in the region (Iran or China), promote energy and strategic partnerships that turn the region toward South Asia or the West, and contribute to political and economic reforms. In 2009, at the same time that the "AfPak" concept was elaborated, the Obama administration undertook a comprehensive review of US strategy in Central Asia and laid out a road map with five goals: "to maximize the cooperation of the states of the region with coalition counterterrorism efforts in Afghanistan (particularly cooperation on hosting US and NATO airbases and on the transit of troops and supplies to Afghanistan along the 'Northern Distribution Network'); to increase the development and diversification of the region's energy resources and supply routes; to promote the eventual emergence of good governance and respect for human rights; to foster competitive market economies; and to increase the capacity of the states to govern themselves, and in particular to prevent state failure in Tajikistan and Kyrgyzstan, including by enhancing food security assistance."[1]

However, these objectives remain very general and only modestly shape everyday realities in Central Asia. The region is important to the narrative of American foreign policy in Eurasia, but marginal in terms of the financial support and diplomatic energy that Washington has committed. Compared to US interests in the Asia-Pacific and the Middle East, Central Asia is not at the top of American priorities or is there by default due to its proximity to Afghanistan. Central Asia's status is therefore subject to changes in the foreign policy of the leading world power, sometimes appearing in the spotlight and sometimes forgotten or relegated to subordinate status.

The United States entered the Central Asian arena rapidly in the 1990s while Russia was in full retreat and China still absent; its influence waned markedly around 2003–2005 and reached a historical low in 2007 and 2008. Since the summer of 2009, the United States has been able to regain some of its geopolitical influence in Central Asia through its transformed involvement in Afghanistan, but the withdrawal in 2014 reduces the chances that the region will remain key on US radar over the long term. The new emphasis of US strategic interests on Asia-Pacific and the maintenance of the focus on a "Greater Middle East," as defined in the 2011 Defense Strategic Review, confirm that the relationship to China and South Asia will be a key element in the American reading of Central Asia's future.[2]

Shifting US Agendas Toward Central Asia

In every state, institutions with differing interests and contradictory priorities determine foreign policy. This feature seems even more applicable in the American case, given how divergent the worldviews of the Pentagon, State Department, Congress, White House, and also of NGOs, lobbies, and private economic actors can be. In addition, the importance assigned to Central Asia has changed significantly in accordance with the various presidents and their administrations, in view of their political orientations, foreign policy priorities, and the policy-making process. Lastly, developments in the global and regional context significantly shape the US viewpoint on Central Asia. Afghanistan dropped from the list of American priorities with the collapse of the Soviet Union, returning to the forefront only in 2001 and probably diminishing again after 2014. Beginning in 2003, the Iraq War diverted some US aid to Central Asia; but it was the institution of the Northern Distribution Network (NDN) in 2009 that assured the region's new place within the architecture of American global security. The US stance on Central Asia is therefore dependent upon several factors, mainly the situation in Afghanistan, the US-Russia bilateral relationship, but also, though to a lesser extent, Washington's view on Iran and China. The region's stance is further conditioned by the American perception of the Caspian Basin's unity and therefore of the links between Central Asia and the Caucasus; and the overall situation in Middle East/West Asia.

With the Soviet Union's disappearance, the United States has concentrated on some major efforts in Central Asia. The first was the oversight of Kazakhstan's process of denuclearization and the prevention of the proliferation of nuclear weapons and weapons of mass destruction. The five states of Central Asia, without military desires of expansion, promptly signed the Nuclear Non-Proliferation Treaty, as well as the Convention on Chemical Weapons. By the end of the 1990s, the goals of the US Cooperative Threat Reduction program—the dismantling of Kazakh nuclear installations and their destruction, among others—were largely reached.[3] Ever since, the program has concentrated on eliminating bacteriological and chemical risks. Between 1998 and 2007, Kazakhstan received US$107 million and Uzbekistan US$79 million to dismantle the infrastructure at Stepnogorsk and on the island of Vozrozhdenie, where Soviet scientists developed and tested pathogenic agents. In 2007, the five Central Asian states ratified the treaty that gave rise to the Central Asian Nuclear Weapon Free Zone (CANWFZ), the first denuclearized zone in the northern hemisphere, bordering atomic powers such as Russia and China, and states on the verge of acquiring nuclear capacity such as Iran.[4] The White House appreciates Kazakhstan's international positioning on this issue: Nursultan Nazarbayev's proposal to elaborate a universal declaration for a denuclearized world, which was put forward at the nuclear security summit held in Washington in 2010, has benefited from American support.[5]

The second historical axis of US engagement in Central Asia, and perhaps the best known and the most controversial among the Central Asian elites, is the aid it has provided for democratization, an objective aimed at the entire post-Soviet space. It took shape via the FREEDOM Support Act (Freedom for Russia and Emerging Eurasian Democracies and Open Markets), today called Assistance to Europe, Eurasia, and Central Asia. These programs provide support for the development of "civil society" by financing the formation of non-governmental organizations, autonomous media organizations, and independent judiciaries. The Silk Road Strategy Acts of 1999 and 2006, focusing largely on promoting democratization and "civil society," quickly ran into difficulties with the Central Asian regimes, who objected overtly to what they interpreted as US interference carried out in the name of human rights. Democracy promotion has experienced declines in funding in any case. From 2000, the budgets for programs to aid "civil society" in Central Asia have been reduced to the advantage of funds for security cooperation.[6]

Democratization is also addressed through aid mechanisms from the US Agency for International Development (USAID). While the aid reaches all the Central Asian states, it is mainly provided to the two poorest, Kyrgyzstan and Tajikistan, with less to Kazakhstan, and very little to Uzbekistan and Turkmenistan. Today Kazakhstan is the first government in Central Asia that contributes financially to the activities of USAID on its own territory. All the US programs, including those such as the Central Asian-American Enterprise Fund (CAAEF), associate democratization with the transition to a market economy on the principle that good governance and the rule of law are essential elements of property rights. The United States has also encouraged the accession of the Central Asian states to the World Trade Organization and signed a framework agreement for trade and investment (Trade and Investment Framework Agreement, TIFA) with all of them in 2005.[7] Trade exchanges rely on the existence of bilateral investment treaties with Kazakhstan and Kyrgyzstan, and on the belonging of Kazakhstan, Kyrgyzstan, and Uzbekistan to the Generalized System of Preferences.

One of the pillars of US engagement in Central Asia, the democracy agenda, has had very paradoxical results. The United States at first supported "shock therapy" strategies that, for the populations concerned, were synonymous with state weakness. By promoting Kyrgyzstan as the "democratic island" of the region, the United States also indirectly fueled the idea that a conjunction exists between the market economy and social chaos, a counterproductive argument that has inadvertently served to validate authoritarian regimes. Eventually, with the "color revolutions" the United States ended up weakening its state-building objectives by giving the impression that street action was more legitimate than established power, the former representing democratic forces, the second authoritarian regimes.[8] The choice of Uzbekistan as a strategic partner in the "war on terror," despite it being one of the most dictatorial regimes in the region, also distorted Washington's political message on democratic values. Similarly, support for the Bakiyev family—in part due to the role of the former president's son, Maksim Bakiyev, in the illegal traffic of jet fuel for the Manas military base through

Table 3.1

Distribution of US Aid to Central Asia per Country and Program in 2011 (in thousands of US$)

	Kazakhstan	Kyrgyzstan	Tajikistan	Turkmenistan	Uzbekistan
Total	**17,567**	**41,364**	**44,482**	**11,012**	**11,335**
Assistance to Europe, Eurasia, and Central Asia (AEECA)	10,400	41,364	40,290	8,500	8,250
Non-Proliferation, Anti-Terrorism, De-Mining and Related Programs (NADR)	1,900	1,550	1,725	1,075	600
Foreign Military Financing (FMF)	2,395	1,496	750	750	0
International Military Education and Training (IMET)	876	820	469	288	289
Global Health, Program (USAID)	1,996	998	1,248	399	2,196
Food for Peace (Title II)	0	0	9,817	0	0

Source: Table based on files per country provided by the US Department of State's Bureau of European and Eurasian Affairs, http://www.state.gov/p/eur/ace/c11609.htm.

Manas Aerofuels and Central Asia Fuels[9]—diminished the image of the country as an advocate for values. Finally, as elsewhere in the world, the war in Iraq accentuated this negative view, in which Washington is suspected of aggression against the Muslim world and of the violation of the universal principles of human rights in the name of its own security interests.[10]

Security as the Main Driver of US Involvement

In the second half of the 1990s a more strictly geopolitical interest in Central Asia developed in Washington, symbolized by Zbigniew Brzezinski's "Grand Chessboard" theory. Brzezinski defined Central Asia and the Caucasus as the "Eurasian Balkans," and construed them as a potential zone of confrontation between great powers. The former security advisor to President Carter claimed that "Eurasia remains . . . the chessboard on which the combat for global primacy will unfold."[11] This is similar to the remark of the British geopolitician Sir Halford Mackinder (1861–1947) that whoever dominates the "Heartland," dominates the world.[12] This overestimation of the region's role in the world global balance may have partly biased US understandings of Central Asia. It has accentuated geostrategic analyses into a "war of influence" with Russia (and, to a lesser extent, with Iran and China), has given a more ideological sense to political evolutions (such as promoting democracy in order to forge a belt of friendly regimes containing Russia), and has cast aside the goals of social and economic development.

At the end of the 1990s, the lack of success in influencing the democratization of Central Asian regimes and the fear of terrorist threats yielded a withdrawal of US economic aid and a focus on military collaboration. Uzbek military personnel participated in numerous bilateral exercises with US troops.[13] In 1998 and 1999 Central Asia was transferred from the jurisdiction of the US Defense Department's Eucom (European Command) to that of Centcom (Central Command), meaning that it was no longer considered part of post-Soviet space, but as part of the "Greater Middle East."[14] After the attacks in Tashkent of February 16, 1999, the Uzbek authorities benefited from aid from the Foreign Military Financing Program and US commando units allegedly spent some time on the ground in order to train Uzbek special forces in the fight against terrorism.[15] Assistance was also concentrated on border securitization. In 2000, the United States instituted the Central Asian Border Security Initiative (CASI), allocating US$3 million to each of the states of the region.[16]

After September 11, 2001, Tashkent's resolutely pro-American engagement gave credence to the notion of Uzbekistan as a key element in the fight against Islamism and a particular case in the Central Asian region.[17] From September 16, the Uzbek authorities declared, despite Russia's pressures, that they were ready to host the Americans on their soil, citing as a reason the country's 137 kilometer-long border with Afghanistan. The ensuing months saw a procession of officials with US Defense Secretary Donald Rumsfeld visiting Tashkent twice in the fall of 2001, while Islam Karimov undertook an official visit to the United States in March 2002. This strategy was win-win for both sides, especially as Tajikistan refused to provide logistical support other than the right to use the Dushanbe airport and Kazakhstan merely opened its air space to US planes.[18] The United States therefore established itself in the Uzbek town of Karshi (Khanabad), opening up its first military base in the former Soviet Union. This American presence offered multiple advantages to Islam Karimov's regime: the maintenance of privileged relations with Washington despite his authoritarian hardening and critiques of the West; a status of regional power compared to its Kazakh rival; US financing to train the Uzbek army; and a legitimization of its discourse concerning the Islamic risk.[19] The United States even pledged its assistance in case of a threat to the independence or integrity of Uzbek territory. However, Washington continued to provide aid to the other countries of the region and furthered its collaboration with an increasingly dynamic Kazakhstan. A second military base opened in Kyrgyzstan at the Manas airfield, close to Bishkek, causing Uzbekistan to lose some of its exclusivity in hosting US forces, although the Karshi base remained more important.

During the first half-decade of the twenty-first century, US influence in Eurasia seemed to have reached its zenith. Among the regional structures being formed with Washington's support, the most prominent was the GUAM, which was supposed to embody the solidarity of post-Soviet states that wanted to leave the Russian fold, and of which Uzbekistan was a member from 1996 to 2001; the group failed, however. In 2003 the United States' reorientation from Afghanistan to the Middle East partly diverted its attention away from Central Asia, disappointing the region's leaders and making them feel as if they had been left to themselves. The start of the war in Iraq ended the consensus in favor of the United States, while the "color revolutions" in Georgia in 2003 and Ukraine in 2004 definitely altered the playing field. The toppling of Kyrgyzstan's Askar Akayev in March 2005 revived fears of forced democratization orchestrated by the United States via NGOs. Since this time, all the Central Asian governments have overtly denounced "Western interference" in their domestic affairs and have developed closer ties with Moscow as well as with Beijing.[20] Even the Kyrgyz government of Kurmanbek Bakiyev, despite being born of the "Tulip revolution," has not concealed its discontent with Western policy. America critiques of the violent repression of May 13, 2005, in Andijan put an end to the privileged alliance between the United States and Uzbekistan, despite Tashkent's interventionist position on Iraq. The Uzbek authorities quickly demanded the closure of the base. Diverse pretexts were advanced for closing it, including the excessive cost for Tashkent, US debt, degradation of access to potable water in the region, and the prejudice of US soldiers toward the local populations.[21]

These developments, linked both to Central Asian domestic situations and the United States' evolving interests, were strengthened by changes to the region's architecture and the rise of the CSTO and the SCO. In 2006, the US Department of State reshuffled its administrative division, transferring Central Asia from the Europe and Eurasia Bureau to the new Central Asia and South Asia one, in an attempt to dynamize the relationship with South Asia.[22] There followed some years during which America proved unable to check the return of Russia's influence and the growing strategic partnership with

China. The only US base in the region, at Manas, was put under constant pressure from Moscow, Beijing, and Tashkent, which requested the departure of the Americans. Washington also had to engage in difficult financial negotiations with the Kyrgyz authorities, for whom the base represented a key element of their foreign currency inflow. In the spring of 2009, the dithering of President Kurmanbek Bakiyev, who was requesting the base's closure, even while he opened a new round of negotiations to maintain it, confirmed the financial as much as strategic stakes of the American presence in Kyrgyzstan.[23]

For the first time since the beginning of the Iraq War, the year 2009 signaled a favorable geopolitical turn for the United States. The Central Asian governments seemed to welcome the presidency of Barack Obama; the second Turkmen president, Gurbanguly Berdymukhammedov, showed interest in negotiating with the West and in searching for new allies, while Uzbekistan, wanting to thwart the Russian-Chinese stranglehold, declared itself open to a renewal of dialogue with Washington.[24] But more importantly, Central Asia's strategic location was enhanced with the establishment of the NDN to supply material to the ISAF (International Security Assistance Force) in Afghanistan. The NDN is a series of logistical arrangements organized by some NATO countries (mainly the United States, Germany, and the United Kingdom), linking the ports of the Baltic and the Caspian with Afghanistan via Russia and the Central Asian states. It allows transit to divert around Pakistan, but at higher cost.

Of the three Central Asian countries bordering Afghanistan, the NDN accords Tashkent a fundamentally central transit role, and Termez has become the key to securing overland access to Afghanistan by the northern route.[25] Flows into Kyrgyz and Tajik territory have all but come to a stop: the route is not operational and too uncertain in terms of security.[26] In 2010, the NDN supplied about 35 percent of all ISAF cargo headed for Afghanistan, and about 60 percent in 2011.[27] Several agreements for reverse supply flows have also been signed with Uzbekistan, Kyrgyzstan and Kazakhstan by ISAF and individual NATO nations.

As the security situation in Pakistan deteriorated, Afghanistan's northern neighbors have regained their forgotten place in the American security architecture for Afghanistan. This has a dual impact: Washington has new arguments for negotiation, since this military cooperation is supposed to accompany a renewal of US economic presence; in return, the Central Asian states have new means of coercion over Washington, which cannot dispense with their support without imperiling its operations in Afghanistan and its withdrawal strategy.[28] In 2010, the Pentagon and US Central Command's Counter-Narcotics Fund announced they would spend over US$40 million on security infrastructure projects in Central Asia, comprising the construction of military training centers in Osh and in the Karategin Valley; a canine training facility and helicopter hangar near Almaty; and border-crossing checkpoints in Uzbekistan, Turkmenistan, and Kyrgyzstan.[29] Other projects related to hard security are likely to be proposed by 2014. Secretary of State Hillary Clinton's tour of Central Asia in October 2011 has allowed Washington to present itself as a key partner in a post-2014 security architecture, but without advancing very concrete proposals. Tashkent in particular seems determined to be restored by the Pentagon as one of the few "fortresses" against possible spillovers from Afghanistan.[30]

Multilateral and Bilateral Strategic Cooperation

The United States has struggled to establish its position with respect to each of the Central Asian states. Turkmenistan and Uzbekistan, as the most active in their attempts to escape the Russian fold, appeared to be promising partners, but they remained closed to the US agenda of promoting democracy and are still today suspicious of encroachments upon their national sovereignty. Ashgabat and Tashkent courted Washington in order to weaken Moscow, but limit any attempt to build a regional, Central Asian unity, and never made any definitive overtures to the United States. In the 1990s, Kyrgyzstan was the most motivated to introduce political and economic reforms to support "civil society" and a market economy, but remained too fragile to become the first US ally in the region. Washington has long considered Kazakhstan to be too close to Moscow and the main driver of Russian influence in the region. However, it is the only country that has also managed to implement a multi-pronged foreign policy, has remained faithful to its multi-vectored principles for two decades, and has avoided the geopolitical subterfuge and quick reversals that characterize its Uzbek neighbor. Today, Astana presents itself as one of Washington's loyal partners, united not only by economic interests but also by a strategic partnership, which has survived despite Russia's revival of influence and China's growing role.

Until the end of the 1990s, the structures of the North Atlantic Treaty Organization served as the main vector of US military cooperation with Central Asia. The five states are members of the Euro-Atlantic Partnership Council and of the Partnership for Peace. However, NATO remains relatively inactive in Central Asia compared with its advances into Ukraine or Georgia. Its aim in the region is not to prepare these countries for membership, but to maintain open lines of communication with the local governments by involving them in joint activities such as military exercises and information exchange. As Simon J. Smith and Emilian Kavalski put it, it was a sort of "cooperation à la carte."[31] In the space of a few years, Kazakhstan has managed to strengthen its strategic weight in the eyes of the Americans,[32] and, much to the annoyance of Uzbekistan, symbolically flaunted this gain by hosting the forum of the Euro-Atlantic Security Council on its territory in June 2009. Kazakhstan is also the only Central Asian state to have created a small peace-keeping force that collaborates with NATO under a UN mandate, the Kazbat battalion, which has been upgraded to the Kazbrig brigade. Astana thereby hopes to obtain interoperability status with NATO in coming years, despite its privileged partnership with Russia.[33]

The United States is also a generous donor of bilateral military aid. This aid is organized through two programs, the Foreign Military Financing program and the International Military Education and Training (ITEM) program. In exchange for often superficial reforms—such as democratic transparency, the professionalism of military personnel, the reduction of the officer corps, collaboration between services, and institutional reform—the Central Asian states can receive substantial sums, enabling them either to subsidize the basic needs of their army corps (Kyrgyzstan, Tajikistan, and Turkmenistan), or to improve military infrastructure and personnel training (Kazakhstan and Uzbekistan). Astana dominates in terms of aid received in the framework of the Foreign Military Financing program, while Bishkek leads in that of the International Military Education and Training program. Ashgabat is absent from the first program because of the nature of its authoritarian regime, and Tashkent remained absent from both of them between 2005 and 2010, when ITEM was revived by Washington.[34]

The United States is keeping a close eye on the militarization of the Caspian Sea, even though US ships cannot patrol it, since this remains a closed area reserved to the five littoral states.[35] The Caspian Sea is considered a strategic sector for US interests in at least three domains: the security of major oil companies participating in international consortiums for the exploitation of hydrocarbons in Azerbaijan and Kazakhstan; the possibility of coming to the aid of the new states if their interests are deemed threatened by Moscow or Tehran; and the security of eastern Turkey and the supervision of export routes from the Caspian to the Black Sea.

The militarization promoted by coastal states is supposed to meet several objectives: the fight against terrorist attacks that might be perpetrated against oil rigs or tankers, the protection of trade ships on the sea, campaigns against poaching sturgeon, and the management of emergency climatic situations.[36] In 2002, Russia gave a sudden boost to the militarization of the Caspian Sea, organizing military maneuvers to simulate counterterrorism and counter-poaching scenarios. The other littoral states, in particular Iran, saw this as a demonstration of force and an assertion of Russian naval superiority.[37] The response was not long in coming. In 2003, the United States launched the Caspian Guard, a training program for a network of special and police forces that would enable Azerbaijan, Kazakhstan, and potentially Turkmenistan to react rapidly and effectively to emergency situations. The most ambitious objective is to establish an integrated regime of air, maritime, and border controls. Endowed with a budget of US$130 million over ten years, the program provides member states with substantial means.[38] However, the military assistance put forward by Moscow and Washington offer is inextricably linked to their own interests: the objective is both geopolitical and commercial, since companies from both countries want to supply military equipment to the Caspian states seeking to modernize or build their fleets.

The main ally of the United States in the Caspian region is quite obviously Azerbaijan, but Washington is also zeroing in on Kazakhstan. However, despite Astana's commitment to NATO structures, relations are more complex than those with Baku, because the Kazakh authorities are less overtly opposed to Moscow. In the early 1990s, the first delegations from the US Coast Guard visited the country and agreements in the sectors of maintenance and training were signed. Financial, technical, and training aid from the United States to the Kazakh military increased after the turn of the century, once Astana made the decision to establish a creditable naval force. After

2004, the United States offered a modernization program for the Kazakh army along with several other components: training officers in the military academies of NATO members, in particular in Turkey, Greece, Italy, and Spain; supplying material for radio and radar surveillance able to monitor both the surface and the depths of the Caspian; and modernizing port infrastructure, in particular at Atyrau.[39] The United States failed to influence the tender bid that the Kazakh Defense Ministry put forward in 2007 for the purchase of large ships designed for the Caspian fleet, but upheld its offer to provide the Kazakh navy with a thousand-ton patrol boat. Baku and Astana also came to an agreement on the training of Kazakh special rapid intervention brigades in Baku, which strengthens tripartite cooperation within the framework of the Caspian Guard.[40]

America's military relations with Turkmenistan are particularly complex and relatively limited. In the 1990s, the US Department of Defense gave several patrol boats to Ashgabat after it announced that it wanted to form its own navy.[41] However, the policy of international defiance that the country's first president, Saparmurat Niyazov, pursued prevented the formalization of closer US ties with the Turkmen army, and showed preference for smaller countries that sought to limit Russian power, such as Ukraine. Ashgabat's interests in potential US support for its Caspian fleet did not develop under the second Turkmen president.

The Economic Rationales of US Involvement

Washington plays a key role in Caspian hydrocarbons and their export routes, despite its notable absence in the other domains linked to mineral resources, with the exception of uranium. Since the early 1990s, it has sought to end the Russian monopoly on Central Asian gas and oil by supporting large international players, such as Chevron and ExxonMobil, in their attempts to establish themselves in Kazakhstan. The United States is also hoping to convince the Turkmen authorities to open their onshore deposits to Western investments, although so far the attempt has been unsuccessful. It supports transport projects that bypass Russia and Iran by linking together Central Asia, the Caucasus, and Turkey.[42] Two main projects supported by the United States, the Baku-Tbilisi-Ceyhan pipeline and the Baku-Tbilisi-Erzerum gas pipeline, have come to life thanks to Turkey's strategic position and Azerbaijan's pro-Western policies. However, Kazakhstan's participation in them is still limited, and that of Ashgabat is even more restricted. Another project, the Turkmenistan-Afghanistan-Pakistan-India gas pipeline, which aims to create an opening toward India and Pakistan with Afghanistan's transformation into a transit zone, has been delayed for more than a decade.[43] The United States also supports the Asian Development Bank (ADB)-led idea of exporting electricity from Tajikistan and Kyrgyzstan toward South Asia. Forging an opening toward South Asia that might enable the region to be steered away from Russian influence will therefore greatly depend on whether Kabul can offer stability. Afghanistan thus remains one of the key elements of the US puzzle in Central Asia.[44]

The bulk of US trade with Central Asia is conducted with Kazakhstan, which has

Table 3.2

The United States' Place in Imports, Exports, and the Trade Total of Central Asian States in 2010 (in millions of US$)

	Imports	Rank	Exports	Rank	Total trade	Rank
Kazakhstan	780.6 (2.7%)	6	1,704.9 (3.7%)	6	2,485.6 (3.3%)	5
Kyrgyzstan	84 (1.2%)	9	3.5 (0.3%)	15	87.5 (1.1%)	9
Tajikistan	91.4 (3.6%)	7	0.1 (0.1%)	25	91.5 (2.5%)	8
Turkmenistan	42.5 (0.8%)	15	43.9 (1.4%)	13	86.4 (1%)	16
Uzbekistan	107.3 (1.3%)	9	60.6 (1.1%)	13	168 (1.2%)	11

Source: 2011 European Commission statistics, http://ec.europa.eu/trade/creating-opportunities/bilateral-relations/countries-and-regions/.

received a total sum of more than US$14 billion in foreign direct investment (FDI) from Washington since 1993.[45] American companies are well established in cutting edge sectors like pharmaceuticals (vaccines, medication) and medical supplies (surgical, diagnostic, and laboratory equipment, test kits), and now are attempting to establish themselves in the domain of telecommunications (digitalization, Internet-related technologies).[46] They are also interested in the oil and gas industries, in which they can anchor their expertise in cutting-edge technologies for deposit exploration, pipeline equipment, purification and ecological upgrade techniques, reviving exhausted fields, laboratory studies, refinery equipment, and the sale of oil products. This also applies in the minerals sector, where they supply excavation and extraction materials, as well as technologies for water decontamination. Many large US companies, such as the United Technologies Corporation, Sikorsky, Kellogg, and General Electric, are active in the promising domain of aircraft technologies, electricity, and railway transport in Central Asia. Lastly, the United States has become Kazakhstan's main partner in agricultural machines and equipment, ahead of Russia, Germany, and Canada, and is targeting the sectors of cereals and biofuel processing, as well as agribusiness.[47]

Nevertheless, on a purely commercial level, American power remains limited. While the United States represented more than 10 percent of Uzbekistan's foreign trade in 1996 and in 2003, this is no longer the case with the appearance of new actors on the Central Asian market. Cotton has long constituted close to 90 percent of American purchases in Uzbekistan, a figure that is declining today following the decision of large companies like Walmart to boycott Uzbek textiles. While the United States was Astana's fifth largest trade partner in 2010, with trade levels of about US$2.5 billion,[48] it ranks between the eighth and the sixteenth partner for the four other states.[49] It accounts for only three percent of Kazakh total trade, and about 1 percent for the other Central Asian countries. As a result, Washington lags far behind China, Russia, and the EU, but is also behind Turkey and Iran, South Korea, and the Ukraine. For the Central Asian governments, this lack of economic engagement is a sign of minimal long-term US commitment in the region.

The role of the United States in Central Asia has proven ambivalent. In the 1990s, in order to weaken Russia, then in the first years of the twenty-first century within the framework of the "War on Terror," Washington was accused of exacerbating antagonisms with other external actors, of forcing local governments to pick a side, of playing the "stick and carrot" game, and of going against its democratic agenda by supporting authoritarian regimes. Its "base politics," as defined by Alexander Cooley,[50] along with an excessive focus on security, have borne bitter fruit for both the American and Central Asian partners. During the Obama administration, the ledger of US activity in the region remained paradoxical. Some objectives were not reached (Moscow again became a major player in the region, and China's economic penetration was more rapid than predicted), while others were obtained but to the detriment of Central Asian economic development (the marginalization of Iran as a regional actor).[51] America's power of attraction and prestige is now negatively impacted by what Central Asian elites interpret as US failure in Afghanistan.

Nonetheless there is room for improvement. To become more influential, the United States must be able to show a commitment to Central Asian societies that goes beyond declarations of goodwill. It must find ways of realizing social and economic development, and demonstrate an ability to listen to Central Asian needs and perspectives. Since 2011 the United States is advancing the "new Silk Road" initiative, which is supposed to direct American investment in Central and South Asia to promote regional trade among Afghanistan's neighbors,[52] but this narrative will probably not lead to fundamental changes, as the region is accustomed to shifts in grand narratives without major consequences for long-term trends.

Regardless of the phases of US interest or disinterest in Central Asia, the feeling that Washington uses the region as a mere pawn in the global game of geopolitics remains dominant in Central Asian public opinion, even if the governments would like to see more US activism as a counter to Moscow and Beijing. The imbalance between the United States' status as a major geopolitical power, but a relatively minor economic actor, works against it and makes Washington appear to have little interest in local realities. It has also been reproached for its absence in the everyday challenges of Central Asian citizens and its weak commitment to development prospects. As Matteo Fumagalli notes, "the impact of U.S. policy on Central Asian state-building has been peripheral."[53] The Central Asian elites, as well as their public opinion, are thus marked by a feeling of disillusion toward the United States and a growing desire to be reassured on Washington's long-term commitment. However, the region remains only of secondary concern for American foreign policy, viewed as it is as part of the "Greater Middle East," the "arc of destabilization" gripping Afghanistan, Pakistan, and Iran, or else in Russia's "sphere of influence." It is therefore questionable what kind of interaction the United States can propose to the Central Asian states, other than being a piece of a more global policy toward Russia, Iran, China, South Asia, r Afghanistan: it is still difficult to pinpoint the rationale behind US engagement in Central Asia, and thus to articulate a long-term policy that is not based on short-term agendas. In addition, the American power of attraction is weakened by the financial and economic crisis, and more crucial theaters like the Middle East, risk make Central Asia a secondary region on the White House radar for the years to come.

Notes

1. As defined by Jim Nichol, *Central Asia: Regional Developments and Implications for U.S. Interests* (Washington DC: Congressional Research Service Report, May 31, 2012), p. 3.

2. *Sustaining US Global Leadership: Priorities for 21st Century Defense*, US Department of Defense, January 2012.

3. T. Kassenova, "Kazakhstan's 'Nuclear Renaissance'," *Stair* 3, no. 2 (2009): 51–74; C. Werner and K. Purvis-Roberts, "After the Cold War: International Politics, Domestic Policy, and the Nuclear Legacy in Kazakhstan," *Central Asian Survey* 25, no. 4 (2006): 461–80.

4. "CANWFZ Treaty Enters into Force," *James Martin Center for Nonproliferation Studies*, March 21, 2009, http://cns.miis.edu/activities/pr090321_canwfz.htm.

5. "Nazarbayev Calls on Countries to Adopt Universal Declaration on Nuclear-Free World," *Interfax*, August 26, 2010, http://www.interfax.com/newsinf.asp?id=185218; "Kazakhstan calls on OSCE States to Adopt Declaration on Nuclear-Free World," *RIA Novosti*, December 12, 2010, en.rian.ru/world/20101201/161573340.html.

6. F. Hill, "A Not-So-Grand Strategy: U.S. Policy in the Caucasus and Central Asia Since 1991," *Brookings*, February 1, 2001, http://www.brookings.edu/articles/2001/02foreignpolicy_hill.aspx.

7. More details on the website of the Office of the US Trade Representative for South and Central Asia, http://www.ustr.gov/countries-regions/south-central-asia.

8. T. W. Simons, Jr., *Eurasia's New Frontiers: Young States, Old Societies, Open Futures* (Ithaca, NY: Cornell University Press, 2008).

9. "Mystery at Manas: Strategic Blind Spots in the Department of Defense's Fuel Contracts in Kyrgyzstan," Report of the Majority Staff, Subcommittee on National Security and Foreign Affairs, Committee on Oversight and Government Reform, U.S. House of Representatives, December 2010.

10. M. Laumulin, "The U.S. Geopolitical Experience in Central Asia: Success or Failure?" in *Great Powers and Regional Integration in Central Asia: A Local Perspective*, ed. M. Esteban and N. de Pedro (Madrid: Exlibris Ediciones, 2009), 53–78.

11. Z. Brzezinski, *The Grand Chessboard: American Primacy and Its Geostrategic Imperatives* (New York: Basic Books, 1998).

12. More in Sengupta, *Heartlands of Eurasia*.

13. J. Nichol, "Central Asia's New States: Political Developments and Implications for U.S. Interests," Congressional Research Service Issue Brief IB93108, May 18, 2001.

14. S. Blank, "The United States and Central Asia," in *Central Asian Security: The New International Context*, ed. R. Allison and L. Jonson (Washington, DC: Brookings Institution Press, 2001), 127–51.

15. M. Djalili and T. Kellner, *Géopolitique de la nouvelle Asie centrale: De la fin de l'URSS à l'après–11 septembre* (Paris: PUF, 2003), 400.

16. R. Giragosian and R. N. McDermott, "U.S. Military Engagement in Central Asia: 'Great Game' or 'Great Gain'?" *Central Asia and the Caucasus*, no. 1 (2004): 53–61.

17. E. Yazdani, "US Democracy Promotion Policy in the Central Asian Republics: Myth or Reality?" *International Studies* 44, no. 2 (2007): 141–55.

18. Turkmenistan has given authorization for American planes to fly over its territory.

19. S. Akbarzadeh, "U.S.–Uzbek Partnership and Democratic Reforms," *Nationalities Papers* 32, no. 2 (2004): 271–86; B. Grodsky, "Direct Pressures for Human Rights in Uzbekistan: Understanding the US Bargaining Position," *Central Asian Survey* 23, nos. 3–4 (2004): 327–44;

J. Heathershaw, "Worlds Apart: The Making and Remaking of Geopolitical Space in the U.S.-Uzbekistani Strategic Partnership," *Central Asian Survey* 26, no. 1 (2007): 123–40.

20. M. Y. Omilecheva, "Western and Central Asian Perspectives on Democracy and Democratization," IREX Scholar Research Brief, August 2011.

21. G. Gleason, "The Uzbek Expulsion of U.S. Forces and Realignment in Central Asia," *Problems of Post-Communism* 53, no. 2 (2006): 49–60.

22. F. Purtas, "The Greater Central Asia Partnership Initiative and Its Impacts on Eurasian Security," *Journal of Central Asian and Caucasian Studies* 3, no. 5 (2008): 115–30.

23. A. Cooley, "U.S. Bases and Democratization in Central Asia," *Orbis* 52, no. 1 (2008): 65–90.

24. M. Brill Olcott, "A New Direction for U.S. Policy in the Caspian Region," Working Paper of the Carnegie Endowment for International Peace, February 2009.

25. D. Tynan, "Uzbekistan: Did Karimov Tantrum Prompt NDN Transit Fee Hike?" *Eurasianet*, February 10, 2011, http://www.eurasianet.org/node/62872.

26. Authors' fieldwork in the Rasht Valley, June 2010.

27. C. J. Radin, "Analysis: The US-Pakistan Relationship and the Critical Factor of Supply," *The Long War Journal*, December 4, 2011, http://www.longwarjournal.org/archives/2011/12/us_pakistani_relatio.php#ixzz22hz30GsU.

28. A. Kuchins, T. Sanderson, and D. Gordon, *The Northern Distribution Network and the Modern Silk Road* (Washington, DC: CSIS, 2009).

29. D. Tynan, "The Pentagon Spreading Wealth in Central Asia," *Eurasianet*, June 19, 2010, http://www.eurasianet.org/node/61434.

30. "SShA i Uzbekistan rasshiriaiut voennoe sotrudnichestvo," *Voice of America*, September 30, 2011, http://www.voanews.com/russian/news/USA-Uzbekistan-2011-09-30-130867828.html; S. Corke, "In Courting Uzbekistan, the United States Stoops too Low," *Freedom House*, November 3, 2011, http://blog.freedomhouse.org/weblog/2011/11/in-courting-uzbekistan-the-united-states-stoops-too-low.html.

31. S. J. Smith and E. Kavalski, "NATO's Partnership with Central Asia: Cooperation *à la carte*," in *The New Central Asia: The Regional Impact of International Actors*, ed. E. Kavalski (Singapore: World Scientific Publishing, 2010), 29.

32. R. N. McDermott, "United States and NATO Military Cooperation with Kazakhstan: The Need for a New Approach," *Journal of Slavic Military Studies* 21, no. 4 (2008): 615–41.

33. R. N. McDermott, *Kazakhstan's Defense Policy: An Assessment of the Trends* (Carlisle, PA: Strategic Studies Institute, US Army War College, 2009).

34. See the section on US Assistance on the Department of State's Bureau of European and Eurasian Affairs website, http://www.state.gov/p/eur/ace/c11609.htm.

35. G. Bahgat, *American Oil Diplomacy in the Persian Gulf and the Caspian Sea* (Gainesville: University Press of Florida, 2003).

36. More details in M. Laruelle and S. Peyrouse, "The Militarization of the Caspian Sea: 'Great Games' and 'Small Games' Over the Caspian Fleets," *China and Eurasia Forum Quarterly* 7, no. 2 (2009): 17–35.

37. A. Tsyganok, "The Power-Keg of Eurasia: Militarization in the Greater Caucasus Could Have Dangerous Consequences," *Nezavisimoe voennoe obozrenie*, no. 5, February 9, 2007, 2.

38. S. L. Quigley, "European Command Transforming to Accommodate New Challenges," *American Force Press Services*, March 9, 2006, http://www.defenselink.mil/news/newsarticle.aspx?id=15224.

39. R. N. McDermott, "Kazakhstan Boosting Caspian Security," *Eurasia Daily Monitor* 3, no. 100, May 23, 2006, http://www.jamestown.org/single/?no_cache=1&tx_ttnews%5Btt_news%5D=31705.

40. "Kto skazal chto voenno-morskomu flotu Kazakhstana prishel konets?" *Aktau Business*, December 30, 2008, http://www.aktau-business.com/2008/12/30/kto-skazal-chto-voenno-morskomu-flotu-kazakhstana.html.

41. J. Nichol, "Turkmenistan: Recent Developments and U.S. Interests," Congressional Research Service Report, May 26, 2011.

42. S. F. Starr and S. E. Cornell, eds., *Baku-Tbilisi-Ceyhan Pipeline: Oil Window to the West* (Uppsala: Silk Road Studies Program, 2005).

43. For more details, see chapter 9.

44. J. Nichol, "Central Asia's Security: Issues and Implications for US Interests," Congressional Research Service Report, February 2009.

45. See the background note on Kazakhstan sheet at the US State Department, http://www.state.gov/r/pa/ei/bgn/5487.htm.

46. According to the data that was available at http://www.buyusa.gov/kazakhstan/en/leading_sectors.html in 2011. The new page at http://export.gov/kazakhstan/index.asp does not provide any more details.

47. Ibid.

48. See the Office of the US Trade Representative, http://www.ustr.gov.

49. 2011 European Commission statistics, http://ec.europa.eu/trade/creating-opportunities/bilateral-relations/countries-and-regions/.

50. A. Cooley, *Base Politics: Democratic Changes and the US Military Overseas* (Ithaca, NY: Cornell University Press, 2008).

51. Brill Olcott, "A New Direction for U.S. Policy."

52. J. Nichol, "Central Asia: Regional Developments and Implications for U.S. Interests," Congressional Research Service Report, October 12, 2011; J. Kucera, "Central Asia: Can Expanded Trade Pacify an Unsettled Region?" *Eurasianet*, October 31, 2011, http://www.eurasianet.org/node/64419.

53. M. Fumagalli, "The United States and Central Asia," in Kavalski, *The New Central Asia*, 177.

4
The European Union
Soft Power or *Realpolitik*?

The European Union has been slow to emerge on the Central Asian scene, and has long delegated the promotion of its interests to the leading country in the region, Germany. However, in the last several years, a common European foreign policy has taken shape and the EU has gained visibility and influence, with the hope to create various niches, both sectoral and geographic, in which it can become a leading actor. Its immediate neighborhood in the Mediterranean and Eastern Europe is naturally privileged, but Central Asia might become a kind of modest extended neighborhood of the EU. Besides the desire to promote a value agenda and soft power strategies, Europe has both economic and security interests in the region: EU relations with Russia and its Near Abroad, the risk of spillovers from Afghanistan, drug trafficking, flows of migrants and refugees, and subsoil riches it would benefit from accessing. However, despite its role as a major commercial partner of Central Asia, the EU hardly has the means to back its ambitions—a situation that is likely to worsen with the 2011 debt crises—and has failed to succeed in reconciling its contradictory agendas and diverse actors. Nonetheless the EU does have long-term advantages in terms of cultural prestige, quality of life, level of education, and specialized know-how, and as a symbol of soft power that searches for synergy rather than conflict.

A Double Challenge: Elaborating Strategies, Delivering Messages

At the beginning of the 1990s, the European Union was managing a full agenda: German reunification and the Franco-German balance, the introduction of the Schengen agreement, the crisis in Yugoslavia, preparing the Central European states for membership, and building new relations with Moscow. The conflicts in the Caucasus and Moldova and the difficult situation in Ukraine also demanded EU attention. Consequently, Central Asia did not constitute a priority; member states were only moderately interested and many of them left Central Asian affairs to their embassies in Moscow and Istanbul. As for the European Commission, it opened a full office in Almaty in 1994, which also had responsibility for the four other republics. It was not until 2010 that the European missions to Kyrgyzstan and Tajikistan were upgraded to full diplomatic delegations, and until 2012 for Uzbekistan. In Turkmenistan the

58

Commission is represented by a so-called Europa House, with no diplomatic status, which takes care of cooperation in policy sectors. Trade and consular questions remain in the hands of the member states' embassies.[1] The objective is to eventually open full representation in Ashgabat once the latter has given authorization.

In the summer of 2007, the German presidency of the EU ratified a "Strategy for a New Partnership with Central Asia," designed to give renewed impetus to relations between the two regions. The project's ambition signals a palpable evolution in European perceptions. The EU made provision for doubling its aid to Central Asia over the period 2007–2013 around three major objectives: stability and security; the fight against poverty; and regional cooperation between the states of Central Asia and the EU in the domains of energy, transport, higher education, and the environment.[2] Even at its most dynamic, the EU Strategy in Central Asia remains small compared to the Eastern Partnership, directed toward Ukraine, Belarus, Moldova, and the three South Caucasian states. The Eastern Partnership is meant to complement the Northern Dimension and the Union for the Mediterranea by providing an institutionalized forum for discussing visa agreements, free trade deals, and strategic partnership agreements with the EU's eastern neighbors, while avoiding the controversial topic of accession to the European Union.[3] Although Kazakhstan's accession to the Eastern Partnership has been discussed informally, especially in 2010 when the country held the chairmanship of the OSCE (Organization for Security and Cooperation in Europe), Central Asia is not meant to be a part of it and the EU's normative impact on the region is destined to remain limited.

Europe involves many different players, which gives it richness, but also limits its capability to act as a unified player and impedes its international visibility. The European Union itself is a complex structure with three heads—the Commission, Council, and Parliament; and with different spokesmen—the governments of the troika (the state that exercises the EU presidency, the one before it and the future one), the president of the Commission, and the higher representatives. It is hindered by internal contradictions among the Commission's administrative services, as well as by the limited resources allocated for the region.[4] The seven priorities that the strategy defines are too general to easily yield results on the ground and moreover, each member state has its own logic of involvement in Central Asia. Some countries—Germany, the UK, Italy, France, the Netherlands—have been present since the 1990s; others are newcomers, like Finland, which arrived in 2009 with a new "Wider Europe" program; still other active countries in the region, like Switzerland, are not part of the EU structure. Member states have conflicting perceptions of their interests in the region. Germany in particular, but also Italy, and to a lesser degree France, have advocated for a clearly utilitarian view of Central Asia, while the UK and the Nordic countries wish to emphasize the values agenda. In addition, the EU collaborates closely with other international organizations, especially those of the UN, and with international donors, and delegates some of its activities. For Central Asian countries, characterized as they are by paternalistic heads of state and a hierarchical and centralized conception of authority, the multitude of European identities and actors is difficult to grasp.

Three elements compete for European interest in Central Asia: the promotion of human rights, civil society, and the rule of law, which is a fundamental part of the EU's value engagement; emerging energy interests that aim to link Turkmenistan to the Southern Corridor; and fostering security in "Greater Central Asia," first through the Western military engagement in Afghanistan since 2001, and now with the preparation of the withdrawal, scheduled for 2014, and the debate about possible spillovers from Afghanistan in Central Asia. In practice, these objectives sometimes compete. The European desire to diversify gas export routes and reduce its dependence on Russia has, for instance, led to a relaxation of human rights pressure on Ashgabat. Although having multiple energy suppliers is a legitimate strategy, Turkmenistan is not reason enough for the jettisoning of the value agenda, and the Central Asian economies need investment and know-how from Europe more than Europe needs Turkmen gas.[5] The Central Asian governments that participate in the Northern Distribution Network, particularly Uzbekistan at its core, also expect to be rewarded for their contribution to the Western intervention in Afghanistan and would like to see Western criticism put aside. The security agenda is therefore paradoxical too, as it is in Central Asia's interest that the international community does not leave Afghanistan unstable. But the EU lacks the means to resolve its internal contradictions. Policy will remain torn between different approaches, but with an already visible trend toward prioritizing energy and security over value-based agenda.

Four major controversies concerning Central Asia have fueled virulent debates among European institutions.[6] First was the vote for sanctions against Uzbekistan following the suppression of the Andijan insurrection in May 2005, which led to an arms embargo and a European travel ban for a dozen senior Uzbek officials.[7] Very quickly, Germany argued for lifting the sanctions, in large part to safeguard its privileged military position at Termez, and has received persons targeted by the sanctions, officially for medical reasons. On the other hand, advocacy groups explained that sanctions could be effective only if all European states applied them equally and that they should target those who stand to lose the most: the leadership of the country with their privileges of overseas travel, European real estate, and investment income concealed in European banks. In the fall of 2009, the sanctions were finally lifted thanks to German lobbying, which was perceived as a victory for the Uzbek government, and a failure in the EU's ability to promote a value agenda.[8]

The second controversy took place from 2007 to 2009, during the campaign for Kazakhstan's candidacy for the chairmanship of the OSCE. Here also, Berlin lobbied in favor of its Central Asian ally without stipulating any conditional agenda of political reform, while Great Britain voiced a much more reserved opinion about the legitimacy of the Kazakh choice and France occupying a position somewhere in-between.[9] Supporters of Astana's candidacy advanced symbolic (Kazakhstan as the first post-communist state leading an organization created during the Cold War) and comparative arguments (Kazakhstan as a country doing well compared to its neighbors). Kazakhstan is indeed an enthusiastic player in international and regional organizations, successfully denuclearized, economically thriving, relatively stable politically, and strikes a geopolitical balance between Russia, China, and the EU. Critics of its candidacy questioned the legitimacy of giving leadership of the OSCE to a country that has not had a free and fair election since 1991, is pursuing no reforms in this area, has had the same leader since 1989, and whose elites shamelessly appropriated national wealth.[10] Kazakhstan's leadership has not fulfilled the hopes of the OSCE: international visibility of the organization has not increased; tensions between its members, in particular between Russia, Armenia, and Azerbaijan, have remained significant; and Kazakhstan has openly flouted OSCE political values by imprisoning journalists and human rights activists in 2010 and by holding early presidential elections in 2011, which Nazarbayev won in Soviet fashion with 91 percent of the vote.[11]

A third controversy was linked to forced child labor employed in Uzbekistan's cotton harvests in Uzbekistan. Sustained pressure from 2008 by human rights organizations eventually resulted in some large European companies refusing to buy Uzbek cotton. This led to Tashkent passing a law banning child labor, although the exploitation of children persists.[12] Then, in 2010 and 2011, a fourth controversy erupted with regard to the ratification of the PCA (Partnership and Cooperation Agreement) with Turkmenistan, which had been pending since 1998. Several European countries wished to ratify it to confirm the place of Ashgabat in European energy strategies and to initiate a dialogue on possible reforms, while opponents criticized the Turkmen regime as authoritarian and refused to make any concessions in exchange for partnership with the EU.[13] Controversies of lesser magnitude are commonplace, for example the refusal of European institutions to admit who was responsible for inviting Uzbek President, Islam Karimov, to visit Brussels in early 2011.[14]

The Joint EU Council and Commission Implementation Report of the EU Strategy for Central Asia, published in June 2010, provided an update on activities since 2007. It recognized these diverging agendas,[15] but without proposing concrete solutions. Some European experts believe that it is impossible to impose democracy from the outside and that it is necessary to "work toward the future" by maintaining a dialogue with the Central Asian regimes, even the most repressive ones. By this logic, the EU will be influential in Central Asia if it is present there, which means building relationships based on common economic and security interests, and leaving aside areas of contention.[16] For others, the EU risks being "on the wrong side of history" by supporting corrupt regimes and thus weakening local supporters of reform. The 2011 Arab Spring supported such a view by gradually forcing an overwhelmed EU to abandon its special relationships with established authoritarian leaders and accept less advantageous geopolitical terms in order to take into account local democratic aspirations.[17] European experts Jos Boonstra and Michael Denison posit that to solve these dilemmas, the driving force of EU engagement with Central Asia should be based on closer links between security and development, with better identified areas of focus (water issues, drug-trafficking, poverty, good governance) and argue that these components are also in the direct interests of the Central Asian states themselves.[18]

A Growing Focus on Security Matters

The EU does not position itself on the international scene as a hard security actor, and its security assistance is often associated with other institutions. Hard security is the domain of NATO, which has its own strategy of engagement with the Central Asian states via Partnership for Peace programs and, for Kazakhstan, a specific Individual Partnership Action Plan (IPAP). Some member states, especially Germany, but also France, have their own bilateral programs (assistance for the training of police and canine brigades, etc.), while soft security is mainly managed by the OSCE, for instance with its border guard training program. Because of the multiplicity of European actors and the fact that EU security mechanisms are too limited and dispersed to be effective, there is no European "grand narrative" on Central Asian security that could compete with that of Russia, China, or the United States. In addition, related security issues are divided into different programs, although in 2006, the establishment of an EU special representative for Central Asia directly linked to the high representative of the Union for Foreign Affairs and Security Policy has helped to create a more centralized dynamic that gives visibility to the security agenda, though partly at the expense of the value agenda.[19]

The 2007 EU Strategy for Central Asia mentions security among its goals, especially border management, the proximity of Afghanistan with its associated challenges, and drug trafficking. The Border Management in Central Asia (BOMCA) Program and Central Asia Drug Action Program (CADAP), both implemented by the United Nations Development Programme (UNDP), are the most well-known EU programs on border securitization. They focus on renovating or building border posts, equipping them with high-tech materiel, training the border guards in search and detection, initiating joint exercises with neighboring countries, and improving cross-border trade.[20] The European countries also encourage many multilateral initiatives, for instance the Central Asia Border Security Initiative (CABSI), a platform for dialogue and discussion initiated by the Austrian Federal Ministry of the Interior with support from the European Union. CABSI meets at regular intervals with members of the international donor community and agencies involved in border security technical assistance, and with, Japan, the Russian Federation, and the United States.[21] The Central Asia Regional Information and Coordination Centre (CARICC) for combating the illicit trafficking of narcotics and psychotropic substances is now operational, and plans to establish links with Interpol.[22] However, due to lack of independent evaluation, it is unclear if these Western-led programs are having a positive impact and if they are sustainable, and thus far, European actions have not resulted in the construction of a regional security architecture.[23]

The June 2010 Joint EU Council and Commission Implementation Report of the EU Strategy for Central Asia recognizes the deficiencies of the strategy in terms of security, and calls for reinforced efforts in "security broadly speaking."[24] It concludes: "It will be necessary to expand the concept of security to include major international and regional challenges such as human security, combating drug trafficking and trafficking in human beings, precursors, nuclear and radioactive materials, uranium tailings, border management, bio-safety, bio-security, combating terrorism and preventing radicalization and extremism, including via a continued emphasis on poverty alleviation. Combating corruption is an important element in countering many of these security challenges."[25] Meanwhile the European Parliament is developing its own position on the implementation of the EU Strategy. The August 2011 draft report on this matter emphasizes the concept of human security. It "takes the view that the cornerstones of the EU's new approach to the region must be human security and genuine regional cooperation,"[26] and calls for the EU to promote "security by meeting the practical day-to-day needs of the population."[27] The EU's new conception of security seems to take greater stock of social and political contexts. It calls for developing a more comprehensive conception of security, promoting good governance principles (the Rule of Law initiative), pushing for more regional cooperation (Water Initiative), and also potentially supporting OSCE calls for security sector reform (SSR).[28]

Bureaucratic Complexities and Limited Effectiveness

Unlike the programs that preceded the 2007 Strategy, which included the five states within the same regional approach, the EU now focuses on bilateral relations in order to better target the specific problems of each country. This dissociation is appreciated locally and analyzed as proof of growing EU pragmatism. In total, between 1991 and 2006, the European Union committed more than 1.3 billion euros in aid to Central Asia, distributed among varied sectors linked to the promotion of democracy and pluralism, to economic modernization, to regional cooperation, to energy, to water, as well as to the struggle against threats such as terrorism, drug trafficking, and human trafficking. With the new Strategy, about 719 million euros are to be spent by 2013 through a detailed Central Asia Indicative Program and a general Regional Strategy Paper for Assistance to Central Asia.[29] Two-thirds of these funds are reserved for EU bilateral assistance toward poverty reduction and sustainable development, while the regional approach, which is the recipient of one third of the budget, is dedicated to all transnational questions, such as organized crime, drug trafficking, and water management.[30]

EU development aid has been significantly refocused on Tajikistan and Kyrgyzstan, in particular through the Food Security Program and the Non-State Actor/Local Authorities Program. The idea is that addressing poverty reduction, improvement of living standards, and rural development will foster social and political stability in these two weak states. In the three other states, the development aid is associated with programs such as cooperation in higher education, water management issues, preparedness for natural disasters, good governance, civil society promotion, and so on.[31] In terms of development, the EU is not the only European actor present in Central Asia, and coordinates its activities with the European Bank for Reconstruction and Development (EBRD), the European Investment Bank (EIB), and with member states' programs: the Deutsche Gesellschaft für Internationale Zusammenarbeit (GIZ), the

German Development Bank (KfW), the UK Department for International Development (DFID). The Swedish International Development Cooperation Agency (SIDA) has closed its offices in the region but the French Agency for Development (AFD) plans to be more involved.[32]

Until 2006 the chief EU aid program, called Technical Assistance to the Commonwealth of Independent States (TACIS), had as its general goal the promotion of the transition to a market economy and democratic governance through support to political and institutional reforms, the development of infrastructure, and minimization of the social consequences of the transition.[33] Aid was offered in three major trends: a regional cooperation program designed to promote good-neighbor relations, the development of energy and transport networks, efficient use of natural resources, and the implementation of international conventions on the environment; a national-level program of aid for Central Asia's integration, the application of trade agreements, and support for educational reforms and professional training; and for the most vulnerable social groups in the Ferghana Valley and the Khatlon region in Tajikistan. This notwithstanding, TACIS did not prove to be a very efficient program: it faced considerable delays, due both to the European bureaucracy and to ratification delays from the Central Asian administrations.[34]

Since the closure of the TACIS program, European aid has been restructured around the Development Cooperation Instrument (DCI), which merges various geographical instruments and issues. It is therefore no longer specific to the post-Soviet states as such and gathers all the institutional tools that the Commission has at its disposal. In the framework of regional cooperation (one-third of the budget), the DCI for Central Asia has defined four main objectives: support for energy and transport networks and integration into the world market; improvement of environmental management, in particular water and forests; border and migration management, including the fight against organized crime; and the promotion of educational exchanges. However, two-thirds of EU aid is given to bilateral programs that are mainly focused on poverty reduction and, to a lesser extent, on good governance and economic reform.[35] The DCI also tries to link up with another financial instrument, the European Neighborhood Policy Instrument, which relates to Mediterranean, East European, and South Caucasus countries.

Apart from the DCI, EU assistance is grounded in four thematic programs: democracy and human rights, nuclear safety, stability, and humanitarian. The second program guarantees EU aid in cases of nuclear threat, while the objective of the third instrument is to support actions for maintaining peace and for helping countries to combat organized crime, terrorism, and transnational menaces. The Humanitarian Office of the European Commission, created in 1992, has been assigned the mission of helping the victims of natural and human catastrophes. However, this aid was reduced after 2004, since the EU decided that the humanitarian situation and the involvement of external actors for development made it possible to focus on other issues. Lastly, the European Union runs three specific economic programs for the region: the Central Asia Invest Program, designed to promote sustainable economic development in the private sector and among small- and medium-size companies; the Interstate Oil and Gas Transport to Europe (INOGATE) program, responsible for facilitating the establishment of an international legal regime around the Caspian Sea and the Black Sea; and the Transport Corridor Europe-Caucasus-Asia (TRACECA) program, aimed at opening up Central Asia and the Caucasus through the creation of a vast transport and communications corridor along an east-west axis.

Paradoxically, despite this multitude of instruments, the EU is not highly visible as a political entity on the Central Asian scene. Like Japan, it is one of the largest donors but also one of the least known, which creates difficulties for unified international action.[36] EU publications are usually upbeat about their successes, particularly in matters such as promoting human rights dialogue and good governance at the local level, as well as support for civil society. However, numerous observers have given far more reserved, and even critical, assessments of the results obtained and the visibility of the EU.[37] For instance, the EU considers the Human Rights Dialogues, established on a bilateral basis with the five states, to be a success, as they exist even with the Uzbek and Turkmen governments, and allow for the discussion of specific cases of imprisoned persons. European political programs concerning the abolition of the death penalty and penitentiary system reforms have also obtained some results. However, the human rights situation in these five states has continued to deteriorate and the dialogue does not really impact on local realities.[38]

The European programs are also roundly criticized by Central Asian actors, both official and unofficial, from different motives. Criticisms include having grandiose objectives but modest means; an absence of transparency in the recruitment of European companies working for the EU in the region; the low level of qualifications of expert agencies selected to provide project feasibility assessments; the disproportionate salaries offered to European expatriates compared to local counterparts; a failure to empower local companies able to benefit from a transfer of technology and know-how through cooperation with European firms; a lack of monitoring of the allocated funds, which favors their misappropriation; and finally, an overly opaque bureaucracy for NGOs and social activists who wish to benefit from the opportunities offered.[39] Broad-ranging EU aspirations tend therefore to work against the focused pursuit of achievable and measurable objectives.

Fostering European Commitment Through the Economy?

Until recently, the European institutions ignored economic issues and regarded them as best dealt with by member states or the private sector. However, the EU increasingly values European economic potential as a driver of its involvement in Central Asia. EU trade relations with Kazakhstan, Kyrgyzstan, and Uzbekistan are governed by a Partnership and Cooperation Agreement (PCA), which is a non-preferential agreement in which the parties grant each other most-favored nation (MFN) status, prohibiting tariffs and quantitative restrictions in bilateral trade. Pending the ratification of the PCA signed with Tajikistan in 2004, an interim agreement on trade and trade-related matters governs EU-Tajik bilateral trade relations. The PCA concluded with Turkmenistan in

Table 4.1

The EU's Place in Imports, Exports, and the Trade Total of Central Asian States in 2010 (in millions of US$)

	Imports	Rank	Exports	Rank	Total trade	Rank
Kazakhstan	6,865.2(23.8%)	2	17,326.2 (37.8%)	1	24,191.4 (32.4%)	1
Kyrgyzstan	284.7(4.1%)	4	18.2 (1.7%)	8	302.9 (3.8%)	5
Tajikistan	251.4(9.8%)	3	41.9 (3.7%)	6	293.3 (7.9%)	5
Turkmenistan	968.6(17.9%)	2	423.8 (13.1%)	2	1,392.4 (16.1%)	3
Uzbekistan	1,683.4(21%)	2	453.6 (8%)	5	2,137 (16.2%)	3

Source: 2011 European Commission statistics, http://ec.europa.eu/trade/creating-opportunities/bilateral-relations/countries-and-regions/.

1998 has not yet been ratified by the EU due to the domestic political situation. As a result, EU-Turkmenistan trade relations are still based on the trade and cooperation agreement signed with the Soviet Union in 1989. All five Central Asian countries are beneficiaries of the EU's generalized system of preferences.

As a whole, the EU is the second-largest trading partner of the Central Asian region, just after China and well before Russia, accounting for more than a quarter of its overall foreign trade.[40] However, if one compares the bilateral trade of Germany with Central Asia to the Russian and Chinese figures, the difference is obviously great: the most prominent European actor's trade with the region has a value of less than US$8 billion, so well below Beijing and Moscow.[41] Kazakhstan positions itself as the principal Central Asian partner of the EU, with trade rising exponentially from US$6.2 billion in 2003 to 24 billion in 2010.[42] Uzbekistan trails in second place, far behind its Kazakh competitor, while Turkmenistan is in third place. Trade with Kyrgyzstan and Tajikistan remains minuscule with a very limited presence of European companies in these two countries often being linked to assistance programs. The economic relations between the EU and Central Asia have therefore a radically imbalanced nature. While the EU constitutes one of the premier commercial partners of Central Asia, the reverse is far from true. In 2010, Kazakhstan represented 1.1 percent of total European imports and 0.4 percent of its exports, placing it thirtieth among the EU's trading partners.

Central Asia's basic wealth consists of its energy resources, some minerals, and its geographical location. EU-Central Asia trade is therefore driven by the energy sector. About 80 percent of EU imports from Kazakhstan are oil products; for Turkmenistan the figure is 90 percent and for Uzbekistan, only 30 percent, even if it remains the first in terms of total value.[43] Investments follow the same pattern: the EU is the largest foreign investor in Kazakhstan with 54 percent of the sum of its FDI, but two-thirds of this are devoted to the mining and extraction sector and one-quarter to geological exploration.[44] A similar profile of investments occurs in Turkmenistan and in Uzbekistan. After hydrocarbons, the nuclear sector constitutes a major component of the European presence in Central Asia, whether through the extraction of Kazakh and

Uzbek uranium, or the construction of nuclear power plants by Areva in partnership with Kazatomprom. Security industries, such as military, aeronautic, and aerospace sectors, also have a rising prominence as Central Asian military budgets have grown steadily since 2007.[45] Additionally, European firms are established in the extraction of precious minerals and metallurgy as well as Central Asia's electric sector, this despite strong international competition.

The EU also has other commercial hands that it can play. The most obvious (but not necessarily the most profitable since it involves sums that are quite modest) concerns what could be called sectors of "national representation," which include traditional industries or industries linked to specific countries: cosmetics, perfumes, and luxury clothes from France, and also, though to a lesser degree, from the rest of Europe; tobacco from Benelux; marble and jewelry from Italy; wood products from Scandinavia and Central Europe; and more generally luxury food, crafts, and alcohol. These quality products have a worldwide reputation to which the Central Asian markets are not impervious, even if their commercial impact remains modest as they are destined for the upper classes, which are not sizeable, even in Kazakhstan.[46]

The EU can also boast of having several areas of excellence capable of rivaling its international competitors. In the industrial domain, the dominant area is probably automobile production, followed by sectors such as chemicals, construction, glass, cement, and cotton. To this can be added certain types of industrial equipment, although they are often too expensive for the Central Asian economies, which prefer to get their supplies from Asian markets. There is also agribusiness, which is becoming increasingly sophisticated, as well as specific agricultural techniques, for example in the treatment of cotton. European know-how in marine industries could also be of interest to Kazakhstan and possibly to Turkmenistan for their national Caspian fleet. Another great strength of the European economy concerns the high-tech sectors linked to technological, scientific, and biological innovation. They include information technologies and telecommunications; optics; biotechnology and the pharmaceutical sector; road, rail, and air transport; nanotechnologies; and renewable energies. Lastly, European firms have a strong worldwide reputation in scientific and applied research, the financial and banking system, strategic advice, financial engineering, and advanced medicines.[47]

In a globalized world, however, Central Asia is not a profitable area for European enterprises. The cost of labor is relatively high, the technical specializations developed in the Soviet era are in the process of disappearing, the investment climate is negative, and the political context fragile. Nonetheless, the activities of European companies in Central Asia ought to be about more than just trade and making profit. Commercial involvement may foster European goals in the region, such as consolidating the overall EU-Central Asian relationship; preventing the Central Asian countries from having to rely too heavily on a few markets; helping to strengthen the institutions of civil society and good governance; and addressing poverty as the root cause of instability. In theory, the EU could make use of its business potential to help disseminate the societal model that it wishes to embody, and choose to privilege business relations that respect the rights of local workers, fight against corruption, promote fair competition and good corporate governance, and recognize the importance of contracts. The long-term objective would be to augment the social responsibility of Central Asian enterprises, something that could have indirect repercussions on the societies themselves insofar as it favors the emergence of a middle class that has political clout.[48]

A stumbling block remains that European private actors do not consider Central Asia to be a profitable region for them. Moreover, large firms, mainly in the energy sector, which shape European economic engagement in Central Asia, do not seek to promote EU values, but rather to build strong alliances with Central Asian leaders to secure their investments. This raises several questions, the answers to which are not unequivocal. Can energy be the driver of EU engagement if energy firms do not support the EU global agenda in the region? Can the promotion of the business sector find a place in the EU's overall strategy without contradicting its value objectives? Should the objective be to promote a sort of committed business strategy, proving that it is possible to support human rights, principles of good governance, and the emergence of the middle class? Should the EU lend its support to business that is principally oriented toward the fight against poverty and sectors involving important ethical issues? Can the EU really promote "clean business" in Central Asia when its own territory is host to financial havens, in particular Luxembourg, where Central Asian heads of state, their families, and the oligarchs stash money away that has been siphoned from the national wealth? Can it emphasize respect for human rights at the same time that in Turkmenistan, French company Bouygues fought to obtain contracts for the pharaonic construction projects of the former dictator Saparmurat Niyazov and also actively participated in the president's personality cult?[49] As is often the case, the envisaged solutions do not so much depend on the type of relations built with Central Asia, but much more on choices internal to the EU and on the ability of member states and European private actors to reconcile their divergent interests.

Member States as the Bearers of Europe's Business Image

As the premier industrial power of Europe, and the fifth-largest economic power in the world, Germany is a key partner driving EU relations with Central Asia, and its direct investment in the region totaled some 250 million euros in 2008.[50] The German-Kazakh partnership is conceived both by Berlin and Astana as a long-term one, and it is based on old, historical links related to the German diaspora in Kazakhstan (close to one million persons at the end of the Soviet Union, but today about 200,000). During the 1990s, most of this diaspora returned to settle in Germany, and in doing so some took advantage of becoming economic go-betweens, seeking to develop bilateral trade relations.[51] Although Berlin is interested in the energy sector, German firms focus mainly on projects with medium infrastructure and high added value such as industrial production, automobile mechanic construction, the electronics industry, agricultural processing industries, and the management and the training of qualified specialists. This interest is mutual. Kazakhstan's strategy for industrial and technological development tries to attract German investors in industrial sectors not related to hydrocarbons, such as transformation technologies and six pilot sectors (construction, tourism, agriculture, transport infrastructure, agribusiness, and the textile industry).[52]

The Italian economy, marked by strong regional contrasts, has many trump cards, including the notoriety of its savoir-faire. Italy is one of Kazakhstan's principal commercial partners, mostly thanks to ENI leadership in the North Caspian Sea Consortium in Kashagan and a growing presence in Turkmenistan. Bilateral exchanges have risen considerably over recent years. Cooperation is developing in very diverse sectors, stretching from the treatment of agricultural and industrial resources to light industry, foodstuffs, and the construction of agricultural equipment.[53] Like France, Italy's exchanges with Uzbekistan have declined over recent years because of Tashkent's policies, but Rome remains interested in Uzbek textiles. French firms have shown some timidity given the difficulties of investing in the region and have reduced their presence in Uzbekistan, but exchanges with Kazakhstan have increased considerably since 2008. Central Asia buys arms from France, as well as nuclear, electric, electronic, and mechanical equipment; basic consumer goods; medications and cosmetics; cars; foodstuffs; and construction materials; and big companies like Total, Areva, Thales, and Alstom are also increasingly involved in the Central Asian market.[54]

In the 1990s, Great Britain was the largest investor in the Kazakh economy after the United States, and over the last decade commercial exchanges between the United Kingdom and Central Asia have risen considerably.[55] British firms are looking to diversify their investments in sectors other than hydrocarbons, such as new technologies, technology and science parks, and agricultural production. London has also supported Astana's wishes to become a regional financial center for the whole Central Asia. These regional exchanges are partly structured by the Scottish city of Aberdeen, which has developed partnerships with Atyrau, Mangistau, and western Kazakhstan.[56] The Netherlands is also one of Central Asia's major investors, especially in Kazakhstan. Dutch companies are particularly interested in foreign investments since their economy is heavily based on foreign trade. The country has been exploring new markets in the post-Soviet space by playing on its central position in air transport, and its status as one of the world's largest exporters of agricultural and market produce. Many projects linked to solar, wind, and hydroelectric power are underway. Between 1993 and 2008, the Netherlands invested more than 7 billion euros in FDI, which makes it Kazakhstan's premier foreign investor. These investments are focused on the energy sector, finance, transport, communications, and transformation industries.[57]

Other European countries, such as Spain, Belgium, Luxembourg, Sweden, Finland, Greece, and Austria, are also involved in Central Asia, but on a more modest scale. They often occupy specific commercial niches, but do not have the same influence as larger countries. Trade exchanges between Central Asia, on the one hand, and Denmark, Portugal, Ireland, Malta, and Cyprus, on the other, are minuscule, or indeed non-existent. By contrast, the countries of Central Europe, former allies of the socialist bloc and now EU member states, offer good opportunities for collaboration with Central Asia. While usually less competitive than Western Europe's, Central Europe's chemical industries (cleaners, fertilizers, pharmaceuticals), transport equipment, and agribusiness are of interest to the Central Asians. In the latter sector, there exists compatibility between the erstwhile socialist countries. Foodstuffs (for example, Czech beer, Hungarian cooked meats) and the wood and furniture sector in Central Europe are aimed at Central Asian middle-class consumers, as their price is better suited to their lower standard of living, and they enjoy a better reputation than those from China.[58]

Poland is one of Central Asia's leading economic partners in Central Europe. Warsaw opened a chamber of commerce and industry in Almaty and the Polish diaspora in Kazakhstan appears active in the development of trade and small joint ventures. Regional cooperation agreements were signed between the regions of Akmolinsk and Mazovia, focusing especially on the construction sector, chemical industry, and agriculture.[59] The Czech Republic has also sharply increased trade with Kazakhstan, and has a well-established presence in Uzbekistan, with interests in the gas, chemical, glass, textile, and water industries. The two countries have cooperated in the mechanical engineering sector, as some of the trolleys and trams in Uzbekistan were manufactured in the Czech Republic.[60] Like other countries of the former Eastern bloc, the Czech Republic purchases much of its cotton from Tashkent, and in 2006, cotton fiber accounted for two-thirds of Czech imports from Uzbekistan.[61] However, this figure will likely decline as the Czech textile industry weakens and as Uzbekistan seeks to process its own cotton. Central Europe and the Balkans also see Central Asia as a future source of energy imports that could reduce their often-total dependence on Russian supplies. Although small compared to Western giants, their national oil companies seek their respective places in the Kazakh market. At the forefront of Central European energy activism, the Romanian company Petrom hopes to establish a cycle of petroleum exploration, extraction, and processing in Kazakhstan and to promote the Romania's location as a crossroads of export routes.[62]

Last but not least, since Soviet times the Baltic states have been one of the principal bases for the export of Central Asian products to Europe, particularly cotton, but also metals. They also specialized in exporting buses, tramways, and carriages, as well as telephones. With the collapse of the Soviet Union, trade relations disappeared, only to take off again at the start of the twenty-first century. Kazakh exports to the Baltic region mostly consist of combustible minerals, oil, and heavy metals, whereas Baltic imports comprise automobiles, pharmaceutical products, electric machines, and products for livestock farming. But the chief aspect of the relationship between the Baltic countries and Central Asia concerns transit. Kazakhstan's "Path to Europe" program states its intention to become one of the main communications hubs between Asia and Europe, while Baltic countries, for their part, hope to benefit from a trade corridor toward the Persian Gulf.[63] In 2003, at the initiative of the Estonian, Latvian, Lithuanian, Russian, and Kazakh railway administrations, a Baltika-Transit project for cargo trains was launched as part of an attempt to reorganize Central Asian transit around the Baltic ports. Since the three Baltic states entered the EU in 2004, exchanges with Central Asia have intensified, in particular in the ports of Riga, Liepaja, and Ventspils. Astana has proposed to Estonia that they create joint ventures in the free trade zone of the Muuga and Tallinn ports.[64] In 2005, Kazakhstan opened a cereals terminal in Ventspils, its first in Europe.[65] Klaipeda also hopes to become one of the export ports for Uzbek agricultural products, which are of interest to the Lithuanian textile industry. However, these relations between the Baltic and Central Asian states depend almost entirely on their common Russian neighbor and the goodwill of its tariff policy.

Despite its status as a major trading partner of Central Asia, the European Union remains insufficiently visible as an independent actor and is sometimes challenged by its own member states, which do not necessarily seek to coordinate their activities among themselves or with Brussels. The Central Asian governments are disappointed by Brussels's lack of enthusiasm, by the small amounts of financing it offers in comparison with the sums invested by China and Russia, and by what they interpret as political "blackmail" in terms of human rights and democratization. They also sometimes have a difficult time understanding the priority the EU gives to the Mediterranean Basin and the Eastern Neighborhood in its partnerships. Central Asian governments always give preference to bilateral over multilateral relations, and prefer to build direct personal connections with the heads of European states over institutionalizing contacts between bureaucracies. Moreover, for nearly two decades, the European approach has been fragmented and aimed at financing multiple projects, rather than at elaborating a genuine strategy. It is founded on a model of regional cooperation that has never functioned, given the reticence of the Central Asian states to work together. In the focus it gives to bilateral relations, the 2007 Strategy does constitute a turning point in the history of EU-Central Asia relations; however, Brussels still has difficulties in surmounting the contradictions of its multiples agendas and actors. It also needs to address the disconnection between policy priorities and actual funding, and focus more on tangible results and development projects.[66] Europe enjoys a particularly high prestige in Central Asia in terms of culture, education, know-how, and quality of life. In hedging its bets on long-term development and focusing on the security-development nexus, Europe could acquire the means to influence the reshaping of Central Asian societies.

Notes

1. J. Boonstra et al., *Into Eurasia: Monitoring the EU's Central Asia Strategy* (Brussels-Madrid: CEPS-FRIDE, 2010), 59.

2. N. Melvin and J. Boonstra, "The EU Strategy for Central Asia @ Year One," Europe-Central Asia Monitoring Policy Brief, no. 1, October 2008.

3. K. Longhurst and S. Nies, "Recasting Relations with the Neighbours—Prospects for the Eastern Partnership," Report of the Institut français des relations internationales (IFRI), Europe Vision, no. 4, February 2009.

4. Authors' interviews with desk officers for Central Asia at the European Commission, Brussels, September 12–16, 2011.

5. For more details, see chapter 9.

6. J. Boonstra, "Defending Human Rights and Promoting Democracy: Euro-Atlantic Ap-

proaches Towards Turkmenistan and Uzbekistan," Fundación para las relaciones internacionales y el diálogo exterior (FRIDE) Activity Brief, December 2008.

7. See "Council Common Position 2005/792/CFS of 14 November 2005 concerning Restrictive Measures Against Uzbekistan," *Official Journal of the European Union*, November 16, 2005, L 299/72; "Council Regulation (EC) No 1859/2005 of 14 November 2005 Imposing Certain Restrictive Measures in Respect of Uzbekistan," *Official Journal of the European Union*, November 16, 2011, L 299/23. See also "Uzbekistan: Europe's Sanctions Matter," International Crisis Group Asia Briefing, no. 54, November 2006.

8. S. Ismailov and B. Jarabik, "The EU and Uzbekistan: Short-Term Interests versus Long-Term Engagement," Europe-Central Asia Monitoring Policy Brief, no. 8, July 2009; "Uzbekistan: Six Years On, No Justice for Andijan Victims," *Human Rights Watch*, May 11, 2011, http://www.hrw.org/news/2011/05/11/uzbekistan-6-years-no-justice-andijan-victims.

9. P. Schriefer, "Kazakhstan as OSCE Chair? Give Us a Break," *Freedom House*, October 31, 2007, http://freedomhouse.org/template.cfm?page=72&release=580.

10. K. James, "Questions Remain over Kazakhstan's Fitness for OSCE Chair," *Deutsche Welle*, January 4, 2010, http://www.dw-world.de/dw/article/0,,4965781,00.html; S. Peyrouse, "La présidence kazakhe de l'OSCE: Un choix avisé?" *Affaires-stratégiques.info*, November 25, 2009, http://www.affaires-strategiques.info/spip.php?article2410.

11. V. D. Shkolnikov, "The 2010 OSCE Kazakhstan Chairmanship: Carrot Devoured, Results Missing," Europe-Central Asia Monitoring Policy Brief, no. 15, April 2011.

12. See the "Stop Child and Forced Labor Cotton Campaign," International Labor Rights Forum, http://ilrf.org/stop-child-labor/cotton-campaign/uzbekistan.

13. "Turkmenistan: Human Rights Prerequisite For Closer EU Ties," *Eurasia Review,* April 20, 2011, http://www.eurasiareview.com/20042011-turkmenistan-human-rights-prerequisite-for-closer-eu-ties; "EU-Turkmenistan Human Rights Dialogue: EU Should Call for Concrete Steps to Improve Civil Society Situation in Turkmenistan," International Partnership for Human Rights, July 6, 2011, http://www.iphronline.org/turkmenistan_20110706_e.html.

14. E. Marat, "Karimov's Brussels Visit Full of Controversy," *Eurasia Daily Monitor* 8, no. 20, January 28, 2011, http://www.jamestown.org/single/?no_cache=1&tx_ttnewspercent-5Btt_newspercent5D=37420; D. Tynan, "Uzbekistan: Karimov's Visit to Brussels Was NATO's Idea," *Eurasianet*, January 20, 2011, http://www.eurasianet.org/node/62740.

15. "Joint Progress Report by the Council and the European Commission to the European Council on the Implementation of the EU Central Asia Strategy," Council of the European Union Report 11402/10, Brussels, June 24, 2010.

16. Authors's interviews with European Commission's desk officers for Central Asia, Brussels, September 12–16, 2010.

17. R. Youngs, "The EU and the Arab Spring: From Munificence to Geo-Strategy," FRIDE Policy Brief, no. 100, October 2011.

18. J. Boonstra and M. Denison, "Is the EU-Central Asia Strategy Running Out of Steam?" Europe-Central Asia Monitoring Policy Brief, no. 17, May 2011.

19. J. Boonstra, "The EU Strategy for Central Asia Says 'Security': Does This Include Security Sector Reform?" Europe-Central Asia Monitoring Policy Brief, no. 10, November 2009.

20. G. Gavrilis, "Beyond the Border Management Programme for Central Asia (BOMCA)," Europe-Central Asia Monitoring Policy Brief, no. 11, December 2009. See also Gavrilis, "Central Asia's Border Woes & the Impact of International Assistance," Open Society Foundations Occasional Paper Series, May 2012.

21. "Central Asian Border Security Issues Discussed in Dushanbe," Press Release, Border Management Programme in Central Asia (BOMCA), March 17, 2011, http://www.bomca.eu/en/news/8.html.

22. See the website for the Central Asia Regional Information and Coordination Center: http://www.caricc.org/index.php?lang=english.

23. Gavrilis, "Beyond the Border Management Programme."

24. "Joint Progress Report by the Council and the European Commission," 6.

25. Ibid., 26.

26. N. Kiil-Nielsen, "Draft Report on the State of Implementation of the EU Strategy for Central Asia," European Parliament Committee on Foreign Affairs, August 2011, 10, http://www.europarl.europa.eu/sides/getDoc.do?pubRef=-//EP//NONSGML+COMPARL+PE-469.951+02+DOC+PDF+V0//EN&language=EN.

27. Ibid., 11.

28. M. Hartog, ed., *Security Sector Reform in Central Asia: Exploring Needs and Possibilities* (Groningen: CESS, 2010).

29. "European Community Regional Strategy Paper for Assistance to Central Asia for the Period 2007–2013," 3.

30. Melvin and Boonstra, "The EU Strategy for Central Asia @ Year One."

31. J. Boonstra and J. Hale, "EU Assistance to Central Asia: Back to the Drawing Board?" Europe-Central Asia Monitoring Working Paper, no. 8, January 2010.

32. The SIDA program for Central Asia closed in 2009, while the AFD began working in the region in 2011.

33. A. Warkotsch, ed., *The European Union and Central Asia* (London: Routledge, 2011).

34. N. Kassenova, "A View from the Region," in *Engaging Central Asia: The European Union's New Strategy in the Heart of Eurasia*, ed. N. J. Melvin (Brussels: Centre for European Policy Studies, 2008), 122–36.

35. "Central Asia: What Role for the European Union?" International Crisis Group Asia Report, no. 113, 2006, 17.

36. N. de Pedro, "The EU in Central Asia: Incentives and Constraints for Greater Engagement," in Esteban and de Pedro, *Great Powers and Regional Integration in Central Asia*, 113–37.

37. More arguments in Melvin, *Engaging Central Asia*.

38. V. Axyonova, "The EU-Central Asia Human Rights Dialogues: Making a Difference?" Europe-Central Asia Monitoring Policy Brief, no. 16, April 2011.

39. "Central Asia: What Role for the European Union?," 15.

40. 2011 European Commission's statistics, http://ec.europa.eu/trade/creating-opportunities/bilateral-relations/countries-and-regions/.

41. See the country fact sheets of the German Federal Foreign Service, http://www.auswaertiges-amt.de/DE/Startseite_node.html.

42. 2011 European Commission's statistics, http://ec.europa.eu/trade/creating-opportunities/bilateral-relations/countries-and-regions/.

43. Ibid.

44. "Investments," Delegation of the European Union to Kazakhstan, http://www.eeas.europa.eu/delegations/kazakhstan/eu_kazakhstan/trade_relation/investments/index_en.htm.

45. J. Kucera, "Central Asia & Caucasus: Governments Spending Heavily on Arms," *Eurasianet*, March 23, 2010, http://www.eurasianet.org/departments/business/articles/eav032410.shtml.

46. "Liuks-riteil ne pustil v Kazakhstane glubokikh kornei," *Arcada.kz*, June 29, 2010, http://www.arcada.kz/rus/presscentr/217; Iu. Melnik, "Roskosh b'et rekordy," *Thenews.kz*, May 12, 2011, http://thenews.kz/2011/05/12/816288.html.

47. S. Peyrouse, "Business and Trade Relationship between the EU and Central Asia," Europe-Central Asia Monitoring Working Paper, no. 1, 2009.

48. Ibid., 11.

49. D. Garcia, *Le pays où Bouygues est roi* (Paris: Danger Public, 2006).

50. See Germany's bilateral relations with each Central Asian country at http://www.auswaertiges-amt.de/EN/Laenderinformationen/LaenderReiseinformationenA-Z_node.html.

51. N. Kadatskaia, "Nemtsy v migratsionnom obmene mezhdu Kazakhstanom i Germaniei: Tendentsii i perspektivy," Central Asian Migration Management and International Coopera-

tion (CAMMIC) Project Working Papers, no. 5, 2008; A. Diener, *Homeland Conceptions and Ethnic Integration Among Kazakhstan's Germans and Koreans* (Lewiston, NY: Edwin Mellen Press, 2004).

52. See "Kazakhstan," German Federal Foreign Service, http://www.auswaertiges-amt.de/EN/Aussenpolitik/Laender/Laenderinfos/01-Nodes/Kasachstan_node.html.

53. "Sotrudnichestvo Respubliki Kazakhstan s Ital'ianskoi Respublikoi," Kazakhstan Ministry of Foreign Affairs, July 8, 2008, http://portal.mfa.kz/portal/page/portal/mfa/ru/content/policy/cooperation/europe_america/23.

54. "Sotrudnichestvo Respubliki Kazakhstan s Frantsuzskoi Respublikoi," Kazakhstan Ministry of Foreign Affairs, September 7, 2009, http://portal.mfa.kz/portal/page/portal/mfa/ru/content/policy/cooperation/europe_america/09.

55. "Cooperation of the Republic of Kazakhstan with the United Kingdom of Great Britain and Northern Ireland," The Embassy of the Republic of Kazakhstan, http://www.kazembassy.org.uk/kazakh_british_relations.html.

56. See Aberdeen City Council's website, http://www.aberdeencity.gov.uk/CouncilNews/ci_cns/pr_atyrau_101008.asp; A. Ferris-Rotman, "A Little Slice of Scotland . . . in Kazakhstan," *Reuters*, October 13, 2008, http://www.reuters.com/article/2008/10/13/kazakhstan-scotland-alliance-idUSLD22195420081013.

57. "Sotrudnichestvo Respubliki Kazakhstan s Korolevstvom Niderlandov," Kazakhstan Ministry of Foreign Affairs, May 6, 2010, http://portal.mfa.kz/portal/page/portal/mfa/ru/content/policy/cooperation/europe_america/15.

58. More in S. Peyrouse, "The Growth of Commercial Exchanges between Central Europe and Central Asia," *Central Asia and Caucasus Analyst*, April 22, 2009.

59. "Sotrudnichestvo Respubliki Kazakhstan s Respublikoi Pol'sha," Kazakhstan Ministry of Foreign Affairs, May 31, 2010, http://portal.mfa.kz/portal/page/portal/mfa/ru/content/policy/cooperation/europe_america/10.

60. "Sotrudnichestvo Respubliki Kazakhstan s Cheshskoi Respublikoi," Kazakhstan Ministry of Foreign Affairs, October 19, 2009, http://portal.mfa.kz/portal/page/portal/mfa/ru/content/policy/cooperation/europe_america/15.

61. "Chekhiia-Uzbekistan: biznes-dialog," *Birzha*, no. 7, January 18, 2011, http://www.mzv.cz/file/577858/czechia.pdf.

62. "Sotrudnichestvo Respubliki Kazakhstan s Rumyniei," Kazakhstan Ministry of Foreign Affairs, September 14, 2009, http://portal.mfa.kz/portal/page/portal/mfa/ru/content/policy/cooperation/europe_america/15; M. Stenesku, "Rumyniia i Kazakhstan: Opyt i perspektivy partnerstva," *Investkz.com*, n.d., http://www.investkz.com/journals/26/406.html.

63. More details in A. Dunn, "Building Bridges between Baltic and Central Asia States," *European Dialogue*, March 20, 2011, http://eurodialogue.org/Building-Bridges-Between-Baltic-and-Central-Asia-states.

64. "Kazakhstansko-estonskie otnosheniia," Kazakhstan Embassy in Estonia, September 11, 2008, http://kazakhstan.embassy.lt/Default.asp?Lang=R&EditionID=48&TopicID=3&SubTopicID=18.

65. "Sotrudnichestvo Respubliki Kazakhstan s Latviiskoi Respublikoi," Kazakhstan Ministry of Foreign Affairs, September 11, 2008, http://portal.mfa.kz/portal/page/portal/mfa/ru/content/policy/cooperation/europe_america/15.

66. See the review of the European Strategy released in 2012, European Council. "Council conclusions on Central Asia," 3179th Foreign Affairs Council meeting, Luxembourg, 25 June 2012, http://www.consilium.europa.eu/uedocs/cms_Data/docs/pressdata/EN/foraff/131149.pdf.

5

Middle Eastern and Gulf Countries Seeking a Role in Central Asia

At the beginning of the 1990s, Central Asia's relationship with Turkey and Iran was a key point of international attention. A biased reading of Central Asia "rediscovering" its cultural and partly linguistic identity with both countries dominated frames of reference both in the West and among the actors themselves. However, the prospect for Central Asia's rapid integration into the Muslim world soon abated. Ankara's hopes in Central Asia were thwarted, and with them those that the United States and Europe placed in Turkey as a counterweight to Russia and Iran. The Turkish political model failed to find any resonance among the authoritarian regimes of Central Asia; narratives on Turkic cultural unity have been marginalized; trade relations have not attained the hoped-for magnitude; and the geopolitics of hydrocarbons has been slow to take off. Likewise, Iran's ability to exert political and religious influence in Central Asia has been overestimated, and the concerns about the expansion in Central Asia of a revolutionary Islam inspired by the Shiite Iranian model have proven to be largely unfounded. In the second half of the 1990s and in the first decade of the twenty-first century, Turkish and Iranian relations with Central Asia seemed to take backstage with the onset of Russian-American tensions in the Caspian Basin, the reassertion of Russian great power, and Beijing's arrival on the Central Asian radar. Yet the two countries remain deeply anchored to the Central Asian region, despite the initial misguided euphoria, and have managed to build long-term influence and pragmatic partnerships with their neighbors. In addition, new partners like the United Arab Emirates and Israel are increasingly visible in the region. The former offers a new, more modern image of the Persian Gulf, while the latter allows the Central Asian states to cultivate their secular distinctiveness within the Muslim world.

Turkey: From Cultural Strategy to Trade Pragmatism

Turkey has long been seen as NATO's sentinel on the southern flank of the socialist bloc. With the end of the Cold War, however, its strategic role weakened, at a time when its relations with the European Union were experiencing difficulties.[1] The Soviet

Union's collapse was thus perceived as a new chance for Turkish regional assertion. Since Kemalism, interest for Central Asia, the Caucasus, Mongolia, the Black Sea, and the Balkans had been limited to the realm of extreme right-wing pan-Turkic circles.[2] The drastic change in the geopolitical environment gave way to the construction of a narrative on the revival of Turkicness. Although Ankara's new infatuation with the region developed among political actors bearing no relation to the extreme right, these actors—quite often unwittingly—adopted certain traits of pan-Turkic logic insofar as they presented the natural element linking all these countries as Turkicness. Thus, the alleged cultural unity stretching "from the Great Wall of China to the Adriatic," according to the formula of President Süleyman Demirel, enjoyed success as a cliché of Turkish public discourse.[3]

This narrative further strengthened within Turkish state organs after 1998, following the European Union's refusal to examine Turkey's dossier for candidacy. The authorities' insistence on the country's role in Eurasia was thus double-edged. Turkey's Eurasian orientation can be presented to Brussels as a bridge across to the Middle East and Central Asia, in terms of hydrocarbons as well as for political influence, but it can also become a means of blackmail in case Turkey's European aspirations are spurned, thus leaving it with new geopolitical alternatives.[4] This last trend has increased under the Recep Tayyip Erdogan governments, with Ankara becoming increasingly detached from European and American interests, and resolutely deciding to engage with the Islamic World and Asia. However, Erdogan's Turkey projects its newly acquired soft power of being both an Islamic and a democratic country more on the Middle-Eastern scene, especially after the Arab Spring, than on the Central Asia one.[5]

Turkey was the first country to recognize the independence of the states of Central Asia and the South Caucasus in January 1992, and to send diplomatic representatives there. It allowed the Central Asian states to join the Economic Cooperation Organization (ECO) created with Pakistan and Iran in 1985, with the aim of strengthening their regional role as Muslim countries.[6] Between 1992 and 1996, Turkish aid represented nearly 90 percent of all assistance that the Central Asian states received, but the figure collapsed to 3 percent in 1997.[7] The Turkish authorities decided to promote cultural proximity in shaping their foreign policy toward the new states, albeit to a lesser degree with Persian-speaking Tajikistan. Ankara hoped to participate actively in local political construction by trying to export its successful model of democracy, secularism, and modernity. However, the naïve optimism of the initial years led Ankara to make errors in its cultural assessment. The Central Asian leaders received Turkey's policies poorly and were quick to denounce the new Turkish "elder brother."[8] Nevertheless, Ankara cannot be considered solely responsible for its failure to capitalize on pan-Turkicness. The authoritarian hardening of the Central Asian states and their lack of goodwill in establishing regional structures massively complicated the Turkish strategy.[9] From the mid-1990s until today, all pan-Turkic sentiments are interpreted in Central Asia as an attempt to question state legitimacy. Accordingly, these ideas have been marginalized from politics and culture, and are limited to dissident milieus.[10] In addition, the two most authoritarian countries, Uzbekistan and Turkmenistan, have regularly accused Ankara of welcoming their political dissidents and have tried to limit Turkish political influence.

Turkey's state projects in Central Asia are managed through the Turkish Agency of International Cooperation, or TIKA (Türkiye İşbirliği ve Kalkınma Ajansı), which is divided into two sections: one arm deals with economic, commercial, and technological matters; the other focuses on society and culture. Ankara also plays a crucial role as a military intermediary, with Central Asian officers, often receiving training in Turkey under the auspices of NATO Partnership for Peace.[11] Turkish "civil society" is also heavily involved in building ties with its "Turkic brothers." Since 1992, the TURKSOY association, a sort of Turkic UNESCO, has held an annual summit of Turkophone countries with a view to promoting unified linguistic and cultural traditions. TURKSOY hoped to create a common Turkic language, encouraging all post-Soviet states that had not already done so to abandon the Cyrillic alphabet in favor of Latin. But the Central Asian states have refused the idea of a common Latinized alphabet, preferring instead to preserve the rationale of linguistic differentiation inherited from the Soviet era, and, for Turkmenistan and Uzbekistan, to institute their own language-specific Latinization.[12] The efforts invested in the reciprocal translation of Turkic literatures and in the reinterpretation of common feast days such as Navruz (Spring festival) have also had little impact in Central Asia. Although they are confined to the cultural sphere, the activities of TURKSOY remain dependent on interstate relations. Thus Uzbekistan, which has become wary of Ankara's political intentions, barely participates in the association. In 2008, Turkey tried to give renewed impetus to its relations with Central Asia through the creation of the Parliamentary Assembly of Turkic Countries, a project backed by Azerbaijan, Kazakhstan, and Kyrgyzstan, but refused by Turkmenistan and Uzbekistan.[13]

Several projects, however, have enjoyed some success on a symbolic level. Ankara, for instance, has been involved in diversifying telecommunications networks. It launched a television channel, Avrasya, with the aid of the Türksat satellite.[14] More recently, it did the same with MTV, which broadcasts uninterrupted music videos throughout the Turkic-speaking space. But the Turkish used by both channels remains predominantly Anatolian and thus inaccessible for most Central Asians, except Turkmen.

Turkey has above all established important school and university curricula, which have had an influence in reconfiguring the Central Asian educational landscape. Each year, a few thousand students from Turkic-speaking countries are given the opportunity to pursue university courses in Turkey, mainly in the hard and applied sciences, but also, although more rarely, in Islamic theology. Turkey has opened co-educational universities in Central Asia such as Hamet Yassavi in Turkestan, and the Manas Turkish-Kyrgyz University in Bishkek. In addition, a large network of private schools (and the Ala Taou private university) has been set up thanks to the activism of the Nurcu movement of Fethullah Gülen, which gathers the disciples of Sait Nursi (1876–1960).

Nurcu doctrine advocates moderate, non-politicized Islam, characterized by the idea of proselytism through exemplarity, which is not devoid of pan-Turkic nationalist accents.[15] Rising suspicions against these Turkish secondary schools, within which Islam is taught as an element of morality, impedes their expansion: Uzbekistan closed them down in 1999; Tajikistan is anxious about the pan-Turkic precepts implied in Nurcu doctrine; Turkmenistan has asked that the theology courses be removed; and Kazakhstan and Kyrgyzstan consider them to be too religious. Nevertheless, they enjoy a good reputation and offer students the kind of training in English, the sciences, and technological subjects with which the public secondary schools cannot compete.[16] Close to the Nurcu movement, the newspaper *Zaman*, published in Turkish, Russian, and the Central Asian languages, promotes the Turkish model in the region with the support of the Turkish authorities.[17]

Ankara failed to spread the idea of Turkic unity, since it was unable to provide a pluralist definition of it in which the states of Central Asia—very sensitive about matters of national cultural heritage—might have been able to recognize themselves. The refusal of the Central Asian leaders to foster supranational regional identities, even those with a religious connotation, has been disappointing for Turkey. But in the first years of the twenty-first century, Ankara has succeeded in readjusting its policies and its objectives to a more modest reality.[18] Central Asia therefore has found a more measured place in Turkey's foreign policy, though much less important than the South Caucasus, the Balkans, or the Black Sea Economic Cooperation Organization.[19]

Like cultural exchanges, trade between Turkey and its Turkic neighbors has not taken the expected turn. Turkey's involvement in the region has little bearing on Turkish global trade. Today Moscow ranks as Ankara's second-largest trading partner after the EU, receiving almost 9 percent of Turkish trade with a value of US$25 billion in 2010, while Kazakhstan is only in sixteenth place with just over 1 percent of Turkish trade.[20] Turkey cannot really match China, the EU, and Russia in their trade with Central Asia as a whole. It is the region's fourth-largest trading partner, but it is only truly important to Turkmenistan. Moreover, its fourth-place ranking should be viewed in the context that Turkey represents only about 5 percent of total Central Asian trade.

Kazakhstan dominates these trade exchanges. Although Turkish companies are well established in Turkmenistan, the dynamism of the Kazakh economy offers them greater opportunities, to the extent that exchanges with Astana are double than those with Turkmenistan. Turkish investments in the Kazakh economy are also significant, and in 2011, they exceeded US$2 billion.[21] Close to 1,600 Kazakh companies see Turkish involvement, the majority of which are in the sectors of commerce, construction, and equipment assembly, as well as in infrastructure, metals, and the oil and chemical industries.[22] Exchanges with the three other republics of Central Asia are much smaller, in particular those with Tajikistan and Kyrgyzstan. While educational relationships between Kyrgyzstan and Turkey are well developed, commercial relations are particularly weak. Although the potential for exchanges with Uzbekistan is superior to that with Kyrgyzstan and Tajikistan, the iciness of Turkish-Uzbek political relations

Table 5.1

Turkey's Place in Imports, Exports, and the Trade Total of Central Asian States in 2010 (in millions of US$)

	Imports	Rank	Exports	Rank	Total trade	Rank
Kazakhstan	869.4 (3%)	5	2,154 (4.7%)	4	3,024.5 (4%)	4
Kyrgyzstan	136.1 (2%)	6	26.6 (2.5%)	7	162.8 (2%)	6
Tajikistan	57.7 (2.3%)	11	361.4 (31.5%)	2	419.1 (11.3%)	3
Turkmenistan	1,207 (22.3%)	1	337.5 (10.4%)	3	1,544.7 (17.9%)	1
Uzbekistan	299.2 (3.6%)	6	755.5 (13.7%)	3	1,054.7 (7.7%)	5

Source: 2011 European Commission statistics, http://ec.europa.eu/trade/creating-opportunities/bilateral-relations/countries-and-regions/.

hampers the development of a partnership. However, since 2007, the exchanges have taken off again with Ankara now ranking as Tashkent's fifth-largest trade partner.[23]

Turkish companies are most involved in the construction sector. Following post-Soviet independence they succeeded in developing dependable relationships and have been thanked by Central Asian governments for having invested considerable sums in the building of government complexes at a time when there were few guarantees of payment. Even though Turkish companies face competition from other foreign builders, they are the undisputed market leaders in this domain throughout the region. They have acquired a reputation for building in record time, and for charging prices that are generally 20 to 25 percent lower than those of their competitors, although their projects are of questionable security and quality. According to the Union of Turkish Industrialists, Turkish construction companies have invested more than US$4 billion in Kazakhstan since 1993.[24] Positive relationships with the Turkmen authorities are also ongoing. Despite competition from the French company Bouygues, Turkish companies received more than US$14 billion worth of contracts from Ashgabat between 1992 and 2008.[25] However, the Turkmen deficit in foreign currency affected this honeymoon period, and in 2011 Ashgabat faced legal action from twenty Turkish construction firms over broken contracts costing them more US$1 billion. Turkish firms have also gained prominence in the textile sector, particularly in Turkmenistan and Uzbekistan.[26] Textiles have become the sector of preference for Turkish businessmen close to Turkmen presidency, such as Ahmet Çalik.

Turkish companies have also invested in the development of the Turkmen electricity sector, as well as in the renovation of transport infrastructure, in particular airports. Additionally, Turkish banks were among the first to set up in Central Asia. But their activities are rather modest, often limited to the financing of bilateral projects involving Turkish companies, so they have not gained a foothold in the real estate and financial markets, nor in individual services. At the beginning of the 1990s, the arrival of Turkish products on the Central Asian market made it possible to compensate partially for the disappearance of industrial and commercial links with the rest of the Soviet Union.

Textiles and household products were the first tangible signs of the opening of the borders and the transition toward a market economy. Turkish supermarkets became heavily involved in food and consumer sundries, the production and distribution of which was always one of the weak points of the Soviet system.[27]

Turkey has built itself a reputation as an efficient partner in commercial matters, but local actors also criticize the Turkish entrepreneurs, as they do all foreign companies operating in Central Asia. Many incidents have tarnished the image of "Turkish business," including building-site accidents; the violation of anti-seismic norms; and giving priority to hiring Turkish expatriates instead of local salaried workers. In Kazakhstan, the Tengiz oil industry has been rocked by skirmishes between Turks and Kazakhs working for the Turkish subcontractors of TengizChevroil.[28] Ankara was one of the first partners of the Central Asian regimes after independence, and the discovery of small business by local actors is often undertaken in partnership, or in competition, with Turkish businessmen.[29] The situation has evolved significantly with the arrival of China, which embodies a new economic modernity. Today Turkish companies have only a few secure commercial niches, namely those in construction, textiles, and foodstuffs. Their presence in other sectors such as energy, transport infrastructure, telecommunications, or banking will be subjected to stiff competition from other actors, especially Chinese ones. In addition, Turkish companies, mainly private and small in size, are discouraged by the investment climate and the complexity of Central Asian administrative formalities.

Geographical distance also remains an essential obstacle to the development of exchanges. While air routes are numerous and very frequent due to the establishment of Turkish Airways throughout the region, road and railway infrastructure remains insufficient and customs passages via Iran or the Caucasus slow down the flows considerably. More than a third of exchanges between Turkey and Kyrgyzstan therefore pass through Russia and Kazakhstan instead of through the southern routes.[30] The transit of hydrocarbons and electricity between Central Asia and Turkey is hampered by geopolitical uncertainties, especially Iran's involvement. So far Ankara has not seen its energy hopes for Central Asia materialize, even if its role as an energy hub is reinforced by the possible completion of European projects such as the Nabucco pipeline. Turkey's geostrategic locations and its relation to Central Asia will evolve in the years to come depending on many factors: the difficult partnership with the European Union and the rise of Euroskepticism among Turkish elites as a result; growing tensions with the West since the war in Iraq and the Arab Spring; Kurdish autonomy in northern Iraq; cooler relations with Israel; a distinct geopolitical rapprochement with Putin's Russia;[31] and the attraction of the Chinese market.

Iran: A Promising Partnership Hampered by Geopolitical Issues

For the Islamic Republic of Iran, the dismantling of the Soviet Union as the main counterweight to American influence drastically modified its geopolitical relation vis-à-vis the West, and its regional neighbors. During Soviet times, Iran was thought of as a buffer state between the USSR, on one side, and pro-Western Turkey and Pakistan, on the other; however, the geopolitical game was turned upside down in the 1990s, with Ankara and Islamabad keen to present themselves as ramparts against the spread of Iranian revolutionary ideas in Central Asia and the Caucasus.[32] The Iranian authorities soon became worried about Turkey's advances into Central Asia: not only was Ankara an ally of the United States, but the return of a pan-Turkic influence would also have jeopardized its role in the regional balance.[33]

Despite many long centuries of proximity, Iran knew little about contemporary Central Asia. Following the independence of the Central Asian republics, Iranian leaders had no specific ideas about what they might hope to achieve in the region, and they did not consider it to be a priority area. Iran's primary concerns were domestic: after emerging from a decade of war with Iraq, the economic and social situation was tense, and the death of Ayatollah Khomeini in 1989 aroused concerns of political destabilization. In the early 1990s, Iran engaged in a program of reforms designed to lead the country toward a more market-oriented economy. Tehran, among other things, encouraged the country's regional administrations to establish relations with neighboring states, which ultimately allowed the Islamic Republic's northern provinces to engage with their former Soviet neighbors. An Iranian province with a Sunni majority, Golestan forged direct relations with Kazakhstan; meanwhile Mazandaran Province extended its links with Turkmenistan.[34] However, it was not until 2001 that the Iranian minister of foreign affairs, Kamal Kharrazi, declared that the region was part of Iranian foreign policy priorities.[35]

The Central Asian states sought, through partnership with Tehran, to escape Russian influence, to diversify economically, and to gain access to open seas in the south. But they were also quite wary about forging a relationship with the Islamic regime and feared that Tehran would seek to export Islamic revolution as it had done in Lebanon, and Palestine. At the time, Central Asian governments also faced mounting pressure from Washington, which sought to prevent the transformation of Iran into a regional power. In 1992, for instance, Kazakhstan was obliged to refuse help offered by Iran for the restoration of the Caspian port of Aktau; instead it chose to work with the Netherlands.[36] Islam Karimov's regime in Uzbekistan, uneasy about Islamist tensions in the Ferghana Valley, decided to curb Iranian influence as early as the first half of the 1990s. Turkmenistan has been open to the development of economic relations with Iran, but has demonstrated a deep reluctance with regard to its religious presence.[37]

Iranian influence was at first predominantly confined to Tajikistan, in light of the two countries linguistic and cultural proximity. It is likely that Iran funded, at least initially, the Party of Islamic Revival of Tajikistan, and indirectly participated in the overthrow of the government of Rakhmon Nabiyev in 1992. Between 1993 and 1997, the Iranian authorities regularly hosted the leaders of the Tajik Islamic opposition.[38] However, Tehran had no interest in destabilizing its neighbor, and has always denied having played a direct role in the Tajik armed conflict; instead it claimed to have understood it as a civil war between regional clans, not a holy war on behalf of Islam. Along with Russia, Iran quickly became involved in the negotiation process. In 1995,

Emomali Rahmon and Nuri Said Abdulloh were invited to Tehran to find a peaceful settlement to the conflict.[39]

In the second half of the 1990s, the Iranian government began to doubt the policy of revolutionary export, with Hashemi Rafsanjani criticizing the preference given to fluid ideological goals at the expense of national interests. From 1997, the export of political Islam was clearly challenged by the rise of the reform-oriented president Mohammad Khatami, who accelerated the removal of Shiite revolutionary ideology from Iran's foreign policy in an effort to bring the country out of international isolation.[40] At the end of the 1990s, Iran tried to strengthen its position in international structures, such as the Organization of the Islamic Conference (OIC), but relations with Israel quickly constituted a point of contention between the Central Asian governments and Tehran. Pressures from Iran, which sought to adopt resolutions against Israel during its 1997–2000 presidency of the OIC, led the Central Asian states to keep their distance from the organization in order to maintain their good relations with Tel Aviv. Iran also sought a leading role in the Economic Cooperation Organization, the only major regional organization to which it belongs.[41] Yet again, the Central Asian states rejected Tehran's attempts at politicization of the organization, which would have put them at odds with the United States. Instead they demanded that the role of the ECO be limited to development assistance and regional transport. The organization has certainly failed to take off and today plays only a marginal role in the development of exchanges between Iran and Central Asia.[42]

In the context of Iran's relations with the Central Asian states, several contentious issues remain unresolved. The main one concerns the legal status of the Caspian Sea: Iran is now the latest actor, along with a hesitating Turkmenistan, to refuse to adopt the majority opinion of the median line (maritime boundaries should conform to a median line equidistant from the shores of neighboring nation-states). If it were to do so, it would see its share of the Caspian Sea drop from 20 to 13 percent.[43] The Iranian nuclear issue is also not without problems for the Central Asian states. They seek to maintain a middle position on this issue, affirming the inalienable right of Iran to use nuclear technology for peaceful purposes and calling for an exclusively diplomatic settlement. A possible US military intervention would indeed threaten the region's geopolitical balance and jeopardize its stability. The Central Asian governments are worried about pressure from Washington and retaliation from Tehran due to their support for the United States. Kyrgyzstan is in a particularly difficult position, given the presence on its soil of the US military base at Manas, and has already declared that it would refuse any American intervention against Iran launched from its territory.[44]

Nor is Tehran's place in regional geopolitical reconfigurations settled. The Iranian regime hopes to break its international isolation by focusing on its Asian neighbors and joining the SCO. It obtained observer status in 2005, but its hopes of becoming a full member are thwarted by the fact that the Central Asian governments, Moscow, and Beijing are against it. In 2003, and then again in 2008, Tehran strongly supported the launch—unsuccessfully, as it has turned out—of an Asian Union, inviting Russia, India, China, and other Asian states to join. The aim was to gather together the major world resources in oil and gas, as well as in people, in order to constitute a counterweight to the United States.[45] Tehran also attempted to foster a new Persian-speaking regional configuration, and Mahmoud Ahmadinejad promoted the Conference of Persian Countries that brought together the presidents of Iran, Tajikistan, and Afghanistan in April 2010.[46] This virtual supranational identity, however, has little chance of realization. Afghanistan is far from being able to fully identify with the Persian-speaking world without arousing the anger of the Pashtuns, and the regime of Hamid Karzai cannot afford to aggravate centrifugal tensions that already threaten Afghan national unity. The question of the Tajik minority is taboo in Uzbekistan, which bills itself as the capital of the Turkic-speaking Turkestani world; Persian-speakers in Armenia and the Azeris of Iran are also rifts in the national identities of these individual states.

Central Asia still holds numerous suspicions linked to Iran's religious orientation. Uzbekistan and Tajikistan regularly accuse the Iranian secret services, or various religious groups, of wanting to destabilize their secular regimes.[47] Twelver Shiism, which is practiced by the Azeri minorities of Central Asia as well as by the Ironis in the Bukhara-Samarkand region, is subject to repression on a regular basis. Shiia is associated with national minorities, equated with Islamism, and therefore with the risk of terrorism or rebellion, and seen as an agent of Iranian influence.[48] Yet almost no Iranian group actively seeks to promote the conversion of Sunni Central Asians to Shiia. The few Shiite-inspired religious groups not belonging to the Azeri or Ironi minorities are the Qadariyya Sufi brotherhoods, which practice an underground faith, often operate as initiatory secret societies, and are unlikely to receive financial support from Iran. Only Tajikistan is experiencing a small trend in the conversion to Shiism, but it is limited specifically to the regions of Khatlon and Kulyab, where the influence of the Islamic Revival Party of Tajikistan is significant. Tajikistan is the only country in Central Asia where pan-Iranian sentiments can be expressed, and where Iran is seen by some as a potential model.[49]

Even if Iran has failed to influence Central Asian geopolitical orientations, Tehran perceives the region as a crossroad for a conflict on two fronts: the traditional conflict with the United States on account of the latter's establishment in the Caspian Basin; and a more recent one with the Sunni fundamentalist currents flowing from the Indian subcontinent and the Persian Gulf, which are gaining ground in Central Asia. While Tehran does not want to interfere with the traditional Sunnism of the Central Asian peoples, it is concerned by the spread of Salafi theories, which it regards as an ideological Arabization harmful to its geopolitical status in the Middle East.[50] Since 2001, the Iranian state has, for instance, been seeking to expand contacts with the Central Asian secret services. This was initially due to the presence of Russian and American bases in the region, but subsequently because of concern with Salafi groups. This situation has led Iran to conduct a paradoxical strategy in Central Asia. It supports Islamic groups that call on Central Asians to become good Muslims in their daily practice as well as in foreign policy by being more critical of the Western (American, Russian, European) presence, while at the same time it seeks to halt Sunni radicalism. These

Table 5.2

Iran's Place in Imports, Exports, and the Trade Total of Central Asian States in 2010 (in millions of US$)

	Imports	Rank	Exports	Rank	Total trade	Rank
Kazakhstan	27.3 (0.1%)	30	123.9 (0.3%)	19	151.2 (0.2%)	19
Kyrgyzstan	8.5 (0.1%)	15	10.8 (1%)	10	19.3 (0.2%)	17
Tajikistan	136.1 (5.3%)	6	57.3 (5%)	4	193.4 (5.2%)	6
Turkmenistan	225.7 (4.2%)	6	153.3 (4.7%)	6	379.1 (4.4%)	6
Uzbekistan	unknown	—	91.3 (1.7%)	10	91.3 (0.7%)	15

Source: 2011 European Commission statistics, http://ec.europa.eu/trade/creating-opportunities/bilateral-relations/countries-and-regions/.

two trends are contradictory because it is precisely these local Islamic groups that are most often inspired by Salafism.

Despite its geographical contiguity with Central Asia via Turkmenistan—an asset that Turkey lacks—Iran's economic exchanges with the region are still limited and even in decline. In 2008 Tehran represented less than 3 percent of the whole of Central Asian foreign trade, with a value of US$3.3 billion; this dropped to less than 1 percent in 2010, with a value only US$834 million. Kazakhstan traditionally dominates the exchanges, followed closely by Turkmenistan, except in 2010 where Tajikistan became second. With the exception of Turkmen and Tajik exports, Iran represents only 0.7 percent of the region's trade.

Iran considers Turkmenistan, with which it shares a 900-kilometer border, as one of its main allies in Central Asia, alongside Tajikistan. It supported Ashgabat in its policy of "permanent neutrality" as an effort to extricate itself from Western influence, but was displeased when it joined the NATO Partnership for Peace program. The two regimes have long had a similar discourse on the methods for sharing the Caspian Sea[51] and have endeavored to simplify visa procedures, a decision that contrasts greatly with Turkmen isolationism toward its former Soviet neighbors. Bilateral relations quickly focused on trade exchanges. More than two hundred Iranian companies or joint ventures currently operate in Turkmenistan, often in the sectors of construction and of basic consumables. In 2005, Niyazov and Khatami inaugurated the largest joint project undertaken by the two countries since Turkmenistan's independence: a dam on the Tedjen River at the border post of Dostluk.[52] However, there has also been numerous grounds for friction. Niyazov regularly changed the export tariffs on Turkmen gas to Iran, pursued a policy of repression against the Shiite minority, and supported the Taliban regime in Afghanistan. Conversely, the situation of the Turkmen minority in Iran (about 3 million people) deteriorated in 2008–2009. Following Niyazov's death in 2006, Irano-Turkmen relations have cooled somewhat.[53] At the end of December 2007, Turkmenistan closed the Korpedje-Kurd Köy gas pipeline for several months, leaving the northern regions of Iran in a dire energy situation. But tensions between

Ashgabat and Gazprom in 2009 brought about a renewal of the gas partnership with Iran, which saw its imports increase rapidly.[54]

Despite its desire to develop relations with Iran, Kazakhstan has had to tread a careful course in order not to provoke objections from the United States. Projects for economic collaboration are numerous, in particular in the sector of commodity transit and in oil swaps, but are still impeded by Iran's marginalization. Nevertheless, Kazakhstan has become one of the major exporters of cereals to Iran and hopes to increase its presence via maritime transportation and the building of cereal terminals in Aktau and the Iranian ports.[55] However, some issues still cause tensions, such as the massive presence of Western firms at Kazakhstan's offshore deposits and the United States' active involvement in the creation of the Caspian fleet.[56] But the scope of Iranian-Kazakh relations has increased in proportion with Astana's increasing self-assertion on the international scene. In 2001, the Kazakh government defined Iran as one of its foreign policy priorities after Russia, China, the United States, and Turkey, and refused to support the United States in its policy of boycotting the Islamic regime.[57] It has not made secret of its interest, in theory at least, to assist the Iranian nuclear power program through the sale of uranium fuel; in 2009, it even offered to host a fuel bank on its territory that Iran could use for civilian purposes.[58] For Astana, Iran is a potentially important customer as a key power in the region, and the international tensions surrounding its nuclear program has had a negative impact on the development of Kazakh civilian nuclear power.[59]

Uzbekistan continues to be the country most reluctant to develop its relations with Iran, a fact which can be attributed to a number of reasons: the Uzbek regime is suspicious of any rival regional power; harbors fears of Islamic insurgency; and promotes itself as the foremost ally of the United States in the region. In 1998, the US-Uzbek Commission even coordinated Tashkent's approaches to Iran with the American State Department.[60] However, Uzbekistan's post-2005 geopolitical reorientation contributed to pacifying relations with Tehran. Trade relations with Tajikistan and Kyrgyzstan have less importance, even if Tajikistan has long been a gateway for Iranian influence in Central Asia. However, while the Tajik and Iranian authorities regularly make a show of their good relations, trade exchanges are limited and Iran acts mainly as an investor in the Tajik economy. Iranian companies are present above all in hydroelectricity, in the purchase of aluminum, and in the agricultural sector.[61]

The partnership between Iran and Central Asia is likely to increase in scope. While the Iranian products that entered the Central Asian markets at the beginning of the 1990s are unable to stave off Chinese competition and are destined to dry up, new sectors of cooperation are developing in which Iranian know-how is appreciated: hydroelectricity, minerals, the industrial treatment of agriculture and textiles, and automobile production. Iran's geographical position is also attractive to the Central Asian states, which are always interested in finding ways to gain access to the southern seas and to the Mediterranean Basin. Projects to connect Central Asian road and railway networks to those of Iran, as well as to those of Turkey and Afghanistan, are numerous, but they are unrealistic given the current geopolitical context, and the flows that circulate on the completed sections are very modest.[62] Nevertheless, Iran's strategic role as a transit zone from the Eurasian continent, on both the east-west and north-south axes, plays in its favor in the long term. But so far geography has not won out in its struggle against geopolitics, and the international community's ostracism of Tehran has cost the Central Asian economies dearly, preventing them from taking full advantage of Iranian proximity and the opportunities this entails.

Unlike in Lebanon, and Palestine, Iran does not play the revolutionary card in Central Asia. The Iranian state presents itself as a pragmatic partner, willing to put aside the ideological differences it has with its Central Asian neighbors—for example regarding Israel or the secular nature of the regimes—in order to promote regional cooperation. It does not seek to exploit Shiite minorities (Azeris and Ironis), and wields relatively little influence over them, unlike the case of the Hazaras in Afghanistan. The Iranian associations and groups most involved in Central Asia, including the Revolutionary Guard, do not broadcast Shiite theories per se, which would bring little agreement in the region; they instead propagate the legacy of the Islamic Revolution and long-term state interests. Beyond theological differences between Shiia and Sunnism, Iran knows that its best hand to play is not that of its Ayatollah-dominated regime, but of a unique religious legitimacy in the Muslim world, and an unambiguous international position vis-à-vis the United States. All these elements are indeed seen positively by some Central Asian Islamic movements, which, although Sunni, are disappointed in the two-faced policies of the pro-Western Islamic regimes like Pakistan and Saudi Arabia. With the likely rise of Salafists in Central Asia, Iran will be forced to engage more substantially in the region through a wide range of activities: supporting traditionalist, anti-Salafi, movements; emphasizing its image as a revolutionary anti-American state; increasing contacts between secret services; and forming networks at the highest state levels.[63]

Alternative Partners: The Gulf Emirates and Israel

In the early 1990s, the only Gulf countries present in Central Asia were Saudi Arabia and Kuwait, which used their vast amount of petrodollars to finance the rebuilding of mosques, the dissemination of copies of the Koran, and the training of imams. This did not endear the two countries to the Central Asian regimes, which quickly clamped down on their presence.[64] Since the first decade of the twenty-first century, the new symbol of the Gulf, the United Arab Emirates (UAE), has gained visibility by positioning itself as an alternative partner. The official visits of heads of state and the exchanges of delegations have increased in recent years,[65] and even if the financial collapse of Dubai in 2009 has slowed implementation, long-term trends are favorable for the Gulf economies. Dubai became for instance Turkmenistan's fifth commercial partner in 2010.

Unlike many other international actors, the UAE has a relatively minor presence in the energy sector. The Abu-Dhabi-controlled International Petroleum Investment Company (IPIC) has been interested for several years in the Caspian Basin, and signed an agreement with KazMunayGas for the construction of a petrochemical complex near Atyrau.[66] A joint venture between the British Petrofac and Abu Dhabi's Mubadala Development Fund, Petrofac Emirates won a contract along with ConocoPhillips for the joint operation of block N in the Caspian Sea.[67] In 2009, Petrofac and Gulf Oil and Gas also entered into an international consortium to operate the Turkmen South Yolotan gas field with CNPC, LG International, and Hyundai Engineering.[68]

Dubai sees Uzbekistan as a hub for the export of cotton, and the Uzbek state holding Uzprommashimpeks attempts to diversify its cotton exports to Asia and the Middle East by building warehouses in Dubai.[69] The UAE also is interested in Uzbek fruits and vegetables, which are exported three times per week on special cargo flights that run to Sharjah and Dubai.[70] Construction projects are numerous. Emirati companies are building a new mosque in southern Kazakhstan, a "knowledge village" in Astana (modeled on one in Dubai), and infrastructure in the capital city. Aktau City, a huge area that will include resorts, apartment buildings, shopping centers, and businesses, is being constructed in large part by Emirati companies, among them Dubai World.[71] With its oil wealth, Abu Dhabi also serves as a model for Kazakhstan, represented by Abu Dhabi Plaza, constructed by Aldar Properties in the Astana special economic zone. In Turkmenistan, Emirati companies have won tenders to build several resorts, in particular in the Avaza tourist area.[72] Last but not least, the UAE has substantial involvement in banking and finance—particularly, though not exclusively, in Islamic finance.[73]

Relations between Central Asia and the UAE include cooperation in less vaunted areas. Uzbek traffic in gold to Dubai benefits from supporters in the ruling elites in Tashkent, who collect illegal revenues from selling it abroad. The illicit hunting of wild animals has grown as well, with rich sheiks coming regularly to hunt prohibited species in Turkmenistan, Uzbekistan, and Kazakhstan.[74] The shuttle trade toward the Emirates began in the early 1990s, and "shop tourism" in Dubai is a must for the Central Asian middle and upper classes. Prostitution rose during the early years of the twenty-first century; women of Slavic and Eurasian origin from Kazakhstan, Uzbekistan, and Tajikistan are in high demand in the Gulf.[75] Airlines have appeared, which run routes from Tajik provincial cities or the Ferghana Valley to Dubai and Abu Dhabi, transporting young women for "sale."[76] In addition, the export of labor seems destined to become a new field of economic cooperation. Central Asian labor migrants, who typically go to Russia and other regional destinations such as Kazakhstan, are starting to travel to the UAE, which is a major consumer of cheap labor. Like Saudi Arabia, Kuwait, and Qatar the UAE is said to have signed formal agreements in this regard with Tajikistan and Turkmenistan.[77]

It is likely that the UAE will maintain high activism in Central Asia. Despite the growing presence of China, it still enjoys status as a transit area between products from South Asia (especially Malaysia and Singapore) and Central Asia.[78] It has a dynamic economy, which features oil as well as new sectors like construction, tourism, and innovation, and presents itself as an alternative ally, especially for Turkmenistan, and in a more limited way for Uzbekistan and Tajikistan. The UAE broadcasts a modern

Table 5.3

The UAE's Place in Imports, Exports, and the Trade Total of Central Asian States in 2010 (in millions of US$)

	Imports	Rank	Exports	Rank	Total trade	Rank
Kazakhstan	42.6 (0.1%)	24	66.8 (0.1%)	23	109.5 (0.1%)	22
Kyrgyzstan	10.5 (0.2%)	14	52.7 (5%)	5	63.3 (0.8%)	11
Tajikistan	58.5 (2.3%)	10	3.8 (0.3%)	14	62.3 (1.7%)	12
Turkmenistan	461.6 (8.5%)	5	230.4 (7.1%)	4	692.1 (8%)	5
Uzbekistan	unknown	—	unknown	—	unknown	—

Source: 2011 European Commission statistics, http://ec.europa.eu/trade/creating-opportunities/bilateral-relations/countries-and-regions/.

image of Islam: this can only please the Central Asian regimes, which are always quick to criticize the political atmosphere in the Middle East for being too conservative, Islamic, and anti-Western. This trend is likely to accelerate in the years ahead: the coming to power of Islamist parties after the 2011 Arab Spring is at odds with the position of the Central Asian states, which are anxious to appear pro-Western and secular.

The partnership with Israel has taken shape in this context of disillusioned relations with the Middle East. Israel has always been well regarded in Central Asia: the overt secularism of the Central Asian governments, links with Soviet Jewish diasporas, which emigrated to Israel in large numbers, and common views on the threat of international terrorism have served to consolidate bilateral ties. Anti-Semitism has traditionally been absent from Central Asian societies, although it has gained some currency as the result of the circulation of conspiracy theories that are in vogue especially in Muslim countries.[79] It became visible in Kyrgyzstan during the turmoil of 2010, when so-called Jewish bankers who were a part of the president's son Maksim Bakiyev's entourage were fiercely denounced in the Kyrgyz press.[80] For Tel Aviv, the stakes of building a positive partnership with Central Asia are high. Alliances with majority Muslim countries are rare, and relations with Turkey and Jordan have deteriorated during the Arab Spring. However, tensions are regular. The Uzbek government has, for instance, asked for the Mossad's assistance in eliminating Islamist groups, but Israel asked for a boycott of Tehran as a condition, which was refused.[81] Despite this conflict, in June 2009, Shimon Peres visited Kazakhstan, Uzbekistan, Turkmenistan, and Azerbaijan, continuing a long tradition of diplomatic exchanges.[82] The Israeli foreign minister, Avigdor Lieberman, the founder and leader of the far-right Beytenou Israel party, has been campaigning since the 1990s for strengthened ties with Central Asia, particularly Uzbekistan.[83]

In 2003, Israel was even the largest foreign investor in Uzbekistan, but bilateral trade has since declined.[84] The Uzbekistani diaspora in Israel is composed of communities of Bukharan and Ashkenazi Jews who play a key role in the development of private trade and are the source of approximately fifty joint ventures. For instance, business-man Khanan Binyaminov, originally from Samarkand and a former vice-mayor of a small suburb of Tel Aviv, who has worked in diamonds for over thirty years, opened two factories in 2009 in Uzbekistan, one for brick production and the other for the fabrication of tubes.[85] The king of diamonds in Israel, Lev Leviev, a native of Uzbekistan and president of the World Congress of Bukharan Jews, also plays the role of commercial mediator between Israel and Uzbekistan.[86] The extraction of minerals and hydrocarbons were the first joint Uzbek-Israeli projects. In the 1990s Bateman Projects Ltd., based in Haifa but part of the South African Bateman Industrial Group, was the main contractor for a recovery plant installed at the mine dumps of Muruntau, near Navoy, and for the Anglo-Uzbek joint venture in extraction industry.[87] But as was the case with their European counterparts, the Uzbek government expelled Israeli firms present in the minerals sector.[88]

At present, cooperative projects have been redirected to other areas such as agriculture, high technology, and training. In agriculture, several Israeli companies are trying to develop drip irrigation that is considered a suitable model for arid regions. Programs to develop milk production were also established through Israeli initiatives; Uzbek cows often produce five to six times less milk than cows in Israel.[89] Since 2007, Israel has been responsible for matters related to agriculture within the Conference on Interaction and Confidence Building Measures in Asia (CICA). Several Israeli high-tech companies are also involved in a project to create an Uzbek industrial park dedicated to new technologies. Bartek has started programming for mobile telecommunications, a booming market in Uzbekistan. Finally, hundreds of Uzbek specialists in the field of agriculture and health have benefited from the training system set up by the Mashav Center for International Cooperation.[90]

In Turkmenistan, some Israeli businessmen have succeeded in building a privileged relationship with President Niyazov and his successor, Berdymukhammedov. Iossif Maiman, a former Mossad agent, was the special representative of "Turkmenbashi" (Saparmurat Niyazov) in the development of gas production. His investment firm, Merhav, became Niyazov's intermediary in his search for foreign investors. Merhav defended Israeli interests and competed with the Russian state monopoly Gazprom for control of the Israeli gas market. In Turkmenistan, the firm was put in charge of several large projects that sought to diminish Iranian and Russian influence to the benefit of Israel and the West. Maiman, for example, played an important role as a consultant in the trans-Caspian gas pipeline construction project. He succeeded in attracting foreign firms to take part in the two main projects run by his company, namely the renovation of Seidi, the country's largest oil refinery, and the construction of a polypropylene factory.[91]

Relationships with Kazakhstan are also growing rapidly. Tel Aviv has a critical need to diversify its oil supplies, as it is in conflict with many producing countries. It has logically turned to Kazakhstan and Azerbaijan for oil, and today a quarter of Israeli's imports of the commodity come from Kazakhstan.[92] However, despite an undeniable economic presence, investments from Israel remain limited.[93] The two countries

Table 5.4

Israel's Place in Imports, Exports, and the Trade Total of Central Asian States in 2010 (in millions of US$)

	Imports	Rank	Exports	Rank	Total trade	Rank
Kazakhstan	64.9 (0.2%)	18	unknown	—	64.9 (0.1%)	29
Kyrgyzstan	0.7 (0.0%)	33	unknown	—	0.7 (0.0%)	38
Tajikistan	0.7 (0.0%)	34	unknown	—	0.7 (0.0%)	36
Turkmenistan	21 (0.4%)	19	unknown	—	21 (0.3%)	25
Uzbekistan	38.5 (0.5%)	15	2.9 (0.1%)	26	41.5 (0.3%)	19

Source: 2011 European Commission statistics, http://ec.europa.eu/trade/creating-opportunities/bilateral-relations/countries-and-regions/.

cooperate in agriculture (modern Israeli agriculture is bound to be appealing in Central Asia), medicine (training of specialists), telecommunications, and new technologies. In 2010, the two countries created a common fund for agricultural research with the support of the Volcani Center, and signed a memorandum of understanding to open an industrial park in Kazakhstan based on the concept of Tefen Park in Galilee, which focuses on agro-technology, energy conservation, water-related technologies, biotechnology, pharmaceuticals, medical equipment, and communications.[94]

Security and military cooperation is also on the rise. In 2008, Astana signed an agreement with two Israeli companies, Soltam and Elbit, to develop new artillery systems with integrated command and control, which Kazakh companies would produce via technology transfer. Israel Aerospace Industries (IAI) is also present on the Kazakh arms market.[95] Russia agreed that Kazakhstan could make the Baikonur Cosmodrome site available to Israel for launches of communications satellites.[96] Despite many cases of corruption and misappropriation of funds around arms sales, Kazakh-Israeli relations are expected to grow in coming years, especially in the areas of security and technology transfer.

Israel has high ambitions in Central Asia at the strategic and commercial levels. Tel Aviv is becoming increasingly interested in partnering with secular Muslim states to compensate for the deterioration of relations with Turkey, and to curb Iran's presence in the region. It looks to Russia, India, and China in order to make up for the loss of influence on Europe and the United States. The relationships benefit from old networks between businessmen and the security services from the former Soviet Jewish diasporas. Israel can draw upon its closeness to the United States in terms of military cooperation and its image as a dynamic economy in the Middle East.

Middle Eastern countries are destined to remain second-class partners in Central Asia without the means to overtake the "big four." In terms of trade, Turkey and Iran largely rank ahead of the United States, though obviously not enough to alter the geopolitical balance in their favor. Moreover, if both Turkish and Iranian commercial niches in the region are well established, growing competition is coming from China. Although the Central Asian elites do not see Turkish and Iranian societies as possible models to emulate, they are not indifferent to their changes. Turkey's domestic evolution, its Islamic conservative modernization, and its rising autonomy from the West may have a significant impact on the political and cultural choices made by the younger generations in Central Asia. Iranian society is closely followed, as well. Internal conflict between conservatives and reformers, the possible victory of the reformers in the years to come, and Iran's potential reintegration into the international order would profoundly affect patterns of Iranian influence in Central Asia. The long-term impact of the 2011 Arab Spring and the rise of Islamic parties as governmental actors are still being studied. China-Iran and China-Turkey relations may also modify the actual regional balance of power, as Beijing considers Iran and Saudi Arabia its two principal partners in the Middle East. India and Pakistan also hope to find a way into Central Asia that bypasses Kabul and look at Iran as an essential partner. Russia, meanwhile, wants to establish itself in Iran and closer to the Indian subcontinent. However, this eventuality of reintegrating Iran into the regional game, where it would respond to geographical and economic logics, remains subject to major geopolitical hazards. This complex situation will evolve in the coming years, and the Central Asian states are well advised to try to diversify their alliances. Both the UAE and Israel can promote a different, renewed image of the Middle East, focused on a dynamic services economy, and not seen as in opposition to the West.

Notes

1. V. Mastny and R. Craig Nation, eds., *Turkey Between East and West: New Challenges for a Rising Regional Power* (Boulder, CO: Westview Press, 1996).

2. J. M. Landau, *Pan-Turkism in Turkey: From Irredentism to Cooperation* (London: C. Hurst, 1981).

3. D. Jung and W. Piccoli, *Turkey at the Crossroads: Ottoman Legacies and a Greater Middle East* (London: Zed Books, 2001).

4. I. Torbakov, "Plans for Turkic Commonwealth," *CEPS European Neighborhood Watch*, no. 19, September 2006.

5. Z. Önis, "Multiple Faces of the 'New' Turkish Foreign Policy: Underlying Dynamics and a Critique," *Insight Turkey* 13, no. 1 (2011): 47–65; E. Alessandri, "The New Turkish Foreign Policy and the Future of Turkey-U.S. Relations," Working Paper of the Instituto Affari Internazionali, no. 1003, 2010.

6. G. Winrow, *Turkey in Post-Soviet Central Asia* (London: Royal Institute of International Affairs, 1995).

7. *Les aides extérieures de la Turquie* (Istanbul: DPT, March 1998).

8. G. E. Fuller and I. O. Lesser, *Turkey's New Geopolitics: From the Balkans to Western China* (Boulder, CO: Westview Press, 1993).

9. Z. Zardykhan, "Turkey and Central Asia: From Fraternity to Partnership," in Esteban and de Pedro, *Great Powers and Regional Integration in Central Asia*, 79–94.

10. The journal *Turkiston Torixi* and opposition parties like Erk and Birlik in Uzbekistan, Jeltoksan in Kazakhstan, Turkmen Ili in Turkmenistan, etc.

11. "Sotrudnichestvo Respubliki Kazakhstan s Turetskoi Respublikoi," Kazakhstan Foreign Affairs Ministry, http://portal.mfa.kz/portal/page/portal/mfa/ru/content/policy/cooperation/europe_america/11.

12. B. Balci, ed., "La Turquie en Asie centrale: La conversion au réalisme (1991–2000)," Report of the Institut Français d'Etudes Anatoliennes, no. 5, 2001.

13. See the Assembly website, http://www.turk-pa.org.

14. S. De Tapia, "Türksat et les républiques turcophones de l'ex-URSS," *Cahiers d'études sur la Méditerranée orientale et le monde turco-iranien*, no. 20 (1995): 399–413.

15. M. Hakan Yavuz and J. L. Esposito, *Turkish Islam and the Secular State: The Gülen Movement* (Syracuse, NY: Syracuse University Press, 2003).

16. B. Balci, *Missionnaires de l'Islam en Asie centrale: Les écoles turques de Fethullah Gülen* (Paris: Maisonneuve & Larose, 2003); B. Balci, "Fethullah Gülen's Missionary Schools in Central Asia and their Role in the Spreading of Turkism and Islam," *Religion, State, and Society* 31, no. 2 (2003): 151–77; C. E. Demir, A. Balci, and F. Akkok, "The Role of Turkish Schools in the Educational System and Social Transformation of Central Asian Countries: The Case of Turkmenistan and Kyrgyzstan," *Central Asian Survey* 19, no. 1 (2000): 141–55.

17. See the *Zaman* website and its Turkmen, Kazakh, and Kyrgyz versions, http://www.todayszaman.com/mainAction.action.

18. G. Yuldasheva, "Turkey's New Foreign Policy Landmarks and Central Asia," *Central Asia and the Caucasus* 49, no. 1 (2008): 51–57.

19. I. Torbakov, "Turkey and Post-Soviet Eurasia: Seeking a Regional Power Status," in *Prospects for Democracy in Central Asia*, ed. B. Schlyter (Istanbul: Swedish Research Institute, 2005), 117–28.

20. 2011 European Commission statistics, http://ec.europa.eu/trade/creating-opportunities/bilateral-relations/countries-and-regions/.

21. H. Kanbolat, "The Future of Kazakhstan for Turkey," *Today's Zaman*, November 28, 2011, http://www.todayszaman.com/columnist-264148-the-future-of-kazakhstan-for-turkey.

22. "Turkey and Kazakhstan Have Words Left to Say, Says Kazakh Ambassador," *Today's Zaman,* December 8, 2011, http://www.todayszaman.com/newsDetail_getNewsById.action?load=detay&link=150056.

23. See the Uzbekistan sheet from the European Commission's statistics office, http://trade.ec.europa.eu/doclib/docs/2006/september/tradoc_113461.pdf.

24. "Sotrudnichestvo Respubliki Kazakhstan s Turetskoi Respublikoi."

25. Press review of the French Embassy in Turkmenistan, January 2009.

26. Press review of the French Embassy in Turkmenistan, March 2008.

27. For more details, see chapter 13.

28. "Posle draki . . . Turetskie rabochie 'begut' iz kazakhstanskogo Atyrau," *CentrAsia*, October 25, 2006, http://www.centrasia.ru/newsA.php?st=1161753120; "Brawl Between Kazakh, Turkish Workers Injures 140," *Radio Free Europe/Radio Liberty*, October 20, 2006, http://www.rferl.org/content/article/1072169.html.

29. M. Sen, "Turkish Islamist Entrepreneurs in Central Asia," in Schlyter, *Prospects for Democracy*, 253–64.

30. "Analysis of Transit Trade Barriers for Kyrgyz Transit Transport through the Republic Kazakhstan," Working Paper of the Corporate Technologies Center of the Asian Development Bank, November 2008, 12.

31. I. Torbakov, "The Georgia Crisis and Russia-Turkey Relations," Jamestown Foundation Occasional Paper, November 2008.

32. S. Hunter, "Iran's Pragmatic Regional Policy," *Journal of International Affairs* 56, no. 2 (2003): 133–47.

33. Ibid.

34. E. Efegil and L. Stone, "Iran's Interests in Central Asia: A Contemporary Assessment," *Central Asian Survey* 20, no. 3 (2001): 353–66.

35. V. Mesamed, "Iran: Ten Years in Post-Soviet Central Asia," *Central Asia and the Caucasus*, no. 1 (2002): 28.

36. K. V. Markov, "Iran i postsovetskie respubliki Tsentral'noi Azii: Tochki pritiazheniia i ottalkivaniia," in *Tsentral'naia Aziia v sisteme mezhdunarodnykh otnoshenii*, ed. V. A. Zair-Bek (Moscow: Institut Vostokovedeniia, 2004), 279–300.

37. S. Peyrouse and S. Ibraimov, "Iran's Central Asia Temptations," *Current Trends in Islamist Ideology* 10 (2010): 82–101.

38. M. Mesbahi, "Tajikistan, Iran, and the International Politics of the 'Islamic Factor'," *Central Asian Survey* 16, no. 2 (1997): 141–58.

39. A. Maleki, "Iran and Turan: Apropos of Iran's Relations with Central Asia and the Caucasian Republics," *Central Asia and the Caucasus*, no. 5 (2001): 89–97.

40. H. Y. Freij, "State Interests vs. the *Umma*: Iranian Policy in Central Asia," *The Middle East Journal* 50, no. 1 (1996): 71–83.

41. Markov, "Iran i postsovetskie respubliki."

42. M. R. Djalili, "L'Iran et la Turquie face à l'Asie centrale," *Journal for International & Strategic Studies*, no. 1 (2008): 13–19.

43. Y. Lee, "Toward a New International Regime for the Caspian Sea," *Problems of Post-Communism* 52, no. 3 (2005): 37–48; P. Mojtahed-Zadeh and M. R. Hafeznia, "Perspectives on the Caspian Sea Dilemma: An Iranian Construct," *Eurasian Geography and Economics* 44, no. 8 (2003): 607–16.

44. "Kirgiziia boitsia stat' zhertvoi Irana esli SShA nachnut s nim voinu," *Vremia.ru*, May 22, 2007, http://www.vremya.ru/2007/86/5/178645.html.

45. N. Swanström, "An Asian Oil and Gas Union: Prospects and Problems," *China and Eurasia Forum Quarterly* 3, no. 3 (2005): 81–97.

46. R. Muzalevsky, "The 'Persian Alliance' and Geopolitical Reconfiguration in Central Asia," *Eurasia Daily Monitor* 7, no. 161, September 9, 2010, http://www.jamestown.org/single/?no_cache=1&tx_ttnews percent5Btt_news percent5D=36799.

47. "Tajikistan and Iran: Is Dushanbe Distancing Itself from Cultural Cousin?" *Eurasianet*, March 7, 2011, http://www.eurasianet.org/node/63021.

48. S. Peyrouse, "Shiism in Central Asia: The Religious, Political, and Geopolitical Factors," *Central Asia and Caucasus Analyst* 11, no. 10 (2009): 9–11.

49. Authors' interviews with anonymous Tajik experts, Dushanbe, March 2008 and June 2010.

50. M. Luomi, "Sectarian Identities or Geopolitics? The Regional Shia-Sunni Divide in the Middle East," Finnish Institute of International Affairs Working Paper, no. 56, 2008; R. Shanahan, "Bad Moon Not Rising: The Myth of the Gulf Shi'a Crescent," Lowy Institute Analysis Paper, September 2008.

51. Djalili and Kellner, *Géopolitique de la nouvelle Asie centrale*, 250–52; more details in Mojtahed-Zadeh and Hafeznia, "Perspectives on the Caspian Sea Dilemma."

52. "Prazdnik na plotine *Druzhba*," *Turkmenistan.ru*, April 19, 2005, http://www.turkmenistan.ru/ru/node/16837.

53. V. Mesamed, "Iran—Turkmenistan: Prodolzhaetsia li aktivnyi dialog?," *Iimes.ru*, August 19, 2007, http://www.iimes.ru/rus/stat/2007/19-08-07c.htm.

54. "Iran to Increase Gas Imports from Turkmenistan," *FARS News Agency*, June 18, 2010, http://english.farsnews.com/newstext.php?nn=8903280609; Peyrouse, *Turkmenistan*, 180–82.

55. "Iran i Kazakhstan podumyvaiut postroit' NPZ," *Rosinvest.com*, December 14, 2006, http://www.rosinvest.com/news/251441/.

56. Mesamed, "Iran: Ten Years in Post-Soviet Central Asia."

57. K. V. Markov, "Iran i postsovetskie respubliki."

58. V. Ivanov, "Iadernyi skandal: Pod zanaves goda Kazakhstan obvinili v nezakonnoi sdelke po uranu s Iranom," *Delovaia Nedelia*, December 31, 2009.

59. For more details, see chapter 10.

60. Mesamed, "Iran: Ten Years in Post-Soviet Central Asia," 30.

61. "Vizit prezidenta Rakhmonova v Iran mozhno nazvat' istoricheskim," *Analitika.org*, February 12 2006, http://www.analitika.org/article.php?story=20060212035915491.

62. For more details, see chapter 12.

63. More in Peyrouse and Ibraimov, "Iran's Central Asia Temptations."

64. M. Haghayeghi, *Islam and Politics in Central Asia* (New York: Palgrave Macmillan, 1996); E. Karagiannis, *Political Islam in Central Asia: The Challenge of Hizb ut-Tahrir* (London: Routledge, 2010).

65. "Sotrudnichestvo Respubliki Kazakhstan s Ob"edinennymi Arabskimi Emiratami," Kazakhstan Ministry of Foreign Affairs, March 2011, http://portal.mfa.kz/portal/page/portal/ mfa/ru/content/policy/cooperation/asia_africa/03; "Sotrudnichestvo Respubliki Uzbekistan so stranami Srednego, Blizhnego Vostoka i Afriki," Uzbekistan Ministry of Foreign Affairs, http:// mfa.uz/rus/mej_sotr/uzbekistan_i_strani_mira/uzbekistan_strani_azii_i_afriki/.

66. "Kazmunaygas, International Petroleum Investment Company Agreed to Cooperate under West Kazakhstan Integrated Gas-Chemical Facility Project," *CIBC News*, http://www. cibcgroup.com/shab_news_en.shtml?cgi-bin/show_news.pl?lang=en&id=2277.

67. S. Carvalho, "UAE's Mubadala, Conoco Agree Kazakh Deal," *Reuters*, October 5, 2008, http://www.reuters.com/article/2008/10/05/emirates-mubadala-conoco-idUSL512067420081005.

68. "CNPC Wins Natural Gas Field Contract in Turkmenistan," China Energy Intelligence and Communication, December 30, 2009, http://www.energychinaforum.com/news/29912.shtml.

69. L. Nolan, "DMCC Finalises Uzbek Cotton Deal," *ArabianBusiness.com*, March 19, 2008, http://www.arabianbusiness.com/property/article/514201-dmcc-finalises-uzbek-cotton deal?limit=20&limitstart=20.

70. "Uzbek Delegation Meets with Dubai Chamber, Looks into Trading Cooperation on Agricultural Produce," *Ameinfo.com*, July 15, 2008, http://www.ameinfo.com/163590.html.

71. A. White, C. Ferris-Lay, and T. Walid, "Ka$hakhstan," *ArabianBusiness.com*, August 10, 2008, http://www.arabianbusiness.com/property/article/526994-kahakhstan/page/2/2.

72. "Kompanii Turtsii i OAE poluchili podriady na zastroiku i blagoustroistvo 'Avazy'," *Turkmenistan.ru*, June 16, 2009, http://www.turkmenistan.ru/?page_id=3&lang_id=ru&elem_ id=15096&type=event&sort=date_desc.

73. "Emirates NBD Seeks Big Uz-buck-istan Ticket in Central Asia," *CPIFinancial.net*, April 6, 2008, http://www.cpifinancial.net/v2/News.aspx?v=1&aid=86&sec=Investment percent20Banking; "Emirates Group and Bank TuranAlem to Promote Islamic Banking in Kazakhstan," *New Horizon*, July 1, 2007, http://www.newhorizon-islamicbanking.com/index. cfm?action=view&id=10439&section=news.

74. For more details, see chapter 14.

75. "Lost Children of Central Asia," *Institute for War and Peace Reporting*, no. 257, November 14, 2005, http://iwpr.net/report-news/lost-children-central-asia; R. Hanks, *Global Security Watch—Central Asia* (Santa Barbara, CA: Praeger, 2010), 110.

76. E. Ivashenko, "Sex Slavery: Personal Story in Detail," *Fergana.news*, December 1, 2011, http://enews.fergananews.com/article.php?id=2728. See also E. Marat, *Labor Migration in Central Asia: Implications of the Global Economic Crisis* (Washington, DC: The Central Asia-Caucasus Institute & Silk Road Studies Program, 2009).

77. "Migratsionnaia sluzhba Tadzhikistana usilivaet voprosy profpodgotovki trudovykh migrantov," *Migration.tj*, November 15, 2011, http://www.migration.tj/ru/index/index/ pageId/511/.

78. Authors' interviews with Central Asian traders, Dordoy, June 6, 2010; Dushanbe's main bazaar, June 24, 2010; and Almaty's main bazaar, September 28, 2010.

79. J. Heathershaw, "Of National Fathers and Russian Elder Brothers: Conspiracy Theories and Political Ideas in Post-Soviet Central Asia," *The Russian Review*, 71, no. 43, (2012): 610–29.

80. "Spetssluzhby vzialis' za samykh 'krutykh' evreev Kirgizii—Gurevicha i Nadelia," *Izrus*, April 11, 2010, http://izrus.co.il/oligarhi/article/2010-04-11/9373.html; G. Mikhailov, "Ty—chuzhoi! Kirgizii privivaiut virus ostrogo natsionalizma," *Nezavisimaia gazeta*, March 5, 2011, http://www.ng.ru/cis/2011-03-04/6_kirgizia.html.

81. Authors' interview with anonymous Uzbek expert in international affairs, Tashkent, March 18, 2008.

82. A. Cohen, "Kazakhstan: Israel's Partner in Eurasia," *Jerusalem Viewpoints*, no. 573 (September-October 2009), http://www.jcpa.org/JCPA/Templates/ShowPage.asp?DBID=1&L NGID=1&TMID=111&FID=443&PID=0&IID=3097; A. Grigoryan, "Priority Directions in the Foreign Policy of Israel: South Caucasus and Central Asia," *Noravank Foundation*, September 22, 2009, http://www.noravank.am/eng/articles/detail.php?ELEMENT_ID=3623.

83. A. Liberman, "Kliuch k Tsentral'noi Azii, bezuslovno, Uzbekistan," *12.uz*, http://www.12. uz/news/show/smi/1816/#.

84. See the European Commission's statistical sheets for previous years.

85. A. Goldenshtein, "Izrail'skii biznesmen perevodit zavody iz Kitaia v Uzbekistan," *Irzus*, March 8, 2009, http://izrus.co.il/dvuhstoronka/article/2009-03-08/3942.html.

86. See Lenta's sheet on Lev Leviev, *Lenta.ru*, n.d., http://lenta.ru/lib/14161564/full.htm.

87. "Zarafshan-Newmont, Uzbekistan," *Mining-Technology.com*, n.d., http://www.mining-technology.com/projects/zarafshan/.

88. For more details, see chapter 10.

89. L. Maarse, "Support to Sustainable Development of Livestock Sector in Uzbekistan: Mid-Term Evaluation," UNDP Evaluation Resource Centre Report, April 21, 2010, erc.undp. org/evaluationadmin/downloaddocument.html?docid=4150; Z. Lerman, "Agricultural Development in Uzbekistan: The Effect of Ongoing Reforms," Hebrew University of Jerusalem Discussion Paper, no. 7 (2008): 13.

90. S. Gonchar, "Mashav Projects in Uzbekistan," *eng.econews.uz*, November 18, 2010, http://eng.econews.uz/index.php?option=com_content&view=article&id=261:mashav-projects-in-uzbekistan&catid=11:eco-education&Itemid=21.

91. S. Rozen and Yu. Juraev, "Mossad Emissary in the Heart of the Muslim East: The Conflict That Didn't Happen," *Axis Globe*, September 20, 2005, http://www.axis globe. com/article.asp?article=389; "Turkmensko-izrail'skie otnosheniia: Istoriia i sovremennost'," *Sankt-Peterburgskii Tsentr izucheniia sovremennogo Blizhnego Vostoka*, http://meast.ru/article/turkmensko-izrailskie-otnosheniya-istoriya-i-sovremennost.

92. R. Medzini, "Peres to Visit Azerbaijan, Kazakhstan," *Ynetnews*, June 28, 2009, http://www.ynetnews.com/articles/0,7340,L-3737906,00.html.

93. "Kazakhstan: Voennye i tekhnologicheskie sviazi s Izrailem krepnut, otmeniat li vizy?" *Izrus*, June 30, 2009, http://izrus.co.il/dvuhstoronka/article/2009-06-30/5170. html#ixzz1g9lCr4cQ.

94. S. Wrobel, "Israelis to Help Build Industry Parks in Kazakhstan," *The Jerusalem Post*, April 16, 2010, http://www.jpost.com/Business/BusinessNews/Article.aspx?id=173297.

95. "IAI Advances Strategic Cooperative Efforts with Kazakhstan," *Israel Aerospace Industries*, June 30, 2009, http://www.iai.co.il/35344-39725-en/MediaRoom_NewsArchives_2009. aspx?PageNum=4.

96. "Israel Could Be A Contender," *Strategy Page*, April 7, 2009, http://www.strategypage. com/htmw/htspace/20090407.aspx.

6

Central Asia Looking East

The Search for Asian Dynamism

In the early years of independence, the Central Asian presidents made positive references to what they saw as an "Asian model," lauding the economic dynamism of Asian countries, but also their political regimes and their allegedly non-Westernized cultural identity. This valorization of Southeast and East Asia, common in the first half of the 1990s, gradually dissipated with the return of Russian influence and the rise of China. Later, at the turn of twenty-first century, Astana translated the symbolism of the Asian dragons (Hong Kong, Singapore, South Korea, and Taiwan) and the Asian Tigers (Thailand, Malaysia, Indonesia, the Philippines, and Vietnam) into Kazakhstan's "snow leopard,"[1] insisting on the prospect for a high-tech future, and rising ties with the Asia-Pacific nations. Whereas Central Asia is often associated to South Asia for geostrategic reasons influenced by the American involvement in Afghanistan and Pakistan and a growing alliance with India, this relationship is minimal in economic terms. Trade and investments ties with Southeast and East Asia are more important, but often unknown as there are seen as having no strategic foundation. If Japan has been the main aid donor to Central Asia until the EU bypassed it, Central Asia is now looking toward South Korea and Malaysia as new reliable long-term partners, and potential models to emulate.

India's Involvement: Hopes and Disillusionment

Upon recognition of Central Asian independence, India felt vested with a new responsibility. Given the cultural and historical ties it has with the region, and because of its tradition of non-alignment, it sees itself as a successful model of modernity after decolonization. The Indian-Soviet friendship made New Delhi very present in the everyday lives of Central Asians via television, movies, music, and cultural exchanges from the 1960s to the 1980s.[2] However, in the 1990s India lost visibility and is now trying to gain back lost cultural influence in the strategic and economic sector. But New Delhi's involvement has been slowed by the complex geopolitical context of Pakistan and Afghanistan, as well as by its own domestic economic and political evolutions, which have prevented it from taking a well-defined stance in Central Asia. The situation changed in the early years of the twenty-first century, but too slowly for the liking of the Central Asian states, which have been disappointed by the broken promises of the Indian elites, as well as by the weak economic presence of their companies.

The Failure of the "Indian Model"

During the 1990s, India did not achieve its ambitions in Central Asia, primarily for economic reasons. It suffered the loss of support from Moscow—in 1990–1991 more than 16 percent of Indian exports went to the Soviet Union and about 6 percent of imports came from it[3]—as well as the disappearance of the Rupee Trade System that allowed India to pay its Soviet imports in Rupee, and not in currency. The Indian economy underwent a significant transformation. Privatization disrupted trade mechanisms, reduced the role and resources of the state—whose capacity for foreign investment was very limited—and altered the political landscape by giving voice to a new merchant class that desired a vastly reduced role for the Byzantine administration that was a legacy of the British empire.[4] New Delhi was also absorbed by domestic political issues, especially the ongoing insurgency in Jammu and Kashmir. The global turmoil associated with the disappearance of socialism and its impact on Nehruvian thought accelerated profound ideological evolutions, after which Hindu nationalism found a new space for expression.[5] In foreign policy, the idea of abandoning the internationalist Nehruvian model in favor of a form of nationalization—meaning "Hinduization"—was also discussed.[6] In addition, India remained focused on its relations with Pakistan and its neighbors in South Asia, Sri Lanka, Bangladesh, and Nepal. This South Asian orientation left little room for post-Soviet Central Asia.[7]

In the first decade of Central Asian independence, diplomatic relations were created, first contacts made and statements of intent issued, initial exchange mechanisms set up, and so on.[8] However, unlike states such as Turkey, Iran, or China, India did not see these early contacts as a constructive step; compared to India-Central Asia relations during the Soviet period, they seemed more like a retreat than an advance.[9] However, the geopolitical context changed drastically in the second half of the 1990s with the establishment of the Taliban regime in Kabul in 1996, the Indian and Pakistani nuclear tests of 1998, the rise of China, and especially the feeling that Pakistan was gaining strength in Central Asia. New Delhi decided therefore to implement a "Look North" policy, based on the model of the "Look West" policy toward West Asia.[10] Traditionally, the Indian elites perceive their neighborhood in terms of widening concentric circles, and divide their Asian interests into different groups in South Asia, East Asia, West Asia, and Central Asia. In the Central Asian case, Indian foreign policy has set specific goals: contain the expansion of Pakistan and prevent the region from becoming Islamabad's strategic stronghold; curb potential terrorist destabilization that would affect Central Asia; gain access to the economic wealth of the region; aim for a possible military rapprochement; and prevent China from becoming too well positioned in the region.[11] These goals have remained unchanged from the end of the 1990s until today.

However, although it is now more focused, Indian policy in Central Asia continues to be marked by indecision and a lack of efficacy.

Another reason for India's failure in the region lies in its lack of a country-specific approach, an error that the European Union also made. Inspired by Nehru's legacy, New Delhi has unsuccessfully called for Central Asia to establish regional mechanisms and has been slow in separating the needs of individual states.[12] Historically, India was closer to Uzbekistan and Tajikistan than to the three other states. However, the Tajik civil war between 1992 and 1997, and more generally the inherent poverty of Tajikistan, reduced New Delhi's prospects in the country. Although Tajikistan was initially conceived of as India's gateway in Central Asia, this relationship did not materialize either in terms of political influence or of economic presence.[13] With Uzbekistan, relations have also proved more difficult than expected. The Uzbek regime's growing isolationism, and an unfavorable climate for foreign investment, have discouraged private Indian firms. Meanwhile, the Karimov regime, particularly in the 1990s, framed itself as an ally of Pakistan, which raised concerns for Indian elites. Turkmenistan has remained closed to India's economic and political interests for too long, even though there has been a resurgence of interest from Ashgabat after the country gradually reopened following the change of president in 2006.[14] While in the 1990s, India, like many other international players, looked at Uzbekistan as the heart of the region, Kazakhstan finally emerged as the major Indian partner in economic terms; it is also likely to become a significant political ally in the future. The signing of a strategic partnership between Astana and New Delhi in 2009 confirmed this tendency and cemented each country's shared expectations.[15]

A Complex Geopolitical Environment

In terms of security architecture, India remains largely uninfluential.[16] Since 2005 New Delhi has been an associate member of the SCO. Despite positive engagement from Moscow and Astana, the prospect of its full membership is still very problematic, especially from Beijing's point of view. Its own statutes prohibit the SCO from admitting states that have not signed the Nuclear Nonproliferation Treaty, which includes India and Pakistan.[17] However, an agreement between India and the International Atomic Energy Agency (IAEA) in 2009 released New Delhi from its "nuclear apartheid," and could theoretically be used as an argument in favor of its membership.[18] But border tensions between China and India have not been settled and therefore would cast a shadow on the main success of the SCO—a peaceful resolution of border disputes with China and the demilitarization of borders. Finally, the fragile state of India-Pakistan relations, particularly the situation in Kashmir, can only worry SCO member states, which do not want territorial disputes between their members.[19] The only regional organization in which both India and the Central Asia states find themselves is the Conference on Interaction and Confidence Building Measures in Asia (CICA), a Kazakh initiative that seeks to broaden the parameters of security in the region by involving other Asian countries, but it has no great influence.[20] The same is true for the South Asian Association for Regional Cooperation (SAARC), which includes Afghanistan and India but not the Central Asian states (at least not yet) and seeks to articulate cooperation between South and Central Asia.[21]

In terms of security, India is far behind Russia, China, the United States, and Europe, and even Turkey. However, India does have some experience in this area. It played a major role in financing and training the anti-Taliban Northern Alliance in the 1990s and has created working groups against terrorism with several Central Asian countries, including Uzbekistan. Officers from all the Central Asian states except Turkmenistan have attended courses at India's premier military institutions, and India has provided infrastructure assistance to the Military Training College in Dushanbe.[22] New Delhi was also a prominent participant in the reconstruction of the Ayni military airbase, where it has tried for many years to open its first overseas base. But in December 2010, the Tajik government announced that Russia was the only country with which it would conduct negotiations for the Ayni base, and Indian personnel deployed there have been evacuated, an important symbolic failure for New Delhi.[23] The former military-technical partnership between India and Soviet Union, now reinvigorated by Indian orders from the Russian military-industrial complex, offers a new field of cooperation with Central Asia. Thanks to the compatibility of their defense equipment, India has become a client for torpedoes and planes built in Kazakhstan and Kyrgyzstan.[24] Delhi could grow in the forthcoming years into a role as an actual security partner, but for now remains so only in embryonic form.

Despite its declarations of intent in favor of Central Asia, Indian foreign policy remains focused on more traditional issues: renewed tensions with Pakistan; geopolitical rapprochement with China; strengthening India's position in South Asia; and building a special partnership with the United States and the European Union. In this context, Central Asia is struggling to distinguish itself. It has become trapped between India's withdrawal from post-Soviet space in general, and from Russia in particular, and security concerns related to the situations in Afghanistan and Pakistan. Nevertheless, there are some developments on the horizon. The Kazakh-Indian Declaration of Strategic Partnership has worked to confirm the qualitative enhancement of their relations and Central Asia's growing perception that India can potentially play a balancing role, which could therefore support the multi-vector foreign policy that all the Central Asian governments hope to build.

Limited, but Promising, Economic Niches

Economically, Indian presence in Central Asia is minimal. Standing at about 0.25 percent of total Indian trade, Central Asia is insignificant for India in trade terms, and is unlikely to exceed more than 1 percent irrespective of developments.[25] In the opposite direction, New Delhi represents only 0.4 percent of Central Asian trade, and ranks from the fifteenth to the twenty-first largest trading partner of each state, while China, its main symbolic competitor, invariably ranks within the top three alongside Russia and the European Union. Trade is growing markedly with Kazakhstan, yet

Table 6.1

India's Place in Imports, Exports, and the Trade Total of Central Asian States in 2010 (in millions of US$)

	Imports	Rank	Exports	Rank	Total trade	Rank
Kazakhstan	155.2 (0.5%)	14	138.9 (0.3%)	18	294.1 (0.4%)	15
Kyrgyzstan	25.7 (0.4%)	13	0.8 (0.1%)	21	26.6 (0.3%)	15
Tajikistan	33.5 (1.3%)	15	0.2 (0%)	23	33.7 (0.9%)	16
Turkmenistan	30.3 (0.6%)	17	11.2 (0.3%)	20	41.5 (0.5%)	21
Uzbekistan	59.7 (0.7%)	13	20.8 (0.4%)	16	80.6 (0.6%)	16

Source: 2011 European Commission statistics, http://ec.europa.eu/trade/creating-opportunities/bilateral-relations/countries-and-regions/.

economic relations with other Central Asian countries are minimal. As was the case in the past, the main goods that India imports from Central Asia consist of raw materials, such as cotton, uranium, zinc, iron, and steel, as well as dried fruits and some furs. By contrast, it exports pharmaceuticals, tea, leather, textiles, rice, and the fruits of modernization—electronic goods, chemical products, and know-how.[26]

The Indian economic presence in Central Asia is hampered by several factors. The majority of India's trade is conducted by sea, and trade relations are developing primarily with South Asia, Europe, and the United States, particularly in the booming information technology sector. Poor relations with Pakistan and the closure of the border with China after the 1962 conflict have impeded continental trade, although Sino-Indian flows are now expanding,[27] and Islamabad and New Delhi have negotiated a preferential trade agreement at the end of 2011.[28] In any case, the space available for Central Asia is limited and does not fit into the current main trends, unless the India-Europe corridor is used, but that is a mainly sea-based route.[29] Moreover, the Indian economy is now largely privatized and the state no longer provides any major incentives. New Delhi cannot force its businessmen to invest in an area deemed unattractive or too unstable, if the state itself does not establish incentive mechanisms that would offset risk-taking. Finally, unlike China, where exports are a key element of growth, the economic strength of India is essentially internal, based on the huge rise of mass consumption in transport and telecommunications, as well as in the service sector.

In the energy sector, India's needs are immense, but its entry into the Caspian Basin has so far been unsuccessful.[30] New Delhi has pinned all its hopes on two gas pipeline projects: the Iran-Pakistan-India (IPI) and the Turkmenistan-Afghanistan-Pakistan-India (TAPI) pipelines, but these have been slow to develop. The American desire to marginalize Russia and Iran, and to hold China back in Central Asia, opens up great opportunities for India, at least in theory, but these expectations have not materialized. In spite of multiple agreements and memoranda of understanding, India fails to rank in the top ten countries involved in the exploitation of oil and gas resources in Central Asia. It will now have difficulties finding a place on this list, considering not only the already established involvement of Russian and Western companies in Central Asia, but also the rapidity of China's growth there. In 2005, despite a memorandum signed between India and Kazakhstan for cooperation in the oil and gas sectors, ONGC Videsh, the subsidiary of ONGC (Oil and Natural Gas Corporation) that looks after foreign purchases, suffered one of its greatest failures after being outbid by the China National Petroleum Company for the acquisition of PetroKazakhstan.[31] In 2009, after several additional years of discussions, ONGC Videsh eventually signed an agreement for joint exploitation of the Satpayev offshore block in the Kazakh part of the Caspian Sea.[32] In 2006, India's Gail and Uzbekneftegaz signed a memorandum providing for the joint exploration and exploitation of Uzbek sites, as well as for the construction of liquid gas and oil factories in the western regions of Uzbekistan.[33] In Turkmenistan, ONGC-Mittal Energy acquired 30 percent of the shares of two oil sites in the Turkmen sector of the Caspian Sea, but it left the blocks after exploratory failures.[34] It is therefore improbable that India will be able to position itself as a major energy player in Central Asia.

To date, Central Asian economies need what the Chinese "world's workshop" has to offer: investment in transport infrastructure and energy production, as well as cheap goods commensurate with the generally low standard of living. With the exception of Kazakhstan, Central Asia's interest in India as the "world's back office" is limited at present. However, sectors where Indian know-how can make an important contribution are numerous: telecommunications and electronics, pharmaceutical and medical equipment, textiles, agribusiness (food processing and packaging) and the modernization of the agricultural sector, chemical and mining industries, and electrical equipment. The economic niches of India are precisely those of the future, and are expected to grow in significance throughout the twenty-first century. Moreover, information technology and services are less "material" than other industries and therefore suffer less from the lack of direct geographical connectivity between India and Central Asia. With Kazakhstan, two key cooperation areas can be added: the space and the nuclear industries (uranium mining, staff training, and fuel supplies).[35]

Two decades after the Soviet Union's disappearance, India is the least powerful of the great powers in Central Asia. It is not in a position to compete with the "big four" on the short to medium-term future: it is a relative latecomer to the region, and is only beginning to establish itself there. Its influence cannot be compared to that of Turkey or Iran, or even to that of countries with an important economic role, such as South Korea or Japan. India has not been able to achieve the objectives that it defined in its "Look North" policy at the end of the 1990s. Despite its efforts to become established in Dushanbe, it has no military presence in the region; it has been unable to prevent China from becoming the new kingmaker in Central Asia; it has not acquired any key place within the regional security architecture; and has been rather disappointing to the Central Asian elites. However, the potential seems significant, and this striking gap between possibility and reality most clearly characterizes the current stage of India-Central Asia relations.

Pakistan: Dashed Hope, Political Suspicion

Central Asia's independence elicited great hopes among the Pakistani elites, who have viewed the region as an Islamic counterweight to India.[36] Since the capture of Kabul by the Taliban in 1996, Islamabad has been dreaming of creating a large zone of influence encompassing Kashmir, Afghanistan, and post-Soviet Central Asia, and offering it the long-awaited "strategic depth" against India. For the landlocked Central Asian states, the key geographical position of Pakistan was seen as an undeniable asset to access to southern seas. The Sino-Pakistani cooperation in Gwadar, the natural end point for the Karakoram Highway, was supposed to transform Pakistan into a key transit zone.[37] The growing influence of Beijing in Central Asia thus strengthened Pakistani elites' belief in shaping a new geopolitical axis between Central Asia, Afghanistan, Pakistan, and China.[38]

However, all these hopes quickly faded. The Central Asian governments have not joined the Pakistani discourse on Islam, which they consider too extreme, did not support the anti-Indian stance of Islamabad, and condemned support for the Taliban. Only Uzbekistan remained pro-Pakistani for a time, before reversing its position once it declared war against the Islamic Movement of Uzbekistan (IMU), and anti-Islamism became the main driver of Karimov's legitimacy.[39] Pakistan's strategic and ideological choices have thus slowed its involvement in Central Asia. Local governments are concerned about the spread of Salafi Islam brought by Pakistani businessmen and seek to halt the spread of proselytizing movements like the Tablighi Jamaat, also stemming from the Indian subcontinent.[40] Moreover, Pakistan and Central Asia do not share many multilateral platforms for discussion. Pakistan must be content with its observer status in the SCO; the Economic Cooperation Organization has failed to demonstrate its effectiveness in the field of transport infrastructure; and the secular Central Asian regimes play but a small role in the Organization of Islamic Cooperation.[41]

In economic terms, Pakistan is very much a secondary actor, positioned seventeenth in terms of trade with the whole Central Asia, and with more modest rankings in terms of bilateral exchanges. The Pakistani economy, dominated by small private firms, is weak and lacks large companies able to carry out massive overseas investment policies. Pakistani businessmen are therefore active mainly in the purchase of cotton, particularly in Uzbekistan, construction materials (cement), food imports, and agribusiness (sugar and flour factories), and trade in traditional products such as leather and jewelry.[42] So far all major projects to link the two regions by transport have failed. Like India, Pakistan is participating in the initiative launched by the Asian Development Bank, the Central-South Asia Transport and Trade Forum (CSATTF), but it has not had much success.[43] The agreement signed in 2004 between Pakistan, China, Kyrgyzstan, and Kazakhstan for transit of goods along the Karakoram Highway has also had little impact.[44] In 2007, during the visit of Prime Minister Shaukat Aziz to Tashkent, a memorandum was signed on the planned energy corridor linking the two countries via Afghanistan: Uzbekistan wants access to the ports of the Indian Ocean, while Pakistan hopes to get the gas and electricity necessary for its growth.

Table 6.2

Pakistan's Place in Imports, Exports, and the Trade Total of Central Asian States in 2010 (in millions of US$)

	Imports	Rank	Exports	Rank	Total trade	Rank
Kazakhstan	4.9 (0.0%)	42	—	—	4.9 (0.0%)	<50
Kyrgyzstan	1.5 (0.0%)	27	0.0 (0.0%)	<50	1.5 (0.0%)	31
Tajikistan	5.8 (0.2%)	23	14.9 (1.3%)	9	20.7 (0.6%)	20
Turkmenistan	0.7 (0.0%)	36	2.4 (0.1%)	23	3.3 (0.0%)	36
Uzbekistan	2.8 (0.0%)	30	1.1 (0.0%)	31	3.9 (0.0%)	32

Source: 2011 European Commission statistics, http://ec.europa.eu/trade/creating-opportunities/bilateral-relations/countries-and-regions/.

Pakistan desperately needs Central Asian energy resources, as the country's growth is significantly hampered by its energy crisis.[45] It does not seek to establish itself directly in Central Asia, but would rather import energy resources, both gas and electricity. However, the TAPI gas pipeline has yet to come to life, and the electricity cooperation in the CASA-1000 framework[46] is very limited. If the two main energy projects are to become a reality, Central Asia-Pakistan relations may become more sustainable, but will need to overcome the security problems around the issue of the Pakistani army's support to the Taliban. Moreover, Pakistan's growing trend toward becoming a failing state serves further to undermine any partnership, and Central Asian governments may remain reluctant to develop cooperation other than in gas and electricity. Any strategic partnership will therefore have to take into consideration Pakistan's position on Afghanistan, which, at present, is at odds with that of the Central Asian capitals.

Japan's Policy in Central Asia: From Idealism to Realism

Since the 1990s, Japan's global foreign policy has been characterized by its push to escape isolationism, to free itself partially from American tutelage, and to appear as an influential power on the international scene, in the hope of getting into the tight circle of permanent members of the UN Security Council.[47] The strategy developed in Central Asia is part of this framework. Since Central Asia's independence in 1991, Japanese elites have seen the region as an arena in which the new Japanese foreign policy can be expressed. Tokyo was a very active partner of the Central Asian states in the 1990s, and did not skimp on investments. But its status as the largest provider of development aid failed to transform into geopolitical influence. Its weak visibility led to difficulties in promoting synergic logic when faced with contending spheres of influence and economic and geopolitical competition. The failure of Japanese ambitions in Central Asia, combined with domestic economic difficulties, has led Tokyo to adopt a more realistic and above all utilitarian stance vis-à-vis the region.

Japan's Narratives on Central Asia

After the collapse of the Soviet Union, Japan formulated a strategy toward the Central Asian states based on aid and development. To this end, it fought for the inclusion of the five countries in development aid programs so that its assistance could be listed as part of its international contribution. In 1993, under pressure from Tokyo, the Organization for Economic Cooperation and Development (OECD) granted the Central Asian states developing country status, and included them in its Development Assistance Program, partly financed by Japan. Tokyo also convinced the Asian Development Bank to admit four of the Central Asian countries (Turkmenistan joined later in 2000) even though they were already members of the European Bank for Reconstruction and Development, which meant that they were able to obtain credit from both of these institutions.[48] Nevertheless, the context of the 1990s was scarcely favorable to the new Japanese foreign policy. The country experienced a significant economic recession and struggled to get involved in any substantial way in Central Asia. Tokyo put off establishing embassies in the region: a liaison office was first opened in Dushanbe only in 2002, and in Ashgabat in 2005.[49]

The hesitations of Japanese policy during the 1990s can also be explained by Japan's misreading of Central Asia. Huge sway was exercised by specific political figures who privileged the development of relations with Kyrgyzstan, which Japan came to perceive as its base of influence in the region.[50] Japanese aid was therefore focused on Bishkek, based on the idea that Askar Akayev was promoting the market economy and democracy more visibly than his neighbors, and that the small size of the country offered Japanese assistance the opportunity for greater effectiveness. However, by the end of the decade Tokyo's interests had shifted to Uzbekistan, a key element of geostrategic stability, and to Kazakhstan, the region's economic driver.[51] Japanese foreign policy is based on the premise that development aid is not conditioned by the political situation. Tokyo believes that democracy cannot be imposed from the outside and that American and European fierce critiques of the lack of democracy can only serve to reinforce anti-Western feelings. It therefore has not had any problems developing relationships with the local authoritarian regimes, took a low profile after the Andijan events of May 2005, and does not favor the development of NGOs that might complicate its relations with the authorities.

In a first phase, extending from 1992 to 1997, Japan sought to present itself as a partner of Central Asia that specifically privileged long-term development and contributed to the stability of the region. Whereas the major international actors were chiefly interested in hydrocarbons, Tokyo insisted on its neutrality in the energy "Great Game" and stressed that it wanted to have a balanced, mutually beneficial partnership with Central Asia. These declarations were not devoid of ambiguity, since Japan actually was in search of energy resources. Within the post-Soviet space, it was especially interested in Siberian resources but was demanding political concessions from Moscow, especially the restitution of the Kuril Islands.[52] Faced with Russian refusal, Tokyo decided to turn its attention to Central Asia, hoping to make Russia yield. In 1993, the Japanese authorities made an open display of their preference for Kazakhstan and Turkmenistan, rather than Siberia, in terms of energy diversification. Despite these official declarations, Japanese companies have proven cautious about investing in a region that they see as potentially unstable.

A second phase of Japanese-Central Asian relations began in 1997 with the "Eurasian diplomacy" of Prime Minister Ryutaro Hashimoto. Arguing that Japanese-American relations constituted one of the foundations of stability in the Asia Pacific region, he put forward an equivalent strategy for the post-Soviet space that included promoting multilateralism, the presence of major international actors, and global objectives of prosperity instead of short-term profitability. Japan thus claimed it was willing to defer its profits for the benefit of Central Asia's long-term development.[53] "Eurasian diplomacy" was also based on the idea of reviving the Silk Roads, and affirming that Japan is one of the main actors in the dialogue between East and West. It sometimes tended to advance "Asianizing" arguments (*Ajia shugi*) on the allegedly specific features of Asian culture, especially the better integration of the individual into the collective. However, this "Eurasian diplomacy" push has had little effect and was limited to issuing slogans. Japanese diplomacy has been hampered by structural elements like the economic crisis, but equally by the administrative reforms that have led to a reduction of the numbers of employees in the Ministry of Foreign Affairs and the embassies.[54]

Cooperation with Central Asia was given fresh impetus in 2004. With the return to economic growth, the Prime Minister Junichiro Koizumi renewed Japan's engagement on the international scene. Tokyo proposed the creation of a "Central Asia + Japan" initiative, designed to establish multilateral dialogue on complex subjects such as economic innovation, the joint management of energy resources, the development of trade via regional transport, and the fight against terrorism and drug trafficking.[55] Taking the positive role played by the ASEAN (Association of Southeast Asian Nations) + 3 (Japan, China, South Korea) initiative as its model, Tokyo argued that only multilateralism could diminish the risks of regional conflict. Since 2005, the Foreign Affairs ministers of member countries of the initiative have met annually, along with Turkmenistan, in spite of its status of permanent neutrality. The former ambassador to Uzbekistan and Tajikistan, Akio Kawato, has for his part suggested creating an OSCE-style pan-continental union that might integrate the "Central Asia + Japan" initiative, the SCO, and other organizations of regional security within a larger framework. This proposition has not interested the Central Asian capitals, even though Tokyo has tried to present itself as an intermediary between, on the one hand, the interests of the United States and the European Union, and on the other, those of Russia and of China.[56]

In 2006, Prime Minister Aso Taro put forward the idea of creating an "arc of freedom and prosperity" in the region,[57] but this came up against the same recurrent question of how this could be realized without involving Moscow and Beijing. The Japanese initiatives cannot, at least for the moment, form any serious counterweight to the Russo-Chinese tandem. Despite having the support of the United States, Japan still has few ways of influencing the Central Asian governments and struggles to push multi-vectored policies to escape the dual Russian and Chinese influence. Long-term cooperation between Japan and Central Asia is therefore partly dependent on the extent of China's ability to impede the economic objectives of its Japanese competitor.[58]

The Mechanisms of Japanese Aid in Central Asia

Between 1992 and 2004, Japan spent more than US$2 billion to support the development of the Central Asian states, making it the biggest donor to the region. However, Tokyo has not managed to turn this investment into a political or cultural asset, and has remained too modest in publicizing it. Moreover, since 2004, development aid has declined significantly. Aid to Kazakhstan and Turkmenistan has been totally eliminated, though for different reasons (economic success for the former, political isolation for the latter), and aid to Uzbekistan has also been drastically reduced.[59] This trend accelerated with the 2008 economic crisis, which reduced Japanese financial capacity, and with the disasters of March 2011, which may relegate Central Asia to a non-priority in Japanese foreign investment for the long term.

Japanese assistance is divided into two categories. The first is the largest and covers long-terms loans at low interest rates called "loans in yen"; the second is of less importance and pertains to the provision of technical assistance for projects. Half the sum invested in Central Asia has been spent under the auspices of Official Development Assistance (ODA), which is run by the Foreign Affairs Ministry. Japanese credits are subject to strict conditions that are sometimes criticized by the Central Asian states, but Tokyo insists on the pedagogical character of the loans, which oblige the authorities to exercise their spending with greater prudence. Two agencies, the Japan International Cooperation Agency (JICA) and the Overseas Economic Cooperation Fund (OECF), contribute to the dispensing of the ODA. Founded in 1974, the JICA's main function is to provide aid to developing countries, in particular in the institutional and social sector and in human development (health, education, conservation of the environment).[60] It distributes the aid allocated by the Department of Economic Cooperation of the Foreign Affairs Ministry. The aid from other ministries, such as Finance, Foreign Trade, Industry, or of the Administration for Economic Planning, often passes through the OECF to the governments and official institutions of recipient countries. The Japanese Bank for International Cooperation (JBIC) contributes its financial support to Japanese companies wishing to settle abroad and manages the credits distributed by the ODA.[61] In addition, Tokyo finances a large part of the projects funded by the Asian Development Bank.

Japan is usually reticent to finance large-scale projects and prefers to commit to medium-sized ones that have more substantial chances of being realized. Aid is broadly diversified: renovating roads, airports, and electricity infrastructures; developing optical fiber equipment; fostering preparedness for management of natural catastrophes; supplying food products; helping agricultural development and water provisioning; and supporting primary schools in villages.[62] Thus, thanks to Japanese assistance,

Table 6.3

Japan's Place in Imports, Exports, and the Trade Total of Central Asian States in 2010 (in millions of US$)

	Imports	Rank	Exports	Rank	Total trade	Rank
Kazakhstan	235.6 (0.8%)	10	532.2 (1.2%)	9	767.8 (1%)	12
Kyrgyzstan	38.4 (0.6%)	12	0.1 (0.0%)	30	38.5 (0.5%)	14
Tajikistan	2.4 (0.2%)	27	0 (0%)	28	2.5 (0,1%)	28
Turkmenistan	26.4 (0.5%)	18	0.1 (0.0%)	35	26.6 (0.3%)	24
Uzbekistan	81.5 (1%)	12	151.9 (2.7%)	8	233.5 (1.7%)	10

Source: 2011 European Commission statistics, http://ec.europa.eu/trade/creating-opportunities/bilateral-relations/countries-and-regions/.

the Kyrgyz government has restored the airport at Manas, as well as the roads from Bishkek to Osh and to Bishkek and Naryn, has trained personnel in green tourism, has modernized its hospital structures, and has opened a Kyrgyz-Japanese Center to promote the learning of Japanese.[63] Uzbekistan has also benefited from Japanese financing for its railway lines.[64]

The Transition to Economic Realism

For many years, Tokyo was perceived as one of the region's largest aid donors, but not as a privileged economic partner. In 2010, it ranked as Central Asia's ninth largest trade partner, with less than 1 percent of the region's trade.[65] Several bilateral committees were created in order to facilitate the development of exchanges. From the Japanese side, these committees bring together political figures such as Iosiro Mori and Taro Aso, high-level state employees from the Foreign Affairs Ministry, and representatives of financial institutions, as well as leaders from the main companies involved in Central Asia (Mitsui, Marubeni, Toshiba, Toyota, and Shimidzu). However, Japanese companies consider the investment climate to be negative, and only major corporations with backing from the political authorities are ready to establish themselves in Central Asia.

Ensuring the security of its supplies has always been at the center of Japan's energy policies, as it is aware of its great vulnerability in this domain. Indeed, the country imports more than three-quarters of its oil and gas, mostly from the Middle East, but also from Malaysia or Indonesia.[66] Tokyo regularly worries about the deteriorating international position of Iran, which is one of its main energy partners, and is looking at alternatives should it need to compensate for the possible loss of the Iranian supplies.[67] Faced with China's rise in power, and its increasing consumption of energy, the Japanese authorities believe that their energy policies cannot be left to the market and that the state must exercise responsibility for long-term energy choices, the programming of investments, and the security of supplies.[68] This position was one of the motives for Japan's commitment in Central Asia and Russia, although it has had mixed success.

At the beginning of the 1990s, Mitsubishi and Japan National Oil Corporation (JNOC) conducted feasibility studies concerning the possible construction of oil and gas pipelines to carry Turkmen and Kazakh hydrocarbons to Japan, via either Russia or China. This project, known as the Energy Silk Road Project, did not get off the ground for reasons of cost, the geopolitical balance between Beijing and Tokyo, and changes in Russo-Japanese relations.[69] In 2002, a Japanese delegation, the Silk Road Energy Mission, visited Central Asia in order to study new prospects for bilateral and regional cooperation in energy matters.[70] Despite Tokyo's hopes, the large Japanese companies have experienced difficulties in establishing themselves in the Central Asian hydrocarbons sector, and are limited mainly to restoring refineries in Kazakhstan, Uzbekistan, and Turkmenistan. The INPEX Corporation is a member of the international consortium at the Kazakh site of Kashagan; Itochu is participating in the exploitation of Azeri deposits in the Caspian Sea; and Nissho Iwai has participated, in partnership with Kellogg and Uzbekneftegaz, in developing the Uzbek oil field of Kokdumalak, on the border with Turkmenistan. With the development of Sakhalin-2 project in the Sea of Okhotsk, two-thirds of whose LNG (liquefied natural gas) production is destined for Japan, Tokyo has finally managed to expand its energy partnership with Russia, despite the Kuril Islands issue.[71] Central Asia appears today as a less necessary partner, and in any case the Caspian Basin is geographically remote from Japan. This notwithstanding, new spheres of cooperation have emerged in the last ten years, such as Japan's import of uranium from Kazakhstan and Uzbekistan.[72]

Both Central Asia and Japan consider their relationship to be good and strong, but non-strategic. The former does not seek Japan as a counterweight to China and is somewhat disappointed that Japanese presence has been more limited than expected in post-Soviet space. Central Asian governments nonetheless appreciate Tokyo's development assistance, its lack of political interference, its alliance with the United States, and its capacity to symbolize modernity while remaining culturally autonomous.[73] The joint reference to the Silk Roads narrative enables both partners to confirm their mutual interest and shared vision of the world, without truly getting beyond the stage of discourse. On the Japanese side, the early enthusiasm for Central Asia has subsided. Much more attention has been turned toward Afghanistan, and goals have been streamlined to increasing energy diplomacy for hydrocarbons and uranium and decreasing development aid. With the absence of small and medium-sized business in the region, and the growing presence of China and other dynamic Asian economies, the Japanese influence in Eurasia has become less visible and is probably destined to remain so.

South Korea: A Discreet but Growing Presence

South Korea, the primary Asian dragon in terms of economic strength, has seen a dramatic phase of growth and integration into the modern global economy. It holds the status of the world's sixth-largest exporter, trading with China, the EU, and the United States. The South Korean economy is based on a close partnership between government and business, and a choice of export-oriented growth. Like Japan, Seoul used the Silk Roads narrative to build bridges with independent Central Asia, and insisted on its privileged partnership with the United States.[74] It has also projected on the region and on Mongolia theories of the "original home" of Koreans, and has sought to build links with the significant Korean diaspora in Kazakhstan (more than 100,000 people).[75] Although they have no direct historical link with Seoul (Koreans deported to Central Asia came from the Russian Far East), they have sought to become cultural and economic intermediaries between the two zones. Korea has also developed migration links with Uzbekistan and is one of the few countries that has signed an official labor agreement with Tashkent.[76] Even if this is not publicized, Seoul now positions itself as the seventh-largest commercial partner of Central Asia, the fourth-largest of Uzbekistan, and will likely play an increasingly important role for the other countries in coming years.

Like Japan, South Korea is a major consumer and importer of energy and seeks to enter the Kazakh and Uzbek markets. The Korean Consortium of the Caspian Oil Project, which includes SK Corporation, LG International, Samsung, and Daesung Industrial, acquired a 27 percent share of the Zhambyl offshore oil block in the Kazakh part of the Caspian Sea.[77] In 2009, Astana and Seoul signed a new investment accord in the fields of energy and technology, worth more than US$5 billion.[78] In Uzbekistan, the Korea National Oil Corporation and Korea Gas Corporation (KOGAS) are exploring and exploiting several fields: the first is also part of an international consortium to explore the Uzbek part of the Aral Sea, alongside Lukoil, Petronas, and CNPC.[79] Daewoo International, which seeks to invest in oil, signed an agreement with Uzbekneftegaz for the exploration of two other blocks on the Ust-Yurt Plateau.[80] Although not established in Turkmenistan, Seoul seeks to boost its presence there, and in 2009, LG and Hyundai won a tender for the construction of a gas processing plant near the massive Yolotan gas field.[81]

South Korea is also looking increasingly to Kazakhstan and Uzbekistan for uranium. The country is dependent on nuclear power for 40 percent of its electricity, has twenty nuclear power plants in operation, and plans to build six more. Since 2008, the Korea Electric Power Corporation (KEPCO) has received uranium from both Tashkent and Astana and this mineral partnership is likely to deepen further.[82] Seoul is also interested in gold, tungsten, and coal. The company Roh is a partner in the Uzbek Zapadno gold mine, while Korea Resources Corporation operates the Uchtepa Ust deposit. Tashkent has granted Seoul the right to mine molybdenum and tungsten at a location 150 kilometers west of Samarkand.[83] South Korea is also involved in the electricity sector with the Korea Electric Power Corporation and Samsung C&T own 65 percent of the new Balkhash power station, which should be operational in 2014 and is expected to reduce energy shortages in southern Kazakhstan.[84]

Kazakhstan is particularly interested in technology transfers. Several memoranda of cooperation have been signed between Samruk-Kazyna and the Hyundai Corporation, Kazakhmys and Samsung, Hyundai and KazMunayGas, and the railway corporations Korail and Kazakhstan Temir Zholy. Korean banks are also interested in their Kazakh

Table 6.4

South Korea's Place in Imports, Exports, and the Trade Total of Central Asian States in 2010 (in millions of US$)

	Imports	Rank	Exports	Rank	Total trade	Rank
Kazakhstan	646.2 (2.2%)	7	294.7 (0.6%)	13	940.9 (1.3%)	9
Kyrgyzstan	110.4 (1.6%)	7	2.2 (0.2%)	17	112.7 (1.4%)	7
Tajikistan	26.4 (1%)	16	0.0 (0.0%)	27	26.5 (0.7%)	17
Turkmenistan	116.3 (2.2%)	10	0.3 (0.0%)	31	116.6 (1.3%)	13
Uzbekistan	1,522.9 (18.5%)	3	19.2 (0.3%)	17	1,542.1 (11.2%)	4

Source: 2011 European Commission statistics, http://ec.europa.eu/trade/creating-opportunities/bilateral-relations/countries-and-regions/.

counterparts. Kookmin Bank purchased 23 percent of the shares of CenterCredit Bank, while Shinhan Bank and Woori Bank also established themselves in the country.[85] But Seoul has also created a unique partnership with Uzbekistan, which is centered on freight infrastructure. Several South Korean companies are now stakeholders of the planned Uzbek logistics center at Navoy. Korean Air is contributing, in partnership with Uzbekistan Airways, to the modernization of Navoy airport into an air hub, and hopes to reap the benefits of being the first on the Uzbek air cargo market, which is expected to grow in coming years.[86] Since 2009 the Hanjin Group has been responsible for coordinating the Navoy logistics center, both in terms of air and land transport. South Korea is also expected to participate in the development of port infrastructure in Turkmenbashi.

The Malaysian Model Emulated in Central Asia

Since the beginning of the 1990s, Central Asian elites, in particular in Kazakhstan and Uzbekistan, have been interested in Malaysia, Indonesia, Brunei, and Singapore. Their objective was to foster alternative partnerships with countries that do not apply geopolitical pressure and can serve as models for economic development. In this context, Malaysia benefits from growing political and economic influence in Central Asia. A country with a Muslim majority that is also multi-ethnic and multi-religious, Malaysia quickly became one of the best performing economies in Asia, and the third largest producer of computer components after the United States and Japan.[87] Thus the Malaysia "model" is one that other states seek to emulate.

The oil company Petronas, which is involved in Turkmenistan and Uzbekistan, is symbolic of Malaysia's energy presence in Central Asia. It was the first foreign company to obtain an onshore PSA (Production Sharing Agreement) in Turkmenistan and has operated the Diyarbekir deposit since the 1990s.[88] In Uzbekistan, Petronas won rights to participate in the exploration and exploitation of deposits on the Ust-Yurt Plateau (Urga, Kuanysh, Akchalak), for which Gazprom had its license revoked in 2009.[89]

Table 6.5

Malaysia's Place in Imports, Exports, and the Trade Total of Central Asian States in 2010 (in millions of US$)

	Imports	Rank	Exports	Rank	Total trade	Rank
Kazakhstan	105.4 (0.4%)	16	−0.6 (0.0%)	<50	106.1 (0.1%)	24
Kyrgyzstan	2.8 (0.0%)	21	0.1 (0.0%)	31	2.9 (0.0%)	26
Tajikistan	1.1 (0.0%)	30	—	—	1.1 (0.0%)	32
Turkmenistan	31.7 (0.6%)	16	0.1 (0.0%)	36	31.8 (0.4%)	23
Uzbekistan	52.6 (0.6%)	14	13.7 (0.2%)	18	66.3 (0.5%)	18

Source: 2011 European Commission statistics, http://ec.europa.eu/trade/creating-opportunities/bilateral-relations/countries-and-regions/.

Other projects in the Sukhandarya region are under consideration. KazTransGas, the subsidiary of KazMunayGas responsible for oil and gas pipelines, has signed cooperation agreements with Petronas, and in 2011, it was decided that Petronas would participate in the exploitation of some Kazakh deposits in exchange for the right of KazMunayGas to work with it on its overseas projects.[90] But the main obstacle to the development of bilateral trade is the lack of transportation corridors. Although some products with high added value are transported by air, most Malaysian exports (electrical and electronic equipment, chemicals, machinery, and palm oil) pass through the UAE, while Central Asia products are directed to the Iranian port of Bandar Abbas before being loaded into containers.[91] Kuala Lumpur has positioned itself as the eighth commercial partner of Turkmenistan and is seeking to develop new trading opportunities in the region.

Relations with Kazakhstan are much stronger than with the other Central Asian states. Kazakh authorities, especially in 2005–2006, showed interest in learning from the Malaysian model. The Kazakh presidential party Nur Otan and the United Malays National Organization (UMNO) established links between their parliamentarians and party structures,[92] and the Malaysian strategy formulated in the Vision-2020 plan is similar to that of Nursultan Nazarbayev's Kazakhstan-2030. The new administrative capital of Malaysia, Putrajaya (located twenty kilometers south of Kuala Lumpur and near the new city of Cyberjaya, which specializes in new technologies), was one of the models that Kazakh authorities considered for Astana. The transformation of KLIA (the Kuala Lumpur International Airport) into a leading aviation hub for Southeast Asia also interests Kazakhstan. Even though Astana failed to become the center of air transit between Europe and Asia, in competition with Tashkent, Malaysia Airports Holdings successfully manages the Kazakh capital's airport.[93] But the most promising areas for bilateral cooperation are in the "multimedia corridor" proposed by Kuala Lumpur, which overlaps with Kazakhstan's development objectives in innovative industries. Kazakhstan Engineering is interested in Malaysian mobile telephone technology; Kazakhstan's Innovation Fund is working with Maybank; Technology Park Malaysia and with Corporation Berhad, and Kazyna with the Multimedia Development

Corporation. Malaysian companies are also well established in the field of interior design for Kazakhstan's new business centers.[94]

Eventually Malaysia seeks also to fill in economic niches related to Islam and to benefit from the suspicion the Central Asian governments harbor toward the Middle East. Many Malaysian companies have established themselves in Kazakhstan in the field of halal food production. Since 2005, the Kazakh authorities have chosen to define their halal standards according to those of Malaysia.[95] Student exchanges have also multiplied in recent years. More than one thousand Kazakh students are enrolled in Malaysian universities, mainly in high technology and multimedia programs. In 2010 a delegation from the Association of Education Officers of Kazakhstan visited the major Malay universities in order to formalize such partnerships. Tourism has also grown: the Kazakh middle classes are attracted to the beaches of Malaysia, but also to Islamic sites. Religious tourism has taken shape, with some people staying for a few months for theological training or participating in pilgrimages (including the *hajj*) from Kuala Lumpur.[96]

For the Central Asian states, the relationship to South Asia has been so far a story of disillusions and fears: India has been a disappointing partner, even if the India-Kazakhstan strategic partnership looks promising; and Pakistan is seen more as a bearer of problems for the whole region than as a constructive ally. Central Asians' pessimism about the post-2014 situation in Afghanistan contributes to reinforce this negative view of the Central Asia-South Asia relationship future. In contrast, ties with East and Southeast Asia are valorized: they are not built on geopolitical constructs but on economic pragmatism; and they are not associated to radical Islamism, even if Malaysia may have a kind of religious agenda to advance in the region. Japan's development aid has not been transformed into an efficient geopolitical leverage tool, but its presence in the region symbolically decreases the dependence on China. This non-Chinese Asia, especially South Korea and Malaysia, therefore stands as an archetypal success, embodied by both modern technology, strong political regime, and cultural sovereignty, corresponding to the ideological projections of Central Asian governments.

Notes

1. S. S. Samubaldin, *Drakony i tigry Azii: Smozhet li kazakhstanskii "bars" proiti ikh tropami?* (Almaty: Gylym, 1998).

2. H. Kapur, *The Soviet Union and the Emerging Nations: A Case Study of Soviet Policy towards India* (London: Graduate Institute of International Studies, Geneva, 1972).

3. G. Sachdeva, "Reviving (Indo-Russian) Economic Interests," *Frontline* 17, no. 21, October 14–27, 2000, http://hindu.com/fline/fl1721/17210170.htm.

4. A. O. Krueger, *Economic Policy Reforms and the Indian Economy* (Chicago: University of Chicago Press, 2002).

5. C. Jaffrelot, *The Hindu Nationalist Movement in India* (New York: Columbia University Press, 1996).

6. S. S. Chaulia, "BJP, India's Foreign Policy, and the 'Realist Alternative' to the Nehruvian Tradition," *International Politics* 39 (2002): 215–34.

7. S. Destradi, *Indian Foreign and Security Policy in South Asia: Regional Power Strategies* (London: Routledge, 2011).

8. K. Warikoo, ed., *Central Asia: Emerging New Order* (New Delhi: Har Anand Publications, 1995).

9. See A. Patnaik, "Framing Indo-Central Asian Relations, 1990s–2000s," in *Mapping Central Asia: Indian Perceptions and Strategies*, ed. M. Laruelle and S. Peyrouse (Burlington, VT: Ashgate, 2011), 91–108.

10. S. N. Bal, *Central Asia: A Strategy for India's Look-North Policy* (New Delhi: Lancer Publishers & Distributors, 2004).

11. Mahapatra, *Central Eurasia.*

12. For more specialized approaches by country, see K. Warikoo and M. Singh, eds., *Central Asia since Independence* (New Delhi: Shipra Publications, 2004).

13. M. Singh, ed., *India and Tajikistan: Revitalizing a Traditional Relationship* (Kolkata: Anamika Publishers & Distributors, 2003).

14. M. Singh Roy, "Strategic Importance of Turkmenistan for India," *Strategic Analysis* 25, no. 4 (2011): 661–82.

15. P. Stobdan, "India and Kazakhstan Should Share Complementary Objectives," *Strategic Analysis* 33, no. 1 (2009): 1–7.

16. E. Kavalski, "India and Central Asia: The No Influence of the 'Look North' Policy," in *The New Central Asia*, 239–60.

17. V. Radiushin, "Seat for India in SCO Put on the Backburner?" *The Hindu*, November 6, 2011, http://www.thehindu.com/news/international/article2604087.ece.

18. In 2008 India agreed on granting inspectors of the International Atomic Energy Agency access to its nuclear energy production sites, along with a moratorium on nuclear tests. In exchange, India gained access to US nuclear technology, ending thirty-four years of embargo on trade in nuclear material. On this agreement see "IAEA Board Approves India-Safeguards Agreement," *IAEA.org*, August 1, 2008, http://www.iaea.org/NewsCenter/ News/2008/board010808.html.

19. "Konflikt Indii i Pakistana meshaet ikh vkhozhdeniiu v ShOS, soobshchil istochnik ShOS," *RIA Novosti*, June 15, 2011, http://ria.ru/world/20110615/388664874.html.

20. See the CICA website, http://www.s-cica.org/page.php.

21. See the SAARC website, http://www.saarc-sec.org.

22. See J. Panda, "India's New Look at Central Asia Policy: A Strategic Review," in Laruelle and Peyrouse, *Mapping Central Asia,* 109–22.

23. R. Muzalevsky, "India Fails to Gain a Military Foothold in Tajikistan," *The Central Asia-Caucasus Analyst*, February 2, 2011, 12, http://www.cacianalyst.org/?q=node/5485.

24. More in S. Peyrouse, "Comparing the Economic Involvement of China and India in Post-Soviet Central Asia," in M. Laruelle et al., eds. *China and India in Central Asia: A New "Great Game"?* (New York: Palgrave Macmillan, 2010), 155–72.

25. See G. Sachdeva, "India-Central Asia Economic Relations," in Laruelle and Peyrouse, *Mapping Central Asia*, 123–41.

26. See G. Sachdeva, "Regional Economic Linkages," in *Reconnecting India and Central Asia: Emerging Security and Economic Dimensions*, ed. N. Joshi (Washington, DC: The Central Asia-Caucasus Institute Silk Road Studies Program, 2010), 115–80.

27. J.-F. Huchet, "India and China in Central Asia: Mirroring Their Bilateral Relations," in Laruelle et al., *China and India in Central Asia*, 97–116.

28. "Pakistan-India Preferential Trade Agreement Will Be a Good Omen," *Pakistan Today*, November 14, 2011, http://www.pakistantoday.com.pk/2011/11/%E2%80%98pakistan-india-preferential-trade-agreement-will-be-a-good-omen%E2%80%99/.

29. For more details, see chapter 12.

30. P. L. Dash, *Caspian Pipeline Politics, Energy Reserves, and Regional Implications* (New Delhi: Pentagon Press and Observer Research Foundation, 2008).

31. R. Dwivedi, "China's Central Asia Policy in Recent Times," *China and Eurasia Forum Quarterly* 4, no. 4 (2006): 139–59.

32. "Note on Satpayev Exploration Block, Kazakhstan," *ONGCIndia.com*, November 18, 2009, http://www.ongcindia.com/press_release1_new.asp?fold=press&file=press417.txt; "Mittal Exits Kazakh Oil Block Exploration," *Thaindian News*, http://www.thaindian.com/newsportal/business/mittal-exits-kazakh-oil-block-exploration_100276700.html#ixzz0fQNF8r62.

33. "Gail to Set Up LPG Plants in Uzbekistan," *Business Standard*, May 8, 2006, http://www.business-standard.com/india/news/gail-to-setlpg-plants-in-uzbekistan/410/on.

34. "ONGC-Mittal Exit Turkmenistan Oil Block," *Indian Times*, January 20, 2010.

35. More in Peyrouse, "Comparing the Economic Involvement of China and India."

36. S. Akbarzadeh, "India and Pakistan's Geostrategic Rivalry in Central Asia," *Contemporary South Asia* 12, no. 2 (2003): 219–28; M. Singh Roy, "Pakistan's Strategies in Central Asia," *Strategic Analysis* 30, no. 4 (2006): 798–833.

37. A. Kazi, "Pakistan," in *The New Silk Roads: Transport and Trade in Greater Central Asia*, ed. S. F. Starr (Washington, DC: Johns Hopkins University-SAIS, 2007), 77–106.

38. S. Singh, ed., *China-Pakistan Strategic Cooperation: Indian Perspectives* (New Delhi: Manohar, 2007).

39. F. Ur-Rahman, "Pakistan's Evolving Relations with China, Russia, and Central Asia," in Akihiro, *Eager Eyes Fixed on Eurasia*, 211–29.

40. B. Balci, "The Jama'at al Tabligh in Central Asia: A Mediator in the Recreation of Islamic Relations with the Indian Subcontinent," in Laruelle et al., *China and India in Central Asia*, 235–47.

41. Even Kazakhstan's presidency in the second half of 2011 did not really foster Central Asia's involvement in the organization, except in terms of financial aid or Islamic financing.

42. A. Saidov, "Pakistan stremitsia v ShOS i k rynkam TsentrAzii cherez Uzbekistan," *Delovaia nedelia*, March 18, 2007, republished at http://www.centrasia.ru/newsA.php?st=1174167060.

43. B. N. Bhattacharyay and P. De, "Restoring the Asian Silk Route: Toward an Integrated Asia," Working Paper of the Asian Development Bank Institute, no. 140, June 2009.

44. On this agreement, see Singh Roy, "Pakistan's Strategies in Central Asia."

45. M. A. Khan and U. Ahmed, "Energy Demand in Pakistan: A Disaggregate Analysis," Pakistan Institute of Development Economics Working Paper, 2009, http://www.pide.org.pk/psde24/pdf/02.pdf; N. Ul Haq and K. Hussain, "Energy Crisis in Pakistan," Islamabad Policy Research Institute Factfile, July 2004.

46. For more details, see chapter 12.

47. J. E. Guzzardi and M. J. Mullenbach, "The Politics of Seeking a Permanent Seat on the United Nations Security Council: An Analysis of the Case of Japan," *Midsouth Political Science Review* 9 (2007–2008): 35–76.

48. K. Akio, "What Is Japan up to in Central Asia?" *Japan's Silk Road Diplomacy: Paving the Road Ahead*, ed. C. Len, T. Uyama, and H. Tetsuya (Washington, DC: Central Asia-Caucasus Institute, 2008), 15–31.

49. D. Walton, "Japan and Central Asia," in Kavalski, *The New Central Asia*, 261–77; T. Yuasa, "Japan's Multilateral Approach toward Central Asia," *Acta Slavica Iaponica*, no. 16 (2007): 65–84.

50. Yuasa, "Japan's Multilateral Approach Toward Central Asia."

51. M. T. Laumulin, "Strategiia Iaponii v Evrazii," in *Kazakhstansko-iaponskoe sotrudnichestvo: Sostoianie i perspektivy* (Almaty: KISI, 2007), 33–47.

52. A. Bukh, *Japan's National Identity and Foreign Policy: Russia as Japan's "Other"* (New York: Routledge, 2009).

53. C. Len, "Japan's Central Asian Diplomacy: Motivations, Implications, and Prospects for the Region," *Central Asia and the Caucasus* 3, no. 3 (2005): 127–49.

54. T. Uyama, "Japanese Policies in Relation to Kazakhstan: Is There a 'Strategy'?," in *Thinking Strategically: The Major Powers, Kazakhstan, and the Central Asian Nexus*, ed. R. Legvold (Cambridge: MIT Press, 2003), 165–86.

55. More details in Len, "Japan's Central Asian Diplomacy."

56. R. Weitz, "Japan Promotes Multilateralism in Central Asia," *Security Watch*, May 7, 2007, http://www.isn.ethz.ch/isn/Current-Affairs/Security-Watch-Archive/Detail/?ots591=4888caa0-b3db-1461-98b9-e20e7b9c13d4&lng=en&id=53231.

57. Taro Aso, "On the 'Arc of Freedom and Prosperity,'" Address on the Occasion of the Twentieth Anniversary of the Founding of the Japan Forum on International Relations, International House of Japan, March 12, 2007, http://www.mofa.go.jp/policy/pillar/address0703.html.

58. N. Kassenova, "Japan's Hesitant Embrace of Central Asia: Will There Be a Strategy?" in Esteban and de Pedro, *Great Powers and Regional Integration in Central Asia*, 95–112.

59. A. King and J. Townsend, "Is Japan's Interest in Central Asia Stagnating?," *The Central Asia and Caucasus Analyst*, May 9, 2007, http://www.cacianalyst.org/?q=node/4685.

60. E. Usubaliev, "Japanese Politics in Central Asia in View of Another Possible Center of Power," *Central Asia and the Caucasus*, no. 5 (2001): 135–40.

61. See the JBIC website, http://www.jbic.go.jp/en/report/.

62. Feffer, "Japan: After Slow Start, Tokyo Engages Central Asia."

63. E. Marat, "Kyrgyzstan: Japan's Prime Partner in Central Asia?" in Len, Uyama, and Tetsuya, *Japan's Silk Road Diplomacy*, 87–100.

64. "Joint Statement between Japan and the Republic of Uzbekistan," website of the Prime Minister of Japan, February 9, 2011, http://www.kantei.go.jp/foreign/kan/statement/201102/09uzbekistan_e.html.

65. Ibid.

66. P. C. Evans, "Japan," Brookings Foreign Policy Studies, Energy Security Series, December 2006.

67. D. Gregor, "Japan-Iran Relations in the Spotlight as UN Sanctions Against the Iranian Regime Approach," *Realité UE*, March 26, 2010, http://www.realite-eu.org/site/apps/nlnet/content3.aspx?c=9dJBLLNkGiF&b=2315291&ct=8133579.

68. S. Valentine, B. K. Sovacool, and M. Matsuura, "Empowered? Evaluating Japan's National Energy Strategy Under the DPJ Administration," *Energy Policy* 39 (2011): 1865–76.

69. C. Len, "Understanding Japan's Central Asian Engagement," in Len, Uyama, and Tetsuya, *Japan's Silk Road Diplomacy*, 35.

70. K. Shimao, "Japan's Energy Strategy Towards West and Central Asia Under Contemporary Globalization," in Len, Uyama, and Tetsuya, *Japan's Silk Road Diplomacy*, 157–74.

71. S. Itoh, *Russia Looks East: Energy Markets and Geopolitics in Northeast Asia* (Washington, DC: CSIS, 2011).

72. For more details, see chapter 10.

73. M. Nurgaliev and T. Shaymergenov, "Japanese Diplomacy Makes New Headway in Central Asia: Its Problems, Expectations, and Prospects," *Central Asia and the Caucasus* 6 (2007): 125–35.

74. K. E. Calder and V. Kim, "Korea, the United States, and Central Asia: Far-Flung Partners in a Globalizing World," *Korea Economic Institute Academic Papers Series* 3, no. 9 (2008).

75. G. Kan, "Koreans in Kazakhstan: Past, Present, Future," *Central Asia and the Caucasus* 13 (2002): 139–47. For more details on the Korean diaspora in Central Asia, see A. Diener, "Diasporic Stances: Comparing the Historical Geographic Antecedents of Korean and German Migration Decisions in Kazakhstan," *Geopolitics* 14, no. 3 (2009): 462–87.

76. See the declarations of the Uzbekistan Agency for Foreign Labor Migration Affairs, *Migration.uz*, November 15, 2011, http://migration.uz/en/news.htm.

77. S. Peyrouse, "South Korea's Advances into Central Asia," *The Central Asia-Caucasus Analyst*, September 1, 2010, http://www.cacianalyst.org/?q=node/5394.

78. "Kazakhstan, S.Korea Sign $5 bln Worth of Deals," *Reuters*, May 13, 2009, http://www.reuters.com/article/2009/05/13/korea-kazakhstan-idUSLD84093020090513.

79. "Energy Cooperation between Korea and Uzbekistan: A Study of the Measures to Promote

Energy Cooperation Between Two Countries," 11, http://www.neasiaenergy.net/nea/e_publications.nsf/xmlcountriesall/A999FC59051BE8EF492575B000099014/$file/cerna2008-21.pdf.
80. S. Li, "Narashchivaiia ekonomicheskii potentsial," *Narodnoe slovo*, January 16, 2009, http://www.ung.uz/ru/press_center/smi/narod/.
81. "LGI and Hyundai Engineering Win a Contract for the Largest Plant in Resource-Rich Turkmenistan," *IR News*, January 11, 2010, http://www.lgicorp.com/jsp/eng/ir/ir_news/news_view.jsp?txtGubun=Q&txtSeqNum=79.
82. For more details, see chapter 10.
83. "Uranium First Acquisition on Official Resource Tour," *Korea Joongang Daily*, May 13, 2008, http://koreajoongangdaily.joinsmsn.com/news/article/article.aspx?aid=2889722.
84. "Sotrudnichestvo Respubliki Kazakhstan s Respublikoi Koreia," Kazakhstan Foreign Affairs Ministry, http://portal.mfa.kz/portal/page/portal/mfa/ru/content/policy/cooperation/asia_africa/13.
85. "Kookmin Bank Buys 23 Percent Stake in Bank CenterCredit," *Silk Road Intelligencer*, August 28, 2008, http://silkroadintelligencer.com/2008/08/28/kookmin-bank-buys-23-percent-stake-in-bank-centercredit/; "Kazakhstan i Koreia: U nas obshchie plany," *Mezhdunarodnyi delovoi zhurnal Kazakhstan*, no. 2 (2011), http://www.investkz.com/journals/77/833.html.
86. L. Blachy, "Navoi Cargo Terminal Opens in Uzbekistan; Korean Air to Expand Cargo Network," *Air Transport World*, August 13, 2010, http://atwonline.com/airports-routes/news/navoi-cargo-terminal-opens-uzbekistan-korean-air-expand-cargo-network-0812.
87. S. Yusuf and K. Nabeshima, *Tiger Economies under Threat: A Comparative Analysis of Malaysia's Industrial Prospects and Policy Options* (Washington, DC: World Bank Publications, 2009).
88. "Malaysian Petronas Chiragli (Turkmenistan) Takes to Extraction of Early Oil in Caspian Sea," *Turkmenistan.ru*, July 14, 2006, http://www.turkmenistan.ru/?page_id=3&lang_id=en&elem_id=8344&type=event&sort=date_desc.
89. "Uzbekistan i Malaziia nachali Ustiurtskii gazovyi proekt stoimost'iu US$500 mln," *CentrAsia*, June 26, 2009, http://www.centrasia.ru/news2.php?st=1246018800.
90. "Petronas to Participate in Kazakh Oil and Gas Project," *Trend.az*, June 6, 2011, http://en.trend.az/capital/energy/1887180.html.
91. Authors' interviews with traders at Dordoi, June 6, 2010; Dushanbe's main bazaar, June 24, 2010; and Almaty's main bazaar, September 28, 2010. More on the role of Bander Abbas in global trade in *Development of The Trans-Asian Railway: Trans-Asian Railway in the North-South Corridor, Northern Europe to the Persian Gulf* (New York: United Nations, 2001).
92. "Delegation of Nur Otan Party to Participate in UMNO General Assembly Work," *Kazinform*, May 15, 2009, http://kazinform.kz/eng/article/2156978.
93. "Malaysia Airports Starts Operating Astana Airport in Kazakhstan," *MalaysiaAirports.com*, May 15, 2007, http://www.malaysiaairports.com.my/index.php/news-archieve/year-2007/121.html; "Aeroport Astany: Idem na vzlet," *Baiterek*, nos. 9–10/56–57 (2011), http://www.baiterek.kz/index.php?journal=30&page=463.
94. "PM's Visit to Kazakhstan Opens Mind to Developments in Central Asia," Office of the Prime Minister of Malaysia, June 2011, http://www.pmo.gov.my/?menu=newslist&page=1731&news_id=7497&news_cat=13.
95. H. Foster, "More Kazakh Meat Producers Offering Islamic-Law-Compliant Products," *Centralasianewswire*, September 13, 2010, http://centralasianewswire.com/Kazakhstan/More-Kazakh-meat-producersnbspoffering-Islamic-law-compliant-products/viewstory.aspx?id=1670.
96. Authors' interview with anonymous experts on Islamism, Almaty, September 24, 2010.

7

The Regional Market

Economic Weaknesses and Political Blockades

Relations between post-Soviet states largely broke down following the collapse of the Soviet system. The former unitary framework was undermined by several factors: neighborly relations often turned sour; underlying territorial or ethno-political conflicts were revealed; a growing competition emerged to retain foreign attention and investments; and divergent, sometimes contradictory strategies of assertion on the international arena developed. With the exception of Russia, post-Soviet countries have economies that are small in size and weak in capacity (Belarus, Moldova, Armenia, Georgia, Tajikistan, Kyrgyzstan), and only Kazakhstan, Azerbaijan, and Ukraine dominate the regional scene, seconded by Turkmenistan and Uzbekistan. Insufficient political will is probably the main factor that seriously hampers the development of regional, intra-Central Asian trade. The Uzbek and Turkmen governments have based much of their foreign policy on preventing Central Asian cooperation. While it may seem logical in the light of the region's economic specializations that priority be given to major external actors, the absence of a regional market has drastically impeded the economic capabilities of Tajikistan and Kyrgyzstan, and weighs on Kazakhstan, Uzbekistan, and Turkmenistan in the critical areas of food security, energy security, and water management.

Preserving CIS Links: Ukraine, Belarus, and Central Asia

Despite the collapse of economic ties between the Soviet republics, Central Asia has kept contacts with Ukraine, and to a lesser extent with Belarus: in 2010 Ukraine positions itself at the region's sixth-largest commercial partner, Belarus as the eighth. The CIS common framework has not helped to maintain these trade exchanges, which are organized instead on a bilateral basis or through Russia-led integrative structures.[1] Belarus has, for instance, been able to continue to trade with Central Asia, particularly Kazakhstan, thanks to its high level of integration in the Russian economy and, until recently, good relations with Moscow. Ukraine, on the contrary, has long been promoted by the Uzbek and Turkmen governments as a means of escape from Russian domination and as an opening to Europe. However, the anti-Russian institution GUAM, which was designed to foster strategic and economic alliance between Georgia,

Ukraine, Azerbaijan, Moldova, and Uzbekistan (when the country was part of it, from 1996 to 2001), has not become efficient enough to change the regional balance.[2] Each of these states currently manages specific and diverse economic partnerships. Since 2010 new political developments in Ukraine toward greater conciliation with Russia did not have any impact on cooperation with Central Asia, which evolves according to commercial needs rather than geopolitical tenets.

Relations with Belarus are limited. Kazakhstan and Uzbekistan provide it with chemicals, especially fertilizers, petroleum products, cotton, and grain, while Belarus exports mechanical engineering (especially related to agriculture such as tractors, transport and electrical materials—in other words, its old Soviet specializations), medicines, and wood products.[3] In the 1990s, cooperation between military-industrial sectors continued, as Belarus offered repairs to equipment and training for Central Asian forces, especially in aviation.[4] In 2010–2011, the regime of Alexander Lukashenko, in the grip of a severe economic crisis and strained relations with its Russian ally, sought new business partners in Kazakhstan and Turkmenistan.[5] Astana is today Belarus's third-largest trading partner after Russia and Ukraine, and their relations are based partly on their common membership in the Customs Union, as well as on the close relationship between the Belarusian and Russian economies on the one hand, and the Kazakh and Russian economies on the other. Minsk is particularly interested in the financial and banking capacity of Kazakhstan (BTA Bank has been present in the country since 2002) and hopes to get Kazakh companies involved in privatization drives initiated by the Belarusian government. It also hopes to produce high-tech military equipment with Astana.[6] In Turkmenistan, Belarus has been solicited to develop the Avaza tourist area and Lukashenko has sought political support from his Turkmen counterpart Berdymukhammedov.

Because of its industrial capabilities, agricultural potential, and access to European markets, Ukraine is a more important partner for Central Asia. The commercial relationship over gas between Kyiv and Ashgabat was a key strategic element of the foreign policies of the two states in the 1990s. Despite their close ties, Ashgabat complained about delays in payments from Ukraine, and Kyiv claimed that it did not receive gas regularly and lived under the threat of supply disruptions.[7] As payment for its gas debts, Ukraine offered its military know-how to Niyazov's regime. This aid materialized in the form of military training for Turkmen officers, the rehabilitation of Turkmenistan's air defense system, and the "key-in-hand" Kolchuga-M station to monitor the Caspian Sea.[8] However, the Russian-Turkmen rapprochement of 2003, and the end of the Turkmen-Ukrainian gas contract in 2006, which was not renewed, have de-escalated bilateral economic relations. Berdymukhammedov seems less interested in a Ukrainian strategy than his predecessor, and Kyiv's relationship with Moscow has evolved to be less oppositional. Between 2007 and 2011, bilateral trade fell to one-twelfth of its original amount, from US\$4.3 billion to only US\$359 million.[9]

Despite the collapse of the Turkmen-Ukrainian gas alliance, hydrocarbons are still the main sector of trade between Ukraine and Central Asia globally. The Ukrai-

Table 7.1

Belarus's Place in Imports, Exports, and the Trade Total of Central Asian States in 2010 (in millions of US$)

	Imports	Rank	Exports	Rank	Total trade	Rank
Kazakhstan	493.7 (1.7%)	8	357.1 (0.8%)	12	850.8 (1.1%)	11
Kyrgyzstan	90.9 (1.3%)	8	7.1 (0.7%)	12	98 (1.2%)	8
Tajikistan	43.4 (1.7%)	12	6.6 (0.6%)	13	50 (1.4%)	13
Turkmenistan	92.1 (1.7%)	11	3 (0.1%)	22	95.1 (1.1%)	14
Uzbekistan	100.7 (1.2%)	11	51.5 (0.9%)	14	152.3 (1.1%)	12

Source: 2011 European Commission statistics, http://ec.europa.eu/trade/creating-opportunities/bilateral-relations/countries-and-regions/.

nian economy heavily depends on Russian and Kazakh oil imports. Eighty percent of Kazakh exports to Ukraine consist of petroleum products and Nazarbayev wants to reconcile with Kyiv in terms of pricing policy for transporting its oil to Europe. Hampered by issues of transit through Russian territory, exchanges are moving now to petroleum equipment. Ukrainian companies have won tenders for the construction of gas turbines in Uzbekistan,[10] while Turkmenistan is interested in the production of pipes and gas compressors, and tends to favor Ukrainian companies rather than Gazprom, with which relations remain difficult.[11]

Ukraine inherited part of its engineering industry from the Soviet Union. It is therefore an important partner of the Central Asian states for the production of heavy metals, chemicals, construction materials, and equipment and transport. Uzbekistan and Ukraine cooperate in the textile sector, non-ferrous metallurgy, and in the transport industries; Tashkent also exports its cotton to Kyiv. In Turkmenistan, several Ukrainian companies have won major contracts in the construction sector.[12] Ukraine is also a significant supplier in terms of food, which accounted for one-sixth of its exports to Kazakhstan in 2007.[13] Ukrainian food products are also well represented on the Turkmen market. In the grain sector, Ukraine, Kazakhstan, and Russia are seeking to develop collective strategies to limit their internal competition, and to establish common mechanisms in case of shortage in one of the three countries (as was the case when drought hit Russia in the summer of 2010) and to succeed in the global grain market.[14] Cooperation between Kazakhstan and Ukraine has grown, with agreements between Karaganda and Dnipropetrovsk, and between Mangystau and Lviv.[15]

Other areas of cooperation are emerging between Ukraine and Kazakhstan. Tripartite ventures with Russia were established in the nuclear sector in order to ensure stable orders for fuel pellets supplied to Ukraine's nuclear reactors. Astana hired Ukrainian companies to upgrade its radar and fleet of tanks, and repair some military aircraft. The Antonov planes built in Ukraine are also sold in Kazakhstan, and in 2011, AeroKz and Antonov signed an agreement for the joint production of aircraft.[16] Finally, cooperation in space ventures has accelerated since 2010. Kazakhstan has acquired a one-third

Table 7.2

Ukraine's Place in Imports, Exports, and the Trade Total of Central Asian States in 2010 (in millions of US$)

	Imports	Rank	Exports	Rank	Total trade	Rank
Kazakhstan	1,380.2 (4.8%)	4	673.8 (1.5%)	8	2,054 (2.7%)	7
Kyrgyzstan	79.2 (1.1%)	10	5.4 (0.5%)	13	84.7 (1.1%)	10
Tajikistan	182.2 (7.1%)	5	10.9 (1%)	10	193.2 (5.2%)	7
Turkmenistan	221 (4.1%)	8	28 (0.9%)	15	249 (2.9%)	7
Uzbekistan	242.9v(3%)	8	71.3 (1.3%)	11	314.2 (2.3%)	9

Source: 2011 European Commission statistics, http://ec.europa.eu/trade/creating-opportunities/bilateral-relations/countries-and-regions/.

stake in Cosmostrans, a Russian-Ukrainian joint venture which uses the Baikonur rocket launch center to send satellites into distant orbits aboard Russia's Dnepr carrier rockets. Both countries have also decided to cooperate on the development of space systems for the exploration of natural resources and environmental monitoring of oil and gas regions in the Caspian Sea.[17] Collaboration is not as substantial with other Central Asian states. Relations with Kyrgyzstan and Tajikistan have always been minimal and Ukraine's former Turkmen and Uzbek geopolitical allies are now less competitive than Kazakhstan.

A Failed Caspian Unity? Central Asia and the South Caucasus

While the Caspian Basin is often conceived of in terms of its hydrocarbon reserves, the Caspian entity has little unity, except in geological terms. Cultural ties between the Caucasus and Central Asia are relatively insignificant, and historical contacts were less frequent than geographical proximity might imply. Despite a promising outlook, the trade exchanges between the South Caucasus and Central Asia remain limited and above all imbalanced. Twenty years after the collapse of the Soviet Union, the viability of a trans-Caspian energy route is not assured, in spite of Western engagement. The infrastructure construction costs involve considerable investments; the completion of the Nabucco gas pipeline is taking more time than expected; and the fragile political situation in the South Caucasus (the Nagorno-Karabakh conflict, and the Russian-Georgian tensions around the secessionist republics of South Ossetia and Abkhazia) serves as a reminder to potentially interested foreign investors to exercise caution. Nevertheless, despite the existence of sometimes divergent interests, and the non-negligible political and economic risks, none of the states of the South Caucasus, nor those of Central Asia, wish to undermine a potential trans-Caspian rapprochement. Indeed both regions are interested in developing not only their bilateral relations, but also a larger regional market: Central Asia would like to reach Turkish and Iranian markets, and the South Caucasus to connect with China.

Kazakhstan and Azerbaijan have emerged as the two main regional powers and the principal partners. Their trade exchanges have experienced constant growth since around 2005, attaining 202 million euros in 2010.[18] The Baku-Tbilisi-Ceyhan oil pipeline, in operation since 2005, materializes Baku's engagement with the West, but Astana is still a modest supplier for this symbol of Western-bound export routes. In 2008, KazMunayGas and Azerbaijan's national company SOCAR signed an agreement for the transport of Kazakh oil to world markets, which permits Azerbaijan to become a key transit country.[19] Kazakhstan's commitment is now stronger, with projects to develop barter systems, tanker shipping, and the building of oil terminals and port infrastructures on its Caspian coast.[20] But despite the enthusiastic official declarations about Kazakh-Azeri cooperation, no Kazakh companies have any shares in the projects for pipelines that run to the West from Baku,[21] and the Azeri share in Kazakh oil transport is important but not decisive, at about 20 percent.[22]

Apart from energy questions, both countries collaborate in the grains sector. Astana has its own wheat silo in the port of Baku, and since 2008, a factory capable of producing 50,000 tons of flour per year.[23] However, the rivalry between shipping companies is growing. The Azeri company Caspar is blocking the expansion of its Kazakh competitor KazMorTransflot, which claims it is being discriminated against by the tariff policies in the ports of the other Caspian states, principally Azerbaijan.[24] In addition, Caspar is the only firm to operate both in the Black Sea and the Mediterranean, and therefore has much more competitive structures than KazMorTransflot. Moreover, on the strictly economic level, the monopolistic position of the Azerbaijan State Shipping Company and the Azerbaijan Railways Company makes tanker-railway transport scarcely profitable because of multiple additional costs.[25] The global rise in competition between Kazakhstan and Azerbaijan has led Astana to diversify its options and gain direct access to the Black Sea by promoting its partnership with Georgia. KazMunayGas has become the owner of the Batumi oil terminal, with a refinery to be built on land adjacent to the terminal.[26] Kazakhstan's involvement in Batumi has caused Baku to bring forward the opening date of its terminal at Kulevi, triggering a price war between terminals.

Although Astana has quickly developed its presence on the Georgian market, bilateral trade remains weak in statistical terms.[27] Most importantly, Kazakhstan has become one of the main suppliers of cereals to Tbilisi. In 2007, both countries signed a contract for the construction of a wheat silo in the port of Poti, designed to facilitate European access to Kazakh cereals.[28] Since 2005, Kazakhstan has become the main post-Soviet investor in Georgia and the third-largest direct foreign investor; between 2006 and 2008, Kazakh companies invested US$300 million in the Georgian economy.[29] Tensions resulting from the Russo-Georgian war of 2008 seem to have slowed, but not stopped, the main Kazakh investment projects, the Poti wheat silo and Batumi oil refinery.[30] But one of the main bilateral projects has collapsed. In 2006, Kaz TransGas, a subsidiary of KazMunayGas, bought the state-run Georgian company for the distribution of gas, Tbilgas; however, the situation turned out to be more complex than first thought following the liberalization of the Georgian gas market in 2008.[31]

Table 7.3

Azerbaijan's Place in Imports, Exports, and the Trade Total of Central Asian States in 2010 (in millions of US$)

	Imports	Rank	Exports	Rank	Total trade	Rank
Kazakhstan	47.2 (0.2%)	23	256.8 (0.6%)	14	304 (0.4%)	14
Kyrgyzstan	44.3 (0.6%)	11	0.8 (0.1%)	22	45.2 (0.6%)	13
Tajikistan	7.8 (0.3%)	21	1.4 (0.1%)	16	9.2 (0.2%)	23
Turkmenistan	222.2 (4.1%)	7	12.1 (0.4%)	19	234.3 (2.7%)	8
Uzbekistan	21.2 (0.3%)	17	10.7 (0.2%)	19	31.9 (0.2%)	20

Source: 2011 European Commission statistics, http://ec.europa.eu/trade/creating-opportunities/bilateral-relations/countries-and-regions/.

KazMunayGas, which is reported to have invested close to US$100 million in the development of the local gas distribution network, announced it was reneging on its commitments and sold its subsidiary.[32] Kazakh businesses, however, have increased their presence in other, more dynamic sectors, such as the Georgian banking industry. Cooperation in the construction sector is also developing, and Kazakh companies are in charge of renovating, modernizing, or building sanatorium, hotels, and business centers in Tbilisi and others cities.

Trade between Kazakhstan and Armenia remains far more modest. Yerevan's very isolated geographical position, remote from the Caspian as much as from the Black Sea, and the double Turkish and Azeri blockade imposed on it, have limited its prospects for trade with Central Asia. Trade exchanges with Kazakhstan—mainly gas—have continuously dropped over recent years to the point that Armenia is Kazakhstan's smallest trading partner in the CIS.[33] Other Central Asian countries have very limited trade with the South Caucasus. Their economies do not complement each other; the geopolitical balance in both regions is fragile; the great powers have very divergent interests; and there are difficulties in opening up landlocked countries, and in diversifying the transit routes that already exist, which run north-south rather than east-west.

All these elements confirm that the establishment of deeper Central Asian-South Caucasian relations is not self-evident. Moreover, trans-Caspian infrastructure is still limited. New terminals are under construction, Caspian commercial fleets are still of small capacity, the cost of transport via tankers and railway is expensive, and the Turkish straits are overcrowded. However, the political will to alter north-south trade flows and the support provided by Europe and the United States to this trans-Caspian axis may influence future developments. The interest of the Caspian states in developing a regional framework has grown. Kazakhstan wishes to promote its Caspian coast and to contribute to the economic opening up of the coastal regions, in particular the Mangystau Peninsula. Turkmenistan also hopes to see the Turkmenbashi region become one of the republic's economic centers. Azerbaijan, for its part, has everything to gain as a country of transit, while Georgia is also banking on using its access to the Black Sea as a driver of development.[34]

Growing Connectivity: Central Asian Businesses in Afghanistan

Albeit Afghanistan is not a CIS country, its relationship with Central Asia relies heavily on a shared Soviet legacy, especially in terms of infrastructures. The proximity between Central Asia and Afghanistan is usually formulated in terms of security challenges, border crossings, the shadow economy, and drug trafficking. Yet Central Asia is much more than a transit region, whether for non-lethal material bound for the ISAF (International Security Assistance Force) troops, or in the opposite direction, for reverse supply in preparation of the 2014 withdrawal. The three border states of Turkmenistan, Uzbekistan, and Tajikistan, as well as Kazakhstan, all play a non-negligible role in providing economic and reconstruction aid, in particular in the northern regions of Afghanistan. In the provinces of Herat, Badghis, Faryab, Jowjzan, Balkh, Kunduz, and Badakhshan, the Afghan populations are more oriented toward their northern neighbors. Throughout the twentieth century, economic and political aid to the Tajiks, Turkmen, and Uzbeks of Afghanistan always came from the north. Today it is largely thanks to Uzbekistan that Kabul has electricity, and to Kazakhstan that Afghan flour supplies did not dry up in 2010 after the floods devastated the fertile fields of Pakistan.

Uzbekistan is positioned as the first Central Asian trading partner of Afghanistan. It benefits from an important Soviet legacy in terms of infrastructures that connected it to its southern neighbor, despite having only 140 km of common borders. As early as 2002 Tashkent reopened the Khairaton Bridge on the Uzbek-Afghan border—the former "friendship bridge," which served as a main transit site for Soviet troops.[35] Uzbekistan's role in the Afghan economy and recovery is central in two sectors: electricity and transportation. Using its Soviet-era infrastructure, since 2007, Uzbekistan's electric state corporation UzbekEnergo has been delivering about 150 megawatts a year to the Afghan capital thanks to a line of more than 400 km stretching from Hairaton to Pul e-Khumri and then to Kabul, built on funds from the Asian Development Bank's Central Asia-South Asia Regional Electricity Market (CASAREM) project.[36] On the level of transportation, Uzbek firms have contributed to restoring motor roads between Mazar-i-Sharif and Kabul, and to reopening eleven bridges along this route.[37] The Uzbek national railway company, Ozbekistan Temir Yollari, also built 75 kilometers of rail line between Hairaton and Mazar i-Sharif.[38] The short-term objective of the new railroad is to increase the role of Uzbekistan in the northern route of supply for the international coalition in Afghanistan and now for reverse supply.[39] Tashkent, however, wants to become a key actor of Afghan rail transport, and hopes to win new tender bids.

Tajikistan, with about 1,400 km of common borders, is in second place for Central Asian–Afghanistan trade. Here again, electricity is the core of the economic partnership between both countries. In 2008, a power purchase agreement was signed for

Table 7.4

Afghanistan's Place in Imports, Exports, and the Trade Total of Central Asian States in 2010 (in millions of US$)

	Imports	Rank	Exports	Rank	Total trade	Rank
Kazakhstan	0.6 (0.0%)	<50	184.7 (0.4%)	16	185.3 (0.2%)	18
Kyrgyzstan	0.6 (0.0%)	36	49.2 (4.6%)	6	49.9 (0.6%)	12
Tajikistan	38.3 (1.5%)	14	50.3 (4.4%)	5	88.5 (2.4%)	9
Turkmenistan	0.6 (0.0%)	37	207.1 (6.4%)	5	207.7 (2.4%)	9
Uzbekistan	0.2*	—	1,087.9**	—	1,294	—

Source: 2011 European Commission statistics, http://ec.europa.eu/trade/creating-opportunities/bilateral-relations/countries-and-regions/.

* B. Anderson, Y. Klimov, "Uzbekistan: Trade Regime and Recent Trade Developments," University of Central Asia Institute of Public Policy and Administration Working Papers no. 4, 2012, http://www.ucentralasia.org/downloads/UCA-IPPA-WP4-Uzbekistan%20and%20Regional%20Trade.pdf, 37.

** Data from the Afghanistan Central Statistics Organization http://cso.gov.af/Content/files/importsbycountry(1).pdf.

the annual export of 300 megawatts of Tajik electricity, but at present exports hover at around 200,000 kilowatts through the only electricity line that links Geran in Tajikistan to Kunduz, initially built in the Soviet period but since renovated.[40] Dushanbe hopes to take advantage of the CASA-1000 project, which finances the connection of the Sangtuda power station to Kunduz and on to Baghlan and Pul e-Khumri, the aim being to link with the line to Kabul.[41] Today, it is this line that enables Dushanbe to compete with Tashkent as an electricity exporter during the summer months, and the electricity it provides are at lower prices than those charged by Uzbekistan. With the exception of these electricity exports, trade exchanges between these two countries are developing on a small scale: the border post of Nizhnii Pianj, rebuilt with international aid, in particular from the United States, is supposed to concentrate the largest part of the freight between the countries, but is very isolated now that the security of the Kunduz region has deteriorated.[42] Further east, several smaller bridges, rebuilt or renovated by the Aga Khan Development Network (AKDN), enable border populations to set up small trade mechanisms to lift them out of poverty.[43] Dushanbe created some cross-border economic zones that are designed to attract foreign investors as well as Afghan entrepreneurs in the Piandj region in the district of Kumsangir, and at the border point of Ishkashim in the Autonomous Gorno-Badakhshan Region.

Turkmenistan, which shares a 750 km-long border with Afghanistan, is also an important partner for Kabul. Electricity exports again constitute the main driver of bilateral trade. In 2002, a bilateral agreement was signed to export about 200 billion kWh (kilowatt hours) per year to Afghanistan. To this end, the state-run electric corporation TurkmenEnergo reconstructed some power stations and 110 kV electric lines in the province of Balkh.[44] The Turkmen authorities have also put back into service a

Soviet-era 2 km cross-border railway between Kushka and Turgundi (Towraghondi) in 2007;[45] and have renovated their own roads from Mary to Serkhetabat (former Kushka) and from Turkmenabat to Kerikichi. Moreover, Turkmenistan provides the Turkmen minority in Afghanistan with financial and technical assistance in the form of medical and school aid, allows them to cross the border to receive treatment in Turkmen hospitals, allocates them various state-funded scholarships, renovates their irrigation infrastructure, and so on.

Despite having no borders with Afghanistan, Kazakhstan also presents itself as a key economic partner for Kabul. It is the only Central Asian country that has published an Assistance Program for the Reconstruction of Afghanistan, with modest projects related to water supply, infrastructure development, delivery of cement, and construction commodities.[46] Astana financed, for instance, the renovation of the Kunduz-Talukan road, the construction of a school and a hospital, for a total of US$2 million. More importantly, Kazakhstan has positioned itself as a major actor in Afghanistan's wheat market, as exports began to take off in 2002. Today, about 20 percent of Afghan wheat and flour imports came from Kazakhstan, and the country even became the major supplier of wheat during the years of Pakistani ban.[47]

Central Asian states play an important but often underestimated role in the economic recovery of Afghanistan. While their trade with Kabul cannot be compared with the much larger volumes of Pakistan or Iran, they remain key actors in terms of electricity supply, of transport, and of food security. This vital role in the supply of electricity to Afghanistan might contribute to developing water management/energy cooperation in Central Asia. Collective water management agreements cannot ignore Afghanistan, which shares with its neighbors the cross-border Amu Darya River, and whose increasing water needs will have an upstream impact. Kazakhstan's growing role as a grain producing power, and its influence on the food security of its Afghan neighbor might also become a driver for broader discussions about food security. The Central Asia-Afghanistan relationship cannot therefore be limited to border security and the transit issue but could include more constructive and cooperative agreements.[48]

Central Asian Cooperation: Interstate Failure, Bazaar Economies

The Central Asian states have never displayed a great eagerness for collaboration. All the attempts at regional economic alliances have stumbled on national sensitivities, on the personal competition between leaders, and on struggles for influence, in particular between Kazakhstan and Uzbekistan. The main regional cooperation mechanisms have been driven by external actors—Russia for the CSTO and China for the SCO—and by international donors, like the Asian Development Bank programs for transport. Difficult regional cooperation is highly detrimental to the development of the whole region. Apart from personal competition between leaders, two of the main issues that jeopardize interstate relations are border and water management.[49]

The Central Asian republics inherited a heavy legacy in their former Soviet borders. Only Kazakhstan has settled its border disputes with all its neighbors. Checkpoints between Kazakhstan and Kyrgyzstan are by and large open and demilitarized, even if tensions reemerge in 2011–2012 with the Russia-Belarus-Kazakhstan Customs Union that isolates Kyrgyzstan. Border relations are especially tense in the Ferghana Valley, where Kyrgyzstan, Tajikistan, and Uzbekistan interweave.[50] Unresolved territoral issues, combined with a lack of regular overland transit between the three countries, contribute to undermine the stability of the valley. Right of movement and access to food, family members, and workplaces are recurring points of contention, as is vehicle traffic. The existence of Uzbek enclaves, mainly Sokh and Shakhimardan, and a Tajik one, Vorukh, in the Kyrgyz part of the valley, complicates interstate relations.[51] The Uzbek-Tajik border has been mined for a decade causing a number of deaths every year. Between Tashkent and Bishkek, apart from the Uzbek enclaves on Kyrgyz territory, more than 400 kilometers of borders remain in dispute. For Kyrgyzstan and Tajikistan, many border zones in the mountains are not delimited and the two countries cannot agree on a demarcation treaty.[52] In the Andijan-Osh-Khudjand-Batken area, border crossings remain a constant subject of tension, all the more as the area is at the heart of numerous illegal smuggling routes, especially those for drug trafficking. Localized clashes between the populations are regular and the relations between border guards tense.[53]

But these chilly interstate relations should not mask the realities on the ground. While official trade figures between Central Asian countries are small, they do not take into account the huge underground market for goods and labor. In border regions, cross-border trade supports much of the local population and offers significant additional revenues. In the 1990s, Kyrgyz living in border areas bought the basic necessities on the Uzbek side that were still largely subsidized there. Significant growth occurred in the trade of vegetables and fruit, cotton, and gas that crossed the border from Uzbekistan to Kyrgyzstan. Subsidized Uzbek oil is still in high demand on the Kyrgyz side and is smuggled in two-hundred-liter containers, while customs agents are bribed to look the other way. The number of Uzbek traders working illegally on the Kyrgyz side has increased, especially in the sale of cotton, as in Kyrgyzstan it can be sold for higher than the Uzbek state price. On the Tajik side, small-scale traffic along the border with Uzbekistan had become very difficult, but exchanges with Kyrgyzstan have been facilitated by the inefficiency of the border control agencies on both sides.[54]

In the early years of the twenty-first century, cross-border trade was increasingly hampered by the many protectionist measures that the Uzbek authorities imposed. From 2009, border crossing was made even more difficult, causing a decline in trade between Uzbekistan and Kyrgyzstan, aggravated by the serious political unrest in Kyrgyzstan in 2010.[55] Freedom of movement is a key issue for the Ferghana Valley as the bazaars play an important economic and social role as sources of employment and sources of private and public revenues. A quarter of all Chinese products entering Kyrgyzstan go through the Karasuu bazaar, near Osh. Only 10 percent of goods are intended for domestic purchase, the rest being reexported to Uzbekistan and Tajikistan.[56] The Uzbek authorities had long been jealous of the Karasuu success, especially since there were many Uzbek traders there. Tashkent has, accordingly, wanted to establish a bazaar on its own territory to accrue transit profits at

Table 7.5

Central Asia's Internal Trade in 2010 (in millions of US$)

	Kazakhstan	Kyrgyzstan	Tajikistan	Turkmenistan	Uzbekistan
Kazakhstan	—	583.9	277	214.1	919.3
Kyrgyzstan	583.9	—	20.7	7	420.5
Tajikistan	277	20.7	—	81.5	77.3
Turkmenistan	214.1	7	81.5	—	150.5
Uzbekistan	919.3	420.5	77.3	150.5	—

Source: 2011 European Commission statistics, http://ec.europa.eu/trade/creating-opportunities/bilateral-relations/countries-and-regions/.

the expense of Kyrgyzstan. In 2009 and 2010, it gave multiple arguments to justify the closing of borders that probably 40,000 people per day had been using. This autarkic policy weakened the whole region, resulting in an 11 percent decrease in Kyrgyz official state revenues in 2010, and a 70 percent reduction in cross-border transit containers.[57]

As a result of the tightening of border restrictions, more flows are being conducted through unofficial channels. The exact figures for illegal trade are obviously not calculable, but its magnitude can be measured by comparing trade figures between the two countries. In 2007, the Kyrgyz border services trade figures were higher than Uzbek statistics by 12.3 percent, by 47.3 percent in 2008, and by a record 75.4 percent in 2009.[58] Differences in national accounting procedures are not sufficient to explain this discrepancy, which must also be attributed to rising illegal traffic and more flexible calculations by the Kyrgyz authorities compared to their Uzbek counterparts. Smuggling has become more professional and better planned. Illegal goods are channeled through official border crossings with the agreement of corrupt customs guards, or clandestinely, by opening new routes along the border. In this latter case traffickers, in the dead of night, steal across trenches that are about five or six meters long and 2.5 meters deep, dug out by the Uzbek authorities.[59] Smuggling has become a source of work in an area plagued by unemployment, especially for women, and a whole series of intermediaries has cropped up that supply various services.[60]

The regular deterioration of interstate relations impacts on the everyday life of the population, but also on the regional geopolitical balance. Uzbekistan has lost its historical status as the commercial hub of Central Asia in favor of Kyrgyzstan and to a lesser extent Tajikistan. Although Uzbek government policies continue to advocate the closure of borders in the name of security, the real issue is not only the balance between security versus trade openness. The rationale at play is also neopatrimonialistic: many high-ranking politicians and security services officers derive substantial personal income from these smuggling practices. Similarly, the Tajik and Kyrgyz groups in power build their local legitimacy on the illegal income derived from this general refusal to normalize border trade relations.[61]

Uzbek-Kazakh Competition for Regional Leadership

Competition between Uzbekistan and Kazakhstan for regional leadership is a major issue for the whole of Central Asia. The personal rivalry between the Uzbek and Kazakh presidents, who have been in place since the years of perestroika, and who want to be granted the status of "first among equals," has been a major challenge for regional cooperation. By the early 1990s, Almaty and Tashkent had entered into symbolic competition.[62] Uzbekistan's Islam Karimov referred to the need for regional unity by reviving the historical name of Turkestan, and promoted an identity based on Turkic and Muslim values that he named Turanism.[63] Nursultan Nazarbayev of Kazakhstan, by contrast, relied on the concept of Eurasia, which situates Central Asia at the crossroads between Europe and Asia. This regional identity would be distinctly less Turkic and Muslim, more open to the Russian heritage, and more predicated on Asian modernity.[64] The external posturing of both states and their strategies of economic development is also somewhat contradictory.[65] When Uzbekistan presents itself as the region's faithful ally of the United States, it criticizes the pro-Russian stance of neighboring Kazakhstan, but when it wants to resist Western influence, it condemns Kazakhstan's economic liberalism, rapprochement with NATO, and greater freedom of the press.

In the second part of the 1990s and first years of the twenty-first century, when Uzbekistan was focused on the idea of being a fortress against Islamism, Tashkent regularly accused Astana of being lax in matters of religious policy and of allowing Islamist terrorists to train on its territory. The tensions were particularly acute at the turn of the millennium, when Kazakhstan harbored a number of Uzbek dissidents whom it refused to extradite.[66] The process of territorial delimitation was also difficult and it was not until 2001 that a treaty determined 96 percent of the Uzbek-Kazakh border.[67] In 2005, outstanding territorial issues in the Saryagash district, where the border ran through properties, were completed, followed by the Maktaaralsk and Chardarinsk districts. The demarcation process along 2,300 kilometers of borders created new problems, and local incidents spiked in 2004–2005, leading to the deaths of several border guards.[68] But in recent years, the two countries have acted to defuse such tensions and have sought to cooperate more. The authoritarian hardening of the Nazarbayev regime and its criticisms of the West have ramped up the efforts at rapprochement. The joint struggle against the "terrorist threat" have also helped to develop a common security narrative: Nazarbayev supported Karimov during the Andijan events in 2005, and agreed to extradite several opponents of the Uzbek regime to Tashkent.[69] The growing instability in Kyrgyzstan led to both presidents denouncing the Kyrgyz "chaos" which they contrasted with the "stability" of their own countries.[70]

Despite the improvement in political relations, trade between the two countries remains very low compared to its potential. Trade collapsed in the 1990s and rebounded in the first decade of the twenty-first century, tripling between 2005 and 2006 to reach US$703 million, but again declined in subsequent years, with less than US$600 million in 2010. An economic cooperation strategy between the two countries was nevertheless signed for the period 2007–2016 in the areas of trade, investment, finance, transport, communications, and cross-border cooperation.[71] Joint ventures increased, as did cross-border trade with the transformation of Shymkent into an outsourcing market for the Tashkent region, but energy trade did not resume. Tashkent remains dependent on the goodwill of Kazakhstan to export oil and gas to Russia and toward China. Tashkent continues episodically to buy oil from Kazakhstan, and Astana purchases gas from its neighbor for its southern regions.

Official figures should not hide the reality of the extent of underground bilateral trade, which is very significant. Uzbeks are used to acquiring in Kazakhstan products that are missing or are more expensive at home. While the Uzbek authorities have declared food self-sufficiency since 2002, they are still forced to import hundreds of thousands of tons of wheat. The village of Dostyk, in the Saryagash district, is known for its flour traffic toward Uzbekistan.[72] Vodka and wood in various forms, from Russia or eastern Kazakhstan, are also sought-after products. Following Tashkent's protectionist measures in 2002, illegal commerce in food soared, pushing the Uzbek authorities to strengthen border controls to prevent trade flows.[73] The Ettysay district, an Uzbek enclave in Kazakh territory, cut off from Shymkent by the Chardara reservoir and accessible only from Uzbekistan, turned into a market of small traders selling Kazakh products to Uzbeks travelling along the road but was abruptly closed.[74] Trade also goes in the opposite direction. Uzbek vegetable growers seek to sell their products on the Kazakh market, at higher prices, prompting retaliation on the part of the Uzbek authorities. "Vegetable wars" are regular, caused by Tashkent's decision to close the border.[75] Border populations play a central role in these underground flows because they can cross borders more easily, and take advantage of their specific territorial status by collecting transit fees. Border villages and border guards have therefore specialized in these activities, particularly those around the Jibek-Joly, Kazygurt, and Kaplanbek checkpoints.[76]

During two decades of independence, the gap between the two largest Central Asian countries has increased. In the Soviet period, Uzbekistan cultivated its status as a regional power, while the Kazakh republic remained comparatively provincial. But by 2010, Kazakhstan had become the economic driver of the whole region. The success of Kazakhstan in terms of increased living standards is embodied in its new status as a migrant-receiving country. After Russia, it is the second-largest destination for migrants in the CIS, and is likely to receive increasing numbers from Uzbekistan and Kyrgyzstan. According to official reports, the country hosts between half a million and one million illegal migrant workers. Taking seasonal flows and shuttle trade into account, a more plausible figure is about two million.[77] Kazakhstan's international visibility has become much larger, and its energy riches seem to guarantee it a more attractive future, than Uzbekistan in spite of the latter's larger population. Even if Tashkent's strategic value is probably greater than, or at least equal to, that of Kazakhstan, the size and youthfulness of the Uzbek population makes any prospect of economic success in the short or medium term difficult.

The Central Asian economies are heavily geared toward major international trading partners. In the context of intra-regional trade, official figures do not reflect reality because they exclude significant underground cross-border trade. Border areas play a key role in small and medium scale exchanges, the Ferghana Valley being an obvious example along with the regions of Tashkent/Shymkent and Bukhara/Turkmenabat. Cotton, horticultural products, flour, and fuel are among the products that pass consistently and allow frontier populations to trade and earn income. Although this commerce is not visible in official statistics, it helps the daily lives of hundreds of thousands of Central Asians. Border trade with Afghanistan is also partly underground. Diasporas also engage in small-scale commerce: about 300,000 Ukrainians, 170,000 Azeris, and about 100,000 Armenians live in Central Asia and conduct trade with their kin state. Although the weakness of trade with the South Caucasus, Ukraine, and Belarus does not bear political consequences, the brakes put on commerce within Central Asia have a direct negative impact on the majority of the population. Moreover, the lack of regional cooperation weakens each state in its negotiations with the major international actors, which can then press home their power differential.

Notes

1. On CIS trade, see L. Freinkman, E. Polyakov, and C. Revenco, *Trade Performance and Regional Integration of the CIS Countries* (Washington, DC: World Bank Publications, 2004).

2. "GUUAM as a Regional Union: The Approaches and Assessments," Razumkov Centre for National Security and Defence Paper, no. 7, 2001, http://www.uceps.org/additional/analytical_report_NSD19_eng.pdf.

3. "Uzbekistan i Belarus' razvivaiut otnosheniia," *Gazeta.uz,* December 10, 2010, http://www.gazeta.uz/2010/12/10/belarus/; "Uzbekistan i Belarus' podpishut soglashenie o zashchite investitsii," *Belarus Regnum,* March 30, 2011, http://belarus.regnum.ru/news/belarus/1389374.html.

4. I. Burnashev, "Specific Features of Kazakhstan-Belarus Relations in Politics, Economics, and Culture," *Central Asia and the Caucasus,* no. 6 (2004): 103–10.

5. On the political situation in Belarus, see B. Bennett, *The Last Dictatorship in Europe: Belarus Under Lukashenko* (New York: Columbia University Press, 2012); S. Parker, *The Last Soviet Republic: Alexander Lukashenko's Belarus* (Bloomington, IN: Trafford Publishing, 2007).

6. "Cooperation of the Republic of Kazakhstan with Belarus," Kazakhstan Ministry of Foreign Affairs, May 6, 2010, http://portal.mfa.kz/portal/page/portal/mfa/en/content/policy/cooperation/CIS/08.

7. M. Sagers, "Turkmenistan's Gas Trade: The Case of Exports to Ukraine," *Post-Soviet Geography and Economics* 40, no. 2 (1999): 142–49.

8. S. Aleksandrov, "Poleznaia strategiia: Turkmenskie orientiry voenno-tekhnicheskogo sotrudnichestva s Ukrainoi," *Nezavisimoe voennoe obozrenie,* May 27, 2005, http://nvo.ng.ru/armament/2005-05-27/6_strategy.html.

9. A. Nosonov, "Zapakh gaza: Ukraina vozvrashchaetsia v Turkmenistan," *Agenstvo strategichnykh doslidzhen',* April 11, 2011, http://sd.net.ua/2011/04/11/print:page,1,zapax-gaza-ukraina-vozvrashhaetsya-v-turkmenistan.html.

10. "Ukrainian-Uzbek Economic Relations on the Rise," Web-Portal of Ukrainian Government, March 10, 2006, http://www.kmu.gov.ua/control/en/publish/article?art_id=30938857&cat_id=3924444.

11. Nosonov, "Zapakh gaza."

12. "Dvukhstoronnie torgovo-ekonomicheskie otnosheniia mezhdu Ukrainoi i Túrkmenistanom," Turkmenistan Embassy in Ukraine, n.d., http://www.ambturkm.org.ua/index.php?option=com_content&view=article&id=82:2011-03-11-12-00-34&catid=7:2011-03-11-10-03-36&Itemid=24.

13. "Kazakhstan i Ukraina: K novomu etapu vzaimootnoshenii," *Ukrrudprom*, March 6, 2008, http://www.ukrrudprom.ua/digest/dfdsfxz060308.html.

14. "Kazakhstan, Ukraina i Rossiia sozdadut zernovoi pul," *Altynsarin.ru*, April 19, 2011, http://www.altynsarin.ru/kaz_news/1678-kazaxstan-ukraina-i-rossiya-sozdadut-zernovoj-pul.html.

15. "Kazakhstan i Ukraina: K novomu etapu vzaimootnoshenii."

16. "Ukraina i Kazakhstan sozdali aviatsionnoe SP," *Rosbalt*, November 24, 2011, http://www.rosbalt.ru/ukraina/2011/11/24/916647.html.

17. "Kazakhstan to Join Russia-Ukraine Space Program," *RIA Novosti*, September 16, 2011, http://en.rian.ru/world/20100916/160614244.html.

18. 2011 European Commission's statistics, http://ec.europa.eu/trade/creating-opportunities/bilateral-relations/countries-and-regions/.

19. "Azerbaijan and Kazakhstan Sign Trans-Caspian Oil Transport Deal," *Gasandoil.com*, November 14, 2008, http://www.gasandoil.com/news/central_asia/dac66870a0b39bda-b21e728e326263cf.

20. For more details, see chapter 9.

21. L. Gusev, "Sotrudnichestvo Kazakhstana s Azerbaidzhanom v sfere energetiki," *Informatsionno-analiticheskii tsentr*, 2009, http://www.ia-centr.ru/expert/3908/.

22. D. Verkhoturov, "Kavkazskii marshrut dlia nefti i gaza," *Ekspert Kazakhstana*, no. 18, May 14, 2007, http://expert.ru/kazakhstan/2007/18/eksport_uglevodorodov/ 23. "Zernovoi terminal i mel'nichnyi kompleks v portu g. Baku, " *Kazagro*, n.d., http://kazagro.kz/index.php/ru/deyatelnost/mezhdunaridnoe-sotrudnichestvo.

24. F. Guliyev and N. Akhrarkhodjaeva, "The Trans-Caspian Energy Route: Cronyism, Competition, and Cooperation in Kazakh Oil Export," *Energy Policy* 37, no. 8 (2009): 3171–82.

25. F. Guliyev and N. Akhrarkhodjaeva, "Transportation of Kazakhstani Oil via the Caspian Sea (TKOC), Arrangements, Actors, and Interests," RussCas Working Paper, Jacobs University, Bremen, 2008.

26. V. Papava, "Georgia's Economic Role in the South Caucasus," *Problems of Economic Transition* 48, no. 4 (2005): 84–92.

27. O. Sidorov, "Kazakhstano-gruzinskie otnosheniia: Nastoiashchee i budushchee," *Gazeta.kz*, October 2, 2008, http://www.gazeta.kz/art.asp?aid=118920.

28. M. Laruelle, "Is Kazakhstan Disengaging from Georgia?," *The Central Asia-Caucasus Analyst*, October 15, 2008, http://www.cacianalyst.org/?q=node/4961.

29. Sidorov, "Kazakhstano-gruzinskie otnosheniia."

30. N. Kassenova, "Kazakhstan and the South Caucasus Corridor in the Wake of the Georgia-Russia War," Europe-Central Asia Monitoring Policy Brief, no. 3, 2009, http://www.eucentralasia.eu/fileadmin/user_upload/PDF/Policy_Briefs/Policy_Brief-3-NK.pdf.

31. J. Daly, "Kazakh Investment in Georgia's Energy Sector," *UPI.com*, April 9, 2009, http://www.upi.com/Energy_Resources/2009/04/09/Analysis-Kazakh-investment-in-Georgias-energy-sector/UPI-81991239300029/2/; F. Sharip, "Are Kazakhstan's Economic Bonds with Georgia the Price of Stronger Ties with Russia?" *Eurasia Daily Monitor* 5, no. 190, October 3, 2008, http://www.jamestown.org/single/?no_cache=1&tx_ttnews%5Btt_news%5D=33993.

32. "Kazakh State Company Says Ready to Sell Tbilisi Gas Grid," *Civil.ge,* March 25, 2009, http://www.civil.ge/eng/article.php?id=20609.

33. "Sotrudnichestvo Respubliki Kazakhstan s Respublikoi Armeniia," Kazakhstan Ministry of Foreign Affairs, 2011, http://portal.mfa.kz/portal/page/portal/mfa/ru/content/policy/cooperation/CIS/09.

34. See S. Peyrouse, "Is There Any Unity to the Trans-Caspian Region? The Economic Relations between Central Asia and the Caucasus," *Asia-Europe Journal* 7, no. 3 (2009): 543–57.

35. V. Paramonov and A. Strokov, "Economic Relations Between Uzbekistan and Afghanistan: Current State, Problems, and Recommendations," in *Afghanistan Stability and Regional Security Implications for Central Asia,* NATO Series, M. Laurelle, ed., (Berlin: Springer, 2012).

36. "Import of Power from Uzbekistan, Tajikistan, and Turkmenistan," USAID Afghanistan Infrastructure and Rehabilitation Program, 2011, https://www.irp-af.com/?pname=open&id=291&type=html&c=5.

37. J.C.K. Daly, "Uzbek Afghanistan Proposal Relevant and Timely," *UPI*, November 5, 2009, http://www.upi.com/Top_News/Analysis/Outside-View/2009/11/05/Outside-View-Uzbek-Afghanistan-proposal-relevant-and-timely/UPI-71691257429600/.

38. F. Mashrab, "Afghan Rail Link Marks a Break-Out Moment," *Asia Times*, January 11, 2012, http://www.atimes.com/atimes/Central_Asia/NA11Ag01.html.

39. J. Kucera, "Pakistan's Gain in Afghan Transit Deal Central Asia's Loss?," *Eurasianet*, May 17, 2012, http://www.eurasianet.org/node/65416.

40. Energy Sector Status Report July – September, 2010, Islamic Republic of Afghanistan Ministry of Economy Inter-Ministerial Commission for Energy (ICE) Secretariat.

41. Central Asia South Asia Electricity Transmission and Trade Project (CASA 1000), http://www.worldbank.org/projects/P110729/central-asia-south-asia-electricity-transmission-trade-project-casa-1000?lang=en.

42. Author's fieldtrip to Nizhnii Pianj check-point in the framework of the OSCE Border Management School, May 19, 2012.

43. S. Peyrouse, "Economic Trends as an Identity Marker? The Pamiri Trade Niche with China and Afghanistan," *Problems of Post-Communism*, 59, no. 4 (2012): 3–14.

44. "Turkmenistan and Afghanistan," *Institute for the Study of War*, n.d., http://www.understandingwar.org/themenode/turkmenistan-and-afghanistan.

45. See for instance the Turkmen propaganda on the repairing of a two-kilometer-long section of the railway crossing the territory of Afghanistan, "A Gift from the Turkmen People to Afghan Brothers," State News Agency of Turkmenistan, February 8, 2008, http://turkmenistan.gov.tm/_eng/2008/02/08/a_gift_front_he_turkmen_people_ to_afghan_brothers.html (accessed August 25, 2010).

46. S. Kozhirova, "The Current Kazakh-Afghan Relations. A Growing Commitment," *Afghanistan Regional Forum*, in Laurelle, *Afghanistan Stability and Regional Security Implications for Central Asia.*

47. 2012 Grain and Feed Annual Afghanistan, USDA Foreign Agriculture Service, http://gain.fas.usda.gov/Recent%20GAIN%20Publications/2012%20Grain%20and%20Feed%20Annual%20_Kabul_Afghanistan_3-12-2012.pdf.

48. More in M. Laruelle, "Involving Central Asia in Afghanistan's future—What Can Europe Do?" Europe-Central Asia Monitoring Policy Brief, no. 20, August 2011, http://www.fride.org/download/PB_EUCAM_20.pdf.

49. For more details, see chapter 11.

50. S. Frederick Starr, ed., *Ferghana Valley: The Heart of Central Asia* (Armonk, NY: M.E. Sharpe, 2011).

51. M. Reeves, "Materialising State Space: 'Creeping Migration' and Territorial Integrity in Southern Kyrgyzstan," *Europe-Asia Studies* 61, no. 7 (2009): 1277–1313; J. Thorez, "Enclaves et enclavement dans le Ferghana post-soviétique," *Cahiers d'études sur la Méditerranée orientale et le monde turco-iranien*, no. 35 (2003), 28–39.

52. G. Gavrilis, *The Dynamics of Interstate Boundaries* (Cambridge: Cambridge University Press, 2008).

53. On localized ethnic tensions at the borders and in the Ferghana enclaves, see the Foundation for International Tolerance Reports, http://fti.org.kg/en/.

54. Authors' fieldwork in the Batken-Khudjand region, June 2010.

55. A. Khamidov, "Closed Kyrgyzstan-Uzbekistan Border Ratcheting Up Tensions," *Eurasianet*, http://www.eurasianet.org/node/63237.

56. Laruelle and Peyrouse, *The "Chinese Question" in Central Asia*.

57. "Posle 7ogo aprelia oboroty konteinerov snizilis' na 70%," *Central Asia Free Market Institute*, n.d., http://freemarket.kg/en/node/446.

58. A. Beshimov et al., *Prigranichnaia torgovlia: Otsenka perecheniia granits mezhdu Kyrgyzstanom i Uzbekistanom* (Bishkek: OSCE-Central Asian Free Market Institute, 2011), 12.

59. Authors' fieldwork at the Uzbek-Kyrgyz border in the Karasuu-Osh region, June 2010.

60. Beshimov, *Prigranichnaia torgovlia*, 22.

61. S. Radnitz, *Weapons of the Wealthy: Predatory Regimes and Elite-Led Protests in Central Asia* (Ithaca, NY: Cornell University Press, 2010); E. McGlinchey, *Chaos, Violence, Dynasty: Politics and Islam in Central Asia* (Pittsburgh, PA: Pittsburgh University Press, 2011).

62. M. Brill Olcott, "Rivalry and Competition in Central Asia," in *Central Asia and the Caucasus: At the Crossroads of Eurasia in the Twenty-First Century*, ed. W. Hermann and J. F. Linn (Thousand Oaks, CA: SAGE, 2011), 17–42.

63. I. Karimov, *Turkistan, nash obshchii dom* (Tashkent: Uzbekiston, 1995).

64. On Kazakh Eurasianism, see Laruelle, *Russian Eurasianism*, 171–88.

65. A. Rustemova, "Political Economy of Central Asia: Initial Reflections on the Need for a New Approach," *Journal of Eurasian Studies* 2, no.1 (2011): 30-39

66. M. Yermukanov, "Astana Yields to Western Pressure over Uzbek Dissident," *Eurasia Daily Monitor* 2, no. 140, July 20, 2005, http://www.jamestown.org/single/?no_cache=1&tx_ttnews%5Btt_news%5D=30678.

67. "Granitsa Kazakhstana s Uzbekistanom opredelena," *Nomad.su*, September 10, 2002, http://www.nomad.su/?a=3-200209100017; "Paritetnyi razmen," *CentrAsia*, September 12, 2002, http://www.centrasia.ru/newsA.php4?st=1031809920.

68. "Kazakhstan usilivaet granitsy s Uzbekistanom," *Nezavisimaia gazeta*, July 21, 2006, http://www.ng.ru/cis/2006-07-21/6_granitsa.html.

69. "Kazakhstan Extradites Kyrgyz Citizen to Uzbekistan," *Radio Free Europe/Radio Liberty*, September 14, 2010, http://www.rferl.org/content/Kazakhstan_Extradites_Kyrgyz_Citizen_To_Uzbekistan/2157056.html.

70. N. Megoran, "The Critical Geopolitics of the Uzbekistan-Kyrgyzstan Ferghana Valley Boundary Dispute, 1999–2000," *Political Geography* 23 (2004): 731–64; Megoran, "Framing Andijon, Narrating the Nation: Islam Karimov's Account of the Events of 13 May 2005," *Central Asian Survey* 27, no. 1 (2008): 15–31.

71. "Kazakhstanskii prem'er K. Masimov podpisal v Tashkente 'dolgosrochnuiu strategiiu sotrudnichestva'," *Centrasia*, July 27, 2007, http://www.centrasia.ru/newsA.php?st=1185529740

72. "Novaia taktika: Kontrabandisty shturmuiut kazakhstano-uzbekskuiu granitsu," *CentrAsia*, May 31, 2007, http://www.centrasia.ru/news2.php?st=1180594380.

73. G. Bukharbaeva, "Uzbekistan: Granitsa s Kazakhstanom na karantine," *Zonakz.net*, January 27, 2003, http://zonakz.net/articles/4print.php?artid=2451.

74. Authors' fieldwork, Ettysay district, Uzbekistan, March 2003 and May 2005.

75. A. Vaiskopf, "Ne po vkusu: Uzbekistan nachal 'ovoshchnuiu voinu' protiv Kazakhstana?" *CentrAsia*, April 28, 2006, http://www.centrasia.ru/newsA.php?st=1146210420; "Pomidory s"edim sami: Uzbekistan neglasno priostanovil eksport ovoshchei i fruktov v RF i Kazakhstan," *CentrAsia*, May 21, 2007, http://www.centrasia.ru/newsA.php?st=1179733860.

76. Authors' fieldwork, Jibek-Joly, Kazygurt, and Kaplanbek checkpoints, June 2005, March 2008.

77. M. Laruelle, "Kazakhstan: Central Asia's New Migration Crossroads," in Laruelle, *Migration and Social Upheaval*.

Part II

Facing Globalization

Strengths and Weaknesses of Central Asia's Economies

Each Central Asian state has its own specific economic potential and there are strong regional contrasts. Kazakhstan's economy boomed in the first decade of the twenty-first century and today its GDP (gross domestic product) represents close to 60 percent of the total GDP of Central Asia. Out of a total five-state GDP of US$387 billion in 2011, Kazakhstan alone generated US$219 billion. Uzbekistan comes in a distant second, with a GDP half Kazakhstan's size, and then comes Turkmenistan, whose GDP is again half as large as Uzbekistan's. Kyrgyzstan and Tajikistan have a minimal share of regional GDP, at less than 5 percent for each. This division is accentuated by each country's share of the region's total commercial exchanges. Kazakhstan dominates the total of Central Asian trade with China, the EU, and Russia: in 2010 it alone generated US$76 billion worth of trade, or about three-quarters of the total, Uzbekistan 12.7 billion, Turkmenistan and Kyrgyzstan 7.5 billion each, and Tajikistan scarcely four billion.[1]

In terms of GDP per capita, Kazakhstan is again at the top, second in the CIS behind Russia (US$15,900) and far ahead of Ukraine (US$6,700). It is followed by Turkmenistan (US$7,500), whose figures are to be viewed with caution since they are provided by the government and calculated at official rates, not at black market rates. Uzbekistan, Kyrgyzstan, and Tajikistan have all stagnated between US$2,000 to 3,000 of GDP per capita. With the exception of Kazakhstan and Turkmenistan, agriculture still represents an important share of the GDP by sector, and provides work for close to half of the population (more than one quarter even in Kazakhstan). The percentages of the population living under the poverty line are still very large in the four southern countries, varying from a quarter to a half, in particular in the two poorest, Kyrgyzstan and Tajikistan. The services domain remains insufficiently developed, even though it generates about half of each country's GDP (with the notable exception of Uzbekistan). But the services available in Central Asia include practically no high value added production. Instead, they represent mainly public service, trade at bazaars, and small everyday services (small boutiques, restaurants, and transport services). In addition, a large share of the informal economic activities and mechanisms of daily survival that result from massive underemployment is concealed by the service economy.

Despite their differences, the Central Asian economies are all stamped by their overreliance in exports on raw materials. They have all maintained the Soviet principle

Table Part 2.1

GDP Purchasing Power Parity per Central Asian Country in 2011 (in billion US$)

Kazakhstan	Kyrgyzstan	Tajikistan	Turkmenistan	Uzbekistan
219	13	16	43	96

Source: CIA World Factbook, https://www.cia.gov/library/publications/the-world-factbook/wfbExt/region_cas.html.

of allocating subsidized fuel to central industries such as metallurgy, textiles, and agriculture. They can therefore be put in the category of economies of rent. Kazakhstan bases its economy on its oil production, which accounts for 60 percent of its exports and over 40 percent of government revenues.[2] Turkmenistan depends on its gas, which accounts for half of its exports, and on oil products, which comprise a third of them.[3] As for Uzbekistan, energy sources and oil products account for 25 percent of its exports, and cotton for about 11 percent of its GDP.[4] The two poorest states, Kyrgyzstan and Tajikistan, have neither hydrocarbon resources, nor an agricultural production capable of export, and are limited to a few types of production. Until recently the main revenue source for foreign currency in Kyrgyzstan was the Kumtor gold mine, which alone represented more than one-third of Kyrgyz exports and 7 percent of its GDP,[5] whereas in Tajikistan, the aluminum produced by the Tursunzoda smelter comprised close to 60 percent of exports.[6] The region's development is therefore exposed to upheavals in the global prices of oil, gas, metals, and cotton, as occurred when the 2008 crisis caused a fall in the prices of these raw materials. Only Kyrgyzstan has developed in a different direction, enabled by China's proximity and the reexport of Chinese products that is now its main source of income.[7]

Apart from the trade in Chinese products, the region remains mostly limited to the traditional sectors of agriculture, hydrocarbons, and minerals, which have been developed over the course of the twentieth century. Under the Soviet regime, a number of industries operated at a loss, as they answered not to commercial logic but to considerations related to the managed economy that prioritized heavy over light industry, or to development, which endowed each republic with an economic niche that contributed to the overall Soviet structure. The transformation industries that survived the fall of the Soviet Union must today contend with Chinese competition and struggle to make a profit despite their aging infrastructures, disrespect of environmental norms, dearth of qualified personnel, and insufficient transport and distribution networks. In addition, the problems of access to energy and of geographical landlockedness impede company operations and entail increased transport costs, thus slowing down the reconversion and modernization of the Central Asian economies.

The region has turned out to be propitious for large-scale subsoil exploitation projects, led by extraction companies that have the backing of the state and its financial institutions and are part of a larger rationale of positioning on the world market. But

Table Part 2.2

Global Economic Structure of Central Asian Countries in 2011

	Kazakhstan	Kyrgyzstan	Tajikistan	Turkmenistan	Uzbekistan
GDP per capita	US$13,200	US$2,400	US$2,100	US$7,900	US$3,300
GDP by sector	agriculture: 5.2% industry: 37.9% services: 56.9%	agriculture: 20.1% industry: 28.8% services: 51.1%	agriculture: 21.4% industry: 21.7% services: 56.8%	agriculture: 7.9% industry: 24.5% services: 67.6%	agriculture: 21.9% industry: 37.7% services: 40.3%
Labor force by occupation	agriculture: 25.9% industry: 11.9% services: 62.2%	agriculture: 48% industry: 12.5% services: 39.5%	agriculture: 49.8% industry: 12.8% services: 37.4%	agriculture: 48.2% industry: 14% services: 37.8%	agriculture: 44% industry: 20% services: 36%
Population below poverty line	8.2%	33.7%	53%	30%	26%

Source: CIA World Factbook, https://www.cia.gov/library/publications/the-world-factbook/wfbExt/region_cas.html.

the regional economy is unfavorable to small and medium-size private companies, since the political environment, the institutional guarantees, and the profitability are often too weak to sustain them. This situation has proven to be an asset for China and Russia, with their state-subsided firms, while it is a handicap for the West, Japan, Turkey, Iran, and India and their mostly private sector. In addition, the Central Asian states are by no means merely passive objects of international covetousness, but are themselves fully fledged actors: they have their own vision of economic development, and believe that certain sectors, such as agriculture, must remain closed to any foreign influence that would be synonymous with interference. They also search for international partnerships to help with exploiting their resources, although there was an evident reassertion of state control after 2005. Tashkent chose to limit exploitation of new deposits and discourage foreign activity, as well as to preserve its hydrocarbons for the future, while Ashgabat has been and still is very cautious regarding foreign investments.

The budgets of the Central Asian countries are as diverse as their economic situations, and their capacities to attract foreign direct investment also diverge in accordance with their openness to the external world and the opportunities that they offer. However, all followed the same trajectory: a lightning drop in GDP in the early 1990s, a timid revival in the second half of the 1990s, a setback caused by the Russian economic crash of summer 1998, and then, between 2000 and 2008, a steady growth of several percent (between 9 and 10 percent for Kazakhstan). This has translated into increased living standards for sections of the population, although the pauperization of those living in rural areas continues apace with the degradation of public services. The 2008 crisis slowed this growth, in particular in the two weakest countries, Kyrgyzstan and Tajikistan; it led to high inflation, to the devaluation of national currencies,[8] and to a drop in FDI from developed countries, in particular for the three producers of hydrocarbons, Kazakhstan, Turkmenistan, and Uzbekistan.[9] The growing instability of Kyrgyzstan—the toppling of the president in April 2010 and the interethnic riots in Osh in June 2010—again contributed to the deterioration of the republic's economic climate, and the country entered in recession.[10]

Despite their divergences, the five countries are all poorly ranked in terms of being countries to do business with. Kazakhstan is the most competitive overall and, in 2010, its position according to *Doing Business* ratings improved by fifteen points. For the first time it headed the list of the top ten countries deemed to have successfully implemented reforms to improve the business climate. Kazakhstan is only surpassed by Kyrgyzstan in *Doing Business* calculations, because Bishkek is a member of the WTO; however, its weak governance subverts all the advantages that it might otherwise draw from its pro-trade legislation. Turkmenistan and Uzbekistan perform so poorly—or are impossible to assess—that they are sometimes not even included in the rankings. Overall, the Central Asian states have a poor business climate, difficulties in raising taxes, and endemic corruption that prevents the state budget from receiving monies it is owed from public companies, exports, and customs. Even if trade barriers such as tariffs are often low, commerce is limited by the opacity of the public service.

Table Part 2.3

Budget Revenues, Expenditures, External Debt, and FDI for the Central Asian Countries in 2011 (in billion US$)

	Kazakhstan	Kyrgyzstan	Tajikistan	Turkmenistan	Uzbekistan
Budget revenues	36.64 billion	1.6 billion	1.84 billion	4.1 billion	14.9 billion
Expenditures	40.52 billion	1.9 billion	1.8 billion	4 billion	14.7 billion
Taxes and other revenues of GDP	20.5%	28.5%	28.3%	16.2%	32.9%
External debt	122.9 billion	3.738 billion	2.202 billion	526 million	4.435 billion
Foreign direct investment	93.0 billion	1.409 billion	0.933 billion	unknown	unknown

Sources: Uzbekistan Newswires, http://www.universalnewswires.com/centralasia/tajikistan/viewstory.aspx?id=13213 and http://www.universalnewswires.com/centralasia/uzbekistan/viewstory.aspx?id=11213 and *CIA World Factbook*, https://www.cia.gov/library/publications/the-world-factbook/wfbExt/region_cas.html.

Table Part 2.4

Main Index of Business Grading of Central Asian States for 2011 by Rank

	Doing Business Report (out of 183)	Global Competitiveness Report (out of 142)	Economic Freedom Index (out of 179)	KOF Index of Globalization (out of 181)*
Kazakhstan	59	72	78	73
Kyrgyzstan	44	126	83	82
Tajikistan	139	105	128	167
Turkmenistan	>183	>142	169	156
Uzbekistan	150	>142	163	152

Sources: Doing Business: World Bank, http://www.doingbusiness.org/reports/global-reports/doing-business-2011/; Global Competitiveness Report: World Economic Forum, http://www3.weforum.org/docs/WEF_GCR_CompetitivenessIndexRanking_2011-12.pdf; Index of Economic Freedom: Heritage Foundation, http://www.heritage.org/index/ranking; KOF Index of Globalization, http://globalization.kof.ethz.ch/.

The institutional environment thus constitutes a major problem: the investment conditions are discouraging for foreign companies, which are critical of the high-risk taxation systems arising from general instability, and the high level of corruption that paralyzes the chain of decision-making.

Corruption is one of the region's endemic evils and is calculated according to an index of perception gauged by local public opinion. The index thus sheds light on daily practices of corruption, but is unable to measure the extent of financial misappropriation carried out at the highest levels. The liberty index, which combines such factors as the electoral process, the autonomy of civil society, the freedom of the press, the independence of the justice system, and governance at the national and local levels, ranks the five states, including the most liberal one, Kyrgyzstan, in the category of "unfree" countries. On this index, Turkmenistan and Uzbekistan are close to the most unfree countries possible. Lastly, the human development index (HDI), which measures life expectancy, literacy, education, and standards of living, confirms the progress made by Kazakhstan. The relatively good results of the other four states should not be taken at face value, however: the higher life expectancy, literacy, and education rates all stem from the Soviet heritage, but are threatened by inadequate amounts of public investment in the domains of health and education. They are also distorted, since the official statistics provided by the governments continue to boast of a literacy rate of 99 percent even though it has collapsed, in particular in Tajikistan, Kyrgyzstan, and Turkmenistan.

Numerous aspects of the Central Asian economy do not appear in these calculations. The shadow economy is obviously not visible; this refers essentially to drug trafficking, which generates considerable revenues for some elite, but also to multiple smuggling activities, in particular in the sectors of metals and of precious minerals.

Table Part 2.5

Corruption, Freedom, and Human Development Index by Central Asian Countries in 2010–2011

	Corruption Perception Index (out of 183)	Freedom House Ranking (degree of freedom 1=highest; 7=lowest)	Human Development Index (out of 187)
Kazakhstan	120	6.43	68
Kyrgyzstan	164	6.11	126
Tajikistan	152	6.14	127
Turkmenistan	177	6.93	102
Uzbekistan	177	6.93	115

Source: Corruption Perception Index: Transparency International, http://cpi.transparency.org/cpi2011/; Freedom House Ranking, http://www.freedomhouse.org/images/File/nit/2011/NIT-2011-Tables.pdf; Human Development Index, UNDP, http://hdr.undp.org/en/reports/global/hdr2011/download/.

This shadow economy has enabled the development of a luxury services market in the capitals (stores selling Western designer brands and precious stones, the building of luxury villas) and also necessitates laundering mechanisms both locally and abroad (integrated banking systems, offshore transfers via front companies, real estate investments in Europe). This shadow economy partly explains the boom in services—in particular in consumption and leisure activities—in the overall structure of the Central Asian economies.

At the other end of the socio-economic chain, the remittances sent by labor abroad are only partially taken into account in national statistics since the money circulates in cash or in Western Union-type systems, which the states are able to tax only minimally or not at all. The remittances sent by Tajik migrants to their families surged during the first years of the twenty-first century, from US$252 million to one billion in 2006 and 2.6 billion in 2011. Kyrgyz remittances were up from US$189 million in 2004 to 1.5 billion in 2011. There are no figures available for Uzbekistan, but as its migrants are the most numerous, the flows of money must be equally substantial. These remittances play a key role in the Tajik and Kyrgyz economies. The World Bank estimates that remittances account for 31.5 percent of Tajik GDP, which means that this country is ranked first in the world in remittances, ahead of the states of Central America and some African states. Kyrgyzstan's figure stands at 20.8 percent, and is surpassed only by Lesotho, Samoa, and Moldova.[11] There are therefore many more mechanisms of interaction with the globalized world than those that we discuss here.

Notes

1. 2011 European Commission statistics, http://ec.europa.eu/trade/trade-statistics/.
2. "Kazakhstan on Road to Recovery, But Banking System Still Weak," *IMF Survey Magazine*, August 17, 2010, http://www.imf.org/external/pubs/ft/survey/so/2010/car081710a.htm.

3. "Turkmenistan," US Bureau of Asian and Central Asian Affairs, State Department, http://www.state.gov/r/pa/ei/bgn/35884.htm.

4. "Uzbekistan," US Bureau of Asian and Central Asian Affairs, State Department, http://www.state.gov/r/pa/ei/bgn/2924.htm.

5. A. Khamidov, "Kyrgyzstan: Could Kumtor Shakedown Backfire on Bishkek?" *Eurasianet*, June 2, 2011, http://www.eurasianet.org/node/63603.

6. "Tajikistan's Aluminium Export Drops 55.36%," *Export.by*, September 18, 2009, http://www.export.by/en/?act=news&mode=view&id=13110.

7. More detailed calculations in Raballand and Kaminski, "Entrepôt for Chinese Consumer Goods."

8. R. Pomfret, "Central Asia and the Global Economic Crisis," Europe-Central Asia Monitoring Policy Brief, no. 7, June 2009.

9. P. K. Mitra, "The Impact of the Global Financial Crisis and Policy Responses: Central Asia and the Caucasus," in Hermann and Linn, *Central Asia and the Caucasus*, 135–71.

10. See the International Monetary Fund note on the Kyrgyz economy, June 21, 2011, http://www.imf.org/external/np/country/notes/kyrgyzrep.htm.

11. World Bank's Migration and Remittances Factbook 2011, http://econ.worldbank.org/WBSITE/EXTERNAL/EXTDEC/EXTDECPROSPECTS/0,,contentMDK:22759429~pagePK:64165401~piPK:64165026~theSitePK:476883,00.html#Remittances.

8

The Weight of the Soil

The Agricultural Sector

The majority of the world's population is now urban, and those living in rural areas are decreasing in number, although they remain the majority in many developing countries. Linked to these urbanization trends, changes in patterns of food consumption impact the agricultural world. In recent decades, the global consumption of cereals has grown exponentially: between 1980 and 2005, consumption of corn rose from 400 to 700 million tons, that of wheat from 480 to 625 million, and that of rice from 450 to 600 million.[1] World agriculture has been undergoing a global phenomenon of centralization since the end of the nineteenth century: for twenty-five of today's thirty most important agricultural products, more than a quarter of world production comes from one country or region. Thirty countries monopolize the major part of production and trade exchanges, in particular for cereals (wheat, corn, sorghum, and barley) and rice.

With its early mastery in antiquity of irrigation techniques, Central Asia has always been an agrarian space, and represents today a vast agricultural area of 306 million hectares.[2] Since the end of the nineteenth century, the "new" countries with vast expanses, such as the United States, Canada, Australia, and the Russian Empire/Soviet Union, have specialized in agriculture. This trend was reinforced after the Second World War as they underwent demographic growth, increased their productivity and exploited resources on an industrial-scale hitherto unseen. For Central Asia this trend was reinforced by the Soviet regime's division of labor, which had the region specialize in agriculture. These processes made Central Asia an important player in terms of world production: Uzbekistan and Turkmenistan are among the ten largest producers of cotton in the world, and Kazakhstan is becoming a major world power in cereals.

Foreign influence in the agricultural sector is limited: seen as the backbone of the Central Asian economies and societies, agriculture remains in the hands of the ruling elites, who are concerned with pocketing the foreign currency benefits from cotton revenues and controlling social stability. Central Asian agriculture, especially in the four southern republics, has multiple structural political and social problems to contend with: unfinished land reforms; a weak growth of productivity; the entrenched corruption of agrarian administration; the opacity of decision-making structures concerning the export of production; a lack of logistical structures for distribution;

and, in some republics, the exploitation of the rural population and child labor. The Central Asian states also all share the climatic hazards linked to agricultural production. Though the Soviet regime made it possible to limit the climatic influences by mechanization and provision of fertilizer, the region is fragile, especially in the context of climate change. Central Asian agriculture poses many environmental problems: the poor condition of irrigation structures, which have particularly high loss rates; overuse of water by farmers; difficulty in demanding payment for its use, given the low rural standard of living; high salinity (according to the World Bank, over 60 percent of irrigated cropland in Central Asia is affected by the problem of salinization);[3] and the degradation of soil quality and its impact on public health. Faced by multiple challenges, the Central Asian agrarian world has been the main loser of the last two decades of changes.

Structural Trends in the Agricultural Sector

By virtue of its size, Kazakhstan is a specific case within Central Asia, and close to Russia and Ukraine in terms of its agriculture. The republic was one of the drivers of Soviet agricultural development, in particular due to the Virgin Lands campaign launched by Nikita Khrushchev in 1954. Despite the failures of this extensive agriculture policy, the Virgin Lands campaign enhanced Kazakhstan's agriculture to the point that it made up as much as 20 percent of the arable land of the entire Soviet Union.[4] In the 1980s, the Kazakh republic exported up to ten million tons of wheat and 300,000 tons of meat, whose revenues constituted one third of its GDP at the time.[5] Other produce was less important on the Soviet scale, but not on the local level, where products such as rice and cotton were cultivated in the southern parts of the republic. In 1991, cotton was the third largest of all Kazakh exports to non-Soviet markets, after mineral fertilizer and coal.[6]

According to official figures from the Ministry of Agriculture, the country now has 222 million hectares of farmland, a majority of which (189 million or 85 percent) is being used as pasture land and twenty-four million (10 percent) as cultivated land. Nearly two-thirds of the latter is devoted to cereals and one-third to fodder crops.[7] However, the extension of agricultural land is no longer a fundamental advantage, as the major stakes are in productivity and integration into global trade circuits. Due to its boom in oil and gas, Kazakhstan has seen agriculture fade rapidly into the background in terms of its share of revenues. Thus, while the primary sector made up almost 13 percent of the national GDP in 1995, it came to represent only 5.4 percent in 2010, and remains small compared to the importance of industry (42.8 percent of GDP) and the tertiary sector (51.8 percent).[8] The trend is similar for exports. In 1988, agriculture accounted for 17 percent of all exports of the Soviet Kazakh republic, but only 6 percent in 2000, while, for the same period, oil jumped from 10 to 50 percent and metal from 19 to 32 percent.[9] This state of affairs is similar to the characteristics of developed countries, in which agricultural production accounts for less than 5 percent of the national wealth; however, in most developed countries farmers represent only

Table 8.1

Arable Lands, Irrigated Lands, Agriculture in GDP Share, and Percentage of the Population

	Kazakhstan	Kyrgyzstan	Tajikistan	Turkmenistan	Uzbekistan
Land area (1,000 ha)	269,970	19,180	13,996	46,993	42,540
Arable land (1,000 ha)	23,400	1,276	742	1,850	4,301
Land equipped for irrigation (1,000 ha)	3,556	1,021	722	1,800	4,281
Share of agriculture in GDP	5.2%	20.1%	21.4%	7.9%	21.9%
Share of the labor force working in agriculture	25.9%	48%	49.8%	48.2%	44%

Source: Table based on FAO figures, http://www.fao.org/countries.

3 to 4 percent of the active population, while in Kazakhstan more than a quarter (28.2 percent) of the working population is still engaged in this sector.[10]

Uzbekistan and Turkmenistan constitute a second category of countries. In both of them, agriculture consists mainly of cotton and much of the population still works in this sector. Despite the many challenges it faces, Uzbekistan is unquestionably the main agricultural power in Central Asia, and even though it has only 43,000 km² of arable land, almost all of it is irrigated.[11] The country produces mostly cotton, but also fruit, vegetables, cereals, and rice in the west (Karakalpakstan and Khorezm), and livestock. These products are intended primarily for domestic consumption, although some are also exported to neighboring countries. The share of agriculture in Uzbekistan's GDP fell from 32 percent in 1995 to about 22 percent in 2010, but the sector still employs 44 percent of the sixteen million people active in the national workforce.[12]

In Turkmenistan, agriculture is also a leading sector, as it employs nearly half the population, but its share of GDP is even more modest than in Uzbekistan, at less than 10 percent as compared with 21 percent for industry and 70 percent for the tertiary sector.[13] Only 5 percent of the surface area of the country is arable, and only 18,000 km² is irrigated. The remaining 95 percent, most of which is desert, is used for grazing livestock or is left undeveloped. The country produces mainly cotton, grain, and livestock. Since independence, the authorities have set goals for grain self-sufficiency, but growth in this area was achieved in part at the expense of fodder crops for animal feed (not without consequences for livestock), cotton, and vegetables.

Kyrgyzstan and Tajikistan have a much smaller agricultural potential due to fact that most of their territory is situated at very high altitudes. However, this sector is one of the few where they have export potential, as well as being a vital area for food security. In Tajikistan, only 6.52 percent of its territory is considered arable and is irrigated. In 2010, agriculture accounted for 19 percent of the country's GDP, and employs half of its workforce.[14] The agricultural sector was particularly hard hit by the collapse of the Soviet Union and then by the civil war; however, by the first half of the 2000s, it returned largely to the same levels of production that it had enjoyed during the final years of the Soviet Union.[15] Tajikistan produces mostly wheat (36 percent), cotton (30 percent) and other cereals (9 percent).[16] Cotton is grown on about 40 percent of the arable land, with more than half the output coming from the southern region of Khatlon and one-third from the northern province of Sogd.[17] Since independence the country's rapid population growth, lack of urban or industrial work opportunities, and rising food insecurity have increased the pressures on the land. Paradoxically, however, the mass migration of people of working age has simultaneously emptied the country and hindered agricultural development: work in the fields is now often left to women, children, and the elderly.

The situation is similar in Kyrgyzstan. Agriculture constitutes 22 percent of the GDP, while industry accounts for 28 percent and services for 51 percent. Of the 2.7 million strong workforce, nearly half (48 percent) work in the agricultural sector, as compared with only 12 percent in industry and close to 40 percent in the tertiary sector.[18] Given the very high overall levels of unemployment and poverty, the agricultural sector is a vital source of income for the population. Kyrgyzstan has become the largest agricultural producer in terms of percentage of GDP after Uzbekistan, but has the smallest amount of arable land, about 12,000 km².[19] In agricultural terms, regional disparities are extremely high. The north has 887,000 hectares of arable land, used mainly for growing wheat, but the south has less than half that area—a mere 415,000 hectares—which serves more than half of the population. The ratio of land per capita is 0.19 hectares in the south, compared to 0.53 hectares in the north.[20] In the south the demographic pressures on the land have direct bearing on the social tensions that became highly visible with the Osh riots in June 2010.

Cotton or Food Self-Sufficiency: A False Dilemma?

Developed since the tsarist period, cotton cultivation picked up after the seizure of power by the Bolsheviks. In Central Asia, the area devoted to cotton increased from 441,000 hectares in 1914, to more than one million in 1940.[21] Cotton's monopoly over the land accelerated after the completion of major irrigation works such as the Ferghana Canal in the 1930s, the canal of the Hunger Steppe between Uzbekistan and Kazakhstan, and the Karakum Canal in the 1950s, which diverts the waters of the Amu Darya to the deserts of Turkmenistan. The area of land covered by cotton continued to increase, reaching 1.4 million hectares in 1960, 1.7 million in 1970, and two million in the early 1980s. In the mid-1970s, the Soviet Union's share in world cotton production was one quarter of global output. However, cotton production declined in the last decade of the Soviet Union and diminished further in the 1990s, due to the financial difficulties incurred by the new states, the lack of inputs, and land degradation. In 2003, the former Soviet Union accounted for only 8 percent of world cotton,[22] and in 2010 Central Asia was raising about 5 percent of world production.

Although maintaining the cotton monoculture obviously allows ruling elites to

Table 8.2

Cottonseed Production in Central Asia and as a Share of Global Production (thousands of metric tons)

	1992	1995	1996	2002	2005	2008	2009	2010
Kazakhstan	141	130	97	198	256	175	145	132
Kyrgyzstan	34	45	45	63	78	63	32	48
Tajikistan	102	242	207	296	246	194	163	205
Turkmenistan	822	780	315	460	655	661	440	650
Uzbekistan	2,451	2,387	1,932	1,900	2,280	2,452	1,800	1,900
Total Central Asia	3,550	3,584	2,596	2,917	3,515	3,545	2,580	2,935
World production	32,855	35,614	32,531	33,684	43,684	41,943	38,601	42,756
% of world production	10.80	10.06	7.98	8.65	8.04	8.45	6.68	6.86

Source: FAO calculations by country and by commodity, http://faostat.fao.org/site/339/default.aspx.

guarantee their own financial benefits, it is also part of a macroeconomic strategy to fund the main public industries, which are largely in deficit.[23] Over two-thirds of Central Asian cotton production is exported, and if the region represents only 6.8 percent of world production, it accounts for 15 percent of world exports.[24] However, significant variance exists between countries. Cotton is one of the major sources of foreign currency for some Central Asian states, especially Uzbekistan and Tajikistan, which benefit from hydrocarbon export only in a limited way or not at all. But it composed a very marginal part of the Kazakh economy. Though Kazakh production decreased during the first half of the 1990s, it more than doubled between 1998 and 2005, in conjunction with the growing acreage allocated to cotton. However, it has been falling since 2005, since priority has been clearly given to cereals. The country thus produced 132,000 tons of cottonseed in 2010, making it eighteenth in the world, but its exports are of secondary importance compared to grain.[25]

In 2009, Uzbekistan was the fifth-largest producer and second-largest exporter of cotton in the world. According to official statistics, it produced an average of 3.4 million tons of cottonseed each year and between one and 1.2 million tons of cotton fiber.[26] However, the figures put forward by foreign organizations are much lower: the Food and Agriculture Organization (FAO) calculated production of only 1.9 million tons of cottonseed for 2010.[27] Since independence, production has been in steady decline: the progressive disappearance of the Aral Sea and exhaustion of the Amu Darya, and the degradation of soil quality have contributed to declining production and falling cotton quality, making it more difficult to export. Moreover, due to child labor, Uzbekistan has also had problems exporting to Western markets in recent years. Bangladesh, the main export market for Uzbek cotton, has suffered from the boycotts of Uzbek cotton imposed by some large Western brands. In addition, Tashkent has been slow to establish a genuine textile industry that would provide work for its population and generate export revenues far greater than those for the raw product.[28]

Tajikistan saw a brutal fall in production during the civil war; however, it picked up again in the early years of the twenty-first century, reaching 296,000 tons of cottonseed in 2004, thereby transforming the country into the world's sixteenth-largest producer and ninth-largest exporter.[29] Its production appears to have declined again, from 246,000 tons in 2005 to 163,000 in 2009, due to a series of bad harvests, but the production improved the following year.[30] The contribution of cotton to the country's overall GDP fell from 37 percent in 1991 to 18 percent by 2008, even while the sector continued officially to employ two-thirds of the total population.[31]

In 2009, Turkmenistan was the eighth-largest cotton producer in the world but, given its wealth in oil, cotton represents only a small share of its GDP. State profits from cotton exports have been steadily falling: they were worth a reported US$791 million in 1995, 332 million in 1996, and only 84 million in 2005.[32] But of all the Central Asian states, Turkmenistan has invested the most in its industrial textile structures, and even so, exports declined 46 percent between 2002 and 2006.[33] As in Uzbekistan, the deterioration in soil quality, as well as of the irrigation systems, the lack of fertilizers, and the general de-mechanization of agriculture—owing in part to the lack of spare parts—have all depressed production and lowered the quality of Turkmen cotton. In 2003, Niyazov announced a record harvest of 2.5 million tons of cottonseed, a largely inflated figure, and more than three million in 2005. Berdymukhammedov has tried to be more realistic and for 2010 announced a harvest of only one million tons.[34] Despite this downward revision, however, specialized international organizations estimate production levels to have been even lower, at around about 650,000 tons,[35] or half of what production levels were at the time of the fall of the USSR.

The Central Asian states have to deal with a fundamental contradiction. They can either prefer cotton and be guaranteed substantial foreign exchange earnings for the state budget, or choose to develop vegetable and grain production for the sake of food self-sufficiency. This issue concerns the four southern states and has now become a particularly sensitive political issue. Indeed, the climate risks (cold winters, excessive rainfall, and drought during the growing season) that make harvests unpredictable, combined with the rising world prices of basic foodstuffs since 2005, are having a direct impact on Central Asia's populations, especially those of Tajikistan and Kyrgyzstan. The region's dependence on a single commodity—wheat—is considerably higher than in other regions that are vulnerable to food insecurity.[36] In 2009, the UN Food Program announced that 2.2 million Tajik citizens faced food insecurity, and that some 800,000 were directly threatened by famine.[37] The country requires 1.2 million tons of grain per year, but the best-case scenario estimates production of just over half this amount. As such, it remains largely dependent on humanitarian aid and grain imports.[38] In Kyrgyzstan, the number of people subject to food insecurity is around one million, and the poorest families tend to spend more than half their income on food. Bishkek's problems in achieving food self-sufficiency require it to rely heavily on grain imports,[39] and with the political turmoil of 2010, the country experienced the largest increase in the world—54 percent—in wheat prices.[40]

In Turkmenistan and Uzbekistan, no reliable figures are available, but cases of food shortage have been confirmed in some provinces.[41] Tashkent has been seeking cereals autonomy since independence, and states to have attained it in the first decade of the twenty-first century. With an official annual wheat production of 6.6 million tons in 2009, it claimed to be self-sufficient, and even now exports some of its production (nineteenth-largest exporter in the world).[42] However, wheat shortages have increased in recent years, particularly in 2008, a year in which Astana agreed to a moratorium on exports, and in 2010, after massive fires in Russia destroyed a large share of the production and forced Moscow to impose a moratorium on cereal exports.[43] The price of bread has soared throughout Uzbekistan and flour is sometimes unavailable, especially in Khorezm and Karakalpakstan.

In Turkmenistan, to ensure autonomy in food production, the authorities need to produce 2.5 million tons of grain each year. Officially, in 2004, grain production reached 2.8 million tons, a figure contradicted by several years of flour shortages and increased wheat imports.[44] The figures announced by Berdymukhammedov do seem more credible than those given by the previous regime. In 2010, the authorities registered a grain production of 1.4 million tons, which is 200,000 tons less than the

150

Table 8.3

Wheat Production in Central Asia as a Share of Global Production (in thousands of metric tons)

	1992	1995	1998	2002	2005	2008	2009	2010
Kazakhstan	18,285	6,490	4,746	12,699	11,198	12,538	17,052	9,638
Kyrgyzstan	679	625	1,203	1,162	950	746	1,056	813
Tajikistan	166	170	388	544	618	659	938	857
Turkmenistan	377	695	1,245	2,326	2,834	2,300	2,900	3,000
Uzbekistan	964	2,347	3,556	4,967	6,057	6,146	6,637	6,730
Total Central Asia	20,471	10,327	11,138	21,698	21,657	22,389	28,583	21,038
World production	565,287	542,603	593,527	574,745	626,867	683,193	686,635	653,654
% of world production	3.62	1.90	1.87	3.77	3.45	3.27	4.16	3.21

Source: FAO calculations by country and by commodity, http://faostat.fao.org/site/339/default.aspx.

amount officially planned by the government, although it was 200,000 tons more than the official yield for the preceding year. This figure, presented in the official media as a success resulting from agricultural reforms, should nonetheless be viewed with caution.[45] Independent estimates put output at 800,000 tons,[46] which would have thus necessitated the import of more than half the country's grain stocks.[47] According to the FAO, about 11 percent of Turkmen children are malnourished to the extent of being underweight and 15 percent to the extent that their growth is stunted.[48]

How is a balance between cotton production and food security to be met? Should cotton be considered a major factor of the food crisis affecting Central Asia? A Mercy Corps study shows that malnutrition is mainly concentrated in cotton growing areas,[49] while in 2004 the World Bank asserted that "in Tajikistan almost three-quarters of the extreme poor live in cotton-growing areas."[50] As an essential source of foreign exchange, cotton is central to the corruption affecting the state apparatus and the lack of wealth redistribution among the population. Control of cotton exports enables the ruling circles to enrich themselves much faster than do the profits obtained from vegetable or grain production, which are minimal and difficult to control. Some international organizations or NGOs, like the International Crisis Group (ICG), therefore argue for a reduction in cotton production in favor of producing more grain and vegetables. To some experts, this position is excessive; more should be done to reform the agricultural sector, upstream and downstream, so that the rural population has access to the riches of cotton, rather than replacing it with other products that would continue to finance the system of coercion imposed by states on their rural populations.[51]

For Kazakhstan, the stakes are very different. It is becoming a major grain exporter —and to a lesser extent, an exporter of fruits and vegetables, in particular to CIS markets—and seeks to become one of the world's major breadbaskets. In 2004, grain production was only nine million tons, but it reached nineteen million in 2007, and a record figure of 22.7 million tons in 2009, before declining to 13.7 million in 2010.[52] Forecasts of wheat production for 2015 could reach 22.0 million tons.[53] According to FAO figures, in 2009 Kazakhstan remained in twelfth position in the world in terms of wheat exports (3.2 million tons) but became the world's second-largest exporter of flour (2.2 million tons).[54] It plays a key role in the food security of its neighbors, and sells to Kyrgyzstan, Uzbekistan, Turkmenistan, Azerbaijan, Afghanistan, and Iran.[55] Tajikistan, for instance, imports more than 90 percent of its flour from Kazakhstan.[56] But as its main customers are rather poor countries, they often have low levels of solvency. This is the reason why the Kazakh authorities want to attain European standards and acquire certification for grain products. They are also moving closer to Russia and Ukraine: these three producer countries envisage setting up common mechanisms permitting them to establish themselves better on the global markets, in particular in Europe and the Middle East, and control about one-third of the world grain market.[57] Kazakhstan's continental climate requires it to engage in extensive farming with low yields. Thus, the record yield attained in 2007 of 1.3 tons of grain per hectare is still less than half that of Canada (2.7 tons of grain per hectare).[58] Nonetheless, due to its dry climate, the country is able to combine several varieties of wheat and durum. The

Table 8.4

Rice Production in Central Asia and as a Share of Global Production (in thousands of metric tons)

	1992	1995	1998	2002	2005	2008	2009	2010
Kazakhstan	467	184	236	199	284	254	307	373
Kyrgyzstan	3	7	11	20	17	17	20	20
Tajikistan	20	21	40	50	62	54	63	76
Turkmenistan	63	78	14	80	120	110	110	144
Uzbekistan	539	327	346	175	171	110	194	207
Total Central Asia	1,092	617	647	524	654	545	694	820
World production	528,568	547,430	579,192	571,386	634,445	689,028	684,595	696,324
% of world production	0.20	0.11	0.11	0.09	0.10	0.07	0.10	0.11

Source: FAO calculations by country and by commodity, http://faostat.fao.org/site/339/default.aspx.

Figure 8.1

Livestock by Country by Year (Cattle, Sheep, and Pigs)

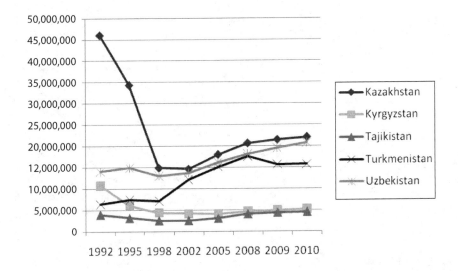

Source: FAO calculations by country and year, http://faostat.fao.org/site/569/default. aspx#ancor.

state-run agricultural holding KazAgro has made massive investments in the domain of storing agricultural products over recent years, and in setting up a distribution network,[59] which enabled it to limit damage during the drought of 2010.

As elsewhere on the planet, the rising living standards and the emergence of middle classes in Central Asia are accompanied by an increase in meat consumption and fresh products to the detriment of bread and starchy foods. The development of livestock farming as a response to growth in consumption requires the growth of animal feed crops. The need to produce between three and seven vegetal kilocalories (kcal) per one animal kcal, depending on the livestock, has triggered worldwide growth in demand for secondary cereals (corn, barley) and cereal substitutes (soya and other proteinaceous vegetables). The development of animal cereal crops, however, is not without risks, as it can impinge on the crops fundamental to food security, as we have seen in sub-Saharan Africa.[60]

Until now, the development of animal feed crops in Central Asia has been limited, and livestock farming, which experienced a decline in the 1990s, has been largely forgotten by state programs and has not regained the production rates of the Soviet period. In Central Asia meat consumption is considered a luxury for the rural and some of the urban population. Very poorly managed after the fall of the Soviet regime, livestock raising is, however, bound to grow in importance. In Kazakhstan, meat production doubled between 2008 and 2009, from 874,000 tons to 1.6 million tons.[61] Beef consumption could grow by 21 percent by 2016.[62] But the increase in production is mainly due to private livestock, not to state-run farms. Supply still fails to meet demand by about 30 percent, and the country requires a significant proportion of its needs. The authorities are well aware of the need to meet domestic consumption, which is growing, but owing to high prices is still below the global average (by about 50 grams of meat per day).[63] Consumption has therefore been focused on poultry, the retail price of which is lower than other types of meat. In the other countries of the region, meat is still considered a luxury by a large part of the population.

The Mixed Results of Land Reforms

While some governments have been more proactive than others in terms of land reform, moving away from the collective economy is far from complete and still faces many obstacles, even in the states with more liberalized economies, namely Kazakhstan and Kyrgyzstan.[64] The Central Asian elites have serious misgivings about land privatization: trained in the Soviet model, they are attached to the principle of land as state property, and are concerned with social stability.[65] Governments have sought to ensure that privatization does not lead to conflict, especially interethnic conflict such as the confrontation between Kyrgyz and Uzbeks in Osh in 1990, triggered by access to land. In Uzbekistan, fear that privatization might lead to massive unemployment, and therefore to social unrest, has paralyzed all reform efforts; and no non-agricultural compensatory economy has developed in rural areas. Moreover, land is a substantial financial resource, and the best parcels of land have generally been allotted to former party elites or former directors of collective farms. Finally, the farmers themselves often express reluctance in regard to privatization. Rural areas have borne the brunt of declining state involvement in social benefits to collective and state farms (food, social and health services, transportation infrastructure, and collective management of expensive equipment and inputs), and are reluctant to let go of the last remaining collective bodies, which stand as symbols of minimal assistance.[66]

Kyrgyzstan is the only country in the region that has resolutely embarked on the conversion of large Soviet farms, guaranteeing the right to private property and creating the legal conditions for an open land market. Its agrarian reforms accelerated after 1994, upon the dissolution of the large collective state-run farms and the shifting of arable lands to the private sector.[67] In 1998, the new constitution introduced the right to own property and today three-quarters of the former collective farms are in the hands of private farmers. Close to 100 percent of agricultural lands in the southern regions are privatized, though the figure is lower for the north, where some large collective farms still operate.[68] The agrarian reforms, however, are not complete, and the reduced acreage of available land has caused conflicts between farmers and the administrative authorities, as well as conflicts between villages in border regions, especially tensions between Tajiks and Kyrgyz over land management and water reserves.[69] Moreover, transhumant herding, which particularly suffered from the collapse of Soviet mechanisms, has been considerably weakened and today still operates thanks only to survival mechanisms.[70]

In Kazakhstan, reforms were initiated quite early but were more limited than in Kyrgyzstan. In the first half of the 1990s, the buying rates for production were still state controlled, but the prices of material inputs had been liberalized, which led to high debt levels among farmers, especially during the droughts of 1996–1998.[71] In 1994, the collective farms were in theory privatized by being split up among employees, although in reality they were reorganized into cooperatives. In 1995, no effective decollectivization occurred, even though the usage of private plots had been guaranteed.[72] In 1998, a new piece of legislation recognized the principle of bankruptcy and thus authorized changes in ownership. Despite ninety-nine-year leases granted to private operators, the ownership of land remains the responsibility of the state. The farms are still very large, a legacy of the Soviet system, and generally managed as collective. Few farms are cultivated on an individual basis. In 2005, individual farms cultivated less than 147,000 hectares out of 222 million hectares, mostly situated in the south and used to grow cotton.[73]

In Uzbekistan, the agricultural sector remains largely in state hands, despite the many existing reform plans, with nobody owning the land they work on. A first plan involved government allocations to farms of a share of the cotton produce or of export receipts to enable farmers to acquire spare parts and the necessary materials and equipment. However, this policy was tightened after some agricultural enterprises allegedly used some of the cotton in exchange for consumer goods. In 1993, collective farms were replaced by cooperatives (shirkat) that only slightly changed the modus operandi of the Soviet regime.[74] Theoretically, 60 percent of shirkat have been transformed into private farms as of 2008. Autonomy remains extremely limited, however. The so-called private operators cannot choose which crops to plant and many are forced to cultivate cotton or wheat almost exclusively. According to the International Crisis Group, farmers who have refused to follow directives have had their water cut off or their land confiscated.[75] The state may also repossess the land, often under opaque conditions, as a sanction for poor performance. In practice, the confiscation of land is part of a system of pervasive corruption, with poor harvests used as a pretext for the confiscation of the best land, which is then redistributed to members of the elite. Whatever the status of land is, the selling price of products is fixed by the authorities, usually at about one-third of the market price; only the surplus can be sold at maximum price. Private farmers (deqhon) have only small farms (0.2 hectares), with leases for periods of ten to fifty years.[76] Despite their small size, these farms are more efficient than the large ones. They represent only 10 percent of the agricultural land in Uzbekistan, but produce about 40 percent of its agriculture. In 2003, over 90 percent of meat, dairy, and potatoes came from private farms.[77]

In Tajikistan, despite the announcement of reforms, little has changed and land remains the property of the state. Individuals may obtain an inheritable right to work an area over their lifetime, but it cannot be sold or purchased. The state also reserves the option to withdraw operators it deems ineffective. Since 2002, a law has authorized the establishment of nominally independent entities for which the operator can choose his crop. In practice, collective farms have simply been re-registered as collective *deqhon*, and farmers are still employees, not shareholders.[78] In 2005, the government officially privatized the last 200 large state-owned farms, but this procedure was widely rigged and half of the applications were refused. A common practice is to force farmers wishing to leave their cooperative commitment to devote 70 percent of their land to cotton, which hampers autonomy. Similar to the situation in Uzbekistan, the smaller farms appear to be the more efficient. Independent *deqhon* with less than 50 hectares produce quantities of cotton that are generally 30 percent higher than collective farms (24 percent more for wheat).[79]

In Turkmenistan, the system has changed much less and continues to be based on respect for the annual state plan. Between 1990 and 1992, the state distributed new irrigated lands to rural families, which allowed many farmers to enlarge their individual plots. The land area has reportedly more than doubled in a few years, from 55,000 to 133,000 hectares. Between 1993 and 1996, a second phase involved the allocation of lands to so-called independent farmers: in 2002, more than 5,000 private farms were inventoried in the country, occupying a total surface area of 81,000 hectares.[80] Nevertheless, these lands are not irrigated: each farmer therefore has the burden of building and maintaining his own irrigation system, which is extremely costly. A third and last phase involved the transformation of state farms into associations of lessors or cooperatives. Under this reform these "peasant associations" were instructed to distribute 90 percent of the arable land (1.5 million hectares) to the total rural population through a lease system. The 350,000 families that now lease the land therefore do not own it, but have the right and duty to work it. Farmers are obliged to complete the harvest, for which planned objectives increase from year to year and the output is bought by the state at prices well below international rates.[81] Although the state remains in control of the selling price, Turkmen farmers are supposed to be independent in acquiring their inputs. As during Soviet times, land plots total only a small area compared to cooperative farms (0.25 hectares compared to 4 hectares allocated to the tenant for growing wheat and cotton), but guarantee a significant share of farmers' revenues.[82]

Political and Social Stakes in the Agrarian Sector

The Central Asian lands were made fertile primarily through human-built irrigation systems, although sometimes from surface waters such as rivers. Across the region, with the exception of Kazakhstan, the pressures placed on the land are much stronger because birth rates remain high in the countryside, where about half the population of the four southern republics lives. In both Turkmenistan and Uzbekistan, a process of ruralization set in during the 1990s (already visible since the 1970s) as a consequence of the difficulties experienced by urban dwellers without work opportunities. Many people preferred to return and resettle in their home villages to work individual plots. Given the land scarcity, however, rural populations also suffer from very high unemployment rates, and the agrarian areas are severely overcrowded.

The situation of farmers differs in each Central Asian country. In Kyrgyzstan and Kazakhstan, farmers are relatively autonomous, and can sell their products at the world market price, but are prisoners to its fluctuations. Rural poverty has not been thwarted by the transition to the market economy. In the most authoritarian states, such as Turkmenistan, Uzbekistan, and Tajikistan, those farmers located at the very beginning of the supply chain benefit very little from their work, the fruits of which are absorbed by the state structure. Here also, rural livelihood is still caught within dynamics of pauperization.[83] The cooperatives serve as essential intermediaries between the state and farmers, and maintain minimal community infrastructure in villages. Production is planned, purchase prices are low and coercion is present at all levels of the system. The regional and local governors (*hokims*) have been made responsible for seeing to it that the plan is respected, even when climate conditions affect the harvest. They receive bribes if they register a higher quantity than that supplied by the farmers, and this, just as in Soviet times, results in the falsification of state statistics.

In Turkmenistan, the regime leaves farmers with little obvious choice. The declines in production experienced by the country have increased pressure on governors who, in turn, exert considerable pressure on farmers to ensure that they meet production quotas. Farmers derive little or no profit from their crops, but receive some compensation from the national company Turkmenpagta, which provides free inputs. In Uzbekistan, cotton is less profitable than other crops, but this varies by region.[84] Prices charged by the state assume that farmers produce at least 2.7 tons of cottonseed per hectare, while production averaged just over 2 tons in the middle of the last decade.[85] The 2002 reform, intended to liberalize state orders, changed little in practice. Under pressure from the IMF, the Uzbek government has begun to align its purchase price to the world market, although these efforts remain modest. Further, in a number of areas, particularly the provinces of Samarkand and Tashkent, the state has offset the increased purchase price of a ton of cotton by tripling property taxes. Moreover, farmers have little control over their earnings. Banks routinely confiscate state-paid monies are only pay fixed cash sums for the purchase of equipment or inputs, but not salaries and or profits. The money is regularly paid late and is not adjusted for inflation. In some cases, Uzbek farmers are paid in kind with oil or flour.[86]

In Tajikistan, although the situation is theoretically more liberalized, an unwritten rule required farmers to grow cotton on more than 80 percent of their plot. Many farmers who have grown other crops have been accused of breach of contract. A decree adopted in 2008, however, guarantees farmers the right to choose their crops, and it appears that cotton has dropped slightly below the 70 percent level.[87] As in Uzbekistan, laws are established to benefit the cotton magnates to the detriment of individual farmers. Amendments to the 2008 land code confirm the complicity of senior officials and landowners, since they can reclaim land from impoverished farmers who are forced to cede them in order to clear their debts. Each year, the Tajik state establishes a production plan that, although presented as a forecast or recommendation, is mandatory in practice. Poor storage and transportation conditions lead to deterioration in the quality of seed cotton, whereby it loses between 20 and 25 percent of its value at harvest. According to the World Bank, the average salary of a cotton farmer in 2004 was US$7 per month, while those who produced anything other than cotton earned eight to thirteen times more.[88] The main cotton-producing area in Tajikistan, Khatlon, with 30 percent of the population, has a 50 percent poverty rate. A witness reported that, in 2008, on a farm in Yavan comprising twenty-three families, the harvest would have yielded a total of no more than US$3,000 regardless of how good it was.[89] While farmers officially receive a salary, many of them are paid in kind with items such as cotton stalks that can be used for fuel.[90]

The work of children and adolescents in the cotton fields, especially during the harvest, is one of the biggest controversies in the Central Asian agricultural sector, especially in Uzbekistan, less so in Tajikistan and Turkmenistan.[91] Officially, the Uzbek regime explicitly prohibited child labor in 2008. However, it is unlikely that this law is being enforced, since without what essentially amounts to a free workforce, the harvest could not be completed and the state would not be able to pocket the profits.[92] Finally, the collapse of the Soviet system led to a rapid de-mechanization of the agricultural sector, aggravating human exploitation. Rising fuel prices, a lack of spare parts, and the problems involved in repairing Soviet tools do not foster technological development. In Turkmenistan, farmers are obliged to use machinery from the state firm Türkmenobahizmat, but the prices for its technical assistance are exorbitant. The Turkmen government spends huge sums to buy foreign equipment—the procurement of which generates many kickbacks—but it remains underutilized due to a lack of technological knowledge, spare parts, or money for upkeep.[93] Moreover, liberalization of input prices makes the use of machines more expensive, which encourages harvesting by hand. Facing high unemployment levels, Uzbekistan deliberately uses de-mechanization to ensure that jobs are available for the largest number of people possible, thus reducing risks of social tension: the share of the mechanized harvest fell from 57 percent in 1990, to 35 percent in 1993, and stands probably at less than 20 percent today.[94]

In border areas, farmers try to circumvent state obligations through smuggling. Uzbek farmers, for example, can sell their cotton in Kyrgyzstan for five times the price they can get at home. In 2003, the purchase price of a ton of cotton in Uzbekistan ranged from US$50 to US$80, while the price ranged between US$250 and US$320 on the Kyrgyz market. According to estimates by ICG, cotton trafficking constituted one-third of the production of the Suzak district near Jalalabad province.[95] Considerable traffic had also been noted along the Turkmen-Uzbek border, where the Uzbek farmers try to sell a portion of their output in exchange for fuel. This trade helps Turkmen farmers and local authorities, under pressure from state planning. During the harvest season, Uzbek farmers also seek to move toward the border with Kazakhstan to work for much more consistent wages.[96]

Although profits from cotton production are expected to help finance other parts of the economy, funds are largely diverted, amputating the expected benefits. In Uzbekistan, most cotton is sold to the state-controlled company Uzpakhtasanoat, which then sells it to government-approved import and export enterprises. Officially private, these companies are under the thumb of the ruling elites, especially the SNB (Committee for National Security). A large majority of local private cotton exporters are members of the ruling elites and manage their business through offshore companies registered in the British Virgin Islands and Cyprus.[97] The corruption of the political elites is equally apparent in Tajikistan. District governors negotiate directly with potential buyers and force farmers to grow cotton.[98] In some cases, governors even have direct financial interests in the local treatment plants.

Central Asia's rural population has to contend with very different realities, depending on the country. In Kazakhstan, public policies are concentrated on the modernization of large farms, the profitability of extensive exploitation, on improvement in distribution mechanisms, and on quality. The rural populations are the great losers of the Kazakh economic boom, from which they have not benefited, but their situation is less precarious than that of peasants in the neighboring countries. In Kyrgyzstan, the main issue is rather to avoid any aggravation of social tensions resulting from the dearth of land and the chronic rural poverty, especially in southern (Osh, Jalalabad, Batken) and mountainous regions (Naryn), and to help farmers to find their place in a largely privatized and deregulated market. In the three other states, Uzbekistan, Turkmenistan, and Tajikistan, several elements of the Soviet agrarian system were kept in place: individual plots of land or the small family farm prove more profitable than collective work because questions of production are left to the users, whose ability to adapt to the local market is greater. Like in the Soviet epoch, the productivity of the large inherited organizations of kolkhozes and sovkhozes is weak, and farmers invest almost solely in their private plots.[99]

The agricultural sector is and will stay a key element of social stability in Central Asia. Poverty alleviation strategies therefore need to be geared toward improving the living and working conditions of a still mostly rural population. Stopping the spiral of deindustrialization and the over-specialization in primary resources would mean, for instance, implementing state policies in favor of developing textile factories and agribusinesses. For the moment, only Turkmenistan and Kazakhstan have succeeded in setting up such logics of industrial modernization, the former in the textile industry, the latter in agribusiness. In addition, the state of agriculture is directly linked to food security, which is no longer assured in Tajikistan or Kyrgyzstan, and not even entirely in Turkmenistan and Uzbekistan, at the same time as risk factors such as demographic growth, drop in yields, and climate change are becoming more severe. Food security can only be ensured by providing international support for producing cereals and produce, by the revival of herding, and the improving of storage and distribution infrastructures, which have always been a weak link in Soviet and post-Soviet economies. Lastly, the extreme corruption of the state apparatuses linked to agriculture (cotton export networks, mafia banking structures, control by the groups in power of the prices of material inputs and mechanical products) aggravates feelings of injustice and sows the seeds of the loss of state credibility.

Notes

1. P. Gauchon, *Le monde: Manuel de géopolitique et de géoéconomie* (Paris: PUF, 2008), 728.

2. R. Deshpande, "Land Reform and Farm Restructuring in Central Asia: Progress and Challenges Ahead," in *Policy Reforms and Agriculture Development in Central Asia*, ed. S.C. Babu and S. Djalalov (New York: Springer, 2006), 131.

3. W. F. Schillinger, "Cropping Systems Research Needs in Uzbekistan: A Report to the World Bank," World Bank Reports, Washington, DC, 2003, 7.

4. S. C. Anninos, "Creating the Market: An Examination of Privatization Policies in Kazakhstan and Egypt" (PhD diss., New York University, 2000), 48.

5. R. Pomfret, "Using Energy Resources to Diversify the Economy: Agricultural Price and Distortion in Kazakhstan," *CASE Networks Studies and Analyses*, no. 335 (2007): 7.

6. Ibid.

7. Ministry of Agriculture of Kazakhstan, http://www.minagri.gov.kz/agro/?ID=5919.

8. See the Kazakhstan fact sheet from the CIA World Factbook, https://www.cia.gov/library/publications/the-world-factbook/geos/kz.html.

9. Pomfret, "Using Energy Resources," 8.

10. Gauchon, *Le monde*, 478.

11. See the Uzbekistan fact sheet from the CIA World Factbook, https://www.cia.gov/library/publications/the-world-factbook/geos/uz.html.

12. Ibid.

13. See the Turkmenistan fact sheet from the CIA World Factbook, https://www.cia.gov/library/publications/the-world-factbook/geos/tx.html.

14. See the Tajikistan fact sheet from the CIA World Factbook, https://www.cia.gov/library/publications/the-world-factbook/geos/ti.html.

15. Z. Lerman, "Tajikistan: An Overview of Land and Farm Structure Reforms," Hebrew University of Jerusalem Discussion Paper, no. 2.08, 2008, 2.

16. D. Gufronov and R. Mizobekova, "Podmochennyi urozhai: Na tadzhikskoe khlopkovodstvo obrushilas' novaia napast'—livni," *CentrAsia*, May 11, 2009, http://www.centrasia.ru/newsA.php?st=1242027900.

17. "The Curse of Cotton: Central Asia's Destructive Monoculture," International Crisis Group Asia Report, no. 93, February 2005, 6.

18. See the Kyrgyzstan fact sheet from the CIA World Factbook, https://www.cia.gov/library/publications/the-world-factbook/geos/kg.html.

19. K. D. Jones, "Land Privatization and Conflict in Central Asia: Is Kyrgyzstan a Model?," in *In the Tracks of Tamerlane: Central Asia's Paths to the Twenty-First Century*, ed. D. L. Burghart and T. Sabonis-Helf (Washington, DC: Center for Technology and National Security Policy, 2003), 262.

20. "General Information About Agro Sector of Kyrgyzstan," Central Asia, Business Project of Kyrgyzstan and Kazakhstan, http://www.rdiland.org/OURWORK/OurWork_Kyrgyzstan.html.

21. M. Spoor, "Cotton in Central Asia: 'Curse' or 'Foundation for Development'?," in *The Cotton Sector in Central Asia: Economic Policy and Development Challenges*, ed. D. Kandiyoti (London: School of Oriental and African Studies, 2007), 56.

22. "Cotton Marketing Systems in Eastern Europe and Central Asia," United Nations Conference on Trade and Development, http://www.unctad.org/infocomm/anglais/cotton/chain.htm.

23. On the global economic policies of Central Asia, see R. Pomfret, *The Central Asian Economies Since Independence* (Princeton, NJ: Princeton University Press, 2006).

24. K. Anderson, E. Valenzuela, and L. A. Jackson, "Recent and Prospective Adoption of Genetically Modified Cotton: A Global CGE Analysis of Economic Impacts," World Bank

Policy Research Working Paper, no. 3917, Washington, DC, May 2006, http://siteresources. worldbank.org/INTRANETTRADE/Resources/GMOcotton0206.pdf.

25. Ministry of Agriculture of Kazakhstan, http://www.minagri.gov.kz/index. php?option=com_content&view=category&layout=blog&id=128&Itemid=118&lang=ru.

26. G. Salimova, "Proizvodstvo khlopka v mire i Uzbekistane," *Birzha*, n.d., http://www. gazetabirja.uz/index.php?option=com_content&task=view&id=21556&Itemid=1.

27. FAO calculations by country and by commodity, http://faostat.fao.org/site/339/default. aspx.

28. For more information, see chapter 13.

29. FAO calculations of country rank by commodity, http://faostat.fao.org/site/339/default. aspx.

30. See the FAO calculations for 2009 and previous years, http://faostat.fao.org/site/339/ default.aspx.

31. Government of Tajikistan, *The Cotton Sector of Tajikistan. New Opportunities for the International Cotton Trade,* April 2007, http://siteresources.worldbank.org/INTTAJIKISTAN/ Resources/MB_300407_E.pdf.

32. R. Pomfret, "Turkmenistan: From Communism to Nationalism by Gradual Economic Reform," *Moct-Most*, no. 11 (2001): 165–76, here 168.

33. A. Saparmuratov and A. Nurbekov, *Focus on Seed Programs: The Seed Industry in Turkmenistan* (Aleppo, Syria: WANA Seed Network Secretariat, 2010), 3.

34. H. Hasanov, "Turkmen President: Use of Child Labor Unacceptable During Cotton Harvest," *Trend.az*, August 12, 2010, http://dailyme.com/story/2010081200001275/ brief-turkmen-president-child-labor-unacceptable.html.

35. "Cotton: World Markets and Trade," US Department of Agriculture Circular FOP 11-10, November 2010, 7.

36. "A Regional View of Wheat Markets and Food Security in Central Asia: With a Focus on Afghanistan and Tajikistan," Report of USAID, UKAID, and the World Food Program, Washington, DC, July 2011, 4.

37. M. Fumagalli, "Food Security in Central Asia: A Priority for Western Engagement," *Central Asia and Caucasus Analyst*, September 15, 2008, http://www.cacianalyst.org/?q=node/4958; Fumagalli, "The 'Food-Energy-Water' Nexus in Central Asia: Regional Implications of and the International Response to the Crises in Tajikistan," Europe-Central Asia Monitoring Policy Brief, no. 2, October 2008.

38. See, for instance, J. F. Linn, "The Compound Water-Energy-Food Crisis Risks in Central Asia: Update on an International Response," Brookings Institution Commentary, August 12, 2008, http://www.brookings.edu/opinions/2008/0812_central_asia_linn.aspx; and the July 2008 UN World Food Program Emergency Food Security Assessments in Urban and Rural Areas of Tajikistan, http://documents.wfp.org/stellent/groups/public/documents/ ena/wfp188192.pdf.

39. J. Lillis, "Kazakhstan: Grain Exports Ban Stokes Inflation Fears Elsewhere in Central Asia," *Eurasianet*, April 16, 2008, http://www.eurasianet.org/departments/insight/articles/ eav041608.shtml.

40. A. Gareginyan, "In Half a Year Wheat Price Has Redoubled," *ArmInfo*, January 19, 2011, http://www.gab-ibn.com/IMG/pdf/Ar24-_In_half_a_year_wheat_price_has_redoubled.pdf.

41. Authors' fieldwork in Turkmenistan and Uzbekistan, March 2008.

42. FAO calculations for wheat in 2009, http://faostat.fao.org/site/339/default.aspx.

43. K. Nurtazina, "Moratorium on Russian Grain Exports Jolts Kazakhstani Wheat Market," *Centralasiaonline*, September 7, 2010, http://centralasiaonline.com/en_GB/articles/caii/features/ main/2010/09/07/feature-02.

44. Saparmuratov and Nurbekov, *Focus on Seed Programs*, 3.

45. "Prazdnik pshenitsy otmetiat v Turkmenistane," *Gundogar*, July 18, 2010, http://www. gundogar.org/?0225000000000000001106201007000#9760.

46. "Turkmenistan: State Hails Food Self-Sufficiency, but Many Say Claim Is Overblown," *Asia News*, July 26, 2010, http://www.asianews.it/news-en/State-hails-food-self-sufficiency,-but-many-say-claim-is-overblown-19037.html.

47. "Turkmen Surplus Appropriation System," *Chronicles of Turkmenistan*, July 13, 2009, http://www.chrono-tm.org/en/?id=1115.

48. See the FAO Turkmenistan fact sheet, http://www.fao.org/countries/55528/en/tkm/.

49. "The Curse of Cotton," 9.

50. In SOAS. 2010 (November). *What Has Changed? Progress in eliminating the use of forced child labour in the cotton harvests of Uzbekistan and Tajikistan.* University of London: Centre for Contemporary Central Asia and the Caucasus, School of Oriental and African Studies; World Bank *PSIA Summary – Tajikistan Cotton Sector, Reform*, 2004, http://go.worldbank.org/NJD5VBE740.

51. Spoor, "Cotton in Central Asia," 54–74.

52. FAO calculations by country and by commodity for 2009 and previous years, http://faostat.fao.org/site/339/default.aspx.

53. Business Monitor International, *Kazakhstan Agribusiness Report Q3 2012*, Industry Report & Forecasts Series, June 2012, 7.

54. FAO calculations for wheat in 2009, http://faostat.fao.org/site/339/default.aspx.

55. D. Prikhodko, "Grain Markets in Kazakhstan, the Russian Federation, and Ukraine," Report of the Food and Agriculture Organization of the United Nations, New York, May 2009, 14.

56. Z. Ergasheva, "To Ensure Food Security Tajikistan Has to Import 250,000 Tons of Grains from Kazakhstan," *News.tj*, September 3, 2010, news.tj/en/printpdf/79841.

57. "Russian, Ukrainian, Kazakh World Grain Market Share Will Rise to 30%, According to OECD," *Global AG Investing*, December 8, 2011, http://www.globalaginvesting.com/news_story.php?id=26293.

58. R. Paxson, "Kazakh Grain Looks Beyond Drought to New Markets," *Reuters*, September 01, 2010, http://www.forexyard.com/en/news/FEATURE-Kazakh-grain-looks-beyond-drought-to-new-markets-2010-09-01T091815Z.

59. "KazAgro Investing 9 Billion Tenge to Build Grain Storage Facilities in 2010," *Interfax News*, June 16, 2010, http://www.interfax.co.uk/kazakhstan-general-news-bulletins-in-english/kazagro-investing-9-billion-tenge-to-build-grain-storage-facilities-in-2010/.

60. Gauchon, *Le monde*, 619.

61. "Kazakhstan—Beef Production Booming," *Meat Trade News Daily*, October 9, 2010, http://www.meattradenewsdaily.co.uk/news/041010/kazakhstan___beef_production_booming_.aspx.

62. Business Monitor International, *Kazakhstan Agribusiness Report Q3 2012*, 7.

63. G. Ia. Guseva, "Razvitie rynka miasa v Kazakhstane—Mnenie uchenogo," *Kazakh Zerno*, March 21, 2011, http://www.kazakh-zerno.kz/index.php?option=com_content&view=article&id=33472%3A2011-03-16-08-34-30&catid=49%3Apopular&Itemid=1.

64. M. Spoor and O. Visser, "The State of Agrarian Reform in the Former Soviet Union," *Europe-Asia Studies* 53, no. 6 (2001): 885–901; Z. Lerman, C. Csáki, and G. Feder, *Agriculture in Transition: Land Policies and Evolving Farm Structures in Post-Soviet Countries* (Lanham, MD: Lexington Books, 2004).

65. T. Trevisani, *Land and Power in Khorezm: Farmers, Communities, and the State in Uzbekistan's Decollectivisation* (Berlin: LIT, 2010).

66. C. Humphrey, *The Unmaking of Soviet Life: Everyday Economies After Socialism* (Ithaca, NY: Cornell University Press, 2002).

67. On agriculture reforms in Kyrgyzstan, see P. C. Bloch, "Kyrgyzstan: Almost Done, What Next?" *Problems of Post-Communism* 49, no. 1 (2002): 53–62; K. Akramov and N. Omuraliev, "Institutional Change, Rural Services, and Agricultural Performance in Kyrgyzstan," International Food Policy Research Institute (IFPRO) Discussion Paper, no. 00904, 2009.

68. K. D. Jones, "Land Privatization and Conflict in Central Asia: Is Kyrgyzstan a Model?," in Burghart and Sabonis-Helf, *In the Tracks of Tamerlane*, 262.

69. See, for example, A. Khamidov, "Kyrgyzstan-Tajikistan: Clashes on Volatile Border Growing Vicious," *Eurasianet,* April 20, 2011, http://www.eurasianet.org/node/63336.

70. S. Jacquesson, *Pastoréalismes: Anthropologie historique des processus d'intégration chez les Kirghiz du Tian Shan intérieur* (Wiesbaden: Reichert, 2010).

71. J. Nazpary, *Post-Soviet Chaos: Violence and Dispossession in Kazakhstan* (London: Pluto Press, 2002).

72. Pomfret, "Using Energy Resources," 15.

73. Ibid., 14.

74. A. Ilkhamov, "Divided Economy: Kolkhozes vs. Peasant Subsistence Farms in Uzbekistan," *Central Asia Monitor* 4 (2000): 5–14; Z. Lerman, "Land Reform in Uzbekistan," in *Land Reform in the Former Soviet Union and in Eastern Europe*, ed. S. Wegren (London: Routledge, 1998), 136–61.

75. "The Curse of Cotton," 3.

76. T. Trevisani, "The Emerging Actor of Decollectivization in Uzbekistan: Private Farming between Newly Defined Political Constraints and Opportunities," in Kandiyoti, *The Cotton Sector in Central Asia*, 151–74.

77. A. S. Salimov et al., *Reorganizatsiia kooperativnykh (shirkatnykh) sel'skokhoziaistvennykh predpriiatii v fermerskie khoziaistva* (Tashkent: Center for Economic Research, 2004), quoted in "The Curse of Cotton," 3.

78. "Desk Study: Rural Sector Reform and Legal Aid in Tajikistan," *KasWag AgriConsulting Worldwide*, June 2008.

79. "The Curse of Cotton," 7.

80. Z. Lerman and I. Stanchin, "Institutional Changes in Turkmenistan's Agriculture: Impacts on Productivity and Rural Incomes," *Eurasian Geography and Economics* 45, no. 1 (2004): 61.

81. Ibid., 60–72. More in Peyrouse, *Turkmenistan*, 143–48.

82. Lerman and Stanchin, "Institutional Changes in Turkmenistan's Agriculture," 64.

83. M. Spoor, "Cotton and Rural Livelihoods in Former Soviet Central Asia," in *The Political Economy of Rural Livelihoods in Transition Economies: Land, Peasants, and Rural Poverty in Transition* (London: Routledge, 2009).

84. Author's interviews with Uzbek experts in Jizzak and Termez, March 2008.

85. "The Curse of Cotton," 4.

86. "White Gold: The True Cost of Cotton; Uzbekistan, Cotton, and the Crushing of a Nation," Report of the Environmental Justice Foundation, London, 2009, 16.

87. D. Rowe, "Agrarian Adaptations in Tajikistan: Land Reform, Water, and Law," *Central Asian Survey* 29, no. 2 (2010): 189–204; see also D. L. Stern, "Tajik Farmers Enslaved Where Cotton Is King," *Farmblogs*, 15 October 2008, http://farmblogs.blogspot.com/2008/10/tajik-farmers-enslaved-where-cotton-is.html.

88. "The Curse of Cotton," 9.

89. Gufronov and Mizobekova, "Podmochennyi urozhai."

90. Kh. Umarov and M. Gafurov, "Finansovyi rynok i khlopkovaia problema," *East Time*, November 11, 2008, http://www.easttime.ru/analitic/1/10/524.html.

91. D. Kandiyoti, ed., *Invisible to the World? The Dynamics of Forced Child Labour in the Cotton Sector of Uzbekistan* (London: School of Oriental and African Studies, 2009).

92. "Uzbekistan: Children Continue to Work on Cotton Fields despite Official Ban," *Fergana. news*, September 16, 2009, http://enews.fergananews.com/article.php?id=2466.

93. "The Curse of Cotton," 11.

94. R. Leroi, "La filière du coton en Asie centrale: Le poids de l'héritage," *Le Courrier des Pays de l'Est*, no. 1027 (2002): 44.

95. "The Curse of Cotton," 5.

96. Authors' fieldwork at the Uzbek-Kazakh border, March 2008.

97. Authors' interviews on KNB corruption with anonymous Uzbek experts, Tashkent, March 17–18, 2008.

98. H. Boboyorov, "Personal Networks of Agricultural Knowledge in the Cotton-growing Communities of Southern Tajikistan," *Demokratizatsiya. The Journal of Post-Soviet Democratization*, no. 4 (2012): 409–435.

99. Deshpande, "Land Reform and Farm Restructuring," 133.

9

Hydrocarbons

At the Core of Central Asia's International Strategies

Since the end of the 1960s, the rhythm of world discoveries of large hydrocarbons deposits slowed down. A number of the new deposits being explored have challenging environments (e.g., the Arctic) and require costly technological feats. Throughout the first decade of the twenty-first century, the planet consumed four times more reserves than those it acquired, whereas in the 1950s this ratio was inverse and about ten to one.[1] However, the oil and gas industry is in the throes of rapid transition. New technology is unlocking unconventional reserves that shift the geography of production and reconfigure import dependencies. The available resources in Central Asia are welcome and represent a pontentially considerable economic advantage for the region. They constitute a formidable asset, in a context where the growing demand for hydrocarbons among rising powers—China, India, Brazil—is transforming the market. In addition, new technologies make it possible to secure a profit on reserves that, some decades earlier, would probably have been abandoned, and to exploit the deposits in a more rational way: currently, on a global scale, between 30 and 35 percent of the oil present in a deposit is exploited, but studies estimate that technological advances will enable as much as half to be extracted in future.

The growth of the hydrocarbon sector is intrinsically linked to the political independence of the Central Asian states, and their role on the international scene. Some reserves were already known about in the Soviet period: the Turkmen and Uzbek gas reserves were modestly exploited, though the Kazakh oil reserves were not, since priority was given to West Siberian sites, which afforded easier extraction, as well as to Azeri oil, which had already been exploited since the beginning of the twentieth century. Central Asian hydrocarbons have great potential, but it is costly to realize. The deposits can sometimes be difficult to access, like those situated in the Ust-Yurt Plateau and the Aral Sea. Some are also environmentally sensitive, like the Kashagan deposit in the Caspian Sea. And others involve unresolved legal conflicts, like the Turkmen offshore deposits, over which there are disputes with Azerbaijan and Iran. Moreover, extraction is technically complex: on most sites the gas is associated with oil; the volume of sulfur and carbon dioxide is large; and the deposits are deep, with high pressure levels. Without the requisite cutting-edge technology and relevant knowledge, the Central Asian national companies are unable to do the work alone, and the Russian companies are less qualified in this regard than the large international majors. The foreign investment necessary for the exploitation of the sites amounts to tens of billions of dollars: the exploitation of the Kashagan oil field in Kazakhstan soared to US$136 billion, making it the costliest project anywhere in the world.[2] Lacking capital and know-how, the Central Asian states are often reliant on foreign partners to develop their hydrocarbons reserves. They then have to contend with the geopolitical game that goes along with the control of resources, although they have been able to develop logics that play external actors off each other.

Reserves and National Companies' Strategies

With almost forty billion barrels of proven reserves, Kazakhstan possesses 3 percent of world oil reserves.[3] It has the second-largest oil reserves as well as the second-largest oil production among the former Soviet republics after Russia. A few years from now, with the exploitation of the gigantic site of Kashagan, the country will come to dominate oil production in the Caspian Basin area, with about 55 percent of the total, followed by Azerbaijan with 32 percent, whereas Russia and Turkmenistan will both produce about 13 percent each.[4] This Caspian production will not by any means replace the Middle East in its role as the world's largest oil supplier, but it will play an important role outside of OPEC, in particular for neighboring countries such as China, and potentially also for consumers like Japan and the Indian subcontinent.

Close to three-quarters of the oil from Kazakhstan is situated in the western regions, which are dominated by three large deposits. The first is the offshore deposit of Kashagan (about thirteen billion barrels) situated close to Atyrau; it is the fifth-largest deposit in the world and the largest oil discovery of the last thirty years. Alone it represents close to half the oil wealth of the country. Its full exploitation, originally planned for 2008, was pushed back to 2011, and then 2013 and finally 2018–2019 (but with a first-phase production in 2013), because the technological challenges turned out to be more complex than first thought.[5] The second deposit is that of Tengiz (about six to nine billion barrels). Discovered in 1979, it is situated onshore on the northeast banks of the Caspian. Tengiz is currently the main site of exploitation in Kazakhstan, and in 2010 produced 560,000 barrels per day.[6] The third site of Karachaganak, also onshore, was discovered around the same time and is situated close to the Russian border. It is mainly rich in gas, but also in oil (eight to nine billion barrels), and has an estimated production capacity of 250,000 barrels per day.[7] In addition, there are many smaller sites (around 200), located in the Kazakh part of the Caspian Sea, in the Atyrau, Mangystau, and Kzyl-Orda regions.

The other Central Asian states are distinctly less oil wealthy. Uzbekistan reportedly has close to 600 million barrels of proven reserves, distributed across more than 170 sites. The main sites are concentrated in the regions of Bukhara and Khiva, which account for 70 percent of oil production. The Ferghana Valley has approximately 15 percent of the inventoried deposits. New sites are being explored in the southwest of the country (Kokdumalak, Shurtan, Olan, Urgin, and South-Tandirchi), as well as on the Ust-Yurt Plateau.[8] The Uzbek authorities also hope to develop their oil shale deposits, estimated at 340 billion barrels. Turkmenistan allegedly has amounts of reserves similar to those of its neighbor, with a little less than 600 million proven barrels, but it has greater chances of discovering new offshore deposits in its section of the Caspian Sea, which could amount to as much as 1.5 million barrels. As is often the case in terms of resources, Kyrgyzstan and Tajikistan are the poor cousins of the region: the former supposedly has proven oil reserves of about forty million barrels, situated mainly in deposits in the Ferghana Valley; and the latter of twelve million barrels, located mostly in the Sogd region.

As with oil, the current revolution in the global gas industry is likely to have collateral implications for Central Asia. Gas is the object of growing desires, particularly in the context of shrinking oil reserves and partial reconsiderations of the nuclear industry after the March 2011 accident in Japan. The growing potential for exploitation of unconventional reserves elsewhere places less of a premium on getting Central Asian supplies. But, as is the case with all extractive resources, the growing Asian demand is the main economic stimulus for the region.

In the natural gas sector, Turkmenistan has managed to steal the show from Kazakhstan, but the precise estimate of its reserves is difficult to arrive at. The first president, Saparmurat Niyazov, continued the Soviet tradition of considering hydrocarbon reserves a state secret and refused all international audits. British Petroleum (BP) estimated the Turkmen reserves at close to 2,700 billion m^3 (bcm), placing the country eleventh in the world, whereas the authorities claimed as much as 26,000 bcm. Niyazov's successor, Gurbanguly Berdymukhammedov, ordered an audit from the British firm Gaffney, Cline, and Associates, which at the end of 2008 announced that the deposits of Yolotan and Osman could contain between 4 and 14 trillion m^3, which would make it the second-largest deposit in the world.[9] BP subsequently readjusted its calculations to 8.6 trillion m^3.[10]

Out of these proven reserves of 8 trillion m^3, three-quarters are believed to be contained in the main deposit of Osman-South Yolotan in the Mary region. The remaining quarter is distributed between the deposits of Dauletabat-Donmez, close to the Iranian border and about a hundred kilometers from Afghanistan, and those of Bagtyiarlyk and Samandepe on the right bank of the Amu Darya. To them must be added the still poorly known deposit of Yashlar, situated in the basin of the Murghab River, whose reserves are estimated at 765 bcm. Discovered in Soviet times, the Dauletabat-Donmez fields were estimated to contain about half of the country's reserves before the discovery of Osman-South Yolotan. Under exploration since 2006, South Yolotan allegedly contains reserves greater than Russia's largest deposit, Shtokman, in the central part of the Russian sector of the Barents Sea. In 2007, the state-run company Turkmengeologia announced its discovery of the geological continuation of South Yolotan, Osman.[11] The most promising deposits are therefore not offshore, as they are in Azerbaijan or Kazakhstan (even

Table 9.1

The Oil Sector in Central Asia in 2010

	Kazakhstan	Kyrgyzstan	Tajikistan	Turkmenistan	Uzbekistan
Production (thousands of barrels per day)	1,757	0.95*	0.22*	216	87
Share of the world reserves	2.9%	less than 0.05%	less than 0.05%	less than 0.05%	less than 0.05%
Consumption (thousands of barrels per day)	262	24*	13*	125	104
Net export-import	1,299*	–23.05*	–12.78*	105.15*	–26.12*
Proven reserves (billion barrels)	39	0.04*	0.01*	0.6	0.6
Refinery capacity	345*	10*	0	237*	222*

Note: * = 2009 Numbers

Source: Table based on US Energy Information Administration (http://www.eia.gov/) and "BP Statistical Review of World Energy 2011," June 2011.

Table 9.2

The Gas Sector in Central Asia in 2010

	Kazakhstan	Turkmenistan	Uzbekistan
Proven reserves in trillion cubic meters	1.8	8.6	1.6
Share of world reserves	1%	4.3%	0.8%
Annual production	33.6	42.4	59.1
Share of world production	1.1%	1.8%	1.8%
Domestic consumption	25.3	22.6	45.5

Note: * = 2009 Numbers
Source: "BP Statistical Review of World Energy," 20–22.

though deposits are also being explored in the Turkmen part of the Caspian Sea, especially Magtymguly), but onshore in the country's east.

Uzbekistan, for its part, has estimated reserves of 1.6 trillion m³, a figure that does not take into account the still poorly known deposits of Ust-Yurt and the Aral Sea. Its main gas sites currently under exploration or exploitation are situated in the region of Kashkadarya (Gazli, Shurtan, Pamuk, Khauzak) as well as around Bukhara. The largest site in operation, the Boyangora-Gadzhak site, was discovered in the 1970s in the Surkhandarya region on the border with Afghanistan. Since 2005, gas production has slowed, and the government has become aware of the need to open its market to foreign investors, declaring that only one-quarter of the potential resources are being exploited.[12] The deposits of the Ust-Yurt Plateau and the Aral Sea seem promising, as do those of the Kandym-Kauzhak-Shady site, whose reserves are estimated at 100 bcm.[13]

Kazakhstan, according to BP, has about 1.8 trillion m³ of proven reserves, but the Kazakh authorities claim 2.5 trillion m³, half of which are contained in the Karachaganak deposit.[14] A modest producer, the country only became an exporter in 2008. There are many specific factors that impede the export of Kazakh gas. This gas is mainly "associated gas" (gas from oil sites), which requires special extraction techniques. About half of it must be sent back to the layers in order to maintain pressure and optimize the oil extraction, but the state company KazMunayGas is developing technologies to enable it to reduce this quantity. In addition, the country must contend with important regional differences in terms of access to gas, since no domestic gas pipeline links the productive regions of the northwest to the consumer regions of the south, which have to import their gas from Uzbekistan. The development of the Amangeldy deposit is designed to remedy these internal imbalances. Lastly, domestic consumption is booming (like Russia, Kazakhstan promotes provision of gas to city), thus reducing short-term export prospects. However, Astana is banking on increasing exports, since the Karachaganak deposit alone is forecast to produce about 25 bcm in the second half of the 2010s, after investments of US$10 billion.[15] The authorities also hope for transit growth, since Turkmen and Uzbek gas bound for Russia and China is forced to cross Kazakh territory.

Tajikistan and Kyrgyzstan are once again the worst off: they are said to have 200 bcm of reserves each, located mainly in the Khatlon region (Khoja Sartez, Qizil Tumshuq) for the former, and in areas difficult for drilling for the latter. However, in late 2010 Gazprom announced that its exploration of the Sarikamysh field, close to Dushanbe, had led to the discovery of a deposit of about sixty bcm, which is the equivalent of fifty years' worth of domestic consumption, and which could, in future, dramatically change the givens of Tajikistan's relationship of dependency on its Uzbek neighbor.[16]

The state of the reserves does not provide an accurate picture of the volumes available for export, which also depend on domestic consumption. The Kazakh oil sector seems set for exponential growth, with production doubling between 2000 and 2008. In 2009, Kazakhstan extracted seventy-eight million tons of oil, and ought to produce more than ninety in 2013 thanks to the two sites of Tengiz and Karachaganak.[17] Thereafter the figures should skyrocket with the giant Kashagan field coming online. The country first planned to produce at least three million barrels per day in 2020,[18] but then announced more realistic forecasts at about two and a half million.[19] Kazakhstan is only placed sixteenth among world exporters, but full development of its major oil fields will make it one of the world's top five oil producers within the next few decades.[20]

In the gas sector, Turkmen production has had difficulties taking off, due to a lack of investments, a dearth of technical competencies, and logistical problems. In the first years of the twenty-first century, production jumped from thirty to forty bcm per year to about sixty-five bcm in 2008 (with only about twenty bcm used for domestic consumption), but collapsed to only forty-two bcm in 2009.[21] It should nonetheless take off in the next decade, allowing Ashgabat to cash in on its future as a "Kuwait of Central Asia."[22] It hopes to sell 125 bcm per year by 2015, and close to 200 bcm by 2020, a prospect that seems somewhat unrealistic given the current conditions of the deposits. Business Monitor International forecasts a production of 95 bcm by 2016, and 150 bcm by 2020.[23] The country is theoretically obliged to honor three export contracts: one with Iran, signed in 1997, whose volume has been increased to 20 bcm in 2010; another with China, signed in 2006, that envisages the export of about 30 bcm, a figure that rose to 65 bcm in 2011; and a third with Russia, signed in 2003, according to which Gazprom is set to receive up to 80 bcm over the next 25 years. In principle, then, the country has guaranteed export markets for an amount of up to 160 bcm, although in reality, production is lower.

Uzbek production has slowly increased to almost 60 bcm in 2009.[24] *Business Monitor International* forecasts a production growth to 86 bcm by 2016 and 105 bcm by 2020.[25] But unlike its Turkmen neighbor, Uzbekistan consumes 80 percent of its gas production, leaving only about ten to fifteen billion m^3 for export: a small share is earmarked for Central Asian neighbors, and the remainder is either bought by Gazprom, or used to feed the pipeline to China. Until the Aral and Ust-Yurt deposits become operational, Tashkent cannot hope to export more than 20 bcm, about 45 bcm by 2020, and has little room to play with in terms of distribution routes.

Figure 9.1

Gas Production in Kazakhstan, Turkmenistan, and Uzbekistan, 1999–2010
(in billion cubic meters)

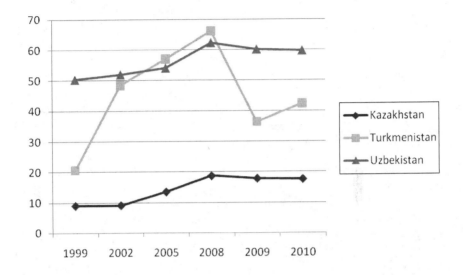

Source: "BP Statistical Review of World Energy 2011," 22.

In order to increase export capacities, the authorities have set in place programs to reduce domestic gas consumption in favor of coal and other types of energy. For its part, Kazakhstan is only just embarking on its future as a gas power. In 2010, its production was 33 bcm, but it is set to increase rapidly to as much as 70 bcm by 2015, and to twice that by 2020, once Tengiz and Karachaganak are operating at full output.

Considered to be a curse by some resource literature, these mineral riches are seen to bear political and social risks. Like other rent economies, Central Asia is distinguished by difficulties associated with redistributing the manna of foreign currency. Hydrocarbons development has paradoxical consequences, such as a deepening of social and regional inequalities; a bolstering of weak institutions; and an absence of real legal constraints or of juridical mechanisms to guarantee that economic decisions are motivated by the public good.[26] However, the governments choose management structures that are part of the historical and political contexts specific to each country. As Pauline Jones Luong and Erika Weinthal state, "mineral-rich states are cursed not by their wealth but rather by the structure of ownership they choose to manage their mineral wealth."[27] These choices are especially important, since today the once obvious idea of ongoing state withdrawal from the extraction sector is being questioned.

On a worldwide scale, four of the five largest oil companies and twelve of the twenty largest oil producers belong either entirely or in the majority to sovereign organizations.[28] Theories according to which the appropriation of deposits upstream was only secondary, since the real opportunities were to be found in the mastery of technologies and having a stranglehold on the downstream sectors of transformation and distribution, have been increasingly questioned: owing to the reduced number of deposits, the desires of large private companies must henceforth be built upon a solid partnership with states, since it is states that control the upstream sectors.[29]

Two models of ownership dominate in Central Asia. At independence, Uzbekistan and Turkmenistan retained the ownership structure inherited from the Soviet regime, and so state companies—Uzbekneftegaz for the former, Turkmengaz and Turkmenoil for the latter—manage the entire chain of production from extraction to distribution. The head of state makes the strategic choices, while his intimates control sections of the chain and ensure contracts are signed to benefit their own private interest. The locating of foreign operators is openly restricted by non-conducive legislation as well as a need to have direct access to political circles. Beginning around 2005, Tashkent tried to relax its system, cognizant of the fact that it lacked foreign investment for exploring and exploiting its deposits, and Ashgabat has also been more receptive to foreign propositions since 2007.[30]

At the start of the 1990s, Kazakhstan, by contrast, opted for a system of private foreign ownership. However, the presence of the international majors has not brought real transparency of decision-making structures in matters of energy, although transparency in spending decisions improved after the turn of the century.[31] Moreover, the sector remains very closely linked to the private interests of the Nazarbayev family and their close circle. The Kazakh government has delayed transforming the national company KazMunayGas into a fully fledged competent state holding like SOCAR in Azerbaijan, and today is trying to shore up shares for it in all exploited deposits. It imposed much stricter rules on foreign companies, reduced excessive value added tax (VAT) exemptions, and reserved the right to cancel a contract if a foreign investor did not respect its commitments, especially in terms of environmental or corporate social responsibility. This recentralization has also reinforced political control over KazMunayGas, which has been placed under the supervision of the president's son-in-law, Timur Kulibayev.[32]

Existing Distribution Routes

For the Central Asian states, the exploitation of new gas and oil deposits constitutes only one plank of their energy policy: the second plank is more complex and necessitates finding profitable export routes that do not entail large extra costs. In terms of the transport of hydrocarbons, Central Asia enjoys few advantages: the globalization of transport networks and of distribution has heightened the growing littoralization of industrial activities. The geographical position of a producer state in relation to these networks is therefore a determining factor in the hierarchy of economic spaces. Though

Central Asia, located at the intersection of several large importers such as China, India, and the European Union, is able to some extent to limit the negative consequences of its landlocked nature, it will never replace the Gulf countries in terms of combining resources and maritime transport (today 75 percent of all oil is transported by sea).[33] The transport of hydrocarbons from isolated continental deposits thus constitutes a challenge in terms of the balance between extraction and transport costs. The construction of pipelines is also being viewed with caution by investors, who are concerned by the volatility of consumption countries, especially as new technologies such as liquefied natural gas (LNG) heighten the flexibility of the global market.

The financial godsend represented by the export of hydrocarbons to the world market does not encourage the upkeep of regional exchanges between Central Asian countries, which are used to paying for energy at low prices and whose enterprises are often insolvent. Since the 1990s, hydrocarbons trade between Russia and Central Asia, as well as between the Central Asian countries themselves has been drastically modified. In 2008, the export of Central Asian gas to Russia exceeded Soviet levels, whereas the import of Russian oil by Central Asia and the exchanges among the five countries remain very limited: today Uzbekistan exports five times less gas to Kyrgyzstan, Tajikistan, and Kazakhstan than in 1990, and imports only very small quantities of oil from Kazakhstan, while Turkmenistan no longer participates in the Central Asian energy market at all.[34] With domestic consumption rising, the increasing emphasis on exporting oil and gas is aggravating the recurrent energy crises in the two weakest states, Kyrgyzstan and Tajikistan, while South Kazakhstan and Uzbekistan also experience regular, although less severe, energy shortfalls.

Russia still dominates the export routes of Central Asian oil. Prior to 1997, Kazakhstan was obliged to export all its production via the only existing Soviet oil pipeline, the Atyrau-Samara, today controlled by Transneft. In 2001, the inauguration of the Caspian Pipeline Consortium (CPC), which links the deposit of Tengiz to the port of Novorossiisk on the shores of the Black Sea, enabled Kazakhstan to enter global markets and to reduce the transit prices asked for by Transneft. The first private oil pipeline to cross Russia, 19 percent of the CPC is controlled by Kazakhstan, 31 percent by Transneft, and 22.5 percent by Chevron ExxonMobil, while Rosneft and Lukoil have had their share increased at the expense of Western investors.[35] Political pressures surrounding the CPC reemerged in 2005, as oil extracted from Tengiz was blocked at Moscow's behest. From 2007, Transneft, which has a monopoly over oil pipelines in Russia, took over management of Russian government interests in the CPC and strived to gain control of it.[36] At the end of 2008, Russia reluctantly accepted the doubling of the capacity of the CPC (from 730,000 barrels per day to 1.4 million, that is, from thirty-two to sixty-seven million tons per year) by 2014 to contend with the oil growth from Tengiz,[37] but the Kazakh authorities and the international consortiums are concerned by the possibility that Russia will cause new delays. The Atyrau-Samara oil pipeline has also been modernized by Rosneft, giving it enough capacity to export 600,000 barrels per day (twenty-five million tons per year), more than half of which comes from Kazakhstan. However, once Tengiz reaches maximum production and

Gas and Oil Pipelines in Central Asia

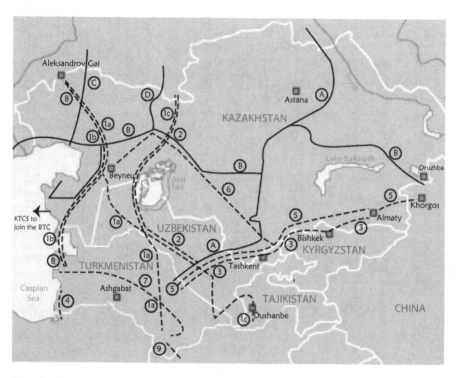

Gas pipelines
1a, 1b, and 1c Central Asia-Center
2 Bukhara-Urals
3 Bukhara-Tashkent-Bishkek-Almaty
4 Turkmen-Iranian
5 Sino-Central Asian

6 Kazakh-Chinese (under
   construction)
7 East-West (under construction)
8 Peri-Caspian (project, to run
   parallel to 1a)
9 TAPI (project)

Oil pipelines
A Chardzhou-Bukhara-Shymkent-Pavlodar-Omsk
B Caspian Sea-Dushanzi (Sino-Kazakh)
C Atyrau-Samara
D Atyrau-Orsk

exploitation of Kashagan gets underway, the two oil pipelines traversing Russia will turn out to be insufficient for Kazakh export needs.[38]

In 2006, Kazakhstan opened its first export route able to bypass Russia, the Atasu-Alashankou pipeline to Xinjiang, with an export capacity of ten million tons per year. It is part of a bigger structure, namely the gigantic oil pipeline linking the shores of the Caspian Sea to China, whose Kazakh section has been constructed in three parts. The first connects the deposit of Kenkiyak to Atyrau; the second the pumping station and the railway terminal of Atasu, in the region of Karaganda, to the Sino-Kazakh border post of Dostyk-Alashankou; while the third links Kenkiyak to the Kumkol fields via the town of Aralsk,. Once the third section is operational, which is case since the end of 2011, the first section can be reversed from west to east to enable the continuous transit of Caspian oil toward China.[39] China will thus have the advantage of an oil pipeline of more than 3,000 kilometers in length connecting the shores of the Caspian to the Dostyk-Alashankou border post, with a capacity for increase to twenty million tons a year.[40]

Though this pipeline is the very embodiment of success in Sino-Kazakh oil sector cooperation, its dimensions nonetheless remain modest and it by no means resolves the problems that both Beijing and Astana are faced with. On the Chinese side, the pipeline's capacity will represent only 5 percent of the country's needs (twenty out of four hundred million tons). After costly optimization works, a volume of forty million tons may be reached, but this will in any case be limited compared with China's real needs and will not undermine the domination of the Middle East as its main supplier.[41] On the Kazakh side, the volumes transported by the pipeline will also remain low: in 2008, they amounted to a mere 10 percent of Kazakh exports (6.3 out of sixty-two million tons).[42] Once production at Kashagan is underway, Astana will not be content with the Chinese line, but will require further export prospects, whether a second oil pipeline to the east, or to new destinations.

In 2007, Kazakh oil exports, which amounted to 1.2 million barrels per day, were distributed in the following directions: half, an amount of 620,000 barrels per day, transited through Russia via the CPC; 408,000 were channeled through different Russian pipelines and railways; 80,000 went to Iran; and 85,000 went to China.[43] Transit via Russia, then, continues to make up the majority of exports. Should its share, as is likely, reduce, Kazakhstan's possibilities for diversification will none-theless remain limited. For Uzbekistan, the leeway is even narrower, since the only operational pipelines are those that remain from Soviet times, which are rather run-down. The totality of Uzbek oil exports is bought by Russia, with the exception of small quantities that are sold to Kyrgyzstan and Tajikistan. Since there are no plans for alternative oil pipelines for the time being, the only means for Uzbek oil to avoid going through Russia would be to go via road transport, railway, or barge. Uzbekistan's situation of double landlockedness is therefore highly disadvantageous, whereas Kazakhstan and Turkmenistan can take advantage of their Caspian shores to develop export via tankers.

In the gas sector, the export capacities of the Central Asian countries are more diversified.[44] They are still largely under Moscow's control, even though Russia is losing influence. In 1995, Turkmenistan terminated Gazprom's monopoly by building a gas pipeline with Iran to link its large Korpetdje deposit to Kurd Köy. This section could potentially form part of a Turkmen-Iranian-Turkish gas pipeline, a project blocked by the American embargo against Tehran. Up until 2004, Turkmenistan had only delivered four bcm of gas to Iran per year, but this figure reached eight billion in 2006 and is supposed to nearly double to fourteen bcm in the years to come. Moreover, a new gas pipeline of only thirty kilometers, linking the Dauleta-bat field to the Serakhs border post and then to the Iranian town of Hangeran, was inaugurated in 2010, with a delivery capacity of six bcm per year.[45] The decision to build it was taken in April 2009 after Gazprom halted its Turkmen imports when a technical incident, which Ashgabat claims Russia caused, led to a deterioration of bilateral relations.[46] For Turkmenistan, there are high stakes in being able to export some twenty bcm to Iran, because Tehran pays in hard currency.

The Russian gas export monopoly came under concerted attack with the inau-guration of the Sino-Central Asian gas pipeline in December 2009. China actually managed the coup of convincing the Turkmen, Uzbek, and Kazakh governments to build a common gas pipeline to transport thirty billion m^3 annually. The gas pipeline draws from the Turkmen reserves of Samandepe, on the right shore of the Amu Darya, then runs 180 kilometers to Gedaim at the Turkmen-Uzbek border, crosses through Uzbekistan for 500 kilometers, and Kazakhstan for more than 1,300 kilometers, to the Chinese border at Khorgos. Each of the three countries is committed to delivering 10 bcm of gas, although Ashgabat and Beijing have signed a contract stipulating the delivery of 30 bcm. Turkmenistan delivered 2.9 bcm of gas to China in 2009 6 bcm in 2010, and 17 in 2011.[47] That year, the two sides announced that by 2015, Turk-menistan will provide a total of 65 bcm to Beijing, which seems unrealistic.[48] The gas pipeline currently in operation does not enable this level of export. Its capacity can be increased to as much as fifty bcm after improvements, but Tashkent and Astana also deliver some of their gas through it. It will therefore be necessary to construct a second trunk to supplement the first, but details about the construction and the route have yet to be discussed.

Faced with Chinese advances and needing to meet its own consumption, Russia has decided to modernize the entire Central Asian gas network, which dates from the Soviet period. The Central-Center Asia gas pipeline, built in the 1960s–1970s, consists of many parallel pipes that originate in Turkmenistan and Uzbekistan, before cross-ing Kazakhstan and entering the station of Alexandrov Gay on the Russian border. In theory, the Central-Center Asia gas pipeline has a total capacity of 90 bcm, but its state of disrepair considerably slows down the flows: it transports forty-five bil-lion m^3 per year at best.[49] Gazprom committed to investing more than US$2 billion in renovating it, but has been slow to put its words into action. In 2008, Uzbekistan agreed to continue to export the large majority of its gas surplus to Russia (since 2002, Gazprom has bought about 10 bcm per year from Uzbekneftegaz) in exchange for a new section to extend the Center-Central Asia gas pipeline and the renovation of the Bukhara-Ural pipeline, which serves the industrial towns of the southern Urals such as Chelyabinsk and Yekaterinburg.[50] The Bukhara-Tashkent-Bishkek-Almaty line has also proven crucial for the transit of regional flows.

In 2007, Russia, Kazakhstan, and Turkmenistan signed an agreement for the construction of a new section that, starting in 2012, should be able to transport about 30 bcm. This Peri-Caspian gas pipeline is planned to run the length of the shores of the Caspian on a south-north axis, with each country overseeing the construction of its own section. However, by the end of 2011, both the distribution of tasks and export prices were still being discussed and the project seemed to be at a stand-still.[51] Consequently, Gazprom has been unable to place itself in a strong position to contend with Chinese and, to a lesser extent, Iranian competition. Nevertheless, for Kazakhstan, a privileged partnership with Russia in gas matters will continue to be unavoidable given the location of its deposits. In 2008, Astana about 15 bcm to Russia and Ukraine, and predicts about 30 bcm will be available by 2020, with the remainder going to meet the rise in local consumption. Starting in 2012, some gas production from Karachaganak will be exported to the Orenburg refinery at a privileged price (US$140 per 1,000 m³) for the next fifteen years, in exchange for which Kazakhstan possesses half the refinery's shares. Gazprom and KazMunayGas control the joint venture, KazRosGas, in charge of this export.[52] Moscow, then, will retain partial control of Kazakh gas, but clearly risks losing the Turkmen market.

Energy Geopolitics: Are the Great Powers Dominating the Game?

For the Central Asian states, the choice of energy partners proves fundamental, be-cause the complexity of the exploitation circuit—upstream and downstream—requires choosing viable allies not only in terms of technological know-how and the export of extracted resources, but also for long-term geopolitical alliances. For a long time it was estimated that the essential asset was not resources as such, but the sophisticated technological capacity to exploit them, which was deemed responsible for Western supremacy. However, deposits have recovered their importance and emergent coun-tries such as China and India are making rapid progress in terms of technology. They will thus probably be able to compete with the large international majors within a few decades, and this will enhance Central Asia's ability to negotiate deals in its own favor.

Though Moscow certainly understands that it can no longer claim a monopoly over Central Asia's hydrocarbons, it continues to be a major actor, especially in terms of export routes. Moscow will remain Kazakhstan's main oil partner. It has not only the means by which it can exert coercion over Astana, for example, by increasing its transit rights on the CPC, but it can also prove to be a solid and reliable partner, guaranteeing Astana access to European markets through the Baltic Pipeline System (BPS). Should Moscow adopt uncooperative policies, it risks accelerating Kazakh desires to find new partners in Asia and to reach Europe via tankers, despite this be-ing more costly than a pipeline. In the gas sector, the Russian monopoly is coming to an end. The price of Central Asian gas is constantly rising: in 2006, Gazprom paid US$44 per 1,000 m³, but two years later this price has more than tripled to US$150. Since 2009, it has had to buy Central Asian gas at world market prices, minus the transit rights, thus reducing the profit that Moscow had been collecting through resale on European markets.[53] Moreover, Russia's financial commitment to remain a key player in the Central Asian energy market has not been borne out: the sums invested by its energy firms, more than 80 percent of which were in Kazakhstan, are limited as compared to those of other international actors. Whereas Russia had pledged to invest some US$10 billion in Central Asia by 2012, mainly in the development of deposits and transport infrastructures,[54] the 2008 economic crisis, as well as Kyrgyz instability and Moscow's difficult relations with Tashkent and Ashgabat, have made it impossible to keep its promise.

In Kazakhstan, Gazprom, Lukoil, and Rosneft are involved in numerous projects. These include geological studies and the development of gas deposits in Karachaganak and Imashevskoe (Atyrau region) and of oil deposits in North Buzachi (Mangystau region) and Karakuduk (Mangystau region); development of oil and gas deposits in North Kumkol (Kzyl-Orda region), Alibekmola and Kozhasay (Aktobe region); and, lastly, development of offshore deposits located in the Kazakh part of the Caspian Sea (Tyub-Karagan, Atashskaya, Kurmangazy, Zhambay, Khvalinskoe, and Tsentralnoe). In Turkmenistan, Russia is only interested in the gas sector. ITERA is the only Russian company directly set up for the exploitation of hydrocarbons, although Lukoil and TNK–BP are trying to enter the Turkmen market. In Uzbekistan, Russian companies, mainly Lukoil, are participating in the development of gas deposits in the following areas: Shakhpakhty and Kungrad in Karakalpakstan, Kandym, Khauzak, and Shady in the Bukhara region; gas and oil deposits in Zhambay in the Uzbek part of the Aral Sea; deposits in the region of Gissar (near Karshi), and in Urga, Kuanysh, and Akhchalak on the Ust-Yurt Plateau. In Kyrgyzstan and Tajikistan, Moscow aims instead to control the sale of oil products, which are very profitable, although Gazprom is also involved in exploring deposits of Tajik gas (Sargazon in the Khatlon region and Rengan and Sarikamysh close to Dushanbe), and of Kyrgyz gas (in the south of the country).[55]

Despite this massive Russian presence, China has succeeded, within the space of a few years, in becoming one of Central Asia's main energy partners. Although they arrived late on the scene, Chinese companies such as China National Petroleum Corporation (CNPC) and its subsidiaries, the China National Offshore Oil Corporation (CNOOC) and the National Oil and Gas Exploration Corporation, as well as the China National Oil Development Corporation (CNODC), and Sinopec (China National Petrochemical Corporation), have devised an offensive strategy, which is reinforced by their acceptance of the rules of the game laid down by KazMunayGas, not to mention the good political relations between the Chinese and Kazakh governments. Today China controls about a third of Kazakh oil production, thanks to its main deposit of Aktobe (AktobeMunayGas), but also through the acquisition of numerous smaller sites situated along the Sino-Kazakh pipeline (North Buzachi, North Kumkol, and Karazhanbas) and of the offshore deposit of Darkhan. Beijing failed in its bid to establish itself on the three main sites of Tengiz, Karachaganak, and Kashagan, and is therefore in a poor position to be able to take advantage of the great oil and gas boom to come. However, at the end of 2009, the CNPC bought MangystauMunayGas, one of the largest oil companies in the country, which exploits or explores thirty-odd sites, in particular those of Kalambas and Zhetybay.[56] Even if China's share of Kazakh oil production increases quickly, due to technical improvements, the exploration of still undiscovered sites, and the purchase of new fields, China's proportional share of total Kazakh oil production will decrease as the exploitation of Tengiz, Kashagan, and Karachaganak increases the size of the pie.

Above all, China has its sights set on Turkmen gas. In 2007 the CNPC pulled off a major feat: it became the only foreign country permitted by Ashgabat (excepting the British company Burren when it signed an agreement with the Turkmen government in the 1990s) to exploit onshore deposit. It now controls shares of Bagtyiarlyk on the right bank of the Amu Darya, whose reserves of 1.3 trillion m^3 are earmarked for the Sino-Central Asian gas pipeline. This Amu Darya natural gas project is China's largest overseas natural gas project so far, but Chinese success does not stop there. In early 2010, Ashgabat announced that the tender bid for US$10 billion to develop South Yolotan had been won by a consortium consisting of the CNPC, LG International, Hyundai Engineering, Gulf Oil & Gas FZE, and Petrofac International. In this framework, CNPC signed a US$3 billion contract, according to which it can produce up to ten bcm per year and retain 3.13 bcm per year to fill the gas pipeline.[57] The Chinese Development Bank, for its part, provided Turkmenistan with a US$3 billion loan for developing South Yolotan, with the provision of another US$4 billion for the completion of the project's first stage.[58] In contrast with projects oriented westward that necessitate an agreement between numerous partners, international majors, transit countries, and destination countries, the projects oriented toward the east concern above all bilateral relations between the Central Asian and Chinese governments and as such are easier to implement.[59]

Western presence in the Central Asian hydrocarbon sector was secured at the beginning of the 1990s with the domination of the large international majors in the exploitation of the two main Kazakh oil deposits, Tengiz and Kashagan. The TengizChevroil joint venture, created in 1993, includes Chevron (50 percent), ExxonMobil (25 percent), and LukArco (5 percent), as well as KazMunayGas, which controls 20 percent of the shares.[60] At Kashagan, the North Caspian Operating Company (NCOC) consortium includes ENI, ExxonMobil, Shell, Total, ConocoPhillips, and INPEX, and KazMunayGas has seen its share increase from 8.33 to 16 percent since the 2007 crisis between the consortium and the Kazakh authorities.[61] ENI is also the main operator of Karachaganak alongside British Gas, with each possessing a 32.5 percent share (Chevron and Lukoil own 20 and 15 percent, respectively). Until 2011 Karachaganak was the only major oil and gas project in which KazMunayGas was not a shareholder, but the Kazakh authorities eventually secured a 10 percent stake in it.[62] Despite their massive presence on the largest sites, the position of Western multinationals has become more fragile in recent years: Russia is reducing the leverage of international operators on the Caspian Pipeline Consortium (CPC), while the Kazakh government has brought in stricter legislation against them, and now demands that the state company KazMunayGas have greater participation.[63]

Other European firms are present on smaller sites: Maersk Oil operates deposits in the Atyrau and Mangystau regions; Agip is involved in the construction of a transformation factory for gas and oil in the Atyrau region; Petrom, bought by OMV, exploits six sites in the Kzyl-Orda and Mangystau regions. Some European companies have also succeeded in establishing themselves in Turkmenistan. Wintershall, a subsidiary of BASF and the first German producer to be directly involved in gas production in Russia, is in the process of conducting seismological studies on blocks eleven and twelve in the Turkmen part of the Caspian in collaboration with Maersk. In 2008, RWE, which forms part of the Nabucco consortium, and its partner OMV, established the Caspian Development Corporation, which brings together various European enterprises seeking to establish themselves in the Central Asian gas sector, and attempts to unify their needs and strategies.[64] Schlumberger, Mannesman, ENEX Process Engineering, and Technofrigo Dell'Orto are present in the transformation of gas and oil products. After the setbacks it suffered in Kazakhstan, ENI bought the shares of British company Burren, which has been the operator of the large Turkmen oil field of Nebit Dag since 1995.

Despite the presence of European companies known for their technological competencies, the European Union has not yet succeeded in establishing mechanisms to encourage Central Asian governments to opt for European export paths. While it is likely that oil routes will diversify, since transport via barges on the Caspian is technologically simple, relatively low in cost, and is not going directly against Russian interests, the gas issue remains more complex. Since the 1990s the project to build a westbound trans-Caspian oil pipeline (Trans-Caspian Pipeline, TCP) has been blocked on multiple levels: legal difficulties (the status of the Caspian Sea is still not settled and Moscow and Tehran continue to maintain that the agreement of all five littoral states is necessary); technical problems (shallow water, unstable climate, frequent storms, and environmental risks); and geopolitical difficulties (Russia and Iran are blocking the development of east-west axes). With the inauguration of the BTC (Baku-Tbilisi-Ceyhan) pipeline in 2005, however, the Caspian energy game entered into a new phase of its history. The pipeline, which concretizes Baku's commitment to the West, represents a dynamic that the European Union and the United States would also like to draw Kazakhstan into. The Kazakh authorities, concerned about incurring Moscow's displeasure, had long been hesitant in making a clear commitment in favor of the BTC, hoping for a rapid capacity expansion through the CPC instead. Russia's ill will on this question, however, forced Astana's hand. In 2006, an intergovernmental agreement between Azerbaijan and Kazakhstan was signed in which Astana committed itself to exporting an initial amount of three million tons of oil via the BTC; the amount is set to rise to seven and then eventually to twenty-five million tons.[65] Turkmenistan has also recently joined the pipeline: since 2010, Ashgabat's purchase of three tankers from Russia have made it possible to transport about 40,000 barrels per day to Baku, that is, 5 percent of the total BTC daily capacity of 800,000 barrels.[66] The long-term solutions, however, are yet to be elaborated. The Azerbaijan International Operating Company (AIOC) hopes to attain a peak production on the Azeri-Chirag-Guneshli site of 1.2 million barrels per day by around 2020, so the BTC will very quickly reach its limits, and increasing its capacity to two million barrels per day would be a long, costly, and scarcely profitable process for foreign companies. Within a decade, Astana will thus have to envisage new routes for transporting its oil to Europe.[67]

In the gas domain, the European Union is seeking to diversify its imports, which are too dependent upon Russia, and to avoid transit issues, since, as demonstrated during the Russo-Ukrainian "gas wars" of 2006 and 2009, they often work to complicate negotiations. However, the importing of Central Asian gas is far from the only solution under consideration: both Nord Stream, which run through the Baltic Sea, and the South Stream project, which will move Russian natural gas through the Black Sea, bypass transit countries, and other alternatives are also being looked into, such as developing LNG, or reducing demand for gas in favor of renewable energies. Central Asia is concerned only by the so-called Southern Corridor, which consists of two gas pipelines: first and foremost is Nabucco, which would link Erzerum in Turkey to Baumgarten an der March in Austria and be able to transport thirty-one bcm, or 5 percent of European demand, as of 2017–2018; and, second, the more limited Turkey-Greece-Italy Interconnector Pipeline (TGII), the capacity of which should increase to eight billion m^3 in 2014.[68] The Southern Corridor will mainly transport Azeri gas extracted from the BP-operated offshore site of Shah Deniz, which has fed the Baku-Tbilisi-Erzerum (BTE) gas pipeline since the end of 2006.

To ensure the viability of Nabucco, an additional eight bcm at least must be secured by 2014, a condition that the site of Shah Deniz II is supposed to fulfill. However, in order to reach thirty-one bcm sometime between 2016 and 2020, a sizably larger volume must be found, whether from the Middle East (Iraq) or Central Asia. Given that Kazakh and Uzbek gas are out of the question, the shortfall in volume could be made up by supplies from Turkmenistan, whether from the offshore deposit of Serdar-Kyapaz—which would cost a rather modest amount to link up to the export network of Shah Deniz, but would require that the territorial conflicts between Ashgabat and Baku are settled—or from the onshore South Yolotan-Osman deposit, in which case the linking costs would be far greater.[69] In March 2009, the Turkmen government put out a tender for the construction of an internal gas pipeline linking this deposit to the Caspian Sea. This could potentially fill one of two competing gas pipelines: either the Moscow-led Peri-Caspian one, or the EU-led Trans-Caspian. To see the latter solution realized, the European Union and the Turkmen authorities will first have to come to an understanding on prices, and then withstand Russian and Iranian pressures, or else transform the gas into LNG so that it can be transported by tankers, a solution that is easier geopolitically but is more costly. By late 2012, the Turkmen authorities had still not officially ratified their agreement to supply ten bcm of gas to Nabucco, even though their leaders said to be committed to it.[70]

Iran, for its part, seems likely to remain a limited actor in the Central Asian energy game, but a major gas partner for Turkmenistan. Only the lifting of the American embargo would enable Tehran to become a genuine transit country for Central Asian hydrocarbons to Turkey or the Indian subcontinent. The project to build a Kazakhstan-Turkmenistan-Iran (KTI) pipeline with a capacity of twenty million tons to link Kashagan to Kharg terminal in the Persian Gulf is at a standstill. So long as the country's geopolitical position remains as it is, Tehran will only be able to collect modest flows of oil from Turkmenistan and Kazakhstan by tanker. Astana and Tehran have, for instance, set up a swap system: in 2007, four million tons of Kazakh oil transited through Iran, and an equal volume was exported to the Persian Gulf from Kharg.[71] The Iranian authorities hope to develop these practices, which they have established with the four Caspian states. In order to do so, they are augmenting capacity at the refineries in Tehran and Tabriz, which receive the oil unloaded from Caspian tankers at the port of Neka.[72] At present, all the projects to build a gas pipeline to India and Pakistan by bypassing Afghanistan via Iran, or to Turkey, remain only speculation.

Lastly, the Turkmenistan-Afghanistan-Pakistan-India (TAPI) gas pipeline has had an eventful history. The project was launched in 1995, then blocked by the Taliban's coming to power, but it has been revived with the support of the Asian Development Bank and the United States. In 2008, the four states concerned signed a heads of agreement (HoA) and a framework agreement (GPFA); in 2010 they gathered together in Ashgabat to sign a new agreement;[73] and in 2011, during a visit by Berdymukhammedov to Islamabad, they announced an agreement on prices, but without giving precise details.[74] The gas pipeline, with a planned length of 1,680 kilometers, will start out from the Dauletabat field, follow the Afghan Herat-Kandahar axis, and then link up again with Quetta and Multan in Pakistan, and eventually with Fazilka in India. An alternative route is reportedly also being examined that runs from Mazar i-Sharif in Kabul to Peshawar, Lahore, and Bikaner.[75] TAPI's transport capacity is forecast to be up to 100 million m^3 per day, which would enable Turkmenistan to supply Pakistan with forty-five bcm per year, with Afghanistan and India sharing the second half of the supply. Security is obviously a key challenge, since the pipeline will go through the province of Kandahar, one of the centers of Taliban activity, and will have to be protected by some 7,000 soldiers from the Afghan security forces; it will also have to pass through the Balochistan region, even though the route has been revised to have it run through sparsely populated areas. Financial questions also have to be discussed: although the Asian Development Bank has committed to financing part of the project, estimated at US$7.6 billion,[76] a considerable share of the funds will have to come from private investors, but few of them have confirmed their commitment.

Non-Chinese Asian partners are modestly involved in Central Asian energy. Malaysian company Petronas is set up in Turkmenistan. The Japanese company INPEX is established on the site of Kashagan and Nissho Iwai participates in the development of the large Uzbek deposit of Kokdumalak, while JGC, Itochu, Nissho Iwai, and Marubeni have won contracts linked to the construction or renovation of refineries in Kazakhstan and Turkmenistan. The South Korean companies KNOC and Korean Gas Corporation (KOGAS) are both active in Uzbekistan, and India's Oil and Natural Gas Corporation (ONGC) Videsh has signed an agreement for the joint exploitation of the Satpayev offshore block in the northern Caspian Sea.[77] Albeit Asian countries, and especially China, are increasingly involved in the Central Asian hydrocarbons, Western firms and Russia remain the main players so far; and China becomes a dominant actor only for Turkmen gas.

Hedging Geopolitics? Transformation Industries and
New Technologies

The maximal exploitation of Central Asian hydrocarbons is impeded by multiple problems ranging from the lack of know-how in new technologies to the functioning of state-run companies that control the oil and gas sectors. The national extraction industries lack qualified personnel and still depend on Soviet equipment that is often outdated. Kazakhstan has been able to take advantage of increasing technology transfers, whereas more isolated countries like Uzbekistan and Turkmenistan have to contend with significant technological and human resource-related difficulties. However, the only strategy that would enable Central Asian states to maximize the profitability of their resources to their own advantage would involve the transformation of primary resources into finished products, the development of alternative systems to pipelines, and the mastering of new CNG (compressed natural gas), GTL (gas to liquids), and LNG (liquefied natural gas) technologies.

Since Soviet times Central Asian countries have been dependent on exporting primary resources in their crude state. Today governments are aware of the need to increase the transformation of crude products into finished products so as to increase their revenues in foreign currency. Kazakhstan has only three refineries on its territory, with a total capacity of 370,000 barrels per day: Pavlodar treats oil from Siberia; Atyrau manages the oil produced in the region; and Shymkent deals with production from the deposits of Kumkol, Aktyubinsk, and Makatinsk. KazMunayGas's purchase of the Romanian refinery of Petromedia, established on the shores of the Black Sea, enabled it to increase its refinery capacity and sell fuel and kerosene on the Central European market. Three gas chemical complexes treat seventeen million m³ per day, not including the half Russian-owned Orenburg refinery. Uzbekistan has three refineries with a total capacity of 220,000 barrels per day: two date from the Soviet period, that of Ferghana, upgraded by Japanese firms, and that of Alty-Aryk; and a third one, built in 1997, is situated in Bukhara. Turkmenistan also has three refineries at its disposal, with a total capacity of 87,000 barrels per day: two of them are state-run, namely Seydi near Turkmenabat, built after independence, and Turkmenbashi, renovated in 2002, whereas the third, built at Khazar, is privately run by Dragon Oil.[78] Kyrgyzstan and Tajikistan have only one refinery each, respectively, that of Jalalabad, which treats Kazakh oil, and the very small refinery of Konibodom. With low oil and gas prices on domestic markets, foreign investors prefer to export rather than sell locally. Central Asia is therefore being pushed further into specializing in primary resources and is finding it hard to create the industrial and human capital required to make its energy riches profitable locally.

For Kazakhstan and Turkmenistan, oil transport by tanker is an alternative that could circumvent pipe geopolitics. However, for it to become a reality, it requires the implementation of programs to develop port and railway infrastructures. Since the end of the 1990s, the Kazakh authorities have sought to skirt the question of a trans-Caspian oil pipeline by developing tanker transport. Oil from Tengiz, for instance, moves as tanker freight from Aktau to Sangachal terminal near Baku and is then transported by railway to the Georgian port of Batumi. Kazakhstan's deliveries to Russia are carried out along a road from Aktau to Makhachkala, whereas the route from Aktau to Neka makes it possible to deliver to Iran.[79] In Turkmenistan, Dragon Oil also delivers oil extracted from the Cheleken Peninsula to Iran by maritime routes.

Banking on the system of trade flow via tankers, Kazakhstan has set up a trans-Caspian transport system (Kazakhstan Caspian Transport System, KCTS), launched in 2007 at a cost of US$3 billion by KazMunayGas, TengizChevroil, and Agip KCO. Initially, it will transport twenty-five million tons each year, later rising to thirty-eight million per year, and is designed to be operational in time for the exploitation of Kashagan.[80] To accomplish this ambitious project, the consortium is building loading terminals on the Kazakh coast and unloading terminals on the Azeri coast. As the northern part of the Caspian Sea is not deep enough for tankers and accumulates ice in winter, the small Kazakh port of Kuryk, situated seventy kilometers to the south of the regional capital of Aktau, was chosen for transformation into a hub of Kazakh oil export. It will be equipped with an oil terminal capable of receiving large capacity tankers and an oil storage and pumping station able to deal with cargos of 500,000 barrels per day. This capacity will be enough to contain Kashagan's initial production as well as part of the flows from Tengiz.[81] New tankers with a capacity of more than 60,000 tons have been ordered. An oil pipeline of 730 kilometers, starting in Eskene, the terminal at which the oil from Kashagan will arrive, will link up with Kuryk and will constitute a major segment of this new export route. Built by KazMunayGas, a subsidiary of KazTransoil and Total, this pipeline will have a capacity of twenty-three million tons per year, which may subsequently be increased to between thirty-five and fifty-six million tons.[82] At the end of 2008, the first tankers loaded with oil extracted from Tengiz started to ply the Aktau to Baku route, and joined up with the BTC pipeline.[83]

The new gas compression and liquefaction technologies will also play a determining role in the future of Central Asian gas. Whereas building gas pipelines results from both commercial stakes and geopolitical strategies, railway and ship transport makes it possible to set aside questions of equilibrium between major powers. Thus, Kazakhstan or Turkmenistan natural gas (CNG) could be transported by tankers across the Caspian Sea in order to skirt the legal problems presented by the status of the sea and by Moscow's recalcitrance regarding the diversification of export routes. However, this solution entails the installation of compression stations along the Kazakh or Turkmen coastline, the equipping of ships, and Azerbaijan's installation of decompression stations in its ports. This possibility, as well as that of Gas to Liquids (GTL), was underlined by the INOGATE program in 2007, but they both require costly investments and political decisions that favor Europe as a recipient market for Central Asian gas.[84] The prospect of exporting Kazakhstan compressed natural gas via the CPC is currently under consideration.

The liquefied natural gas (LNG) solution is also being increasingly discussed in Central Asia. Better grasping of liquefaction technologies and the rapid development of a fleet able to transport LNG, in particular cryogenic vessels, have already caused prices to fall drastically. These two factors have thus opened new prospects for the transport of gas, prospects that have already been exploited by Qatar, Japan, South Korea, and Europe.[85] However, for Central Asia, this technological turn is difficult to take. At present only Kazakhstan has managed to begin production of LNG, with 1.4 million metric tons in 2007,[86] and six million metric tons in 2009.[87] Kazakh LNG is mainly produced by TengizChevroil, which exports to Turkey and Europe. New liquefaction plants are under construction, and the CNPC at Zhanazhol will also produce approximately 500,000 tons of LNG in the years to come.[88] The cost of production of Central Asian hydrocarbons is already relatively high and its products are only of interest when the world prices are high. The expansion of LNG thus highlights the weaknesses of the Central Asian market: none of the countries concerned possess the necessary technologies or know-how to exploit LNG. Furthermore, the region's land-locked character works against its market development. Indeed, LNG is particularly profitable for sites with access to open oceans and thus plays to the advantage of the Russian deposits in the Barents Sea and Sakhalin, while Central Asian production once again finds itself at a disadvantage due to its lack of access to international waters.

As in Africa or Latin America, hydrocarbons can be both a boon and bane for states endowed with a rich subsoil. The extraction sector is volatile: while periods of strong economic growth intensify demand for primary materials, economic crises, such as the one in 2008, can lead to a considerable drop in demand and drastically curtail state revenue. These industries thus prove more highly sensitive to fluctuations in the world economy than other sectors. Moreover, issues of over- or under-capacity can also come to the fore. Central Asia has so far succeeded in avoiding the spiral of violence linked to the poor redistribution of oil and gas wealth, but it will have to contend with the risk of a "Dutch disease" given the expected growth of Kazakh and Turkmen production over the coming decade.[89] Social tensions resulting from the poor distribution of oil wealth in West Kazakhstan have already increased in magnitude. An institutional environment that guarantees some degree of wealth redistribution, and one that also protects foreign investors' rights, has yet to be established in Kazakhstan, let alone Uzbekistan or Turkmenistan. However, the financial stakes are such that the international majors as well as the global and regional powers are all interested in establishing themselves in the Central Asian hydrocarbon sector.

As such, the Central Asian governments have genuine leeway, since they can play on the competition in terms of selling prices as well as in export routes, and they have been doing so rather successfully: Russia is losing its control of gas and oil exports, China is rising in power, Western companies are well established in the Kazakh oil industry and hope to break into that of Turkmen gas. Moreover, more modest actors, such as Iran, Japan, South Korea, Malaysia, and India, are also being welcomed to help reduce the geopolitical pressure from within the Russia-China-Western triangle. The Central Asian governments believe that production must be nationalized, at least in part, as it supports long-term geopolitical and financial autonomy. But for the time being, they are also losing out, since they are being cemented in the economic logic of primary resource extraction, and, with the exception of Kazakhstan, are failing to master the technologies that would enable them to make the transition to transformation. Their future as world-class export countries will therefore prove difficult: they are subject to the upheavals of international markets and the global geopolitical balance; they have to contend with competition from technologies such as LNG and new shale resources; and they are unable, at least for the time being, to use oil and gas to create new industrial wealth and invest in their human capital.

Notes

1. Gauchon, *Le monde*, 572.
2. R. Orange, "Shell Shuts Caspian Office, $50bn Kashagan Project on Ice," *Telegraph*, May 24, 2011, http://www.telegraph.co.uk/finance/newsbysector/energy/oilandgas/8530144/Shell-shuts-Caspian-office-50bn-Kashagan-project-on-ice.html.
3. "BP Statistical Review of World Energy 2010," June 2010, 6.
4. "Caspian Energy and Transport Issues Expand into Military-Political Confrontation," *Nezavisimoe voennoe obozrenie*, May 18, 2007, English translation available at http://www.gab-ibn.com/IMG/pdf/Re11-_Caspian_Energy_And_Transport_Issues_Expand_Into_Military-Political_Confrontation._Microsoft_Word.pdf.
5. R. M. Cutler, "Kashagan Feels Growing Pains," *Kazworld.info*, November 17, 2011, http://kazworld.info/?p=17829.
6. J. Roberts, "The Barrel: A Tricky Question for Kazakh Oilmen," October 11, 2011, http://www.platts.com/weblog/oilblog/2011/10/11/tricky_question.html.
7. S. M. Yenikeyeff, *Kazakhstan's Gas: Export Markets and Export Routes* (Oxford: Oxford Institute for Energy Studies, 2008), 23–27.
8. See the 2011 fact sheet for Uzbekistan, http://www.globalsecurity.org/military/world/centralasia/uzbek-energy.htm.
9. "Gaffney, Cline & Associates Confirms Turkmenistan Possesses Giant Natural Gas Reserve," *Central Asian News*, October 16, 2008, http://en.ca-news.org/news/103781.
10. See "BP Statistical Review of World Energy 2011," 22.
11. G. Ulmishek, "Petroleum Geology and Resources of the Amu-Darya Basin, Turkmenistan, Uzbekistan, Afghanistan, and Iran," US Geological Survey Bulletin 2201-H, Reston, VA, 2004.
12. M. Barry, "The Development and Use of Production Sharing Agreement Law in Uzbekistan Oil and Gas," *Central Asia and the Caucasus*, no. 5 (2006): 47–59; M. Kenisarin, "The Energy Sector of Uzbekistan: Present State and Problems," *Central Asia and the Caucasus*, no. 3 (2004): 172.
13. G. F. Ulmishek, "Petroleum Geology and Resources of the North Ustyurt Basin, Kazakhstan, and Uzbekistan," US Geological Survey Bulletin 2201-D, Reston, VA, 2001; Ulmishek, "Petroleum Geology and Resources of the Amu-Darya Basin."
14. Yenikeyeff, *Kazakhstan's Gas*, 19.
15. "Oil & Gas Opportunities in Kazakhstan," UK Trade and Investment Sector Briefing, 3, http://pdfuri.com/oil-gas-opportunities-in-kazakhstan.
16. B. Pannier, "Tajikistan on Road to Energy Self-Sufficiency, Dicier Relations With Tashkent," *Radio Free Europe/Radio Liberty*, December 20, 2011, http://www.rferl.org/content/tajikistan_gas_uzbekistan/2253993.html.
17. "KazMunaiGas EP to Buy New Assets, Invest in Output," *Kazworld*, October 21, 2011, http://kazworld.info/?p=17254.
18. G. Raballand and R. Gente, "Oil in the Caspian Basin: Facts and Figures," in *The Economics and Politics of Oil in the Caspian Basin: The Redistribution of Oil Revenues in*

Azerbaijan and Central Asia, ed. B. Najman, G. Raballand, and R. Pomfret (London: Routledge, 2007), 9–29.

19. Business Monitor International, *Kazakhstan Oil & Gas Report Q3 2012*, Industry Report & Forecasts Series, May 2012, 23.

20. See the Energy Information Administration Kazakhstan fact sheet, http://www.eia.gov/countries/analysisbriefs/Kazakhstan/pdf.

21. "BP Statistical Review of World Energy 2011," 24.

22. More details in Peyrouse, *Turkmenistan*, 169–92.

23. Business Monitor International, *Turkmenistan Oil & Gas Report Q3 2012*, Industry Report & Forecasts Series, May 2012, 5.

24. "BP Statistical Review of World Energy 2011," 24.

25. Business Monitor International, *Uzbekistan Oil & Gas Report Q3 2012*, Industry Report & Forecasts Series, May 2012, 5.

26. T. L. Karl, *The Paradox of Plenty: Oil Booms and Petro-States* (Berkeley: University of California Press, 1997).

27. P. Jones Luong and E. Weinthal, *Oil Is Not a Curse: Ownership Structure and Institutions in Soviet Successor States* (Cambridge: Cambridge University Press, 2010), 6.

28. P. Dicken, *Global Shift: Mapping the Changing Contours of the World Economy* (New York: Guilford Press, 2011), 260.

29. Gauchon, *Le monde*, 563.

30. P. Jones Luong and E. Weinthal, "Two Versions of Rentierism: State Ownership with Control in Turkmenistan and Uzbekistan," in *Oil is Not a Curse*, 77–120.

31. Jones Luong and Weinthal, "Revisiting the Obsolescing Bargain: Foreign Private Ownership in Kazakhstan," in *Oil Is Not a Curse*, 259–98.

32. S. Peyrouse, "The Kazakh Neopatrimonial Regime: Balancing Uncertainties Among the 'Family,' Oligarchs and Technocrats," *Demokratizatsiya. The Journal of Post-Soviet Democratization*, 20, no. 4 (2012): 345–370.

33. Gauchon, *Le monde*, 587.

34. V. Paramonov and A. Strokov, *Russia-Central Asia: Existing and Potential Oil and Gas Trade* (Shrivenham: Defence Academy of the United Kingdom, 2008), 7.

35. See the CPC website, http://www.cpc.ru.

36. "Transneft to Manage Caspian Pipeline Consortium for $0.04 a Year," *Kommersant*, May 02, 2007, http://www.kommersant.com/p763111/r_500/Transneft_CPC_Transnefteproduct/.

37. R. Paxson and M. Gordeyeva, "Caspian Oil Shipments to Fall amid Work on Pipeline," *Reuters*, October 6, 2011, http://af.reuters.com/article/energyOilNews/idAFL5E7L-61WE20111006.

38. T. Babali, "Prospects of Export Routes for Kashagan Oil," Energy Policy, no. 7 (2009): 1298–1308.

39. S. Peyrouse, *The Economic Aspects of the Chinese-Central-Asia Rapprochement.* (Washington, DC: The Central Asia-Caucasus Institute Silk Road Studies Program, 2007), 57–58.

40. "Sino-Kazakh Pipeline Transports 20 Million Tons of Oil to China," *China Daily*, January 25, 2010, http://www.chinadaily.com.cn/bizchina/2010-01/25/content_9374000.htm.

41. Zhang Jian, "China's Energy Security: Prospects, Challenges, and Opportunities," *Brookings*, July 2011, http://www.brookings.edu/research/papers/2011/07/china-energy-zhang.

42. R. Demytrie, "Struggle for Central Asian Energy Riches," *BBC News*, June 3, 2010, http://www.bbc.co.uk/news/10175847.

43. "Kazakhstan Country Analysis Brief," Energy Information Administration, February 2008, 5, http://www.eia.gov/countries/cab.cfm?fips=KZ.

44. "Perspectives on Caspian Oil and Gas Development," International Energy Agency Working Paper Series, December 2008, 12.

45. J. Humphries, "Construction of Turkmen-Iran Pipeline Complete," *Oil and Gas*, November 12, 2009, http://www.ngoilgasmena.com/news/turkmen-iran-pipeline-complete/;

"Turkmenistan: New Pipeline to Iran Set to Open," *Eurasianet*, January 4, 2010, http://www.eurasianet.org/departments/news/articles/eav010510.ahtml.

46. V. Socor, "Turkmenistan Pressured by Gazprom's Halt on Turkmen Gas Imports," *Eurasia Daily Monitor* 6, no. 215, June 30, 2009, http://www.jamestown.org/single/?no_cache=1&tx_ttnews%5Btt_news%5D=35193.

47. Business Monitor International, *Turkmenistan Oil & Gas Report Q3 2012*, 5.

48. R. M. Cutler, "Turkmenistan to Boost Gas Exports to China," *Asia Times*, December 1, 2011, http://www.atimes.com/atimes/Central_Asia/ML01Ag01.html.

49. R. M. Cutler, "Moscow and Ashgabat Fail to Agree Over the Caspian Coastal Pipeline," *The Central Asia-Caucasus Institute Analyst* 11, no. 7 (2009), www.cacianalyst.org/?q=node/5080.

50. "Russia and Uzbekistan: Oil and Gas Cooperation," *RIA Novosti*, July 7, 2010, http://en.rian.ru/international_affairs/20100720/159879904.html.

51. K. Simonov, "Russian-Turkmen Relations: Clearing the Way for Gas Pipes," *RIA Novosti*, October 28, 2010, http://en.rian.ru/analysis/20101028/161115262.html.

52. "Kazakhstan Country Analysis Brief," 9.

53. D. Bochkarev, "'European' Gas Prices: Implications for Gazprom's Strategic Engagement with Central Asia," *Pipeline and Gas Journal* 236, no. 6 (2009), http://www.pipelineandgasjournal.com/%E2%80%9Ceuropean%E2%80%9D-gas-prices-implications-gazprom%E2%80%99s-strategic-engagement-central-asia?page=show.

54. V. Paramonov and A. Strokov, *Russian Oil and Gas Projects and Investments in Central Asia* (Shrivenham: Defence Academy of the United Kingdom, 2008), 2 and 7.

55. Ibid., 9.

56. "KazMunayGas and CNPC E&D Close Deal for Purchase of 100% Stake in MangistauMunayGas," *Visor Capital*, November 25, 2009, http://www.visocap.com/ShowNews.aspx?NewsId=280.

57. S. Bierman and A. Shiryaevskaya, "CNPC, LG Win $9.7 Billion of Turkmen Gas Contracts," *Bloomberg*, December 30, 2009, http://www.bloomberg.com/apps/news?pid=newsarchive&sid=a41E4ecIpaTY.

58. Ia. Khummedov, "Kitai pokupaet Turkmenistan," *Gundogar*, July 19, 2010, http://www.gundogar.org/?013049709000000000000011000000.

59. P. Ipek, "The Role of Oil and Gas in Kazakhstan's Foreign Policy: Looking East or West?" *Europe-Asia Studies* 59, no. 7 (2007): 1179–99.

60. See the TengizChevroil website, http://www.tengizchevroil.com/en/.

61. In August 2007, Astana announced the three-month suspension of the ENI's activities on the Kashagan site, officially for failing to respect ecological norms, in reality to manifest its discontent over the report announcing the start of production, which has been pushed back from 2005 to 2008, then to 2010 (today to 2017). The Kazakh authorities sought to obtain rapid financial compensation and to guarantee KazMunayGas a share of the revenues from the deposit without having to foot the costs for exploitation and the management of risks.

62. J. Kilner, "Kazakhstan Shores Up Control Over Its Energy Industry," *Telegraph*, December 14, 2011, http://www.telegraph.co.uk/news/worldnews/asia/kazakhstan/8955933/Kazakhstan-shores-up-control-over-its-energy-industry.html.

63. M. B. Olcott, "KAZMUNAIGAZ: Kazakhstan's National Oil and Gas Company," Paper of the James A. Baker III Institute for Public Policy, Rice University, 2007.

64. M. Denison, "The EU and Central Asia: Commercializing the Energy Relationship," Europe-Central Asia Monitoring Policy Papers, no. 2, 2009, 9.

65. L. Gusev, "Sotrudnichestvo Kazakhstana s Azerbaidzhanom v sfere energetiki," Informatsionno-analiticheskii tsentr, February 2009, http://www.ia-centr.ru/expert/3908/.

66. "Turkmen Oil Starts Flowing Through BTC Pipeline," *Radio Free Europe/Radio Liberty*, August 12, 2010, http://www.rferl.org/content/Turkmen_Oil_Starts_Flowing_Through_BTC_Pipeline/2126224.html.

67. E. C. Chow and L. E. Hendrix, "Central Asia's Pipelines: Field of Dreams and Reality," Special Report of the National Bureau of Asian Research, no. 23, September 2010.

68. M. Giuli, "Nabucco Pipeline and the Turkmenistan Conundrum," *Caucasian Review of International Affairs* 2, no. 3 (2008): 124–32.

69. Denison, "The EU and Central Asia," 9.

70. R. M. Cutler, "Turkmen Boost for Nabucco," *Asia Times*, June 9, 2011, http://www.atimes.com/atimes/Central_Asia/MF09Ag01.html.

71. "Astana, Tehran to Swap Oil Rights," *Zawya*, October 27, 2008, http://www.zawya.com/story.cfm/sidZAWYA20081027061449/?relcontent=ZAWYA20110823054703.

72. "Perspectives on Caspian Oil and Gas Development," 35.

73. "Presidents Sign Accord in Ashgabat on TAPI Pipeline," *Radio Free Europe/Radio Liberty*, December 11, 2010, http://rferl.org/content/tapi_pipeline_approved/2245135.html.

74. M. Gurt, "Turkmenistan Agrees Gas Price with Pakistan," *Reuters*, November 16, 2011, http://uk.reuters.com/article/2011/11/15/gas-turkmenistan-pakistan-idUKL5E7M-F0LK20111115.

75. "Perspectives on Caspian Oil and Gas Development," 36–39.

76. "New Route for Gas Flow," *Turkmenistan.ru*, January 24, 2011, http://www.turkmenistan.ru/en/articles/14522.html.

77. More details on India's involvement in chapter 5.

78. "Turkmenistan's Crude Awakening: Oil, Gas, and Environment in the South Caspian," Report by Crude Accountability, January 2009, 10.

79. More in Guliyev and Akhrarkhodjaeva, "Transportation of Kazakhstani Oil via the Caspian Sea."

80. "Trans-Caspian Gas Pipeline and Caspian Oil Transport System Can Become CAREC Part," *Kazworld.info*, November 28, 2011, http://kazworld.info/?p=18038.

81. Guliyev and Akhrarkhodjaeva, "Transportation of Kazakhstani Oil via the Caspian Sea," 6.

82. Kassenova, "Kazakhstan and the South Caucasus Corridor," 2.

83. S. Primbetov, "Vse soglasheniia po Kazakhstanskoi Kaspiiskoi Transportnoi Sisteme budut zakliucheny v etom godu," *Nomad.su*, April 8, 2009, http://www.nomad.su/?a=3-200902060024.

84. "The INOGATE Programme," http://www.inogate.org.

85. For Asia, see, for instance, H. Hashimoto, "Evolving Roles of LNG and Asian Economies in the Global Natural Gas Markets," Advance Summit Paper from the 2011 Pacific Energy Summit, February 21–23, 2011, Jakarta, Indonesia.

86. Yenikeyeff, *Kazakhstan's Gas*, 49.

87. "Kazakhstan's LNG Production Decreases," *Trend.az*, December 13, 2011, http://en.trend.az/capital/energy/2050332.html.

88. "First Line of the Third Zhanazhol Oil and Gas Processing Plant Becomes Operational," *CNPC*, December 13, 2007, http://www.cnpc.com.cn/en/press/newsreleases/2007/12-13-2.htm.

89. R. Pomfret, "Kazakhstan's Economy Since Independence: Does the Oil Boom Offer a Second Chance for Sustainable Development?" *Europe-Asia Studies* 57, no. 6 (2005): 859–76.

10
Mineral Wealth
Export Strategies Versus State Sovereignty

The Central Asian subsoil is rich in minerals. The southern parts of Kazakhstan, Uzbekistan, Kyrgyzstan, and Tajikistan all include the rocky formations of the Tian Shan Mountains, the Pamirs, whereas Turkmenistan is part of another geological zone. Kazakhstan's central regions around Karaganda and eastern regions in the Altay have also proven rich in minerals. Working gold and silver has been a traditional livelihood for artisans in sedentary Turkestani societies and has been used in the animal art of nomads. It was not until the Russians came to the region in the nineteenth century that the first large-scale extraction industries took shape. The Soviet Union's thirst for energy and the priority it gave to heavy industry hastened the development of the extraction sector. Minerals such as bauxite, chrome, zinc, manganese, and copper were used by Soviet industries in abundance; Central Asian uranium has been used since the end of the 1940s for nuclear experiments on the Semipalatinsk site; and its gold was sold on international markets. In the last decade, rare minerals such as titanium, beryllium, tantalum, cobalt, and cadmium have become increasingly sought after for the production of new technologies.[1] But the Central Asian minerals market is highly political: production is strategic since it provides a share of foreign currency reserves for the state budget, feeds key national industrial sectors, and enables the governing circles to reap additional revenues. As a result, the financial transactions and rationales for exploitation are opaque, and, with the exception of the uranium sector, foreign companies have lost their influence in the face of a reassertion of state sovereignty.

Kazakhstan's Mineral Eldorado and Its Oligarchs

Kazakhstan exceeds its Central Asian neighbors in terms of its mineral wealth and its possession of industrial structures, established during the Soviet period, required to exploit it. Its reserves of ferrous minerals are considerable, estimated to be about 16.6 billion tons, or 8 percent of the world's reserves. In addition, two-thirds of the 8.8 billion tons already explored are considered to be easy to access, and so are available for a modest price.[2] Kazakhstan is second in the world for manganese reserves (600 million tons), eighth in iron reserves (12.5 billion tons), and has close to one-third of the world's chrome deposits. Within the CIS, it has the most reserves of chrome and

190

lead, ahead of Russia, takes second place in manganese, nickel, silver, and zinc, and third in coal, gold, and tin.[3] It furthermore produced 101 million tons of coal in 2009, making it the world's ninth-largest producer.[4]

During Soviet times, 95 percent of the chrome produced in the Soviet Union came from Kazakhstan. The republic's two main metallurgy plants, SSGPO (Sokolov-Sarbai Mining Production Association) and KarMet, represented close to a quarter of Soviet production capacity.[5] At the start of the 1990s, facing rapid industrial decline, the Kazakh authorities banked on foreign investments, even if the idea of opening these strategic sectors to foreigners was politically contentious, and whet the appetites of local oligarchs. Some international companies have succeeded in rapidly acquiring sites at very modest prices, hoping for short-term profits, in particular in the iron and steel industry, as well as, more modestly, in that of manganese and chrome. However, the difficulties involved in setting up sites and disillusionment over their profitability quickly curbed international enthusiasm. Several transactions turned out to be of little interest for foreign companies.

In 1996, in order to remedy the decline of the SSGPO, Kazakhstan entrusted the management of the sites to Ivedon International, a joint venture between Trans World Group and the Eurasian Group of the Kazakh oligarch Alexander Mashkevich, who succeeded in obtaining the full percentage of its shares in 2000.[6] The Karaganda metallurgical complex, KarMet, was also the object of several transactions that resulted in losses for some European firms. During Soviet times, KarMet was the largest company in the Soviet Kazakh republic: it represented 5 percent of total steel production of the entire Soviet Union, more than 10 percent of the Kazakh GDP, and was the place where President Nursultan Nazarbayev began his career.[7] Developments surrounding its privatization in the 1990s and the change in attitude of the political authorities toward the involvement of foreign investors in its management, including the Austrian company Voestalpine as well as Japanese companies, attest to the difficulties involved in securing foreign investments in the extraction sector.[8]

In 1995, Ispat International, which belongs to Indian billionaire Lakshmi Mittal and is the eleventh-largest global producer of steel, bought KarMet and, in so doing, became one of the first foreign companies to successfully manage the restructuring of a major Soviet enterprise in Central Asia. Today ArcelorMittal Temirtau is the largest company in the Kazakh metallurgical sector, treating the majority of the steel and cast iron produced in the country.[9] Thanks to EBRD support, Mittal initially invested US$500 million to revive production, which had nearly stopped.[10] In the first decade of the twenty-first century, the Temirtau complex has undergone a progression from exports via a barter system to a regime of strong foreign currency. This success has allowed other investments to be generated, in particular from the World Bank and EBRD. Today, Kazakhstan's largest industrial giant includes six steelworks, coke plants, steel factories, laminate factories, cast iron factories, several production cycles for metal tubes and aluminum, zinc, and polymer coating, two electricity stations, and it exploits ten mines and twelve surface extraction sites.[11]

However, tensions between the Kazakh authorities and ArcelorMittal, which benefits from significant financial privileges negotiated at the time of settlement, grew in magnitude. Kazakh ministries hurled diverse accusations: failure to respect environmental legislation, unpaid back tax payments on profits, and a lack of corporate responsibility. For instance, the group has not maintained the social benefits devolved to employees from the Soviet period and has delegated this task to the municipal administrations, whose budgets do not allow for the administration of social welfare. Several fatal accidents in the coal mines have shaken Kazakh public opinion, which has accused the company of not modernizing obsolete security systems.[12] In 2008, the Kazakh government threatened to take Mittal's license away, but in reality it cannot permit any such loss in production or the loss of thousands of jobs in what is an already depressed region. Astana hopes for a review of the contract signed with Lakshmi Mittal, and then Prime Minister Karim Masimov has explicitly noted that the times of the 1990s, when the country welcomed investors regardless of the cost, are well and truly past.[13] In order to defuse the conflict, ArcelorMittal has announced that it will increase output in steel production from five to ten million tons, modernize the Atasu iron mine, acquire self-sufficiency in iron ore, and make investments of US$1.2 billion to improve security for employees.[14]

With the exception of Mittal, the major foreign companies have lost ground in the Kazakh extraction sector due to the rise in power of national companies such as the Eurasian National Resources Corporation (ENRC), also known as the Eurasian Group. This group is controlled by a "trio" of oligarchs from Kazakhstan, including Alexander Mashkevich, Patokh Shodiev, and Alizhan Ibragimov, who are listed each year in *Forbes'* rankings,[15] and who have close relations with the ruling circles and with President Nazarbayev himself. Thanks to their networks, both national and international, they have built one of the largest commercial empires in all of Central Asia. They control Alferon Management, the group's main London-based company and holder of several mines in various countries throughout the world (Sub-Saharan Africa, Indonesia, Kosovo, and Russia), as well as Kazchrome, Aluminum of Kazakhstan, the industrial and mining complexes of Zhairem and SSGPO, the Eurasian Energy Corporation, and ENRC Marketing.

One of the largest producers of ferrous alloy, Kazchrome is third on the world market for ferrochrome. It owns the Donskoy mine, which has been worked since 1943 and was considered the largest producer of chrome minerals in the world during Soviet times, as well as three factories: Aktobe (Aktiubinsk region), Aksu (Pavlodar region), and KazMarganets (Karaganda region). The management of Kazchrome was initially delegated to the Japan Chrome Corporation, and then to Trans World Group, before falling into the hands of the Eurasian Group.[16] Aluminum of Kazakhstan specializes in the extraction of bauxite and its transformation into aluminum. It is distributed across five sites: the Pavlodar factory, the Torgay and Krasnooktiabrsk bauxite mines, the Keregetas limestone mine, and the Pavlodar thermal station.[17] The Kazakhstan Aluminum Smelter, a cutting-edge blast furnace, is also currently under construction in the Pavlodar region by a parity joint venture created with RusAl. The Zhairem mine and the factory related to it specialize in manganese and ferrous manganese. The mine is one of the largest of Kazakhstan, with reserves of close to four million tons of

193

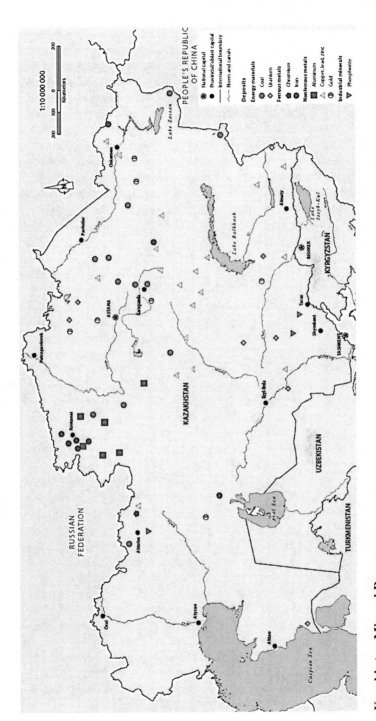

Kazakhstan Mineral Resources

iron ore, and significant deposits of zinc, silver, and barium sulfate. The metals from Zhairem are reputed to have particularly low levels of phosphorus and sulfur, which assure an easier transformation.[18]

SSGPO is a world leader in the extraction and transformation of iron ore. The company owns several open-cut iron ore mines (Sarbay, Sokolov, Kachar, and Kurzhunkul), as well as limestone and dolomite mines.[19] In order to master transformation processes and to increase the group's competitiveness, the "trio" has also set up the Eurasian Energy Corporation, one of the country's main private energy producers, which specializes in electricity and coal. It supplies Kazchrome and SSGPO with low-priced electricity and the group's other factories with coal. It includes the Aksu electricity station, which links the electricity networks of Central Siberia, the Altay, and the Kazakh Northeast, with the open-cut coal mine of Vostochny.[20] Last but not least, the group has created Swiss-based ENRC Marketing, the sole supplier of its products, with offices in the United Arab Emirates, Russia, China, the United States, and Kazakhstan. ENRC Marketing is a leading operator of the Kazakh railways and has its own freight terminals at ports on the Caspian, the Black Sea, the Baltic Sea, and the Sea of Azov, as well as at several Chinese and Iranian ports.[21]

The Eurasian Group is in competition with another holding, Kazakhmys, headed by Vladimir Kim, a member of the Korean community of Kazakhstan and often ranked by *Forbes* as Kazakhstan's premier businessman. Very close to Nazarbayev, he is suspected of concealing the interests of the president and those in his close circle; this is in contrast to the status of Kazakhmys, which is listed on the London Stock Exchange.[22] Kazakhmys is Kazakhstan's main copper producer, the tenth largest in the world for the production of cathodic copper and fifth in the production of silver.[23] The company also produces gold (more than 5,000 kg annually), zinc, copper-plated wire, and enameled wire. In 2008, Kazakhmys bought part of the shares of the Eurasian Group and now possesses 18.8 percent of its competitor.[24] Though the country's two main oligarchs, Mashkevich and Kim, seek to keep their industrial wealth separately, the Kazakh government, which owns shares in both their companies, views a rapprochement between the two holdings favorably, which might result in the unification of their international strategies.[25] The largest Kazakh producer of zinc, KazZinc, was born in 1997 from the merger of the three main non-ferrous metal combines in the eastern part of the country, Ust-Kamenogorsk, Leninogorsk, and Zyrianovsk, with which the hydroelectric station of Bukhtarma is associated. The majority of KazZinc's shares were ceded by the state to Swiss company Glencore International AG, which is also established in other mineral extraction sectors in Central Asia.[26]

The 2008 global crisis has had the effect of drastically reducing the profitability of Kazakh mining and metallurgic complexes: in 2008, ArcelorMittal had to reduce its Kazakh production by 30 percent and cut the work hours of its employees, and has complained about the lack of profit from the Temirtau complex since the fall of metal prices.[27] Kazakhmys and the Eurasian Group lost billions of dollars due to the drop in metal prices, but announced that production levels had almost regained previous levels at the end of 2009, although the volatility of world prices continues to worry them.[28] Despite the presence of international actors such as Mittal and of large holdings that have backing from the political authorities, such as the Eurasian Group and Kazakhmys, the Kazakh metallurgical sector has to contend with the challenges posed by post-Soviet industry: its machinery is outdated and has to be imported due to a lack of local production; provisions for environmental protection are largely inadequate; upgrading to international norms is costly; and logistical problems and social pressures weigh heavily. However, despite the hazards of prices on the world market and the pressures the government exerts to have a share in these assets, too rapidly privatized, there are profits for the taking.

This metallurgical sector is considered to be crucial for Kazakhstan's future since metallurgical resources constitute 35 percent of its total exports, and account for 19 percent of industrial jobs.[29] According to Business Monitor International, Kazakhstan's mining industry value could reach US$36 billion by 2016, with a growth led mostly by the coal, iron ore and copper sectors.[30] The vast majority of this ferrous production is exported (85 percent), a particularly high rate that can be explained by weak domestic demand in the construction and mechanical industries after the fall of the Soviet Union. Between 2002 and 2008, the country experienced average annual growth of 4 percent for the extraction of minerals and metallurgy.[31] Despite the 2008 global crisis and falling prices, Kazakhstan banks on a rapid growth in its extraction industry: compared to its Russian or Western competitors, Kazakh metallurgy retains privileged markets since one of its main clients, China, continues to be a major consumer of metals of all sorts.[32]

The same highly politicized management of large metallurgical companies occurs in Tajikistan.[33] The aluminum smelter at Tursunzoda, TALCO, which accounts for 70 percent of the country's exports, is an example of the difficulties involved in modernizing Soviet heavy industrial infrastructures, which are fairly unprofitable and devour energy. TALCO consumes about 40 percent of Tajikistan's electricity, but does not pay its electric bills to the state-run electricity company Barki Tojik, which places a major strain on the state budget.[34] It provides very little in the way of revenue for the Tajik state, in large part due to financial misappropriations linked to the ruling circles, a fact revealed by an audit requested by the International Monetary Fund. Indeed, TALCO's main commercial partner, CDH, a shell company based in the British Virgin Islands that was in charge of exporting its aluminum production, was used by intimates of the presidential family as a means of personal enrichment, and these practices seem to be continuing with the new TALCO Management Ltd.[35] The foreign companies that have sought to acquire TALCO, in particular the Russian metallurgical holding RusAl, have all retreated due to its functional opacity and its lack of profitability, which has been further exacerbated by the dearth of raw materials to treat.[36]

Rare Earth Metals: Will Kyrgyzstan and Kazakhstan Compete with China?

In addition to the traditional metals, a new global race is shaping up for so-called rare earth metals (REMs), that is, the seventeen metals used in technological applications

Table 10.1

Main Mines in Central Asia, their Owners, Production, and World Ranking in 2010 and 2011

	Country	Main owner	Annual production in tons	World ranking
Tortkuduk	Kazakhstan	Katco JV/Areva	2,608	4
Budenevskoye 2	Kazakhstan	Karatau JV/Kazatomprom-Uranium One	2,175	7
Inkai	Kazakhstan	Inkai JV/Cameco	1,602	9
South Inkai	Kazakhstan	Betpak Dala JV/Uranium One	1,548	10
Central Mynkuduk	Kazakhstan	Ken Dala JSC	1,242	14
East Mynkuduk	Kazakhstan	Stepnoe RU	1,029	15
Akdala	Kazakhstan	Betpak Dala JV/Uranium One	1,027	16
Karamuran	Kazakhstan	Kazatomprom	1,017	17
Myunkum	Kazakhstan	Katco JV	889	18
Uchkuduk Northern Mining	Uzbekistan	Navoy		19
Zafarabad-Central Mining	Uzbekistan	Navoy		20
Nurabad-South Mining	Uzbekistan	Navoy	Total 2,400	21
Zarechnoe	Kazakhstan	Zarechnoe JV/Uranium One	778	23
Irkol	Kazakhstan	Semizbai JV/Kazatomprom	750	24
Budenevskoe 1 & 3	Kazakhstan	Akbastau JV/Kazatomprom	740	25
Kanzhugan	Kazakhstan	Tauken/Kazatomprom	562	30

Source: "World Uranium Mining," *World Nuclear Association*, December 2011, http://www.world-nuclear.org/info/inf23.html.
Note: 2011 statistics for the first ten mines, 2010 statistics for the others.

like televisions, mobile phones, and PC monitors, which are also necessary for the manufacture of green energy products. REMs are found in nature in dispersed forms, present in hundreds of minerals. The main accessible concentrations are found in China, where more than 95 percent of production currently takes place. Beijing takes advantage of its near-monopoly situation to force up world prices. In 2010 it drastically cut exports by 70 percent and in 2011 announced that it would reduce them by 10 percent, two decisions that helped to raise the value of its REM exports by 376 percent.[37] Global demand is set to grow considerably: it could reach between 185,000 and 210,000 tons in 2015, leading to a strong price increase, while they have already risen more than 300 percent in price between 2008 and the end of 2010.[38] According to some sources, prices for rare earths could multiply by two or three over the next twenty years.[39]

However, China's decisions have caused the relevant industries in Japan, South Korea, Europe, and the United States to consider alternative products and suppliers. The search for new, economically viable deposits spans the entire globe from Greenland and South Africa, to the CIS countries and North America. India plans to take stock of the value of its reserves, but they do not appear to be very significant. With the second largest explored rare earth reserves in the world, maybe the first in terms of potential reserves, Russia could also challenge the Chinese monopoly.[40] Kyrgyzstan and Kazakhstan have also thrown their hats into the ring.

Canada's Stans Energy Corporation, which also works with the Research Institute of Chemical Technology (VNIIHT) on Russian deposits, obtained a twenty-year extraction license for the Kutessay II mine, located north of Lake Issyk-Kul in Kyrgyzstan, near the Kazakh border. Exploited since the beginning of the 1960s, the mine produced 80 percent of the Soviet Union's rare earth supply. Moscow used it to supply its nuclear program with about 750 tons a year of rare earth metals. Kutessay contains the fifteen main REMs and its reserves of dysprosium represent 6.7 percent of total rare earths, with terbium making up 1.15 percent and neodymium representing 8.5 percent.[41]

Kazakhstan's reserves have also drawn attention of other countries, in particular from two of its biggest partners, Germany and Japan. The Federation of German Industries (BDI) hopes to gain access to Kazakh REMs in order to secure its supply and limit its dependency on China.[42] As the world's largest uranium producer, Kazakhstan has the technical capacity to extract REMs from uranium ore at a reasonable cost. The country plans to more than double its production of beryllium through 2014. At present, three-quarters of Kazakh ores are exported to Russia and 20 percent to China, but other international players want to prevent Kazakhstan's reserves from flowing toward Beijing. In April 2011 the state company Kazatomprom announced an investment of US$800 million to develop rare-earth metal mining in Kazakhstan through a joint venture with Rosatom, Toshiba, and Sumitomo. Set up in 2010, the Kazatomprom-Sumitomo joint venture plans to extract molybdenum and rhenium from uranium ore, while the joint project with Toshiba may produce niobium, rhenium, wolfram, tantalum, and beryllium.[43]

Finally, Tajikistan would like to be seen as a contender and has indicated that the

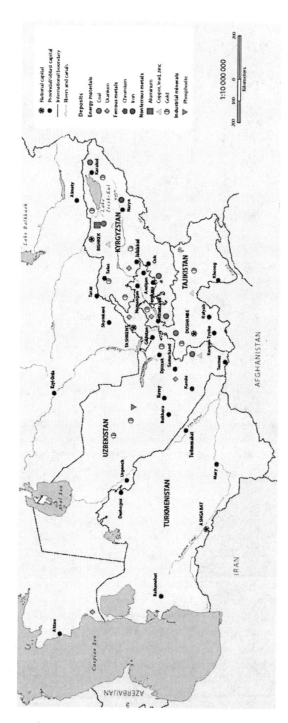

Mineral Resources in Kyrgyzstan, Tajikistan, Turkmenistan, and Uzbekistan

former Vostokredmet mining complex, near Khudjand, could potentially participate in this world race for REMs. Kazyna Capital Management recently set up the Kazakh-Tajik Private Equity Fund, which is intended to finance investments in REMs. The Russian-based Converse Group also plans to start production of recycled vanadium at Vostokredmet, but the conditions for extracting new minerals seem too complex to be financially viable, at least for now.[44]

The necessity for those industrialized states most dependent upon rare earths to find new sources of supply opens up several new economic opportunities to Central Asian countries, opportunities that will nevertheless contain substantial risk concerning environmental situations and often dysfunctional logics of development. It is desirable that Kazakhstan, and Kyrgyzstan, succeed in finding some balance between the urgency to gain access to a new financial manna, environmental preservation, and their requirements in technology transfers.

Central Asia's Gold Riches

Along with hydrocarbons and uranium, gold constitutes one of Central Asia's main riches, as the region is traversed by the Tian Shan mountain range, one of the largest and richest auriferous belts in the world. The mountain range begins in Uzbekistan, crosses through Tajikistan and Kyrgyzstan, and extends to China's northwest, over a distance of more than 1,500 kilometers.[45] While gold production is almost non-existent in Turkmenistan and rather modest in Tajikistan, it is significant in the three other states—Kazakhstan, Kyrgyzstan, and especially Uzbekistan. The cumulative extraction from these three producer republics is reported to be about 120 tons of gold per year.[46]

During the Soviet period, these resources were left practically unexploited, since Moscow gave priority to Siberia. For the newly independent states, the possession of gold constitutes a real opportunity, but the boom in the gold industry has come late in comparison with that of hydrocarbons, for several reasons. First, extraction requires considerable financial investments, which the Central Asian governments can only rarely raise without foreign help. Second, multiple fluctuations in the gold rate in the 1990s have led the states to adopt a cautious attitude. However, after the 2008 crisis, when gold prices skyrocketed, Central Asian hopes were revived by the prospect that the national markets might attract new investors. Third, the gold market is at the core of several political-financial intrigues, which have implicated highly placed figures. The information on these issues is scant, but the exploitation of these mines has provoked conflicts between foreign investors, state-run companies, and political power brokers.

With more than eighty tons extracted per year, Uzbekistan lies in ninth place in the international extraction of gold and is second behind Russia among the CIS countries. The country possesses about 600 mineral extraction sites, forty of which contain gold, but only nine deposits are being exploited and fifteen are still undergoing exploration. The estimated reserves stand at around 3,300 tons, including 2,000 confirmed, which guarantees Tashkent several more decades of substantial revenues.[47] The Uzbek extractive industry enjoys possession of the immense Navoy mining combine (NGMK), the world's second largest after that of Grasberg in Indonesia, which is today considered as one of the emblems of Uzbek industry bestowed by the Soviet regime, and employs more than 60,000 people.[48] A second metallurgical combine, Almalyk (AGMK) in the Tashkent region, produces 90 percent of the country's silver and also has a gold treatment factory. Thanks to Almalyk, Uzbek gold has been taken as the benchmark by the arbitration laboratory of the London Metal Exchange and has the good fortune to be cheap, which aids its export. Navoy produces sixty of the eighty-five tons manufactured each year in Uzbekistan, the remainder coming from the Almalyk combine.[49]

Uzbek reserves are distributed across three main regions along the western range of the Tian Shan: in the Kyzylkum desert close to the Zaravshan River, in the Samarkand region, and in that of Tashkent near the Chatkal River. The Amantaytau region, to the north of Navoy city, is site of the main deposits of Muruntau, Amantaytau, Daugystau, Vysokovoltnoe, Tsentralnoe, and Asaukak. These deposits are situated close to the railway and road networks, which give them a considerable advantage compared with the other Central Asian mines, which are often situated high in the mountains in landlocked zones. Muruntau, one of the world's largest mines with estimated reserves of about 80,000 tons of gold, is the country's premier gold supplier, and has never been privatized.[50]

One of Kyrgyzstan's rare riches is gold, of which it has the third-largest reserves among CIS countries, behind Russia and Uzbekistan. Confirmed reserves are around 1,000 tons, distributed over several sites, including the Kumtor mine, which accounts for more than half (about 700 tons). Situated in the Tian Shan Mountains close to the Chinese border, it alone represents 40 percent of Kyrgyz exports and about 10 percent of the country's GDP, bringing in about US$30 million to the state coffers each year.[51] From 1992 to 1996, Kyrgyzstan extracted about 1.5 tons per year, and then embarked on a more intensive exploitation of about fifteen tons per year. However, the extraction conditions are difficult, making Kyrgyz gold relatively unprofitable: one ounce costs more than US$450, which is two to three time more expensive than Russian or Uzbek gold.[52] But while more than forty deposits have been discovered in the country, Kumtor has long been the only mine that has really been exploited. The resources of the Makmal site were exhausted around 2005. The country's second- and third-largest mines, Taldybulak Levoberezhny (2,000 tons of gold) and Jerooy (1,500), will start production in 2013. Kyrgyzstan has other gold reserves in the Talas region. Although they are situated at an altitude of between 1,800 and 3,000 meters, these sites are accessible all year round by road, and four mines are in the process of exploration and exploitation.[53]

With 9 percent of Soviet production in 1991, Kazakhstan was the third-largest Soviet gold manufacturer,[54] and today occupies fourth position in the CIS, having been overtaken by Kyrgyzstan. Yearly gold production between 1995 and 2004 attained an average of ten tons per year: it reached a peak in 2000 with 16.4 tons extracted, but this figure was halved in 2007.[55] In 2010, Kazakhstan produced 13.3 tons of refined gold and 29.9 tons of unprocessed gold,[56] and aims to raise production to seventy tons annually to become the second-largest CIS producer after Russia.[57] Compared to other mineral resources, Kazakh gold was barely exploited by the Soviet regime. The assessments of Kazakh reserves were for a long time contradictory, but today estimates seem to have converged on a total of 800 tons.[58] However, the gold industry is slowed by the dispersion of its sites, which number more than 200 in total, are spread across the whole territory, and are too small to justify the necessary investments. Close to two-thirds of the gold extracted in the country comes from sites of small or medium size, and 41 percent of them are considered unprofitable. Moreover, close to half of the reserves are difficult to enrich and contain impurities, in particular arsenic and antimony.[59]

At independence, the authorities had their hopes set on the exploitation of the two large deposits of Akbakay, close to Jambul, and Vasilkovskoe, in the northeast of Kokchetau. They also envisaged developing refinery capacities, non-existent during the Soviet Union, to make it possible to export a better quality, and therefore more expensive, finished product.[60] The majority of the small-size mines have been opened to foreign investors and, at the end of the 1990s, were held by foreign companies such as Orsu Metals, Polymetall, Ivanhoe Mines, Hambledon Mining, Eurasia Gold, Alhambra Resources, Data Mining, Celtic Resources Holdings, and Frontier Mining. The companies have, however, experienced serious difficulties, heightened by the fall of gold prices on the world markets.[61] The tense relations between foreign investors and state authorities have also weakened the country's ability to attract new investors: gold has turned out to be the least attractive commodity on the Kazakh market for foreign investors. Most of the exploitation licenses have therefore been resold many times over, some having come back under the control of the state-run corporation Altynalmas. The only large gold mine that has not been privatized is that of Akbakay, whose reserves are estimated at ninety-five tons of gold.[62] Today Altynalmas, as well as two Kazakh companies, ABC Balkhash and Kazakhaltyn, alone account for two-thirds of the gold extractions undertaken in the country, even if nearly a hundred other companies hold exploitation licenses.[63]

Tajikistan also has gold resources; however they are a lot smaller than those of its three neighbors. It has close to thirty deposits, with total reserves estimated at about 430 tons, and each year produces three tons of gold. Jilau is the main Tajik mining site, part of a group of auriferous deposits that also include Taror, Chor, and Kirhona, all owned by the Metallurgical and Enrichment Combine (ZGC).[64] This state-run combine controls reserves estimated at 11.3 million ounces of gold, but only 5.6 million of them—around half—are held to be in conformity with international criteria. In 2007, the joint venture exploiting Jilau, the Zeravshan Gold Company, once controlled in part by Nelson Resources and then acquired by Avocet Mining, was bought by one of the largest Chinese gold companies, Zijin Mining Group. The group plans to make significant investments to develop its production.[65] Many other sites of modest size are being exploited in joint ventures by the Tajik government and Western companies, such as Gold and Mineral Excavation, Kryso, and Gulf International Minerals, but they are struggling to find the necessary finances for undertaking new explorations or for development and exploitation.

Central Asian gold resources have been associated with a number of controversies. Above all, the working conditions of the miners, not to mention their remuneration, create discontent in public opinion. Several incidents have arisen in the last few years: in 2007, for instance, the miners of Akbakay went on strike to demand payment of their salaries, which had not been paid for three months.[66] Ecological questions also provoke turmoil in the local media. In Kyrgyzstan, also in 2007, the inhabitants of Talas blocked the road that provided access to the Jerooy mine on several occasions in order to stop the transport of workers and equipment. The villagers argued that the region collected no dividends from the mine despite the leaking of cyanide used to extract pure gold from the ore. Some modest measures were taken to oblige extraction companies to give some of their revenues to the Issyk-Kul social development fund.[67] In addition, the gold mines must regularly contend with clandestine exploitation. In 2007, in Kazakhstan, several law suits were opened against gold mine directors by Akmola region prosecutors, who accused them of exploiting small, abandoned reserves. More than 17,000 tons of gold ore are believed to have been illegally smuggled outside of the country.[68] Mines under license can also be subject to clandestine exploitation, such as that of Bestube: a database of 1,500 clandestine miners with photos and precise information had to be compiled before it was revealed that one and a half ton of gold had allegedly been stolen, constituting nearly 70 percent of the gold extracted from this mine over the course of four years.[69]

In Kyrgyzstan, Kumtor's position has been beset by many shake-ups linked to corruption and the struggles for power. Exploitation began in 1992 by a joint venture, Kumtor Gold Company, created between government-run Kyrgyzaltyn and Canadian corporation Cameco. Under this agreement, the Kyrgyz government secured itself a percentage calculated not in terms of the number of tons of extracted gold, but of the profits made through their sale.[70] Since the 1990s, the country has therefore seen its share of revenues melt away in accordance with increases in exploitation costs and the necessary infrastructure investments (extraction, treatment, construction of roads, the financing of environmental programs, etc.). In 2004, Cameco's shares were resold, without Bishkek's agreement, to another Canadian company, Centerra Gold. Ever since, conflicts between Centerra and the Kyrgyz state, which aims to have its share of the profits increased, have served to impede the functioning of the mine. In addition, some Kyrgyz deputies believe that Kyrgyzstan ought to have control of at least half of Kumtor's shares, as it is one of the state's primary sources of revenue, and make regular calls for the mine to be nationalized.[71]

However, factors such as Kyrgyzaltyn's technological inability to be able to run the mine alone, the risks of misappropriation of funds by the high functionaries in charge of running it, and the general lack of transparency in the extraction industry, make the idea of nationalization problematic.[72] In 2009, an agreement was reached that was designed to put an end to this long conflict and give investors a better image of Kyrgyzstan. The Kyrgyz state's share in the manufacture of gold from Kumtor increased considerably, from 15.6 to 33 percent, in exchange for which the Gold Company was exempted from part of its taxes.[73] But the political events of 2010 have further weakened the Canadian presence and nationalist political figures have stirred up debates about nationalizing Kumtor.[74] Looking for compromise solutions, the government then decided to impose a ban on the export of ore after 2012, with the hope of forcing in-country processing and having exporters pay extra tax.[75]

In Uzbekistan, the government has tried for several years to expel Western firms from the ore market, and little by little they have pulled out. In 2006, it published a decree announcing that several companies with foreign capital working in the domain of extraction would no longer benefit from the tax relief that had formerly been accorded to them.[76] The main enterprise targeted by this law was the Anglo-Uzbek joint venture Amantaytau Goldfields, which lost its exploitation license to Zeromax, a company allegedly controlled by Karimov's eldest daughter, Gulnara Karimova.[77] Oxus Gold had then been the last foreign company to have remained in the Uzbek gold market, albeit having ceded half of its Amantaytau assets to Zeromax. But it was forced to close its operations in Uzbekistan in spring 2011 and has seen its former chief metallurgist condemned to twelve years in prison.[78] The precious mineral extraction sector is therefore subject to multiple pressures from the Central Asian elites, who seek to renegotiate the contracts signed in the 1990s on more advantageous terms both for themselves and for the country, and consider the exploitation of natural resources as a matter of state sovereignty.

Uranium: Resources, Extraction, and Transformation Factories

During the 1990s, the uranium riches of Central Asia and the existence of a nuclear arsenal were only brought up in the context of the denuclearization efforts that followed the collapse of the Soviet Union. Even today, the Soviet legacy continues to be a heavy burden:[79] the Central Asian societies are often critical of any return to nuclear industries in the region; the ecological risks are especially great since the environment is already significantly damaged; and the management of radioactive waste (more than ten million tons) could not be more problematic. In addition, there are potential risks of nuclear proliferation or of bioterrorism in a region in which some states are weakened by internal tensions and by a fragile geopolitical environment. However, while the international companies have concentrated on the oil and gas resources, the region has rediscovered its uranium riches and the role that nuclear energy could play in a zone chronically lacking in energy. The exponential growth of the nuclear industry worldwide can only attract the attention of Central Asian states seeking to increase their energy potential and state revenues.

The uranium extracted from the Central Asian deposits does not meet the international standards of the Joint Ore Reserves Committee (JORC) or the Canadian National Instrument (NI) 43–101, and therefore costly technologies are required to bring it up to international norms. The reserves are large enough, however, to make upgrading technology to achieve international norms worthwhile. Kazakhstan ranks as

Table 10.2

World Rankings of Producer Countries of Uranium (in tons)

	2003	2005	2007	2009	2010
1. Kazakhstan	3,300	4,357	6,637	14,020	17,803
2. Canada	10,457	11,628	9,476	10,173	9,783
3. Australia	7,572	9,516	8,611	7,982	5,900
4. Russia	3,150	3,431	3,413	3,564	3,562
5. Uzbekistan	1,598	2,300	2,320	2,429	2,400

Source: "World Uranium Mining," *World Nuclear Association*, December 2011, http://www.world-nuclear.org/info/inf23.html.

Figure 10.1   **Main World Producers of Uranium** (in tons)

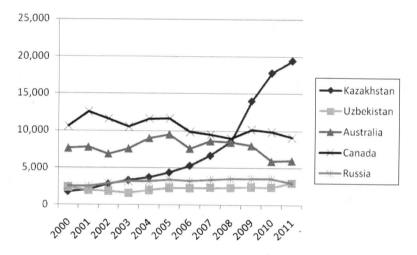

Source: World Nuclear Association, http://world-nuclear.org/info/uprod.html.

the second-largest country in the world for its uranium reserves, after Australia, with between 16 and 19 percent of global reserves, that is, between one and one-and-a-half million tons. Since 2009, it has been the world's largest producer ahead of Canada and Australia.[80] The extraction programs, which slowed in the 1990s (production fell by a quarter between 1991 and 1997), were revived in the following decade: 2,000 tons were produced in 2000, 8,500 in 2008, about 13,000 tons in 2009,[81] and 19,900 tons in 2011. After more than tripling its output of uranium in four years, Kazakhstan has stabilized production to around 20,000 tons annually in order to avoid further depressing prices but forecasts the extraction of 25,000–30,000 tons by around 2020.[82]

Kazakhstan has about fifty deposits spread across six provinces. The main ones of Budenovskoe, Zarechnoe, Moinkum, Mynkuduk, and Inkay are situated in the region of South Kazakhstan (in particular in the Sozak district), which contains more than 60 percent of the reserves. Other zones contain more modest deposits: Khorassan in the Kzyl-Orda region; Kyzyltu in the Akmola region; and Semizbay, which straddles Semizbay and North Kazakhstan province. Other sites, near the Syr Darya, the Ili, and the Caspian perimeter, also have small amounts of resources.[83] For the majority the world's sites, uranium is extracted from underground mines or in open-cut mines where the onsite leaching possibilities are marginal. In Kazakhstan, by contrast, more than half the reserves can be extracted by onsite leaching, a procedure that is cheaper and more environmentally friendly.[84] However, the Kazakh deposits necessitate considerable quantities of sulfuric acid given the significant presence of carbonate.

On the industrial level, Kazakhstan still benefits from its Soviet heritage but has established international partnerships to modernize its infrastructures. The country's main combine, Ulba, close to Ust-Kamenogorsk, was created in 1949 to treat uranium, beryllium, tantalum, and various precious metals necessary for the Soviet nuclear industry and in particular to exploit the site of Semipalatinsk. The combine currently functions at only 30 percent of its capacity, but will undergo a substantial modernization that will make it into one of the most efficient transformation factories in the country.[85] Kazakhstan has a second combine, Stepnogorsk, which is much newer, having been constructed in 2004; its function is to treat uranium and molybdenum extracts from neighboring mines and includes a plant for sulfuric acid production.[86] Another acid production plant, situated in Zhanakorgan around Kzyl-Orda, should be operational in order to treat the uranium extracted from the Khorassan deposits. Although Kazakhstan produces uranium, it does not itself use nuclear power: the country's only nuclear power station, situated in Aktau, operated between 1972 and 1999, producing 135 MW, or 0.1 percent of the country's electricity.[87] Its production was mainly used for heating some parts of the Mangystau Peninsula and for the desalination of water from the Caspian Sea.

Kazakhstan is the only Central Asian state to have set up an ambitious development program for its nuclear energy industry. KATEP, an agency that gathered together all Kazakh enterprises linked to the nuclear industry, was replaced by Kazatomprom in 1997, a symbol of Astana's ambitions in the nuclear domain. Not only will the country remain the world's foremost exporter of uranium, but by 2015, it wants to control 30 percent of the global fuel fabrication market, which would enable it to collect significant profits.[88] It also wants to export small and medium size reactors (from 50 to 100 MW) to countries that need nuclear electricity without wanting to invest in the whole production cycle. Although they are above all focused on export, Kazakh objectives have a domestic dimension, since the authorities plan to revive nuclear power to overcome chronic electricity shortfalls and to reduce the carbon emissions involved with other types of energy. A new nuclear power plant of 600 MW is planned for Aktau, to be built on the site of the former Soviet station: the first reactor should be operational in 2016, the second in 2017. With feasibility studies still incomplete, it is difficult to estimate the project cost, but it is likely be in the vicinity of US$2 billion.[89]

With the exception of the phases of conversion and enrichment, Kazatomprom controls the entirety of the nuclear cycle from deposit exploration, uranium extraction to its transformation into yellow cake. The subsequent phase, which manufactures fuel pellets, is also carried out in the Ulba factory, but these pellets are manufactured to Soviet norms that are still applied in Russia. With the aid of its foreign partners, Kazakhstan is acquiring technology which is allowing it to produce pellets to international standards and to master a new stage of the cycle, conversion (transformation of uranium oxide into uranium hexafluoride), thanks to the construction of a factory capable of producing up to 12,000 tons of hexafluoride gas per year.[90] The fuel pellets will then be sent to Russia where they will be enriched and put into fuel rods. A new line of construction allowing for their assemblage into rods is planned to begin in Ulba in the near future. The resulting rods will be used in the construction of reactors. Because of its extreme sensitivity, only the last enrichment phase, which in theory makes a military use of uranium possible, is carried out abroad and will remain so. In order to avoid international concerns over risks of nuclear proliferation, Astana has made it clear that it will not seek to acquire enrichment technology.[91]

The other Central Asian states are not as richly endowed in uranium and do not have any nuclear energy program. During Soviet times, Uzbekistan produced a significant amount of uranium for the military-industrial complex, with an annual production that attained 3,800 tons in the mid-1980s. Production collapsed in the 1990s, however, and has not recovered to its Soviet levels, since in 2010 Uzbekistan reportedly produced only 2,400 tons of uranium.[92] The Uzbek reserves—destined entirely for exports—are much more modest than those of Kazakhstan: estimated at between 111,000 tons and 185,000 tons, they nevertheless put the country in seventh position worldwide.[93] The main deposits are situated in the desert around Navoy and are grouped in five production units, Zarafshan, Uchkuduk, Zafarabad, Nurabad, and Krasnogorsk, all of which are dependent on the Navoy mining combine. Modernization of the uranium extraction industry is planned in order to increase the production of sulfuric acid, which is necessary to treat uranium. Exploitation of seven new deposits is also planned, including the sites of North Kanimekh, Meilysay, and Tutlinskaya.[94]

Kyrgyzstan also has uranium resources, but a much smaller quantity.[95] Many sites are located in the Ferghana Valley near Uzbekistan and Tajikistan, as well as in the region of Naryn. A number of them were exploited during the Soviet period, in particular Mailuu-Suu in the province of Jalalabad, where more than 10,000 tons were extracted between 1946 and 1967.[96] All the uranium mines were closed after independence. The Kara Balta Combine (KBGK) near Bishkek, commissioned in the 1950s for the treatment of uranium extracted from Kyrgyz and Kazakh mines, continued to treat about 200 tons of uranium ore tailings, which are extremely radioactive, until 2005.[97] For the time being, new sites' prospecting and exploration is taking place, but no mining is planned for quite some years. The sites that are not exhausted are considered to be too difficult to exploit, since they are dangerous and highly radioactive. Turkmenistan's uranium was also mined between 1952 and 1967, mainly the deposit of Chernoe, which reportedly produced between 5,000 and 7,000 tons, but at present the country allegedly has no extractable resources.[98]

Tajikistan is not traditionally ranked in the list of countries possessing uranium.

Nevertheless, the former chemical and mining combine of Leninabad, Vostokredmet, founded in 1945, was the first uranium treatment factory in the Soviet Union, and it treated uranium from the Ferghana Valley for half a century.[99] Today it works only on uranium tailings and other rare metals. In 2007–2008, Tajik scientists identified several uranium deposits in the north in the Mogoltay-Karamazara region, in the east in the Hissar Mountains and the Karategin Valley, as well as in the Pamirs and Tian Shan Mountains. According to these analyses, the Pamirs are supposed to be particularly rich, with sixty deposits containing rare minerals and at least five containing uranium, in particular on the perimeter of Lake Sasyk-Kul, whose water is known to have traces of uranium.[100] However, to turn these riches into profit, Tajikistan must change its legislation. In 2008 the parliament allowed foreign companies to extract uranium ore, but the local context still greatly impedes foreign participation in strategic sectors such as that of uranium.[101]

International Partners and Central Asian Uranium: A Shift Toward Asia?

Russia occupies a privileged place in Central Asian uranium, for the obvious historical reason that this sector was promoted during the Soviet period. Its main partner in the region continues to be Kazakhstan. In 2006, Moscow and Astana signed an interstate cooperation program in the nuclear energy sector that included several cooperation agreements worth a total of about US$10 billion. The first agreement, reached between Kazatomprom and Atomstroyexport, created the Atomnye Stantsii joint venture, whose mission is to construct the Aktau reactor and to set up the production and sale of small and medium-size VBER-300 reactors to third party countries.[102] Moscow made clear that it hesitated to transfer the property rights of the reactors, but a final agreement was reached. The second contract concerns the exploitation of two Kazakh uranium sites, namely, Zarechnoe in the Otrar district, and Budenovskoe in the Sozak district.

A third contract established a center for uranium enrichment with a fifty-fifty share between Kazatomprom and Tekhsnabexport. The new installation, located at the International Uranium Enrichment Centre (IUEC) in Angarsk, is planned to produce approximately 750 kilos of low-enriched uranium by 2013.[103] Afterward, this uranium will be used by Kazakhstan to supply its power stations, or to be sold abroad. The factory will be a "black box" for Kazakh technicians, who will have no access to the enrichment methods. The contract specifies that Russia will benefit from the priority purchase of 6,000 tons of uranium extracted from Zarechnoe and Budenovskoe for the fueling of Angarsk.[104] Kazatomprom has also acquired 10 percent of the capital of the IUEC, which enables an internationalization of the nuclear production cycle to ensure control over enrichment. This fuel bank is able to enrich uranium for partner countries such as Ukraine, Armenia, Mongolia, and perhaps South Korea.[105]

Russia also aims to establish itself in Uzbekistan, although in a more limited fashion, since Uzbek state control over the uranium market is not favorable to international cooperation and the Uzbek authorities have always worked to prevent Russia from achieving a stranglehold over this sector. In 2006, Moscow and Tashkent signed a

memorandum of understanding for the creation of a joint venture, the Uranium Mining Company (UMC), between Tekhsnabexport and Rusburmash on the Russian side,
and the Navoy combine and the State Committee for Geology and Mineral Resources
on the Uzbek side. The aim was to develop the Aktau deposit, whose resources are
estimated at about 4,400 tons. However, the project has not been realized for the time
being, nor has the possible participation of Uzbekistan in the International Enrichment
Center at Angarsk.[106]

In Kyrgyzstan, the Russian investment group Renova purchased 72.28 percent of
the shares of the Kara Balta Combine from the Kyrgyz state in 2007. Renova hopes to
be able to make Kara Balta operational, together with the Minkush deposit, currently
mined but many environmental problems remain unresolved, and the security of the
infrastructure has not been ensured.[107] Moreover, for want of Kyrgyz deposits, Kara
Balta could be revived only by the arrival of uranium from Kazakhstan.

After the disappearance of the Soviet Union, the major Western companies established themselves on the Central Asian market and were well received by the governments, which were eager to collaborate with new partners. Nearly all of Uzbekistan's
uranium production has been exported since 1992 by Nukem, the world's premier
uranium operator. Between 1992 and 2008, Nukem sold close to 45,000 tons of Uzbek
uranium to the United States, Canada, Argentina, Europe, and Asia.[108] In Kazakhstan,
General Electric signed a memorandum of understanding for the extraction of uranium
and nuclear production, but this has not led yet to concrete partnerships. Since 2007 a
privileged alliance between Kazatomprom and the American company Westinghouse
has been consolidated—Westinghouse is the second-largest constructor of nuclear
power plants after Areva and supplies close to half the world's reactor market. Having bought 10 percent of Westinghouse's shares from Toshiba, Kazatomprom now
delivers nuclear fuel to the American company, which will equip the reactors with it,
and China will be the first country to buy such a reactor.[109]

Canadian companies have also invested in Central Asia. In Kazakhstan, Cameco,
the world's largest producer of uranium oxide, has been developing the Inkay site in
collaboration with Kazatomprom, and has undertaken a feasibility study concerning
the construction of a uranium treatment factory. In 2008, both partners announced the
birth of a second joint venture, Ulba Conversion, which is in charge of building the
Ulba hexafluoride plant.[110] Uranium One (formerly UrAsia Energy) is also established
on several sites through its 70 percent control of the Betpak-Dala joint venture and its
30 percent stake in Kyzylkum.[111] An interstate treaty of nuclear cooperation between
Kazakhstan and Canada is currently being considered. Two large Australian companies are also active in the region: Monaro Mining, which entered the Kyrgyz market
with the purchase of eight exploration licenses for deposits containing uranium,[112]
and Nimrodel, which is exploring many sites in the Mailuu-Suu region in central
Kyrgyzstan, as well as a deposit in the Batken region.[113]

France has also entered the Central Asian market, chiefly in Kazakhstan. In 1996,
Cogema (now Areva) and Kazatomprom created a joint venture, Katco (51 percent
owned by Areva, 49 percent by Kazatomprom), which obtained the license for the

Moinkum site in 1999 and began extraction in 2005. According to a new agreement signed in 2008, Katco is authorized to produce 4,000 tons of uranium per year and will manage sales until 2039.[114] In 2009, during a visit by Nicolas Sarkozy to Kazakhstan, the joint venture Ifastar was established to manage the sale of integrated fuel packages to Asian countries and to create a new fuel manufacturing line with a capacity of 400 tons of uranium per year as part of the Ulba combine.[115] After Nigeria and Canada, Kazakhstan now ranks as France's third-largest partner for uranium exploitation. Through this partnership, Areva will be able to target Asian markets, in which Kazatomprom has established a solid foothold.

In Asia, Japan was the first country to grasp the importance of the Kazakh, and, to a lesser extent, Uzbek markets. Since 2006, when Tokyo defined a new energy strategy that forecast the development of the nuclear industry, the country has sought to diversify its supplies: Kazakhstan should ultimately be able to secure a quarter of Japan's uranium requirements, and possibly as much as 40 percent.[116] In 2005, a first joint venture called APPAK was created that groups together Kazatomprom, Sumitomo, and Kansai Electric Power for the exploitation of the Mynkuduk West site, with a full capacity of 1,000 tons per year, the majority of which is exported to Japan.[117] In 2007, the Energy Asia consortium, which includes Marubeni, Tokyo Electric Power Company, Chubu, and Tohoku, obtained majority shares in two of Kazatomprom's subsidiaries, Kyzylkum and Baiken-U, both of which exploit two Khorassan sites in the Kzyl-Orda region, where combined production is forecast to reach 5,000 tons annually by 2014.[118] Toshiba appears set to top the list of Japanese companies established in Kazakhstan, as Marubeni has transferred to it 22.5 percent of its shares in Kyzylkum and Baiken-U.

Further, Japan has not limited itself to uranium mining: in 2007, it signed twenty new projects, including one for technical assistance for fuel manufacture and nuclear reactor construction.[119] In 2009, Kazakhstan's National Nuclear Center signed an agreement with the Japan Atomic Energy Agency (JAEA) to begin building a nuclear reactor. Toshiba has also committed to helping in the important domain of technologies for uranium treatment and the initial stages of enrichment. Mastering these technologies will permit Astana to make and sell a product that meets with international norms.[120] Japan also has its sights set on Uzbekistan: the Uzbek State Committee for Geology and Mineral Resources has signed a cooperation agreement with Japan Oil, Gas, and Metals National Corporation (JOGMEC) for the joint exploration of four deposits, as well as an agreement with Mitsui for the creation of a joint venture to explore the resources of the Kokpatasskaya mines 300 kilometers to the northeast of Navoy.[121]

To contend with its exponential growth and energy consumption, China is also looking to develop its nuclear sector and plans a nearly five-fold expansion by 2020.[122] The Chinese authorities prioritize partners with whom they have already established global economic cooperation, like Kazakhstan. In 2006 and 2007, several cooperation agreements were signed between Kazatomprom and the Guangdong Nuclear Power Group (CGNPC). In 2008, a tripartite strategic partnership between the Kazakh national company and two Chinese state companies, CGNPC and China National

Nuclear Corporation (CNNC), propelled Kazakhstan to the position of China's main foreign supplier of uranium, ahead of its traditional partner, Areva.[123] Both Chinese companies have invested considerable sums of money in three extraction joint ventures, and Kazakhstan has agreed to supply a total of about 24,000 tons of uranium to China by 2020. As a symbol of this increasing partnership, Kazatomprom opened a representative office in Beijing in the fall of 2009.[124] Astana is also setting up in the Chinese market in the construction of nuclear reactors. A first feasibility study was completed during 2009 and a joint venture should see the light of day in the near future. Kazakhstan will then be in charge of supplying Beijing with VBER-300 reactors as well as fuel for a whole series of new reactors. The Guangdong Nuclear Uranium Corporation is also active in Uzbekistan, and in 2009 it signed an agreement with the State Committee of Geology and Mineral Resources to establish a joint venture, Uz-China Uran, for the exploration of the Boztauskoe deposit in the Navoy region, whose uranium will be sold by the Chinese company.[125]

South Korea arrived somewhat late on the Central Asian market. For the time being, at least, it does not aim to set itself up in the extraction sector, but instead in uranium imports so as to meet its growing needs. For this reason, the national company Korea Electric Power Corporation (KEPCO) signed a purchase agreement with Tashkent in 2008 for 2,600 tons of uranium (about 9 percent of its total consumption) by 2015 at a total cost of US$400 million.[126] In the same year, Seoul reached an agreement with Kazakhstan to import just over 3,000 tons of uranium between 2011 and 2017.[127]

The situation is different for India, long marginalized from the uranium world market for its refusal to adhere to the Non-Proliferation Treaty. Today, thanks to an agreement signed with the International Atomic Energy Agency, India has established itself on the world market and the nuclear domain is seen as one of the major areas of Indo-Kazakh partnership. In 2009 both governments increased their cooperation over civil nuclear energy and in 2011 signed an agreement for "Cooperation in Peaceful Uses of Atomic Energy" that envisages supply of fuel, construction and operation of atomic power plants, exploration and joint mining of uranium, exchange of scientific and research information, reactor safety mechanisms, and use of radiation technologies for healthcare. Nazarbayev also announced that Kazatomprom would supply India with 2,100 tons of uranium.[128]

Dominated by Russia, Canada, and Australia in the 1990s, the Central Asian uranium sector has been increasingly invested in by Asian countries, mainly Japan and China, more modestly South Korea and India. These Asian actors are progressively undermining Russian and Western supremacy on the Central Asian market and confirm Asia's importance in the civil nuclear industry boom.

After hydrocarbons, minerals have been heralded as one of Central Asia's trump cards in positioning itself on the world market. Basic ferrous and non-ferrous minerals are in increasing demand with the "explosion" of industrial capacities in emerging countries, in particular China and India, and the REMs seem destined to be the drivers of technological progress in the years to come, though they can probably be replaced over the long term. As for coal, it is unlikely to become a major export since deposits are found across the globe; it nonetheless serves a purpose in domestic Central Asian energy production. Lastly, gold, as a safe investment in the face of the current crises affecting the euro and the dollar, continues to have a promising global market that will generate revenues for Central Asian state budgets. Despite an unattractive investment climate, uncompetitive salaries in comparison with some Asian or African countries, and often outdated equipment, the Central Asian metallurgical industries continue to yield profits, and are increasingly recentralized in the hands of the local ruling elites rather than foreign investors.

For Kazakhstan, the advantages of its status as the world's number one producer of uranium are not solely financial, but power-related. The fact that, in the space of a decade, Astana succeeded in setting up a civil nuclear program confirms its long-term ambitions on the international scene. Although the country still lacks the human and technological resources to realize its ambitions, Kazakhstan has succeeded in diversifying its partnerships and in developing genuine future prospects. Despite the question surrounding the nuclear sector after the Fukushima catastrophe in March 2011 and the announcement made by some countries, in particular Germany, that they will quit nuclear energy, the region's two extractor countries, Uzbekistan and Kazakhstan, have no intention of cutting back on a financial manna of such importance. The international community still harbors many concerns, however. A member of the Central Asian Nuclear Weapon Free Zone, Kazakhstan has agreed not to import radioactive waste and to reduce that which is situated on its own territory. But the Kazakh authorities are poorly prepared for the consequences of a growth in uranium exploitation and currently lack the human and technological capacities to deal with the treatment of waste or with a possible nuclear accident. With no experience in waste management, and despite the fact that regional stability is somewhat fragile, the Central Asian governments have been handling these dangerous elements themselves.

The international concerns that Central Asia could well be turned into a zone for trafficking radioactive products are increasing, especially given the high levels of state corruption and the absence of stability in Kyrgyzstan and Tajikistan. Although Kazakhstan takes the norms of the Non-Proliferation Treaty very seriously and cannot be suspected of wanting to acquire a nuclear military arsenal, the rise in power of a new nuclear actor, even a civil one, in a particularly sensitive zone of the world, can only provoke questions and concerns. None of the states of Central Asia have signed a partnership with Tehran in the nuclear sector, but Kazakhstan does not conceal its possible desire to support Iran's civil nuclear program through the sale of uranium and fuel. Furthermore, Kazakhstan's main partners, Russia and China, are pursuing policies somewhat favorable to the reintegration of Iran into the international fold. This in turn heightens concerns about the potential for Kazakhstan's forcible recruitment into a Russia-China-Iran nuclear triangle that Western countries deem dangerous.

Notes

1. For a general overview of mineral resources in the CIS, see R. M. Levine and G. J. Wallace, "The Mineral Industries of the Commonwealth of Independent States," in *Minerals Yearbook 2005* (Reston, VA: US Geological Survey, 2007).

2. "Iron and Steel Industry in Kazakhstan," *Yqyq.net*, http://yqyq.net/49067-Chernaya_metallurgiya_Kazahstana.html.

3. Levine and Wallace, "The Mineral Industries of the Commonwealth of Independent States."

4. "Kazakhstan Mining Crusher Equipment," *SBM*, August 26, 2011, http://www.crusher-supply.com/kazakhstan-mining-crusher-equipment.html.

5. A. Peck, *Economic Development in Kazakhstan: The Role of Large Enterprises and Foreign Investment* (London: RoutledgeCurzon, 2004), 104.

6. A. Peck, "Industrial Privatization in Kazakhstan: The Results of Government Sales of the Principal Enterprises to Foreign Investors," *Russian and East European Finance and Trade* 38, no. 1 (2002): 31–58.

7. Peck, *Economic Development in Kazakhstan*, 104.

8. Ibid., 105.

9. S. Smirnov, "Kazakh Metallurgy under the Control of International Corporations," *Kazakhstan International Business Magazine*, no. 2 (2008), http://www.investkz.com/en/journals/56/467.html.

10. See "Mittal Steel," Bank Information Center, http://www.bicusa.org/en/Project.63.aspx.

11. See the company website: http://arcelormittal.kz/about/o_kompanii/.

12. Marsh, "Arcelor Mittal in Talks Over Kazakh Safety Fears," *Financial Times,* January 21, 2008, 0000779fd2ac.html#axzz1gR2QCNAk.http://www.ft.com/cms/s/0/667ccaba-c84b-11dc-94a6–0000779fd2ac.html#axzz23vaTmWvi.

13. N. Antelava, "Threat to Investors in Kazakhstan," *BBC News*, September 27, 2007, http://news.bbc.co.uk/2/hi/7015361.stm.

14. "ArcelorMittal Plans to Double Output of Temirtau Plant," *ArcelorMittal*, June 10, 2008, http://www.arcelormittal.com/corp/news-and-media/press-releases/2008/jun/10-06-2008.

15. See the *Forbes* website and their ranking in 2011, http://www.forbes.com/lists/.

16. Y. Kalyuzhnova, *The Kazakhstani Economy: Independence and Transition* (London: St. Martin's Press, 1998), 79–83.

17. "Aluminium of Kazakhstan JSC to Increase Alumina Production till Year-End to 20–25 th. Tons," *Kazahstanskaia fondovaia birzha*, February 3, 2006, http://www.kase.kz/news/show/187416.

18. "Kazakhstan is in the Spotlight," *Invest.kz*, n.d., http://www.investkz.com/en/openkz/14.html; "Zhairemskii GOK," *Kazakhstanskaia fondovaia birzha*, http://www.kase.kz/ru/emitters/show/JGOK.

19. R. M. Levine and G. J. Wallace, "The Mineral Industries of the Commonwealth of Independent States," in *Minerals Yearbook 2006* (Reston, VA: US Geological Survey, 2009), 7 and 9.

20. See the ENRC website, http://www.enrc.com/en-GB/Our-Divisions/Energy/.

21. More details in "Unlocking Resources," Annual Report and Accounts 2010 of the Eurasian Natural Resources Corporation, http://www.enrc.com/Documents/Reports/ENRC_Annual%20Report%202010.pdf.

22. "Risky Business: Kazakhstan, Kazakhmys PLC, and the London Stock Exchange," Global Witness Report, July 2010, http://www.globalwitness.org/sites/default/files/pdfs/gw_risky_business.pdf.

23. See the Kazakhmys website, www.kazakhmys.com.

24. E. Onstad, "Kazakhstan Seeking Kazakhmys-ENRC Partnership," *Mineweb*, April 11, 2008, http://mineweb.com/mineweb/view/mineweb/en/page504?oid=50573&sn=Detail.

25. U. Kozhantaeva, "Mednye liki i zheleznye vzgliady ne skhodiatsia," *Delovaia nedelia*, April 10, 2009.

26. U. Kozhantaeva, "Tsinkovye barony molchat: Sdelki s zolotom i tsinkom ostaiutsia zakrytymi," *Delovaia nedelia*, May 27, 2011; A. Hotter, "Glencore: Kazzinc Buyout Is Opportunistic Deal," *Wall Street Journal*, April 15, 2011, http://online.wsj.com/article/SB10001424052748704116404576264003766081470.html.

27. "ArcelorMittal Temirtau Reaches Deal with Workers," *Silk Road Intelligencer*, June 2, 2009, http://silkroadintelligencer.com/2009/06/02/arcelormittal-termirtau-reaches-deal-with-workers.

28. C. Nuttal, "Mining a Rich Seam," *Silk Road Intelligencer*, May 10, 2011, http://silkroadintelligencer.com/2011/05/10/mining-a-rich-seam/; U. Kozhantaeva, "Otrezannyi lomot': Lobbiruia interesy osnovnykh vladel'tsev, metallurgiia stanovitsia vse bolee zakrytoi," *Delovaia nedelia*, February 4, 2011.

29. See the CIA World Factbook's Kazakhstan fact sheet, https://www.cia.gov/library/publications/the-world-factbook/geos/kz.html.

30. Business Monitor International, *Kazakhstan Mining Report Q3 2012*, Industry Report & Forecasts Series, May 2012, 5.

31. Smirnov, "Kazakh Metallurgy Under the Control of International Corporations."

32. See, for instance, J. Li, "China's Rising Demand for Minerals and Emerging Global Norms and Practices in the Mining Industry," USAID/Foundation for Environmental Security and Sustainability Working Paper, no. 2, 2006.

33. More in Heathershaw, "Tajikistan Amidst Globalization," 157–61.

34. "Tajikistan: On the Road to Failure," International Crisis Group Asia Report, no. 162, February 12, 2009, 14–15.

35. "Wikileaks: Komu prinadlezhit 30% doli Talco Management?" *CentrAsia*, June 6, 2011, http://www.centrasia.ru/newsA.php?st=1307377740; "Talko: Bermudskii treugol'nik na tadzhikskoi zemle," *Tjknews.com*, November 6, 2011, http://tjknews.com/?p=3864.

36. "Aliuminievyi spor prodolzhaetsia," *Ariana*, December 9, 2008, http://www.ariana.su/?S=4.0812091256; J. Helmer, "Tajikistan Struggles for Power," *Asia Times*, October 3, 2007, http://www.atimes.com/atimes/Central_Asia/IJ03Ag02.html.

37. M. Montgomery, "Russia May Challenge China's Rare Earth Dominance," *Rare Earth Investing News*, February 28, 2011, http://rareearthinvestingnews.com/2971/russia-may-challenge-chinas-rare-earth-dominance/.

38. "La Chine et les terres rares: bataille mondiale pour les métaux précieux," *La Tribune*, November 10, 2010, http://www.latribune.fr/actualites/economie/international/20101110trib000571640/la-chine-et-les-terres-rares-bataille-mondiale-pour-les-metaux-precieux.html.

39. Sergei Smirnov, "Redkie metally i zemli daiut GMK redkii shans," *Investkz.com*, no. 3, 2011, http://www.investkz.com/journals/78/863.html; A. Babkina, "Kazakhstan Steps Up Activity in Rare-Metals Market," *Central Asia Online*, October 17, 2011, http://centralasiaonline.com/en_GB/articles/caii/features/main/2011/10/17/feature-01.

40. Montgomery, "Russia May Challenge China's Rare Earth Dominance."

41. "Kyrgyzstan Holds Potential for Major Heavy Rare Earth Supplies," *Metàlminer*, April 27, 2010, http://agmetalminer.com/2010/04/27/kyrgyzstan-holds-potential-for-major-heavy-rare-earth-supplies/.

42. "Kazakhstan to Enter Race for Rare Earth Elements," *Silk Road Intelligencer*, September 27, 2011, http://silkroadintelligencer.com/2011/09/27/kazakhstan-to-enter-race-for-rare-earth-elements/; "Germany Working on Rare Earth Partnership with Kazakhstan," *Global Rare Earth Elements News*, February 1, 2011, http://rareearthdigest.com/ree-news/news-global/95-newsglobal2011020101.html.

43. S. Rogers, "Sumitomo, Kazatomprom Sign Agreement," *Central Asia Online*, March 25, 2010, http://www.centralasiaonline.com/en_GB/articles/caii/newsbriefs/2010/03/25/newsbrief-12.

44. "Race for Rare Earths in Central Asia," *Silk Road Intelligencer*, February 22, 2011, http://silkroadintelligencer.com/2011/02/22/race-for-rare-earths-in-central-asia/.

45. "The Tien Shan Belt: Golden Heart of Central Asia," *Gangue*, no. 88, January 2006.

46. "Dobycha zolota v Tsentral'noi Azii sopostavima s rossiiskimi ob"emami," *Iuvelinet*, http://www.juvelinet.ru/process/news.html?id=9497.

47. "Zolotye novosti: Rastushchii zolotoi potentsial Uzbekistana," *Otraslevoi obzor, Avesta Investment Group*, February 28, 2005, 2. According to other sources, the amount is 5,300 tons: "Gold Mining in Uzbekistan," *Mbendi*, n.d., http://www.mbendi.com/indy/ming/gold/as/uz/p0005.htm.

48. For more information, see the NKMK website, http://www.nkmk.uz.

49. "Mining, the Golden Sector," *World Investment News*, http://www.winne.com/uzbekistan/cr04.html.

50. "Zarafshan-Newmont, Uzbekistan," *Mining Technology*, n.d., http://www.mining-technology.com/projects/zarafshan/.

51. A. Khamidov, "Kyrgyzstan: New Agreement on Kumtor Divides Kyrgyz Elites," *Fergana. news*, April 30, 2009, http://enews.fergananews.com/article.php?id=2529.

52. "Kumtor Gold Mine, Kyrgyzstan," *Mining Technology*, n.d., http://www.mining-technology.com/projects/kumtorgoldminekyrgyz/.

53. More information on Orsu Metals website, http://www.orsumetals.com/talas.aspx.

54. Peck, *Economic Development in Kazakhstan*, 127.

55. "Dobycha zolota v Tsentral'noi Azii."

56. "Gold Production in Kazakhstan Rises 60% in First Half," *Silk Road Intelligencer*, July 15, 2011, http://silkroadintelligencer.com/2011/07/15/gold-production-in-kazakhstan-rises-60-in-first-half.

57. "Kazakhstan May Build New Gold Refinery to Help Boost Output," *Silk Road Intelligencer*, July 5, 2011, http://silkroadintelligencer.com/2011/07/05/kazakhstan-may-build-new-gold-refinery-to-help-boost-output/.

58. R. M. Levine, "The Mineral Industry in Kazakhstan," *Minerals Yearbook 2009* (Reston, VA: US Geological Survey, 2011), 4.

59. "Gold Mining in Kazakhstan. Overview," *Mbendi*, http://www.mbendi.com/indy/ming/gold/as/kz/p0005.htm.

60. M. J. Sagers, "Gold Production in Central Asia," *Post-Soviet Geography and Economics* 39, no. 3 (1998): 125–50.

61. Peck, *Economic Development in Kazakhstan*, 128.

62. V. Lebedev, "Precious Gift to the Country: The Reconstructed Akbakay Gold Processing Plant is Set to Annually Produce 2.8 Tons of Gold Bullions Dore," *Kazakhstanskaia pravda*, July 14, 2007, http://kazpravda.kz/c/1310644186.

63. Adil' Bekzatov, "Zoloto Kazakhstana: Kratkii obzor," *Mezhdunarodnyi delovoi zhurnal Kazakhstan*, no. 1 (2004), http://www.investkz.com/journals/38/236.html.

64. "Dobycha zolota v Tsentral'noi Azii."

65. "Kitaiskaia Zijin Mining kupila mestorozhdenie zolota v Tadzhikistane za $55 mln," *CentrAsia*, June 30, 2007, http://www.centrasia.ru/newsA.php?st=1183147500; "Zijin Mining Invests Abroad as Gold Shines," *China Daily,* July 31, 2007, http://www.chinadaily.com.cn/bizchina/2008-07/31/content_6893900.htm.

66. "Zabastoval Akbakaiskii GMK v Kazakhstane: Zoloto est,' deneg—net . . . ," *CentrAsia*, June 30, 2006, http://centrasia.ru/newsA.php?st=1183190160.

67. V. Bogdetsky, K. Ibraev, and J. Abdyrakhmanova, "Mining Industry as a Source of Economic Growth in Kyrgyzstan," World Bank Reports, Bishkek, 2005.

68. L. Dubrovina, "AO 'GMK Kazakhaltyn' reshilo borot'sia so stikhiinoi dobychei zolota," *Zakon.kz*, July 10, 2009, http://www.zakon.kz/142932-ao-gmk-kazakhaltyn-reshilo-borotsja-so.html.

69. Ibid.

70. E. Marat, "Kyrgyz Government, Parliament Refuse to Prolong Contract with Canadian Gold Company," *Eurasia Daily Monitor* 5, no. 112 (2008), http://www.jamestown.org/single/?no_cache=1&tx_ttnews%5Btt_news%5D=33714.

71. A. Khamidov, "Kyrgyzstan: New Agreement on Kumtor Divides Kyrgyz Elites," *Turkish Weekly*, May 2, 2009, http://www.turkishweekly.net/news/75212/kyrgyzstan-new-agreement-on-kumtor-divides-kyrgyz-elites.html.

72. E. Marat, "Nationalization of Kumtor Gold Mine Sparks Controversy in Kyrgyzstan," *The Central Asia-Caucasus Analyst* 9, no. 10 (2007): 16–17.

73. Khamidov, "Kyrgyzstan: New Agreement on Kumtor Divides Kyrgyz Elites."

74. A. Khamidov, "Kyrgyzstan: Could Kumtor Shakedown Backfire on Bishkek?" *Eurasianet*, June 2, 2011, http://www.eurasianet.org/node/63603.

75. "Kyrgyzstan to Stop Exporting Gold Ore," *Commodity Online*, August 27, 2011, http://www.commodityonline.com/news/kyrgyzstan-to-stop-exporting-gold-ore-41970-3-1.html.

76. "Financing Development: Project Finance Case Study—Zarafshan-Newmont Joint Venture," Institute for International Law and Justice Case Study, http://www.iilj.org/courses/FDProjectFinanceCaseStudy.asp ; "The Uzbek Authorities Intend to Revise Their Tax Relations with Newmont of the United States," *Fergana.news*, March 29, 2006, http://enews.fergananews.com/article.php?id=1347.

77. "Voskhod i zakat imperii Zeromaks," *Uznews.net*, September 22, 2011, http://www.uznews.net/article_single.php?lng=ru&cid=36&aid=844.

78. "Uzbekistan Jails Former Metallurgist at British Mining Company for Spying," *Telegraph*, August 11, 2011, http://www.telegraph.co.uk/news/worldnews/asia/uzbekistan/8695231/Uzbekistan-jails-former-metallurgist-at-British-mining-company-for-spying.html.

79. Werner and Purvis-Roberts, "After the Cold War."

80. "Record Year for Kazakh Uranium," *World Nuclear News*, February 1, 2011, http://www.world-nuclear-news.org/C-Record_year_for_Kazakh_uranium-0102117.html.

81. "Progress in Kazakh Ambitions," *World Nuclear News*, August 12, 2009, http://www.world-nuclear-news.org/ENF-Progress_in_Kazakh_ambitions-1208095.html; "Kazakhstan vykhodit na pervoe mesto v mire po dobyche urana," *RIA Novosti*, December 15, 2009, http://ua.rian.ru/CIS_news/20091215/78255073.html.

82. "New Uranium Mining Projects—Kazakhstan," *WISE Uranium Project*, October 8, 2011, http://www.wise-uranium.org/upkz.html.

83. E. Vinokurov, "Integratsiia atomno-energeticheskikh kompleksov Rossii i Kazakhstana," *Atomnaia strategiia*, no. 8 (2007): 24–26; "Kazakhstan Eyes Top Spot in Uranium Output," *World Nuclear News,* July 23, 2008, http://www.world-nuclear-news.org/ENF-Kazakhstan_eyes_top_spot_in_uranium_output-2307084.html.

84. "World Uranium Mining," *World Nuclear Association*, December 2011, http://www.world-nuclear.org/info/inf123.html.

85. "Ul'binskomu metallurgicheskomu zavodu—60 let," *Yk.kz*, October 29, 2009, http://www.yk.kz/news/show/4880; "Uranium and Nuclear Power in Kazakhstan," *World Nuclear Association*, November 2011, http://world-nuclear.org/info/inf89.html.

86. "Stepnogorsk Mining-Chemical Complex," *Kazatomprom*, n.d., http://www.kazatomprom.kz/en/pages/stepnogorsk_mining-chemical_complex.

87. "Aktau Nuclear Power Station," *International Nuclear Safety*, http://insp.pnl.gov?-profiles-aktau-ak.htm.

88. "Uranium and Nuclear Power in Kazakhstan," *World Nuclear Association*, http://world-nuclear.org/info/inf89.html.

89. T. Kassenova "Kazakhstan's Nuclear Ambitions," *Bulletin of the Atomic Scientists*, April 28, 2008, http://www.thebulletin.org/web-edition/features/kazakhstans-nuclear-ambitions. See also: "Kazakhstan: Energy Report," Economist Intelligence Unit Report, January 10, 2011, http://www.eiu.com/index.asp?layout=ib3Article&article_id=397763224&pubtypeid=1142462499&country_id=300000030&category_id=775133077&rf=0.

90. Kassenova, "Kazakhstan's 'Nuclear Renaissance,'" 55.

91. Ibid., 56–57.

92. "World Uranium Mining."

93. "New Uranium Mining Projects—Uzbekistan," *WISE Uranium Project*, October 6, 2011, http://www.wise-uranium.org/upuz.html.

94. "Uzbek NMMC to Invest $124 Million to Increase Uranium Mining," *Times of Central Asia*, December 1, 2011, http://www.timesca.com/index.php/m-news-by-category/business-and-market-news/744-uzbek-nmmc-to-invest-124-million-to-increase-uranium-mining.

95. M. Sevcik, "Uranium Tailings in Kyrgyzstan: Catalyst for Cooperation and Confidence-Building?," *Nonproliferation Review* 10, no. 1 (2003): 147–54.

96. Ibid., 149.

97. More on the Kara Balta Combine in V. Bogdetsky, ed., "Mining Industry and Sustainable Development in Kyrgyzstan," Report of the Mining, Minerals, and Sustainable Development Project of the International Institute for Environment and Development, no. 110, November 2001.

98. *Uranium 2003: Resources, Production, and Demand* (International Atomic Energy Agency and OECD, 2004), 223–24.

99. V. Kasymbekova, "Uranovyi khvost," *Oasis*, no. 10 (2009): 1–3.

100. V. Panfilova, "Syr'e dlia Irana: Tegeran ishchet partnerov v uranovom biznese," *Nezavisimaia gazeta*, January 11, 2011, http://www.ng.ru/energy/2011-01-11/15_iran,html.

101. R. M. Levine, "The Mineral Industry in Tajikistan," in *Mineral Yearbook 2009*, 3.

102. "Atomnaia stantsiia VBER-300," *Kazatomprom*, http://www.kazatomprom.kz/ru/pages/Atomnaya_stantsiya_VBER-300; Tulekbaeva, "Stroitel'stvo atomnoi stantsii v Kazakhstane planiruet'sia v 2011 godu," *Kazinform*, November 21, 2010, http://www.investkz.com/articles/2458.html.

103. Kassenova, "Kazakhstan's Nuclear Ambitions." See also "Kazakhstan i Rossiia sozdaiut mezhdunarodnyi tsentr po obogashcheniiu urana," *Regnum*, http://www.regnum.ru/news/825275.html#ixzz!gXgUQcYv; and "Obogoschenie," *Kazatomprom*, n.d., http://www.kazatomprom.kz/ru/pages/obogaschenie.

104. Kassenova, "Kazakhstan's Nuclear Ambitions."

105. More information on the IUEC website: http://eng.iuec.ru.

106. M. Starchak, "Uranovyi potentsial Uzbekistana," *Tsentr strategicheskikh otsenok i prognozov*, November 6, 2011, http://www.csef.ru/print/2079/.

107. "Partners Agree to Develop Kara Balta Mill," *World Nuclear News*, October 20, 2008, http://www.world-nuclear-news.org/IT-Partners_agree_to_develop_Kara_Balta_mill-2010085.html.

108. "Obzor pressy," *Polpred.com*, February 20, 2011, http://polpred.com/?ns=1&ns_id=292455.

109. D. Diello, "China Forges Ahead with Nuclear Energy," *Scientific American*, March 28, 2011.

110. Kassenova, "Kazakhstan's 'Nuclear Renaissance,'" 56.

111. More information on the Uranium One website, http://www.uranium1.com/index.php/en/.

112. *Minerals Yearbook 2008*, vol. 3, *Area Reports: International* (Reston, VA: US Geological Survey, 2010), section 4.10.

113. "Nimrodel Starts Drilling at Batken Oblast," *Mineweb*, August 12, 2008, http://www.mineweb.com/mineweb/view/mineweb/en/page674?oid=59407&sn=Detail.

114. "Fast Track: Meeting the Challenge of Producing 4,000 Tons in 2012," *Areva*, n.d., http://www.areva.com/EN/operations-3948/fast-track-meeting-the-challenge-of-producing-4000-tons-in-2012.html

115. "Areva and Kazatomprom Sign a Fuel Marketing Joint Venture Agreement," *Areva*, October 6, 2009, http://www.areva.com/EN/news-7989/areva-and-kazatomprom-sign-a-fuel-marketing-jointventure-agreement.html.

116. "Uranium and Nuclear Power in Kazakhstan," *World Nuclear Association*, December 2009, http://world-nuclear.org/info/inf89.html.

117. "APPAK," *Kazatomprom*, n.d., http://www.kazatomprom.kz/en/pages/aPPak.

118. "Baiken," *Kazatomprom*, n.d., http://www.kazatomprom.kz/en/pages/baiken-u; and "Kyzylkum," *Kazatomprom*, n.d., http://www.kazatomprom.kz/en/pages/kyzylkum.

119. "Uranium and Nuclear Power in Kazakhstan."

120. On the Kazakh-Japanese Partnership, see S. A. Apikyan and D. J. Diamond, eds., *Nuclear Power and Energy Security* (Dordrecht: Springer, 2009), 232.

121. "Uzbekistan: Glittering Prospects of Uzbek Uranium," *Uranium.kg*, June 24, 2009, http://www.uranium.kg/archives/759.

122. A. McDonald, "Nuclear Power Global Status," *IAEA*, 2011, http://www.iaea.org/Publications/Magazines/Bulletin/Bull492/49204734548.html; M. Ragheb, "The Global Status of Nuclear Power," Working Paper of the University of Illinois at Urbana-Champaign, 28, https://netfiles.uiuc.edu/mragheb/www/NPRE%20402%20ME%20405%20Nuclear%20Power%20Engineering/The%20Global%20Status%20of%20Nuclear%20Power.pdf.

123. "Press Release on Signing of Agreements for Strategic Partnership between Kazatomprom, CNNC, and CGNPC," *Kazatomprom*, November 6, 2008, http://www.kazatomprom.kz/en/news/2/Press_Release_on_Signing_of_Agreements_for_Strategic_Partnership_Between_Kazatomprom_CNNC_and_CGNPC.

124. "In September Kazatomprom to Open Office in Beijing," *Nuclear.ru*, September 8, 2009, http:///www.nuclear.ru/eng/press/other_news/2113776.

125. "Uzbekistan i Kitai sozdaiut uranovoe SP," *Gazeta.uz*, August 31, 2008, http://www.gazeta.uz/2009/08/31/uranium/.

126. J. C. K. Daly, "Analysis: Uzbek Uranium Exports Increase," *UPI*, July 10, 2008, http://www.upi.com/Science_News/Resource-Wars/2008/07/10/Analysis-Uzbek-uranium-expoerts-increase/UPI-51681215740150.

127. "South Korea Scouts for Energy in Central Asia," *World Nuclear News*, May 12, 2008, http://www.world-nuclear-news.org/ENF-South_Korea_scouts_for_energy_in_Central_Asia_1205081.html; Na Jeong-ju, "S. Korea to Import 3,140 Tons of Uranium From Kazakhstan," *Korea Times*, May 14, 2008, http://www.koreatimes.co.kr/www/news/nation/2009/11/113_24203.html.

128. "India-Kazakhstan Nuclear Cooperation Agreement Signed," *World Nuclear Association*, April 18, 2011, http://www.world-nuclear-news.org/NP-India_Kazakhstan_nuclear_cooperation_agreement_signed-1804118.html.

11
A Driver of Development
The Electricity Sector

In theory, the Central Asian region should not be suffering large energy shortages: some states are rich in gas, oil, and coal, while others have significant hydroelectric potential. The reality, however, is more complex and can be traced to the Soviet heritage and a lack of regional cooperation. Central Asia's economic priorities as part of the Soviet Union centered on large energy-consuming industries. Accordingly, collective mechanisms of water and electricity management were set up. But Central Asian governments no longer want to maintain this joint management system: each, in their own way, tends to privilege their energy autonomy by reducing imports and exports and prioritizing domestic needs. The transition to the market economy has also turned out to have paradoxical effects. Ageing installations and obsolete distribution networks required costly investments that the states could not finance without international aid. Their markets, however, have proved relatively unattractive for potential foreign investors: administrative apparatuses are riddled by corruption, governments' keep electricity prices low to avoid social discontent, and bankrupt companies or others considered strategic are reluctant to pay their electricity bills. In addition, the established elites pay little attention to long-term questions of profitability or sustainable development; they privilege quick revenues in foreign currency, and therefore centralized, large-scale projects that are more likely to enable them to gain from bribery. Lastly, the energy choices made by the Central Asian governments are highly politicized: they often rely on rationales that valorize national sovereignty, without much connection to economic rationality. The complexity and diversity of these problems, compounded by the further deterioration of interstate relations, as well as the escalation in official discourse, that systematically associates energy negotiations with state security, makes finding nuanced decisions particularly difficult.

Wavering Central Asian Cooperation

With the collapse of the Soviet Union, multiple disputes over energy set the Central Asian states at loggerheads with one another, despite their theoretical complementarity (three countries produce gas and oil, and two produce hydroelectricity). The energy exchanges between them halved between 1990 and 2000 and have never regained their

Soviet levels: According to the Asian Development Bank, regional electricity trade declined from 25 GWh (gigawatt hours) in 1990 to 4 GWh in 2008.[1] Negotiations over the exchange of water for oil and gas regularly break down, through participants questioning the contractual terms. Moreover, the stakes are not exclusively economic; for there is also a geopolitical dimension involved. Until now, the countries downstream of the large rivers, the Amu Darya and the Syr Darya, have been in a position of strength relative to the two water-rich countries of Kyrgyzstan and Tajikistan. By transforming water into a geopolitical weapon—Kyrgyzstan controls 70 percent of Uzbekistan's supply of water—both Kyrgyzstan and Tajikistan hope to strengthen their position vis-à-vis Tashkent. A part of the regional balance is therefore dependent on the future of the water-electricity axis.[2]

According to the UN Convention on the Non-Navigational Uses of International Watercourses, adopted in 1997, upstream countries are prohibited from selling water; they can only trade with services linked to water, such as delivery and storage.[3] The Tajik and Kyrgyz authorities find it unacceptable that they should be responsible for the enormous costs of maintaining and upgrading hydroelectric stations without receiving any financial compensation, especially when the energy gains are only slim. For its part, Tashkent believes that construction on cross-border rivers requires the prior agreement of all countries in the region, and asks to be systematically included in all negotiations, while denouncing all interventions by third-party countries.[4] Kyrgyzstan refuses to yield to this request concerning the hydroelectric stations of Kambarata[5], while Tajikistan claims that the Rogun station is situated on the Vakhsh, itself not a cross-border river, but whose tributaries—the Amu Darya and the Panj—are shared by several countries.[6] For Tashkent, the real challenge is to avoid the growing autonomy of Bishkek and Dushanbe, currently reliant on its gas, and to maintain Uzbekistan's leverage on its neighbors. However, since 2009, under international pressure, the Uzbek authorities have agreed to discuss the idea that stations be constructed under UN control, though no breakthroughs have yet been made.[7]

In terms of water-energy balance, two interstate agreements, the first signed in February 1992, the second in March 1998, were created to maintain the system inherited from the Soviet era. The Intergovernmental Irrigation Agreement (IGIA) of 1998 prevents countries upstream from producing electricity whenever they so desire: water releases are a priority for satisfying the needs of downstream agricultural countries, in exchange for which Kyrgyzstan and Tajikistan are supposed to receive gas and oil during the winter to compensate for their lack of electricity. However, the authorities of both countries have contested the fact that they must pay for their energy imports while the water is distributed without charge. In 2001, Kazakhstan, Kyrgyzstan, and Uzbekistan reached an agreement to settle part of their mutual energy debts through energy barter. The remainder of the exchanges are at a lower price than those of the world market. Thus, in 2007, Bishkek bought gas from Tashkent at about US$150 per 1,000 m^3, but in 2009 Uzbekistan demanded that these tariffs be doubled.[8] The sudden changes in oil and gas prices are detrimental to these exchanges: either Tashkent balks at delivering energy at such a cheap price, or Bishkek declares that it will not pay such high prices.[9] In the last several years, Uzbekistan has regularly cut its energy deliveries to its two neighbors in order to exert pressure on them. The Uzbek authorities complain that their summertime water deliveries are insufficient and that their arable lands are flooded in winter, due to the water released from either the Kyrgyz or Tajik side to produce electricity.

Regional structures were created in order to develop mechanisms of cooperation for water management, such as the Water Energy Consortium (WEC), but they have proven largely ineffective. Some experts argue that the way to settle these conflicts would be to create a water-energy consortium involving all the states of the region, an option raised, without success, under the auspices of the Central Asian Cooperation Organization and then the Eurasian Economic Community.[10] Since the 2007 energy crises, Bishkek and Dushanbe have decided to override the Uzbek blockade and encourage the construction of large stations. In 2008, Islam Karimov noted the risk of interstate conflicts over water and insisted on the danger presented by the building of new dams: any further reduction in the flow of the Amu Darya would have a catastrophic impact on the country's cotton production. Diplomatic tensions have therefore risen, despite the holding of regular summits, and negotiations held in order to resolve the disputes have been made more complex since Uzbekistan has adopted an empty-chair policy.

In the domain of electricity distribution, the disappearance of the Soviet Union spelled the end of the unified electricity network that linked Central Asia to Russia. For Kazakhstan, this situation has proven especially complex, since its northern grid is connected to the Russian network, and its southern grid to the Central Asian network, called the Central Asian Power System (CAPS). At the end of the 1990s, the Russian authorities reestablished the interconnection of electricity networks to enable the state-run company Unified Energy System (UES) to enter the post-Soviet electricity market. Kazakhstan declared that it was in favor of this proposal, which was designed to enable a better regional balance. In 2000, the Russian and Kazakh, and the Kazakh and CAPS networks were reconnected. As a result, the Central Asian network is again able to exchange electricity with Russia via a number of high-tension lines that connect northern and southern Kazakhstan.[11]

In the framework of their common electric grid, the Central Asian states possess equal parts of a public company based in Tashkent, the Central Asian Central Dispatch Center, which is responsible for the upkeep of the balanced and synchronized system of transfer and distribution of electricity for all member countries.[12] In fact, the imbrication of electricity networks practically obliges all the states to import and export electricity in some of their border regions. However, the unified Central Asian system is in the process of disappearing. In 2000, Turkmenistan announced its exit from CAPS in favor of connecting itself to the Iranian power system, which would enable it to collect much more substantial profits. In 2009, Kazakhstan and Uzbekistan both declared their desire to end their participation in CAPS. KEGOC (Kazakhstan Electricity Grid Operating Company) complained about the illegal misappropriation of electricity by Tajikistan, which risked creating large shortfalls in the southern regions of the country. In Uzbekistan, meanwhile, CAPS was believed to be a source of interstate conflict, and the national company UzbekEnergo wanted to make Kyrgyzstan pay for the transit of electricity. Kazakhstan has given its assurances that it will uphold its commitments to Bishkek, but the withdrawal of Uzbekistan, which produces half the electricity redistributed by CAPS, could have disastrous consequences for Kyrgyzstan and Tajikistan.[13] However, these threats have not been carried out and electricity exchanges continue to occur, albeit with regular interruptions.

A Difficult Balance Between Production and Consumption

While electricity shortages were common throughout Central Asia in the 1990s, each country faces its own particular electricity-related challenges, though all also have to contend with similar problems inherited from the Soviet Union. The large Central Asian electricity installations were built in the 1960s–1970s and today have grown obsolescent, though no real replacement or refurbishment programs have begun. None of these countries produces the necessary equipment for the modernization or the construction of new power stations. All are therefore dependent on external production: with the exception of China, no country is able to supply them with the necessary material cheaply and quickly, which suggests there will be difficulties in years to come.[14]

In Kazakhstan, electricity production declined significantly in the first years of independence. It rose again in the first decade of the twenty-first century and exceeded domestic consumption from 2003 on. In 2010, production reached eighty-three billion kWh, but remains a few billion below forecasts.[15] Thanks to Kazakhstan's economic dynamism, electricity consumption has increased each year between 5 and 7 percent, and may reach ninety-seven billion kWh in 2013, and 140 in 2020.[16] The government forecasts a production increase to 150.2 TWh (terrawatt hours) by 2030, with power demand rising to almost 145TWh over the same period, but with shortages expected in coming years.[17] These shortages will be especially acute, since the 2008 financial crisis has slowed the construction of new power stations and has further limited the maintenance of existing structures. In addition, the imbalance in consumption remains extremely large between urban and rural zones, as well as between regions: Kazakh citizens consume an average of 10 kWh (kilowatt hours) of electricity per day and per person, but in six regions of the country, they receive only 2 kWh.[18] The northern regions, which are well connected to the Russian electricity network, suffer fewer shortages than the southern and western regions. However, being the most industrialized, the north is also the biggest consumer and therefore does not escape from chronic deficits. In rural zones, the deterioration of the electricity network inherited from the Soviet Union negatively affects agriculture and whole villages still await their connection to the network.[19]

With seventy-one electric power stations, Kazakhstan has a total production capacity of 18,500 MW. Close to 80 percent of the electricity is produced by coal thermal

Table 11.1

Electricity Production, Consumption, Import, and Export in Central Asia in 2011 (in GWh)

	Production	Consumption	Import	Export
Kazakhstan	86.2	88.1	1.8	3.7
Kyrgyzstan	14.9	7.4	0.535	2.6
Tajikistan	16.1	16.7	0.338	4.4
Turkmenistan	15.5	13	1.4	2.5
Uzbekistan	47.4	40.1	11.44	11.5

Source: Table based on the CIS World Factbook, https://www.cia.gov/library/publications/the-world-factbook/wfbExt/region_cas.html.

power stations, established mainly in the country's north,[20] and 12 percent by six hydroelectric stations.[21] Like other republics, Kazakhstan inherited outdated installations: 90 percent of the cogeneration factories reached the official limit of their life in 2010. If the country does not proceed to rapid modernization, the production of these stations could fall by a third by 2015.[22] According to KEGOC, US$3 billion would be necessary to upgrade the old installations, to construct new ones, and to generate an additional 1,500 MW.[23] In 2007, the government launched a development plan for the electricity industry for 2015, which lists all the factories that are in need of modernization, renovation, or construction. Irrespective of the decisions taken to develop this sector, the wait required to see any impact is relatively long: once the decision is made to build a new production unit, about five years are needed for its construction, often more in the case of hydroelectric stations. Thus, the first power stations with a sufficient production to be able to counter the imbalance between supply and demand are anticipated in 2014 at the earliest.[24]

With a production capacity of 11,580 MW in 2008, Uzbekistan is the second-largest producer of electricity in the region after Kazakhstan. Uzbek electricity is produced by forty-two power plants, including eleven thermal ones with a total capacity of 9,870 MW, and thirty-one hydroelectric stations with a capacity of 1,700 MW.[25] More than two-thirds of the electricity produced comes from thermal gas plants, 7 percent from oil plants, 3.5 percent from coal plants, and 12.5 percent from hydroelectric stations.[26] Like the neighboring states, the whole of the network has deteriorated; the stations are thirty-odd years old or more and require substantial repairs. The country has also suffered a drop in production in recent years, which underlines the urgent need to refurbish the entire system, from the stations to the transmission and distribution networks. A reconstruction and development program for the electricity sector for 2001–2010 was supposed to determine an operational end date for the existing electric power plants and to construct new ones in order to increase production,[27] but few changes can be observed. In the new state program "Priorities for the Development of Industry in Uzbekistan 2011–2015," the state company UzbekEnergo has been tasked with oversight of the vast program of modernization in production and power distribution networks through forty-four new electric projects totaling US$5.2 billion.[28]

In Kyrgyzstan, it was not until 2006 that electricity production regained and then exceeded its Soviet levels, at 14.5 billion kWh. However, it has fallen again in recent years, dropping to 10.5 billion kWh in 2007 and to 8.8 billion in 2008.[29] Out of a total production capacity of 3,700 MW, close to 80 percent is produced by sixteen hydroelectric stations, which are highly concentrated: the Toktogul Reservoir and the Naryn Falls make up 97 percent of hydroelectric capacity and 78 percent of the country's total electricity capacity. Kyrgyzstan only has two gas, oil, and coal stations, which produce only a little more than a billion kWh per year. Here again, all the production plants built under the Soviet regime require considerable maintenance and renovation work, the estimated cost of which is at least US$180 million.[30] More than half the country's electric system is considered to be substantially deteriorated. The power lines and the substations are almost permanently overloaded, with demand far outstripping supply. Despite some initiatives, the sums invested remain insufficient: in 2007, Bishkek could make a mere US$13 million available for the renovation of the plants.[31] Instead of seeking to develop modest but effective strategies for energy efficiency, the Kyrgyz authorities set themselves grandiose and unattainable objectives: a strategy for the energy and fuel complex for 2025 forecast a growth in the country's production capacity of close to 40,000 MW, among other means by the construction of the Kambarata I and II hydroelectric stations.[32]

Despite its considerable hydroelectric potential, Tajikistan produces only 4,000 MW a year, most of which comes from the Vakhsh River Falls and the Dushanbe electric power plant.[33] In winter, shortages are exacerbated by the water releases necessary to supply the Tursunzoda aluminum factory, TALCO, which absorbs 40 percent of the country's yearly electricity production. The factory is not adapted to the current electricity production and does not aim to produce more in summer and consume less in winter.[34] Tajikistan's water storage is thus not adapted to meet total electricity demand. In the winter of 2008–2009, the drop in the level of the main reservoir at Nurek led to a decline in electricity production, a mere six billion kWh between January and June 2009, that is, 10 percent less than the preceding year.[35] As in the winter of 2007–2008, the national company, Barki Tojik, was compelled to ask the government to impose restrictions on households and businesses to avoid drawing from the reservoir.[36] To remedy these difficulties, instead of prioritizing the rapid construction of small plants for local supply, the Tajik authorities have banked on large hydroelectric sites such as Sangtuda I and II, and Rogun, which necessitate years of work and complex geopolitical negotiations.

With its low human density, Turkmenistan has an electricity production capacity that exceeds its domestic consumption. In 2000, it produced 9.3 billion kWh, including 7.7 billion for the domestic market, leaving a surplus of 1.6 billion for export.[37] Production appears to have been continuing to increase throughout the decade: according to the International Energy Agency, based on Turkmen statistics, the country produced 15 billion kWh in 2008.[38] Almost all Turkmen electricity is generated by thermal factories.

For several years now, the government has ramped up the number of renovations and modernizations: new turbines in the hydroelectric stations of Abadan and Balkanabat, a new gas plant with a capacity of 250 MW designed to increase the electricity security of the capital, Ashgabat, and the Ahal region, and, since 2009, the construction of new gas plants at Ahal and in the tourist areas of Avaza and Balkanabat.[39]

The methods of electricity production diverge between the two upstream countries, Kyrgyzstan and Tajikistan, which are developing their hydroelectric potential, and the three downstream states, Kazakhstan, Turkmenistan, and Uzbekistan, most of whose electricity is produced by thermal power stations. Despite these differences, all Central Asian states are similar in that they must not only manage the Soviet legacy, but also deal with issues of sustainable development. Gas and oil, widely used in the Soviet period, have today become too expensive for the average living standard of Central Asian populations. Moreover, the lack of cooperative relationships between the states also complicates the picture; indeed, Uzbekistan regularly holds up gas deliveries headed for its neighbors. The governments thus tend to want to privilege national resources in order to avoid complex negotiations with neighbors.[40] Coal is foremost among them. Widely distributed across the world, it represents more than one quarter of global energy consumption, and will doubtless still account for a fifth of consumption by 2020. From this standpoint, the post-Soviet space is well placed, with about 250 Gt (billion tons) of estimated reserves, behind the United States but ahead of China and India.[41] In Central Asia, coal is viewed as a major energy source for the production of electricity, making it possible to reserve the gas stocks for export. All the Central Asian governments are therefore planning to build new coal-fired power plants.

Management Bodies, Transmission Networks, and Export Strategies

Each country subscribes to different degrees of economic reform in regard to the production and distribution of electricity. The two more liberalized economies, Kazakhstan and Kyrgyzstan, have sought to privatize part of the market, while electrical energy is still state controlled in the three other republics. The low profitability of the Central Asian electric system and the social implications of energy policies (electricity is sold cheaply and it is difficult to install individual meters) do not favor market privatization. Governments aim to keep their hold over this strategic sector and corruption is considerable: the highest-placed Kyrgyz and Tajik officials have been implicated in misappropriating and illegally selling electricity.[42] Lastly, there are very few private investors for the additional reason that electricity production is seen as a matter of national security by the governments involved, and therefore remains under state control, a situation that does not favor its privatization at either the national or local levels.

In Kazakhstan, while the vast majority of power plants have been privatized, the distribution networks remain in state hands. KEGOC, created in 1997, administers the electrical system at the national level (high-tension lines, substations, and a central distribution apparatus) while it accords various private companies the rights for local management. Numerous problems remain, in particular an insufficient legislative framework. In addition, the municipal administrations are poorly equipped to manage public service matters connected with electricity and its daily distribution.[43]

In Kyrgyzstan, the management of energy is divided into different ministries and state agencies. The former Ministry of Water Management has been merged with the Ministry of Agriculture, whereas others sectors were transferred to the Ministry of Ecology and of Emergency Situations, or to the public company "Electric Utilities" (*Elektricheskie stantsii*), which has control over all of the country's waterfalls and hydroelectric and thermal power stations.[44] Deliveries of heat and electricity are the responsibility of the Kyrgyz Public Corporation, while gas purchases are handled by Kyrgyzgas. The absence of a unified decision-making body slows the development of the energy sector. The law is only rarely applied and public or private organizations that consume more than their daily quota go practically unpenalized. The regional distribution of electricity is divided into four companies, each of which is in charge of a part of the country: Oshelektro (the Osh region), Jalalabadelektro (the Jalalabad region), Vostokelektro (east), and Severelektro (north).[45] Only the last of these has been privatized, for an amount of US$3 million, which is probably far below its real worth. The hydroelectric plants are in fact scheduled to be gradually privatized so that the very costly maintenance operations can be passed on to the private sector, something which nonetheless necessitates private investors to come forward and stump up the money.

In Uzbekistan, despite some restructuring, the energy sector, the coal industry, the regional heating systems, and the distribution systems of liquid fuel remain under state control. The Energy Ministry has been transformed into a national company, UzbekEnergo, which seeks to develop joint ventures with foreign investors, while retaining the controlling shares. The success of this partial privatization strategy has been very limited: in 2006, Tashkent had to acknowledge the failure of the tender bid for the Navoy and Tahiatash power plants due to a lack of potential candidates. Between 2005 and 2007, tenders were put out for six electrical power plants, once again without attracting foreign investors, who were put off by the retroactive measures of the Uzbek government and its low-price policy for selling electricity.[46] UzbekEnergo plans to gradually make the distribution of electricity profitable. Since 2010, it has been launching the installation of meters, at first in business and commercial structures, and then for consumers. During the first six months of 2011, more than 260,000 meters were installed.[47]

In Tajikistan, the electricity sector is under the control of a state-run company, Barki Tojik, and all the parties involved in the regulation of the sector are financed through the state budget. The selling price of electricity is decided by the president himself. The difficulty involved in initiating a private market for electricity resides partly in the fact that a single waterfall generates the majority of the country's electricity.[48] In Turkmenistan, the system remains entirely under state control.

Despite its more advanced state of economic development, Kazakhstan, due to its huge size, faces problems in electricity transmission. Its electricity distribution is divided into three somewhat interconnected networks. Two networks, situated in the north, are connected to Russia and function thanks to the region's coal stations, while the third, in the south, is connected to the Central Asian Power System. The southern network is only connected to those of the north by two lines of 220 kV (kilovolt) and a line of 500 kV.[49] Kazakhstan is therefore obliged to import electricity from Kyrgyzstan and Uzbekistan for its southern regions. Currently experiencing rapid economic development due to its oil boom, the west of the country is also suffering from shortages. The country suffers large losses of electricity during transport and distribution: In 2009, about 15 percent of the electricity was reportedly lost before reaching the consumer.[50] A state program was set up to modernize the national electricity grid in two phases, with the first finishing in 2009, and the second phase lasting from 2008 to 2017, for a total cost of around US$800 million. The loans are being provided by Islamic Development Bank and EBRD in partnership with the Development Bank of Kazakhstan.[51] The stated objectives are twofold: the first, to construct a new north-south line of 500 kV, so that imports from Uzbekistan and Kyrgyzstan are no longer required; the second, to increase the efficiency of production and distribution in the north in order to sell at more competitive prices to local metal and petrochemical industries.[52]

Kazakhstan hopes its production surplus will grow from 10.2 billion kWh in 2008 to 21 in 2013, giving it more prospects for export, in particular with Russia.[53] In 2008, Astana also reached an agreement with Bishkek to export 250 million kWh to Kyrgyzstan. However, Kazakhstan is cautious about exporting large quantities and prefers to reduce its imports, which are too costly and are sensitive on the geopolitical level. Thus, in 2008, the export of electricity diminished by more than a third and the imports by close to a quarter, reflecting the preference of the authorities for local consumption.[54] In addition to its own production, Kazakhstan places hopes in its role as a transit country: the Kambarata and Sangtuda projects are planned to export electricity to Russia, which will enable Astana to amass considerable transit fees.[55] The construction of a second high-tension line connecting the north and the south of the country contributed to a realignment in favor of the southern regions of the country, but will also serve as a site of transit for Central Asian electricity to Siberia. Aware of the importance of distribution, the Kazakh government insists on the fact that henceforth all projects for the construction of new power stations be accompanied with transmission lines.

Kyrgyzstan's electrical grid is also complex, since it was designed to circumvent the Tian Shan Mountain range dominating the center of the country. Its state of dilapidation and the dearth of financing available to renovate it preclude its profitability and results in recurrent electricity breakdowns, such as the one in August 2009, which caused majors blackouts in the Chui region and the capital, Bishkek.[56] The losses of electricity are large: while they were allegedly 11 percent in 1991, they reached 40 percent in 2004, before falling to 31 percent in 2008.[57] With a view to developing export potential, two important projects have been launched: the first is the construction of a transmission line of 500 kV, the Datka-Kemin, which will connect the north to the south of the country, for a cost of US$170 million;[58] and the second is the overall renovation of the southern transmission system. Loans from the World Bank and the IMF should improve the southern electrical grid by decongesting specific lines, increasing supply in winter, and putting a halt, at least partially, to imports from Uzbekistan. For some years already, Kyrgyzstan has been putting its electricity surpluses up for auction: about 15 percent of its total electricity production becomes exportable in the summer months. The Kyrgyz authorities try to play off the competition in order to obtain better prices. In 2007, they exported 200 million kWh to Kazakhstan at 1.52 cents per kWh. In the summer of 2009, Kazakhstan again became the destination for more than 540 million kWh at a price of 4.6 cents per kWh.[59]

In Uzbekistan, the state of the Central Asian Power System and the Central Asian United Dispatch Center is so dilapidated that it has become difficult to maintain reliable operations in the country, let alone to develop a regional electricity market. In 2010, UzbekEnergo put 300 kilometers of new lines into service, and 1,000 kilometers more are expected to be operational by 2015. It also launched the construction of a second turbine in the Sukhan substation in the south of the country, and began constructing a line of 500 kV connecting Guzar to Sukhan, as well as another connecting the thermal station of Novo-Angren near Tashkent to the Ferghana Valley.[60] Uzbek electricity exports are sent to neighboring countries: Tajikistan and Kyrgyzstan during the winter, Afghanistan the whole year round. In 2009, thanks to a loan from the Islamic Development Bank, an electricity line enabling Uzbekistan to export up to 300 MW of electricity to Kabul was set up, to complement the railway line linking both countries.[61]

Tajikistan's electricity system is also divided into a northern grid, in the Khudjand region, and a southern grid near Dushanbe. These operate almost without interconnection and are both linked up to Uzbekistan. The majority of energy transfers between the two regions are carried out by a 500 kV transmission line that crosses Uzbek territory. Given the state of relations between the two countries, this is not without problems. One of Barki Tojik's priorities was thus to construct two new lines, one between Lolazor and Obi Maror in the Khatlon region in the south, and another of 500 kV connecting the north and the south of the country and capable of transferring eight billion kWh. The second, built by Chinese companies, is now operational. As for the Gorno-Badakhshan Autonomous Region (GBAO), it functions in near autonomy because of a third network, Pamir Energy, a station built by the Aga Khan Foundation.[62] The interconnection of the electrical grids of the north of Tajikistan with those of Uzbekistan obliges both countries to undertake continual import-export exchanges. Trade in electricity could potentially develop with Bishkek, and like its neighbor, Tajikistan has an electricity surplus in the summer months that it wants to sell to Afghanistan.

Since the turn of the century, Turkmenistan has been upgrading its lines in order to remedy its considerable energy losses, and its transmission network has been mostly modernized. It has thus become one of the largest Central Asian electricity exporters (close to 2.5 billion kWh in 2009)[63] and one of the only ones to have significantly diversified its partnerships. Whereas in the 1990s, Kazakhstan was its only client, in 2003 Ashgabat succeeded in signing a tripartite cooperation agreement with Iran and Turkey. The Iranian-Turkmen part (Balkanabat-Gonbad) of the new transmission line was constructed in 1999 by the Iranian company Tavanir and the Iranian-Turkish part (Hoj-Bashkal) in 2003 by the Turkish company Tetas.[64]

The Turkmen authorities are targeting the countries of South Asia. In 1999, an agreement was signed with Islamabad for the construction of a transmission line via Afghanistan, but the project has been postponed. In 2002, a bilateral agreement was signed for the export of about 200 million Turkmen kWh per year to Afghanistan. Relations with its Central Asian neighbors remain difficult since Ashgabat is obliged to transit via the Uzbek electricity grid if it wants to sell electricity to Tajikistan and Kyrgyzstan. In 2007, it signed a five-year agreement with Dushanbe for the annual delivery of 1.2 billion kWh.[65] Uzbekistan authorized the use of its grid for the transit of Turkmen electricity, but seems to have asked for particularly high transit fees (10 percent of the price).[66] Not having obtained an agreement on the fee, Tashkent interrupted deliveries in January 2009 claiming a problem with the operation of the Karakul substation, but refused to allow Tajik engineers access to diagnose the problem and help repair it.[67] Electricity deliveries resumed after a meeting of the Tajik-Uzbek Economic Cooperation Commission but remain subject to frequent interruptions.

Apart from satisfying their own growing needs, the Central Asian states hope to export their seasonal surpluses to neighboring countries Russia and China (especially Xinjiang), as well as to Afghanistan and its southern neighbors, Pakistan and India. The World Bank has encouraged the governments to sign interregional agreements concerning the transit of electricity and to open up the region to export markets. This cooperation is bound to exceed a bilateral framework and become multilateral. Several summits of the Shanghai Cooperation Organization have confirmed the willingness of member states to develop a common strategy on matters pertaining to electricity and a working group has been set up. Barki Tojik even affirmed that the SCO could create a collective department and be transformed into an OPEC-style electricity organization.[68]

With the Asian Development Bank support, the CASA-1000 project (Central Asia-South Asia), the first phase of a regional project known as Central Asia-South Asia Regional Electricity Market (CASAREM), envisages the export of electricity to Afghanistan and Pakistan via Kyrgyzstan and Tajikistan thanks to the construction of an interconnection line of 500 kV between Kyrgyzstan and Tajikistan, and of another between Tajikistan and Pakistan via Afghanistan, allowing 1,300 MW to be exported, 300 MW for consumption in Afghanistan and 1,000 MW in Pakistan.[69] The Uzbek authorities do not hide their concerns about the increasing competition from Tajik sales of electricity to Afghanistan in winter, and at rates far lower (3.5 cents) than those offered by UzbekEnergo (7.5 cents). The construction of a thermal power plant in the Sukhandarya region, on the border with Afghanistan, is one of the Uzbek government's responses to this competition, along with the railway blockade Tashkent organized to halt the construction of Rogun.[70] However, like the pipeline projects, these electricity corridors come up against the Afghan question: an essential transit country for any southward expansion, its instability severely impedes cooperation with Pakistan and India. In 2009, Washington exerted pressure on Islamabad and Kabul and a new report confirming the CASA-1000 project's viability was released in 2011, despite the unresolved questions of transit tariffs and purchase prices.[71] Given the shortages that the export countries themselves suffer, their capacity to supply substantial energy surpluses in the short term leaves many experts skeptical.

The Challenges of Developing Hydroelectricity

Renewable energies have been in the Western media spotlight, but in Central Asia they are only taking their first faltering steps. In spite of many development programs, they are too costly for local budgets and require substantial foreign investments and onsite high-tech training. Moreover, many energy alternatives are too diffuse (e.g., solar energy) or only exploitable on particular sites (geothermal energy). On a global scale, interest is centered mainly on hydroelectricity, wind energy, and biomass, but here again there are obstacles to their development: one agricultural hectare is necessary, for example, to produce one toe (ton of oil equivalent) of bio-fuel. In Central Asia, as elsewhere, the production of bio-energies thus competes with human food requirements.[72] Despite these reserves, renewable energies would serve a purpose in Central Asia, in particular in remote areas like in Kazakhstan, where the construction of electricity power lines to villages populated by only a few hundred inhabitants make standard electricity projects unprofitable.

More than solar energy, wind energy, or biomass, hydroelectricity appears likely to be a major renewable energy for Central Asia's future. In terms of hydroelectric potential, Tajikistan (530 billion kWh per year) and Kyrgyzstan (142 billion kWh) rank as the second- and third-largest countries of the CIS, behind Russia.[73] However, despite the promises made by the local authorities in developing this sector further, many thorny questions must first be resolved. Local geographical conditions are difficult, seismic risks are high, the environmental balance is precarious, and risks of river pollution owing to the construction of dams must be taken into account. Tajik and Kyrgyz dams dating from the Soviet era were constructed to supply water to agricultural zones situated downstream and not to produce electricity: their structures lack the storage capacities necessary for production in winter, which results in frequent load shedding of water. The governments have thus concentrated on building new dams. As the life span of a hydroelectric dam is estimated at about 300 years, at least for the larger ones, the grand projects envisaged must be viewed on a long temporal scale.

In Kyrgyzstan, the share of hydroelectric stations in total production has risen from 67 to 94 percent, while that of thermal stations has dropped from 32 to 6 percent.[74] However, most experts believe that Kyrgyzstan at best exploits only 9 percent of its hydroelectric potential.[75] The largest stations are situated on the Naryn River: Toktogul (1.2 million kWh), Kurpsay (800,000 kWh), Tash-Kumyr, Atabashin, Alamedin, and Uchkorgon. The country's main reservoir, Toktogul, holds several years' worth of water

Table 11.2

Hydroelectric Potential of the Countries of Central Asia

	In millions of tons of oil equivalent	Percentage in relation to total potential in Central Asia
Kazakhstan	2.3	5.2
Kyrgyzstan	14	31.1
Tajikistan	27.3	60.5
Turkmenistan	0.2	0.4
Uzbekistan	1.3	2.9
Total	45.1	100

Source: A. Kazantsev, "Perspektivy razvitiia gidroenergeticheskogo i uglevodorodnogo sektorov ekonomik tsentral'noaziatskikh gosudarstv: Vozmozhnye posledstviia dliia politiki Rossii," *Analiticheskie zapiski* 2, no. 31 (2008): 5.

stocks for indispensable agricultural irrigation downstream. Under the Soviet regime, three-quarters of load shedding was done in summer, a quarter during winter. Today the ratio have practically been inverted, with 36 percent of load shedding being done in summer and 62 percent in winter.[76] While the winter of 2007–2008 was very difficult in terms of harsh weather, the winter of 2008–2009, despite its milder temperatures, was accompanied by a worsening of the dire energy situation. The volume of water in the Toktogul reservoir fell drastically from nineteen billion m³ of water in 2005 to only 9.5 billion.[77] This significant loss approached the threshold of five billion m³, below which the generators of the hydroelectric station can no longer function. The hydroelectric plants have been heavily affected, with some industries witnessing production as a result. The impact on agriculture was particularly visible: 30 percent less water, even if this level was irregular, caused a 40 percent reduction in crop yields. In the summer of 2009, the level rose partially and the reservoir reached a threshold of twelve billion m³.[78] It regained its normal level in 2010–2011.

Since the plant at Toktogul is generally insufficient to heat the country in winter and supply agriculture in summer, Kyrgyzstan has placed a lot of hope in the construction of the hydroelectric stations of Kambarata I (1,900 MW) and Kambarata II (300 MW) on the Naryn River, which could also make available surpluses for export. Despite objections from the Uzbeks, in 2009 President Kurmanbek Bakiyev announced his decision not to delay the start of construction any further. However, government information remains imprecise about the progress of work on Kambarata I and about the real financing available for Kambarata II, whose construction costs will be particularly high.[79] The dearth of competent specialists, experts as well as technicians, also hinder Kyrgyzstan's prospects for success. The first turbine of Kambarata II, which was delivered by Moscow, was put into operation in November 2010. While the second and third turbines are still pending, the real issue is that of the future realization or otherwise of Kambarata I. The rather high construction costs have put the viability of this dam into question: 2009 estimates projected a budget of US$1.7 billion, but this

Table 11.3

Main Hydroelectric Power Stations and their Production on the Naryn River

	Installed capacity, MW	Output million kWh
Kambarata 1	1,900	5,088
Kambarata 2	360	1,148
Upper Naryn Cascade	352	1,600

Source: E. Vinokurov, "Financing Infrastructure in Central Asia: Water and Energy Nexus," *World Finance Review* (Spring 2007): 137.

was revised markedly upwards in 2011 to as much as US$3 or 4 billion, owing to the need for building with reinforced concrete instead of ballast.[80] The associated extra cost will considerably increase the price of a kilowatt hour to as much as fourteen cents, whereas current market price is only two to three cents. The future of Kambarata I is therefore far from assured if its profitability is in question, and the production of Kambarata II will remain limited if Kambarata I does not operate upstream.

Like Kyrgyzstan, Tajikistan has based its long-term development strategies on hydroelectricity, which produces about 90 percent of the country's total energy. The Nurek power plant is the country's largest at 3,000 MW; it is situated on the Vakhsh, a river with an estimated power potential of more than 9,000 MW.[81] Located at the top of the falls, its reservoirs enable a seasonal regulation of the river flows. The other hydroelectric stations, with much more limited production, are those of Golovnaya and Baypasin on the Vakhsh, Karakum on the Syr Darya in the north of the country, and the Varzob Falls in the south. All date from the Soviet period and are in need of modernization. Like Kyrgyzstan, Tajikistan lacks water storage to enable sufficient production during winter, and would like to export to procure foreign currency revenues. Nevertheless, the weakness of the Tajik economy makes any rapid exploitation of the hydroelectric potential difficult in the short or medium term. Necessary investments are very high in relation to the limited state budget, and therefore foreign investments are required. The hydroelectric station of Sangtuda I on the Vakhsh, with a capacity of 670 MW, was officially inaugurated in 2009 at a cost of US$500 million. Sangtuda I is set to produce 12 percent of the country's electricity, if the reservoir is full and the plant can function at total capacity. The Sangtuda II plant (220 MW) was inaugurated by presidents Rahmon and Ahmadinejad in September 2011.[82]

However, Tajikistan's major project remains the construction of the hydroelectric station and reservoir of Rogun on the Vakhsh, whose production is estimated to reach 3,600 MW. After the breakdown in negotiations with Russian company RusAl, the Tajik government decided to construct the power plant and reservoir without international participation by fleecing its own population (the project needs more than twenty years of financing from the state budget), forcing it to buy shares of the Rogun public company.[83] Under international pressure, Dushanbe eventually has agreed to undergo an external evaluation by the World Bank that should be made public in the first half of 2013. The World Bank has already pointed out the risks of building a dam at the maximum height requested by the Tajik authorities (335 meters) in a seismic zone.[84] In addition, the considerable amount of sediment carried by the Vakhsh River could block the tunnels and seriously disrupt the hydroelectric system. The international experts therefore have suggested a more modest structure of around 120 meters high, almost two-thirds lower than that desired by the Tajik government. Dushanbe replied that such a dam would not be economically viable or cover the costs incurred.[85] President Emomali Rahmon now finds himself between a rock and a hard place: political pressure on the population regarding the Rogun project has been so strong in recent years that the failure of the project would probably undermine the president's legitimacy.

The Rogun project is also extremely expensive. The consulting firm Lahmeyer International estimated that it would be necessary to reconstruct almost the entire structure put in place by the Soviets in the late 1980s, which would significantly increase the final budget. The Tajik government continues to be extremely optimistic, anticipating the opening of the first two generators in 2013, while Lahmeyer calculates that it will take eight to fifteen years to fill the reservoir.[86] In response to criticism from Uzbekistan and Kazakhstan, the Tajiks have argued that the water levels of the Vakhsh will return to normal once the reservoir is filled and that any lower levels will be offset by the possibility of importing cheap electricity. But the conditions for the sale of electricity and its price are also very vague; neither the Ministry of Energy nor the national electric company Barki Tojik has provided any hard data on this.[87] International experts are now mulling over the increasing number of alternative proposals: the construction of a dam with a lower height; the construction of smaller hydroelectric facilities on the Zeravshan, Panj, and Gunt Rivers, a project that the Tajik government suspended in favor of focusing on Rogun; investment in solar panels; or a program to drastically reduce electricity losses from industry and homes. All of these programs cost less than the construction of Rogun, would have a minor impact on the environment, decrease the risks of failure or an accident, and limit tensions with Tashkent. Faced with so many uncertainties, it is likely that the debate over Rogun is not yet over.

For both Kyrgyzstan and Tajikistan, a dilemma has emerged: should large power stations be privileged on account of the fact that they would guarantee both countries substantial export revenues, or is this outweighed by the cons that include their exorbitant cost (several billion dollars), the environmental damage caused, and interstate tension? Arguing in favor of smaller power stations is the fact that they are relatively cheap, are less politically contentious regarding neighboring countries, and provide more for local populations? The Asian Development Bank endorses decentralized electricity production in rural and isolated areas that avoids the need for electricity grids to cover vast expanses of territory. Small hydroelectric power stations, including even wind and solar energy, in fact seem to provide potentially interesting solutions for some areas of Central Asia. Moreover, their development would perhaps enable

Table 11.4

Main Hydroelectric Power Stations and their Production in Tajikistan

	Location	Installed capacity, MW	Output million kWh
Sangtuda 1	Vakhsh	679	—
Sangtuda 2	Vakhsh	220	—
Rogun	Vakhsh	3,600	13,100
Shurob	Vakhsh	850	987
Zeravshan Falls	Zeravshan	unknown	Up to 20,000
Panj Falls	Panj	300 to 4,000	Up to 86,300

Source: Vinokurov, "Financing Infrastructure in Central Asia," 137.

a halt to be put to ongoing deforestation: impoverished rural populations are increasingly using wood as fuel for heating, a trend which is having significant environmental consequences in already ecologically fragile areas.[88]

Despite a much more limited potential, Turkmenistan and Uzbekistan are also trying to develop hydroelectricity to supply more poorly served regions and reduce their gas consumption so that it can be reserved for export. In Uzbekistan, the largest hydroelectric stations are those of Charvak (620 MW)[89] and Khodjikent. The total hydroelectric potential is estimated to be about 20,000 MW, including 30 percent by small-size stations. At present, only a third of this potential is reportedly being utilized. Aware of the stakes, the Uzbek government has set aside, with backing from the Asian Development Bank, a budget of US$250 million for the construction of a new power plant on the Chatkal River (100 MW), several small-sized power plants (and new irrigation networks), as well as a solar power plant in the Tashkent region.[90]

Contrary to Kyrgyzstan and Tajikistan, hydroelectricity makes up only a small portion of Kazakhstan's production of electricity—about 14 percent. After the fall of the USSR, two-thirds of the country's electricity was generated by coal stations. Close to 400 small hydroelectric stations with an annual production capacity of six billion kWh allegedly went into disuse in the 1990s. Three hydroelectric stations currently produce 10 percent of the country's electricity demand: those of Bukhtarma and Ust-Kamenogorsk on the Irtysh and that of Kapchagay on Lake Balkhash. Taking its economic power into account, Kazakhstan is interested in water more for the purposes of agriculture than for generating electricity. Though its hydroelectric sector remains relatively undeveloped, Astana is planning to invest more in it in the coming decade: from now until 2018, the country's electricity production is planned to increase by 83 percent, with a significant amount of that increase coming from hydroelectricity.[91] The Kazakh government has thus set out on the search for international financing for some hydroelectric projects such as the Moynak station about 200 kilometers east of Almaty, the power station on the Khorgos River (a tributary of the Irtysh that forms the international border with China), and the modernization of the Aksu station.[92]

Does Central Asia Have a Geopolitics of Electricity?

Russia continues to be the largest foreign investor in the electricity sector of Central Asia: UES controls half of Kazakhstan's main coal power plant, Ekibastuz II, and runs the Sangtuda I hydroelectric station in partnership with the Tajik authorities. RusHydro is set to invest US$800 million in the hydro-power stations to be constructed along the Naryn River, though Kyrgyzstan's domestic political situation has slowed down Russian investment.[93] Russia was also in charge of constructing Rogun, but the partnership established between Dushanbe and RusAl fell apart in 2007.[94] Thanks to the existence of a common electricity grid, UES imports cheap Kyrgyz and Tajik electricity for some parts of Siberia, and delivers electricity to the north of Kazakhstan. More generally, Moscow has not hidden its interest in a north-south energy bridge that would enable it to develop a Eurasian market and to export to Asia via the Central Asian network.[95]

China has rapidly imposed itself as the second-largest electricity partner of the Central Asian governments. The Sino-Kazakh strategic partnership signed in 2005 makes provision for cooperation between KEGOC and the GRID Corporation of China, and is encouraging the construction of an "electricity bridge" between both countries.[96] This could become reality in a few years with the construction of a new coal-powered plant at Ekibastuz and a high-tension line of 800 kV spanning more than 4,000 kilometers, which Beijing would take complete responsibility for, in exchange for which it would acquire all the electricity produced.[97] Chinese companies are also actively involved in two hydroelectric projects, the Dostyk station close to the Khorgos border post, and Moynak, the first large-scale Sino-Kazakh project in the domain of non-mineral resources. In Tajikistan, China seems to have decided to invest mainly on the Zarafshan River, in the Penjikent region. The state-run Sinohydro Corporation won the tender for the Yavan power station, but the project has been suspended for the moment under pressure from Uzbekistan. China hopes to get involved in Kyrgyzstan with the construction of high-tension lines to Xinjiang but the project has not yet been finalized. Chinese financing is being floated for three mid-size hydroelectric stations, built on cross-border rivers running down from the Kyrgyz glaciers toward China.[98] Lastly, in Uzbekistan, UzVodEnergo set up a partnership with the China National Electric Equipment Corporation (CNEEC) for the construction of two small hydroelectric stations at Andijan and Ahangaran for a cost of US$17 million, which includes the delivery of equipment and the assembly of the two blocks, as well as personnel training.[99]

Other external actors are also present on the Central Asian power market, but with more modest levels of involvement. The US company AES bought Kazakhstan's largest electric power station, Ekibastuz I, and invested more than US$60 million in it over a course of a decade. In 2008, however, it resold it to Kazakhmys for nearly one and a half billion dollars, and Kazakhmys itself was obliged to cede 25 percent of it to the state holding Samruk Kazyna in 2009 in order to finance part of its debts.[100] As for the American company General Electric, it settled in Turkmenistan through its partnership with Turkish company Çalyk Energy, which has a close relationship to the Turkmen authorities. In collaboration with Çalyk, it has constructed two power plants in Dashoguz, has equipped several other power stations and has been engaged in the training of personnel.[101] Lastly, Tehran is financing the construction of the Sangtuda II hydroelectric station, whose production will be exported to Iran. The exploitation and profits are reserved for Tehran for a period of twelve years, after which the station will be returned to the Tajik state.[102]

None of the great powers can therefore claim to have a monopoly over the Central Asian market. The financial weakness of Kyrgyzstan and Tajikistan often necessitates the alliance of several foreign investors in order to guarantee the feasibility of what are often costly projects. The idea of creating large international consortiums regularly appears on the table during international discussions about Kambarata and Rogun, with the support of major international financial institutions and the European Union. Since the potential is immense and still vastly underexploited, relations between the Russian, Iranian, and Chinese companies calls for cooperation and sharing of tasks rather than competition.

The issue of electricity is multi-layered. It is international, because the prospect of exporting electricity to Russia and South Asia constitutes a potential that the Central Asian governments intend to turn to their advantage in the decades to come. It is regional, because the regulation of electricity exchanges between Central Asian countries depends on the ability or inability of the governments to come to an agreement, and today constitutes the main reason for interstate tensions. It is national, because the imbrication of the networks between republics and the lack of connections between regions within a country raises the issue of securing national sovereignty over power circulation and creates large domestic disparities. It is local, because the public administrations, in rural as well as urban areas, are unable to cope with consumption needs and tend to distort distribution by siphoning off power illegally or by not paying their bills. The debate on electricity is therefore multidimensional. It is economic, because businesses and services are penalized by the short supply of electricity, which also deters foreign investors. It is environmental, as the question of sustainable development is particularly acute in a region as environmentally fragile as Central Asia: the populations are, for example, forced to chop down trees for fuel, and some industries are lobbying the government for a return to coal. It is social, for it is the people that are first to suffer from the inefficiency of the current system: in Tajikistan and some regions of Kyrgyzstan, the energy crisis has compounded the already existing food crisis; in Uzbekistan, more than one million people are still waiting to be connected to the electricity grid; and throughout the entire region, Kazakhstan included, the shortages in rural areas have not been stamped out.

Despite the fragile state of the current system, the export potential of Central Asian electricity is something that ought to be taken into account. A large number of local industries will never recover from the collapse of the Soviet Union, so consumption is bound to remain modest compared with production potential. However, the costly reforms of the electric system cannot be carried out without the aid of foreign investors. They will therefore not be accomplished unless the sector becomes more transparent on the administrative level and more financially profitable. Once again, the authorities have a certain number of cards up their sleeves that they do not necessarily deal out for reasons concerning their direct involvement in the predation of natural resources. A major field of development, the electricity sector brings to light the functioning of the post-independence regimes, their difficulties in thinking in terms of long-term rationales, and the priority they give to state prestige and symbolic strategic security to the detriment of improving the living standards of their populations. The real issue is thus that of operational efficiency, and of transactional transparency, which seem difficult to achieve given that Central Asian governments have constantly manipulated the water/energy nexus as a foreign policy tool and as a strategy of ensuring their domestic legitimacy.

Notes

1. M. Cain, "Dilemmas for International Donors and Autocrats: Obstacles to Energy Reform in Central Asia" (unpublished paper, April 2011), 6.
2. T. Dadabaev, "Water Politics and Management of Trans-Boundary Water Resources in Post-Soviet Central Asia," in Schlyter, *Prospects for Democracy*, 169–84.
3. P. Wouters, ed., *Codification and Progressive Development of International Water Law: The Work of the International Law Commission of the United Nations* (London: Kluwer Law, 1998).
4. There is an abundant literature on water and the conflicts linked to hydraulic questions in Central Asia. Worth mentioning are: V. A. Dukhovnyi and J. de Schutter, *Water in Central Asia: Past, Present, Future* (Boca Raton, FL: CRC Press, 2011); "Central Asia: Water and Conflict," International Crisis Group Asia Report, no. 34, May 2002; Z. Karaev, "Water Diplomacy in Central Asia," *Middle East Review of International Affairs* 9, no. 1 (2005): 63–69; S. Hodgson, "Strategic Water Resources in Central Asia: In Search of a New International Legal Order," Europe-Central Asia Monitoring Policy Brief, no. 14, May 2010; M. Spoor and A. Krutov, "The 'Power of Water' in a Divided Central Asia," *Perspectives on Global Development and Technology* 2, nos. 3–4 (2003): 593–614; K. Wegerich, "Water Resources in Central Asia: Regional Stability or Patchy Make-Up?," *Central Asian Survey* 30, no. 2 (2011): 275–90; for a more specific approach on Uzbekistan see, among others, J. Azam and G. Makhmejanov, "Isolationism in Uzbek Economic Policy as an Obstacle for Water-Energy Consortium," Working Paper of the Toulouse School of Economics, May 2010.
5. "Kyrgyzstan to Build Hydroelectric Stations Despite Opposition," *People's Daily Online*, April 18, 2009, http://english.peopledaily.com.cn/90001/90777/90851/6639779.html.
6. M. Laldjebaev, "The Water-Energy Puzzle in Central Asia: The Tajikistan Perspective," *International Journal of Water Resources Development* 26, no. 1 (2010): 23–36.
7. B. R. Eshchanov et al., "Rogun Dam—Path to Energy Independence or Security Threat?" *Sustainability*, no. 3 (2011): 1573–92; K. Wegerich, O. Olsson, and J. Froebrich, "Reliving the Past in a Changed Environment: Hydropower Ambitions, Opportunities, and Constraints in Tajikistan," *Energy Policy*, no. 35 (2007): 3815–25.
8. A. Roul, "The Elusive Yet Abundant Hydropower in the Kyrgyz Republic," *Ecoworld*, January 15, 2009, http://www.ecoworld.com/fuels/hydropower-in-kyrgyzstan.html.
9. A. Saidov, "Ultimatum Tashkenta," *Press.uz*, September 17, 2009, http://www.press.uz/article.php?&&article=1410.
10. M. A. Olimov, "Ispol'zovanie vodnykh resursov v Tsentral'noi Azii: Problemy i ugrozy,"

in *ShOS v poiskakh novogo ponimaniia bezopasnosti*, ed. B. K. Sultanov et al. (Almaty: Kazakhstanskii institut strategicheskikh issledovanii, 2008), 73–74.

11. G. Gleason, "Russia and the Politics of the Central Asian Electricity Grid," *Problems of Post-Communism* 50, no. 3 (2003): 42–52.

12. See the "Regional Energy Security, Efficiency, and Trade (RESET) Program, Central Asia," *USAID RESET Monthly Electronic Bulletin*, April 2011, http://ca-reset.org/library/EBulletins/RESETAprilBulletin2011.pdf.

13. S. Peyrouse, "The Central Asian Power Grid in Danger?," *The Central Asia-Caucasus Analyst* 11, no. 23 (2009): 9–11; V. Naumova, "Kazakhstan May Pull Out of Central Asia's Power System Soon," *Asia Plus*, October 27, 2009, republished at http://tajikwater.net/docs/091028_AsiaPlus2.htm.

14. R. Iakutkin, "Energetika Kazakhstana: V ozhidanii chuda," *Kazakhstan*, nos. 5–6 (2008), http://investkz.com/journals/58/593.html.

15. C. Nuttal, "Coal to Remain Kazakhstan's Top Energy Source," *Silk Road Intelligencer*, June 1, 2011, http://silkroadintelligencer.com/2011/06/01/coal-to-remain-kazakhstans-top-energy-source/.

16. "Kazakhstan Power Report," *Business Monitor International*, July 2009, http://www.mindbranch.com/Kazakhstan-Power-Q3-R302-7380/; Iakutkin, "Energetika Kazakhstana."

17. Business Monitor International, *Kazakhstan Power Report Q2 2012*, Industry Report & Forecasts Series, Mach 2012, 5.

18. See papers presented at the conference "Renewable Energy in Central Asia: Creating Economic Sustainability to Solve Socio-Economic Challenges," November 10, 2009, Dushanbe, Tajikistan, Carnegie Endowment for International Peace, http://carnegieendowment.org/2009/11/10/renewable-energy-in-central-asia-creating-economic-sustainability-to-solve-socio-economic-challenges/3hx.

19. K. Suleimenov, "The Future of Electrical Power in the Republic of Kazakhstan," in Burghart and Sabonis-Helf, *In the Tracks of Tamerlane*, 305–18; Z. Atakhanova and P. Howie, "Electricity Demand in Kazakhstan," *Energy Policy*, no. 35 (2007): 3729–43; U. Kozhantaeva, "Trevozhnye trendy: Proizvodstvo elektroenergii otstaet ot ee potrebleniia," *Delovaia nedelia*, May 27, 2011.

20. "EIA Kazakhstan Electricity," *Silk Road Intelligencer*, January 10, 2008, http://silkroad-intelligencer.com/2008/01/10/eia-kazakhstan-electricity/.

21. "Country Analysis Brief: Kazakhstan," *US Energy Information Administration*, November 2010, http://www.eia.gov/countries/cab.cfm?fips=KZ.

22. Iakutkin, "Energetika Kazakhstana."

23. "Country Analysis Brief: Kazakhstan," 11.

24. Iakutkin, "Energetika Kazakhstana."

25. "Electricity Sectors in CAREC Countries: A Diagnostic Review of Regulatory Approaches and Challenges," Report of the Asian Development Bank, Manila, 2005, 80.

26. "Uzbekistan—The Electric Power Sector," *AllBusiness.com*, October 6, 2008, http://www.allbusiness.com/energy-utilities/utilities-industry-electric-power/11604901-1.html.

27. J. Kakharov, "Uzbekistan Power Generation Sector Overview," US and Foreign Commercial Service and US Department of State, January 2008, http://www.nema.org/gov/trade/briefs/uzpowergen.pdf.

28. "Uzbekenergo do 2016 realizuet 44 investproekta na 5,2 milliarda dollarov," *RusCable.ru*, May 3, 2011, http://www.ruscable.ru/news/2011/05/03/Uzbekenergo_do_2016_goda/.

29. "Rost elektroenergetiki respubliki," *Mykyrgyzstan.ru*, February 10, 2009, http://mykyrgyzstan.ru/geography/20-rost-jelektrojenergetiki-respubliki.html. On electricity in Kyrgyzstan, see also S. Juraev, "Energy Emergency in Kyrgyzstan: Causes and Consequences," Europe-Central Asia Monitoring Policy Brief, no. 5, February 2009; N. Abdyrasulova and N. Kravsov, *Electricity Governance in Kyrgyzstan: An Institutional Assessment* (Bishkek: Civic Environmental Foundation UNISON, 2009).

30. A. Zozulinsky, "Kyrgyzstan: Power Generation & Transmission," Report of the US Department of State, US Embassy Bishkek, October 2010, 2, http://photos.state.gov/libraries/kyrgyzrepulic/328656/pdfs/Kyrgyz%20Power%20Industry%20Report%20_2_.pdf.

31. A. Zozulinsky, "Kyrgyzstan: Power Generation & Transmission," Report of the US Department of State, US Embassy Bishkek, March 2007, 1, http://bishkek.usembassy.gov/uploads/images/rXcSjKDyhKkWIbSpUUIegg/KG_07_Power_Generation_Report.pdf.

32. Roul, "Elusive Yet Abundant Hydropower."

33. "Electricity Sectors in CAREC Countries," 69. See also R. G. Musayeva et al., "Electricity Governance in Tajikistan: Applying the EGI Indicator Toolkit in Tajikistan," Report of the Electricity Governance Initiative, Dushanbe, 2009, http://electricitygovernance.wri.org/publications/54.

34. See Wikileaks note, "Tajikistan—Back in the USSR at Talco," US Embassy in Tajikistan, April 14, 2008, http://dazzlepod.com/cable/08DUSHANBE516/.

35. B. Slay, "Energy in Central Asia: Questions Looking for Answers," Report of the UN Development Programme, Bureau for Europe and the CIS, July 20, 2009, http://europeandcis.undp.org/uploads/public1/files/vulnerability/Senior%20Economist%20Web%20site/Slay_energy.pdf.

36. M. J. G. Cain, "Tajikistan's Energy Woes: Resource Barriers in Fragile States," *Washington Review of Turkish and Eurasian Affairs*, January 2011, http://www.thewashingtonreview.org/articles/tajikistans-energy-woes-resource-barriers-in-fragile-states.html; "Tajikistan Introduces Restrictions on Power Consumption," *Akipress*, September 2, 2008, republished at http://www.thefreelibrary.com/Tajikistan+introduces+restrictions+on+power+consumption.-a0184359724.

37. "Turkmenistan—The Power Sector," APS Review Downstream Trends, September 18, 2006, http://www.thefreelibrary.com/TURKMENISTAN+-+The+Power+Sector.-a0152080732.

38. "Electricity/Heat in Turkmenistan in 2008," International Energy Agency Turkmenistan Fact Sheet, http://www.iea.org/stats/electricitydata.asp?COUNTRY_CODE=TM.

39. J. C. K. Daly, "Turkmen Wind Power," *Eurasia Daily Monitor* 5, no. 157, August 15, 2008, http://www.jamestown.org/programs/edm/single/?tx_ttnews%5Btt_news%5D=33893&tx_ttnews%5BbackPid%5D=166&no_cache=1. See also E. Vinokurov, "Obshchii elektroenergeticheskii rynok SNG," Report of the Eurasian Development Bank, Astana, July 2008; "Central Asia Regional Electricity Export Potential Study," Report of the World Bank, Washington, DC, 2004.

40. On this issue, see M. M. Rahaman and O. Varis, eds., *Central Asian Waters: Social, Economic, Environmental, and Governance Puzzle* (Helsinki: Helsinki University of Technology, 2008); J. Allouche, "The Governance of Central Asian Waters: National Interests versus Regional Cooperation," *Disarmament Forum*, no. 4 (2007): 45–55.

41. "Where Is Coal Found?," *World Coal Association*, http://www.worldcoal.org/coal/where-is-coal-found/.

42. For the Kyrgyz case, see E. Marat, "Corruption in the Hydro-Energy Sector Becomes Clearer in Kyrgyzstan," *Eurasia Daily Monitor* 5, no. 184, September 25, 2008, http://www.jamestown.org/single/?no_cache=1&tx_ttnews%5Btt_news%5D=33970.

43. Iakutkin, "Energetika Kazakhstana."

44. N. Abdyrasulova and N. Kravtsov, "Upravlenie sektorom elektroenergetiki v Kyrgyzstane: Institutsional'nyi i prakticheskii analiz," Report of the World Resources Institute and the Prayas Energy Group, Washington, DC, 2009.

45. See E. Suhir, "What Matters in Privatization is Process—Lessons Not Yet Learned by Kyrgyzstan," *Center For International Private Enterprise*, February 24, 2010, http://www.cipe.org/blog/?p=4365.

46. Kakharov, "Uzbekistan Power Generation Sector Overview."

47. "Uzbekenergo Supplies 20.8 Billion K.W.H. of Electricity to Consumers in 1H," *Uzdaily.com*, July 21, 2011, http://www.uzdaily.com/articles-id-15071.htm.

48. More on this issue in Musayeva, "Electricity Governance in Tajikistan."

49. "Electricity Sectors in CAREC Countries," 43.

50. C. Nuttall, "Temporary Respite for Kazakhstan's Electricity Generation Sector," *Silk Road Intelligencer*, March 18, 2009, http://silkroadintelligencer.com/2009/03/18/temporary-respite-for-kazakhstans-electricity-generation-sector/.

51. Iakutkin, "Energetika Kazakhstana."

52. "Kazakhstan: World Bank Supports Electricity Transmission to South," World Bank Press Release, October 27, 2005, http://web.worldbank.org/WBSITE/EXTERNAL/PROJE CTS/0,,contentMDK:20700434~menuPK:64282137~pagePK:41367~piPK:279616~theSiteP K:40941,00.html.

53. "Kazakhstan Power Report."

54. Iakutkin, "Energetika Kazakhstana."

55. T. Sabonis-Helf, "Notes for Russia/Kazakhstan: The Energy Issues, TOSCCA Workshop, Kazakhstan between East and West," Lecture Notes, St. Anthony's College Oxford, November 28, 2005, http://www.toscca.co.uk/lecture%20notes/SabonisKazRusEnergy.doc.

56. E. Marat, "Kyrgyzstan to Begin Electricity Rationing Next Month," *Eurasia Daily Monitor* 6, no. 175, September 24, 2009, http://www.jamestown.org/programs/edm/single/?tx_ttnews%5Btt_news%5D=35531&tx_ttnews%5BbackPid%5D=27&cHash=e0c419c32e; D. Gullette, "Resurrecting an Energy Tariff Policy in Kyrgyzstan," OSCE Academy and GCS Central Asia Security Policy Brief 1, November 29, 2010.

57. M. Levina, "Kyrgyzstan Seeks New Approach to Reduce Loss in Electricity Supply," *Times of Central Asia*, May 28, 2009.

58. "Electric Power Sector," US Trade and Development Agency, http://www.ustda.gov/program/sectors/electricpower.asp.

59. "Kyrgyzstan perenapravil v Kazakhstan elektrichestvo, kotoroe ne vykupil Uzbekistan," *CentrAsia*, July 8, 2009, http://www.centrasia.ru/newsA.php?st=1247058120.

60. Saidov, "Ultimatum Tashkenta."

61. "Uzbekistan Implements Big Project on Electricity Export to Afghanistan," *Asia Plus*, October 28, 2009, http://en.ca-news.org/news:107271/.

62. B. Renouvin, "La conception ismaélienne du développement: L'exemple du Pamir," *Mondes en développement* 132 (2005): 129–38.

63. See the Turkmenistan CIA fact sheet, https://www.cia.gov/library/publications/the-world-factbook/geos/tx.html.

64. "Turkmenistan Starts Electricity Export Supplies to Turkey Through Iran," *Turkmenistan.ru*, October 15, 2003, http://www.turkmenistan.ru/en/node/2599.

65. "Turkmenistan Begins Electricity Supplies to Tajikistan," *Global Energy Network Institute*, December 3, 2007, http://www.geni.org/globalenergy/library/technical-articles/transmission/bbc-monitoring/turkmenistan-begins-electricity-supplies-to-tajikistan/index.shtml; "Tajikistan s 1-ogo maia perestal importirovat' elektroenergiiu iz Turkmenistana i Uzbekistana," *CentrAsia*, May 6, 2009, http://www.centrasia.ru/newsA.php?st=1241591880.

66. V. Naumova and P. Chorshanbiyev, "Uzbekistan Agrees to Offer Its Power Systems for Transiting Turkmen Electricity to Tajikistan," *Asia Plus*, August 19, 2008, http://www.asiaplus.tj/en/news/31/55992.html.

67. S. Mehtan, "Tajikistan Left Without Energy Assistance as Winter Approaches," *Central Asia Online*, November 12, 2009, http://centralasiaonline.com/en_GB/articles/caii/features/2009/11/12/feature-01.

68. "Expert: SCO's Energy Club Will Become the OPEC Alternative," *Regnum*, June 18, 2006, http://www.regnum.ru/english/658559.html.

69. More details on the project in V. Vucetic and V. Krishnaswamy, "Development of Electricity Trade in Central Asia—South Asia Region," Report of the World Bank, Washington, DC, 2005.

70. F. Najibullah, "Tajikistan's Transportation Challenge: Ending Dependency on Uzbek

Transit Routes," *Eurasia Daily Monitor* 8, no. 207, November 9, 2011, http://www.jamestown. org/single/?no_cache=1&tx_ttnews%5Btt_news%5D=38643&tx_ttnews%5BbackPid%5D=7 &cHash=4d52df7a228753ffc1e871cb3bdb50a1.

71. "Central Asia-South Asia Electricity Transmission and Trade (CASA-1000) Project Feasibility Study Update," SNC Lavalin Transmission and Distribution Divison Report, February 2011, http://www.energo.gov.kg/doc/Final%20feasibility%20Report.pdf.

72. On bioenergies, see C. S. Harwood, A. L. Demain, and J. D. Wall, eds., *Bioenergy* (Washington, DC: ASM Press, 2008).

73. Roul, "Elusive Yet Abundant Hydropower."

74. Ibid.

75. More in "Developing the Potential for Energy Efficiency and Alternative Energy in the Kyrgyz Republic," Report of the Jefferson Institute, Washington, DC, 2009.

76. Levina, "Kyrgyzstan Seeks New Approach."

77. Juraev, "Energy Emergency in Kyrgyzstan."

78. Il'ias Davydov, "V predstoiashchem osenne-zimnem periode shkoly Kyrgyzstana ot podachi elektroenergii otkliuchat' ne budem," *Zamandash*, July 7, 2009, http://www.zpress. kg/news/news_only/3/8959.ru.

79. E. Marat, "Towards a Water Regime in the Syr Darya Basin," *The Central Asia-Caucasus Analyst*, November 12, 2008, http://www.cacianalyst.org/?q=node/4980.

80. E. Karybekov, "Kyrgyzstanu nevygodno stroitel'stvo GES Kambarata 1," *CentrAsia*, May 28, 2011, http://www.centrasia.ru/newsA.php?st=1306308480.

81. "Electricity Sectors in CAREC Countries," 69. See also "Energetiki Tadzhikistana otmechaiut 50-letie goroda Nurek," *Asia Plus*, December 22, 2010, http://tjknews.ru/news/862.

82. "GES Sangtuda-2 do sikh por ne vyrabatyvaet elektroenergiiu," *Toptj*, December 15, 2011, http://www.toptj.com/m/news/2011/12/15/ges_sangtuda_2_do_sikh_por_ne_vyrabaty-vaet_elektroenergiyu; "Iranian Built Sangtuda 2 Hydropower Plant Inaugurated in Tajikistan," *Presstv.ir*, September 6, 2011, http://www.presstv.ir/detail/197629.html.

83. "Tajikistan: Forced Rogun Payments Sowing Discontent Among Impoverished Tajiks," *Eurasianet*, January 4, 2010, http://www.eurasianet.org/departments/business/articles/ eav010510.shtml. See also S. Olimova, "Tajikistan, January–February 2010," *Central Asia Observatory Newsletter*, Barcelona, March 2010.

84. S. Majidov, "World Bank Advises Tajikistan to Halt Construction of Hydropower Station," *The Central Asia-Caucasus Analyst* 13, no. 16 (2011): 15–16.

85. O. Tutubalina and Z. Ergasheva, "Spetsialisty VB zatiagivaiut sroki: Ili oni ne spetsialisty," *Asia Plus*, August 22, 2011, http://news.tj/ru/news/spetsialisty-vb-zatyagivayut-sroki-ili-oni-ne-spetsialisty.

86. Eshchanov, "Rogun Dam," 1579.

87. J. C. K. Daly, "Tajikistan: The Future is Hydroelectricity—or Perhaps Not," *Oilprice. com*, August 30, 2011, http://oilprice.com/Alternative-Energy/Hydroelectric-Energy/Tajikistan-The-Future-is-Hydroelectricity-or-Perhaps-Not.html.

88. "Tajikistan: Energy Shortage Accelerates Deforestation," *Eurasianet*, December 8, 2011, http://www.eurasianet.org/node/64660.

89. "Uzbekistan—The Electric Power Sector."

90. "Uzbekenergo to Build HP in Tashkent Region," *Hydroworld.com*, October 19, 2011, http://www.hydroworld.com/index/display/news_display.1523568978.html.

91. "Kazakhstan Power Report."

92. More in S. Peyrouse, "The Hydroelectric Sector in Central Asia and the Growing Role of China," *The China and Eurasia Forum Quarterly* 5, no. 2 (2007): 131–48.

93. "Russian Company to Invest $750 Million in Kyrgyz Hydropower," *Central Asia Newswire*, March 24, 2011, http://www.universalnewswires.com/centralasia/viewstory. aspx?id=3631.

94. B. Pannier, "Tajikistan: Dushanbe Scraps Contract with Russia's RusAl," *Radio Free Europe/Radio Liberty*, August 30, 2007, http://www.rferl.org/content/article/1078431.html.

95. More on Russian regional strategies in "Obshchii elektroenergeticheskii rynok SNG."

96. "Prisutstvie Kitaia v Kazakhstane: 'Dostizheniia' i 'perspektivy'," *PostBackUSSR*, February 10, 2006, http://www.pbussr.ru/index.php?razdel=5&condition=show_news&id=8992.

97. S. Smirnov, "'Kitaiskie' megavatty," *Ekspert Kazakhstan* 32, no. 134 (2007), http://www.expert.ru/printissues/kazakhstan/2007/32/kazahstanskiy_tek/.

98. More in Peyrouse, "The Hydroelectric Sector in Central Asia."

99. "Uzvodenergo to Commission Two Small Hydro Power Stations," *Uzbekistan Daily*, September 25, 2009, http://www.uzdaily.com/articles-id-7224.htm.

100. "Kazakhmys to Receive $339 Million Through 25% Stake Sale of Ekibastuz Power Plant," *Proactive Investors*, October 13, 2009, http://www.proactiveinvestors.co.uk/companies/news/9058/kazakhmys-to-receive-339-million-through-25-stake-sale-of-ekibastuz-power-plant-9058.html.

101. See Wikileaks cables, "GE Turbines Boost Electricity Capacity in Turkmenistan," *Cablegatesearch.net*, November 24, 2009, http://www.cablegatesearch.net/cable.php?id=09ASHGABAT1498.

102. "Pochemu Sangtuda-2 ne proizvodit elektroenergiiu, i kodga zakrutitsia vtoroe koleso GES?," *Nezavisimoe mnenie*, December 2, 2011, http://nm.tj/economy/1181-pochemu-sangtuda-2-ne-proizvodit-elektroenergiyu-i-kogda-zakrutitsya-vtoroe-koleso-ges.html.

12

Landlocked

The Transport Challenge

Central Asia's development is consistently hampered by the transport question. In tsarist times, the construction of the trans-Caspian railway made it possible to open up the region and to integrate it further into the flows of people and commodities arriving from Russia. Later the Soviet regime invested considerable amounts in the railway network, one of the flagships of national industry, as well as in roads and the development of air links. Nevertheless, even within the unified Soviet economic system, the elevated cost of Central Asian products was partly explained by their transport. With independence, the situation became worse, and high transport costs further contributed to Central Asia's economic overspecialization and the disappearance of a whole set of products.[1] Traffic within the Central Asian region grew significantly less and the governments begrudged the maintenance of their public transport networks. Whereas periods of crisis are traditionally unfavorable to the development of transport networks, considering the heavy investments that are needed, poor interstate relations and the desire of the Turkmen and Uzbek governments to restrict the free travel of their citizens have aggravated the situation. Even if international aid has enabled improvements in transport on arterial roads, people are still impeded in their daily movements and in their implementation of informal commercial mechanisms; and the large export sectors are hampered by excessive transport costs, a fact that also scares off a number of foreign investors. Today the major international financial institutions are concentrating their activities on improving transport in the region, which tends to ascribe to Central Asia the status of being at the crossroads of world trade, although it in large part omits mention of the daily challenges of development.

State of the Road, Rail, and Air Networks

Roads are the primary mode of transport for people and commodities in Central Asia: for example, in 2007 in Uzbekistan, road freight amounted to close to 755 million tons or 85 percent of all freight.[2] In Kyrgyzstan, as much as 95 percent of transportation is by road.[3] Due to its economic dynamism and its immense territory, Kazakhstan is the only country where a majority of commodities and passengers are transported by train and plane, instead of by road. Kazakhstan is also the only state to have devised a strategy for transport development by 2015, for which an investment of US$25 billion is to be set aside. This includes privatization of a number of sectors designed to be financially self-sufficient, such as the major airports, the port terminals, and some of the railway stations.[4] By contrast, the central road and rail network as well as the river infrastructure will remain under state control. The other Central Asian countries have kept the entire transport domain under their control for political as much as economic reasons.

In the early 1990s, the servicing of rural areas by public transport collapsed. Today this is compensated for by a system of collective taxis that ensure city-country links and transfers between regions. However, their schedule is irregular and unpredictable and they are prohibitively expensive for the poorest classes. Mobility in rural areas has thus been widely hindered, both in mountainous regions as well as in remote areas such as Karakalpakstan or the Mangystau Peninsula.[5] The system of transport links between the republics has also been hampered by tensions at the borders: collective taxis can no longer cross at Chernyaev, the busiest border post between Kazakhstan and Uzbekistan, obliging passengers to change vehicles.[6] The demarcation of the borders has aggravated the situation by transforming roads that once crossed over into the territory of neighboring countries into cul-de-sacs; and the villages affected are unable to secure alternative roads from their governments.[7] Due to a lack of financing, the condition of the roads has deteriorated: while the major routes linking the capitals have been repaired, as have the routes considered strategic for state security, numerous regional and local roads have lost their bitumen surfacing. The reduction in the number of coaches and their replacement by smaller collective taxis has slowed the informal exchanges of commodities. In 2000, the level of Central Asian road freight was no higher than 5 percent of the 1990 level.[8] The stock of private automobiles has been partly renewed by imports or local products, such as those from the Daewoo factory in Uzbekistan, but freight stocks are still made up of aged Soviet vehicles, even if a new generation of Kamaz (Russia's main brand of truck) has been introduced. Existing logistical systems are not adapted to the efficient transportation of commodities. Small private vehicles, operating over long distances, represent an abnormally high percentage of road freight, a sign of the absence of any public strategy in this area.[9]

Kazakhstan has close to 90,000 kilometers of roads, including 23,000 classified as motorways, but two-thirds are deteriorated and require significant work.[10] The major towns located on the transit axes between China and Russia are relatively well serviced, as are Astana and Almaty, which are linked together by a road that was refurbished at the beginning of the twenty-first century. However, isolated and sparsely populated regions, such as Mangystau or Jezkazgan, have not benefited from important state subsidies in the roads sector, and the Kzyl-Orda region has the lowest road density in the country.[11] Despite a significant individual market of used cars from Japan, about 40 percent of the 90,000 common transport vehicles registered for the entire country are more than fifteen years old.

The situation is similar in neighboring countries. In 2007, Uzbekistan had a little more than 84,000 kilometers of roads, but only 3,200 of them were classified as motorways.[12] Most of the asphalted roads are in the Tashkent region and the Ferghana Valley, while the west and the north of the country are serviced by much poorer quality roads. About 200 kilometers of new roads are built every year, in particular in Khorezm and Karakalpakstan, where a bridge over the Amu Darya now facilitates trips into these regions.[13] Two large sections are under renovation: Gulistan-Akhangaran (Angren) and Samarkand-Tashkent, whose route was changed after the Uzbek authorities demanded that Kazakh territory be bypassed. The road linking Tashkent to Ferghana, important for the economy and for security, has also been restored and new tunnels have been laid through the Kamchik and Rezak peaks.[14] Turkmenistan, for its part, has been able to finance nearly all of its transport network: by 2001, the country is said to have had 18,000 kilometers of asphalted roads out of a total of 22,000.[15] The new road linking Ashgabat to Dashoguz, which runs alongside the railway, including a 300-meter bridge over the Amu Darya, is now operational.

Kyrgyzstan and Tajikistan are the worst off in terms of transport and the unity of their national territory is not yet assured. Their networks, already limited in the Soviet period, have deteriorated for want of financing and both have had to cope with specific altitude-related problems. Tajikistan has about 30,000 kilometers of roads, which today have largely deteriorated. Iran's construction of the Anzob tunnel has made it possible to keep the link open between north and south, which until recently had to be closed during winter because it was impossible to cross the mountain peaks. The missing sections that will enable the bypassing of Uzbekistan are under construction.[16] China financed two other tunnels designed to aid traffic flows between the capital and the main Tajik cities: the Shar-Shar tunnel on the Dushanbe-Kulyab road, and the Shakhristan tunnel on the road leading to Khudjand, both of which are today operational.[17] Despite this progress, some regions remain totally cut off from the rest of the country during winter and intra-Tajik economic trade is limited.

Kyrgyzstan has 18,500 kilometers of roads, most covered by asphalt, but only 140 kilometers are considered motorways. The north and the south are connected by the Bishkek-Osh-Batken arterial, which hitherto had been difficult to pass in winter. Thanks to international financing from the Asian Development Bank and the Japan International Cooperation Agency, its renovation now enables traffic to circulate without interruption throughout the year, which is an important element for the rather fragile unity of the country. Some works are also being carried out on the economically vital roads linking the country's two largest cities, Bishkek and Osh, to the border posts with China (Bishkek-Torugart and Osh-Sary Tash-Irkeshtam). Lastly, the Jambul-Talas-Suusamyr road that links the regions of Osh, Jalalabad, and Chui, and provides access to Kazakhstan, is also due for new asphalt.[18]

While the railway sector was relatively well-developed during the Soviet period, the continuous effacement of the network has had detrimental effects on the development of rail freight, which is much less costly than road transport, and has also hindered the opening up of isolated regions. Indeed, without any railway links, the exploitation of mineral resources has seen the cost price skyrocket: Two-thirds of the cost price for a ton of coal extracted from the Kavak Basin in Kyrgyzstan can be put down to the cost of transport alone.[19] Investments initiated in railways after independence have been limited, and the Central Asian rail network has not been upgraded since Soviet times. Even in Kazakhstan, according to the Transport Ministry, rail infrastructure has aged considerably with 50 to 80 percent of railway equipment having markedly deteriorated.[20] On some lines, the speed of trains cannot exceed 30 kilometers per hour, so bad is the state of the tracks. The degradation of the infrastructure, considerable logistical problems, and the lack of funds and capacity for upgrading have resulted in soaring cost increases in railway transport.

The Soviet Central Asian republics used to import their railway material from the German Democratic Republic or Belarus, and today must either buy equipment new at higher international prices, or acquire production industries. Russia tries to maintain its former dominance over the equipment purchases of the Central Asian states, but they are increasingly looking toward China, which supplies them with cheaper wagons and locomotives.[21] Most of the Central Asian railway lines are not electrified and have only a single track. The exceptions to this are the major trans-Soviet lines like the Trans-Caspian and the Turksib: the first runs along a west-east axis from the Turkmen shores of the Caspian to Semipalatinsk, and then to central Siberia; and the second along a north-south axis from Russia to the north of Kazakhstan and then Almaty. Upon independence, only 300 kilometers of Uzbekistan's tracks, out of 3,600 in total, were electrified. In the first years of the twenty-first century the Uzbek authorities set about electrifying close to 1,000 kilometers more, in particular sections with economic viability, such as those near Navoy, and the Tashkent-Samarkand-Bukhara line, which serves to promote tourism.[22] In Kazakhstan, important economic routes, such as that linking Ekibastuz to Pavlodar, were only recently electrified.[23] As for Kyrgyzstan, it only began the electrification of its major line—that connecting Bishkek to the Kazakh border—as late as 2008.[24]

Railway flows have markedly decreased in the whole region and their revival is uncertain. Several passenger lines have been eliminated, in particular those connecting provincial towns; the frequency of trains has considerably diminished; and the international lines that have to cross borders have had to be rerouted.[25] The former Almaty–Tashkent line has ceased operating, since Uzbekistan refuses to let Kazakh trains enter its territory, obliging passengers to disembark at Shymkent and proceed by bus to the Uzbek capital. The intra-Central Asia passenger network consists of only five major train lines that, for the most part, link towns located in the same republic by passing through foreign territory. With the exception of a few regional links, such as Almaty-Nukus or Nukus-Aktau, only the trains bound for Russia count as international traffic.[26] In the first decade of the century, there were only fifteen convoys each week traveling between Russia and Central Asia, whereas on the eve of the break-up of the Soviet Union, there were as many as 150.[27] Rising labor migration flows contribute to an increase in this sector, mainly in the direction of Russia, but the border crossing remains too much of a bureaucratic obstacle to bring about a real renewal of the railways, once again with the sole exception of Kazakhstan, which is better integrated in transcontinental transport networks.

In Kazakhstan, the authorities have launched a modernization program for railway transport that forecasts the construction of 1,600 kilometers of new lines and the electrification of 2,700 kilometers.[28] The network, which encompasses over 14,000 kilometers, is run by the state company, Kazakhstan Temir Zholy, but part of the freight activities, the passenger transport, and the maintenance has been handed over to private subsidiaries.[29] A shortfall of about 500 wagons has led to a reduction in the proposed services of the Kazakh railway system. Two-thirds of the passenger carriages reportedly require repair: of the 2,000 in service in the country, only 140 are less than ten years old.[30] More than a third of the freight wagons (that is, 30,000 units) are in the private domain, but the companies that own them are small (about 190 firms, a third of which only possess five wagons each) and are often unable to modernize their stock. Only the state and a few major freight companies working at the international level can afford to have a purchasing policy for new railroad cars. The same holds for the locomotives, two-thirds of which have exceeded their official life span.[31] In order to compensate for these problems, a number of steps have been taken: a locomotive factory has been constructed in partnership with General Electric;[32] Spanish Talgo trains have been put into circulation between the former and the new capital; contracts have been signed with France's Alstom and Russia's TransMashHolding; and multiple purchases have been made from China.[33] Modernizing the railway sector ought to make it possible to reduce costs, to triple the transit of cargo—set to reach thirty-two million tons by 2015—and to increase the speed of transportation. Some new railway lines are under construction in the western regions of Kazakhstan in order to develop maritime freight via the Caspian.[34]

In the other countries, the situation is just as difficult. Uzbekistan has a network including close to 4,000 kilometers of standard tracks. Railway freight remains minor compared with road transport: in 2007, it amounted to only fifty-eight million tons, or 6.5 percent of the total.[35] With the gradual tightening of borders, new lines have been put into service. Halfway through the 1990s, the blockade on the train linking Tashkent with Urgench via Bukhara, which passed several times over onto the left bank of the Amu Darya and therefore into Turkmen territory, accelerated the construction of a new line across the desert via Navoy and Uchkuduk that links up with Nukus. Further to the south, the Karshi-Termez line, which also bypasses Turkmenistan thanks to the new Guzar-Kumkurgan section, is designed to facilitate transport to the Afghan border by crossing Kashkadarya and Sukhandarya. Lastly, a line that circumvents Tajik territory—thanks to a new section between Angren and Pap and several tunnels—is planned to link the Ferghana Valley with the Tashkent region. The 2008 economic crisis has, however, obliged the government to push back the project completion date. Additionally, the railway linking Kungrad to Aktau has been revitalized in the hope of increasing Uzbek exports via the Kazakh Caspian port.

Turkmenistan, for its part, has 2,500 kilometers of railways, largely concentrated in the border zones with Uzbekistan and Iran. However, it has invested considerable sums in the construction of more than 700 kilometers of new lines since independence. Turkmenabat, on the border with Uzbekistan, will now be linked to Atamurat, in the

Lebap region, and a small section has also served Kerkichi on the border with Afghanistan since 2011.[36] Nevertheless, the country's key railway achievement remains
the trans-Karakum line, opened in 2006, which links Ashgabat directly to Dashoguz
via the desert, avoiding the detours of Mary and the Uzbek border. This line halves
the travel time between the north and the south of the country.[37] The authorities have
purchased equipment from China, and have also signed contracts with several European companies to buy equipment for the construction of the Turkmen section of the
railway line that will link Kazakhstan to Iran in the years to come.

Once again, Kyrgyzstan and Tajikistan are the farthest behind, since their networks
were not designed by the Soviet regime as specific entities within their republics. As a
result, Kyrgyzstan has been left with six sections of rail that are not linked up to one
another, across a total length of 470 kilometers, many of which have become dead
ends following the closure of the borders.[38] The only operational railway network
is that of the Chu Valley, which serves several industrial enterprises and runs along
the Kazakh border. Some analysts plead in favor of developing the railways in order
to revive the economy, but in view of the major financing required to construct new
lines, the government has little motivation.[39] Tajikistan is also particularly badly off
in terms of its railway network, which comprises less than 500 kilometers of, often
unconnected tracks. Projects are rarely put forward to revive railway traffic, although
a new line was opened between Kulyab and Kurgan-Tepe in 2000. The train linking
the capital with the Sogd province in the north and Khatlon in the south continues to
have to pass through Uzbekistan, a trip of more than thirty hours, one-third of which
is spent undergoing customs formalities. The Tajik authorities hope to open a section
enabling them to bypass Uzbekistan and connect Dushanbe with Khudjand directly.[40]
Until 2006, the country possessed no factory for rail-related repairs and had to send
its cars and locomotives to Uzbekistan or Ukraine, at significant expense.[41]

Air transport, which was significantly developed during Soviet times, has also been
drastically reduced. Within the Central Asian region, the number of flights operated
shrank drastically: in 1996, the network was limited to five regular routes.[42] While
Tashkent was linked to twenty-seven other Central Asian towns in 1989, there were
no more than six Central Asian destinations available in 2005.[43] Tensions between
the republics weigh heavily on air transport: Ashgabat and Tashkent are linked by
very few weekly flights, revealing of the state of their relations, and there are none
between Tashkent and Dushanbe, because of Uzbekistan's refusal to provide services
to Tajikistan since the end of the 1990s. Except for Kazakhstan, flights between
provincial towns are rare and often require a transfer in the capital. Those between
provincial towns of different countries are very few, here again with a few exceptions
such as Almaty, thanks to its status as a former capital, or Atyrau, Kazakhstan's oil
capital. Starkly reduced in the 1990s, the connections between Central Asia and Russian cities underwent a rapid expansion during the following decade due to migration
flows. The towns serviced in Russia are those that welcome considerable numbers of
migrants: flights linking Yekaterinburg, Novosibirsk, Saratov, Samara, Tyumen, and
Krasnoyarsk to the Ferghana Valley, Khudjand, Kurgan-Tyube, Bishkek, Jalalabad,

and Osh are multiplying, in particular in the springtime and the end of the fall, during the migration season.[44] Several public or private regional companies specialize in the transport of Central Asian migrants, for example, Atlant-Soyuz, the Moscow municipality's public company.

Even if the regional connections have not been revived, international links have developed and market-capture strategies have been put into place by some companies. For Kyrgyzstan and Tajikistan, the costs of maintaining a fleet of aircraft are very high. Both their national companies only offer a reduced range of services and their aged planes inherited from the Soviet Union often do not meet the norms of the International Civil Aviation Organization. Some small private companies have charter flights abroad, serving pilgrims traveling to Mecca for instance. Each of the two states has nearly forty airports, which are often no more than runways, and only those of the capitals can take the larger carriers that require runways of more than 3,000 meters.[45] The major international organizations are financing the modernization of the main airports and are upgrading consistent with international security norms.

The three other countries have tried to develop their international fleet. Air Astana, 51 percent owned by the government and 49 percent by British company BAE Systems Ltd., has experienced rapid growth and regularly expands its number of destinations; its fleet consists entirely of Boeing or Airbus planes. But the Kazakh network (twenty-two airports) requires upgrading to international standards, and only five airports (Astana, Almaty, Aktobe, Atyrau, and Karaganda) can take large carriers. The country has about fifty airlines, most of which are very small, including thirty that operate in the sectors of passenger and commodity transport, while the others undertake aerial work, mainly chemical spraying of crops.[46] Turkmenistan remains very isolated from global air networks and mostly depends on the services offered by Turkish Airlines. Despite the weak traffic this entails it has completely renewed its fleet and substantially modernized some of its airports, although only the capital is able to receive large carriers.[47]

Uzbekistan has the largest international visibility in the air sector, having won its gamble to become the aerial freight hub for Central Asia; Lufthansa, for instance, uses it en route to Asia. The national airline, Uzbekistan Airways, serves more than twenty cities in the CIS and a further twenty in Europe, on the North American continent, in Asia, and in the Middle East. It has opted to target the sector of cheap tourist flights from Western Europe to Southeast Asia, but it has lost out to competition from low-cost Thai and Vietnamese airlines and to the high-quality service provided by the Emirati companies. Uzbekistan Airways is not merely an airline company: it runs the nation's entire organization of air transport, from airport infrastructure to air traffic control.[48] Domestic air freight, however, remains extremely limited, since in 2007 it represented only 0.001 percent of all freight, or 6.5 million tons transported by plane.[49] Six airports are able to receive large carriers, but few foreign companies are authorized to serve provincial towns. Today Tashkent hopes to develop its status as an air hub for international freight with a grand project for logistical center at Navoy, which is being built in partnership with South Korea.

Table 12.1

Airports, Railroads, Roads, and Waterways in 2011 (in km)

	Airports paved runways	Railways	Paved roadways	Unpaved roadways	Total routes	Waterways
Kazakhstan	64	15,079	84,100	9,512	93,612	4,000
Kyrgyzstan	18	470	—		34,000 (2003)	600
Tajikistan	17	680			27,767 (2000)	200
Turkmenistan	21	2,980	47,577	11,015 (2002)	58,592	1,300
Uzbekistan	33	3,645	75,511	10,985 (2000)	86,496	1,100
Total	153	22,854			300,376	7,200

Source: Table based on the CIA World Factbook sheets, https://www.cia.gov/library/publications/the-world-factbook/wfbExt/region_cas.html.

The International Community's Focus on Transcontinental Transport Corridors

As China has become the European Union's largest trading partner, all the Central Asian countries dream of becoming a trade crossroads between the two zones and seek to emphasize their potential as a transit site between Europe and Asia. Even if they are a conduit for much less trade than their situation on a map seems to merit, the prospect of accruing considerable transit rights motivates local governments eager to generate revenues in foreign currency. In 2007, for instance, Kazakhstan reportedly collected about US$500 million in transit fees and could see this figure double by 2015 if continental transit reaches US$1,000 billion.[50] Like the Central Asian governments, the main regional organizations and international donors have also placed their bets on transport to revive the economies of the region.

All the regional organizations, or programs, to which the Central Asian states belong are in theory occupied with the transport corridors, but very few have obtained any tangible results. Moreover, as Johannes Lynn notes, the plurality of organizations, each having different members and their own underlying rationales, leads to a duplication of programs, which creates a certain number of problems.[51] The Economic Cooperation Organization and the UN Special Program for the Economies of Central Asia have only had a limited impact on the transport issue, as has the Shanghai Cooperation Organization, since Chinese advances on transport matters have been made above all at the bilateral level. Only the Eurasian Economic Community, and now the Customs Union, might influence the flows of transport. The Eurasian Development Bank, which has expertise on the situation of Europe-Asia transport, has invited governments to attach more importance to these questions.[52] Transport via road, which makes up between two-thirds and three-quarters of the transportation total of freight within the Eurasian Community, should continue to exceed rail freight.

At the international level, successive programs have attempted to inject some dynamism into transcontinental transport. In 1993, the European Union set up TRACECA (Transport Corridor Europe-Caucasus-Asia), a program that aims to open up Central Asia and the Caucasus by the creation of a vast transport and communication corridor along an east-west axis. Endowed with a budget of 110 million euros between 1993 and 2002, it has financed the modernization of the ports of Ilyichevsk, Poti, Batumi, Turkmenbashi, Baku, and Aktau, as well as the Kungrad-Beineu-Aktau railway, and has established the boat-railway link between Varna to Batumi and Baku to Aktau.[53] Originally, TRACECA involved the five countries of Central Asia and the three South Caucasian states, but it has been strengthened by the addition of Moldova, Ukraine, Turkey, Romania, and Bulgaria. The program is now increasingly connected with pan-European road projects planned in the framework of the EU Neighborhood Policy.

However, twenty years after having been launched, TRACECA has still not redirected trade flows. The conflicts that rocked the Caucasus in the 1990s, and the suspicions harbored by Central Asian states against one another, have significantly impeded the integration of national transport networks. Moreover, the reduced budgets proposed by the EU (on average two million euros per project) were too limited to achieve such ambitious tasks. Last, and above all, the economic profitability of the route is contested: not only does transport through Russia save considerable time, but the numerous taxes demanded by too many transit states reduce the margins. According to the Eurasian Development Bank, the tariffs enforced by the Russian railway company are 1.7 times less than those of TRACECA for cereals and cotton, and 1.2 times less for oil and non-ferrous metals.[54] Presently, the corridors that are subsidized by TRACECA mainly transport oil products from Kazakhstan and Turkmenistan, as well as cotton from Uzbekistan, but not goods from China. The infrastructure is far from operating at maximum capacity: the Batumi-Poti-Ilyichevsk ferry line transports about one million tons per year, and that between Baku and Turkmenbashi two million, whereas they were designed to carry between fifteen and twenty million.[55]

A similar route was endorsed by the United States through a Silk Road Strategic Act initiated in 1999 and renewed in 2006.[56] The symbolic route of these new "Silk Roads" connects Lianyungang, on the shores of the China Sea, to the Bulgarian port of Constanta, crossing Xinjiang, Kazakhstan, Uzbekistan, Turkmenistan, Azerbaijan, Georgia, and then the Black Sea. This east-west axis was supposed first to reduce the dependence of the South Caucasus and Central Asia on Russia, second to avoid Iran becoming a hub of regional commerce, and third to bolster Turkey's role as a crossroads between Asia and Europe. Though the United States has always supported these east-west projects, in the new century it has sought to increase the status of another form of east-west axis, this time linking South Asia to Central Asia.[57] The "East" sought after here is therefore no longer China but rather India, Washington's new strategic partner, and the United States is looking to build an Afghanistan-Pakistan trade axis in an effort to stabilize both countries. Consequently, in 2011 Secretary of State Hillary Clinton launched a Silk Road Strategy, presented by the White House as one of its major contributions to the post-2014 period in Afghanistan, and designed to direct American investment to favor regional trade linking South and Central Asia.[58] Trade along this axis remains extremely limited, however.

The Western-backed Silk Road narrative is rivaled by Russian strategies developed through the Eurasian Economic Community and the Customs Union, but also by the so-called North-South Corridor. Marginalized from the east-west routes in the 1990s, Russia, Iran, and India have been seeking to give life to their potential economic complementarity. The North-South Transport Corridor Agreement, signed in 2000 in Saint Petersburg, plans to establish a road and rail corridor linking Russia to the Persian Gulf.[59] An agreement for a new railway line running along the Caspian through Uzen-Gyzylgaya-Bereket-Etrek-Gorgan was also signed between Russia, Kazakhstan, Turkmenistan, and Iran in 2007. If built, it will connect the Russian railway grids to the Persian Gulf, reduce the existing link that passes through Serakhs by 600 kilometers, and permit the transport of about 5 million tons in its first year, a figure that is ultimately intended to reach ten million tons yearly.[60] A motorway with international status is also planned to run alongside the railway. India is therefore, at least on paper, part of two competing strategies of regional integration, one supported by Washington, the other by Moscow.

But here again, the viability of such a route is not guaranteed. Due to Tehran's international political isolation, all projects with a focus on Iran have hitherto enjoyed only limited success and a connection between the Central Asian railway network and the Persian Gulf or Turkey has remained on paper only. The project for a southern corridor linking Istanbul to China via Iran, Turkmenistan, Uzbekistan, and Kyrgyzstan is also a recurrent theme, but, again, for want of political and financial support has failed to get off the ground. In 2002, while a railway line connecting Almaty, Tashkent, Turkmenabat and Tehran was triumphantly opened (financed in part by the Economic Cooperation Organization), its operation was suspended just a few weeks later, with Uzbekistan refusing to accede to a regular schedule for trains transiting across its territory.[61]

Even at the level of Iranian-Turkmen bilateral relations, which are less fraught by tensions, the interconnection of transport networks is proceeding hesitantly. As early as 1992 both countries indicated their intention to connect their lines, and the first Tejen-Serakhs-Mashhad railway link was inaugurated in 1996.[62] Officially, the line was supposed to be able to transport half a million persons, but in practice it is not open to passenger transport. In one decade (1996–2006), it transported more than fourteen million tons of goods, providing Ashgabat with associated revenues. In 2006, the transit volume is reported to have been close to three million tons.[63] Products can now travel, at least in theory, from Dashoguz in the north of Turkmenistan to the Iranian port of Bandar Abbas. Turkmenistan also invested in the construction of a road that connects to the Mashhad-Tehran motorway network, but passenger traffic is again highly constrained by the lack of travel freedom. The transport of goods is not as restricted, however: A new road terminal was opened at the main Iranian-Turkmen border post thirty kilometers from Ashgabat in 2007, which can accommodate up to eight trucks simultaneously.[64] The flow of goods from Iran plays an important role in meeting domestic consumption in Turkmenistan, but has no great impact on continental traffic as a whole, and not even on regional Central Asian traffic.

These two east-west and north-south corridors, predicated more on the geostrategic vision of the great powers than on hard-nosed economic realities, have not yet succeeded in becoming real trade corridors. This east-west north-south opposition tends, moreover, to have been rendered obsolete by several programs. This is the case, for example, with the Central Asian Regional Economic Cooperation program (CAREC)—while it does not include Russia among its members, it does include it in its transport projects. Set up in 1997, the program includes the five Central Asian states, China, Afghanistan, Pakistan, Mongolia, and Azerbaijan, as well as six international institutions (the ADB, the EBRD, the IMF, the Islamic Development Bank, the World Bank and the UNDP). CAREC is not only involved in envisioning and building new transport corridors (feasibility studies, financing for the renovation or construction of missing sections), but also seeks to modify the commercial policies of the member states and their legislation in order to facilitate traffic flows. Its projects include initiatives to harmonize customs procedures, simplify documents, encourage information sharing between states, and so on.[65]

In contrast with other programs, CAREC supports the whole set of transport projects, both east-west and north-south. They are grouped under six large corridors: the first, Europe-East Asia, links the EU to China via Russia, Kazakhstan, and Kyrgyzstan; the second, Mediterranean-East Asia, connects the Caucasus to Central Asia and then to China; the third, Russia-Middle East and South Asia, links Russia to the Persian Gulf via Central Asia and Afghanistan; the fourth envisions Mongolia as a point of linkage between Siberia and China; the fifth, East Asia-Middle East-South Asia, links China to Pakistan via Kazakhstan, Kyrgyzstan, Tajikistan, and Afghanistan; and the sixth includes three roads linking Russia to the Arabian Sea and the Persian Gulf. Most of these corridors consist of two or three routes in some places, and are trying to combine maximum rail and road capacities. More than a third of the 8,640 kilometers of axial roads included in the CAREC corridors require substantial renovation.[66]

From the point of view of road transport, the artificial opposition between the east-west and south-east axes is undermined by the development of the NELTI corridor (New Eurasian Land Transport Initiative), financed by CAREC and the International Road Transport Union, which groups road freight associations from the transited countries. The objective is to increase road freight from China to the ports of the Baltic and Poland, which includes about 8,800 kilometers of transit through Kazakhstan and Russia. In contrast with the usual corridor of Moscow-Yekaterinburg-Omsk-Novosibirsk-Irkutsk-Nakhodka, cutting through Kazakhstan and utilizing the Dostyk-Alashankou border post with China will shave 670 kilometers off the Moscow-Lianyungang route and 860 kilometers off the Moscow-Hong Kong route.[67] While the other Central Asian states are not included in this corridor, bifurcations in their direction are envisaged. The project cost is put at US$2.3 billion and the official announcement of the start of construction was held in 2009.[68] To complement Kazakhstan's status as a transit road hub, in 2010 the ADB confirmed a US$800 million loan to upgrade the country's road network.

NELTI will have to contend, however, with two major challenges. First, the extreme length of the route, which, to be profitable, presumes that the trucks will also travel at night. It is therefore likely that this corridor will be used mainly for medium distances within post-Soviet space, and that it will not really be able to compete with railway freight in terms of continental transit. Then, as with all commerce between Europe and Asia, the differential ratio by direction is an acute issue: the amount of goods transiting in the west-bound direction is twice that going the other way. The profitability of all continental freight, rail and road, will therefore remain limited so long as the question of returning empty containers from Europe to Asia is unresolved.[69] Another possible route, not included in CAREC or TRACECA, but supported by the Eurasian Development Bank, is the "pan-central European" route. Starting out from China and crossing Kazakhstan, it joins up with Ukraine and Central Europe through the north of the Caspian. This route takes advantage of already existing Soviet infrastructure, in particular of double-track electrified railway, and runs alongside agricultural regions seeking export markets. For the EU, it could provide better service to the new member states by taking advantage of their former connections with Ukraine and Central Russia.[70]

China is obviously the economic driver of these trans-Eurasian corridors. Although Beijing through its contributions to the ADB, participates in the CAREC projects, it has also developed its own specific regional and bilateral strategies with the Central Asian countries. It promotes two international projects and one that is more regionally based. The first one is a "Western Europe-Western China" corridor from China's production sites on its eastern coast to Russia and Europe, with Kazakhstan as a main transit country.[71] The road and railway terminal at the two main border posts, respectively at Khorgos and Dostyk-Alashankou, have been modernized and their storage capacity has also been increased. Part of this logic, the Trans-Kazakhstani Trunk Railways program plans to reduce the journey between China and Europe to less than ten days owing to the tracks using the same standard gauge as Chinese and European tracks.[72] The second international corridor heads toward Afghanistan and then the Gulf countries, and will complement Chinese continental logics already underway in Pakistan with the Karakoram Highway and the port at Gwadar.[73] It includes Tajikistan, and, to a lesser degree, Kyrgyzstan, as transit countries between Xinjiang and Afghanistan. Beijing and Bishkek have recognized seventeen roads as having corridor status, while for the time being Tajikistan enjoys only one, but several sections are undergoing renovation aided by Chinese financing.[74]

The regional project concerns Uzbekistan. China hopes to link up with it as directly and rapidly as possible, via rail and road, so that its goods can reach the comparatively large Uzbek market. Beijing and Tashkent back the idea of a thousand-kilometer road linking Kashgar to the Uzbek capital via Osh and Andijan. A part of the section lying in Kyrgyzstan requires substantial reconstruction, to be financed by the ADB, but as yet no political solution has been found to the question of crossing the difficult Uzbek-Kyrgyz border.[75] The project for a railway linking Kashgar to Andijan has come up against multiple problems over the past fifteen years, including divergences of opinion and technical difficulties. During a meeting in 2008, the tripartite Sino-Kyrgyz-Uzbek Commission reached agreement on a winding route of close to 270 kilometers. Starting in Kashgar, the proposed route would pass through Torugart, in the Naryn region, and then join the Arpa Valley and the Ferghana Mountains on its way to Uzgen and, most importantly, Karasuu in the Osh region, before crossing the Uzbek border in the direction of Andijan. If it ever becomes operational, this line will not only play a key role in the development of Sino-Uzbek trade relations, as well as in opening up Kyrgyzstan.[76] However, almost no progress has been reported since 2008.

Beyond Geopolitical Grand Narratives: The Reality of Transport

Offering an "easy" grand narrative to frame the growing integration of Central Asia into world markets, transport quickly became a flagship issue from the 1990s for international financial institutions, external state actors, and local governments alike.

However, the challenges involved are often far more complex than declarations of intention might indicate. First, the supposed objectivity of the actors involved is questionable. The World Bank or the Asian Development Bank have every interest in selling lines of credit to the Central Asian states, since that is their raison d'être, and they will not be held responsible if the projects fail to be economically viable. They are thus not neutral in promoting transit corridors and do not ask whether private shipping companies are ready to commit to using them. As for external state actors, they seek to influence the regional geopolitical balance. Preparations for the withdrawal from Afghanistan in 2014 have for instance, witnessed competition between the Russian-led Eurasian and the American-led Silk Road strategies reemerge. Moreover, although governments of the region are promoting showcase transport projects that sound impressive to their local populations, as well as to international financial institutions and external actors, all these construction projects land local high-level senior officers considerable bribes, an advantage that none of them want to lose.[77]

With the opening of the maritime route in the sixteenth century, the continental routes lost their appeal. Furthermore, in a little less than half a century, or since 1950, maritime exchanges have increased seven-fold, and they now represent three-quarters of the volume and two-thirds of the value of world trade.[78] Since the invention of port containers, the increase in ship transport capacity has considerably lowered costs, and the world fleet continues to adapt quickly to the growing demands of international transport by such means as specialized ships for agricultural and truck farming. In addition, deregulation on a global scale has lowered transport costs, with the result that an increasing number of ships are registered in developing countries that are less strict in terms of taxation, security, and recruitment. At an average of US$59 per ton of merchandise, the cost of maritime transport represents less than 5 percent of the value of transported goods for wholesale products such as oil or metals, whereas the margin is even much smaller (a few cents) for sophisticated industrial products and technology.[79] In cost terms, distances have been largely abolished, and world space has become fluid. This increasing maritimization of the global economy, in particular in the Pacific region, is not to the advantage of Central Asia.

Today, 99 percent of the commodities circulating between Asia and Europe take maritime routes, leaving about 1 percent of the trade, to the continental route.[80] It is highly unlikely that the dominance of maritime trade will be threatened. The competitiveness of freight is usually calculated on the basis of three commercial components: time, service, and tariffs. Maritime traffic offers many advantages. Transportation costs are reduced, since the maritime companies offer tariffs that are at least half those of railway freight. Moreover, ships traveling between Asia and Europe have huge storage capacities that make train and truck transport rather unprofitable. The client service is also generally superior since the innumerable hazards linked to border crossings and the endemic corruption of the transit countries are avoided. It is more complex to dissociate the process of customs formalities, border crossings, and final customs clearances in continental trade than it is to carry out these operations simultaneously in ports for maritime trade.[81] Only delivery time is longer in maritime trade than by a

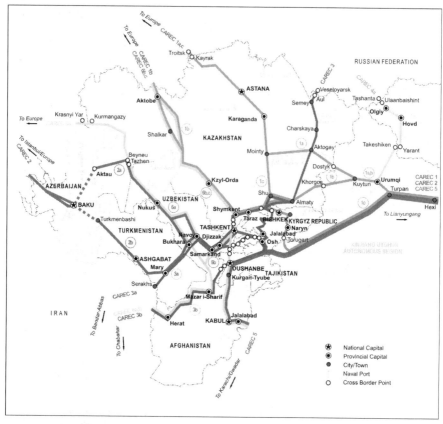

CAREC Transportation Corridors

continental route, but it can be guaranteed, which is not the case for road or railway freight. Transport between Europe and Asia is seventeen days by road, about thirty-five days by the Suez Canal, and forty-five days via the Cape of Good Hope. For the moment, the track gauge difference between the former Soviet Union, Europe, and China means that railway transport, which takes approximately six weeks, is still too slow. Compared to products going from Western Europe to Moscow, the time factor increases by 80 percent from Moscow toward Central Asia.[82] It can be presumed that this journey times will become shorter, but tariffs and services will never be competitive with maritime trade.

CAREC has set itself the rather ambitious target of 5 percent of global Asia-Europe trade passing along continental routes.[83] While this would be an immense success (revenues generated from this figure would be enormous for transit states), it is hard to seriously envisage a significant rerouting of maritime trade in favor of continental routes. Among all the corridors envisaged for Central Asia, the EU-led TRACECA east-west projects are the least profitable, since they transit through too many countries with conflictual relationships and different customs systems, and must change transport modes twice along the way (railway and ship). The American-led Silk Road strategy of linking Central Asia to South Asia requires that Afghanistan can be crossed in total security, which is not presently the case and will not be the case anytime soon. The North-South Corridor could potentially be developed, especially as the Suez Canal tends to be saturated and Russia, as well as Central Asia, aspires to gain access to the southern seas. But it is blocked by Iran's marginalization on the international scene and the absence of any real coordination between Russia and India. The most promising corridors are the rail and road networks promoted by China that would link Chinese ports to Russia and Europe via the Sino-Kazakh border, often presented as the "Eurasian bridge" or the "northern trans-Eurasian corridor." These corridors benefit from the political support of Moscow, Beijing, and Astana, and from their strategic rapprochement; they also have Chinese financial backing. The roads and railways are being rapidly modernized, the logistical difficulties have been factored in, and the private companies, mainly Chinese and Russian, involved in continental transit, have the advantage of avoiding detours via the Russian Far East. Continental commerce between China and Europe is therefore bound to pass mainly through Russia and Kazakhstan, and not through the other Central Asian states and South Caucasus.

The development of continental trade must also contend with geographical realities that political will cannot modify. Though the Siberian and Kazakh Steppes are without any mountainous obstacles and lend themselves to transit, in the past the landscape of what was formerly Turkestan was suited for trade only by camel caravans. The topography of Kyrgyzstan and Tajikistan is not conducive to the construction of major roads or railways: the technological feats required to build tunnels and bridges cause construction costs to skyrocket; landslides are a regular occurrence; the high altitude requires a particularly heavy treatment of surfacing in order to cope with the climatic conditions; and the routes are not sufficiently wide to take large-size trucks or high-speed trains. These geographical realities are not technologically insurmountable, but they reduce the profitability of continental routes and are important for rationales of development rather than commerce.

Geography is not the sole source of problems, and the state of transport networks weighs heavily, too. First, the economic crisis following the dissolution of the Soviet Union caused a drastic reduction in the state budgets for public transport and road maintenance. Road surfaces deteriorated, and some disappeared altogether, while often only a single track of the railway network, if any, was electrified. Second, in most cases the new states were not equipped with industries that would enable them to repair, modernize, and produce transport material, and were incapable, for budgetary reasons, of investing large sums in this area. National transport were obliged to rent railroad cars and containers from neighboring countries or to continue using outdated material.[84] The necessity of purchasing transport material over the coming decade will add to the already high price of continental transport. Third, logistics always comprised one of the weak links in the Soviet economy, and they remain so in Central Asia. The age of the infrastructure, the lack of storage sites and terminals able to manage large flows, the dearth of modern trucks or refrigerated containers, the lack of computerized systems—all these elements combine to make continental transit unreliable in the short and medium run. Containers may get lost en route, be held up for obscure administrative reasons for months, or be stolen. Goods can disappear, or arrive spoiled or damaged. Here again, solutions to these problems are available, but will take a long time to implement since they require large budgets, as well as human capital. Central Asia still has a severe shortage of technical professionals, and today the independent states are finding it difficult to plug this generational gap and pass on the required knowledge.

Political factors must also be taken into account. While intra-Central Asian travel was still relatively unrestrictive in the first half of the 1990s, the reduction and deterioration of transport networks between 1996 and 2002 coincided with a relative improvement in the economic situation and a phase of tightening border controls. First Turkmenistan and then Uzbekistan put an end to the free circulation of people and goods, set up visa systems, and decided that the opening of borders constituted a threat to their sovereignty. This allowed them not only to have more control over their populations, but also to multiply the fiscal barriers and raise more tax revenues. While Turkmenistan's decisions had only a limited impact on neighboring states, Uzbekistan's isolationist policies upset the entire regional balance in terms of transport. Even today, the negative interstate climate impedes the prospects for connecting infrastructure networks. Administrative problems have even multiplied in the last decade, including a visa system demanding that trucks change driver upon entering a new country; overly complex customs formalities; great disparities in transit tariffs; excessive taxation on imports into Uzbekistan; a refusal to unify the opening hours of border posts; a lack of posts open to international traffic, and so on.

Corruption also undermines the advantages of continental trade: it increases transit costs, makes waiting times unpredictable, and slows down traffic flows. Blockages at the borders are a direct source of corruption: In 2005, Kyrgyz trucks transiting through Uzbek territory had to pay between US$150 and 200 in bribes, in addition to the US$450 of compulsory customs duties, if they did not want to remain parked at the border posts for several days.[85] The cost of bribes is now even higher. Vehicles that manage to cross the border posts are easily identifiable by their license plates and become privileged targets of a corrupt police force, which ensures that they pay bribes all throughout the journey. This corruption is difficult to stop because it is enmeshed in highly placed political networks and is an integral part of the functioning of institutions like the Customs Committees.[86] The circulation of people and commodities does not therefore depend only on the existence of routes, but also on fulfilling a set of conditions that would make such routes more viable to travel on: guarantees of security, ease of crossing border posts, procedural simplifications, and less corruption.

Finally, geopolitical factors are also at play. Kazakhstan, for instance, is trying to suffocate Kyrgyzstan economically in order to control trade flows from China, while Tashkent has been engaged in a systematic policy of obstructing continental trade to weaken Dushanbe. Only a change of development strategy would allow Tashkent to benefit from the trade flows that, today, are trying to bypass this refractory country.

The regional imbalance between Central Asian states in terms of trade is therefore bound to grow. With the exception of Kazakhstan, which is increasingly integrated into Chinese strategies to reach Russia and Europe, the Central Asian states have been left with the smallest share of regional trade flows. European and American transport strategies have not materialized and local elites can only hope that they will be able to open up to Iran and Afghanistan thanks to Chinese dynamism.

The metanarrative on the "new Silk Road" has probably been detrimental to Central Asia, insofar as it has magnified theories that bear little connection to reality and so help to avoid addressing real challenges such as weak governance. As Richard Pomfret states, "dramatic images of new silk roads or continental crossroads present a misleading picture. Central Asia's location advantages are not those of the fourteenth century."[87] Indeed, continental trade is not at all likely to dethrone maritime trade and Central Asia has little chance of capturing a significant share of global Asia-Europe trade. However, the resources at Central Asia's disposal will continue to be highly sought after, especially in a context of dwindling primary resources and proximity to the Chinese and Indian markets. But trade outside of hydrocarbons, energy, and minerals will remain minimal. The only country with real transit potential in Central Asia, essentially via railway, is Kazakhstan. Moreover, the exchanges of non-energy-related goods between China and Central Asia are, for the greatest part, those between Xinjiang and Kazakhstan. Even if one pictures an optimistic scenario in regard to Afghanistan, the trade dynamic will come from China much more than from India, at least over the next decade. The transport network will therefore essentially be regional, which presumes that the countries of the region have complementary economies rather than competitive ones, and that Afghanistan can be secured.

Trade and the establishment of trading routes is not solely a commercial enterprise with profitability as its primary objective, but it has also to do with development. The Karakoram Highway between the Pakistani port of Gwadar and Chinese Xinjiang does not make much difference to trans-Eurasian commerce, since the flows remain minimal, but it facilitates access to the products of remote mountain regions. A similar logic is visible in Sino-Tajik trade to Afghanistan, in the opening of routes between Central Asia and Xinjiang, and indeed in those, if only on paper, between Central Asia and Kashmir.[88] The aim is to offer development opportunities to these isolated populations, without concern for large world trade flows. This development-oriented perspective on the transport issue is probably more relevant to Central Asia's long-term prospects than the grand narrative on transcontinental trade. As G. Raballand, A. Kunth, and R. Auty have shown, "the generally low density of economic activity . . . renders scale-sensitive freight costs disproportionately high in rural areas compared with the larger centers. . . . Consequently, intra-country trade flows are becoming concentrated on routes between the larger cities to the detriment of economic prospects in the more rural areas, where most citizens still reside. . . . We call this effect the low-income trap: it further intensifies the risk that high transportation costs will dissipate the potential for economic catch-up."[89]

Notes

1. G. Raballand, A. Kunth, and R. Auty, "Central Asia's Transport Cost Burden and Its Impact on Trade," *Economic Systems* 29, no. 1 (2005): 6–31.

2. "Secteur des transports en Ouzbékistan," *Mission Economique UBIFRANCE*, April 28, 2008.

3. B. B. Uulu, "Zheleznodorozhnyi tupik," *CA-News*, July 15, 2010, http://www.ca-news.org/news/435421.

4. See "Transport Strategy of the Republic of Kazakhstan," Government of the Republic of Kazakhstan, http://en.government.kz/resources/docs/doc5.

5. On the impact of the Soviet collapse on transport, see J. Thorez, "Flux et dynamiques spatiales en Asie Centrale: Géographie de la transformation post-soviétique" (PhD diss., Paris 10 Nanterre, 2005); J. Linn, "First Eurasia Emerging Markets Forum: 'Connecting Central Asia with the World'," *Global Journal of Emerging Market Economies*, no. 1 (2009): 241–58.

6. Authors' regular fieldwork at the Chernyaev border post from 2002 to 2005, and in March 2008.

7. M. Reeves, "Fixing the Border: On the Affective Life of the State in Southern Kyrgyzstan," *Environment and Planning D: Society and Space* 29, no. 5 (2011): 905–23.

8. Raballand, Kunth, and Auty, "Central Asia's Transport Cost Burden," 21.

9. E. Vinokurov, M. Jadraliyev, and Y. Shcherbanin, "The EurAsEC Transport Corridors," Eurasian Development Bank Sector Report, no. 5, Astana, March 2009, 30.

10. "Trans-European North-South Motorway (TEM) Project," Report of the United Nations Economic Commission for Europe, Geneva, 2005, 238.

11. C. Grigoriou, "Landlockedness, Infrastructure, and Trade: New Estimates for Central Asian Countries," World Bank Development Research Group Policy Research Working Paper, no. 4335, August 2007, 8.

12. More details in "Uzbekistan: Road Rehabilitation Project," Asian Development Bank Evaluation Report, December 2010.

13. Kh. Salimov, "V Uzbekistane ezhegodno prokladyvaiutsia ili rekonstruiruiutsia 150–200 km dorog," *Natsional'noe Informatsionnoe Agentsvo Uzbekistana*, February 2, 2008, http://uza.uz/ru/business/2078/.

14. Authors' fieldwork, Uzbekistan, March 2008; "Active Measures Taken to Improve Quality of Roads in Uzbekistan," Uzbek Embassy in Belgium, August 8, 2008, http://www.uzbekistan.be/press-releases/72-2008.html.

15. "Country Profile: Turkmenistan," Library of Congress Federal Research Division, Washington, DC, February 2007, 10.

16. More in "Country Profile: Tajikistan," Library of Congress Federal Research Division, Washington, DC, January 2007.

17. Authors' fieldwork, Tajikistan, June 2010.

18. "Zavershen proekt 'Reabilitatsiia avtodorogi Taraz-Talas-Suusamyr,' Faza II, km 52–73," Ministry of Transport and Communication of the Kyrgyz Republic, September 9, 2011, http://www.mtc.gov.kg/index.php?option=com_content&view=article&id=722:-l-r-ii-52–73&catid=1:latest-news&Itemid=53.

19. Uulu, "Zheleznodorozhnyi tupik."

20. Vinokurov, Jadraliyev, and Shcherbanin, "The EurAsEC Transport Corridors," 42.

21. See the Council for Rail Transport in the CIS, whose president is Vladimir Yakunin, head of the Russian railways, http://www.sovetgt.org/default.htm.

22. "Uzbekistan nameren realizovat' proekt elektrifikatsii zheleznykh dorog stoimost'iu $600 mln," *Delovaia Pressa*, no. 33, August 20, 2002.

23. M. Kozachkov, "Zheleznaia doroga dolzhna stat' lokomotivom ekonomiki," *Liter*, April 19, 2005, http://www.nomad.su/?a=4-200504200220.

24. A. Kutueva, "V Kyrgyzstane v 2008 nachnetsia elektrifikatsiia zheleznoi dorogi," *CIS News*, January 18, 2008, http://www.cis-news.info/read/41006/.

25. Thorez, "Flux et dynamiques spatiales en Asie centrale."

26. Ibid., 373.

27. Ibid.

28. S. Smirnov, "Transport Kazakhstana: Uzly na rel'sakh," *Mezhdunarodnyi delovoi zhurnal Kazakhstan*, nos. 5–6 (2008), http://www.investkz.com/journals/58/594.html.

29. M.S. Ashimbaev and R.I. Krumm, *Perspektivy Tsentral'noi Azii kak tranzitnogo mosta mezhdu Evropoi i Kitaem: Sbornik materialov mezhdunarodnoi konferentsii* (Almaty: Kazakhstanskii Institut Strategicheskikh Issledovanii, 2005), 29.

30. Smirnov, "Transport Kazakhstana."

31. Ibid.

32. "GE Signs Agreement for 150 Shunter Locomotives in Kazakhstan," *General Electric*, April 11, 2010, http://www.genewscenter.com/Press-Releases/GE-Signs-Agreement-for-150-Shunter-Locomotives-in-Kazakhstan-273a.aspx.

33. "Kazakhstankie passazhiry peresiadut v kitaiskie zh.d. vagony?" *Centrasia*, January 15, 2006, http://www.centrasia.ru/newsA.php?st=1137299340.

34. Vinokurov, Jadraliyev, and Shcherbanin, "The EurAsEC Transport Corridors," 39.

35. "Secteur des transports en Ouzbékistan."

36. "First Passenger Train Crossed Amu Darya River Along Railway Bridge," *Turkmenistan. ru*, June 30, 2011, http://www.turkmenistan.ru/en/articles/15061.html.

37. "Trans-Karakum Railway Finished," *International Railway Journal*, April 2006, http://www.highbeam.com/doc/1G1-144930812.html.

38. "Country Profile: Kyrgyzstan," Library of Congress Federal Research Division, Washington, DC, 2007.

39. Uulu, "Zheleznodorozhnyi tupik."

40. "Tadzhikistan postroit zheleznuiu dorogu v obkhod Uzbekistana," *Fergana.ru*, October 16, 2008, http://www.fergana.ru/news.php?id=10429.

41. "Tadzhikskaia zheleznaia doroga—Vchera, segodnia, zavtra," *Evraziia Vesti*, no. 11 (2008), http://www.eav.ru/publ1.php?publid=2008-11a06.

42. Thorez, "Flux et dynamiques spatiales en Asie centrale."

43. Ibid.

44. J. Thorez, "Transport-Traffic-Transfer: Migration Networks between Russia and Central Asia," Paper presented at the conference "National Identity in Eurasia II: Migrancy & Diaspora," Wolfson College, University of Oxford, July 10–12, 2009.

45. "Country Profile: Tajikistan"; A. Zozulinsky, "Transportation, Distribution, and Warehousing Services in the Kyrgyz Republic," US & Foreign Commercial Service and US Department of State Report, November 2006.

46. S. Smirnov, "Civil Aviation: Takeoff or Letdown?" *International Business Magazine Kazakhstan*, no. 2 (2007), http://www.investkz.com/en/journals/52/408.html.

47. "Air Transport: Passengers Carried in Turkmenistan," *Trading Economics*, http://www.tradingeconomics.com/turkmenistan/air-transport-passengers-carried-wb-data.html.

48. "Secteur des transports en Ouzbékistan," 2.

49. Ibid., 1.

50. "CAREC Transport and Trade Facilitation: Partnership for Prosperity," Asian Development Bank/CAREC Report, Manila, 2009.

51. J. Linn and O. Pidufala, "Lessons from Central Asia: Experience with Regional Economic Cooperation," Wolfensohn Center for Development Working Paper, no. 4, October 2008, 13.

52. M. Emerson and E. Vinokurov, "Optimisation of Central Asian and Eurasian Trans-Continental Land Transport Corridors," Europe-Central Asia Monitoring Working Paper, no. 7, December 2009, 7.

53. "Progress Report II," TRACECA Co-ordination Team Report, December 1, 2002, annex 3, 2.

54. Vinokurov, Jadraliyev, and Shcherbanin, "The EurAsEC Transport Corridors," 23.

55. Ibid.

56. Kavalski, *The New Central Asia*, 180–81.

57. S. F. Starr, *Afghanistan beyond the Fog of Nation Building: Giving Economic Strategy a Chance*. (Washington, DC: The Central Asia-Caucasus Institute Silk Road Studies Program, 2011) and S. F. Starr and A. C. Kuchins, *The Key to Success in Afghanistan: A Modern Silk Road Strategy,* Washington, DC: The Central Asia-Caucasus Institute Silk Road Studies Program, 2010.

58. A. Kuchins, "Laying the Groundwork for Afghanistan's New Silk Road: How Washington and Kabul Can Turn a Vision into a Plan," *Foreign Affairs,* December 5, 2011, http://www.foreignaffairs.com/articles/136714/andrew-c-kuchins/laying-the-groundwork-for-afghanistans-new-silk-road?page=show; J. Kucera, "The New Silk Road?," *Diplomat,* November 11, 2011, http://the-diplomat.com/2011/11/11/the-new-silk-road/.

59. R. Spector, "The North-South Transport Corridor," *The Central Asia-Caucasus Analyst,* July 3, 2002, http://www.cacianalyst.org/newsite/?q=node/165.

60. "Turkmenistan Approved the Funding of the Railway North-South," *Baku Today,* June 26, 2011, http://www.bakutoday.net/turkmenistan-approved-the-funding-of-the-railway-north-south.html; "Mezhdunarodnyi transportnyi koridor Sever-Iug," *RZhD Cargo,* n.d., http://cargo.rzd.ru/static/public/cargo?STRUCTURE_ID=5130&.

61. R. Abazov, *Historical Dictionary of Turkmenistan* (Lanham, MD: Scarecrow Press, 2005), 52; "O sotrudnichestve mezhdu Respublikoi Kazakhstan i Organizatsiei Ekonomicheskogo Sotrudnichestva," Kazakhstan Ministry of Foreign Affairs, July 28, 2009, http://portal.mfa.kz/portal/page/portal/mfa/ru/content/policy/inegration/ECO.

62. A. Maleki, "Iran," in Starr, *The New Silk Roads*, 182.

63. A. Kurtov, "Turkmenistan i Iran: Vzaimootnosheniia sosedei," *Gündogar*, January 14, 2007, http://gundog.newhost.ru/?0212043745000000000000013000000.

64. Authors' fieldwork, Ashgabat, April 2008.

65. More on the CAREC website, http://beta.adb.org/countries/subregional-programs/carec.

66. "CAREC Transport and Trade Facilitation," 1.

67. Emerson and Vinokurov, "Optimisation of Central Asian and Eurasian Trans-Continental Land Transport Corridors," 8.

68. Vinokurov, Jadraliyev, and Shcherbanin, "The EurAsEC Transport Corridors," 28.

69. Y.H.V. Lun, Kee-hung Lai, and T.C.E. Cheng, *Shipping and Logistics Management* (New York: Springer, 2010).

70. Emerson and Vinokurov, "Optimisation of Central Asian and Eurasian Trans-Continental Land Transport Corridors," 9.

71. "Mintranskom Kazakhstana ne dovolen tempami stroitel'stva dorogi Zapadnaia Evropa-Zapadnyi Kitai," *Today.kz,* September 29, 2011, http://www.today.kz/ru/news/kazakhstan/2011–09–29/51416.

72. "Kazakh Railways: Back to the Future," *Kazworld,* December 21, 2009, http://kazworld.info/?p=5153.

73. R. Weitz, "Afghanistan in China's Emerging Eurasian Transport Corridor," *China Brief* 10, no. 14 (2010): 10–14.

74. More in Laruelle and Peyrouse, *The "Chinese Question" in Central Asia*, 89–91.

75. M. Parkash, "Connecting Central Asia: A Road Map for Regional Cooperation," Asian Development Bank Report, Manila, 2006.

76. S. Peyrouse, "The Growing Trade Stakes of the Chinese-Kyrgyz-Uzbek Railway Project," *The Central Asia-Caucasus Analyst* 11, no. 5 (2009): 9–12.

77. On bribery in the construction sector, see *The Construction Sector Transparency Initiative*, http://www.constructiontransparency.org.

78. Gauchon, *Le monde*, 502.

79. J. Korinek and P. Sourdin, "Maritime Transport Costs and Their Impact on Trade," Report of the Organization for Economic Co-operation and Development, Paris, August 2009, 2.

80. Emerson and Vinokurov, "Optimisation of Central Asian and Eurasian Trans-Continental Land Transport Corridors," 5.

81. J. Arvis, G. Raballand, and J. Marteau, "The Cost of Being Landlocked: Logistics Costs and Supply Chain Reliability," World Bank Working Paper, no. 4258, June 2007.

82. Raballand, Kunth, and Auty, "Central Asia's Transport Cost Burden," 27.

83. "CAREC Transport and Trade Facilitation," 12.

84. On the lack of containers, see Vinokurov, Jadraliyev, and Shcherbanin, "The EurAsEC Transport Corridors."

85. N. Megoran, G. Raballand, and J. Bouyjou, "Performance, Representation, and the Economics of Border Control in Uzbekistan," *Geopolitics* 10, no. 4 (2005): 712–40.

86. For examples of corrupt schemes at the border with China, see S. Ibraimov, "China-Central Asia Trade Relations: Economic and Social Patterns," *China and Eurasia Forum Quarterly* 7, no. 1 (2009): 47–59.

87. R. Pomfret, "Trade and Transport in Central Asia," in Hermann and Linn, *Central Asia and the Caucasus*, 49.

88. See, for instance, S. Peyrouse, "Economic Trends as an Identity Marker?"; "The Pamiri Trade Niche with China and Afghanistan," *Problems of Post-Communism* 59, no. 4 (2012): 3–14; and M. Kaw, "Restoring India's Links with Central Asia across Kashmir: Challenges and Opportunities," in Laruelle and Peyrouse, *Mapping Central Asia*, 179–97.

89. Raballand, Kunth, and Auty, "Central Asia's Transport Cost Burden," 25.

13
A Structurally Weakened Industrial Base

In Soviet times, Central Asia specialized in agriculture and heavy industries, and had a very limited industrial base apart from extraction. A few light industries operated as links in a larger chain of production that often began and ended in European Russia, Siberia, or Ukraine, but most finished products arrived—in small amounts—from other republics. This entire industrial base collapsed in the first half of the 1990s, due to the disappearance of linkages between republics, the unprofitability of factories, and the opening up to foreign markets. Even Kazakhstan was unable to safeguard the majority of its light industries. The industrial base is therefore structurally weak in Central Asia, and helpless when faced with competition from China, which supplies all kinds of products at ultra-competitive prices. However, some industrial niches did survive or have been reconstituted: chemical and pharmaceutical industries are attempting to modernize; Russia has revived the military-industrial complex; the automobile sector, one of the region's last remaining mechanical industries, has taken off in Uzbekistan; the textile sector is developing, with more success in Turkmenistan than in Uzbekistan; the construction market is going through an unprecedented boom; and the food processing and distribution sectors are restructuring.

The Soviet Legacy: The Chemical and Pharmaceutical Industries

The Central Asian chemical industry was developed by the Soviet regime in response to the agricultural needs of the Kazakh, Uzbek, and Turkmen republics. Today the sector is difficult to revive: its technologies are outdated, the specialists have left, and its output is well below international quality standards. However, the Central Asian governments insist on reviving the chemical industry for three main reasons: (1) importing fertilizer is very costly for their agricultural systems; (2) refined hydrocarbons can be exported at far higher prices than raw material; and (3) pharmaceutical security necessitates a national production capability. So, despite the difficulty of emerging from the—environmentally damaging—Soviet industrial system, the Central Asian chemical industry has a future. The subsoil is rich in materials awaiting chemical

264

transformation, agriculture will remain a primary revenue source for Uzbekistan and Turkmenistan, and the authorities want to attain the largest possible autonomy in terms of pharmaceutical production.

Thanks to its subsoil reserves, Kazakhstan possesses significant chemical industrial potential. The consumption of fertilizer rose considerably during the Virgin Lands campaign, up from 170,000 tons in 1965 to more than one million in 1986.[1] A factory was set up along the Begun and Shayan Rivers to manufacture the anti-parasitic drug Santonin, refinement factories were constructed at Karatau and Aktyubinsk to handle large reserves of phosphate rock, and the Aral phosphate factory has become the base of the republic's glass industry. Kazakhstan also has significant reserves of potassium salt, borates, bromine, sulfates, phosphate rock, and sulfur from pyrites. It produces synthetic detergent, mineral fertilizers, microbiological proteins, chemical fibers and threads, and synthetic plastics. It also has an unexploited potential for petrochemical synthesis, in particular of ethylene, polypropylene, and resin.[2]

The Kazakh chemical industry went through a grave crisis after the fall of the USSR, but began to pick up in the first years of the twenty-first century thanks to state aid such as subsidies for railway tariffs.[3] The authorities redoubled their efforts to encourage foreign investment in a bid to cover their financial burdens and to invest in modern technologies. In 2009, Kazakhstan launched a state program for the development of the petrochemical and chemical industry by 2015, with an earmarked investment of US$9 billion.[4] The objective is above all to boost the local production of agricultural fertilizers: since 2005, the country has only produced 10 percent of the chemical products required for agriculture, although it is capable of providing for 100 percent of its needs in phosphate fertilizers.[5] In this context, in 2009 the Samruk-Kazyna Fund created the United Chemical Company, which was tasked with increasing the share of the chemical sector in the country's GDP by helping large firms like Kazfosfat, Kazazot, and the Caustic and Mineral Resource Mining Company, to get back on their feet.[6] As the spearhead of the Kazakh chemical sector, Kazfosfat controls several factories, including Novojambul for yellow phosphorus, the Taraz mineral fertilizer factory, the complexes of Janatas and Karatau for mineral ore treatment, the Stepnogorsk chemical factory, and the Shymkent detergents factory. The arrival on the Kazakh market of Eurokhim, one of Russia's and Europe's main producers of phosphate minerals and nitrogen, means that the market for phosphate fertilizers is now more competitive, which forces Kazfosfat to direct itself toward exports. The company already exports to the Baltic countries and to Moldova, but aims increasingly at markets further afield such as India, Southeast Asia, and Latin America.[7]

The Uzbek chemical sector was formed in the 1930s, as fertilizers and pesticides were in high demand as the cotton sector developed, although the largest factory, Navoyazot, which today captures half the market, dates only from the 1960s.[8] The chemical industry is divided into three large sectors: non-organic materials and fertilizers; organic chemicals, artificial filaments, and polymers; and reactive chemicals for energy, gold mines, and the chemical industry. The sector is influenced by the needs of engineering companies (plastic and glass), the textile industry (fibers and paint), agriculture (fertilizers and pesticides), transport (fuels, lubricants, rubber), and construction (protective films, glass, and plastic). It employs about 40,000 people and enjoys an advantage over the industry in Kazakhstan in that the gas needed for transformation is easy to access and cheap. As a consequence, Uzbekistan produces enough fertilizer to meet the needs of its domestic markets and can even export part of its production.[9] Today the country aims to be the largest producer of sal ammoniac, carbamide, ammonium nitrate, ammonium sulfate, and superphosphate in Central Asia.[10] Production is managed by the state-run company Uzkimyosanoat (Uzkhimprom in Russian), which combines twenty-nine companies, some of which are in the process of modernizing thanks to partnerships with the Dubai-based International Petroleum Investment Company (IPIC) and the German MAN Ferrostaal. The Uzbek state seeks to privatize its chemical enterprises, and between 2006 and 2008, it opened competition for nine of them, or nearly half of its capacity, but the outcome was disappointing because the Russian and Chinese firms balked at the Uzbek tenders.[11]

Though the Turkmen chemical industry was not greatly developed in Soviet times, in the first decade of the twenty-first century the authorities decided to reduce the amount of fertilizer imported by promoting national production. In 2007, a state-run corporation, Turkmenkhimia, was created to oversee the country's main chemical factories. The country's largest production enterprise, Maryazot, was modernized through a joint venture with the Chinese Citic Group, which is also setting its sights on other companies in this market.[12] Turkmenistan also plans to specialize in iron sulfate, which is used for water purification, and wants to develop the production of potassium salts, because the country has notable reserves close to Magdanly in the Lebap region.

In addition to agricultural fertilizers, one of the most promising branches of the chemical industry is undoubtedly the pharmaceutical sector, which has grown considerably all over the CIS. In Kazakhstan, health expenditure increased by 27 percent between 2006 and 2007, and by 42 percent between 2007 and 2008.[13] But consumption is still six to ten times lower than that of developed countries at approximately US$60 per capita, a level equivalent to Russia (in developed countries this figure varies from between US$350 and US$700).[14] The Central Asian market is dominated by low-range products, but with rising living standards, part of the population is asking for more complex medications. Products from India and China, and local pharmaceutical industry, which has specialized in simple preparations, are unable to meet the growth in domestic demand of expensive and more sophisticated medicines.

Pharmaceutical security is therefore under question. While in Uzbekistan, six of the ten largest pharmaceutical firms are foreign-based, Kazakhstan distinguishes itself by its high degree of national production: The five largest companies, Khimfarm, Global Farm, Romat, Nobel AFF, and Nur-May Farm, yield between 80 and 90 percent of Kazakh domestic production.[15] Khimfarm alone controls nearly half the national market and the state-run corporation SK Farmatsiia, created by the Samruk-Kazyna Fund, is the country's sole pharmaceutical distributor.[16] The share of national production on the market is 34 percent, a rate higher than the strategic security rate of 20 percent.[17] But the distribution networks are inadequate: in 2010, several regions such as Mangystau suffered from shortages due to failures in procurement of medicines.[18] Lastly, the country is very short of qualified personnel, but is trying to set up new pharmaceutical education courses with the help of foreign companies.

Beyond CIS countries such as Russia, Germany, France, and India are well established in the local pharmaceutical sector. But foreign companies still face high protectionist barriers, since national companies lobby hard to preserve their monopoly. However, measures have been taken in recent years to make transactions more transparent and to reduce the black market. There is stiff competition between firms, distributors, and resellers that makes it possible to keep medications at reasonable prices. Kazakhstan grants such importance to the development of the pharmaceutical sector not only for the epidemiological aim of protecting the health of its citizens, but also in hopes of rapid export growth to its Uzbek and Kyrgyz neighbors, and eventually to Afghanistan.[19] In this domain as well as in others, Astana hopes to become a regional leader for the whole of Central Asia.

The Revival of the Military-Industrial Complex

At the collapse of the Soviet Union, all the Central Asian firms linked to the military-industrial complex practically shut down. However, in the last decade or so, Moscow has decided to revalorize its Soviet legacy by reviving its military-industrial ties with the region. While Turkmenistan and Tajikistan did not inherited any military industries, in the three other countries, Moscow and the local governments have a shared interest in rebuilding this sector. Central Asian military budgets have increased by more than 50 percent between 2007 and 2010.[20] Kazakhstan's defense spending increased from US$206 million in 1999 to 855 million in 2008, and Kyrgyzstan's went from US$44 million to 79 million over the same period.[21] Kazakhstan is obviously leading in military investments, even if all of the region's states are trying to bolster their spending, in accordance with their means. They are also contemplating joint exports to third countries, as many of the military items produced in Central Asia have export potential, especially to China and India.[22]

The Kazakh military industries have looked to promote their wares, doing so successfully during the yearly KADEX exposition of weapons systems and military equipment in 2010.[23] The state corporation tasked with the import and export of military material, Kazspetseksport, has not concealed its main objective: to become an essential partner of those foreign companies that set their sights on the Central Asian market, and even on other Asian countries, such as China and India.[24] Kazakhstan Engineering, entirely controlled by Samruk-Kazyna, acts as an umbrella for about twenty companies in the country linked to the military industry. Five Russo-Kazakh joint ventures dominate. The Granit Office of Technological Construction, in charge of information security, supplies warning systems to the Kazakh armed forces, is involved in the computerization of information and decision-making in the air force, and in antimissile defense. The Kirov mechanical engineering works produces torpedo submarines, while Zenit (Automobile Construction Company of West Kazakhstan, ZKMK) based in Uralsk specializes in the construction of minehunters and minesweepers, and also produces specific parts for torpedoes. It collaborates with Tatar factories, which specializes in the construction of large tonnage vessels (between 500 and 1,000 tons) for the Kazakh Caspian fleet. Two other firms are based in Petropavlovsk in the north of the country: the first, ZIKSTO, formerly the Kuibyshev mechanical factory, produces anti-ship mines; and the second, the Kirov factory, is in charge of equipment for naval communications.[25] The growing role given to telecommunications companies like Nat Kazakhstan and Astel, and the new Kazakh Center of Geoinformation Systems confirm Kazakh military's commitment to the domain of new technologies.[26]

In Kyrgyzstan, Russia is most active at Karakol on the southern shore of Lake Issyk-Kul, not far from the border with China. The Ozero factory, today a Russo-Kyrgyz joint venture 95 percent owned by Moscow, has been part of the production chain for Dagdizel torpedoes since 1943, when it was relocated from Dagestan during the Second World War. The Kremlin considers this site strategic, since it also hosts the Koi-Sary naval military base, often referred to as the "submarine Baikonur."[27] The Dastan factory in Bishkek, which makes VA-111 Shkval torpedoes—allegedly able to attain higher speeds than NATO submarine missiles—constitutes another important part of the Russo-Kyrgyz military-industrial complex. In 2009, Bishkek agreed to cede its majority shares in Dastan to Russian state-run company Rosatom for a sum of about US$30 million.[28] In exchange for this, Russia has committed to developing the company, and its export capacities are growing. In addition, the Ainur Russo-Kyrgyz joint venture in Bishkek produces munitions for infantry forces, while Zhanar, also situated in the capital city, has been reconverted and now produces electronic material, radar, and magnetic sensors for use in border protection.[29]

Uzbekistan has also tried to revive its military-industrial sector, but the Chkalov aviation factory, TAPO, one of the flagship industries of independent Uzbekistan, has experienced several setbacks since the fall of the USSR. During Soviet times it was famous for its production of large military Il-76 transporters (though it also produced smaller Il-114 planes and the wings of the An-70 military planes). Whereas close to a thousand military transport planes were built there during the Soviet period, only ten new units—bound for the Indian military-industrial complex—have been produced since independence. Tensions between TAPO and the aviation company Ilyushin came to a head in 2006 over the delivery of the Il-76 (90 percent produced in Russia but completely assembled in Tashkent) to the Chinese army. These tensions were in part resolved by the cession of 50 percent of TAPO shares to the Russian United Aircraft Corporation, which oversees the main Russian aviation producers, including Mig, Sukhoy, Ilyushin, and Tupolev.[30] Uzbekistan is important for the Russian military-industrial complex: Tashkent remains the only site in the former Soviet Union where the fourth-generation Il-76 MF is constructed to Western environmental standards, as

Russia possesses only older generation planes, nearly all of which are prohibited to fly over European airspace. For the Russian state consortium Rosoboronexport, the Tashkent factory should concentrate on export orders, whereas the Ulyanovsk factory is reserved for the needs of the domestic military-industrial complex. In 2007, a new Russian-Uzbek joint venture, UzRosAvia, was created to carry out repairs on Russian military helicopters at the Chirchik factory close to Tashkent.[31] But at the end of 2010, TAPO, unable to pay its debts, was declared bankrupt and the legal procedures for closure were begun in 2011.[32] Should they be carried to term, TAPO's total closure will put a large dent in Tashkent's hopes of remaining an industrial power and of maintaining the expertise it accumulated during the Soviet period.

The future of the military industrial sector in Central Asia is therefore closely linked to the relationship to Russia. With the exception of Kazakhstan, the other Central Asian countries are destined to remain buyers of military production, but not producers of it.

One of the Last Mechanical Industries: The Uzbek Automobile Sector

Although Uzbekistan risks losing its aviation factory, it has another trump card up its sleeve, unique in Central Asia—namely its automobile industry. The global automobile sector alone represents close to 10 percent of world trade in manufactured products. Although the United States, Japan, and the EU control about 80 percent of world export,[33] Tashkent hopes to take advantage of regional export circuits, especially as cars are highly in demand among several of its neighbors, in particular Kazakhstan and Russia. Uzbekistan's car industry is therefore one of the few sectors not related to extractive industries that have actually been successfully developed since independence. It accounts for over one-third of the country's mechanical production.[34]

Two large plants share the market: formerly UzDaewoo, today GM Uzbekistan, which produces cars, and SamAuto, the Samarkand-based automobile plant, which specializes in commercial transportation vehicles. Launched in early 1990 in the small village of Asaka, near Andijan, the famous Uzbek-South Korean Daewoo joint venture has long been seen as a symbol of the Karimov regime's modernizing aims and its opening up toward Asia. Hundreds of thousands of cars have been sold, under three main brands: the smaller-sized Tico, the more luxurious Nexia, and the minibus Damas. UzDaewoo production has transformed the Uzbek automobile market, which has very little access to the used cars from Japan or South Korea, and is otherwise dominated by old Soviet brands.[35] Daewoo's shares were acquired by the state agency Uzavtosanoat in 2005.[36] Three years later the Uzbek authorities, undesirous of managing the sector alone, accepted an offer from General Motors to acquire a 25 percent stake; GM, if it so wishes, is permitted to acquire up to 40 percent of the joint venture.

GM Uzbekistan has so far looked primarily to foreign markets, and was among the top ten most-traded cars in Russia in 2010.[37] The car market in neighboring Kazakhstan has changed rapidly thanks to the import of European, Japanese, and South Korean car brands, but Uzbekistan has nevertheless succeeded in setting up there.[38] The Tajik and Kyrgyz markets also have potential because purchasing new cars has been slow, but small salaries, border closures, and Tashkent's isolationism have prevented such growth. UzDaewoo was already exporting as far away as Azerbaijan and Moldova, and the Uzbek authorities do not hide their regional ambitions, in particular their desire to enter the promising Afghan market. Over the years, they have prioritized foreign sales for GM, but since 2009, with a reduction in the sales tax, the joint venture has focused increasingly on the Uzbek domestic market.[39] This is reflected in changes in production and rapid growth of new models, such as economy cars. The partnership between GM and Uzavtosanoat is considered a success given the difficult investment climate for foreign companies in Uzbekistan. A second joint venture has even been established: GM Power Train Uzbekistan builds engines and casting parts in the Tashkent region.[40] Although the bankruptcy of GM in 2009 reduced the production of the Asaka plant by 14 percent that year, the situation has stabilized and GM Uzbekistan introduced its new Chevrolet Spark model in 2010. The plan is for 50,000 cars to be built per year, including 20,000 for export to the Asian market.[41]

The Uzbek authorities have bolstered some other international partnerships. In 2010, Uzavtosanoat signed an agreement with India's Ashok Minda Group to create the Uzminda joint venture for the production of speedometers and security systems in the Navoy free industrial zone, in which the South Korean joint venture Chasys had already invested.[42] The Uzbek authorities also plan to develop the production of buses and trucks. SamAuto formed a joint venture with the German group MAN to manufacture about one thousand heavy commercial vehicles per year, and another with Germany's Daimler to build six hundred Mercedes-Benz buses per year.[43] This promising automobile market is specific to Uzbekistan, which, for once, has an advantage over its arch-competitor Kazakhstan.

Is the Potential of the Textile Industry Still Unexploited?

A major cotton producer, Central Asia is trying to establish its place on the world textile market. Uzbekistan, and to a lesser extent Turkmenistan, Kazakhstan, and Tajikistan are important cotton producers, but they have few industrial structures for processing. A growing textile production might nonetheless open up some prospects both in economic and social terms. Cotton processing has a high added value: while a kilo of cotton purchased on the domestic market is worth US$1.4, knitted products cost an average of 5.4 and finished products US$16.[44] Moreover, this sector could create many jobs in rural regions, in particular for women, and therefore have a positive impact on rural development.

The present-day textile market in Central Asia is largely dominated by Turkmen and Uzbek production. Ashgabat has heavily invested in its industrial textile structures. From 1991 to 2002, it saw production fall, plunging from 430,000 to 170,000 tons of fiber per year, yet local treatment rose from 4 percent to 35 percent.[45] Today more than half of the cotton produced is treated locally, yielding a considerable increase in sales revenues, since the majority (more than 90 percent) is exported to Turkey. Foreign companies, mainly Turkish ones (the best known of which is Gap Inshaat, owned by businessman Ahmet Çalyk), have invested more than a billion dollars in the Turkmen textile industry. Textiles are the preferred sector for Turkish businessmen: They are allowed to buy goods in Turkmen *manat* at black-market prices, and then convert the money into dollars at official prices, which reaps them substantial profits.[46] In total, about twenty Turkish-Turkmen joint ventures have been created in the textile sector. In 2008, of the US$328 million of direct foreign investment from Turkish companies in the country, 256 million were ploughed into the textile industry.[47]

Other companies, many of them European, are also present. Swiss company Bezema AG has succeeded in acquiring a good share of the market in chemical products and dyes, and is established at the main production sites in Ashgabat, Gök-Tepe, Gypjak, and Bayramali. In collaboration with the Ministry of the Textile Industry, the Belgian company NVA & A Demeilenaere & Co opened a textile services center in the capital in 2009 in order to set up direct contacts with foreign partners. Wool production has not yet returned to its Soviet levels, but Turkmenistan has tried to maintain the production of traditional Astrakhan fur. A share of silk production (which, according to official figures, increased by 50 percent in 2007 from 2006 figures, reaching 6.5 million meters of fabric and 110 tons of thread[48]) is also earmarked for the Turkish market, not to mention the rugs produced at the Halash factory. And thanks to the efforts of the company 5M Inshaat Textil Ithalat Sanayi, silk production partly revived in Turkmenabat in 2008. But if Turkmenistan wants to remain competitive at an international level, its textile industry needs to equip itself with the means to redevelop its wool sector (a cooperation agreement with China was signed in this area), and more importantly, to develop the capacity to produce artificial fibers and to improve its chemical dyeing facilities.

Uzbekistan also has considerable potential, but the share of the textile sector in its economy is only 2 to 2.5 percent. The Uzbek textile holding, O'zbekengilsanoat, has doubled its production between 2004 and 2009.[49] In 2005, the government stated that it would invest heavily in the treatment of raw cotton in order to double the share of processed products. It offered a number of investment advantages to foreign companies, facilitated access to capital for textile companies, and exempted equipment imports from customs duty.[50] But, as in other sectors, retroactive measures and broken promises have tarnished Tashkent's image in the eyes of foreign investors. The revocation, as of January 1, 2011, of the promise to reduce export taxes and to provide a 15 percent discount on the purchase of cotton has led some Chinese companies to terminate their projects. Among them is the Shandong Yuncheng Hengshi Textile Company, which had invested US$1.3 million in the construction of a textile mill.[51] Moreover, despite the rhetoric of promoting cotton processing, the Uzbek authorities continue to pursue a policy that encourages the export of raw cotton to earn foreign currency. Between 2005 and 2007, only 20 percent of cotton production was sold domestically, and in 2008 and 2009, the share of domestic sales of cotton yarn and fabrics declined significantly.[52] Textile exports remain very weak, and in 2008 amounted to just US$500 million, compared to US$23 billion for Turkey or India, and US$12 billion for Bangladesh. Uzbek production is well below its real potential: the country accounts for 12.2 percent of cotton sales on the international market and 4 percent of world production, but less than 0.5 percent of finished products.[53]

Currently, some two hundred companies are involved in the national textile industry, including Daewoo Ferghana Textile, which alone accounts for 20 percent of the country's textile production. New construction projects have been set up, such as the Namimpeks Tekstil plant in Namangan, with the goal of producing eight million meters of cotton cloth per year and 500,000 units of readymade garments.[54] Several foreign companies have responded to the calls of the Uzbek government for investment. Two Indian firms, Spentex and Ginni International, plan to invest US$35 million by the end of 2012 for the setting up of textile spinning and weaving in the region of Syr Darya. In 2009, Spentex acquired the Margilan textile conglomerate which, after large investments, is set to reach production levels of thirteen million meters of finished fabric and 16,500 tons of cotton yarn.[55] Turkish companies have long been active on the scene, especially Tarmak Tekstil, which has invested in the production of spun textiles.

In the meantime, domestic producers continue to face multiple challenges. Uzbek companies are forced to buy cotton at the world market prices listed by the Liverpool Cotton Exchange, with a discount of 15 percent for the cost of transportation. The Uzbek manufacturers must also pay for the cotton in foreign currency, which is a handicap for them given the difficulty in converting the Uzbek *som*, and this was particularly so during the 2008 global financial crisis. In addition, the quality of the raw materials is often poor, and this reduces the competitiveness of domestic production. The technology possessed by local manufacturers is often outdated and therefore energy-inefficient and of poor quality. Finally, the interest rates that banks offer are too high and act as a disincentive for companies to take long-term loans. Although Tashkent has promised to invest US$1.7 billion in the textile industry by 2015 and has issued statements of intent to support the industry, and although there are a number of foreign and national investors, the current situation is far removed from the official, optimistic picture.[56]

While it might be possible to rectify these difficulties in the investment climate over the long term, the real problem of the Central Asian textile industry will remain the stiff competition it faces from China and its Southeast Asian neighbors. The textile industry was the industrializing industry par excellence of the Far East, and today China ranks as the world's largest exporter, and the only country able to carry out all the phases of production on its own territory. Owing to the sharp reduction in the costs of global transportation, combined with a Southeast Asia's considerable and cheap labor force, it will be very tough for Central Asia to compete. At US$200 per month, the cost of labor in Uzbekistan is much higher than among the main Asian producers.[57] In addition, as the quotas in the framework of the MFA (Multi-Fiber Arrangement), which governed the world trade in textiles and garments from 1974 through 2004, have been eliminated, Asian exports have flooded all the world markets.[58] On the other hand, the demand for finished products such as clothes is growing less quickly than revenue: as a result, clothes makers and retailers require a stimulation of demand, but this involves greater expenditures and marketing operations than the Central Asian producers cannot afford. Domestic production has also already entered into competition with the "made in China" phenomenon. It is nonetheless possible to envisage a Central Asian textile industry that specializes in specific designs and produces better quality products with a view to export to European markets.

The Construction Market Boom: Changes in Political Architecture and Real Estate

The construction market is one of the most dynamic sectors of the Central Asian economies outside hydrocarbons and minerals. The region can take advantage of two phenomena: the explosion of "political architecture" symbolizing the new statehood, and the demand for real estate. This so-called political architecture is particularly pronounced in Astana and Ashgabat the former having been built from the ground up, the latter having had its urban landscape totally reconceived in the 1990s.[59] Such architecture is also present in Tashkent and Almaty, but on a more modest scale. "Political architecture" represents a gold mine for foreign construction companies, and its financial interest for the ruling elites is also significant, as the—extremely opaque—process of awarding contracts is a way for them to pocket substantial bribes. The housing market, long a typical symbol of Soviet supply shortages, is also booming. The new urban middle classes seek to move into new residences with better quality services, while the elites flaunt their wealth in new palatial villas. In rural regions, the demand for improved family homes is just as high, even though it requires significantly lower investment, and there is a push to construct larger houses to accommodate the arrival of new generations. Across Central Asia, the housing infrastructure in place is in bad shape, especially the buildings dating from the Khrushchev era. In Kazakhstan, of the 276 million m^2 of real estate available in 2011, more than one-third (105 million m^2) was considered to be in poor condition.[60]

Until now, the public construction market has been dominated by three large competitors: a collection of Turkish and Russian firms, and the French company Bouygues, though UAE companies are gaining a foothold, and Chinese companies, hitherto confined to large infrastructure projects, will probably quickly enter the market. Turkish companies dominate in Turkmenistan, where they share the market with Bouygues, while in Kazakhstan they have to compete with Russian firms.

According to the Union of Turkish Industrialists, Turkish construction companies have invested more than US$4 billion in Kazakhstan since 1993.[61] They have acquired a reputation for building in record time, and for charging prices that are generally 20 to 25 percent lower than those of their competitors, although the security and quality of the constructions is questionable. In Turkmenistan, despite competition from Bouygues, Turkish companies are the undisputed market leaders: Between 1992 and 2008, they received more than US$14 billion worth of orders from Ashgabat.[62] However, the Turkmen deficit in foreign currency affected this honeymoon period, and in 2011 Ashgabat faced legal action from twenty Turkish construction firms over broken contracts costing them more US$1 billion.[63]

Rational considerations sometimes seem to be relegated to the background, demoted in favor of ideological excesses and schemes of corruption. Avaza, the alleged Turkmen "tourism Mecca" near Turkmenbashi on the shores of the Caspian, is a case-in-point. It is supposed to have sixty hotels, restaurants, and shopping centers, recreational activities, a seven-kilometer artificial river, six artificial lakes with beaches and islands, four acres of wooded parks, sports complexes, a theme park, a planetarium, an aquarium, and even an ice rink, as well as a free trade area to promote market entry for foreign companies.[64] However, with no market study having been undertaken prior to launching the project, it is far from being realized. The zone is not favorable to the development of tourism: the sea there is cold while the climate is too hot during summer months and too cold the rest of the year; road and railway infrastructure as well as air links are minimal (a new airport and motorways are supposed to be built); and the country requires visas that are difficult to obtain. The site is ecologically unfavorable to tourist activity (nauseating fumes and various pollutions) because it is close to oil complexes and opposite an offshore extraction platform. In addition, services do not at all meet international standards due to the absence of heating, the irregular hot water, the mediocre cuisine, and an almost total absence of training in tourism professions.[65]

The Turkmen authorities would like to turn Avaza into a small Caspian Emirate based on the model of Dubai, with avant-garde architecture and advantageous conditions for foreign investors. It hoped that the majority of investment, estimated at US$5 billion, would be provided by foreign companies and would allow the authorities to extract immense building-sector bribes. But the disappointment has been great: foreign firms are reticent and only get involved under duress, such as when their contracts are at stake. Their participation is simply a commercial gesture to the Turkmen authorities in order to obtain further construction contracts. None of them want to take up the management of these hotel complexes once they are operational, as they will not be profitable.[66] The majority of construction is therefore initiated by the government itself, which obliges each ministry and large state corporation to possess its own hotel or sanatorium so that it can send its personnel there.[67]

The severe impact of the 2008 economic and financial crisis slowed down the real estate market in all of Central Asia, and especially in Kazakhstan. Commercial real estate, offices, and luxury spaces were less affected, but supply has nevertheless continued to be in excess of demand: at the start of 2010, 70,000 m^2 were released on the market, 80 percent of which still lay empty at the year's end.[68] On Astana's high-end left bank, the price per square meter has dropped by a third, down from US$3,000 to 2,000.[69] In Almaty, though the price per square meter has also fallen, it is still way too high (US$1,700) compared to the financial means of the population. The sites on which construction halted due to the crisis were, for the most part, operational again in 2010: the municipal authorities have refused to grant new construction permits to any firm still in the process of completing buildings, yet a certain number of projects deemed unrealistic have been officially abandoned. The South Korean project of Apple Town in Almaty, set up by Woolim, was based on a price per square meter of US$4,500 and had to be scaled down in order to find clients, who often refuse to buy uncompleted apartments.[70]

The Kazakh market is paradoxical, as it has a surplus of luxury and commercial real estate, but a shortage of cheap housing. Indeed, both capitals have significant migration flows but lack rental space for new arrivals. In Almaty the population increased 12 percent between 2003 and 2009 (from 1,150,000 to 1,382,000 habitants), and in Astana it is rising quickly due to the arrival of thousands of new state employees each year.[71] The capital's housing deficit reached 908,000 m^2, and if priority continues to be given to office buildings rather than housing construction, the figure could reach 1,130,000 m^2 by 2015.[72] In 2010, the Kazakh government and the state bank Zhilstroisberbank launched a new development program for the rental market. Thus, in the years to come, both Almaty and Astana will have to meet the challenge of developing affordable housing. Almaty's G4 city project has been given the go-ahead and four satellite towns will be built to provide affordable housing to newcomers. This project is designed to absorb the excess population, but it might be decades before it is completed.[73]

This construction boom has had a direct impact on the cement market. In Soviet times, cement production was quantitatively impressive, but often of mediocre quality. The largest of the Kazakh and Uzbek cement factories collapsed in the 1990s, but later revived thanks to domestic demand as well as growing prospects on the regional market. Kazakhstan has been the spearhead in matters of cement production and consumption in Central Asia. Most of cement is bound for those areas experiencing expansion such as Atyrau and Mangystau, South Kazakhstan, and Astana and Almaty, which, in 2007, all together represented 60 percent of all new construction and 52 percent of newly built residences.[74] Regional disparities have generated a clear differentiation in prices: those regions far from production sites and where demand is high, primarily in the north, experience prices far higher than those in the south.[75] The global economic crisis has affected demand, inducing a fall in the price per ton of cement, down from US$90 to 57, as well as the bankruptcy of several cement works.[76] Caught in a vicious cycle, the Kazakh authorities then had to take drastic measures to revive real estate construction, and forced producers to sell cement at factory prices.[77] The state program for developing the building materials sectors for 2010–2014 envisages a rise in production to as much as 13.5 million tons by 2014, and to eighteen million by the end of the decade.[78] It also makes provision for significant infrastructure development such as roads, railways, and energy transmission that, combined with industrial growth, will entail a sharp increase in demand for cement. New cement factories situated closer to consumption needs are under construction, and a network of clinker (one of the main ingredients of cement) terminals is being developed on a countrywide scale. Despite this progress, Kazakhstan will continue to import some of its cement needs from Russia, Uzbekistan, and China.[79]

Uzbekistan is the second-largest cement producer in Central Asia. Industrial and infrastructure projects have contributed to stimulate demand, which has more than doubled in a single decade: up from 3.28 million tons in 2000 to 7 million in 2010, it is predicted to reach 8 to 8.5 million tons in 2012.[80] The Uzbek authorities have launched a program for the technological upgrading of construction companies and plan to invest close to US$350 million in it. The investments are to go into the modernization of Soviet-era cement works, mainly Kyzylkum, but also, to a more limited extent, Bekabad, Kuvasay, and Ahangaran.[81] The Kyzylkum and Ahangaran factories, which specialize in a type of cement required for the oil industry, are the main suppliers for Uzbekneftegaz, but their production is inadequate and will soon be supplemented by the new Sherabad factory.[82]

Production is far smaller in the three other countries, although demand is also increasing. In Kyrgyzstan, the Kant factory, established in 1964, is said to have a production output potential of 1.1 million tons per year, but this figure is inflated and the factory cost-price is so high that it must regularly lay off employees. Production at the Technolin factory, set up in the Chu region in the 1970s, is also inadequate for current needs. As a result, the country opened its newest and largest cement works in 2009 in Kyzyl-Kiia, run by an international consortium including Chinese, Ukrainians, Kazakhs, and South Kyrgyz Cement. The cement that it produces will be used for building the new hydroelectric stations in the Batken region, which until now had to be supplied by imports from the Uzbek Kuvasay factory.[83] In Tajikistan, Tojikcement, which allegedly produces 500,000 tons per year, remains the largest national producer, but current energy conditions and its aging infrastructure limit production.[84] Dependent on Tashkent's goodwill in selling it gas, it will probably be converted for coal utilization. Many other small cement factories have opened up in other regions. Lastly, Turkmenistan has kept particularly quiet about its cement production, deeming that industrial production figures are state secrets. It is estimated that several new cement factories have increased the country's capacity to about 1.5 million tons, but in view of the building frenzy of the Turkmen authorities, this figure would seem to err on the low side.[85]

Cement production is not only a domestic issue, but is also part of global export rationales. The reconstruction of Afghanistan, for example, looms as a considerable potential market and Central Asian proximity could take advantage of it. Production costs in Central Asia remain relatively low: between 2005 and 2008, Russia sold a ton of cement for US$166, whereas Kyrgyzstan offered a ton for 100.[86] Uzbekistan is the region's main exporter, having sold 1.3 million tons abroad in 2009, notably to Kazakhstan, Tajikistan, and Afghanistan.[87] Kazakhstan, however, is the only country in the region to have invested in cement outside its own borders: the United Cement Group is also the owner of two cement factories in Russia, and the Kazakhstan Investment Fund possesses shares in South Kyrgyz Cement.[88] This two-pronged strategy of increasing local consumption and creating a regional market has attracted foreign companies. China has taken advantage of the situation and in just a few years has become one of the major partners of the Central Asian cement market. Eximbank, for example, granted Bishkek a loan of US$70 million for the construction of the Kyzyl-Kiia factory and Chinese companies are also involved in building the new

Yangi-Yul plant close to Tashkent.[89] Beijing has also pledged to invest some US$600 million to build a large cement plant in Tajikistan's southern district of Shahritus. Several large Russian companies such as BaselCement, one of the holdings of the aluminum oligarch Oleg Deripaska, have developed strategies to enter the Kazakh market.[90] Numerous European companies are also involved, as well as Omani and Malaysian firms.[91] All complain, however, about the corruption of the local official suppliers, who operate in close cooperation with the state.

Sectors of the Future: Agribusiness and Distribution

Economic development and demographic growth have helped to stimulate the development of a food processing industry. While only in its infancy when the Central Asian countries emerged from the Soviet Union, the industry was in a state of collapse until very recently: in 2009 the Kyrgyz food industry was only 15 percent of its 1991 level.[92] In rural regions, the main objective is food security: to improve the distribution networks is one of the key elements for ensuring better supplies. In the large towns and the regions experiencing economic boom, the outlook for the food processing industry is promising. The increase in living standards has brought about an evolution in consumption habits accompanied by a reduction of the time required to prepare food at home thanks to processed and packaged food, and the discovery of new Western-style food products. Central Asia is also dealing with an overall evolution in production methods in which biotechnologies (fertilizer, herbicides) are increasingly used, and that local producers have to learn to master. It requires enormous capital investments, which confer on transnational food producers as well as large retailers considerable power. With its potential for production, Central Asia hopes to enter more global export circuits, although in this sector as in others it remains subject to competition from neighboring countries. China alone represents 38 percent of the world production of fruit and vegetables and is one of the world's three largest chicken producers, along with the United States and Brazil. Though a large part of Chinese production is locally consumed, part of it goes to Central Asia, and the authorities perceive this as a threat to local production, their export potential, and also food sovereignty.[93]

Of all the Central Asian countries, Kazakhstan has banked the most on the development of its agribusiness sector, particularly in cereals. Nazarbayev has made it a priority to diversify the country's economy and ensure food security. A 2003–2005 state program for the agribusiness sector came with an injection of some US$2 billion to reduce the export of unprocessed in favor of processed products.[94] Hence, although in 2003 flour only represented 10 percent of total wheat exports, this share rose by close to half in 2009.[95] The EBRD granted a loan of US$35 million to Kazeksportastyk, one of the main agrarian holdings and one of the largest Kazakh cereal producers, to develop a program for advanced agricultural technologies and practices.[96] China has also declared itself willing to invest in the local agribusiness sector.[97] The Kazakh president has set the particularly ambitious objective that national production will come to constitute more than 80 percent of the food products consumed by 2014. This goal is probably unattainable given the growing number of foreign food products on the Kazakh market, and the domestic difficulties related to outdated equipment and a coefficient of capacity utilization that is still too low—in the dairy industry, for example, it is a mere 25 percent.[98]

In the other countries, the outlook for developing the food processing sector is more limited, but not totally bleak. Kyrgyzstan, for example, is looking to export its dairy products (fermented milk, yogurt) to neighboring markets, as well as to China and Europe, with the support of Swiss firms.[99] The regional market for alcohol is also considerable: the Samarkand and Tashkent wine factories have been producing red wine since Soviet times, not to mention liquors such as cognac, albeit of low quality. A beer boom is in full swing, with several foreign companies having invested in the Central Asian market in recent years: Russia's Baltika Breweries is prominent in this market, but there is also competition from UzCarlsberg, from a new joint venture between Heineken and Efes Breweries, and from SAN InBev, the Russian subsidiary of a large international beer consortium.[100] The advantage of being based in Tashkent is linked to the regional nature of the market, which can also be routed to link up with Kyrgyzstan and Tajikistan.

The transition to the market economy and the improving living standards have also created a new, previously non-existent economic niche—that of supermarkets. This sector remains rather small, however: whereas the large chains control about 40 percent of consumption in Russia, the figure is only 25 percent in Kazakhstan, and is even lower in the neighboring countries.[101] In Kazakhstan, there is fierce competition between supermarket brands competing against one another; between national brands often owned by oligarchs close to the authorities and foreign brands, mainly Turkish or Russian; and lastly, between supermarkets and bazaars. In Kazakhstan the supermarkets are established in the wealthy cities like Almaty and Astana where consumption habits have evolved, but also in cities such as Aktau and Aktobe, where supermarkets constitute close to half the market, as well as Atyrau, where they control 80 percent of it.[102] In the other countries, supermarkets are less present. While operating in Bishkek, they are scarce outside of the capitals and practically non-existent in Tajikistan and Turkmenistan.

After independence, Turkish companies were the first to establish themselves in the sectors of food distribution and basic goods, whose production and distribution was always a weak point of the Soviet system. The Turkish supermarkets Ramstor (in Kazakhstan) and Beta (in Kyrgyzstan) were among the first to open stores. Russian supermarkets followed (Vester Group), as did the German group Metro, and the Middle-Eastern group Spinneys. Beta is in direct competition with two national chains, Narodnyi and Stolichnyi, which were run by the Akayev clan during many years.[103] In Uzbekistan, Turkish business is also facing growing difficulties, and in 2011, the security services closed down the four-level Turkish supermarket Turkuaz in central Tashkent, as well as other Turkish brands like Gunesh Café and Kaynak, all of which were accused of disseminating banned Islamic literature. These well-established Turkish supermarkets are increasingly facing stiff competition from new shopping centers like Poitaht Savdo Markazi, and the 32,000 m^2 Mega Planet supermarket complex, controlled by the children of the Uzbek political elite.[104]

In Kazakhstan, Ramstor, which is controlled by the Turkish Koc Holding, piqued the interest of Walmart, Carrefour, and Auchan, as well as Russian Seventh Continent and X5 Retail.[105] While Ramstor remains the example of a success story in Kazakhstan, other national chains controlled by Kazakh businessmen (often of Russian origin) divide the market among themselves, whether by securing a fief in the former capital Almaty, or developing niche strategies in discount or local minimarkets. Inter Gros, for example, has close to twenty stores, half in Almaty, and aims to establish itself across the entire market, from large supermarkets to local minimarkets; Astykzhan has been present in Astana, Karaganda, and Kostanay, again in various formats; Anvar dominates the market in Aktobe, with subsidiaries in Atyrau, Aktau, and Uralsk; Tau-Market specializes in discount stores, but had to close ten of them in provincial towns in 2009; and Dastarkhan and Tian-Shan operate only in the local minimarket niche.[106] In the other Central Asian countries, the bazaars continue to occupy a very large share of the market.

In Central Asia the predominance of the agricultural sector, the mineral wealth of the subsoil, neighboring China, and uncompetitive labor costs, do not allow much room for maneuver to develop new industrial production. Some industries that are still operational, such as the chemical industry, are directly linked to the nature of the Central Asian subsoil. Others are a heritage of Soviet history, such as the military-industrial complex, which will probably disappear in the coming decades, except in Kazakhstan, if Russia's interest in it fades. Still others are based on small national niches, such as Turkmen textiles, or Uzbek automobiles. They target a regional market (Central Asia, Afghanistan, Turkey, and Iran), but will not be able to rival the industrial giants that have been established in other global regions. The value of some sectors is not solely commercial but is also related to national security, such as pharmaceutical production and the food processing industry. Like the majority of developing countries, Central Asian governments are very sensitive to the non-traditional threats linked to food self-sufficiency and epidemics. It is therefore most likely that they will continue to invest in sectors adjudged strategic. However, beyond hydrocarbons, minerals, and cotton, the future of the region and its ability to insert itself in the world market will partly reside in the service sector and the postindustrial economy.

Notes

1. "Chemical Industry," *Sario* 1, http://www.sario.sk/userfiles/file/sario/zo/teritoria/kazachstan/kz_chemical_industry.pdf.

2. "Chemical Industry of Kazakhstan," Report by Kaznex, Almaty, 2008; "Chemical Industry," *Invest in Kazakhstan*, n.d., http://www.invest.gov.kz/?option=content&section=6&itemid=92; "Chemical and Petrochemical Industry," Report of the Ministry of Commerce of the RPC, European Department, n.d., http://ozs.mofcom.gov.cn/table/kaza/chemical.pdf.

3. S. Domin, "Khimicheskaia rekonkista," *Ekspert Kazakhstan*, June 20, 2011, http://expert.ru/kazakhstan/2011/24/himicheskaya-rekonkista/.

4. "Kazakhstan to Inject over $9 Billion in Chemical Industry in Seven Years," *HRS Group*, March 3, 2009, http://www.hrs-group.net/news/en/2009/03/03/kazakhstan-to-inject-over-9-billion-in-chemical-industry-in-seven.aspx.

5. N. Galmor, "Kazphosphate: Reviving a Giant of the Kazakhstani Economics," *International Business Magazine Kazakhstan*, no. 4 (2002), http://www.investkz.com/en/journals/33/233.html.

6. C. Nuttall, "New Focus on 'People's IPO' Following Election," *Silk Road Intelligencer*, May 15, 2011, http://silkroadintelligencer.com/2011/05/15/new-focus-on-peoples-ipo-following-election/.

7. E. Britskaia, "EvroKhim i Kazfosfat podeliat rynok Kazakhstana," *Kursiv.kz*, October 16, 2008, http://www.kursiv.kz/anonses/1195201461-evrokhim-i-kazfosfat-podeljat-rynok.html.

8. "Obzor osnovnykh ekonomicheskikh sobytii," Avesta Investment Group Report, August 24, 2007, 2.

9. See the Uzkimyosanoat website, http://www.uzkimyosanoat.uz.

10. "Chemical Industry," *Uzinfoinvest*, n.d., http://www.investuzbekistan.uz/eng/investment_opportunities/by_industry/chemical_industry/; "Uzkimyosanoat Enterprises Produce Goods for 980.9bn Soums," *Silk Road Economy and Business Report*, February 28, 2011, 16.

11. M. Fadeyev, "Uzbekistan Is Selling Objects of the National Chemical Industry," *Fergana. news*, November 1, 2006, http://enews.fergana.ru/article.php?id=1674.

12. "CITIC Reconstructing Maryazot Plant for $266 Mln," *Times of Central Asia*, no. 35, August 31, 2006.

13. V. Gus'kov, "Sostoianie i prognoz razvitiia farmatsevticheskogo rynka Kazakhstana," *BTA Analitika*, December 2008, 20.

14. "Farmatsevticheskii rynok Kazakhstana," *Amanat*, April 1, 2008, http://amanat.kz/kazakhstan_news/961/.

15. "V poslednie gody v Kazakhstane nabliudaiutsia vysokie tempy rosta vnutrennego farmatsevticheskogo rynka," *Kazinform*, October 30, 2009, http://www.inform.kz/rus/article/2208754.

16. "Riad regionov Kazakhstana ispytyvaiut defitsit lekarstvennykh sredstv," *Amanat*, February 20, 2010, http://amanat.kz/kazakhstan_news/3823/.

17. "Kazakh Government Maintains Ambitious Plans for Pharma Sector Development as Hospital Market Grows 53% Y/Y in H1," *IHS*, December 15, 2011, http://www.ihs.com/products/global-insight/industry-economic-report.aspx?ID=1065931975. The 34 percent needs to be taken with a grain of salt, as some experts calculate the share of national production at only 10 to 12 percent: Gus'kov, "Sostoianie i prognoz razvitiia."

18. "Riad regionov Kazakhstana ispytyvaiut defitsit lekarstvennykh sredstv."

19. "Analizi prognoz farmatsevticheskogo rynka Kazakhstana," *Abercade*, 2010, http://www.abercade.ru/research/industrynews/3387.html.

20. J. Kucera, "Central Asia and Caucasus: Governments Spending Heavily on Arms," *Eurasianet*, March 23, 2010, http://www.eurasianet.org/departments/business/articles/eav032410.shtml.

21. Ibid.

22. In 2011 India passed China as the world's top arms importer. See "SIPRI Yearbook 2011: Armaments, Disarmament, and International Security," Report of the Stockholm International Peace Research Institute, Stockholm, 2011.

23. See the KADEX website, http://www.kadex.kz/node/25.

24. Kazakhstan has its own program to develop a military-industrial complex, which it launched in 2007: "V Kazakhstane utverzhdena gosprogramma razvitiia vooruzheniia, voennoi tekhniki i oboronno-promyshlennogo kompleksa do 2015 goda," *Pravitel'stvo respubliki Kazakhstan*, http://ru.government.kz/site/news/2007/03/48.

25. "Petropavlovskoe aktsionernoe obshchestvo 'Ziksto' otmetilo 70-letie," *Kazinform*, August 13, 2011, http://www.inform.kz/rus/article/2398445; N. Limov, "Period zastoia zakon-

chilsia, vperedi bol'shaia rabota," *Izvestiia Kazakhstana*, July 25, 2008, http://www.izvestia. kz/node/6822.

26. J. Kucera, "Kazakhstan's Military-Industrial Complex Struts its Stuff," *Eurasianet*, May 26, 2010, http://www.eurasianet.org/node/61162.

27. More in Peyrouse, "Russia-Central Asia."

28. I. Tezz, "Kyrgyzstan: Russia Set to Take Major Stake in Kyrgyz Torpedo Plant," *Eurasianet*, March 31, 2009, http://www.eurasianet.org/departments/insightb/articles/eav040109c. shtml.

29. Paramonov and Stolpovskii, "Rossiia i Tsentral'naia Aziia," 10.

30. "TAPOiCH voidet v sostav OAK k kontsu 2008 g.," *Vzgliad*, September 20, 2007, http:// vz.ru/news/2007/9/20/110855.html.

31. "OAO Vertolety Rossii i OOO UzRosAviia razvivaiut servisnoe obsluzhivanie rossiiskikh vertoletov v Tsentral'no-aziatskom regione," *Novosti VPK*, December 7, 2009, http://vpk.name/ news/34377_oao_vertoletyi_rossii_i_ooo_uzrosavia_razvivayut_servisnoe_obsluzhivanie_ rossiiskih_vertoletov_v_centralnoaziatskom_regione.html.

32. "OAK otkazalas' ot sotrudnichestva s Tashkentskim aviazavodom," *Lenta.ru*, June 2, 2011, http://readers.lenta.ru/news/2011/06/02/tapoich/.

33. Gauchon, *Le monde*, 738.

34. "Ob avtomobil'noi promyshlennosti Uzbekistana," *Vsia AvtoMoskva*, August 27, 2009, http://www.adb.ru/reviews/review/604673109.

35. C. Park, "Daewoo Globalization: Uz-Daewoo Auto Project," Harvard Business School Brief 9–568–065, March 23, 1998.

36. "GM and UzAvtoSanoat Move Closer to GM-Uzbekistan Joint," *East Europe Auto*, February 26, 2008, http://www.easteurope-auto.net/article.php?article_id=22.

37. "Russian Sales of GM Uzbekistan Cars Increase Sharply," *Radio Free Europe/Radio Liberty*, July 18, 2011, http://www.rferl.org/content/russian_sales_of_gm_uzbekistan_cars_ increase_sharply/24269481.html.

38. "GM Uzbekistan Sells 372 Cars in Kazakh Market," *Uzbekistan Daily*, November 21, 2011, http://www.uzdaily.com/articles-id-16515.htm.

39. A. Davydov, "GM Uzbekistan Cars Become More Readily Available to Uzbeks," *Central Asia Online*, March 17, 2009, http://centralasiaonline.com/en_GB/articles/caii/ features/2009/03/17/feature-03.

40. "GM Opens Engine Plant in Uzbekistan," *GM News*, November 15, 2011, http:// media.gm.com/content/media/us/en/gm/news.detail.html/content/Pages/news/us/en/2011/ Nov/1115_uzbek.

41. "Uzbekistan: GM Uzbekistan's Uncertain Future amid Talk of a Takeover," *Eurasianet*, June 4, 2009, http://www.eurasianet.org/departments/news/articles/eav060509b.shtml; "GM Uzbekistan Stakes on New Mini Car," *Uzinfoinvest*, September 3, 2011, http://www.uzinfoinvest. uz/eng/news/gm_uzbekistan_stakes_on_new_mini_car.mgr.

42. "Automobile Industry of Uzbekistan Gradually Develops," *Uzbekistan Daily*, September 10, 2010, http://www.uzdaily.com/articles-id-11403.htm.

43. "Uzbekistan Plans to Increase Production of Cars," *Uzbekistan Daily*, January 18, 2011, http://www.uzdaily.com/articles-id-12848.htm.

44. Iu. V. Naumov, I. L. Pugach, and Iu. B. Yusupov, "Uzbekistan's Textile Industry: How to Implement Development Potential?," United Nations Development Programme Policy Brief 14, no. 1 (2010), 5.

45. A. Strokov and T. Davlatmirzo, "Tekstil'nyi kompleks gosudarstv Tsentral'noi Azii: Upushcheniia, dostizheniia, perspektivy," *Rynok legkoi promyshlennosti*, no. 37 (2004), http:// rustm.net/catalog/article/418.html.

46. "Turks—The Only Minority Facing No Problems in Turkmenistan," *Chronicles of Turkmenistan*, August 5, 2006, http://archive.chrono-tm.org/en/?id=717.

47. Press Review of the French Embassy in Turkmenistan, March 2008.

48. "Textile Industry of Turkmenistan," *Export.by*, n.d., http://www.export.by/en/?act=s_docs&mode=view&id=10584&type=by_class&indclass=40958&mode2=archive&doc=64.

49. Naumov, Pugach, and Yusupov, "Uzbekistan's Textile Industry," 4.

50. More details in "Problemy i perspektivy razvitiia tekstil'noi promyshlennosti Uzbekistana," United Nations Development Programme Policy Brief, no. 5, 2006.

51. "Chinese Textile Mills Withdraw Investment in Uzbekistan," *Textile Today*, March 31, 2011, http://www.textiletoday.com.bd/index.php?pid=36&news=NEWS000971.

52. Naumov, Pugach, and Yusupov, "Uzbekistan's Textile Industry," 10.

53. Ibid., 5.

54. "Namimpeks-Tekstil LLC to Build Textile Plant in Uzbekistan," *Fibre2Fashion*, February 24, 2011, http://www.fibre2fashion.com/news/industrial-textiles-news/newsdetails.aspx?news_id=96153.

55. "Indian Companies to Create Textile Plant in Syrdarya Region," *Uzbekistan Daily*, January 20, 2011, http://www.uzdaily.com/articles-id-12876.htm.

56. "Investments to Textile Industry of Uzbekistan to Hit US$1.7bn by 2015," *Uzbekistan Daily*, October 13, 2011, http://www.uzdaily.com/articles-id-16063.htm.

57. "Textile Industry of Uzbekistan: Potential to Rise & Opportunity to Invest," *O'zbekyengilsanoat*, 2011, 17.

58. Dicken, *Global Shift*, 305.

59. S. Anacker, "Geographies of Power in Nazarbayev's Astana," *Eurasian Geography and Economics* 45, no. 7 (2004): 515–33; A. Fauve and C. Gintrac, "Production de l'espace urbain et mise en scène du pouvoir dans deux capitales 'présidentielles' d'Asie Centrale," *L'espace politique* 8, no. 2 (2009), http://espacepolitique.revues.org/index1376.html; C. Gintrac and A. Fénot, *Achgabat, une capitale ostentatoire: Autocratie et urbanisme au Turkménistan* (Paris: L'Harmattan, 2006).

60. A. Amalbaev, "Luchshii drug stroitelei," *Oasis*, no. 7 (2011), 1.

61. "Sotrudnichestvo Respubliki Kazakhstan s Turetskoi Respublikoi."

62. Press Review of the French Embassy in Turkmenistan, January 2009.

63. "Turkmenistan Dismisses Claims Turkish Companies Troubled by Unpaid Bills," *Today's Zaman*, July 17, 2011, http://www.todayszaman.com/newsDetail_getNewsById.action?load=detay&newsId=250694&link=250694.

64. S. Agayeva, "Avaza to Become Turkmenistan's Int'l Tourism Centre," *Turkish Weekly*, May 29, 2009, http://www.turkishweekly.net/news/78702/-quot-avaza-quot-to-become-turkmenistan-s-int-l-tourism-centre.html.

65. Author's interviews with representatives of European firms in Ashgabat, March 2008.

66. Ibid.

67. "Seashore Paradise," *Turkmenistan.ru*, August 13, 2008, http://www.turkmenistan.ru/en/node/7289.

68. Authors' interviews with real estate experts, Astana, September 28, 2010.

69. G. Zhakimbaeva, "Rynok nedvizhimosti Kazakhstana ozhivaet," *Ism.kz*, April 21, 2010, http://www.insur.kz/index.php?option=com_content&view=article&id=1093:2010-04-28-17-48-29&catid=1:latest-news&Itemid=18.

70. C. Nuttall, "A Thaw in Kazakhstan as Real Estate Prices Rise Again," *Silk Road Intelligencer*, January 19, 2010, http://silkroadintelligencer.com/2010/01/19/a-thaw-in-kazakhstan-as-real-estate-prices-rise-again/.

71. "Zastroishchiki snova daiut pozitivnye prognozy po rynku nedvizhimosti," *Gazeta.kz*, August 13, 2010, http://articles.gazeta.kz/art.asp?aid=318493.

72. Zhakimbaeva, "Rynok nedvizhimosti Kazakhstana ozhivaet."

73. C. Nuttall, "Kazakhstan Gambles on Kapchagay Development," *Silk Road Intelligencer*, October 22, 2008, http://silkroadintelligencer.com/2008/10/22/kazakhstan-gambles-on-kapchagay-development/.

74. "Analiz proizvodstva i rynok tsementa, 2003–2008 gg.," *Mir Finantsov*, May 28, 2009, http://www.wfin.kz/node/1432.

75. Ibid.

76. O. Pavlovskaya, "Global Financial Crisis Hits Kazakhstan's Cement Industry," *Central Asia Online*, January 31, 2009, http://centralasiaonline.com/cocoon/caii/xhtml/en_GB/features/caii/features/2009/01/31/feature-05.

77. "Tsementnye zavody Kazakhstana zastavliaiut prodavat' tsement po sebestoimosti," *Nezavisimyi stroitel'nyi portal*, May 25, 2009, http://www.nsp.su/news/2009-05/4143/.

78. "Kto kontroliruet rynok tsementa," *Profinance.kz*, April 23, 2010, http://profinance.kz/2010/04/23/u-ucsn-u-ninb.html; D. Kazakov, "Rynok tsementa v Kazakhstane," *BRIF Research Group*, June 23, 2010, http://www.brif.kz/blog/?p=725.

79. "Rossiia iavliaetsia osnovnym importerom tsementa v Kazakhstan," *Profinance.kz*, April 16, 2010, http://profinance.kz/2010/04/16/yoyosya-yaecyanyoya-yoei-sini-ninb-e-ubpbxyob.html.

80. "Uzbekistan's Cement Production Has Doubled in 9 Years," *Cemweek*, http://www.cemweek.com/news/volume-a-pricing/10173-uzbekistans-cement-production-has-doubled-in-9-years.

81. "Growing Market of Construction Materials of Uzbekistan," *Uzbekistan Today*, July 14, 2008, http://www.uzinfoinvest.uz/eng/news/growing_market_of_construction_materials_of_uzbekistan.mgr; V. Luchkin, "Proizvodstvo tsementa v Uzbekistane: Postupatel'noe razvitie," *Advanced Financial Solution*, n.d., http://www.afs-research.com/ru/article/3203/.

82. "Some 600,000 Tonnes of Cement Exported through UzEX in 2010," *Uzbekistan Daily*, January 19, 2011, http://www.uzdaily.com/articles-id-12868.htm.

83. "Tsementnyi 'skvozniak' v Kirgizii: Na iug strany kontrabandnyi tsement vvozitsia, a s severa—vyvozitsia," *Fergana.news*, August 13, 2008, http://www.fergananews.com/article.php?id=5283.

84. "China Intends to Fund Construction of Cement Plant in Tajikistan," *Asia Plus*, September 10, 2010, http://www.asiaplus.tj/en/news/31/38422.html. Some experts calculate more limited production: "In Tajikistan, Produced More Than 240 Thousand Tons of Cement," *Avesta.tj*, October 10, 2011, http://www.avesta.tj/eng/business/703-in-tajikistan-produced-more-than-240-thousand-tons-of-cement.html.

85. "Analiz proizvodstva i rynok tsementa, 2003–2008 gg."

86. Ibid.

87. "Bekabadcement to Produce 1.9m Tonnes of Cement a Year by 2012," *Uzbekistan Daily*, November 24, 2010, http://www.uzdaily.com/articles-id-12318.htm.

88. "Kazakh-Backed Kyrgyz Cement Producer to Invest $75 Million in New Plant," *Silk Road Intelligencer*, July 15, 2009, http://silkroadintelligencer.com/2009/07/15/kazakh-backed-kyrgyz-cement-producer-to-invest-75-million-in-new-plant/.

89. Kassenova, "China as an Emerging Donor in Tajikistan and Kyrgyzstan," 18.

90. C. Nuttall, "International Companies Get Stuck into Kazakh Cement," *Silk Road Intelligencer*, June 10, 2008, http://silkroadintelligencer.com/2008/06/10/international-companies-get-stuck-into-kazakh-cement/.

91. "New Cement Capacity Under Construction in Uzbekistan," *World Cement*, August 12, 2010, http://www.worldcement.com/sectors/cement/articles/New_cement_capacity_under_construction_in_Uzbekistan.aspx; M. Zhumadil, "Steppe Cement: Hostage of the Macro," *Halyk Finance*, October 27, 2011, 4.

92. "Rynochnaia model' razvitiia agrarnoi ekonomiki Kyrzgyzstana v perekhodnyi period," *Novye Issledovaniia Tuvy*, no. 3 (2009), http://www.tuva.asia/journal/issue_3/462-temirbaev.html.

93. Laruelle and Peyrouse, *The "Chinese Question" in Central Asia*, 169.

94. G. Kaliev, "Agropromyshlennyi kompleks Kazakhstana," *Ekonomicheskii portal*, June 12, 2008, http://institutiones.com/agroindustrial/125-2008-06-12-18-00-19.html.

95. "Razvitie agropromyshlennogo kompleksa iavliaetsia vazhnym segmentom diversi-fikatsii ekonomiki Kazakhstana," *KazInform*, February 2, 2010, http://www.inform.kz/rus/article/2238334.

96. "EBRD Boost for Kazakh Agri-sector," *Trade Finance*, March 29, 2012, http://www.tradefinancemagazine.com/Article/3004021/EBRD-boost-for-Kazakh-agri-sector.html.

97. "Kazakhstan: Food & Drink Report," Business Monitor International Report, London, 2009; "Kitai gotov investirovat' v agropromyshlennyi kompleks Kyrgyzstana," *For.kg*, December 3, 2007, http://for.kg/ru/news/50988/.

98. Kaliev, "Agropromyshlennyi kompleks Kazakhstana."

99. *Enhancing the Prospects for Growth and Trade of the Kyrgyz Republic* (Washington, DC: World Bank, 2005), 49. See also "Kazakhstan Lifts Ban on Importing Dairy Products from Kyrgyzstan," *Caspionet*, December 15, 2011, http://www.caspionet.kz/eng/business/Kazakh-stan_lifts_ban_on_importing_dairy_products_from_Kyrgyzstan_1323924743.html.

100. "Rynok piva Uzbekistana: Itogi oseni," *Avesta Research*, December 11, 2008, http://research.uz/pages/10; "Rossiia: 'SAN InBev' nachala eksportnye postavki v Uzbekistan, Litvu i Armeniiu," *Uzbekistan Daily*, February 1, 2010, http://www.uzdaily.uz/articles-id-1300.htm.

101. "Kazakh Supermarket Chains Stake Their Claims," *Silk Road Intelligencer*, May 6, 2010, http://silkroadintelligencer.com/2010/05/06/kazakh-supermarket-chains-stake-their-claims/; "Hidden Heroes: The Next Generation of Retail Markets," *Deloitte Audit*, 2011, 5–7, http://www.deloitte.com/view/en_GX/global/aae970613d792310VgnVCM3000001c56f00aRCRD.htm.

102. Authors' interviews with Kazakh experts on the food distribution market, Almaty, September 30, 2010.

103. Authors' interviews with Kyrgyz experts on the food distribution market, Bishkek, June 7, 2010.

104. "Tashkent's Major Shopping Centre Closed Down," *Uznews.net*, March 3, 2011, http://www.uznews.net/news_single.php?lng=en&sub=&cid=2&nid=16526.

105. Authors' interviews with Kazakh experts on the food distribution market, Almaty, September 30, 2010.

106. Ibid.

14
The Future of the Services Sector

In the Soviet period, Central Asia was not considered a propitious zone for tertiary economies: Although its education level was high, as everywhere else in the Union, the region lacked technical and industrial knowledge and relied heavily on support from qualified specialists from Russia and the European republics (Ukraine, Belarus, Baltic countries). At the fall of the USSR, this handicap increased: the technical specialists, who often belonged to the European minorities, left the region or went into retirement without passing on their knowledge; and the last remaining specialists moved into other, more profitable professional niches. The region still pays a high price for this brain drain, especially in a world economy characterized by information technologies, cutting-edge industries, and the need for continuous industrial innovation. A global economy in which knowledge has become more important than capital and labor does not work in Central Asia's favor as the region is hampered by its distinct dearth of senior managers, its poor connectivity with the rest of the world, and weak public investments in education and research.

While the service sector has increased its weight in all Central Asian GDPs, it consists mainly in supplying everyday services. Trade is a central element: except for Kazakhstan, the bazaars are still the backbone of the local economies. The changes in consumption habits of the middle and upper classes have also given rise to new economic niches: restaurants, cafés, resorts, technical maintenance of residential buildings, private transport, and the like, all of which supplies employment to numerous strands of the workforce. The service sector is therefore consumption-related; it is much less developed in the more productive areas such as finances and real estate (although Kazakhstan is an exception), science and technology, administrative and support services, education, and health. Even so, several sectors have nonetheless emerged: Kazakhstan is on the way to becoming the financial center of the whole region; the telecommunications market, in particular for mobile phones, is booming; Astana has begun to put into place high-tech procurement strategies; and the region has a burgeoning tourism potential.

285

Building the Banking System from Scratch

At the fall of the Soviet Union, each republic inherited elements of the Soviet banking system, comprising the state bank (*gosbank*) and a few industrial banks; individuals, however, were unused to using banking services. As was the case in several other areas, the evolution of the banking sector depended upon the activism of some governments and the reticence of others to undertake vast economic reforms.[1] The disparities are therefore considerable between the totally state-run Turkmen banking sector, and the Kazakh one, which, like its Russian counterpart, is well integrated into global financial flows.

The Kazakh system is by far the most sophisticated of the region, thanks to the economic dynamism the country has known since the turn of the century. In 1993, the national currency, the tenge, was put into circulation, the national bank of Kazakhstan was transformed into a central bank, and the industrial banks were turned into anonymous companies. In 1996, the government launched a reform program imposing international standards in matters of capitalization, ratios, and liquidities.[2] The reforms accelerated in 1999 with the nomination of Grigorii Marchenko to the head of the National Bank of Kazakhstan, whose mission was to stabilize the national banking system, which, like its Russian neighbor, was affected by the crash of summer 1998. Banks with insufficient capital were obliged to close: between 1996 and 2007, their number fell by 65 percent, down from 101 to 33.[3] In 2001, the Kazakhstan Development Bank was created in a bid to boost the country's industrial development. In only a few years, the efficient regulation carried out by the Central Bank and its regulatory body for monitoring markets and financial organizations, have made Kazakhstan one of the CIS countries' most distinguished banking systems.

In Kyrgyzstan, the National Bank assumed the responsibility for granting licenses and supervising second tier banks in 1992. Along with very liberal reforms, the granting of banking licenses proceeded apace: by 1995, the country already had nineteen commercial banks, five of which were state run, and the other fourteen private.[4] However, half of them had to report to the National Bank a net negative situation, which brought about the first wave of reforms in the sector. In 1996–1997, with the support of the World Bank, two specialized state-run banks and four private banks were closed, two other specialized banks were restructured, and a state-run agency (Debt Equity and Bank Restructuring Agency—DEBRA) was founded to shore up the assets of the liquidated banks.[5]

Widely affected by the Russian financial crisis of 1998 and growing economic instability, Kyrgyz banks had a tendency to underestimate the risks linked to credit and the fluctuations of foreign exchange rates: in 1999, a total of 30 percent of loans were found to be unprofitable. Six banks went bankrupt, two were restructured, and their funds were transferred to DEBRA, whereas their responsibilities were given to a new state bank, Kairat, which took possession of one-third of the Kyrgyz banking sector.[6] The 1998 crisis also caused a change in attitudes toward foreign investors, who had previously been limited to controlling 30 percent of a bank's shares, with the exception of Demir Bank, the only totally foreign-held bank (Turkish) at the time. From 2002, foreign presence in the Kyrgyz banking system grew, in particular Kazakh investments: Energobank was taken over by ATF Bank, Inksimbank by BTA, and Autobank was absorbed by Kazkommerzbank, while Kairat came under the control of Halyk Bank. At the end of 2005, the share of foreign capital in the Kyrgyz banking system reached 60 percent, and the only financial institution still owned by the state was the Savings and Settlement Company.[7]

Uzbekistan embarked on much more hesitant banking reforms than its Kazakh and Kyrgyz neighbors, curbing foreign presence, while the non-convertibility of the national currency, the som, has not helped to dynamize the sector.[8] The Uzbek banking sector has declined proportionally since 2005: the ratio of total capital to GDP fell from 37 to 34.7 percent between 2005 and 2006, and today the banking system remains one of the most opaque in the entire former Soviet Union. The total number and value of portfolios held by Uzbek banks is no longer published; according to analysts this is a sign of the deterioration of the system.[9] During 2009, decreed the year of development of the agricultural sector, two new banks were created, the Qishloq Qurilish bank, which specialized in rural housing, and Agrobank, a merger of the former Galla-Bank and Pakhta Bank, also tasked with financing agricultural projects.[10] In 2010, the country had a total of twenty-nine banks, a low figure in comparison with the other CIS countries.[11] Moreover, several of them are sectoral, as was the case during the Soviet epoch, and the state controls at least half their shares. Their resource base is limited, since it comprises little more than corporate accounts and funds contributed by the government, both in the form of liquidity and capital. Most Uzbek citizens try to avoid opening a bank account, as opening one invites the inquisitive gaze of the authorities into their revenues.

The Tajik banking system is particularly uncompetitive, and remains one of the least developed in the EBRD region.[12] The Banking Development Strategy for 2010–2015, designed in collaboration with international financial institutes, has little chance of success, even if some signs of improvements are visible.[13] In 2011 Tajikistan had a two-tier banking system that is composed of fourteen banks with 260 branches, two non-bank credit institutions, and 123 micro-financing institutions.[14] The banking sector is concentrated around four large banks: Agroinvestbank, which controls the agricultural sector; Orionbank, which is in the hands of intimates of the presidential family and attracts the most profitable corporate accounts; and Amonatbank and Tojik-sodirotbank. All of them have very low volumes of loans and offer very high interest rates; the deposits of natural persons and legal entities are used as resources for these loans; and savings, pensions, and insurance funds are minimal.[15] Micro-finance is a growing sector as one of the strategies to alleviate rural poverty, while remittances sent by migrants arrive either in cash, or via Western Union-style banks.

Turkmenistan kept the Soviet system in place until very recently.[16] During his first year in power, in 2007, president Berdymukhammedov announced a new financial policy in macroeconomic matters and to this end created the Institute for Strategic Planning and Economic Development. Some improvements were made to the banking sector. The Central Bank of Turkmenistan, for example, allowed commercial banks to engage in formerly prohibited activities, such as managing international banking operations, opening accounts in foreign banks, and accessing to SWIFT (Society for Worldwide Interbank Financial Telecommunication) transactions.[17] Some exchange bureaus, closed under Niyazov, were reopened. Positive steps have included the unification of the dual exchange rates into a single official exchange rate, and the establishment of a stabilization fund. The country now has five state-owned banks, three joint stock banks, and one joint venture, but the domestic economy remains cash-dominated.[18]

The impact of the 2008 crisis on Central Asian banks varied greatly. The Turkmen banks did not suffer, since they are poorly integrated into the world economy; while the Tajik and Kyrgyz banking sectors, which were fundamentally weak, were above all affected by the drop in remittances sent by migrants. In Uzbekistan, the fall of bank revenues and the increase of unprofitable bank loans, estimated at between 15 and 25 percent of total loans, was a sign that the country had been hard-hit.[19] In the fall of 2008, the Uzbek government had to inject close to US$300 million into the six banks that it deemed the most important, extending the share of the state in the banking system to 71 percent. The state also exerts a strong influence on the supposedly private banks, whose directors are often closely connected to the presidential family. The first report published by Moody's on the Uzbek banking system in 2008 noted that the predominance of the state, the volatility of the environment, and the strict limits imposed on banks dampen the interest of foreign investors.[20]

The arrival on the Central Asian market of Islamic finance has been accelerated by the world crisis. The Islamic banking system, which aims to attract devout Muslims, functions in accordance with *sharia* and prohibits usury and financial investments in sectors deemed to be illegal (gaming, tobacco, alcohol, etc.). Islamic banks project themselves not only as mere suppliers of funds, but as partners of the entrepreneur, since they apply the principle of shared risk with their clients.[21] The cultural reception of these Islamic products in Central Asia is questionable, in particular in Kazakhstan and Kyrgyzstan, in which *sharia* law is quite unknown and very broadly associated with Islamic radicalism. Islamic financial services, mainly available in Almaty and Bishkek, are being offered to populations that are largely secularized and Russified, while it is likely potential customers could be found in the Ferghana Valley or in Tajikistan. But in countries where the banking institutions are not regarded as reliable, Islamic banks inspire confidence in customers because they share the risks with them.

Kyrgyzstan hoped to become the regional leader in this new Islamic banking sector. In 2007, the privately owned Ekobank, which in the 1990s had been controlled by the Russian bank Rossiiskii kredit and Kyrgyz businessmen, was transformed into the first *sharia*-based bank in partnership with the Islamic Development Bank. It organized the first ever meeting of the CIS Sharia Council, which fixed the norms for Islamic financing in the region.[22] Several investment funds from Persian Gulf countries have also raised the prospect of committing one and a half billion dollars to the Kyrgyz economy in the sectors of agriculture, health, transport, and communications.[23] In 2009, President Kurmanbek Bakiyev declared that he would like to create a cultural and financial Islamic center in Bishkek for the purpose of training personnel.[24] Islamic finance has also arrived in Uzbekistan: the Islamic Corporation for the Development of the Private Sector, a section of the Islamic Development Bank, has offered a loan of forty-two million dollars to three Uzbek banks: Ipoteka Bank (private), Asaka Bank, and Uzpromstroibank (public).[25] The first two have received fifteen million dollars each and the third twelve million, for the purpose of undertaking modernization projects in the domains of agriculture and transport. The Uzbek government has also signed a memorandum of cooperation with the Islamic Corporation that lays down the financing plan for new economic projects that meet Islamic norms.

Kazakhstan's Success Story: Central Asia's Rising Financial Center

Kazakhstan's immense resources have attracted considerable capital, heightened by the real estate sector boom that started about 2005. In terms of total capital to GDP ratio (used to evaluate a country's banking system), Kazakhstan was already the undisputed CIS leader in 2006 (101.7 percent), way ahead of Ukraine (63.5 percent), Russia (52.8 percent), and Moldova (51.7 percent).[26] This performance was especially remarkable as in Eastern Europe only the Czech Republic and Croatia had a higher coefficient. Thanks to the extraction industries, the finance sector has been one of the main beneficiaries of Kazakh dynamism. The explosion of consumer credit, mortgages, and loans for medium and small businesses has accentuated its considerable development. In 2005 total credit recorded an increase of 74 percent and in 2006 an increase of 82 percent, whereas credits to individuals rose 129 percent.[27] Kazakhstan has thus become Russia's main rival in the CIS financial sector.

Until the 2008 world crisis, the Kazakh banking sector comprised three groups of actors: the dominant trio of Halyk Bank, TuranAlem Bank, and Kazkommertsbank controlled 60 percent of banking assets; a small number of mid-sized banks, with a significant hold over retail trade and the financing of small and medium-sized enterprises, had 15 percent of the assets; and several small, often specialized banks, divvied up the remainder.[28] Though the Kazakh banking system concentrated largely on the financing of companies (with more than 55 percent of its assets), it diversified after 2005, enabling banks such as Allianz Bank and ATF Bank to enter the consumer sector and to rival the three giants by drawing on cheap foreign credit.[29] Compared with their counterparts in the other republics, the Kazakh banks had satisfactory profitability and high liquidity. A reform implemented in 2007 brought the system into greater conformity with international standards and its degree of transparency was relatively high for a CIS country. In addition to their presence on the Kyrgyz market, the Kazakh banks were also established in other CIS countries.[30]

However, despite the low level of risk, the stable course of the tenge, and low inflation, there were already several elements of concern before the crisis: overconcentration (the ten largest banks of the country controlled 94 percent of total capital), over-sized loans for mid-sized banks, and overly high credit rates for preinvestment.[31] The explosion of retail trade and the financing of small and mid-sized companies led many observers to question the reliability of the loans and to express concern at the over-exposure of some banks to the real estate market. Boosted by oil money and on the lookout for quick profits, the Kazakh banks also borrowed substantial sums from their American counterparts that were linked to hedge funds.[32] Kazakh banks have thus been exposed to the volatility of exchange rates and interest rates because of little diversification in terms of activities; the elevated degree of concentration of loans; investment in other, much less reliable CIS markets; overly rapid growth in the volume of banking operations abroad and in currency.

In the summer of 2007, the American subprime crisis hit the Kazakh real estate market, and a few months later the whole of the banking sector. Real estate fell 60 percent in the first quarter of 2008.[33] Inflation exceeded 9.5 percent through 2008 and 7.3 percent in 2009, while the national currency was devalued by 25 percent relative to the dollar after an announcement about the nationalization of several banks.[34] This devaluation limited foreign capital flight, but increased the cost of paying back foreign debt. At the end of 2008, Kazakhstan's foreign debt-service hit a level of 42 percent of the country's exports. In 2009, the debt parameters worsened due to the global economic crisis, but this drop was in line with that of exports.[35]

For the first time since the 1998 crash, the Kazakh authorities had to manage a large-scale shock that gave them a measure, in real time, of the solidity of the country's most dynamic sectors, but also of the efficiency of mechanisms of state intervention. They reacted rapidly, playing the role of regulator and stabilizer. When Standard and Poor's and Moody's Investors Service downgraded Kazakh banks in the summer of 2008, the government decided to invest eleven billion dollars in the national economy, or close to a quarter of its Central Bank reserves, in order to avoid loans from abroad.[36] A stability fund of four billion dollars that guaranteed liquidities was also set up, but this did not suffice to reassure foreign investors when Renaissance Capital's Rencasia Index for Central Asia collapsed in September 2008 after the announcement of the Lehman Brothers bankruptcy.[37] In 2009, the stabilization measures taken by the state widened in scope. Nursultan Nazarbayev released an additional ten billion dollars in aid: four billion were earmarked to stabilize the financial sector, three billion the badly hit real estate sector, one billion was transferred to small business, and another billion to infrastructure development projects.[38] In the post-crisis period, the republic opted to limit foreign borrowing and to strengthen domestic influence through the state funding of important programs (housing, roads, etc.), which has been achieved thanks to the development of public-private partnerships, individual investment, and Islamic financing.[39] In total, more than twenty-five billion dollars, or one-quarter of the GDP, were injected into the national economy to battle the crisis.[40]

During the crisis, the country's main banks endured an unprecedented drop in their capital, in particular the National Bank, Kazkommertsbank, and Astana Finance. The ATF Bank was the first to carry out a major reclassification of its assets in 2008. In the first semester of 2009, the Kazakh banking sector suffered astronomical losses of 1.6 billion dollars and a negative balance of 3.1 billion, and six of the country's ten main banks lost substantial sums (some were able to minimize losses, like HSBC Kazakhstan).[41] Risk assets continued to grow and reached a sum of twenty billion dollars: they counted for about one-third of the assets of Kazakh banks, but hit a record figure of 60 percent for BTA and Alliance Bank. The largest bank, BTA, which was very badly hit since it was heavily involved in the construction sector, lost fourteen billion dollars of capital in the first three quarters of 2009, or three-quarters of its portfolio.[42] In February 2009, Astana practically nationalized BTA and Alliance Bank, the leader of the retail credit market, and took over 25 percent of the shares of the second- and third-largest banks of the country, Kazkommertsbank and Halyk Bank, as they were deemed "too big to fail."[43] The crisis also facilitated the increase of foreign banks on the Kazakhstan market, which had formerly only owned 15 percent. UniCredit (Italy), Kookmin (South Korea), Alnair Capital (Abu Dhabi), Hapoalim (Israel), HSBC (London), and of course Russia's premier bank, Sberbank, jostled for position on the Kazakh market, while the German Raiffeisen International and Bank of Tokyo Mitsubishi opened offices in Almaty.[44]

In riding the crisis Kazakhstan has proven its overall financial solidity over the short run, but the long-term picture remains to be seen. As elsewhere, the crisis has resulted in a much stronger presence of the state in the banking sector. In addition, state influence on the banking system has become fundamental: 60 percent of the corporate deposits on which the banks subsist come from state-run companies. However, though the banking sector was bailed out by public money, these measures remain insufficient for long-term development: governmental financing cannot be their main revenue source. This situation does have a positive aspect, namely the cleaning up of the system, and an increase in banking revenues based on the country's domestic resources. Significant debt restructuring markedly reduced Kazakh banks' reliance on foreign debt to 24 percent of total liabilities at year-end 2010 from a pre-crisis peak of over 50 percent. At the end of 2011, the country was rewarded for its good financial behavior: Standard and Poor's ratings services raised its long- and short-term foreign currency ratings from "BBB/A-3" to "BBB+/A-2," singling out "Kazakhstan's improving fiscal and external flexibility as a result of its twin surpluses, strong economic growth driven by rising oil production and prices, prudent fiscal policy, and consistently high foreign direct investment inflows."[45]

Kazakhstan continues to pursue its goal of becoming the financial heart of the Central Asian region. To this end, the government established the Regional Financial Center of Almaty (RFCA) in 2006.[46] Its aim is to transform the former capital into a global financial center in order to facilitate the integration of the Kazakh financial industry with the international stock market. The hope is that establishing international market regulation standards and strategies will attract private investors, a prerequisite for the export of Kazakh capital. Almaty is in a favorable position: The central offices of major national financial institutions are there, as are the country's major regulatory and oversight institutions, such as the National Bank of

Kazakhstan, the Kazakhstan Agency for Regulation and Supervision of Financial Markets and Financial Organizations, and the Kazakhstan Stock Exchange. Initially, the Kazakh market was directed mainly toward London. In 2006, the London Stock Exchange and the RFCA signed a cooperation agreement to formalize bilateral ties.[47] The London Stock Exchange saw Kazakhstan as an important market: it listed ten Kazakh companies between 2005 and 2007, and hoped to serve as a hub for international investment in Kazakhstan.[48] However, the global financial crisis and Almaty's excessive dependence on British capital led Kazakh officials to diversify their strategies. Grigorii Marchenko, the president of the Kazakh National Bank, argued that Kazakhstan had relied too much on London, which held 95 percent of its stock market listings, and that it was time to shift operations to Asia.[49] The Kazakh government encouraged Kazakhmys and the Eurasian National Resources Corporation to list in Hong Kong and urged more companies to make their initial public offering in other financial centers.

Since 2008 Almaty has also sought to assert its status as a regional Islamic financial center, particularly during its presidency of the Organization of Islamic Cooperation in 2011. The Kazakh authorities have been impressed with the sustainability of Islamic finance during the global financial crisis. As flows of foreign direct investment to the country dropped by 20 percent in 2009, the government announced its intention to seek ten billion dollars of Islamic financing over a period of five to seven years.[50] Kazakhstan's interest in Islamic finance is not new: in 1994, the Saudi group Al Baraka opened its first subsidiary in the country. In the first decade of the twenty-first century, Islamic banks granted loans to several major Kazakh banks: 50 million dollars in 2005 and 2006 to BTA Bank, 38 million in 2006 and 2007 to the CenterCredit Bank, and 150 million between 2007 and 2009 to a partnership between the Alliance Bank and Calyon Bank/Abu Dhabi.[51] For its part, Kazakhstan has a number of *sharia*-friendly organizations such as Fattah Finance (one of the first companies to provide financial services compliant with Islamic standards), Istisna'a Corporation (one of the leading companies in terms of Islamic financial consulting), and Halal Mutual Insurance Takaful.[52]

With the crisis, Nazarbayev sought to accelerate this Islamic financial presence in Kazakhstan. In 2010, he ratified an agreement between the Abu Dhabi Investment Board and the Kazakh government for establishing Al Hilal as the first Islamic bank in the country, with offices in Almaty, Astana, and Shymkent. The bank primarily seeks to obtain projects for large corporations under Islamic *murabaha* contracts; in 2010 it invested 250 million dollars in the Kazakh economy and is expected to invest one billion by 2012–2013.[53] In August 2010, Kazakhstan's Road Map for the Development of Islamic Finance was approved, consisting of a better regulation of Islamic finance, attracting investments in accordance with *sharia* from Islamic Cooperation Organization members, the introduction of Islamic financial standards, and the establishment of micro-finance institutions in accordance with *sharia*. Nazarbayev also proposed that the Organization of Islamic Cooperation and the Islamic Development Bank create specific banking mechanisms for small and medium businesses.[54]

A Booming Mobile Telecommunications Market

According to mobile telephone companies, there are now 140 mobile phones per 100 inhabitants in Russia.[55] The Central Asian market, modeled on Russia's, also appears to be booming. The poor quality of the services on offer for landline telephones favors the rapid expansion of mobile market. Landline telephones are still dependent upon state companies that lack the means to modernize their networks and have not liberalized their prices. Mobile phones, which are much less expensive, enable a large part of the population, including those living in isolated regions, to communicate, and have become essential for Central Asian migrants living abroad to keep contact with their families. Since personal computers are still limited and Internet cafes are uncommon outside of major urban centers, mobile phones are becoming the primary means of accessing the Internet, with an enormous potential market.

Central Asia's main neighbors, China and Russia, have been classified by the British telecommunications regulator OFCOM as two of the chief driving forces of the world telecommunications market.[56] Another Central Asian neighbor, Iran, has also manifested an undeniable infatuation for mobile phones. For the Chinese, the Iranians, and the Central Asians alike, the mobile phone constitutes not only a technological advance, but also a way to circumvent political coercion and to disseminate local information in real time. In Central Asia as well, especially after the Arab Spring, the potential role of the Internet as a vector of political change has led the authorities to find ways to tighten control over access to it and all forms of new social media.[57] This could transpire with the help of China: although the software services in Central Asia are by and large owned by Russian companies, the suppliers of technology are mainly Chinese (China Telecom, Shanghai Bell-Alcatel, ZTE, and Huawei Technologies).

In Kazakhstan fixed landlines account for only 25 percent of the market with the mobile market making up the rest. The authorities support plans to modernize the country through information technology, and are concerned about the low share of the communication sector in the GDP (2 percent only). At the end of 2011, Kazakhstan approached market saturation with 15.7 million mobile phone subscribers out of a total population of sixteen million.[58] For major companies operating in the country, the challenge now is to boost market adoption of new technologies. Availability of broadband services and third- and fourth-generation (3G and 4G) technology is growing. However, the disparity between rural and urban areas remains significant. The networks are still in the hands of the state-run agency Kazakhtelecom, which was late in installing digital switches, fiber-optic lines, and Demand Assigned Multiple Access (DAMA) in sparsely populated areas. The whole country should be ready for digital switchover by 2015, especially thanks to the KazSat 2 satellite, which will allow private companies to invest in the under-served rural market.[59]

The six companies that share the market for fixed lines are also expected to upgrade their systems in order to bring down prices and offer better call quality, especially abroad. Most of them are related to large state-run companies, such as Kazakhstan Temir Zholy, which created Transtelecom, and KazMunayGas, which has its own

294

Table 14.1

Mobile Phones and Internet Users in Central Asia in 2011

	Kazakhstan	Kyrgyzstan	Tajikistan	Turkmenistan	Uzbekistan
Mobile cellular	19.768 million	5.275 million	5.941 million	3.198 million	20.952 million
Internet users	5.299 million	2.195 million	700,000	80,400	4.689 million

Source: Table based on the CIA World Factbook, https://www.cia.gov/library/publications/the-world-factbook/wfbExt/region_cas.html.

telephone company, KazTransCom. The state agency Kazakhtelecom has a virtual monopoly in sparsely populated rural areas unattractive to private operators. The mobile sector is shared by four private companies, two of which are major, competing players: GSM-Kazakhstan and Kar-Tel. GSM-Kazakhstan (49 percent of its shares are held by Kazakhtelecom) cooperated with the Turkish company Turkcell before joining the largest Scandinavian telecommunications holding company, TeliaSonera.[60] It now controls half of the Kazakh market with more than 7.5 million subscribers under the trademark K'Cell. Given Kazakhstan's huge size and sparse population, the objective is to provide services to the most isolated regions, and K'Cell hopes to offer services in areas with fewer than one thousand inhabitants by 2012.[61] Kar-Tel, which the Russian company Vimpelcom purchased, is in second place with just under seven million subscribers to K-Mobile and Beeline.

The Uzbek mobile phone market is one of the most dynamic in the region. In 2010, Uzbekistan had about 21.9 million subscribers out of a total of twenty-seven million inhabitants, meaning that more than three-quarters of the population were reachable via mobile.[62] As a result, prices have fallen: a mobile telephone can now be bought for twenty dollars and the least costly monthly subscriptions begin at three dollars.[63] A marketing offensive has multiplied the offers of specific services, especially those linked to Islam (prayer time, etc.). Trying to prevent market saturation, companies today are targeting remote rural areas, which are still poorly connected to the networks, and are accelerating the transition to 3G technologies. This has resulted in increased competition to control the Uzbek market, mainly between the two largest Russian operators, MTS and Beeline. In 2009, MTS serviced 50 percent of the Uzbek market, and Beeline 35 percent, leaving little room for the three national companies, Uzdun-robita, Unitel, and Coscom, while Perfectum mobile and UzMobile, a subsidiary of the national company Uzbektelecom, had a rather modest share of the market.[64]

The market in Tajikistan has also remained dynamic compared with the other sectors of the national economy. At the end of 2009, out of a total of seven million inhabitants, more than five million persons possessed a mobile phone. Here again, the Russian companies are firmly entrenched. Since 2005 Vimpelcom has owned 60 percent of the shares in Takom, which it commercialized under the Beeline brand. However, its ambitious objective to attain 80 percent coverage of the Tajik population has proved unachievable so far.[65] The Russian company Megafon, for its part, possesses three quarters of Megafon-Tajikistan, while TajikTelecom owns the remaining quarter.[66] Megafon today controls one-third of the Tajik market, its main rival being the American-Tajik joint venture Indigo Somonkom, which has close to one and a half million subscribers.

The Kyrgyz market was more sluggish in taking off, but today appears to be following the example of its neighbors. In 2009–2010 subscriber growth was about 50 percent and, in 2013, the country is expected to have as many mobile phones as inhabitants.[67] Disparities between regions are still important: in 2009 more than 80 percent of the inhabitants of the capital, Bishkek, possessed at least one mobile phone, while in the Batken region only 35 percent did, but the rural areas that have been behind are making up ground. Five operators share the market, with 85 percent of subscribers shared between Sky Mobile, which belongs to Vimpelcom and trades under the Beeline brand, and Alpha Telecom.[68]

Lastly, in Turkmenistan, the market has taken longer to get off the ground, but estimates are that more than half of the population (almost three million out of five million inhabitants) had a mobile phone in 2011. At the end of 2010, the Turkmen government expelled the Russian company MTS—which had 80 percent of the market with 2.4 million subscribers—provoking tensions between Moscow and Ashgabat, and leaving a large part of the country without access to mobile telephones for several months.[69] The aim of the authorities was both political and financial: to prevent Turkmen citizens from easily accessing the Internet from their mobile phones, to privilege the state company, Altyn Asyr (which only had a little more than 300,000 subscribers in 2009), and to reap the revenues of this booming market.[70]

Kazakhstan and New Technologies

The sudden and brutal collapse of the Soviet system of scientific education at the start of the 1990s, the disappearance of public financing for training and research, and the brain drain of Soviet-educated experts abroad, resulted in reinforcing the over-specialization of the Central Asian economies. In the first decade of the twenty-first century, Kazakhstan, aware of the backwardness of its high-tech industries, used its oil revenues to try to set up the institutional structures required to dynamize this sector. It has every interest in seeing its potential in new technologies develop: its agricultural sector has a high demand for transformation industries; its territory is favorable for renewable energies; its chemical and pharmaceutical industries are in need of modernization; and its space program is idle and awaiting innovation. But Kazakh ambitions were revised downward following the 2008 crisis, and the objectives of the "Strategy for the Development of Innovation Industries by 2015" are unlikely to be met.

Some mechanisms are operational, however. The state holding Parasat is supposed to ensure the link between basic and applied research. It unites several of the major Kazakh communication companies, such as Kazsatnet for cable and satellite technology, Kazteleradio, KazPost, the Foundation for Science, and the National Center for Informatization.[71] Four sectors of activity have been made a priority: the development of e-government (government electronics databases, making administration and public services accessible online); providing support for the new technologies market and the protection of intellectual property rights; the development of digitized infrastructures for the media; and the technological modernization of postal services. The mobile phone and Internet companies are also very interested in Kazakhstan's involvement in the "information highway" and the development of ADSL, Wi-Fi, Wi-Max, 3G, and 4G networks throughout the country.[72] As in Russia, the state remains the main driving force of this economic reorientation, while foreign investors are still cautious.

The Almaty Institute of Energy and Communications and the Al-Farabi National University have, for instance, set up a "Kazakh nano-electronics initiative," but the

financing provided by the Ministry of Education is too limited to train the new generation of scientists.[73] The Kazakh "Silicon Valley"—the Alatau technological park—
which is situated in the free economic zone surrounding Almaty, has also been slow
to come to life. Inaugurated with great pomp in 2003 by President Nazarbayev, it still
faces basic problems such as electricity shortages and poor access to water to carry out
experiments.[74] Three technological parks in Uralsk, Karaganda, and Ust-Kamenogorsk,
as well as the center of biological technologies in Astana, are also hoping to see the
government's promises implemented. In 2008, a national laboratory for nanotechnologies called Nanofab was created in Shymkent. Its objective is to serve as a unifying
platform for the country's ten university engineering laboratories and to consolidate
international cooperation. The laboratory is designed to function autonomously using solar energy and will employ robotized systems. On the international level, it has
made contact with major Californian and German centers, with cutting-edge Japanese
nanotechnology companies such as ULVAC, JEOL, and Seki Technotron, as well as
with the Indian Ministry of Sciences and Technologies, which has promised to supply
the laboratory with equipment.[75]

The space sector is seen as a motor for high-tech development. Having its own
space program is a question of national branding, since the space race is viewed as
a technological challenge that confirms a rise to great power status and sharpens a
country's international image. Kazakhstan already proudly boasts Talgat Musabayev,
the last Soviet cosmonaut to go into space, in 1991, and the first Kazakh to do so. He
subsequently participated in three space missions through the Russian program and is
now the director of the state agency Kazkosmos.[76] Despite its great power ambitions,
Kazakhstan has struggled to live up to the ambitions of its space program. Affected
by the economic crisis, Kazkosmos in 2009 had to postpone a plan to send one of its
own cosmonauts to the International Space Station. That same year, it managed to
avoid much more substantial problems. Control over the first Kazakh satellite KazSat,
launched into orbit in 2006, was lost in 2008, and the country risked having to pay
huge fees if it collided with other satellites. Fortunately, with help from the Moscow-
based Khrunichev State Research and Production Center that had built it, the satellite
was maneuvered into an inactive area.[77] Then, at the end of 2010, Kazkosmos was
forced to acknowledge that it was having trouble repaying a budgetary loan whose
grace period had expired.[78]

The situation improved in 2011. The second satellite, KazSat 2, whose launch was
postponed due to technical complications, took off successfully in March 2011 and
should remain in service for a decade, providing Kazakhstan with new possibilities in
satellite technologies.[79] Kazakhstan is also part of an international consortium tasked
with the creation of the World Space Observatory Ultraviolet (WSO/UV), led by
Roskosmos with the assistance of Spain, Italy, China, and Ukraine, to be operational
in 2012.[80] Cooperative ventures have developed with other partners, for example the
Indian Space Research Organization (ISRO). The two countries share very similar
goals in space, although India is far closer to achieving them. Kazkosmos and ISRO
have planned the construction of a landing site in Kazakhstan, the launch of Indian

IRS rockets, which are known for the high quality of images they take in space, and the use of a radar complex on Kazakh territory.[81] Astana also signed a new agreement for two earth observation satellites with the European EADS-Astrium, along with documents allowing for the construction of an Assembly, Integration, and Test Center (AIT) in Astana.[82]

Although Astana benefits from having the Baikonur Cosmodrome on its territory and the ability to rent it to Russia, it faces many challenges in developing its own space program. Russia and Kazakhstan have allocated 223 million dollars each for the construction of Baiterek, a new launch pad designed to launch Angara carrier rockets that are capable of delivering twenty-six metric tons of payload to low-Earth orbits.[83] The Soyuz, Cosmos-3M, Rockot, and Tsyklon rockets are currently launched from the Plesetsk Cosmodrome, near the Arctic, but the heavy Proton and Zenit rockets can only be launched from Baikonur. However, Moscow has announced plans to launch Angara rockets from Plesetsk in 2013, which would undermine the profitability of Baikonur, and in coming decades, it is expected to give priority to the Vostochnyi Cosmodrome in the Amur region.[84] Moscow and Astana, despite their close association, have also been through tense times related to their respective space strategies. For example, the draft version of a new space technology development program, approved by Astana in October 2010, supposes Kazakhstan's full operational control over the Baikonur Cosmodrome in a few decades with the progressive retreat of Russia.[85] Although Moscow is ready to have its Kazakh partner increasingly involved in Baikonur, the Kremlin does not plan to fully replace it with the Far Eastern launch sites, for symbolic historic reasons as well as for economic ones: Baikonur is closer to the equator than any of the other existing or projected Russian cosmodromes, which is essential for saving fuel in satellite launches.[86] Further, Russia does not want to have Kazakhstan as a new competitor in the space race.

It is clear that for Kazakhstan, Baiterek will become the main center for training cosmonauts and the specialized staff involved in space flights. Astana envisages Baiterek becoming not only the main launch site for manned space missions, but also Eurasia's communications hub through the expansion of its fixed satellite communications and satellite navigation services. Kazakhstan's strategy to become a global communications hub for road, rail, and air requires advanced telecommunications systems and space-based satellite communications. Last but not least, Kazakhstan hopes that the space race pays off in producing a new generation of high-tech workers and scientists. In 2008, the government approved the foundation of a National Center for Space Research and Technologies, the aim being to promote technical and science-applied research.[87]

The Potential for Tourism

Eventually the countries of Central Asia are banking on developing their tourism potential, though here again the chances of success are quite variable. The first tourism developed in the region during the Soviet period: foreign teams were climbing the great peaks of the Tian-Shan (the Peak of Communism and the Peak of Victory are both above 7,400 meters) in the 1970s and 1980s. From the beginning of the 1990s, the Kyrgyz government promoted this mountain tourism, as well as ecotourism, with the aid of Swiss NGOs, among others.[88] This market has helped to open up very remote regions and provide supplementary incomes for local people, especially those in the Naryn region, which has specialized in serving Western tourists who wanted to experience the "nomadic way of life" (yurts, herding). This tourist market has suffered from the country's image of instability, in particular during the political crises of 2010. Tajikistan has also tried to develop mountain ecotourism in the autonomous region of Gorno-Badakhshan, but with limited success.[89]

Uzbekistan, on the other hand, benefited from a major tourist boom in the second half of the 1990s and into the new century: its architectural wealth and a fashion for the theme of the Silk Roads throughout Europe earned the country a significant flow of tourists, in particular French and Italians, but also Israelis, on the Khiva-Bukhara-Samarkand circuit.[90] At first, this tourism was very beneficial to the Uzbek population who were able to offer bed-and-breakfast style lodging, sell arts and crafts, as well as providing various services (car rentals, guides, translators) to supplement their usual income. However, from approximately 2005, the Uzbek state tried to exploit the tourist trade by imposing various taxes and obliging providers to register their services, as well as to restrict communication between Uzbek citizens and foreign tourists.[91] Turkmenistan permits only group tourism via Western travel agencies working in partnership with local ones, along an itinerary that includes Dashauz, Merv, Niva, and the archeological sites of the Karakum desert.[92] Kazakhstan ventured into tourism late, and banks on ecotourism, the observation of migrating birds, some pre-historic sites, and the retracing of the nomadic past.[93] Some programs, of modest scale, also aim to promote the country's Soviet past, in particular the Gulag camps around Karaganda.[94]

Hunting tourism is also growing throughout the region. A luxury and individualized type of tourism, it is almost exclusively reserved for foreigners. Companies like the Central Asian Hunting Club and ProfitHunt specialize in this lucrative sector, which the state supports due to the significant income generated by the sale of licenses. Kyrgyzstan in particular has become a center of attraction for international trophy hunting tourism, and more than eighty companies are working in this sector.[95] Among the most-hunted animals in the region are the famous Marco Polo sheep, Tian Shan sheep, Siberian ibex, wolves, wild boar, Karatau sheep, red deer, antelope and gazelle, red marmot, migratory geese and ducks, and Hungarian partridge. Local species are also sought, such as the trans-Caspian Urial sheep in Turkmenistan, and trout as large as ten pounds in Lake Issyk-Kul. For the best-known mammals such as the Marco Polo sheep and Siberian ibex, buying a trophy license costs several thousand dollars.[96]

While many of these tourists meet the conditions set by local law, the legal boundary between hunting and international animal smuggling is blurred, and corruption can easily circumvent official regulations. Not only can these protected species be hunted for several thousand dollars, but the black market for hunting tourism is also booming.[97]

Turkmenistan has, for example, specialized in hosting hunters from the United Arab Emirates. They arrive by private jet and their budgets allow them to obtain multiple permits (usually a hunter is only allowed to kill one animal), including for animals that are not supposed to be hunted. In the Tian Shan Mountains in Kyrgyzstan, the snow leopard is threatened with extinction from hunting for its fur and bones, and cases of illegal hunting of Himalayan brown bears have been reported.[98] Although Western and Gulf countries dominate Central Asian hunting tourism, growing contacts with Asia have given birth to hunting and poaching tourism related to medicinal products. Chinese, Japanese, and Koreans value the skins, musk, horns, tongue and other animal parts from wolves, antelopes, bears, and deers that are traditionally held in high regard for their medicinal value.[99] The market is therefore destined to expand quickly with this new wave of Asian tourists in search of wild animals from the Eurasian space.

Central Asian societies have found it difficult to catch up from the lost post-Soviet decades in terms of education and research. In an increasingly competitive world, and as neighbors of a booming Asia in terms of new technologies and higher education, they have little chance of developing competitive skills. Moreover, the cost of Central Asian labor is too high for foreign firms to be able to take advantage of relocating there. Only Kazakhstan, thanks to its oil revenues, will be able to make a transition to new technologies, that is, provided that it follows strategies similar to those applied in the United Arab Emirates, where the oil rent is largely reinvested in the knowledge economy, and that it invests much more than it currently does in education. Though higher education has partially rebounded since its collapse after the fall of the USSR, the academy, and particularly applied technical research, is still moribund. Turkmenistan, which envisages itself as a Central Asian Emirate, still has a long way to go before even approaching this model, which would presuppose its opening up to the outside world. Uzbekistan, with its strong demographic growth, has little chance of providing prospects for widespread entry into higher education or of becoming a leader in new technologies, even if Tashkent has targeted a few niches of excellence, such as in solar energy.[100] Lastly, Kyrgyzstan, and to a lesser extent Tajikistan, are being transformed into service economies only thanks to the impact of Chinese trade, which has turned them into sites of trade and re export.

Notes

1. On the CIS banking system, see, for instance, the Research Center of CIS Banking Systems, http://cisbankingresearch.com. See also I. Golodniuk, "Financial Systems and Financial Reforms in CIS Countries," Center for Social and Economic Research (CASE) Network Studies and Analyses, no. 306, Warsaw, 2005.
2. D. Terlikbayeva, "Le secteur bancaire au Kazakhstan," Economic Mission, French Embassy in the Republic of Kazakhstan, August 2007, 1.
3. Ibid.
4. M. Brown et al., "The Impact of Banking Sector Reform in a Transition Economy: Evidence from Kyrgyzstan," *Journal of Banking and Finance*, no. 33 (2009): 1677–87, here 1678.

5. "Kyrgyz Republic: Financial Sector Assessment," Report of the World Bank Financial Sector Assessment Program, Washington, DC, April 2003.

6. Brown, "The Impact of Banking Sector Reform."

7. Ibid., 1679.

8. A. V. Akimov and B. Dollery, "Uzbekistan's Financial System," *Problems of Economic Transition* 48, no. 12 (2006): 6–31.

9. M. Mizuno, "The Finance in the Capital Market and Credit Rating in Uzbekistan," Research Paper of the Nihon University Center for China and Asian Studies, Tokyo, 2009.

10. K. Ruziev and D. Ghosh, "Banking Sector Development in Uzbekistan: A Case of Mixed Blessings?" *Problems of Economic Transition* 52, no. 2 (2009): 3–41; "Financial Analysis," Asian Development Bank Housing for Integrated Rural Development Investment Program, n.d., http://www.adb.org/Documents/RRPs/UZB/44318/44318-013-uzb-fa.pdf; A. Vakhabov and T. Bobakulov, "Uzbekistan's Banking System and Its Role in Implementing the Anti-Crisis Program," *Central Asia and the Caucasus*, nos. 4–5 (2009): 91–105.

11. C. Nuttall "Moody's Puts Uzbekistan's Banking Sector on Negative Outlook," *Business New Europe*, August 12, 2009, http://www.bne.eu/story1725/rencap.swf.

12. "Developing the Banking Sector in Tajikistan," *European Bank for Reconstruction and Development*, June 8, 2011, http://www.ebrd.com/pages/project/case/asia/tajikistan_abtj.shtml.

13. J. Stenga, "Demand and Challenges of Accessing Saving Products in Tajikistan Microfinance Institutions" (MA thesis, Université Libre de Bruxelles, 2010), 3.

14. The Tajik Agricultural Finance Framework (TAFF) was set up by the EBRD, http://www.taff.tj/en/background/tajikistan-in-a-snap-shot.html.

15. Z. Ergasheva, "Tajikistan's Banking System Does Not Satisfy the Needs of Country's Economy, ABT Experts," *Asia Plus*, June 24, 2010, http://news.tj/en/news/tajikistan-s-banking-system-does-not-satisfy-needs-country-s-economy-abt-experts.

16. G. O. Khalova, "The Banking System and Monetary Policy in Turkmenistan," *Russian and East European Finance and Trade* 35, no. 5 (1999): 45–74; J. Šír, "*Halk Maslahaty* in the Context of the Constitutional Evolution of Post-Soviet Turkmenistan," *Perspectives on European Politics and Society* 6, no. 2 (2005): 321–30.

17. J. Šír, "Turkmenistan—A Promised Land for Making Business? Macroeconomic Reforms under Berdymukhammedov," *China and Eurasia Forum Quarterly* 8, no. 3 (2010): 67–92.

18. P. Puhl, "Financial Sector in Turkmenistan and Deutsche Bank in Turkmenistan," *Deutsche Bank AG*, Ashgabat, May 19, 2011.

19. "State Involvement in Banks Doing Little for Uzbekistan," *Times of Central Asia*, November 27, 2011, http://mx1.timesca-europe.com/index.php/m-news-by-category/economy-finance-and-investment-news/889-state-involvement-in-banks-doing-little-for-Uzbekistan.

20. Nuttall, "Moody's Puts Uzbekistan's Banking Sector on Negative Outlook."

21. G. Gresh, "Promoting Prosperity: The Islamic Development Bank and the Rise of Islamic Banking and Finance in Central Asia," *Central Asia and the Caucasus*, no. 1 (2008): 135–46; "Central Asia: Governments, Banks Gradually Open Up to Islamic Banking," *Eurasianet*, July 12, 2007, http://www.eurasianet.org/departments/insight/articles/pp071307.shtml.

22. "History of Ekobank," *EkoIslamikBank*, n.d., http://www.ecobank.kg/ecob/history.html.

23. "Islamic Corporation Opened in Kyrgyzstan Credit Line for Development of Small and Mid-Sized Business," *Times of Central Asia*, September 28, 2008.

24. "K. Bakiev zaiavil o zainteresovannosti v sozdanii Islamskogo obrazovatel'nogo, kul'turnogo i finansovogo tsentra v KR," *For.kg*, November 9, 2009, http://www.for.kg/ru/news/101712/.

25. "Uzbekskii Ipoteka-bank beret kredit v \$10 mln u Islamskoi korporatsii razvitiia chastnogo sektora," *EkoIslamikBank*, August 3, 2008, http://www.ecobank.kg/index.html?subaction=showfull&id=1249274099&archive=&start_from=&ucat=8&.

26. A. Buzdalin, "Banking Sector of Kazakhstan Displayed an Impressive Growth All over the Commonwealth in 2006," *Fergana.news*, April 9, 2007, http://enews.ferghana.ru/article.php?id=1916.

27. Terlikbayeva, "Le secteur bancaire au Kazakhstan," 1–2.

28. "Consolidation of Kazakhstan's Banking Sector Likely," *Silk Road Intelligencer*, February 13, 2008, republished on http://www.speroforum.com/a/14562/Consolidation-of-Kazakhstan-banking-sector-likely.

29. Ibid.

30. E. Vinokurov, "Vzaimnye investitsii v bankovskom sektore," *Evraziiskaia ekonomicheskaia integratsiia* 3, no. 2 (2009): 141–47.

31. Buzdalin, "Banking Sector of Kazakhstan Displayed an Impressive Growth."

32. M. Laruelle, "Kazakhstan Challenged by the World Financial Crisis," *The Central Asia-Caucasus Analyst,* November 12, 2008, http://www.cacianalyst.org/?q=node/4979; Pomfret, "Central Asia and the Global Economic Crisis," 2.

33. "Kazakhstan Shakes Up Banking Sector," *Banker*, February 9, 2009, http://www.the-banker.com/News/Kazakhstan-shakes-up-banking-sector.

34. J. Lermusiaux, "Key Factors Behind the February 2009 Devaluation of the Tenge," *Visor Capital*, April 2009, http://www.visocap.com/media-feb2009.html; "Kazakhstan: The National Bank Devalued the Tenge by 25%," *Fergana.news*, February 4, 2009, http://enews.fergananews.com/news.php?id=988.

35. "Vneshnii dolg Kazakhstana v I kvartale vpervye sokratilsia na $2,7 mlrd—Natsbank," *Zakon.kz*, July 16, 2009, http://fin.zakon.kz/143343-vneshnijj-dolg-kazakhstana-v-i-kvartale.html.

36. S. Barisitz and M. Lahnsteiner, "From Stormy Expansion to Riding Out the Storm: Banking Development in Kazakhstan," Oesterreichischen Nationalbank Financial Stability Report, no. 19, June 2010, 62–71.

37. On this RENCASIA Index, see centralasia.rencap.com.

38. S. Barisitz, et al., "Crisis Response Policies in Russia, Ukraine, Kazakhstan, and Belarus—Stock-Taking and Comparative Assessment," *Focus on European Economic Integration*, no. 4 (2010): 48–77.

39. N. Ramazanov, "Kontseptsiia postkrizisnogo razvitiia," *Delovaia nedelia*, November 27, 2009.

40. L. Leutskii, "O krizise i momente istiny v nyneshnikh usloviiakh strany," *Delovaia nedelia*, July 31, 2009.

41. O. Maslov, "Financial Crisis Makes the State Bankruptcy of Kazakhstan Just a Matter of Time," *Huliq*, n.d., http://www.huliq.com/2893/72569/financial-crisis-makes-state-bankruptcy-kazakhstan-just-matter-time.

42. "Kazakhstan Will Not Provide State Guarantees for Bank Debt Restructuring," *Silk Road Intelligencer*, April 22, 2009, http://silkroadintelligencer.com/2009/04/22/kazakhstan-will-not-provide-state-guarantees-for-bank-debt-restructuring/.

43. J. Lillis, "Kazakhstan: With Financial System Stressed, Astana Takes Over Banks, Devalues Currency," *Eurasianet*, February 3, 2009, http://www.eurasianet.org/departments/insightb/articles/eav020409.shtml.

44. C. Nuttall, "Foreign Banks Seize the Moment in Kazakhstan," *Silk Road Intelligencer*, September 12, 2008, http://silkroadintelligencer.com/2008/09/12/foreign-banks-seize-the-moment-in-kazakhstan/.

45. "Standard & Poor's Raises Kazakhstan's Sovereign Rating," *Regional Financial Center Almaty*, November 8, 2011, http://www.rfca.kz/en/news/1001741.

46. See the RFCA website, www.rfca.kz.

47. "London Stock Exchange and Regional Financial Centre of Almaty, Kazakhstan, Sign Co-Operation Agreement," *London Stock Exchange*, November 21, 2006, http://www.londonstockexchange.com/about-the-exchange/media-relations/press-releases/2006/exchange-andregionalfinancialcentreofalmatykazakhstansignagreement.htm.

48. "Kazakh IPOs in London: Past and Future," *Silk Road Intelligencer*, March 14, 2008, http://silkroadintelligencer.com/2008/03/14/kazakh-ipos-in-london-past-and-future/.

49. R. Orange, "Kazakhstan Shuns London for Hong Kong," *Telegraph*, November 15, 2010, http://www.telegraph.co.uk/finance/newsbysector/banksandfinance/8132583/Kazakhstan-shuns-London-for-Hong-Kong.html.

50. "Kazakhstan Embraces Non-Traditional Financial Instruments," Kazakhstan Embassy in the Netherlands, n.d., http://www.kazakhembassy.nl/index.php?option=com_content&view=article&id=203:kazakhstan-embraces-non-traditional-financial-instruments-&catid=35:general&Itemid=86.

51. "Islamic Finance Will Grow in Kazakhstan," Kazakhstan Embassy in India, n.d., http://www.kazembassy.in/news.php?newsid=117.

52. "Kazakhstan Embraces Non-Traditional Financial Instruments."

53. "Al-Hilal Plans Islamic Bank in Kazakhstan," *A1SaudiArabia.com*, September 21, 2009, http://www.a1saudiarabia.com/10179-al-hilal-plans-islamic-bank-in-kazakhstan/.

54. "Second Islamic Finance Forum in Astana Raises Business Awareness," *Kazworld*, September 22, 2011, http://kazworld.info/?p=16679.

55. See the Russia sheet by Econstats, which synthesizes World Bank and World Development indicators, http://www.econstats.com/wdi/wdic_RUS.htm.

56. "Emerging Markets: Brazil, Russia, India, and China," *OFCOM*, n.d., http://stakeholders.ofcom.org.uk/market-data-research/market-data/communications-market-reports/icmr07/overview/emerging/.

57. B. Dufour and F. Tuhbatullin, "Central Asia: Censorship and Control of the Internet and Other New Media," Report of the International Partnership for Human Rights, Brussels, 2011.

58. "Almost Every Resident in Kazakhstan Is a Mobile Phone User," *Interfax Kazakhstan*, December 15, 2011, http://www.interfax.kz/?lang=eng&int_id=in_focus&news_id=13.

59. "Kazakhstan uspeshno zapustil sputnik sviazi KazSat-2," *Today.kz*, July 16, 2011, http://www.today.kz/ru/news/kazakhstan/2011-07-16/47207.

60. "TeliaSonera to Increase Its Stake in GSM Kazakhstan," *Tengrinews*, October 18, 2011, http://en.tengrinews.kz/companies/4628/.

61. "Competition Grows in Kazakhstan's Mobile Market," Kazakh Chamber of Commerce in the USA, September 7, 2011, http://kazcham.com/competition-grows-in-kazakhstan%E2%80%99s-mobile-market/.

62. Sh. Ganiev, "Sotovaia sviaz' Uzbekistana—Itogi 2010," *TsentrAziia*, June 20, 2011, http://www.centrasia.ru/newsA.php?st=1308548940.

63. Authors' fieldwork, Tashkent, March 2008.

64. More details in "Central Asia Telecom Industry Report, 2008–2009," Report of the Research in China Institute, Beijing, 2009.

65. Z. Ergasheva, "Beeline planiruet pokryt' territoriiu, gde prozhivaet 80% naseleniia Tadzhikistana," *Toptj*, September 12, 2006, http://www.toptj.com/m/news/2006/09/12/beeline_planiruet_pokryt_territoriyu_gde_prozhivaet_80_naseleniya_tadzhikistana.

66. "Brend 'MLT' poluchil novoe imia—'Megafon-Tadzhikistan'," *Asia Plus*, July 20, 2011, http://news.tj/ru/news/brend-mlt-poluchil-novoe-imya-megafon-tadzhikistan.

67. "V Kyrgyzstane prognoziruetsia rost chisla abonentov sotovoi sviazi," *Profit.kz*, July 20, 2009, http://www.profit.kz/news/5026-V-Kirgizstane-prognoziruetsya-rost-chisla-abonentov-sotovoj-svyazi/.

68. "V Kyrgyzstane snizilis' tempy prirosta abonentov sotovoi sviazi," *Mobinfo.uz*, February 19, 2010, http://mobinfo.uz/3237-v-kyrgyzstane-snizilis-tempy-prirosta-abonentov.html.

69. "Turkmenistan Suspends License of Largest Mobile Operator," *Radio Free Europe/Radio Liberty*, December 21, 2010, http://www.rferl.org/content/turkmenistan_suspends_russian_phone_provider_mts/2254591.html.

70. A. Berdyeva, "Internet v Turkmenii—Dorogoe udovol'stvie i nekachestvennaia sviaz'," *Deutsche Welle*, April 22, 2011, http://www.dw-world.de/dw/article/0,,15014186,00.html;

C. Fitzpatrick, "Huawaei and Nokia Siemens Step in to Gap Left by Russia's MTS in Turkmenistan," *Eurasianet*, http://www.eurasianet.org/node/63272.

71. See the Parasat website, http://www.parasat.com.kz; "Glava MON RK opredelil glavnye zadachi dlia kholdinga 'Parasat'," *Kazinform*, May 27, 2011, http://www.inform.kz/rus/article/2383365.

72. More in "Broadband for Central Asia and the Road Ahead: Economic Development through Improved Regional Broadband Networks," ESCAP Technical Paper, Information and Communications Technology and Disaster Risk Reduction Division, Bangkok, October 2009.

73. "Fundament dlia proryva," *Kazakhstanskaia pravda*, July 18, 2009, http://www.kazpravda.kz/print/1247860038; "Obshchie svedeniia," *Kazakhstanskii natsional'nyi universitet imeni Al'-Farabi*, http://kaznu.kz/ru/9723.

74. "Nanotekhnologiia v Kazakhstane: PR-aktsiia ili spasatel'nyi krug dlia ekonomiki?," *Delovaia nedelia*, November 13, 2009.

75. "Nauchno-tekhnologicheskii tsentr 'NANOFAB'," *Nanotekhnologii*, n.d., http://sgm-lab.ru/nanotechnology-in-electronics/nauchno-texnologicheskij-centr-nanofab/; Iu. Mel'nik, "Nanotekhnologii: Ne panatseia, no nano," *Mezhdunarodnyi delovoi zhurnal Kazakhstan*, no. 5 (2009), http://www.investkz.com/journals/69/694.html.

76. See his biography, "Talgat Amangeldievich Musabaev," *SpaceRef*, http://www.spaceref.com/focuson/tito/musabaev.html.

77. "Full Truth About KazSat-1," *Tengrinews*, April 19, 2011, http://en.tengrinews.kz/science/Full-truth-about-KazSat-1-1044/.

78. "Kazakh Space Agency Seeks Extra Funding for New Baikonur Launch Pad," *RIA Novosti*, June 12, 2010, http://en.rian.ru/science/20101206/161645920.html.

79. "Proton Successfully Launches Two Geostationary Satellites," *Space News*, July 18, 2011, http://www.spacenews.com/launch/110718-proton-launches-sats.html; G. Delaney, "Giant Step for Kazakhstan as Kazsat-2 Satellite Goes into Orbit," *Kazakhstan Live*, July 27, 2011, http://www.kazakhstanlive.com/2.aspx?ProdID=84f2313a-08a7-442f-b84f-88e704418ecc&CatID=9f9f8034-6dd6-4f7e-adcf-0f6a7c0406d9&sr=100&page=1.

80. A. Raimov, "Kazakh Space Agency Sets Sights beyond Solar System," *Central Asia Online*, January 27, 2009, http://www.centralasiaonline.com/en_GB/articles/caii/features/2009/01/27/feature-03.

81. "Delegatsiia Natsional'nogo kosmicheskogo agentstva Kazakhstana nakhoditsia s rabochei poezdkoi v Indii," *Kazinform*, September 29, 2007, http://www.inform.kz/rus/article/188228.

82. "Astrium to Fully Equip Kazakhstan's Satellite Integration and Test Centre," *EADS*, October 27, 2010, http://www.astrium.eads.net/en/press_centre/astrium-to-fully-equip-kazakhstans-satellite-integration-and-test-centre-.html.

83. "Kazakh Space Agency Seeks Extra Funding for New Launch Pad at Baikonur," *RIA Novosti*, December 6, 2010, http://www.interspacenews.com/FeatureArticle/tabid/130/Default.aspx?id=5691.

84. "Angara Launch Vehicle," *Globalsecurity.org*, April 20, 2011, http://www.globalsecurity.org/space/world/russia/angara.htm.

85. M. Sieff, "New Kazakh Space Program is Ambitious but within Reach," *Central Asia Newswire*, October 18, 2010, http://www.universalnewswires.com/centralasia/viewstory.aspx?id=2046.

86. "Launching Satellites," *EUMETSAT*, http://www.eumetsat.int/Home/Main/Satellites/SatelliteProgrammesOverview/SP_20100427133512861?l=en.

87. "Space Research and Technologies Center Set Up in Kazakhstan," *Central Asian News*, January 16, 2008, http://en.ca-news.org/news/2459.

88. T. Watanabe et al., "Tourism in the Pamir-Altai Mountains, Southern Kyrgyz Republic," *Geographical Studies*, no. 84 (2009): 3–13; N. J. Palmer, "Economic Transition and the Struggle for Local Control in Ecotourism Development: The Case of Kyrgyzstan," *Journal of Ecotourism* 5, nos. 1–2 (2006): 40–61.

89. Authors' interview with the representative of the Milal-Inter Association for Promoting Tourism, Khorog, June 29, 2010.

90. C. Werner, "The New Silk Road: Mediators and Tourism Development in Central Asia," *Ethnology* 42, no. 2 (2003): 141–59; D. Airey and M. Shackley, "Tourism Development in Uzbekistan," *Tourism Management* 18, no. 4 (1997): 199–208.

91. Authors' fieldwork in Uzbekistan, May 2005, April 2008.

92. Authors' fieldwork in Ashgabat, April 2008.

93. X. Li, Z. Wang, and N. Kerimbay, "Cooperative Study on Eco-tourism Based on Transport Corridor in China and Kazakhstan," ADB-CAREC Research Grants Program, June 2008; "O kontseptsii razvitiia turizma v respublike Kazakhstan," http://www.kazatur.narod.ru/zakon/1. HTML; A. Tonkobaevoi, *Rukovodstvo po razvitiiu ekologicheskogo turizma v Kazakhstane* (Almaty: Aziatsko-Amerikanskoe partnerstvo, 2009). See also the current research done by Guillaume Tiberghien on "Authenticity and Tourism in Kazakhstan and Its Application to Neo-Nomadic Culture within a Post-Soviet Heritage" at the New Zealand Tourism Institute, nztri.org.

94. Authors' fieldwork, Kazakhstan, September 2010.

95. "Kyrgyzstan: Nature Conservation in the Tien Shan Mountains," *Nature and Biodiversity Conservation Union*, n.d., http://www.nabu.de/en/themen/international/laender/kirgistan//.

96. Ibid.

97. "V Kyrgyzstane pytaiut'sia iskorenit' brakon'erstvo," *Huntfishing.ru*, October 11, 2011, http://huntfishing.ru/index.php?action=news&id=41.

98. "Kyrgyzstan: Nature Conservation."

99. Authors' interview with Kyrgyz and Kazakh firms organizing exports of medicinal products to Asia, Almaty, and Bishkek, February 2008.

100. R.A. Zakhidov and M.S. Saidov, "Renewable Energy in the Early Twenty-First Century and Prospects for Development of Solar Engineering in Uzbekistan," *Applied Solar Energy* 45, no. 1 (2009): 1–6.

Conclusion

As a "buffer zone" between big powers, Central Asia's autonomy is based on a balance between multiple "smaller" and "greater" actors. If the region is viewed as a site for competition and rivalry, local governments are forced to choose a "camp" and to play exclusively (one external actor against another) rather than complementarily (all external actors coexisting). If the region is thought of in development terms, then geo-economic logics become more complementary. The development needs are such that competition disappears, or remains limited to classic market mechanisms. Tajik and Kyrgyz hydroelectric projects, for instance, are still struggling to find investors, as are some gold mines in Kazakhstan, old extraction complexes in Uzbekistan, and transformation industries in the whole region. Even Russian and Chinese companies, which are backed by their governments and supported by their own financial institutions, are hesitant about committing to overly risky operations. As programs like CAREC show, development needs are so costly that only joint international strategies and investments make it possible, even if only partially, to meet the expectations of Central Asian societies. These countries have therefore been left with the impression that they are unattractive to foreign interests, and that their human capital is not valuable.

Competition among external actors does exist in some areas. Turkmen gas is coveted by China, Russia, Europe, and South Asia; Kazakh uranium by Russia, China, Japan, and South Korea; Kazakh oil by Russia and China; and in the coming years, rare earth metals will probably be sought by Europe, Russia, and China, and Kazakhstan's space potential by Russia, India, and China. Competition is also growing in political terms. The United States and the European Union champion the democratization of the regimes, which Moscow and Beijing reject, while other states such as India, Japan, and South Korea refuse to issue normative discourses on the nature of regimes. Less visible competition between different understandings of Islam is also present. Pakistan and Saudi Arabia are pushing for the dominance of conservative Salafi Islam, while Tehran, threatened by this ideological "Arabization" or "Pakistanization," prefers to promote traditionalist Islam—Sufi and depoliticized—that does not call into question Iran's status as a rising regional power. Finally, strategic competition has also taken shape. The EU and the United States, through NATO and other institutions, would like to have more powerful mechanisms for security cooperation with the Central Asian governments, and tend to see the CSTO and SCO as competitors. However, the West does not offer Central Asia a comprehensive regional security architecture, and must be content with multiple uncoordinated initiatives. Competition between the CSTO and SCO has also become more visible since 2005, when Moscow hampered Chinese attempts to build an integrated economic space and to be more involved in strategic issues, and made it clear that it does not envisage further integration, despite official discourse by the Kremlin on the excellent health of Russian-Chinese relations.[1] The Russian-Chinese competition grew in magnitude with Putin's new dynamics of regional integration, that have the clear but not formulated goal of hampering Chinese advances in Central Asia.

The Central Asian arena has become very diversified in two decades of independence. Russia still remains one of the main relevant partners, even for reluctant Uzbekistan and Turkmenistan, and the rise of other external actors is perceived by Western pundits to be largely at Moscow's expense. But the former imperial metropole no longer enjoys a monopoly in the region: After losing political control over Central Asia at the beginning of the 1990s, Russia found a way to reconquer certain economic and strategic niches and now conceives of its status in Central Asia in terms of its competition and complementarity with other powers. The shared Soviet past, cultural influence, and contemporary migration flows form the bases of Russia's legitimacy in the region. However, in coming decades Moscow will have to fundamentally reshape its relations with Central Asia if it wishes to continue to have decisive influence over it. It will remain a major actor in Kazakhstan and Kyrgyzstan, but will lose influence in Turkmenistan and Uzbekistan; and it will have to promote soft security issues rather than hard ones. However, it can remain a model for Central Asian societies if it succeeds in its own political and social transformation. Its territorial proximity to and cultural and economic interaction with the region will not disappear, but will be reformulated. This will likely create a better balance between Russia and Central Asia, making Central Asia a more respected partner in the Kremlin.

China will remain the foremost economic power in Central Asia. The latter's dependence on the Chinese is probably one of the biggest changes that has occurred in the region since independence, although it has had paradoxical effects. In a sign of China's leverage capacity, the Central Asian elites feel that they would be penalized by more Chinese presence (loss of autonomy and possible challenges to sovereignty), but also by less of it. If for some reason China collapsed politically or shrank economically, the consequences for Central Asian societies would be huge. By imposing itself so quickly as Central Asia's most influential external actor after Russia, Beijing has had to tackle new challenges, in particular its weakness in terms of security influence and its lack of success in becoming an attractive cultural partner. This security influence may grow at the expense of Russia's, but for the time being, Beijing prefers to leave Moscow as the policeman of its economic interests in the region. The Chinese authorities have also been unable to set up cultural diplomacy and to generate a discourse to promote "Chineseness." The pro-Chinese gamble of the new Central Asian generations, who see a pragmatic opportunity in their great neighbor, could modify the situation in the next decade, when all things Chinese will have become synonymous with a successful professional career and a substantial income. The replacement of the old Soviet elite, in particular through the education abroad of the young generations of the middle and upper classes, constitutes one of the drivers of change. However, the differential of power risks feeding an already well-established Sinophobia. Whatever its success in meeting these challenges, China has nevertheless emerged as the main "measuring stick" for the other external actors in Central Asia.

These other external actors will face difficulties competing with Russia and China. Their lack of territorial contiguity and of influence that can be expressed simultaneously in the political, security, economic, and cultural realms limits their impact. China's grand strategy is not subject to short-term geopolitical developments and is planned over the long-term. Territorial contiguity also works in favor of Russia's long-term interests, even if the demographic decline points away from any new leverage capacity in Central Asia. However, this does not mean that the region will necessarily remain dominated by a Russian-Chinese tandem—whether friendly or competitive—because the combination of several other actors like the United States, EU, Japan, South Korea, India, or Turkey, could curtail the influence of Moscow and Beijing. On paper, India has the possibility of greater influence, as would an Iran that had been reintegrated into the international community, finally allowing it to play its natural role as a regional link between Central Asia and the Persian Gulf. Faced with the weight of geography and economic transformations due to globalization processes, the United States and Europe are a priori losers in terms of long-term influence. The economic crises of 2008 and debt crises of 2011 signaled the probable slow decline of Western foreign policies, and their withdrawal toward more modest goals, which will leave more room for maneuver to the "emerging powers."

Central Asia is therefore part of current global trends that are changing the world power balance. It stands as a symbol in the new geopolitical paradigms: the end of the last empire, the Soviet Union; projections by China and India of their own foreign policy and strategic culture; rising regionalism in Eurasia and Asia; the testing of the EU as a normative power; post–Cold War negotiations and growing cooperation between Moscow and Washington; and competition between different conceptions of Islam from Iran, the Gulf States, Malaysia, and Pakistan. The region also illustrates changes in the world economy. The economic swing toward China and more generally toward Asia is obvious, but other features can also be mentioned: the Kazakh example demonstrates the growing power of state energy companies, the willingness of governments to regain at least partial control of resource deposits, and the development of sovereign funds. The purpose of this "state capitalism," seen as the engine of modernization from above, is not only to curb the profits of big multinationals or to obtain more attractive financial benefits for states. It also suggests the use of resources in terms of sustainable development, both for the environment and as part of a legacy for future generations. But the choices made by the Central Asian governments depend heavily on the logics shared by the elites in power: Should immediate income be forgone in order to avoid new social crises, or to preserve wealth for the future of the nation? Should purely commercial rationales be pursued, or those that reinforce state sovereignty? Should private interests be promoted in order to maintain intra-elite consensus, or to try to develop a more transparent investment climate?

Central Asia will not suddenly become a driver of Eurasian continental economic dynamism. Its geographic location between three BRIC countries does not mean it will automatically benefit from Chinese, Indian, or Russian economic might. The political will of governments or international donors does not create development and wealth per se, and proximity on a map is not a sufficient means to an end. In many ways, Central Asia will remain a periphery of the globalized world, which does not mean that it will not be integrated with it on many levels. Labor migration, shadow economies, energy resources, uranium, gold, cotton, and wheat are its principle elements of integration. Kazakhstan can expect more: a regional financial center, production of nuclear and potentially space technologies, and a trans-Eurasian hub for commerce and communications. But hopes for Central Asia as a whole to become a logistical node can only be achieved on a very modest scale. With the exception of Kazakhstan, which can capture rail traffic flowing from China to Europe via Russia, other states are unlikely to become transit hubs—except possibly for air cargo in Uzbekistan. The region will capture only a small portion of land traffic between Asia and Europe (probably 2 or 3 percent), even if it manages to improve governance and effectively fight corruption. The same is true for energy resources. Oil and gas revenues can transform the future of Kazakhstan and Turkmenistan, and possibly Uzbekistan, but are not enough to build a positive future if these resources are not used properly. The model to follow is not that of Nigeria, but that of the Emirates, which invested oil revenues to build a post-industrial, service-oriented growth.

Overall, landlocked countries are more subject to geographical preconditions than countries with coastlines: they cannot easily access distant markets or create new trade niches and production alternatives for themselves. Thus Chinese competition more clearly disadvantages Central Asia than it does Southeast Asia. The Central Asian states must therefore transform their economies in order to take advantage of their Chinese neighbor, rather than to suffer under it, hence the necessary transition from industry to services. Over-specialization in the export of raw materials is in many respects harmful to the economies. It works to reinforce the rent-seeking tendencies, inequalities of distribution, and the predatory rationales of the ruling elites. It also accelerates deindustrialization and migration, since millions of people no longer have any professional prospects. The rural population cannot cope with agrarian overpopulation and the urban middle classes are not experiencing the social and economic advancement they expect. With the exception of Kazakhstan, the Central Asian economies offer few niches for potential middle classes.

However, despite the social anxieties provoked by Beijing's growing influence in Central Asia, China's proximity has also proven a guarantee of development and access to world markets. As Kyrgyzstan has shown, the reexport of Chinese products throughout the rest of Central Asia, Russia, and potentially the Middle East, makes it possible to set up new dynamics that transform the social fabric. A whole range of new professions are being structured, all linked to the service economy: transport, freight, logistics, translation, legal and commercial services, foreign sales networks, and so forth. This niche of services is bound to develop throughout the entire region and could act to curb, at least partially, the brain drain due to migration flows.

The transition to a service economy, however, demands that the governments recognize that knowledge in general—whether theoretical knowledge or technical competence—is a key element of economic development in the twenty-first century. The maintenance of a quality educational system, free and accessible to all, will prove to be the essential condition for the successful transformation of societies, especially as the Soviet Union left behind a very broadly literate and well-educated population. As governments seem relatively unaware of the importance of the issue, it is unknown whether they will address critical human capital and competence-building issues.[2] Used to collecting rent revenues from primary materials, the Central Asian regimes have not really placed their bets on this service economy, which does not offer the same opportunities for financial control; on the contrary, it accentuates the autonomy of society against the state. However, the change of generation that is taking shape throughout the region will have significant repercussions. Those under the age of fifteen years represent 24 percent of the population in Kazakhstan, 33 percent in Uzbekistan, and 38 percent in Tajikistan.[3] The new elites and middle classes are pushing for change, and the structuring of new economic niches will have, in one way or another, a political impact.

Central Asian societies expect stability and development from their governments. None of these countries, with the exception of Kazakhstan, are able to meet these expectations without foreign help. Even Kazakhstan is not free from risks. Its poor distribution of wealth from oil revenues has led to social tensions, especially in the large cities in the west like Atyrau, Aktau, and Aktobe, and to the worst unrest the country has seen since independence, in Zhanaozen, at the end of 2011. Terrorist attacks perpetrated by radical Salafi groups, which have easily recruited youths frustrated by their lack of access to wealth, are another sign of policy failure. On the political front, the inability of Nursultan Nazarbayev to prepare his succession and to obtain the consensus of oligarchic and bureaucratic elites around an heir could create serious tensions in the years ahead if the distribution of wealth among elites is challenged. Although the country has successfully managed the post-Soviet challenges of the 1990s—like the risk that the large Russian minority would secede—it will face new challenges in the coming decade. Kazakh nationalism is much more pronounced among the younger generations, the role of Islam in public life must be discussed rather than ignored as it is now, and the financial windfall being directed to the higher education system will by itself not reverse the declining quality of primary and secondary education and the massive corruption present in higher education.

In the four other countries, the governments are unable or unwilling to meet the needs of their populations. Turkmenistan will be unable to make itself into a "Central Asian Emirate" unless it duly recognizes and invests in its human capital. Its gas riches and small population are not sufficient for sustainable growth; it is necessary to invest further in its primary wealth, that is, human beings. An "Emirate future" implies a literate population that is educated in foreign languages, has contacts abroad, and is able to respond to an international presence; a population that is trained in technological professions in order to better shape the country's strategic choices, and one which is competitive in terms of the service and knowledge economy. While the Turkmen regime has so far succeeded in insulating the country from external pressures and in guaranteeing domestic impermeability, no sustainable development will be credible without a liberalization of society and greater permeability vis-à-vis its interactions with the rest of the world.

Uzbekistan has found itself in a situation that could be compared to that of Egypt in Mubarak's final years: an authoritarian regime that has hardened over the years, losing its popular legitimacy; an aging dictator, incapable of initiative, leaving the country's wealth to be divided up not only by family members, but also by the security services, which constitute both a "state within a state" and a business empire; law enforcement agencies that terrorize the population, track down those deemed dissidents, and engage in torture; an opaque and corrupt judicial system; and an economic situation that continues to deteriorate for the rural population and the middle classes, who seek to emigrate en masse. The legitimacy of the Karimov regime, which sees itself as the last "fortress" of secularism and pro-Western international positions in the face of an impending "Islamic wave," is a long-term dead end. The young age of the Uzbek population, the high levels of unemployment, the injustice of the regime, and the successful social roots of Islamism as the only alternative narrative are supporting prospects of change on the model of the Arab Spring.

Tajikistan and Kyrgyzstan are both fragile countries, often presented as on the road to state "failure." National wealth is more limited than in other states; remittances now constitute one of the primary sources of income for citizens, accentuating dependence on Russia; drug trafficking has corrupted state structures, in particular the law enforcement agencies; and consensus among elites, especially between the center and regions, is weak and frequently called into question. Kyrgyzstan remains nonetheless a unique experiment in Central Asia: despite flaws and weaknesses its parliamentary system has prevented the emergence of overly absolute presidential authority, and forced the elite to re-organize in a more innovative, and more democratic, way the management of their relations with their constituencies.

The Central Asian states will have to confront sizeable security challenges in the years to come. The dangers they face, however, are not conventional ones. Russia, Iran, and Afghanistan have all recognized the borders left from the Soviet era and have not sought to dispute them. As for China, it has signed border delimitation treaties and demilitarization agreements with the Kazakh, Kyrgyz, and Tajik governments. Among the Central Asian states themselves, there are still some border tensions, mainly between Kyrgyzstan and Tajikistan, but a priori the national armies have no need to prepare themselves for the type of conflict typically linked to territorial issues. The only issue that seems to be able to provoke military tensions is water, and Islam

Karimov has repeatedly brandished the threat of sending his troops into Tajikistan and Kyrgyzstan if there is a significant disruption in the water supply. The lack of regional integration may not be resolved with the coming to power of a new generation, because intra-Central Asia competition is a long-term given,[4] but it does not portend any kind of military conflict between states. Nevertheless, the security pressures on the region are important, although they relate to non-conventional threats: organized crime, drug trafficking, corruption, localized insurgencies, uncontrolled migration flows, food security, pandemics, and environmental risks. All these potential dangers reveal low-intensity forms of conflict, and confirm that the region now figures significantly in globalized logics.

This situation requires that the Central Asian states move their focus from hard security (conventional defense) to soft security (security in a broader sense). It also requires the establishment of mechanisms for improved governance and risk-prevention strategies based on intelligence and logistics, and the enhancement of human capital. In all three areas, the Central Asian countries are faring badly. Weak governance is a long-term problem that is difficult to address, as it requires not only improvement of the rule of law and the accountability of the government to the people, but also combating high-level corruption, recruitment of the best and brightest for public posts, and the effectiveness of law enforcement agencies. Risk prevention also has been slow to take shape as the Central Asian governments operate in a reactive, not a preventive, manner, and find it difficult to delegate time and budget for events that are only prospective. In addition, their logistical capabilities are weak and they do not have effective emergency situations ministries, as Russia does. Their intelligence services in areas as diverse as meteorology, geology, industrial risk, and social unrest are just as bad; they both refuse to address difficult issues and lack capacity. This relates to a third and key issue—that of human capital and competence building. The Central Asian states remain slow to develop their primary wealth in human capital, which, of course, is an essential element of successful integration into a globalized world.

Notes

1. Blank, "Toward a New Chinese Order in Asia."
2. M. Laruelle, "The Growing Illiteracy in Central Asia: A Challenge for the EU," Europe Central-*Asia Monitoring Commentary*, no. 6, December 2009.
3. See the Population Reference Bureau statistics, http://www.prb.org/DataFinder/Topic/Rankings.aspx?ind=10.
4. Olcott, "Rivalry and Competition in Central Asia," 19.

Bibliography

Abashin, S., and S. Gorshenina, eds. *Le Turkestan russe: Une colonie pas comme les autres?* Tashkent and Paris: Editions Complexe, 2009.

Abazov R., *Historical Dictionary of Turkmenistan*. Lanham, MD: Scarecrow Press, 2005.

Abdrakhmanov, A., and A. Kaukenov. "Otnosheniia Kitaia i stran Tsentral'noi Azii glazami kazakhstanskikh ekspertov." *Kazakhstan v global'nykh protsessakh*, no. 3 (2007): 119–28.

Abdyrasulova, N., and N. Kravsov. *Electricity Governance in Kyrgyzstan: An Institutional Assessment*. Bishkek: Civic Environmental Foundation UNISON, 2009.

———. "Upravlenie sektorom elektroenergetiki v Kyrgyzstane: Institutsional'nyi i prakticheskii analiz." Report of the World Resources Institute and Prayas Energy Group, Washington, DC, 2009.

Airey, D., and M. Shackley. "Tourism Development in Uzbekistan." *Tourism Management* 18, no. 4 (1997): 199–208.

Akbarzadeh, S. "India and Pakistan's Geostrategic Rivalry in Central Asia." *Contemporary South Asia* 12, no. 2 (2003): 219–28.

———. "U.S.–Uzbek Partnership and Democratic Reforms." *Nationalities Papers* 32, no. 2 (2004): 271–86.

Akihiro, I., ed. *Eager Eyes Fixed on Eurasia*. Sapporo: Hokkaido University, 2007.

Akimov, A. V., and B. Dollery. "Uzbekistan's Financial System." *Problems of Economic Transition* 48, no. 12 (2006): 6–31.

Akramov, K., and N. Omuraliev. "Institutional Change, Rural Services, and Agricultural Performance in Kyrgyzstan." International Food Policy Research Institute (IFPRO) Discussion Paper, no. 00904, 2009.

Alessandri, E. "The New Turkish Foreign Policy and the Future of Turkey-U.S. Relations." Working Paper of the Instituto Affari Internazionali, no. 1003, 2010.

Allison, R., and L. Jonson, eds. *Central Asian Security: The New International Context*. Washington, DC: Brookings Institution Press, 2001.

Allouche, J. "The Governance of Central Asian Waters: National Interests versus Regional Cooperation." *Disarmament Forum*, no. 4 (2007): 45–55.

Anacker, S. "Geographies of Power in Nazarbayev's Astana." *Eurasian Geography and Economics* 45, no. 7 (2004): 515–33.

Anceschi, L. *Turkmenistan's Foreign Policy: Positive Neutrality and the Consolidation of the Turkmen Regime*. London: Routledge, 2008.

Anderson B., and Y. Klimov. "Uzbekistan: Trade Regime and Recent Trade Developments." University of Central Asia Institute of Public Policy and Administration Working Papers no. 4, 2012.

Anderson, K., E. Valenzuela, and L. A. Jackson. "Recent and Prospective Adoption of Genetically Modified Cotton: A Global CGE Analysis of Economic Impacts." World Bank Policy Research Working Paper 3917, Washington, DC, May 2006.

Anninos, S. C. "Creating the Market: An Examination of Privatization Policies in Kazakhstan and Egypt." PhD diss., New York University, 2000.

Apikyan, S. A., and D. J. Diamond, eds. *Nuclear Power and Energy Security.* Dordrecht: Springer, 2009.

Aris, S. *Eurasian Regionalism: The Shanghai Cooperation Organisation.* New York: Palgrave Macmillan, 2011.

Arvis J., G. Raballand, and J. Marteau. "The Cost of Being Landlocked: Logistics Costs and Supply Chain Reliability. World Bank Working Paper, no. 4258, June 2007.

Ashimbaev, M., and G. Chufrin, eds. *ShOS: Stanovlenie i perspektivy razvitiia.* Almaty: Institut mirovoi ekonomiki, 2005.

Ashimbaev M. S., and R. I. Krumm. *Perspektivy Tsentral'noi Azii kak tranzitnogo mosta mezhdu Evropoi i Kitaem: Sbornik materialov mezhdunarodnoi konferentsii.* Almaty: Kazakhstanskii Institut Strategicheskikh Issledovanii, 2005.

Asian Development Bank. "Electricity Sectors in CAREC Countries: A Diagnostic Review of Regulatory Approaches and Challenges." Report of the Asian Development Bank, Manila, 2005.

Aslund, A. "Why Doesn't Russia Join the WTO?" *Washington Quarterly* 33, no. 2 (2010): 49–63.

Atakhanova, Z., and P. Howie. "Electricity Demand in Kazakhstan." *Energy Policy*, no. 35 (2007): 3729–43.

Averre, D. "Russian Foreign Policy and the Global Political Environment." *Problems of Post-Communism* 55, no. 5 (2008): 28–39.

Axyonova, V. "The EU-Central Asia Human Rights Dialogues: Making a Difference?" Europe-Central Asia Monitoring Policy Brief, no. 16, April 2011.

Azam, J., and G. Makhmejanov. "Isolationism in Uzbek Economic Policy as an Obstacle for Water-Energy Consortium." Working Paper of the Toulouse School of Economics, May 2010.

Babali, T. "Prospects of Export Routes for Kashagan Oil." *Energy Policy*, no. 7 (2009): 1298–308.

Babu, S. C., and S. Djalalov, eds. *Policy Reforms and Agriculture Development in Central Asia.* New York: Springer, 2006.

Bahgat, G. *American Oil Diplomacy in the Persian Gulf and the Caspian Sea.* Gainesville: University Press of Florida, 2003.

Bal, S. N. *Central Asia: A Strategy for India's Look-North Policy.* New Delhi: Lancer Publishers & Distributors, 2004.

Balci, B. "Fethullah Gülen's Missionary Schools in Central Asia and Their Role in the Spreading of Turkism and Islam." *Religion, State, and Society* 31, no. 2 (2003): 151–77.

———. *Missionnaires de l'Islam en Asie centrale: Les écoles turques de Fethullah Gülen.* Paris: Maisonneuve & Larose, 2003.

———, ed. "La Turquie en Asie centrale: La conversion au réalisme (1991–2000)." Report of the Institut Français d'Etudes Anatoliennes, no. 5, 2001.

Barisitz, S., H. Holzhacker, O. Lytvyn, and L. Sabyrova. "Crisis Response Policies in Russia, Ukraine, Kazakhstan, and Belarus—Stock-Taking and Comparative Assessment." *Focus on European Economic Integration*, no. 4 (2010): 48–77.

Barisitz, S., and M. Lahnsteiner. "From Stormy Expansion to Riding Out the Storm: Banking Development in Kazakhstan." Oesterreichischen Nationalbank Financial Stability Report, no. 19, June 2010.

Barry, M. "The Development and Use of Production Sharing Agreement Law in Uzbekistan Oil and Gas." *Central Asia and the Caucasus*, no. 5 (2006): 47–59.

Becker, S. *Russia's Protectorates in Central Asia: Bukhara and Khiva, 1865–1924.* London: RoutledgeCurzon, 2004.

Bennett, B. *The Last Dictatorship in Europe: Belarus Under Lukashenko.* New York: Columbia University Press, 2012.

Benson, S. "The MAGAI Construct and the Northern Distribution Network." Washington, DC: Center for Strategic and International Studies, 2009.

Beshimov, A., O. Abdykaimov, B. Radzhapov, and N. Tashbekov. "Prigranichnaia torgovlia: Otsenka peresecheniia granits mezhdu Kyrgyzstanom i Uzbekistanom." Working Paper of the OSCE-Central Asian Free Market Institute, 2011.

Bhattacharyay, B. N., and P. De. "Restoring the Asian Silk Route: Toward an Integrated Asia." Working Paper of the Asian Development Bank Institute, no. 140, June 2009.

Blank, S. "Toward a New Chinese Order in Asia: Russia's Failure." National Bureau of Asian Research Special Report, no. 26, March 2011.

Bloch, P. C. "Kyrgyzstan: Almost Done, What Next?" *Problems of Post-Communism* 49, no. 1 (2002): 53–62.

Boboyorov, H. "Personal Networks of Agricultural Knowledge in the Cotton-growing Communities of Southern Tajikistan." *Demokratizatsiya. The Journal of Post-Soviet Democratization*, 20. no. 4 (2012): 409–435.

Bogdetsky, V., ed. "Mining Industry and Sustainable Development in Kyrgyzstan." Report of the Mining, Minerals, and Sustainable Development Project of the Internationl Institute for Environment and Development, no. 110, November 2001.

Bogdetsky, V., K. Ibraev, and J. Abdyrakhmanova. "Mining Industry as a Source of Economic Growth in Kyrgyzstan." World Bank Reports, Bishkek, 2005.

Boonstra, J. "Defending Human Rights and Promoting Democracy: Euro-Atlantic Approaches towards Turkmenistan and Uzbekistan." Fundación para las relaciones internacionales y el diálogo exterior (FRIDE) Activity Brief, December 2008.

———. "The EU Strategy for Central Asia Says 'Security': Does This Include Security Sector Reform?" Europe-Central Asia Monitoring Policy Brief, no. 10, November 2009.

———. "Russia and Central Asia: From Disinterest to Eager Leadership." *EU-Russia Centre Review*, no. 8 (2008): 70–79.

Boonstra J., and M. Denison. "Is the EU-Central Asia Strategy Running Out of Steam?" Europe-Central Asia Monitoring Policy Brief, no. 17, May 2011.

Boonstra, J., M. Emerson, N. Hasanova, M. Laruelle, and S. Peyrouse. *Into Eurasia: Monitoring the EU's Central Asia Strategy*. Brussels-Madrid: CEPS-FRIDE, 2010.

Boonstra, J., and J. Hale. "EU Assistance to Central Asia: Back to the Drawing Board?" Europe-Central Asia Monitoring Working Paper, no. 8, January 2010.

British Petroleum. "BP Statistical Review of World Energy 2011." June 2011.

Brown, M., M. Rueda Maurer, T. Pak, and N. Tynaev. "The Impact of Banking Sector Reform in a Transition Economy: Evidence from Kyrgyzstan." *Journal of Banking and Finance*, no. 33 (2009): 1677–87.

Brzezinski, Z. *The Grand Chessboard: American Primacy and Its Geostrategic Imperatives.* New York: Basic Books, 1998.

Bukh, A. *Japan's National Identity and Foreign Policy: Russia as Japan's "Other."* New York: Routledge, 2009.

Bukhanov, A. "Aktual'nye voprosy kazakhstansko-rossiiskikh otnoshenii glazami kazakhstanskikh ekspertov." *Kazakhstan v global'nykh protsessakh*, no. 4 (2006): 92–99.

Burghart, D. L., and T. Sabonis-Helf, eds. *In the Tracks of Tamerlane: Central Asia's Paths to the Twenty-First Century*. Washington, DC: Center for Technology and National Security Policy, 2003.

Burnashev, I. "Specific Features of Kazakhstan-Belarus Relations in Politics, Economics, and Culture." *Central Asia and the Caucasus*, no. 6 (2004): 103–10.

Business Monitor International. *Kazakhstan Agribusiness Report Q3 2012*. Industry Report & Forecasts Series, June 2012.

Business Monitor International. *Kazakhstan Mining Report Q3 2012*. Industry Report & Forecasts Series, May 2012.

Business Monitor International, *Kazakhstan Oil & Gas Report Q3 2012*. Industry Report & Forecasts Series, May 2012.

Business Monitor International, *Kazakhstan Power Report Q2 2012*. Industry Report & Forecasts Series, March 2012.

Business Monitor International, *Turkmenistan Oil & Gas Report Q3 2012*. Industry Report & Forecasts Series, May 2012.

Cabestan, J. *La Politique internationale de la Chine: Entre intégration et volonté de puissance*. Paris: Presses de Sciences Po, 2010.

Calder, K. E., and V. Kim. "Korea, the United States, and Central Asia: Far-Flung Partners in a Globalizing World." Korea Economic Institute Academic Papers Series 3, no. 9, 2008.

Castets, R. "Opposition politique, nationalisme et islam chez les Ouïghours du Xinjiang." *Les Etudes du CERI*, no. 110, 2004.

Causarano, P., V. Galimi, et al., eds. *Le XXe siècle des guerres*. Paris: Éd. de l'Atelier, 2004.

Chaulia, S. S. "BJP, India's Foreign Policy, and the 'Realist Alternative' to the Nehruvian Tradition." *International Politics* 39 (2002): 215–34.

Chow, E. C., and L. E. Hendrix. "Central Asia's Pipelines: Field of Dreams and Reality." Special Report of the National Bureau of Asian Research, no. 23, September 2010.

Cooley, A. *Base Politics: Democratic Changes and the US Military Overseas*. Ithaca, NY: Cornell University Press, 2008.

———. *Great Games, Local Rules: The New Great Power Contest in Central Asia*. Oxford: Oxford University Press, 2012.

———. "The Stagnation of the SCO: Competing Agendas and Divergent Interests in Central Asia." PONARS Eurasia Policy Memo, no. 85, September 2009.

———. "U.S. Bases and Democratization in Central Asia." *Orbis* 52, no. 1 (2008): 65–90.

Council of the European Union. "Joint Progress Report by the Council and the European Commission to the European Council on the Implementation of the EU Central Asia Strategy." Council of the European Union Report 11402/10, Brussels, June 2010.

Courmont, B. *Chine: La grande séduction; Essai sur le soft power chinois*. Paris: Editions Choiseul, 2009.

Crane, K., D. J. Peterson, and O. Oliker. "Russian Investment in the Commonwealth of Independent States." *Eurasian Geography and Economics* 46, no. 6 (2005): 405–44.

Crow, S. *The Making of Foreign Policy in Russia Under Yeltsin*. Munich: RFE/RL Research Institute, 1993.

Crude Accountability. "Turkmenistan's Crude Awakening: Oil, Gas, and Environment in the South Caspian." Report by Crude Accountability, January 2009.

Cutler, R. M. "Moscow and Ashgabat Fail to Agree over the Caspian Coastal Pipeline." *The Central Asia-Caucasus Institute Analyst* 11, no. 7 (2009): 3–5.

Dabrowski, M. "The Reasons of the Collapse of the Ruble Zone." Center for Social and Economic Research (CASE) Network Studies and Analyses, no. 58, Warsaw, 1995.

Dash, P. L. *Caspian Pipeline Politics, Energy Reserves, and Regional Implications*. New Delhi: Pentagon Press and Observer Research Foundation, 2008.

Demir, C. E., A. Balci, and F. Akkok. "The Role of Turkish Schools in the Educational System and Social Transformation of Central Asian Countries: The Case of Turkmenistan and Kyrgyzstan." *Central Asian Survey* 19, no. 1 (2000): 141–55.

Denison, M. "The Art of the Impossible: Political Symbolism and the Creation of National Identity and Collective Memory in Post-Soviet Turkmenistan." *Europe-Asia Studies* 61, no. 7 (2009): 1167–87.

———. "The EU and Central Asia: Commercializing the Energy Relationship." Europe-Central Asia Monitoring Policy Papers, no. 2, 2009.

Destradi, S. *Indian Foreign and Security Policy in South Asia: Regional Power Strategies*. London: Routledge, 2011.

De Tapia, S. "Türksat et les républiques turcophones de l'ex-URSS." *Cahiers d'études sur la Méditerranée orientale et le monde turco-iranien*, no. 20 (1995): 399–413.

Dicken, P. *Global Shift: Mapping the Changing Contours of the World Economy.* New York: Guilford Press, 2011.

Diener, A. "Diasporic Stances: Comparing the Historical Geographic Antecedents of Korean and German Migration Decisions in Kazakhstan." *Geopolitics* 14, no. 3 (2009): 462–87.

———. *Homeland Conceptions and Ethnic Integration Among Kazakhstan's Germans and Koreans.* Lewiston, NY: Edwin Mellen Press, 2004.

Djalili, M. "L'Iran et la Turquie face à l'Asie centrale." *Journal for International & Strategic Studies*, no. 1 (2008): 13–19.

Djalili, M., and T. Kellner. *Géopolitique de la nouvelle Asie centrale: De la fin de l'URSS à l'après 11 septembre.* Paris: PUF, 2003.

Dollfus, O. *La mondialisation.* Paris: Presses de Sciences Po, 2001.

Dufour, B., and F. Tuhnatullin, "Central Asia: Censorship and Control of the Internet and Other New Media." Report of the International Partnership for Human Rights, Brussels, 2011.

Dukhovny, V. A., and J. de Schutter. *Water in Central Asia: Past, Present, Future.* Boca Raton, FL: CRC Press, 2011.

Dunlop, J. "Reintegrating 'Post-Soviet Space'." *Journal of Democracy* 11, no. 3 (2000): 39–47.

Dwivedi, R. "China's Central Asia Policy in Recent Times." *China and Eurasia Forum Quarterly* 4, no. 4 (2006): 139–59.

Eberstadt, N. "Russia's Peacetime Demographic Crisis: Dimensions, Causes, Implications." National Bureau of Asian Research Project Report, Seattle, May 2010.

Efegil, E., and L. Stone. "Iran's Interests in Central Asia: A Contemporary Assessment." *Central Asian Survey* 20, no. 3 (2001): 353–66.

Emerson M., and E. Vinokurov. "Optimisation of Central Asian and Eurasian Trans-Continental Land Transport Corridors." Europe-Central Asia Monitoring Working Paper, no. 7, December 2009.

Environmental Justice Foundation. "White Gold: The True Cost of Cotton; Uzbekistan, Cotton, and the Crushing of a Nation." Report of the Environmental Justice Foundation, London, 2009.

ESCAP. "Broadband for Central Asia and the Road Ahead: Economic Development through Improved Regional Broadband Networks." ESCAP Technical Paper, Information and Communications Technology and Disaster Risk Reduction Division, Bangkok, October 2009.

Eshchanov, B. R., M. Grinwis Plaat Stultjes, S. K. Salaev, and R. A. Eshchanov. "Rogun Dam—Path to Energy Independence or Security Threat?" *Sustainability*, no. 3 (2011): 1573–92.

Esteban, M., and N. de Pedro, eds. *Great Powers and Regional Integration in Central Asia: A Local Perspective.* Madrid: Exlibris Ediciones, 2009.

"The Eurasian Union Project." *Russian Analytical Digest*, no. 112, April 20, 2012.

European Council. "Council Conclusions on Central Asia." 3179th Foreign Affairs Council Meeting, Luxembourg, June 25, 2012.

Fauve, A., and C. Gintrac. "Production de l'espace urbain et mise en scène du pouvoir dans deux capitales 'présidentielles' d'Asie Centrale." *L'espace politique* 8, no. 2 (2009).

Foot, R. "Chinese Strategies in a US-Hegemonic Global Order: Accommodating and Hedging." *International Affairs* 82, no. 1 (2006): 77–94.

Freij, H. Y. "State Interests vs. the *Umma*: Iranian Policy in Central Asia." *Middle East Journal* 50, no. 1 (1996): 71–83.

Freinkman, L., E. Polyakov, and C. Revenco. *Trade Performance and Regional Integration of the CIS Countries.* Washington, DC: World Bank, 2004.

Frolenkov, V. S. *Sovremennye torgovo-ekonomicheskie otnosheniia KNR s tsentral'noaziatskimi stranami-chlenami ShOS i Turkmenistanom.* Moscow: Institut Dal'nego Vostoka RAN, 2009.

Fuller, G. E., and I. O. Lesser. *Turkey's New Geopolitics: From the Balkans to Western China.* Boulder, CO: Westview Press, 1993.

Fumagalli, M. "The 'Food-Energy-Water' Nexus in Central Asia: Regional Implications of and the International Response to the Crises in Tajikistan." Europe-Central Asia Monitoring Policy Brief, no. 2, October 2008.

———. "Food Security in Central Asia: A Priority for Western Engagement." *The Central Asia and Caucasus Analyst*, September 15, 2008.

Garcia, D. *Le pays où Bouygues est roi*. Paris: Danger Public, 2006.

Garver, J. W. "Development of China's Overland Transportation Links with Central, South-West, and South Asia." *China Quarterly*, no. 185 (2006): 1–22.

Gauchon, P. *Le monde: Manuel de géopolitique et de géoéconomie*. Paris: PUF, 2008.

Gavrilis, G. "Beyond the Border Management Programme for Central Asia (BOMCA)." Europe-Central Asia Monitoring Policy Brief, no. 11, 2009.

———. "Central Asia's Border Woes & the Impact of International Assistance." Open Society Foundations Occasional Paper Series, May 2012.

———. *The Dynamics of Interstate Boundaries*. Cambridge: Cambridge University Press, 2008.

Gill, B. *Rising Star: China's New Security Diplomacy*. Washington, DC: Brookings Institution Press, 2007.

Gintrac, C., and A. Fénot. *Achgabat, une capitale ostentatoire: Autocratie et urbanisme au Turkménistan*. Paris: L'Harmattan, 2006.

Giragosian, R., and R. N. McDermott. "U.S. Military Engagement in Central Asia: 'Great Game' or 'Great Gain'?" *Central Asia and the Caucasus*, no. 1 (2004): 53–61.

Giuli, M. "Nabucco Pipeline and the Turkmenistan Conundrum." *Caucasian Review of International Affairs* 2, no. 3 (2008): 124–32.

Gleason, G. "Russia and the Politics of the Central Asian Electricity Grid." *Problems of Post-Communism* 50, no. 3 (2003): 42–52.

———. "The Uzbek Expulsion of U.S. Forces and Realignment in Central Asia." *Problems of Post-Communism* 53, no. 2 (2006): 49–60.

Global Witness. "Risky Business: Kazakhstan, Kazakhmys PLC and the London Stock Exchange." Global Witness Report, July 2010.

Goldstein, A. *Rising to the Challenge: China's Grand Strategy and International Security*. Stanford: Stanford University Press, 2005.

Golodniuk, I. "Financial Systems and Financial Reforms in CIS Countries." Center for Social and Economic Research (CASE) Network Studies and Analyses, no. 306, Warsaw, 2005.

Gresh, G. "Promoting Prosperity: The Islamic Development Bank and the Rise of Islamic Banking and Finance in Central Asia." *Central Asia and the Caucasus*, no. 1 (2008): 135–46.

Grigoriou C. "Landlockedness, Infrastructure, and Trade: New Estimates for Central Asian Countries." World Bank Development Research Group Policy Research Working Paper, no. 4335, August 2007.

Grodsky, B. "Direct Pressures for Human Rights in Uzbekistan: Understanding the US Bargaining Position." *Central Asian Survey* 23, nos. 3–4 (2004): 327–44.

Guliyev, F., and N. Akhrarkhodjaeva. "The Trans-Caspian Energy Route: Cronyism, Competition, and Cooperation in Kazakh Oil Export." *Energy Policy* 37, no. 8 (2009): 3171–82.

———. "Transportation of Kazakhstani Oil via the Caspian Sea (TKOC): Arrangements, Actors, and Interests." RussCasp Working Paper, Jacobs University, Bremen, 2008.

Gullette, D. "Resurrecting an Energy Tariff Policy in Kyrgyzstan." OSCE Academy and Geneva Centre for Security Central Asia Security Policy Brief, no. 1, 2010.

Guzzardi, J. E., and M. J. Mullenbach. "The Politics of Seeking a Permanent Seat on the United Nations Security Council: An Analysis of the Case of Japan." *Midsouth Political Science Review* 9 (2007–2008): 35–76.

Haghayeghi, M. *Islam and Politics in Central Asia*. New York: Palgrave Macmillan, 1996.

Hakan Yavuz, M., and J. L. Esposito. *Turkish Islam and the Secular State: The Gülen Movement*. Syracuse, NY: Syracuse University Press, 2003.

Hale, E. "Regime Cycles: Democracy, Autocracy, and Revolution in Post-Soviet Eurasia." *World Politics* 58 (October): 133–65.

Hanks R. *Global Security Watch—Central Asia.* Santa Barbara, CA: Praeger, 2010.

Hanova, S. "Perspectives on the SCO: Images and Discourses." *China and Eurasia Forum Quarterly* 7, no. 3 (2009): 63–82.

Hartog, M., ed. *Security Sector Reform in Central Asia: Exploring Needs and Possibilities.* Groningen: CESS, 2010.

Harwood, C. S., A. L. Demain, and J. D. Wall, eds. *Bioenergy.* Washington, DC: ASM Press, 2008.

Hashimoto, H. "Evolving Roles of LNG and Asian Economies in the Global Natural Gas Markets." Advance Summit Paper from the 2011 Pacific Energy Summit, February 21–23, 2011, Jakarta, Indonesia.

Heathershaw, J. "Tajikistan Amidst Globalization: State Failure or State Transformation?" *Central Asian Survey* 30, no. 1 (2011): 147–68.

———. "Worlds Apart: The Making and Remaking of Geopolitical Space in the U.S.-Uzbekistani Strategic Partnership." *Central Asian Survey* 26, no. 1 (2007): 123–40.

Hedenskog, J., and R. L. Larsson. *Russian Leverage on the CIS and the Baltic States.* Stockholm: Swedish Defense Research Agency, 2007.

Hermann, W., and J. F. Linn, eds. *Central Asia and the Caucasus: At the Crossroads of Eurasia in the Twenty-First Century.* Thousand Oaks, CA: SAGE, 2011.

Hill, F. "In Search of Great Russia: Elites, Ideas, Power, the State, and the Pre-Revolutionary Past in the New Russia, 1991–1996." PhD diss., Harvard University, 1998.

———. "A Not-So-Grand Strategy: U.S. Policy in the Caucasus and Central Asia Since 1991." *Brookings,* February 1, 2001. http://www.brookings.edu/articles/2001/02foreignpolicy_hill.aspx.

Hill, F., and K. Jones. "Fear of Democracy or Revolution: The Reaction to Andijan." *Washington Quarterly* 29, no. 3 (2006): 111–25.

Hodgson, S. "Strategic Water Resources in Central Asia: In Search of a New International Legal Order." Europe-Central Asia Monitoring Policy Brief, no. 14, May 2010.

Hopkirk, P. *The Great Game: The Struggle for Empire in Central Asia.* New York: Kodansha International, 1992.

Humphrey, C. *The Unmaking of Soviet Life: Everyday Economies after Socialism.* Ithaca, NY: Cornell University Press, 2002.

Hunter, S. "Iran's Pragmatic Regional Policy." *Journal of International Affairs* 56, no. 2 (2003): 133–47.

Ibraimov S. "China-Central Asia Trade Relations: Economic and Social Patterns." *China and Eurasia Forum Quarterly* 7, no. 1 (2009): 47–59.

Ilkhamov, A. "Divided Economy: Kolkhozes vs. Peasant Subsistence Farms in Uzbekistan." *Central Asia Monitor* 4 (2000): 5–14.

International Atomic Energy Agency. *Uranium 2003: Resources, Production, and Demand.* International Atomic Energy Agency and OECD, 2004.

International Crisis Group. "Central Asia: Water and Conflict." International Crisis Group Asia Report, no. 34, May 2002.

International Crisis Group. "Central Asia: What Role for the European Union?" International Crisis Group Asia Report, no. 113, 2006.

International Crisis Group. "The Curse of Cotton: Central Asia's Destructive Monoculture." International Crisis Group Asia Report, no. 93, February 2005.

International Crisis Group. "Tajikistan: On the Road to Failure." International Crisis Group Asia Report, no. 162, February 12, 2009.

International Crisis Group. "Uzbekistan: Europe's Sanctions Matter." International Crisis Group Asia Briefing, no. 54, November 2006.

International Energy Agency. "Perspectives on Caspian Oil and Gas Development." International Energy Agency Working Paper Series, December 2008.

Ipek, P. "The Role of Oil and Gas in Kazakhstan's Foreign Policy: Looking East or West?" *Europe-Asia Studies* 59, no. 7 (2007): 1179–99.

Ismailov, S., and B. Jarabik. "The EU and Uzbekistan: Short-Term Interests versus Long-Term Engagement." Europe-Central Asia Monitoring Policy Brief, no. 8, July 2009.

Itoh, S. *Russia Looks East: Energy Markets and Geopolitics in Northeast Asia*. Washington, DC: CSIS, 2011.

Iwashita, A., ed. *Eager Eyes Fixed on Eurasia*. Hokkaido: Slavic Research Center, Hokkaido University, 2007.

Jackson, N. J. *Russian Foreign Policy and the CIS: Theories, Debates, and Actions*. London: Routledge, 2003.

Jacquesson, S. *Pastoréalismes: Anthropologie historique des processus d'intégration chez les Kirghiz du Tian Shan intérieur*. Wiesbaden: Reichert, 2010.

Jaffrelot, C. *The Hindu Nationalist Movement in India*. New York: Columbia University Press, 1996.

Jefferson Institute. "Developing the Potential for Energy Efficiency and Alternative Energy in the Kyrgyz Republic." Report of the Jefferson Institute, Washington, DC, 2009.

Jones Luong, P., and E. Weinthal. *Oil Is Not a Curse: Ownership Structure and Institutions in Soviet Successor States*. Cambridge: Cambridge University Press, 2010.

Jonson, L. *Vladimir Putin and Central Asia: The Shaping of Russian Foreign Policy*. London: I.B. Tauris, 2004.

Joshi, N., ed. *Reconnecting India and Central Asia: Emerging Security and Economic Dimensions*. Washington, DC: The Central Asia-Caucasus Institute Silk Road Studies Program, 2010.

Jung, D., and W. Piccoli. *Turkey at the Crossroads: Ottoman Legacies and a Greater Middle East*. London: Zed Books, 2001.

Juraev, S. "Energy Emergency in Kyrgyzstan: Causes and Consequences." Europe-Central Asia Monitoring Policy Brief, no. 5, February 2009.

Kadatskaia, N. "Nemtsy v migratsionnom obmene mezhdu Kazakhstanom i Germaniei: Tendentsii i perspektivy." Central Asian Migration Management and International Cooperation (CAMMIC) Working Papers, no. 5, Toyama City, Japan, 2008.

Kalyuzhnova, Y. *The Kazakhstani Economy: Independence and Transition*. London: St. Martin's Press, 1998.

Kaminski, B., and G. Raballand. "Re-Export Flows through Bazaars in Kyrgyzstan: Magnitude and Implications for Country's External Performance." Unpublished Paper, 2010.

Kan, G. "Koreans in Kazakhstan: Past, Present, Future." *Central Asia and the Caucasus* 13, no. 1 (2002): 139–47.

Kandiyoti, D., ed. *The Cotton Sector in Central Asia: Economic Policy and Development Challenges*. London: School of Oriental and African Studies, 2007.

———, ed., *Invisible to the World? The Dynamics of Forced Child Labour in the Cotton Sector of Uzbekistan*. London: School of Oriental and African Studies, 2009.

Kapur, H. *The Soviet Union and the Emerging Nations: A Case Study of Soviet Policy Towards India*. London: Graduate Institute of International Studies, Geneva, 1972.

Karaev, Z. "Water Diplomacy in Central Asia." *Middle East Review of International Affairs* 9, no. 1 (2005): 63–69.

Karagiannis, E. *Political Islam in Central Asia: The Challenge of Hizb ut-Tahrir*. London: Routledge, 2010.

Karimov, I. *Turkistan, nash obshchii dom*. Tashkent: Uzbekiston, 1995.

Karl, T. L. *The Paradox of Plenty: Oil Booms and Petro-States*. Berkeley: University of California Press, 1997.

Kassenova, N. "Aide au développement: La percée chinoise au Tadjikistan et au Kirghizstan." Report of the Institut français des relations internationales (IFRI), Russie.NEI.Visions, no. 36, January 2009.

————. "Kazakhstan and the South Caucasus Corridor in the Wake of the Georgia-Russia War." Europe-Central Asia Monitoring Policy Brief, no. 3, 2009.

Kassenova, T. "Kazakhstan's 'Nuclear Renaissance'." *Stair* 3, no. 2 (2009): 51–74.

Kasymbekova, V. "Uranovyi khvost." *Oasis*, no. 10 (2009): 1–3.

Kavalski, E., ed. *The New Central Asia: The Regional Impact of International Actors.* Singapore: World Scientific Publishing, 2010.

"Kazakhstan: Gold Mining Industry." Kazakhstan Investment Report, July 2003.

Kazakhstansko-iaponskoe sotrudnichestvo: Sostoianie i perspektivy. Almaty: KISI, 2007.

Kellner, T. "Le Dragon et la tulipe: Les relations sino-afghanes dans la période post-9/11." Brussels Institute of Contemporary China Studies, Asia Paper 4, no. 1, 2009.

————. *L'Occident de la Chine: Pékin et la nouvelle Asie centrale, 1991–2001.* Paris: PUF, 2008.

Kenisarin, M. "The Energy Sector of Uzbekistan: Present State and Problems." *Central Asia and the Caucasus*, no. 3 (2004): 172–8.

Khalova, G. O. "The Banking System and Monetary Policy in Turkmenistan." *Russian and East European Finance and Trade* 35, no. 5 (1999): 45–74.

Kiil-Nielsen, N. "Draft Report on the State of Implementation of the EU Strategy for Central Asia." European Parliament Committee on Foreign Affairs, August 2011. http://www.europarl.europa.eu/sides/getDoc.do?pubRef=-//EP//NONSGML+COMPARL+PE-469.951+02+DOC+PDF+V0//EN&language=EN.

King, A., and J. Townsend. "Is Japan's Interest in Central Asia Stagnating?" *The Central Asia-Caucasus Institute Analyst*, May 9, 2007. http://www.cacianalyst.org/?q=node/4685.

King, C., and N. J. Melvin. *Nations Abroad: Diaspora Politics and International Relations in the Former Soviet Union.* Boulder, CO: Westview Press, 1999.

Korinek, J., and P. Sourdin. "Maritime Transport Costs and Their Impact on Trade." Report of the Organization for Economic Co-operation and Development, Paris, August 2009.

Kramer, M. "Russian Policy Toward the Commonwealth of Independent States: Recent Trends and Future Prospects." *Problems of Post-Communism* 55, no. 6 (2008): 3–19.

Krueger, A. O. *Economic Policy Reforms and the Indian Economy.* Chicago: University of Chicago Press, 2002.

Kuchins, A., T. Sanderson, and D. Gordon. *The Northern Distribution Network and the Modern Silk Road.* Washington, DC: CSIS, 2009.

Lai, H. *The Domestic Sources of China's Foreign Policy: Regimes, Leadership, Priorities, and Process.* London: Routledge, 2010.

Laitin, D. *Identity in Formation: The Russian-Speaking Populations in the Near Abroad.* Ithaca, NY: Cornell University Press, 1998.

Laldjebaev, M. "The Water-Energy Puzzle in Central Asia: The Tajikistan Perspective." *International Journal of Water Resources Development* 26, no. 1 (2010): 23–36.

Landau, J. M. *Pan-Turkism in Turkey: From Irredentism to Cooperation.* London: C. Hurst, 1981.

Larrabee, F.S. *Foreign and Security Policy Decisionmaking Under Yeltsin.* Santa Monica, CA: Rand, 1997.

Laruelle, M. "Beyond the Afghan Trauma: Russia's Return to Afghanistan." Jamestown Foundation Occasional Paper, August 2009.

————. "The Growing Illiteracy in Central Asia: A Challenge for the EU." Europe-Central Asia Monitoring Commentary, no. 6, December 2009.

————. *In the Name of the Nation: Nationalism and Politics in Contemporary Russia.* New York: Palgrave Macmillan, 2009.

————. "Involving Central Asia in Afghanistan's Future—What Can Europe Do?" Europe-Central Asia Monitoring Policy Brief, no. 20, August 2011.

————. "Is Kazakhstan Disengaging from Georgia?" *The Central Asia-Caucasus Analyst*, October 15, 2008: 3–4.

————, ed. *Migration and Social Upheaval as the Face of Globalization in Central Asia.* London: Brill, 2013.

————. *Russian Eurasianism: An Ideology of Empire.* Washington, DC: Woodrow Wilson Press/Johns Hopkins University Press, 2008.

————. *Russian Policy on Central Asia and the Role of Russian Nationalism.* Washington, DC: The Central Asia-Caucasus Institute Silk Road Studies Program, 2008.

————. "Russia's Perceptions and Strategies in Afghanistan and Their Consequences for NATO." NATO Research Paper, no. 69, November 2011.

Laruelle, M., J. Huchet, S. Peyrouse, and B. Balci, eds. *China and India in Central Asia: A New "Great Game"?* New York: Palgrave Macmillan, 2010.

Laruelle M., and S. Peyrouse. *The "Chinese Question" in Central Asia: Domestic Order, Social Change, and the Chinese Factor.* New York and London: Columbia University Press/ Hurst, 2012.

————. "Cross-Border Minorities as Cultural and Economic Mediators Between China and Central Asia." *China and Eurasia Forum Quarterly* 7, no. 1 (2009): 93–119.

————, eds. *Mapping Central Asia: Indian Perceptions and Strategies.* Burlington, VT: Ashgate, 2011.

————. "The Militarization of the Caspian Sea: 'Great Games' and 'Small Games' over the Caspian Fleets." *China and Eurasia Forum Quarterly* 7, no. 2 (2009): 17–35.

Lee, Y. "Toward a New International Regime for the Caspian Sea." *Problems of Post-Communism* 52, no. 3 (2005): 37–48.

Legvold, R., ed. *Thinking Strategically: The Major Powers, Kazakhstan, and the Central Asian Nexus.* Cambridge: MIT Press, 2003.

Len, C. "Japan's Central Asian Diplomacy: Motivations, Implications, and Prospects for the Region." *Central Asia and the Caucasus* 3, no. 3 (2005): 127–49.

Len, C., T. Uyama, and H. Tetsuya, eds. *Japan's Silk Road Diplomacy: Paving the Road Ahead.* Washington, DC: Central Asia-Caucasus Institute, 2008.

Leonard, M. *What Does China Think?* London: Fourth Estate, 2008.

Lerman, Z. "Agricultural Development in Uzbekistan: The Effect of Ongoing Reforms." Hebrew University of Jerusalem Discussion Paper, no. 7, 2008.

————. *Tajikistan: An Overview of Land and Farm Structure Reforms.* Hebrew University of Jerusalem Discussion Paper, no. 2.08, 2008.

Lerman, Z., C. Csáki, and G. Feder. *Agriculture in Transition: Land Policies and Evolving Farm Structures in Post-Soviet Countries.* Lanham, MD: Lexington Books, 2004.

Lerman, Z., and I. Stanchin. "Institutional Changes in Turkmenistan's Agriculture: Impacts on Productivity and Rural Incomes." *Eurasian Geography and Economics* 45, no. 1 (2004): 60–72.

Leroi, R. "La filière du coton en Asie centrale: Le poids de l'héritage." *Le Courrier des Pays de l'Est,* no. 1027 (2002): 40–51.

Les aides extérieures de la Turquie. Istanbul: DPT, March 1998.

Levine, R. M. "The Mineral Industry in Kazakhstan." In *Minerals Yearbook 2009.* Reston, VA: US Geological Survey, 2011.

————. "The Mineral Industry in Tajikistan." *Minerals Yearbook 2009.* Reston, VA: US Geological Survey, 2011.

Levine, R. M., and G. J. Wallace. *Minerals Yearbook 2005.* Reston, VA: US Geological Survey, 2007.

————. *Minerals Yearbook 2006: Commonwealth of Independent States.* Reston, VA: US Geological Survey, 2009.

Li, J. "China's Rising Demand for Minerals and Emerging Global Norms and Practices in the Mining Industry." USAID/Foundation for Environmental Security and Sustainability Working Paper, no. 2, 2006.

Li X., Z. Wang, and N. Kerimbay. "Cooperative Study on Eco-tourism Based on Transport

Corridor in China and Kazakhstan," ADB-CAREC Research Grants Program, June 2008.

Lieven, A. *Chechnya: Tombstone of Russian Power*. New Haven: Yale University Press, 1998.

Linn J., "First Eurasia Emerging Markets Forum: 'Connecting Central Asia with the World'." *Global Journal of Emerging Market Economies*, no. 1 (2009): 241–58.

Linn J., and O. Pidufala, "Lessons from Central Asia: Experience with Regional Economic Cooperation." Wolfensohn Center for Development Working Paper, no. 4, October 2008.

Lo, B. *Axis of Convenience: Moscow, Beijing, and the New Geopolitics*. Washington, DC: Brookings Institution Press, 2008.

———. *Vladimir Putin and the Evolution of Russian Foreign Policy*. London: Royal Institute of International Affairs, 2003.

Longhurst, K., and S. Nies. "Recasting Relations with the Neighbours—Prospects for the Eastern Partnership." Report of the Institut français des relations internationales (IFRI), Europe Vision, no. 4, February 2009.

Lun Y. H. V., Kee-hung Lai, and T. C. E. Cheng. *Shipping and Logistics Management*. New York: Springer, 2010.

Luomi, M. "Sectarian Identities or Geopolitics? The Regional Shia-Sunni Divide in the Middle East." Finnish Institute of International Affairs Working Paper, no. 56, 2008.

Mackerras, C., and M. Clarke, eds. *China, Xinjiang, and Central Asia: History, Transition, and Crossborder Interaction into the Twenty-First century*. New York: Routledge, 2009.

Mahapatra, D. A. *Central Eurasia: Geopolitics, Compulsions, and Connections; Factoring India*. New Delhi: Lancer's Books, 2008.

Majidov, S. "World Bank Advises Tajikistan to Halt Construction of Hydropower Station." *The Central Asia-Caucasus Analyst* 13, no. 16 (2011): 15–16.

Makhonina, M. *Voenno-politicheskoe sotrudnichestvo mezhdu Rossiei i Tadzhikistanom, 1993–1999*. Dushanbe: Akademiia Nauk, 1999.

Maleki, A. "Iran and Turan: Apropos of Iran's Relations with Central Asia and the Caucasian Republics." *Central Asia and the Caucasus*, no. 5 (2001): 89–97.

Marat, E. *Labor Migration in Central Asia: Implications of the Global Economic Crisis*. Washington, DC: The Central Asia-Caucasus Institute and Silk Road Studies Program, 2009.

———. "Nationalization of Kumtor Gold Mine Sparks Controversy in Kyrgyzstan." *The Central Asia-Caucasus Analyst* 9, no. 10 (2007): 16–17.

———. "Soviet Military Legacy and Regional Security Cooperation in Central Asia." *China and Eurasia Forum Quarterly* 5, no. 1 (2007): 83–114.

Mastny, V., and R. Craig Nation, eds. *Turkey between East and West: New Challenges for a Rising Regional Power*. Boulder, CO: Westview Press, 1996.

McDermott, R. N. *Kazakhstan's Defense Policy: An Assessment of the Trends*. Carlisle, PA: Strategic Studies Institute, US Army War College, 2009.

———. "United States and NATO Military Cooperation with Kazakhstan: The Need for a New Approach." *Journal of Slavic Military Studies* 21, no. 4 (2008): 615–41.

McGlinchey, E. *Chaos, Violence, Dynasty: Politics and Islam in Central Asia*. Pittsburgh, PA: Pittsburgh University Press, 2011.

Megoran, N. "The Critical Geopolitics of the Uzbekistan-Kyrgyzstan Ferghana Valley Boundary Dispute, 1999–2000." *Political Geography* 23 (2004): 731–64.

———. "Framing Andijon, Narrating the Nation: Islam Karimov's Account of the Events of 13 May 2005." *Central Asian Survey* 27, no. 1 (2008): 15–31.

Megoran N., G. Raballand, and J. Bouyjou. "Performance, Representation, and the Economics of Border Control in Uzbekistan." *Geopolitics* 10, no. 4 (2005): 712–40.

Megoran, N., and S. Sharapova, eds. "On the Centenary of Halford Mackinder's Geographical Pivot of History." *Central Asia and the Caucasus* 34, no. 4 (2005).

Melvin, N., ed. *Engaging Central Asia: The European Union's New Strategy in the Heart of Eurasia.* Brussels: Centre for European Policy Studies, 2008.

Melvin, N., and J. Boonstra. "The EU Strategy for Central Asia @ Year One." Europe-Central Asia Monitoring Policy Brief, no. 1, October 2008.

Mendikulova, G. M., and B. Zh. Atanbaeva. *Istoriia migratsii mezhdu Kazakhstanom i Kitaem v 1860–1960-e gg.* Almaty: Izd-vo SaGa, 2008.

Mesamed, V. "Iran: Ten Years in Post-Soviet Central Asia." *Central Asia and the Caucasus,* no. 1 (2002): 27–35.

Mesbahi, M. "Tajikistan, Iran, and the International Politics of the 'Islamic Factor'." *Central Asian Survey* 16, no. 2 (1997): 141–58.

Meyer, K., and S. B. Brysac. *Tournament of Shadows: The Great Game and the Race for Empire in Central Asia.* Washington, DC: Counterpoint, 1999.

Millward, J. A. *Eurasian Crossroads: A History of Xinjiang.* New York: Columbia University Press, 2007.

Mizuno, M. "The Finance in the Capital Market and Credit Rating in Uzbekistan." Research Paper of the Nihon University Center for China and Asian Studies, Tokyo, 2009.

Mojtahed-Zadeh, P., and M. R. Hafeznia. "Perspectives on the Caspian Sea Dilemma: An Iranian Construct." *Eurasian Geography and Economics* 44, no. 8 (2003): 607–16.

Morgan, G. *Anglo-Russian Rivalry in Central Asia, 1810–1895.* London: Frank Cass, 1981.

Muzalevsky, R. "India Fails to Gain a Military Foothold in Tajikistan." *The Central Asia-Caucasus Analyst* 13, no. 2 (2011): 12–14.

Myant, M., and J. Drahokoupil. "International Integration and the Structure of Exports in Central Asian Republics." *Eurasian Geography and Economics* 49, no. 5 (2009): 604–22.

Nadyrov, Sh. "Sin'tszian-uigurskii avtonomnyi raion v dinamike ekonomicheskikh i politicheskikh otnoshenii RK i KNR." *Kazakhstan-Spektr,* no. 1 (2006): 14–25.

Najman, B., G. Raballand, and R. Pomfret, eds. *The Economics and Politics of Oil in the Caspian Basin: The Redistribution of Oil Revenues in Azerbaijan and Central Asia.* London: Routledge, 2007.

Naseleniia Respubliki Uzbekistan 2005. Tashkent: Goskomstat, 2005.

Naumkin, V. V. *Radical Islam in Central Asia: Between Pen and Rifle.* Lanham, MD: Rowman & Littlefield, 2005.

Naumov, Iu. V., I. L. Pugach, and Iu. B. Yusupov. "Uzbekistan's Textile Industry: How to Implement Development Potential?" United Nations Development Programme Policy Brief 14, no. 1 (2010).

Nazarbaev, N. *Evraziiskii soiuz: Idei, praktika, perspektivy, 1994–1997.* Moscow: Fond sodeistviia razvitiiu sotsial'nykh i politicheskikh nauk, 1997.

Nazpary, J. *Post-Soviet Chaos: Violence and Dispossession in Kazakhstan.* London: Pluto Press, 2002.

Nichol, J. "Central Asia: Regional Developments and Implications for U.S. Interests." Congressional Research Service Report, October 12, 2011.

———. "Central Asia: Regional Developments and Implications for U.S. Interests." Congress Research Service, May 31, 2012.

———. "Central Asia's New States: Political Developments and Implications for U.S. Interests." Congressional Research Service Issue Brief IB93108, May 18, 2001.

———. "Central Asia's Security: Issues and Implications for US Interests." Congressional Research Service Report, February 2009.

———. "Turkmenistan: Recent Developments and U.S. Interests." Congressional Research Service Report, May 26, 2011.

Nikitin, A. "Post-Soviet Military-Political Integration: The Collective Security Treaty Organization and Its Relations with the EU and NATO." *China and Eurasia Forum Quarterly* 5, no. 1 (2007): 35–44.

Nurgaliev, M., and T. Shaymergenov. "Japanese Diplomacy Makes New Headway in Central

Asia: Its Problems, Expectations, and Prospects." *Central Asia and the Caucasus* 6 (2007): 125–35.

Nygren, B. *The Rebuilding of Greater Russia: Putin's Foreign Policy towards the CIS Countries.* London: Routledge, 2007.

Ohayon I. "La déportation des peuples punis en Asie centrale." in *Le XXe siècle des guerres,* edited by P. Causarano, V. Galimi, 172–81, Paris: Éd. de l'Atelier, 2004, 172–81.

Olcott, M. B. "KAZMUNAIGAZ: Kazakhstan's National Oil and Gas Company." Paper of the James A. Baker III Institute for Public Policy, Rice University, 2007.

———. "A New Direction for U.S. Policy in the Caspian Region." Working Paper of the Carnegie Endowment for International Peace, February 2009.

Omilecheva, M. Y. "Western and Central Asian Perspectives on Democracy and Democratization." IREX Scholar Research Brief, August 2011.

Ong, R. "China's Security Interests in Central Asia." *Central Asian Survey* 24, no. 4 (2005): 425–39.

Önis, Z. "Multiple Faces of the 'New' Turkish Foreign Policy: Underlying Dynamics and a Critique." *Insight Turkey* 13, no. 1 (2011): 47–65.

Orr, M. J. "The Russian Garrison in Tajikistan—201st Gachina Twice Red Banner Motor Rifle Division." Conflict Studies Research Center Occasional Brief 85, 2011.

Palmer, N. J. "Economic Transition and the Struggle for Local Control in Ecotourism Development: The Case of Kyrgyzstan." *Journal of Ecotourism* 5, nos. 1–2 (2006): 40–61.

Papava, V. "Georgia's Economic Role in the South Caucasus." *Problems of Economic Transition* 48, no. 4 (2005): 84–92.

Paramonov, V., and O. Stolpovski. *Russia and Central Asia: Bilateral Cooperation in the Defence Sector.* Shrivenham: Defence Academy of the United Kingdom, 2008.

———. *Russia and Central Asia: Multilateral Security Cooperation.* Shrivenham: Defence Academy of the United Kingdom, 2008.

Paramonov, V., and A. Strokov. *Economic Involvement of Russia and China in Central Asia.* Swindon: Defence Academy of the United Kingdom, 2007.

———. *Ekonomicheskoe prisutstvie Rossii i Kitaia v Tsentral'noi Azii.* Shrivenham: Defence Academy of the United Kingdom, 2007.

———. *The Evolution of Russia's Central Asia Policy.* Shrivenham: Defence Academy of the United Kingdom, 2008.

———. *Russia-Central Asia: Existing and Potential Oil and Gas Trade.* Shrivenham: Defence Academy of the United Kingdom, 2008.

———. *Russian Oil and Gas Projects and Investments in Central Asia.* Shrivenham: Defence Academy of the United Kingdom, 2008.

Parkash M. "Connecting Central Asia: A Road Map for Regional Cooperation." Asian Development Bank Report, Manila, 2006.

Parker, J. W. "Russia's Revival: Ambitions, Limitations, and Opportunities for the United States." Institute for National Strategic Studies Strategic Perspectives, no. 3, 2011.

Parker, S. *The Last Soviet Republic: Alexander Lukashenko's Belarus.* Bloomington, IN: Trafford Publishing, 2007.

Peck, A. *Economic Development in Kazakhstan: The Role of Large Enterprises and Foreign Investment.* London: RoutledgeCurzon, 2004.

———. "Industrial Privatization in Kazakhstan: The Results of Government Sales of the Principal Enterprises to Foreign Investors." *Russian and East European Finance and Trade* 38, no. 1 (2002): 31–58.

Perovic, J. "From Disengagement to Active Economic Competition: Russia's Return to the South Caucasus and Central Asia." *Demokratizatsiya. Journal of Post–Soviet Democratization.* no. 1 (2005): 61–85.

Peyrouse, S. "Business and Trade Relationship between the EU and Central Asia." Europe-Central Asia Monitoring Working Paper, no. 1, 2009.

———. "The Central Asian Armies Facing the Challenge of Formation." *The Journal of Power Institutions in Post-Soviet Societies*, no. 11 (2010): 2–16.

———. "The Central Asian Power Grid in Danger?" *The Central Asia and Caucasus Analyst* 11, no. 23 (2009): 9–11.

———. *The Economic Aspects of the Chinese-Central-Asia Rapprochement.* Washington, DC: The Central Asia-Caucasus Institute Silk Road Studies Program, 2007.

———. "Economic Trends as an Identity Marker? The Pamiri Trade Niche with China and Afghanistan." *Problems of Post-Communism* 59, no. 4 (2012): 3–14.

———. "Flowing Downstream: The Sino-Kazakh Water Dispute." *China Brief* 7, no. 10 (2007): 7–10.

———. "The Growing Trade Stakes of the Chinese-Kyrgyz-Uzbek Railway Project." *The Central Asia-Caucasus Analyst* 11, no. 5 (2009): 9–12.

———. "The Growth of Commercial Exchanges Between Central Europe and Central Asia." *Central Asia and Caucasus Analyst*, April 22 (2009) 6–8.

———. "The Hydroelectric Sector in Central Asia and the Growing Role of China." *China and Eurasia Forum Quarterly* 5, no. 2 (2007): 131–48.

———. "The Kazakh Neopatrimonial Regime and Its Actors: Balancing Uncertainties Among the 'Family,' Oligarchs and Technocrats," *Demokratizatsiya. The Journal of Post-Soviet Democratization*, no. 4 (2012): 345–37.

———. "Is There Any Unity to the Trans-Caspian Region? The Economic Relations Between Central Asia and the Caucasus." *Asia-Europe Journal* 7, no. 3 (2009): 543–57.

———. "Military Cooperation between China and Central Asia: Breakthrough, Limits, and Prospects." *China Brief* 10, no. 5 (2010): 10–14.

———. "Rare Earth Metals in Central Asia and Mongolia: A Promising but Paradoxical Agenda." *Central Asia Economic Paper*, no. 1, August 2012.

———. "Russia-Central Asia: Advances and Shortcomings of the Military Partnership." In *Central Asian Security Trends: Views from Europe and Russia*, S. Blank, ed. Carlisle, PA: Strategic Studies Institute, US Army War College, 2011, 1–34.

———. "The Russian Minority in Central Asia: Migration, Politics, and Language." Kennan Institute Occasional Papers, no. 297, 2008.

———. "Shiism in Central Asia: The Religious, Political, and Geopolitical Factors." *Central Asia and Caucasus Analyst* 11, no. 10 (2009): 9–11.

———. "Sino-Kazakh Relations: A Nascent Strategic Partnership." *China Brief* 8, no. 21 (2008): 11–15.

———. "South Korea's Advances into Central Asia." *The Central Asia-Caucasus Analyst*, September 1, 2010, 6–8.

———. *Turkmenistan: Strategies of Power, Dilemmas of Development.* Armonk, NY: M.E. Sharpe, 2011.

Peyrouse, S., and S. Ibraimov. "Iran's Central Asia Temptations." *Current Trends in Islamist Ideology* 10 (2010): 82–101.

Pi, Y. "China's Boundary Issues with the Former Soviet Union." *Issues and Studies* 28, no. 7 (1992): 63–75.

Piatigorsky, J., and J. Sapir, eds. *Le grand jeu—XIXe siècle, les enjeux géopolitiques de l'Asie centrale.* Paris: Autrement, 2009.

Pomfret, R. "Central Asia and the Global Economic Crisis." Europe-Central Asia Monitoring Policy Brief, no. 7, June 2009.

———. *The Central Asian Economies Since Independence.* Princeton, NJ: Princeton University Press, 2006.

———. "Kazakhstan's Economy Since Independence: Does the Oil Boom Offer a Second Chance for Sustainable Development?" *Europe-Asia Studies* 57, no. 6 (2005): 859–76.

———. "Turkmenistan: From Communism to Nationalism by Gradual Economic Reform." *Moct-Most*, no. 11 (2001): 165–76.

————. "Turkmenistan's Foreign Policy." *China and Eurasia Forum Quarterly* 6, no. 4 (2008): 19–34.

————. "Using Energy Resources to Diversify the Economy: Agricultural Price and Distortion in Kazakhstan." Center for Social and Economic Research (CASE) Network Studies and Analyses, no. 335, Warsaw, 2007.

Prikhodko, D. "Grain Markets in Kazakhstan, the Russian Federation, and Ukraine." Report of the Food and Agriculture Organization of the United Nations, New York, May 2009.

Purtas, F. "The Greater Central Asia Partnership Initiative and Its Impacts on Eurasian Security." *Journal of Central Asian and Caucasian Studies* 3, no. 5 (2008): 115–30.

Raballand, G., and A. Andrésy. "Why Should Trade between Central Asia and China Continue to Expand?" *Asia-Europe Journal* 5, no. 2 (2007): 235–52.

Raballand, G., and B. Kaminski. "Entrepôt for Chinese Consumer Goods in Central Asia: The Puzzle of Re-Exports Through Kyrgyz Bazaars." *Eurasian Geography and Economics* 50, no. 5 (2009): 581–90.

————. "La Déferlante économique chinoise et ses conséquences en Asie centrale." *Monde chinois*, no. 11 (2007): 129–34.

Raballand G., A. Kunth, and R. Auty. "Central Asia's Transport Cost Burden and Its Impact on Trade." *Economic Systems* 29, no. 1 (2005): 6–31.

Radin, C. J. "Analysis: The US-Pakistan relationship and the Critical Factor of Supply." *Long War Journal*, December 4, 2011.

Radnitz, S. *Weapons of the Wealthy: Predatory Regimes and Elite-Led Protests in Central Asia.* Ithaca, NY: Cornell University Press, 2010.

Rahaman, M. M., and O. Varis, eds. *Central Asian Waters: Social, Economic, Environmental, and Governance Puzzle.* Helsinki: Helsinki University of Technology, 2008.

Rangsimaporn, P. *Russia as an Aspiring Great Power in East Asia: Perceptions and Policies from Yeltsin to Putin.* New York: Palgrave Macmillan, 2009.

Razumkov Centre for National Security and Defence. "GUUAM as a Regional Union: The Approaches and Assessments." Razumkov Centre for National Security and Defence Paper, no. 7, 2001.

Reddaway, P., and D. Glinski. *The Tragedy of Russia's Reforms: Market Bolshevism Against Democracy.* Washington, DC: United States Institute of Peace Press, 2001.

Reeves M. "Fixing the Border: On the Affective Life of the State in Southern Kyrgyzstan." *Environment and Planning D: Society and Space* 29, no. 5 (2011): 905–23.

————. "Materialising State Space: 'Creeping Migration' and Territorial Integrity in Southern Kyrgyzstan." *Europe-Asia Studies* 61, no. 7 (2009): 1277–1313.

Renouvin, B. "La conception ismaélienne du développement: L'exemple du Pamir." *Mondes en développement* 132 (2005): 129–38.

Research in China Institute. "Central Asia Telecom Industry Report, 2008–2009." Report of the Research in China Institute, Beijing, 2009.

Ross, R. S., and A. I. Johnston, eds. *New Directions in the Study of China's Foreign Policy.* Stanford: Stanford University Press, 2006.

Ross, R. S., and F. Zhu, eds. *China's Ascent: Power, Security, and the Future of International Politics.* Ithaca, NY: Cornell University Press, 2008.

Rowe, D. "Agrarian Adaptations in Tajikistan: Land Reform, Water, and Law." *Central Asian Survey* 29, no. 2 (2010): 189–204.

Rumer, B., ed. *Central Asia: A Gathering Storm?* Armonk, NY: M.E. Sharpe, 2002.

Rumer, E., D. Trenin, and H. Zhao. *Central Asia: Views from Washington, Moscow, and Beijing.* Armonk, NY: M.E. Sharpe, 2007.

Rustemova A., "Political Economy of Central Asia: Initial Reflections on the Need for a New Approach." *Journal of Eurasian Studies* 2, no. 1 (2011): 30–39.

Ruziev, K., and D. Ghosh. "Banking Sector Development in Uzbekistan: A Case of Mixed Blessings?" *Problems of Economic Transition* 52, no. 2 (2009): 3–41.

Sagers, M. "Gold Production in Central Asia." *Post-Soviet Geography and Economics* 39, no. 3 (1998): 125–50.

———. "Turkmenistan's Gas Trade: The Case of Exports to Ukraine." *Post-Soviet Geography and Economics* 40, no. 2 (1999): 142–49.

Samubaldin, S. S. *Drakony i tigry Azii: Smozhet li kazakhstankii "bars" proiti ikh tropami?* Almaty: Gylym, 1998.

Saparmuratov, A., and A. Nurbekov. *Focus on Seed Programs: The Seed Industry in Turkmenistan.* Aleppo, Syria: WANA Seed Network Secretariat, 2010.

Schillinger, W. F. "Cropping Systems Research Needs in Uzbekistan: A Report to the World Bank." World Bank Reports, Washington, DC, 2003.

Schlyter B., ed. *Prospects for Democracy in Central Asia.* Istanbul: Swedish Research Institute, 2005.

Sengupta, A. *Heartlands of Eurasia: The Geopolitics of Political Space.* Lanham, MD: Lexington Books, 2009.

Sevcik, M. "Uranium Tailings in Kyrgyzstan: Catalyst for Cooperation and Confidence-Building?" *Nonproliferation Review* 10, no. 1 (2003): 147–54.

Shanahan, R. "Bad Moon Not Rising: The Myth of the Gulf Shi'a Crescent." Lowy Institute Analysis Paper, September 2008.

Shearman, P., ed. *Russian Foreign Policy Since 1990.* Boulder, CO: Westview Press, 1995.

Shkolnikov, V. D. "The 2010 OSCE Kazakhstan Chairmanship: Carrot Devoured, Results Missing." Europe-Central Asia Monitoring Policy Brief, no. 15, April 2011.

Simons, T. W., Jr. *Eurasia's New Frontiers: Young States, Old Societies, Open Futures.* Ithaca, NY: Cornell University Press, 2008.

Singh, M., ed. *India and Tajikistan: Revitalizing a Traditional Relationship.* Kolkata: Anamika Publishers and Distributors, 2003.

Singh Roy, M. "Pakistan's Strategies in Central Asia." *Strategic Analysis* 30, no. 4 (2006): 798–833.

———. "Shanghai Cooperation Organisation and Afghanistan: Scope and Limitation." Strategic Analysis 34, no. 4 (2010): 545–61.

———. "Strategic Importance of Turkmenistan for India." *Strategic Analysis* 25, no. 4 (2011): 661–82.

Singh, S., ed. *China-Pakistan Strategic Cooperation: Indian Perspectives.* New Delhi: Manohar, 2007.

Šír, J. "*Halk Maslahaty* in the Context of the Constitutional Evolution of Post-Soviet Turkmenistan." *Perspectives on European Politics and Society* 6, no. 2 (2005): 321–30.

———. "Turkmenistan—A Promised Land for Making Business? Macroeconomic Reforms Under Berdymukhammedov." *China and Eurasia Forum Quarterly* 8, no. 3 (2010): 67–92.

Spoor, M. "Cotton in Central Asia: 'Curse' or 'Foundation for Development'?" In *The Cotton Sector in Central Asia: Economic Policy and Development Challenges*, ed. D. Kandiyoti. London: School of Oriental and African Studies, 2007, 54–74.

———, ed. *The Political Economy of Rural Livelihoods in Transition Economies: Land, Peasants, and Rural Poverty in Transition.* London: Routledge, 2009.

Spoor, M., and A. Krutov. "The 'Power of Water' in a Divided Central Asia." *Perspectives on Global Development and Technology* 2, nos. 3–4 (2003): 593–614.

Spoor, M., and O. Visser. "The State of Agrarian Reform in the Former Soviet Union." *Europe-Asia Studies* 53, no. 6 (2001): 885–901.

Starr, S. F. *Afghanistan Beyond the Fog of Nation Building: Giving Economic Strategy a Chance.* Washington, DC: The Central Asia-Caucasus Institute Silk Road Studies Program, 2011.

———, ed. *Ferghana Valley: The Heart of Central Asia.* Armonk, NY: M.E. Sharpe, 2011.

———, ed. *The New Silk Roads: Transport and Trade in Greater Central Asia.* Washington, DC: Johns Hopkins University-SAIS, 2007.

———, ed. *Xinjiang: China's Muslim Borderland.* Armonk, NY: M.E. Sharpe, 2004.

Starr, S. F., and S. E. Cornell, eds. *Baku-Tbilisi-Ceyhan Pipeline: Oil Window to the West.* Uppsala: Silk Road Studies Program, 2005.

Starr S. F., and A. C. Kuchins. *The Key to Success in Afghanistan: A Modern Silk Road Strategy.* Washington, DC: The Central Asia-Caucasus Institute Silk Road Studies Program, 2010.

Stenga, J. "Demand and Challenges of Accessing Saving Products in Tajikistan Microfinance Institutions." MA Thesis. Université Libre de Bruxelles, 2010.

Stern, J. P. *The Future of Russian Gas and Gazprom.* Oxford: Oxford University Press, 2005.

Stobdan, P. "India and Kazakhstan Should Share Complementary Objectives." *Strategic Analysis* 33, no. 1 (2009): 1–7.

Strauss, J. C., and M. Saavedra, eds. "China and Africa: Emerging Patterns in Globalization and Development." *China Quarterly*, no. 199 (2009).

Sultanov, B. K., ed. *ShOS v poiskakh novogo ponimaniia bezopasnosti.* 18 Almaty: Kazakhstanskii institut strategicheskikh issledovanii, 2008.

Sultanov, B., and R. Krumm, eds. *Problemy ekonomicheskogo i finansovogo sotrudnichestva v ramkakh ShOS.* Almaty: Kazakhstanskii institut strategicheskikh issledovanii, 2006.

Sultanov, B. K., and L. M. Muzaparova, eds. *Stanovlenie vneshnei politiki Kazakhstana: Istoriia, dostizheniia, vzgliad v budushchee.* Almaty: IWEP, 2005.

Swanström, N. "An Asian Oil and Gas Union: Prospects and Problems." *China and Eurasia Forum Quarterly* 3, no. 3 (2005): 81–97.

———. "Shanghai Cooperation Organization and the Aftermath of the Russian Invasion of Georgia." *China and Eurasia Forum Quarterly* 6, no. 3 (2008): 3–7.

Syroezhkin, K. L. *Problemy sovremennogo Kitaia i bezopasnost' v Tsentral'noi Azii.* Almaty: Kazakhstanskii Institut Strategicheskikh Issledovanii (KISI), 2006.

Tabata, S., and A. Iwashita, eds. *Slavic Eurasia's Integration into the World Economy and Community.* Sapporo: Slavic Research Center, Hokkaido University, 2004.

Tellis, A. J., and M. Wills, eds. *Strategic Asia 2005–06: Military Modernization in an Era of Uncertainty.* Seattle: National Bureau of Asian Research, 2005.

Thorez, J. "Enclaves et enclavement dans le Ferghana post-soviétique." *Cahiers d'études sur la Méditerranée orientale et le monde turco-iranien*, no. 35 (2003): 28–39.

———. "Flux et dynamiques spatiales en Asie Centrale: Géographie de la transformation post-soviétique" (PhD diss., Paris 10 Nanterre, 2005).

———. "Transport-Traffic-Transfer: Migration Networks Between Russia and Central Asia," Wolfson College, University of Oxford, Paper presented at the conference "National Identity in Eurasia II: Migrancy & Diaspora," July 10–12, 2009.

Tonkobaevoi A., *Rukovodstvo po razvitiiu ekologicheskogo turizma v Kazakhstane.* Almaty: Aziatsko-Amerikanskoe partnerstvo, 2009.

Torbakov, I. "The Georgia Crisis and Russia-Turkey Relations." Jamestown Foundation Occasional Paper, November 2008.

———. "Plans for Turkic Commonwealth." *CEPS European Neighborhood Watch*, no. 19, September 2006.

"Trans-European North-South Motorway (TEM) Project." Report of the United Nations Economic Commission for Europe, Geneva, 2005.

Trenin, D. *The End of Eurasia: Russia on the Border Between Geopolitics and Globalization.* Washington, DC: Carnegie Endowment for International Peace, 2002.

———. "Russia's Spheres of Interest, Not Influence." *Washington Quarterly* 32, no. 4 (2009): 3–22.

———. "Southern Watch: Russia's Policy in Central Asia." *Journal of International Affairs* 56, no. 2 (2003): 119–31.

Trevisani, T. *Land and Power in Khorezm: Farmers, Communities, and the State in Uzbekistan's Decollectivisation.* Berlin: LIT, 2010.

Tsygankov, A. *Russia's Foreign Policy: Change and Continuity in National Identity.* Lanham, MD: Rowman & Littlefield, 2006.

Ul Haq, N., and K. Hussain. "Energy Crisis in Pakistan." Islamabad Policy Research Institute Factfile, July 2004.

Ulmishek, G. "Petroleum Geology and Resources of the Amu-Darya Basin, Turkmenistan, Uzbekistan, Afghanistan, and Iran." US Geological Survey Bulletin 2201-H. Reston, VA, 2004.

———. "Petroleum Geology and Resources of the North Ustyurt Basin, Kazakhstan, and Uzbekistan." US Geological Survey Bulletin 2201-D. Reston, VA, 2001.

United Nations. *Development of the Trans-Asian Railway: Trans-Asian Railway in the North-South Corridor, Northern Europe to the Persian Gulf.* New York: United Nations, 2001.

United Nations Development Programme. "Water Resources of Kazakhstan in the New Millennium." Report of the United Nations Development Programme, UNDPKAZ 07, Almaty, 2004.

United Nations Office on Drugs and Crime. "Illicit Drug Trends in the Russian Federation." United Nations Office on Drugs and Crime, Paris Pact Initiative Report, April 2008.

———. "World Drug Report 2010." United Nations Office on Drugs and Crime, Vienna, 2010.

US Department of Agriculture. "Cotton: World Markets and Trade." US Department of Agriculture Circular FOP 11–10, November 2010.

US Department of Defense. *Sustaining US Global Leadership: Priorities for 21st Century Defense*, January 2012.

US Department of State. "International Narcotics Control Strategy Report 2008." US Embassy Moscow, 2008.

US Geological Survey. *Minerals Yearbook 2008*, vol. 3, *Area Reports: International.* Reston, VA: US Geological Survey, 2010.

USAID. "A Regional View of Wheat Markets and Food Security in Central Asia: With a Focus on Afghanistan and Tajikistan." Report of USAID, Washington, DC, July 2011.

Usubaliev, E. "Japanese Politics in Central Asia in View of Another Possible Center of Power." *Central Asia and the Caucasus*, no. 5 (2001): 135–40.

Vakhabov, A., and T. Bobakulov. "Uzbekistan's Banking System and Its Role in Implementing the Anti-Crisis Program." *Central Asia and the Caucasus*, nos. 4–5 (2009): 91–105.

Valentine, S., B. K. Sovacool, and M. Matsuura. "Empowered? Evaluating Japan's National Energy Strategy under the DPJ Administration." *Energy Policy* 39 (2011): 1865–76.

Vinokurov, E. "Financing Infrastructure in Central Asia: Water and Energy Nexus." *World Finance Review* (Spring 2007): 135–39.

———. "Integratsiia atomno-energeticheskikh kompleksov Rossii i Kazakhstana." *Atomnaia strategiia*, no. 8 (2007): 24–26.

———, ed. "Mezhdunarodnye transportnye korridory EvrAzES: Bystree, deshevle, bol'she." Report of the Eurasian Development Bank, Astana, March 2009.

———, ed. "Obshchii elektroenergeticheskii rynok SNG." Report of the Eurasian Development Bank, Astana, July 2008.

———. "Vzaimnye investitsii v bankovskom sektore." *Evraziiskaia ekonomicheskaia integratsiia* 3, no. 2 (2009): 141–47.

Vinokurov E., M. Jadraliyev, and Y. Shcherbanin. "The EurAsEC Transport Corridors." Eurasian Development Bank Sector Report, no. 5, Astana, March 2009.

Vucetic, V., and V. Krishnaswamy. "Development of Electricity Trade in Central Asia—South Asia Region." Report of the World Bank, Washington, DC, 2005.

Warikoo, K., ed. *Central Asia: Emerging New Order.* New Delhi: Har Anand Publications, 1995.

Warikoo, K., and M. Singh, eds. *Central Asia Since Independence.* New Delhi: Shipra Publications, 2004.

Warkotsch, A., ed. *The European Union and Central Asia.* London: Routledge, 2011.

Watanabe, T. et al. "Tourism in the Pamir-Altai Mountains, Southern Kyrgyz Republic." *Geographical Studies*, no. 84 (2009): 3–13.

Wegerich, K. "Water Resources in Central Asia: Regional Stability or Patchy Make-Up?" *Central Asian Survey* 30, no. 2 (2011): 275–90.

Wegerich, K., O. Olsson, and J. Froebrich. "Reliving the Past in a Changed Environment: Hydropower Ambitions, Opportunities, and Constraints in Tajikistan." *Energy Policy*, no. 35 (2007): 3815–25.

Wegren, S., ed. *Land Reform in the Former Soviet Union and in Eastern Europe*. London: Routledge, 1998.

Weitz R. "Afghanistan in China's Emerging Eurasian Transport Corridor." *China Brief* 10, no. 14 (2010): 10–14.

Werner, C. "The New Silk Road: Mediators and Tourism Development in Central Asia." *Ethnology* 42, no. 2 (2003): 141–59.

Werner, C., and K. Purvis-Roberts. "After the Cold War: International Politics, Domestic Policy, and the Nuclear Legacy in Kazakhstan." *Central Asian Survey* 25, no. 4 (2006): 461–80.

Wilson, J. L. "The Legacy of the Color Revolutions for Russian Politics and Foreign Policy." *Problems of Post-Communism* 57, no. 2 (2010): 21–36.

Winrow, G. *Turkey in Post-Soviet Central Asia*. London: Royal Institute of International Affairs, 1995.

World Bank. "Central Asia Regional Electricity Export Potential Study." Report of the World Bank, Washington, DC, 2004.

———. *Enhancing the Prospects for Growth and Trade of the Kyrgyz Republic*. Washington, DC: World Bank, 2005.

Wouters, P., ed. *Codification and Progressive Development of International Water Law: The Work of the International Law Commission of the United Nations*. London: Kluwer Law, 1998.

Wu, H., and C. Chen, "The Prospects for Regional Economic Integration between China and the Five Central Asian Countries." *Europe-Asia Studies* 56, no. 7 (2004): 1059–80.

Yazdani, E. "US Democracy Promotion Policy in the Central Asian Republics: Myth or Reality?" *International Studies* 44, no. 2 (2007): 141–55.

Yenikeyeff, S. M. *Kazakhstan's Gas: Export Markets and Export Routes*. Oxford: Oxford Institute for Energy Studies, 2008.

Youngs, R. "The EU and the Arab Spring: From Munificence to Geo-Strategy." Fundación para las relaciones internacionales y el diálogo exterior (FRIDE) Policy Brief, no. 100, October 2011.

Yuasa, T. "Japan's Multilateral Approach Toward Central Asia." *Acta Slavica Iaponica*, no. 16 (2007): 65–84.

Yuldasheva, G. "Turkey's New Foreign Policy Landmarks and Central Asia." *Central Asia and the Caucasus* 49, no. 1 (2008): 51–57.

Yusuf, S., and K. Nabeshima. *Tiger Economies Under Threat: A Comparative Analysis of Malaysia's Industrial Prospects and Policy Options*. Washington, DC: World Bank, 2009.

Zair-Bek, V. A., ed. *Tsentral'naia Aziia v sisteme mezhdunarodnykh otnoshenii*. Moscow: Institut Vostokovedeniia, 2004.

Zakhidov, R. A., and M. S. Saidov. "Renewable Energy in the Early Twenty-First Century and Prospects for Development of Solar Engineering in Uzbekistan." *Applied Solar Energy* 45, no. 1 (2009): 1–6.

Zhang, J. *China's Energy Security: Prospects, Challenges, and Opportunities*. Washington, DC: Brookings Institution Press, 2011.

Zhao, H. "Kitai, Tsentral'naia Aziia i Shankhaiskaia Organizatsiia sotrudnichestva." Carnegie Moscow Center Working Paper, no. 5, 2005.

Index

Foreign policy *(continued)*
Japan, 104–7
Malaysia, 110
Pakistan, 102
Russia, 10–14
South Korea, 108–9
Turkey, 76–78
Ukraine, 117–18
United States, 44–45, 46*t*, 47
France, 59, 60, 62, 64, 69, 208–9
FREEDOM Support Act, 45

Gaidar, Egor, 10
Gap Inshaat, 270–71
Gas resources. *See* Hydrocarbons
Gas to Liquids (GTL), 183, 184
Gazprom
in Kazakhstan, 17–18, 177, 178
in Kyrgyzstan, 17
in Tajikistan, 17, 170
in Turkmenistan, 17, 175, 176
in Uzbekistan, 17–18, 110, 176
General Electric, 53, 208, 234–35, 246
Generalized System of Preferences, 45
Georgia
color revolution (2003), 13, 48
foreign policy, 120
future prospects, 122–23
political background, 120
trade
banking sector, 122
construction industry, 122
food production, 121
hydrocarbons, 121–22
Kazakhstan, 121–22
Germany, 59, 60, 62, 63–64, 68–69
Glencore International AG, 194
Globalization impact
borderless concept, xiii
budget expenditures, 139*t*
budget revenues (2011), 139*t*
business behavior, 138, 140
business grading (2011), 140*t*
China, 307–8, 309–10, 311–12
economic competition, 306–7
economic dimension, xiii–xiv
economic structure per country (2011), 137*t*
external debt, 139*t*

Globalization impact *(continued)*
foreign direct investment (2011), 139*t*
geopolitics, 309–10
global trends, 308–9
government corruption, 140, 141*t*
government stability, 310–12
gross domestic product (GDP)
per capita, 135, 137*t*
per country, 135–36, 137*t*
per sector, 136, 137*t*
human development index (2010), 140, 141*t*
international organizations, xvii
labor force by occupation, 137*t*
labor migration, 141
liberty rating (2010), 140, 141*t*
poverty level, 135, 137*t*
purchasing power per country (2011), 136*t*
regional dimension, xiv
Russia, 307
service sector, 310
trade, 135–36
GM Uzbekistan, 269–70
Gold, 87, 109, 190–91, 194, 199–203
Great Britain, 59, 60, 63–64, 69
Great Game theory, xix, xv, 3, 5–7, 306
Gross domestic product (GDP)
globalization impact
per capita, 135, 137*t*
per country, 135–36, 137*t*
per sector, 136, 137*t*
GUAM (Georgia-Ukraine-Armenia-Moldova), 12, 48, 117–18
Gulf Oil and Gas, 87, 179

Hashimoto, Ryutaro, 105
Hu Jintao, 38, 39
Humanitarian Office of the European Commission, 64
Human rights
European Union (EU), 60, 61, 62–63, 64, 65
United Arab Emirates (UAE), 87
Uzbekistan, 158
Human Rights Dialogue, 65
Hunting, 87, 299–300

About the Authors

Marlene Laruelle is Director of the Central Asia Program and a Research Professor of International Affairs at the Institute for European, Russian and Eurasian Studies, Elliot School of International Affairs, George Washington University.

Sebastien Peyrouse is a Research Professor of International Affairs at the Institute for European, Russian and Eurasian Studies, Elliot School of International Affairs, George Washington University.

Both have co-authored *The Chinese Question in Central Asia: Domestic Order, Social Changes and the Chinese Factor* (2012), and co-edited *China and India in Central Asia: A New "Great Game"?* (2010), and *Mapping Central Asia: Indian Perceptions and Strategies* (2011).